# Object-Oriented Concepts, Databases, and Applications

# ACM PRESS

**Editor-in-Chief:**

Peter Wegner, *Brown University*

ACM Press books represent a collaboration between the Association for Computing Machinery (ACM) and Addison-Wesley Publishing Company to develop and publish a broad range of new works. These works generally fall into one of four series.

*Frontier Series.* Books focused on novel and exploratory material at the leading edge of computer science and practice.

*Anthology Series.* Collected works of general interest to computer professionals and / or society at large.

*Tutorial Series.* Introductory books to help nonspecialists quickly grasp either the general concepts or the needed details of some specific topic.

*History Series.* Books documenting past developments in the field and linking them to the present.

In addition, ACM Press books include selected conference and workshop proceedings.

# Object-Oriented Concepts, Databases, and Applications

Edited by

**Won Kim**

Microelectronics and
Computer Technology Corporation

and

**Frederick H. Lochovsky**

Computer Systems Research Institute
Department of Computer Science
University of Toronto

ACM PRESS
New York, New York

▼▲ ADDISON-WESLEY PUBLISHING COMPANY
Reading, Massachusetts • Menlo Park, California
New York • Don Mills, Ontario • Wokingham, England
Amsterdam • Bonn • Sydney • Singapore
Tokyo • Madrid • San Juan

ACM Press Frontier Series

Many of the designations used by manufacturers and sellers to distinguish their products are claimed as trademarks. Where those designations appear in this book, and Addison-Wesley was aware of a trademark claim, the designations have been printed in caps or initial caps.

The programs and applications presented in this book have been included for their instructional value. They have been tested with care, but are not guaranteed for any particular purpose. The publisher does not offer any warranties or representations, nor does it accept any liabilities with respect to the programs or applications.

## Library of Congress Cataloging-in-Publication Data

Object-oriented concepts, databases, and applications, / [edited] by
  Won Kim, Frederick H. Lochovsky.
    p.  cm.
  Includes bibliographies and index.
  ISBN 0-201-14410-7
  1. Object-oriented programming (Computer science) 2. Data base management.  I. Kim, Won.  II. Lochovsky, Frederick H.
  QA76.6.024 1989
  005.74—dc19

        88-31839
        CIP

Reprinted with corrections September, 1989

CDEFGHIJ-AL-89

# Contributors

**J. Annevelink**
Hewlett-Packard Laboratories
Palo Alto, CA

**Nat Ballou**
Microelectronics and
    Computer Technology
    Corporation
Austin, TX

**D. Beech**
Oracle Corporation
Belmont, CA

**Anders Björnerstedt**
Department of Computer and
    Systems Sciences
University of Stockholm
Stockholm, Sweden

**Robert Bretl**
Servio Logic Development
    Corporation
Beaverton, OR

**Michael J. Carey**
Computer Sciences Department
University of Wisconsin
Madison, WI

**Hong-Tai Chou**
Microelectronics and Computer
    Technology Corporation
Austin, TX

**E. Chow**
Hewlett-Packard Laboratories
Palo Alto, CA

**T. Connors**
Hewlett-Packard Laboratories
Palo Alto, CA

**Alfred Dale**
Department of Computer Sciences
University of Texas
Austin, TX

**J.W. Davis**
Hewlett-Packard Laboratories
Palo Alto, CA

**Dominique Decouchant**
Laboratoire de Genie Informatique
Universitie de Grenoble
Grenoble, France

**David J. DeWitt**
Computer Sciences Department
University of Wisconsin
Madison, WI

**Jim Diederich**
Department of Mathematics
University of California
Davis, CA

**Clarence A. Ellis**
Microelectronics and Computer
  Technology Corporation
Austin, TX

**D.H. Fishman**
Hewlett-Packard Laboratories
Palo Alto, CA

**Jorge F. Garza**
Microelectronics and Computer
  Technology Corporation
Austin, TX

**Simon J. Gibbs**
Microelectronics and Computer
  Technology Corporation
Austin, TX

**W. Hasan**
Hewlett-Packard Laboratories
Palo Alto, CA

**C.G. Hoch**
Hewlett-Packard Laboratories
Palo Alto, CA

**Christer Hultén**
Department of Computer and
  Systems Sciences
Stockholm, Sweden

**W. Kent**
Hewlett-Packard Laboratories
Palo Alto, CA

**Kyung-Chang Kim**
Department of Computer Sciences
University of Texas
Austin, TX

**Won Kim**
Microelectronics and Computer
  Technology Corporation
Austin, TX

**Roger King**
Department of Computer Science
University of Colorado
Boulder, CO

**S. Leichner**
Hewlett-Packard Laboratories
Palo Alto, CA

**Henry Lieberman**
Visible Language Workshop
Media Laboratory
Massachusetts Institute of
  Technology
Cambridge, MA

**Frederick H. Lochovsky**
Computer Systems Research
  Institute
University of Toronto
Toronto, Canada

**P. Lyngbaek**
Hewlett-Packard Laboratories
Palo Alto, CA

**B. Mahbod**
Hewlett-Packard Laboratories
Palo Alto, CA

**David Maier**
Department of Computer Science
  and Engineering
Oregon Graduate Center
Beaverton, OR

**Fred Mellender**
Advanced Computing Laboratory
Eastman Kodak
Rochester, NY

**Jack Milton**
Department of Mathematics
University of California
Davis, CA

**David A. Moon**
Symbolics Corporation
Cambridge, MA

**J. Eliot B. Moss**
Department of Computer and
    Information Science
Lederle Graduate Research Center
University of Massachusetts
Amherst, MA

**M.A. Neimat**
Hewlett-Packard Laboratories
Palo Alto, CA

**Oscar Nierstrasz**
University of Geneva
Geneva, Switzerland

**Allen Otis**
Servio Logic Development
    Corporation
Beaverton, OR

**Jason Penney**
Servio Logic Development
    Corporation
Beaverton, OR

**Joel E. Richardson**
Computer Sciences Department
University of Wisconsin
Madison, WI

**Steve Riegel**
Advanced Computing Laboratory
Eastman Kodak
Rochester, NY

**T. Risch**
Hewlett-Packard Laboratories
Palo Alto, CA

**David M. Russinoff**
Microelectronics and Computer
    Technology Corporation
Austin, TX

**Mark Scheevel**
Microelectronics and Computer
    Technology Corporation
Austin, TX

**Bruce Schuchardt**
Servio Logic Development
    Corporation
Beaverton, OR

**M.C. Shan**
Hewlett-Packard Laboratories
Palo Alto, CA

**Eugene J. Shekita**
Computer Sciences Department
University of Wisconsin
Madison, WI

**Andrea H. Skarra**
Department of Computer Science
Brown University
Providence, RI

**Jacob Stein**
Servio Logic Development
    Corporation
Beaverton, OR

**Lynn Andrea Stein**
Department of Computer Science
Brown University
Providence, RI

**Andrew Straw**
Advanced Computing Laboratory
Eastman Kodak
Rochester, NY

**Mark A. Tarlton**
Microelectronics and Computer
    Technology Corporation
Austin, TX

**P. Nong Tarlton**
Microelectronics and Computer
    Technology Corporation
Austin, TX

**Chris Tomlinson**
Microelectronics and Computer
    Technology Corporation
Austin, TX

**D.C. Tsichritzis**
University of Geneva
Geneva, Switzerland

**David Ungar**
Computer Systems Laboratory
Electrical Engineering Department
Stanford University
Stanford, CA

**Yair Wand**
Management Information Systems
Faculty of Commerce and Business
    Administration
University of British Columbia
Vancouver, Canada

**Steven P. Weiser**
Computer Systems Research Institute
University of Toronto
Toronto, Canada

**W.K. Wilkinson**
Hewlett-Packard Laboratories
Palo Alto, CA

**E. Harold Williams**
Servio Logic Development Corporation
Beaverton, OR

**Monty Williams**
Servio Logic Development Corporation
Beaverton, OR

**Darrell Woelk**
Microelectronics and Computer
    Technology Corporation
Austin, TX

**Stanley B. Zdonik**
Department of Computer Science
Brown University
Providence, RI

# Preface

Object-oriented systems are receiving wide interest these days in a number of areas of computer science. Object-oriented systems have their roots in programming languages (e.g., Simula and Smalltalk), and the object paradigm was subsequently adopted and extended by artifical intelligence. More recently, the object paradigm has generated particular interest in the area of database management systems. This interest resulted from the requirements of new application areas of database systems, such as office information systems and computer-aided design. These application areas require data modeling capabilities and transaction execution models not supported by current implementations of database management systems. Accordingly, a major focus of this book is on the representation of and support for object-oriented concepts in database management systems and the use of these systems in addressing the data management needs of application areas.

This book is divided into five parts containing 24 chapters on a broad spectrum of topics on object-oriented systems, with an emphasis on object-oriented database management systems. The five parts correspond to the five topical areas the chapters address:

- object-oriented concepts as embedded in object-oriented programming languages and semantic data models
- object-oriented applications
- object-oriented database systems
- architectural issues in object-oriented systems
- directions for future research and development in object-oriented concepts and systems

Part 1 of the book consists of five chapters, and is intended to introduce the reader to a number of interesting aspects of object-oriented concepts. In Chapter 1, Oscar Nierstrasz provides *A Survey of Object-Oriented Concepts*, and discusses the use of object concepts in a number of application contexts. In Chapter 2, *My Cat Is Object-Oriented*, Roger King identifies fundamental similarities and differences between object-oriented concepts and semantic data modeling concepts, in an attempt to dispel some of the confusion about object-oriented databases. Lynn Stein, Henry Lieberman, and David Ungar provide in Chapter 3, *A Shared View of Sharing: The Treaty of Orlando*, some important insight into the sharing and organization aspects of object-oriented concepts in their discussion of the concepts of delegation and prototypes, which have been proposed as alternatives to the conventional concepts of inheritance and classes. In Chapter 4, David Moon provides an overview of *The COMMON LISP Object-Oriented Programming Language Standard*. This is the first effort to standardize object-oriented extensions to COMMON LISP. This standard is expected to have a major impact on the future of object-oriented concepts and systems, and to go a long way in settling the debate about "what objects mean." The survey of *Concurrent Object-Oriented Programming Languages* in Chapter 5 by Chris Tomlinson and Mark Scheevel points to one important direction of future research in object-oriented systems, namely application and extensions of object-oriented concepts to programming languages and systems for parallel and distributed environments.

Part 2 consists of four chapters that show object-oriented concepts in action, by featuring significant operational applications from a number of important application domains, including artificial intelligence, office information systems, database design systems, and graphical representation systems. David Russinoff describes the object-oriented approach to organizing knowledge, rules, and base facts in an expert system shell in Chapter 6, *Proteus: A Frame-based Nonmonotonic Inference System*. Mark and Nong Tarlton describe the object-oriented approach to representing and manipulating graphics in Chapter 7, *Pogo: A Declarative Representation System for Graphics*. In Chapter 8, *Objects, Messages, and Rules in Database Design*, Jim Diederich and Jack Milton discuss a database design system in which the entities of interest to the designers of a relational database are organized in terms of objects. In Chapter 9, Oscar Nierstrasz and Dennis Tsichritzis describe an object-oriented approach to addressing the information modeling, run-time support, and software engineering needs of *Integrated Office Systems*.

Part 3 features the architectures and functionality supported in some of the operational object-oriented database systems. Our intent is to highlight the similarities and differences among different systems. The COMMON LISP Object-Oriented Programming Standard (CLOS) is a first attempt by the object-oriented programming language community to standardize object-oriented concepts and language features. The database community is expected, in the near future, to attempt to standardize the object-oriented data model to support not only object-oriented programming languages but also various data-intensive, object-oriented application systems. The similarities in the object-oriented data models supported by the systems described here may serve as a basis for initiating the standardization effort for an object-oriented data model within the database community. Part 3 highlights only four object-oriented database systems. There are a few additional noteworthy operational systems, including V-Base from Ontologic, Inc. and Avance from the University of Stockholm, among others. For a number of reasons, including corporate confidentiality, the chapters in Part 3 do not provide detailed descriptions of the architecture and performance of each system; instead they provide fairly high-level views of important aspects of the systems. In Chapter 10, Dan Fishman et al. provide an *Overview of the Iris DBMS* prototyped at Hewlett-Packard. Iris has adopted the functional data model (one of the semantic data models), and has implemented the object manager on top of a relational database system. One important aspect of Iris is its attempt to provide an object-oriented query language that is compatible with the SQL relational database language. In Chapter 11, Won Kim et al. present the *Features of the ORION Object-Oriented Database System* prototyped at MCC. ORION provides a number of database features, including transaction management, queries, dynamic schema evolution, versions, composite objects, and multimedia data management. The ORION interface is an object-oriented extension to COMMON LISP. However, it is not compatible with the CLOS; it lacks some important features of CLOS, such as metaclasses and method combination, but provides important features that CLOS lacks, including transactions, queries, indexes, and versions. Robert Bretl et al. describe in Chapter 12 the features of *The GemStone Data Management System* developed at Servio Logic Corporation. Along with V-Base, GemStone is one of the early commercial object-oriented database systems. One major aspect of GemStone is the integration of database support for the Smalltalk language system. Steve Weiser and Fred Lochovsky describe in Chapter 13 *OZ+: An Object-Oriented Database System* prototyped at the University of Toronto. The system was designed specifically to support and facilitate the implementation of integrated office information systems.

Part 4 consists of six chapters that feature the results of recent research into a number of major issues in object-oriented database architecture, including storage techniques for objects, indexing techniques for the evaluation of complex object-oriented queries, concurrency control, message passing, extending the object-oriented database with a model of versions, and distributed object management. Michael Carey et al. discuss data structures and storage management algorithms for arbitrary-size objects in Chapter 14, *Storage Management for Objects in EXODUS*. The approach is an interesting extension of the B-tree organization, and is efficient in supporting incremental updates to portions of a very large object. In Chapter 15, *Indexing Techniques for Object-Oriented Databases*, Won Kim, K.C. Kim, and Al Dale describe an indexing technique that extends conventional indexing techniques to the class hierarchy in object-oriented databases. The proposal is based on the observation that in object-oriented systems, attributes of a class are inherited into its direct and indirect subclasses; as such, it may be better to maintain just one index on an attribute (or a combination of attributes) for a class and all its subclasses, rather than a separate index on the class and each of the subclasses. Andrea Skarra and Stan Zdonik discuss concurrency control and transaction management issues in object-oriented databases in Chapter 16, *Concurrency Control and Object-Oriented Databases.* They review techniques for increasing concurrency by exploiting the semantics of objects, and also point out the relevance of research into long-duration transactions because of the use of object-oriented databases in interactive design and engineering environments. In Chapter 17, *Optimizing Smalltalk Message Performance*, Fred Mellender, Steve Riegel, and Andy Straw discuss performance enhancements in the areas of message passing and garbage collection in a Smalltalk-based object manager called Alltalk under development by Eastman Kodak. This chapter addresses very important problems for object-oriented programming systems, which perhaps have not received enough attention in the literature. Anders Björnerstedt and Christer Hultén present the semantics and uses of versions in the Avance object management system in Chapter 18, *Version Control in an Object-Oriented Architecture.* They discuss the semantics and uses of versions from both the user and the system perspectives with the system using versions as a concurrency-control mechanism. In Chapter 19, *A Distributed Object Manager for the Smalltalk-80 System*, Dominique Decouchant describes the design of a prototype distributed object manager, and addresses a number of issues in distributed object management, including the problem of object migration and garbage collection in a network.

Part 5 consists of five chapters that provide the reader with a rare collection of relatively well-thought-out opinions about the directions for future research and development in object-oriented systems. The subject matter includes overall research directions, active objects, formalization of object-oriented concepts, performance issues, and integration of languages and database systems. In Chapter 20, *Directions in Object-Oriented Research*, Dennis Tsichritzis and Oscar Nierstrasz discuss both fairly conservative extensions to the traditional research directions and radical departures from them. Yair Wand, in Chapter 21, makes *A Proposal for a Formal Model of Objects.* His proposal is based on ontology, the philosophy of science that deals with modeling the existence of things in the world. Skip Ellis and Simon Gibbs announce the impending demise of object-oriented programming as we know it today, and predict the coming of active objects in Chapter 22, *Active Objects: Realities and Possibilities.* Active objects are objects that may be activated not only by messages but also by any type of event, including timer interrupts, updates to the state of an object, and so on. They point out that active objects are natural for modeling parallel and distributed applications. David Maier discusses his views on *Making Database Systems Fast Enough for CAD Applications* in Chapter 23. Eliot Moss discusses the issues of unifying programming languages and database in Chapter 24, *Object-Orientation as Catalyst for Language-Database Integration.*

Won Kim
Frederick H. Lochovsky

# Contents

## Part 1 Introduction to Object-Oriented Concepts

**Chapter 1** A Survey of Object-Oriented Concepts    3
Oscar Nierstrasz

**Chapter 2** My Cat Is Object-Oriented    23
Roger King

**Chapter 3** A Shared View of Sharing: *The Treaty of Orlando*    31
Lynn Andrea Stein, Henry Lieberman, David Ungar

**Chapter 4** The COMMON LISP Object-Oriented Programming Language
Standard    49
David A. Moon

**Chapter 5** Concurrent Object-Oriented Programming Languages    79
Chris Tomlinson, Mark Scheevel


## Part 2 Object-Oriented Applications

**Chapter 6** Proteus: A Frame-Based Nonmonotonic Inference System    127
David M. Russinoff

**Chapter 7** Pogo: A Declarative Representation System for Graphics    151
Mark A. Tarlton, P. Nong Tarlton

**Chapter 8** Objects, Messages, and Rules in Database Design    177
Jim Diederich, Jack Milton

**Chapter 9** Integrated Office Systems    199
Oscar Nierstrasz, D.C. Tsichritzis

# Part 3 Object-Oriented Database Systems

**Chapter 10** Overview of the Iris DBMS    219
D.H. Fishman, J. Annevelink, D. Beech, E. Chow, T. Connors,
J.W. Davis, W. Hasan, C.G. Hoch, W. Kent, S. Leichner, P. Lyngbaek,
B. Mahbod, M.A. Neimat, T. Risch, M.C. Shan, W.K. Wilkinson

**Chapter 11** Features of the ORION Object-Oriented Database
System    251
Won Kim, Nat Ballou, Hong-Tai Chou, Jorge F. Garza,
Darrell Woelk

**Chapter 12** The GemStone Data Management System    283
Robert Bretl, David Maier, Allen Otis, Jason Penney, Bruce Schuchardt,
Jacob Stein, E. Harold Williams, Monty Williams

**Chapter 13** OZ+: An Object-Oriented Database System    309
Steven P. Weiser, Frederick H. Lochovsky

# Part 4 Architectural Issues in Object-Oriented Systems

**Chapter 14** Storage Management for Objects in EXODUS    341
Michael J. Carey, David J. DeWitt, Joel E. Richardson, Eugene J. Shekita

**Chapter 15** Indexing Techniques for Object-Oriented Databases    371
Won Kim, Kyung-Chang Kim, Alfred Dale

**Chapter 16** Concurrency Control and Object-Oriented Databases    395
Andrea H. Skarra, Stanley B. Zdonik

**Chapter 17** Optimizing Smalltalk Message Performance    423
Fred Mellender, Steve Riegel, Andrew Straw

**Chapter 18** Version Control in an Object-Oriented Architecture    451
Anders Björnerstedt, Christer Hultén

**Chapter 19** A Distributed Object Manager for the Smalltalk-80
System    487
Dominique Decouchant

# Part 5 Future Research and Development in Object-Oriented Systems

**Chapter 20** Directions in Object-Oriented Research    523
D.C. Tsichritzis, Oscar Nierstrasz

**Chapter 21** A Proposal for a Formal Model of Objects    537
Yair Wand

**Chapter 22** Active Objects: Realities and Possibilities    561
Clarence A. Ellis, Simon J. Gibbs

**Chapter 23** Making Database Systems Fast Enough for CAD
Applications    573
David Maier

**Chapter 24** Object Orientation as Catalyst for Language-Database
Integration    583
J. Eliot B. Moss

**Index**    593

# 1 Introduction to Object-Oriented Concepts

# 1

# A Survey of Object-Oriented Concepts

Oscar Nierstrasz

## INTRODUCTION

The explosion of interest in object-oriented approaches in the last few years has led to a proliferation of definitions and interpretations of this much-used and much-abused term. As a consequence, it can be very difficult for a newcomer to understand and evaluate what is meant by a claim that a programming language or a piece of software or a user interface is "object-oriented." Do they all mean the same thing?

In this chapter we shall survey object-oriented approaches as they appear in programming languages and systems today. We shall see that what these approaches have in common is that they all exploit *encapsulation* or "packaging" in various interesting ways. Encapsulation has traditionally been important in computer science for the simple reason that it is necessary to decompose large systems into smaller encapsulated subsystems that can be more easily developed, maintained, and ported. Object-oriented languages and systems formalize encapsulation and encourage programming in terms of "objects" rather than "programs" and "data." Each of these approaches adopts a particular object model, depending on which properties of objects they need to encapsulate. A complete definition of what it means to be object-oriented is therefore not possible, though we can perhaps judge when one system or language is "more" object-oriented than another.

In the following sections we shall first survey object models as manifested by various object-oriented programming languages. Object-oriented concepts such as instantiation via object classes, class inheritance, polymorphism, genericity, and strong-typing in object-oriented languages will be shown to depend ultimately on object encapsulation. We shall then briefly consider systems that provide run-time support for objects and for programmers building object-oriented applications.

## 1.1 Object-oriented Programming Languages

The first appearance of the notion of an *object* as a programming construct was in Simula, a language for programming computer simulations [Birtwistle et al. 1973]. This is not surprising, since it is quite natural to model the objects of a simulation directly as software "objects." More surprising is the discovery that software objects can be useful not only for programming simulations, but also for prototyping and application development. This is the direction that was pursued by the Smalltalk system [Goldberg and Robson 1983], building upon the concept of an *object class* introduced in Simula.

Since object-oriented programming has been popularized mainly through the Smalltalk effort, it is extremely tempting to adopt a *de facto* definition of an object-oriented programming language as one that supports both object classes and class inheritance (discussed below). We feel that this view is too restrictive, however, since there are many arguably object-oriented approaches that do not depend on class inheritance. We therefore suggest that any programming language that provides mechanisms that can be used to exploit encapsulation is (at least to some degree) object-oriented. By using such a loose definition, we do not feel obliged to answer difficult questions like, "Are Ada and Modula object-oriented?" Instead, we say that you should ask, "In what *ways* are Ada or Modula object-oriented (or not)?" By analogy, it is not so interesting whether Prolog is "declarative" or "procedural," but in which ways it is declarative, and where the paradigm breaks down.

In passing, we should point out that another important way in which one language can be "more" object-oriented than another is in how *homogeneous* the object model is. Is "everything" an object? Are object classes themselves objects? Is there a distinction between "user objects" and "system objects," or between "active objects" and "passive objects?" These distinctions are important if we wish to apply object-oriented mechanisms (like class inheritance) and discover that they are not valid for certain kinds of "objects."

Object models for programming languages often encapsulate objects in terms of a set of *operations* as a visible interface, while hiding the object's *realization* (i.e., its data structures and the implementation of the operations). To emphasize object independence, one often speaks of objects as communicating by *message passing*. This is not so much an implementation strategy as it is a paradigm for communication: one may not manipulate or view an object's hidden data; instead one sends a "message" to an object, and the object itself selects the *method* by which it will react to the message.

Once objects are encapsulated in this fashion, we can exploit encapsulation to provide, for example, the possibility of multiple object instantiation, behavioral sharing through various inheritance mechanisms, verification of correct object usage through strong-typing, and structuring of resources in concurrent applications. Object-oriented programming languages make it easier to program with objects by providing language constructs for defining useful kinds of objects. Our discussion will center on the issues of software reusability, object types, and concurrency.

### 1.1.1 Reusability

Encapsulation of procedures, macros, and libraries has been exploited for many years to enhance the reusability of software. Object-oriented techniques achieve further reusability through the encapsulation of programs and data. The techniques and mechanisms we shall discuss here are primarily concerned with paradigms for packaging objects in such a way that they can be conveniently reused without modification to solve new problems.

**Instantiation and Object Classes** Instantiation is perhaps the most basic object-oriented reusability mechanism. Every programming language provides some built-in data types (like integers and floating-point numbers) that can be instantiated as needed. Objects may be either statically or dynamically instantiated. Statically instantiated objects are allocated at compile time and exist for the duration that the program executes. Dynamically instantiated objects require run-time support for allocation and for either explicit deallocation or some form of garbage collection.

The next step is to provide a way for programmers to define and instantiate their own objects. This can be done by providing the programmer with a facility to define *object classes*, as is the case in Smalltalk. An object class specifies a set of visible operations, a set of hidden *instance variables,* and a set of hidden *methods* that implement the operations. The instance variables can be modified only indirectly by invoking the operations. When a new instance of an object class is created, it has its own set of instance variables, and it shares the operations' methods with other instances of its class.

A simple example is the class *ComplexNumber*. The programmer would define an interface consisting of the arithmetic operations that complex numbers support, and provide the implementation of these operations and the internal data structures. It would be up to the programmer to decide, for example, whether to use a representation based on Cartesian or polar coordinates.

An alternative approach to instantiation is to use *prototypical objects* [Lieberman 1986] rather than object classes as the "template" from which new instances are forged. This is exactly what we do when we make a copy of a text file containing a document composed in a formatting language like $T_EX$ or troff: we re-use the structure of the old document, altering its contents and possibly refining the layout. This approach is useful to avoid a proliferation of object classes in systems where objects evolve rapidly and display more differences than similarities. The difference between object classes and prototypical objects is brought out sharply when viewed in terms of applicable inheritance mechanisms (discussed next).

**Inheritance**   Inheritance has many forms, depending on what we wish to inherit and when and how the inheritance takes place. In most cases, however, inheritance is strictly a *reusability* mechanism for sharing behavior between objects, not to be confused with *subtyping*, which will be discussed in a later section. (Many of the "problems" with inheritance arise from the discrepancy between these two notions.) The differences between the various forms of inheritance can be loosely summed up in terms of the following issues:

- Does inheritance occur statically or dynamically (at run time)?
- What are the clients of the inherited properties (i.e., classes or instances of classes)?
- What properties can be inherited (e.g., instance variables, methods, rules, values)?
- Which inherited properties are visible to the client?
- Can inherited properties be overridden or suppressed?
- How are conflicts resolved?

We shall proceed with a brief overview of the more common kinds of inheritance, starting with class inheritance and concluding with what we will call *dynamic inheritance*.

Class inheritance is often represented as the fundamental feature that distinguishes object-oriented from other programming languages. Although this may be a useful and simple guide, it overemphasizes the importance of just one aspect of object-oriented programming and therefore devalues the contributions of other languages that do not provide an explicit mechanism for class inheritance. Nevertheless, class inheritance is an important mechanism that, when properly applied, can simplify large pieces of software by exploiting the similarities between certain object classes.

The key idea of class inheritance is to provide a simple and powerful mechanism for defining new classes that inherit properties from existing classes. With *single inheritance*, a *subclass* may inherit instance variables and methods of a single *parent* class, possibly adding some methods and instance variables of its own. Suppose, for example, that we want to display our complex numbers on a two-dimensional grid. We could then define a subclass *GraphicComplexNumber* that inherits from *ComplexNumber* and adds a *display* operation.

A natural extension to simple inheritance is *multiple inheritance*, that is, inheritance of a subclass from multiple parent classes. In this case we would view our *GraphicComplexNumber* as, say, a subclass of both *GraphicObject* and *ComplexNumber*. Some languages that support multiple inheritance include LISP with flavors [Moon 1986], Mesa with Traits [Curry et al. 1982], Trellis/Owl [Schaffert et al. 1986], and Eiffel [Meyer 1986].

At this point we get into some interesting fine points concerning class inheritance. First, not all languages with class inheritance support multiple inheritance (Smalltalk-80, for example). Although multiple inheritance is not frequently required, it can be quite clumsy to make do without it. Second, it is important to be able to override inherited methods. A *display* operation is quite specific to an object, and may have to be re-implemented or altered for a subclass that inherits it.

Third, subclasses may or may not be permitted direct access to inherited instance variables. Should a subclass, as a client of the parent class it inherits from, be allowed to see what is normally hidden from regular clients of its parent? When a subclass adds a method that accesses inherited instance variables, it effectively violates encapsulation of that parent. Consider our *Graphic-ComplexNumber*. If its *display* operation makes use of inherited instance variables, then we are no longer free to alter the internal representation of the parent *ComplexNumber*. On the other hand, if *display* makes use of only inherited operations, such as *xvalue* and *yvalue* (which may in fact be computed from polar coordinates), then we achieve greater independence between subclass and parent.

A fourth point is the issue of name clashes in the presence of multiple inheritance. If we inherit two *display* operations, which method do we take? Actually, this is a non-problem that can easily be resolved by indicating precisely what is to occur when a *display* operation is invoked. Either the system provides default rules for selecting one method or for combining inherited methods, or it requires the programmer to make an explicit choice. Similarly, inheritance of identically named instance variables from multiple parents poses no real problem, provided we separately inherit each variable, and we have a means to distinguish them in new methods (for example, by prefixing them with their parent class name).

The difficulties with access to "hidden" inherited properties and with resolving inheritance clashes are most pronounced when we must consider the possibility of changes to the class hierarchy. If we wish to change the definition or implementation of an object class, how will this affect inheriting subclasses? Will the rules for resolving name clashes adversely affect subclasses? Principles for evaluating "good" and "bad" inheritance mechanisms are discussed in [Snyder 1986b]. Supporting modifications to class definitions is especially problematic when the existing instances of the modified classes and subclasses must be preserved. This problem is known as *schema evolution* in object-oriented databases, by analogy with schema evolution in relational and other database systems. An approach to schema evolution used in the ORION object-oriented database is described in [Banerjee et al. 1987b].

Inheritance has a slightly different flavor in the field of knowledge representation. Object classes may then represent knowledge or beliefs rather than software packages. (See also [Russinoff 1988] in this book.) An instance of a subclass, then, has all the properties of its parents, and possibly more. A subclass is viewed as a *specialization* of its parents. For example, everything that we know to be true about mammals also holds for humans, but not vice versa. Note that this means that every instance of a subclass is also effectively a member of its parent classes. This points out how specialization is distinct from *aggregation*. It is *not* valid to define a class *Car* that inherits from *Body*, *Frame*, *Wheels*, and similar classes, since a car is not a wheel. A *GraphicComplexNumber*, however, is at once both a *GraphicObject* and a *ComplexNumber*. Inheritance in this case serves not only as a reusability mechanism, but also as a conceptual structuring mechanism.

An interesting variation on class inheritance is what we call *partial inheritance*. In this case we inherit some properties and suppress others. For example, we may define a *Queue* to inherit from a *List* by inheriting instance variables and a *length* operation. However, we suppress the *insert* and *delete* operations, replacing them with, say, *getfirst* and *putlast*. In this case neither *Queue* nor *List* is a subclass of the other, but they are undeniably related. Partial inheritance is therefore arguably convenient for code sharing, but it can create a mess of a class hierarchy. This mechanism is provided by both C++ [Stroustrup 1986] and CommonObjects [Snyder 1986a].

Class inheritance is essentially a *static* form of inheritance: new classes inherit properties when they are defined rather than at run time. Once a class has been defined, the properties of its instances (instance variables and methods) are determined for all time. Note that if we permit the redefinition of object classes at run time (i.e., schema evolution), then instances and subclass instances will effectively inherit new properties. We do *not* consider this an example of dynamic inheritance, however, because class redefinition is not an operation on objects. By analogy, modifying a database schema is not normally considered a database transaction. We must temporarily step out of the object model in order to make dynamic changes to the inheritance hierarchy.

We will use *dynamic inheritance* to refer to mechanisms that permit objects to alter their behavior in the course of normal interactions between objects. Dynamic inheritance, as opposed to schema evolution, occurs *within* the object model. We can distinguish two fundamentally different forms of dynamic inheritance, which we will call *part inheritance* and *scope inheritance*. The key difference is that the former occurs when an object explicitly changes its behavior by accepting new parts from other objects, whereas the latter occurs indirectly through changes in the environment.

Basically, part inheritance is nothing more than an exchange of value between objects: an object that modifies an instance variable necessarily changes its behavior, although in a way that is limited by its object class. But part inheritance is far more interesting if we consider instance variables and methods themselves as values. In such a model, an object may dynamically inherit new instance variables and methods from other objects. An example of this kind of inheritance occurs in a system for distributed problem-solving using "knowledge objects" [Tsichritzis et al. 1987; Casais 1988]. Evolving active objects can acquire new rules and methods in response to events occurring in their environment.

Scope inheritance is more common. In this case an object's behavior is determined in part by its environment or its acquaintances. When changes in the environment occur, the behavior of the object changes. A simple example is that of a paragraph in a document that inherits its font, type style, point size, and line width from its enclosing environment. If the same paragraph is moved to a footnote or a quotation, new properties will be inherited.

Both forms of dynamic inheritance are possible within systems based on prototypical objects [Lieberman 1986]. An object may have instance variables and methods, but it may also *delegate* certain messages to an acquaintance, called a prototypical object. Part inheritance occurs when an object replaces an acquaintance to which it delegates messages. Scope inheritance occurs when a prototype changes its behavior, implicitly affecting all the objects that delegate to it. Modification of a prototype is analogous to modifying a class in a class-based language, but requires no changes to the inheriting instances.

To illustrate that dynamic inheritance is not limited to prototypical objects, let us consider a new mechanism called *dynamic subclassing*. Suppose we have an instance of a *ComplexNumber*, and we want to display it. Unfortunately it does not have a *display* method. What we really want is an instance of *GraphicComplexNumber*. With dynamic subclassing, we would temporarily repackage the original *ComplexNumber* as a *GraphicComplexNumber*, perform the *display* operation, and then discard the shell. Although dynamic subclassing is not supported by any object-oriented language, it can easily be simulated by implementing a *GraphicComplexNumber* as an object containing the identifier of a *ComplexNumber*, and delegating all messages other than *display*. When we enter the scope in which we want to display the object, we create a new *GraphicComplexNumber* initialized to point to the old *ComplexNumber*, and simply release it when we are done. (The point of dynamic subclassing is to be able to provide a standard mechanism for extending the behavior of objects at run time in a way that is independent of the application that uses it: the new *display* operation can be added to any *ComplexNumber* anywhere.)

**Polymorphism and Overloading**   A polymorphic function is one that can be applied uniformly to a variety of objects. For example, the same notation may be used to add two integers, two floating-point numbers, or an integer and a float. Similarly, the addition function for a programmer-defined complex number type may also be able to cope with the addition of complex numbers to integers or floats, provided that the handling of these combinations is defined. In these cases the "same" operation maintains its behavior transparently for different argument types.

On the other hand, the operation *open* may apply to both data streams and windows. Here we are concerned with two operations that coincidentally share a name, and otherwise have completely different behavior. This is *ad hoc* polymorphism, or "mere" overloading of operation names [Cardelli and Wegner 1985]. This kind of polymorphism is useful, but can lead to unpleasantness if abused. It is up to programmers to choose meaningful names for operations, and to avoid reusing names that can be misinterpreted.

Class inheritance is closely related to polymorphism. The same operations that apply to instances of a parent class also apply to instances of its subclasses. Of course, it is possible to have support for polymorphism without class inheritance. In Unix, for example, the paradigm of a file (or data stream) is omnipresent: the operations *open*, *read*, *write*, and *close* apply polymorphically to any "stream" object. In each case different methods are used to implement these operations. In an object-oriented Unix, every stream object class would inherit methods from a generic stream class, and would tailor those specific to the new kind of stream.

Polymorphism enhances software reusability by making it possible to implement generic software that will work not only for a range of existing objects, but also for objects to be added later. A *Sorter* will sort any list of objects that support a comparison operator, just as software written for Unix streams will continue to work if we add a new kind of stream object.

Polymorphism may or may not impose a run time overhead, depending on whether *dynamic binding* is permitted by the programming language. If all objects are statically bound to variables, we can determine the methods to be executed at compile time. For example, the addition of an integer expression to a floating-point expression is normally detected by the compiler, which then generates the appropriate code for that kind of addition. In this case polymorphism is little more than a syntactic convenience. On the other hand, if variables can be dynamically bound to instances of different object classes, some form of *run-time method lookup* must be performed. In Smalltalk, for example, it may be necessary to search through the class hierarchy at run time to find the method of an inherited operation. The cost of dynamic binding can be much lower, of course, with the result that there will be more work involved when modifying a method inherited by many subclasses. In both Simula and C++, the designer of an object class may decide that dynamic binding is to be permitted, and thus declare certain operations as *virtual functions*. Subclasses can specify implementations of virtual functions, and invocation of these functions on instances will be resolved at run time on the basis of the class to which the instance belongs.

**Generic Classes**    Whereas the mechanism of class inheritance achieves software reusability by factoring out common properties of classes in parent classes, generic object classes do so by partially describing a class and parameterizing the unknowns. (For a good discussion of the relationship between inheritance and genericity in a strongly-typed setting, see [Meyer 1986].) These parameters are typically the classes of objects that instances of the generic classes will manipulate. There are basically two categories of generic object: homogeneous "container" objects, like arrays and lists, that operate on any kind of object, and "tool" objects, like sorters and editors, that can operate only on certain object classes.

In the case of tool objects, the parameter must be constrained to indicate the required parent class of the parameter. A generic sorter, for example, could sort only objects with a comparison operator, that is, instances of some subclass of the class *TotallyOrdered*. The sorter object can then exploit polymorphism to apply uniformly to all objects that satisfy the constraint. This idea of constrained parameters works well in a typed object-oriented language, as we shall see shortly.

Even when the parameter is not important for the generic object itself, it can be useful for maintaining homogeneous collections. A *List* object, for example, may be capable of storing any kind of object, but when it is used by the *Sorter* object, it is important to guarantee that only *TotallyOrdered* objects are inserted in the list.

Depending on the nature of the parameters, it may or may not be possible to compile generic classes before the parameters are bound. For example, the code for a *List* object could be precompiled if implemented using pointers to the elements, but the *Sorter* object might need to bind the comparison operator statically in order to achieve reasonable performance. In the latter case, a generic class is similar to a macro.

## 1.1.2 Object Types

An *object type* is superficially the same thing as an object class. The difference is that when we manipulate typed objects, we would like to verify statically that we are doing so in a consistent fashion. With static type-checking we can eliminate the need for objects to protect themselves from unexpected messages.

Languages like Clu [Liskov and Guttag 1986] and Ada [ANSI 1983] support the definition of *abstract data types* but provide no mechanisms for class inheritance. In other words, there are languages that are legitimately "object-oriented" (i.e., oriented toward programming in terms of objects), yet support a very different style of programming from that encouraged by languages like Smalltalk or LISP with flavors. More recently several attempts have been made to unify object classes and object types. Languages like C++, Trellis/Owl, and Eiffel are object-oriented in the Smalltalk sense as well as being strongly-typed.

The traditional approach to type-checking in languages with user-defined object types is to insist that the types of expressions supplied to operation invocations and to assignments must correspond exactly to the expected type. In object-oriented languages with polymorphic operations and dynamic binding, we must cope with the fact that some types may be equivalent to others, or included in other types. In this case, the declared types of variables and of arguments to operations serve as *specifications* for valid bindings and invocations. Informally, one type *conforms* to a second if some subset of its interface is identical to that of the second. We also say that the first is a *subtype* of the second. They are *equivalent* if they conform to one another. What constitutes the interface of an object type depends on the particular type model chosen for a language, but normally includes operation names and the types of the arguments and return values. These issues are discussed in detail in the context of functional programming languages in [Cardelli and Wegner 1985].

We can more clearly interpret the difference between object classes and object types if we view the latter purely as specifications. In the presence of dynamic binding it is (in general) impossible to determine statically the class of a variable, but with the appropriate type rules we can still perform type-checking. For example, if we consider the expression:

$$x \leftarrow y + z$$

then we can statically determine whether this expression is type-correct, without knowing the classes of the instances to which $x$, $y$, and $z$ will be bound (they may change). First, we examine the declared type of $y$ and see whether it supports the operator $+$. If so, we check whether the type of $z$ is valid for an argument. Then, the type information of $y$ will tell us the type of $y + z$ (but not its class). If this type conforms to the type of $x$ (i.e., if $y + z$ supports *at least* the interface required by $x$), then the expression is type-correct.

Many variations on this basic scheme are possible. If dynamic binding is not supported then an object type will always uniquely determine an object class. For primitive objects (like integers) one may also insist on information about the representation of instances. At the opposite extreme, in an "untyped" object world all objects have the same type, *object*, and will accept any message, though their responses may be unpredictable.

Note that class hierarchies are *not* the same as type hierarchies, although they may overlap. Two classes may be equivalent as types, although neither inherits anything from the other.

Type information can be extremely useful for generic object classes. For example, our generic *Sorter* object will be able to sort only *TotallyOrdered* classes. This constraint is in fact a type constraint, since we do not care what class the objects to be sorted belong to, only whether a total order is defined. Our programming language should then verify that whenever a *Sorter* is instantiated, the type parameter is bound to an object class that satisfies the constraint, e.g.:

**var** s : Sorter of integer ;

where the class *integer* conforms to the type *TotallyOrdered*.


### 1.1.3 Concurrency

There are two ways in which programming languages have traditionally dealt with concurrency and communication:

1. Active entities (processes) communicate indirectly through shared passive objects.

2. Active entities communicate directly with one another by message passing.

The first approach is typical of languages like Modula-2 [Wirth 1983], whereas the second is adopted by, for example, Thoth [Gentleman 1981] and various Actor languages [Agha 1986]. (See [Andrews and Schneider 1983] for an excellent survey of concurrent programming languages and notations.) These same approaches are used in object-oriented programming languages in order to structure concurrent applications, although they result in different object models.

If we adopt the first approach, it is quite natural to structure the shared memory as a collection of passive objects and to view a process as a special kind of active *Process* object. We require that actions on the passive objects be performed according to their declared interface. For this approach to work, we must have some mechanism whereby the active objects may synchronize their accesses to the shared objects. This may be through the use of semaphores or locks as in Smalltalk and Trellis/Owl [Moss and Kohler 1987], or through the use of monitors (as in Modula-2) or transactions as in Avance (formerly OPAL) [Ahlsen et al. 1985]. This approach is necessarily nonhomogeneous, that is, the object model contains two fundamentally different kinds of objects:

active and passive. Furthermore, it is not possible to interact directly with the active objects, at least not by the same paradigms for interaction that apply to passive objects; two active objects can communicate only through a passive intermediary. Finally, it is not possible to extend this model to a distributed environment without employing some form of hidden message passing. This suggests that the second approach is in some sense more general.

Considering the second approach, we permit any object to communicate with any other object. Objects become "active" in response to a communication. In effect, threads of control are determined implicitly by message passing, whereas in the first approach each thread of control was localized in an explicit *Process* object. Explicit synchronization is not required since message passing packages both communication and synchronization, but we must make a choice as to what style of message passing to adopt. For example, message passing may be synchronous as in POOL-T [America 1987] or buffered, as between top-level objects in Hybrid [Nierstrasz 1987]. Similarly, we may permit unidirectional message passing as in Act-1 [Lieberman 1987], or we may insist on a *call/return* protocol as in Hybrid and ConcurrentSmalltalk [Yokote and Tokoro 1986]. We may also find it useful to provide an *express* mode of message passing for interrupting active objects as in ABCL/1 [Yonezawa et al. 1986].

In either case, it is possible to accommodate the various reusability mechanisms we have discussed as well as an extendible type system. With the message-passing model we interpret strong-typing to mean that a message-passing expression is type-correct if the message being sent is guaranteed to be valid for the recipient. Similarly, we can support an untyped view, if all objects are prepared to handle any message sent to them. Run-time support for concurrent applications can be quite different for these two object models, as we shall see in the following section. For a more detailed look at approaches to concurrency in object-oriented languages, see [Tomlinson and Scheevel 1988] in this book.

## 1.2 OBJECT-ORIENTED SYSTEMS

Our discussion thus far has focused on object-oriented programming language constructs and mechanisms, without consideration for run-time support for objects, or for tools to aid programmers in constructing object-oriented applications. In this section we shall provide a brief overview of two important kinds of object-oriented system: those that provide run-time support for object-oriented applications, and those that form an environment for object-oriented software development.

### 1.2.1 Object Management

Object management refers to a mixed bag of run-time issues such as object-naming, persistence, concurrency, distribution, version control, and security.

The amount of support provided or required depends very much on the intended application domain. At the low end we have single-user, single-thread applications with minimal persistence requirements, and at the high end we have distributed, concurrent, multiuser applications with support for evolving software. In either case objects reside in a "workspace" that may be local and private, or distributed and shared.

Minimal object management support is provided for C++ objects. Objects may be allocated and freed in virtual memory. Memory addresses serve as object identifiers. There is no support for garbage collection, persistence, concurrency, or distribution. The result is a very lean language and object environment that imposes very little run-time overhead for objects, without preventing the programmer from defining various extensions (for persistence, concurrency, etc.).

Smalltalk and LISP additionally provide for automatic garbage collection, and implement a trivial form of persistence by permitting users to save the (single-user) object workspace. Since there is no provision for communication between objects in different workspaces, there is no need to worry about maintaining global consistency in a distributed environment. Persistence for distributed object applications must cope with the possibility of local failures: if a message sent between workspaces is lost, or if either the sender or receiver is accidentally destroyed, then we risk a global inconsistency. Means for dealing with these problems are suggested by two traditional fields: operating systems and database systems.

An object-oriented operating system may provide support for persistence, resilience, reliable communication, or distributed object-naming at a low level. For example, Chorus [Zimmermann et al. 1984] and Mach [Jones and Rashid 1986] provide kernel support for distributed object-oriented systems. Argus is a programming language with operating system support for persistence, encapsulation, and distribution through the concept of *guardians* [Liskov and Scheifler 1983]. LOOM provides a large object-oriented memory for Smalltalk systems [Krasner 1983].

Most of the object management issues we have mentioned are addressed in some way by traditional database technology. It is therefore natural to try to see whether this technology can be transferred to the problem of managing objects. An *object-oriented database* is therefore a system that provides database-like support (for persistence, transactions, querying, etc.) for *objects*, that is, encapsulated data and operations. Some examples are the GemStone system from Servio Logic [Maier et al. 1986; Purdy et al. 1987], ORION from MCC [Banerjee et al. 1987a], and Iris from Hewlett-Packard Labs [Derrett et al. 1985; Fishman et al. 1987].

Although object-oriented databases are being built and have clearly practical applications, there are several open problems in this area. First, there is no agreement as to a standard data model for object-oriented databases. We do not have the equivalent of relational algebra for an object-oriented data model, and we therefore have no standard guidelines for designing object-oriented databases. This is to be expected, since we have no corresponding agreement as to what mechanisms belong in an object-oriented programming language, or what the rules for encapsulation or inheritance should be. For this reason it is also difficult to decide on a standard query language for objects. Should we be permitted to query on attributes (i.e., instance variables), and if so, how does that square with the principle of encapsulation? (With typical applications for which object-oriented databases have been designed, like CAD/CAM, querying on attributes may be precisely what we want to do, but what about other application domains?) Finally, should we consider object-oriented databases as providing a complete picture of executing applications, or are they better seen as repositories for persistent objects? In particular, can we view active objects as executing *within* the database (as they do inside a Smalltalk workspace) or should we adopt a more traditional database view in which running applications (i.e., threads) are explicitly *outside* the database?

### 1.2.2 Object-Oriented Programming Environments

Another significant category of object-oriented systems is that of tools and environments for application development. Object-oriented programming promises a great deal in terms of easing the cost of building applications; our ability to realize this promise depends largely on whether objects are truly reusable. This implies that we need not only powerful mechanisms and paradigms for reusability (such as those provided by object-oriented languages), but tools to help us design objects, to select and reuse objects, and to manage an evolving software base.

Object design is a software engineering issue: how should we decompose our application into objects in such a way as to best exploit the object-oriented paradigms available to us? This task can be supported to some extent by applying conceptual modeling techniques from the database area to object design. An example of such an approach is described in [Loomis et al. 1987]. See also [Diederich and Milton 1988] in this book.

The next major problem is that of selecting objects from the software base that may be useful for building your application (ideally this would be carried out in tandem with the design task). Here a programmer would normally rely on three things: personal expertise, software documentation, and *browsing* tools. Smalltalk, Trellis [O'Brien et al. 1987], and Cedar [Swinehart et al. 1986] are examples of programming environments that provide tools for browsing the available software base. The real difficulty is that human expertise cannot realistically cope with a large, evolving software base. Perhaps one can manage to remember the 300 fundamental Smalltalk object classes, or even a couple of thousand generally useful object classes, but how are we to cope with tens of thousands of object classes, perhaps available from different vendors? The object selection problem is similar to that of performing a literature search. We depend heavily on services to classify objects and to maintain cross-references in the face of updates.

Finally, an object-oriented programming environment must cope with evolution of the software base. There are two ways in which it can do so. The first is by providing software management tools that maintain global consistency. When changes are made to the software base, it is important to ensure that these changes are properly distributed. The problem of managing software evolution in object-oriented systems is especially interesting in the face of class inheritance and subtyping [Skarra and Zdonik 1986]. As long as the interface to an object class is not modified, we have considerable freedom in modifying its realization. When the interface is changed, however, we fall into a snake pit of invalidated references between object classes.

The second problem with evolution is essentially Darwinian: how do we encourage "survival of the fittest"? If prototyping and application development are really much easier with a well-designed software base, how do we make sure that the right objects end up there? This suggests that we should take more of a long range view of application development: whenever we can't find the objects we need to solve our problem in the software base, either we need new objects, or we need to modify old ones. What we do not know is how to make sure that the new objects not only will solve our problem, but will also give us a "better" software base.

## SUMMARY

We have put forward the proposition that the term *object-oriented* is best interpreted as referring to any approach that exploits encapsulation or "packaging" in the process of designing and building software. With this premise in mind, we have surveyed object-oriented techniques in programming languages to enhance software reusability, to enhance maintainability and robustness through extendible type systems, and to ease the development of concurrent and distributed applications. We have also given a brief overview of the issues in providing run-time support for objects, and in providing programming environments for the development of object-oriented software.

We have not discussed other applications of object-oriented concepts, for example, in the area of user interfaces. (Direct manipulation interfaces provide the user with the illusion that the objects of the application are being "directly" manipulated by a set of polymorphic operators: move, copy, delete, resize, etc.)

Object-oriented languages and systems are a developing technology. There can be no agreement on the set of features and mechanisms that belong in an object-oriented language, since the paradigm is far too general to be tied down. (What features belong in a declarative language?) The idea of using objects to model software is a natural one that will inevitably appear and reappear in various forms; we can expect to see new ideas in object-oriented systems for many years to come.

## REFERENCES

[ANSI 1983] American National Standards Institute, Inc., *The Programming Language Ada Reference Manual*, Lecture Notes in Computer Science 155, Springer-Verlag, New York, 1983.

[Agha 1987] G.A. Agha, *ACTORS: A Model of Concurrent Computation in Distributed Systems*, The MIT Press, Cambridge, MA, 1987.

[Ahlsen et al. 1985] M. Ahlsen, A. Björnerstedt, and C. Hultén, "OPAL: An Object-Based System for Application Development," *IEEE Database Engineering*, vol. 8, no. 4, pp. 31–40, 1985.

[America 1987] P. America, "POOL-T: A Parallel Object-Oriented Language," in *Object-Oriented Concurrent Programming*, ed. A. Yonezawa and M. Tokoro, pp. 199–220, The MIT Press, Cambridge, MA, 1987.

[Andrews and Schneider 1983] G.R. Andrews and F.B. Schneider, "Concepts and Notations for Concurrent Programming," *ACM Computing Surveys*, vol. 15, no. 1, pp. 3–43, 1983.

[Banerjee et al. 1987a] J. Banerjee, H. Chou, J.F. Garza, W. Kim, D. Woelk, N. Ballou, and H. Kim, "Data Model Issues for Object-Oriented Applications," *ACM Transactions on Office Information Systems*, vol. 5, no. 1, pp. 3–26, 1987.

[Banerjee et al. 1987b] J. Banerjee, W. Kim, H.-J. Kim, and H.F. Korth, "Semantics and Implementation of Schema Evolution in Object-Oriented Databases," *Proceedings of the ACM SIGMOD '87*, vol. 16, no. 3, pp. 311–322, 1987.

[Birtwistle et al. 1973] G. Birtwistle, O. Dahl, B. Myhrtag, and K. Nygaard, *Simula Begin*, Auerbach Press, Philadelphia, 1973.

[Cardelli and Wegner 1985] L. Cardelli and P. Wegner, "On Understanding Types, Data Abstraction, and Polymorphism," *ACM Computing Surveys*, vol. 17, no. 4, pp. 471–522, 1985.

[Casais 1988] E. Casais, "An Object-Oriented System Implementing KNOs," *Proceedings of the Conference on Office Information Systems (COIS)*, pp. 284–290, Palo Alto, March 1988.

[Curry et al. 1982] G. Curry, L. Baer, D. Lipkie, and B. Lee, "TRAITS: An Approach for Multiple Inheritance Subclassing," *Proceedings of the ACM SIGOA, SIGOA Newsletter*, vol. 3, no. 12, 1982.

[Derrett et al. 1985] N. Derrett, W. Kent, and P. Lyngbaek, "Some Aspects of Operations in an Object-Oriented Database," *IEEE Database Engineering*, vol. 8, no. 4, pp. 66–74, 1985.

[Diederich and Milton 1988] J. Diederich and J. Milton, "Objects, Messages, and Rules in Database Design," in *Object-Oriented Concepts, Applications, and Databases,* ed. W. Kim and F. Lochovsky, Addison-Wesley, Reading, MA, 1988.

[Fishman et al. 1987] D.H. Fishman, D. Beech, H.P. Cate, E.C. Chow, T. Connors, J.W. Davis, N. Derrett, C.G. Hoch, W. Kent, P. Lyngbaek, B. Mahbod, M.A. Neimat, T.A. Ryan, and M.C. Shan, "Iris: An Object-Oriented Database Management System," *ACM Transactions on Office Information Systems,* vol. 5, no. 1, pp. 48–69, 1987.

[Gentleman 1981] W.M. Gentleman, "Message Passing Between Sequential Processes: The Reply Primitive and the Administrator Concept," *Software—Practice and Experience,* vol. 11, pp. 435–466, 1981.

[Goldberg and Robson 1983] A. Goldberg and D. Robson, *Smaltalk-80: The Language and its Implementation,* Addison-Wesley, Reading, MA, 1983.

[Jones and Rashid 1986] M.B. Jones and R.F. Rashid, "Mach and Matchmaker: Kernel and Language Support for Object-Oriented Distributed Systems," *Proceedings of the First ACM Conference on Object-Oriented Programming Systems, Languages and Applications, SIGPLAN Notices,* vol. 21, no. 11, pp. 67–77, 1986.

[Krasner 1983] G. Krasner, *Smalltalk-80: Bits of History, Words of Advice,* Addison-Wesley, Reading, MA, 1983.

[Lieberman 1986] H. Lieberman, "Using Prototypical Objects to Implement Shared Behavior in Object-Oriented Systems," *Proceedings of the First ACM Conference on Object-Oriented Programming Systems, Languages and Applications, SIGPLAN Notices,* vol. 21, no. 9, pp. 214–223, 1986.

[Lieberman 1987] H. Lieberman, "Concurrent Object-Oriented Programming in Act 1," in *Object-Oriented Concurrent Programming,* ed. A. Yonezawa and M. Tokoro, pp. 9–36, The MIT Press, Cambridge, MA, 1987.

[Liskov and Scheifler 1983] B. Liskov and R. Scheifler, "Guardians and Actions: Linguistic Support for Robust, Distributed Programs," *ACM Transactions on Programming Languages and Systems,* vol. 5, no. 3, pp. 381–404, 1983.

[Liskov and Guttag 1986] B. Liskov and J. Guttag, *Abstraction and Specification in Program Development,* The MIT Press, Cambridge, MA, 1986.

[Loomis et al. 1987] M.E.S. Loomis, A.V. Shah, and J.E. Rumbaugh, "An Object Modeling Technique for Conceptual Design," *Proceedings of the European Conference on Object-Oriented Programming,* pp. 325–335, Paris, France, 1987.

[Maier et al. 1986] D. Maier, J. Stein, A. Otis, and A. Purdy, "Development of an Object-Oriented DBMS," *Proceedings of the First ACM Conference on Object-Oriented Programming Systems, Languages and Applications, SIGPLAN Notices,* vol. 21, no. 11, pp. 472–482, 1986.

[Meyer 1986] B. Meyer, "Genericity versus Inheritance," *Proceedings of the First ACM Conference on Object-Oriented Programming Systems, Languages and Applications, SIGPLAN Notices,* vol. 21, no. 11, pp. 391–405, 1986.

[Moon 1986] D.A. Moon, "Object-Oriented Programming with Flavors," *Proceedings of the First ACM Conference on Object-Oriented Programming Systems, Languages and Applications, SIGPLAN Notices,* vol. 21, no. 11, pp. 1–8, 1986.

[Moss and Kohler 1987] J.E.B. Moss and W.H. Kohler, "Concurrency Features for the Trellis/Owl Language," *Proceedings of the European Conference on Object-Oriented Programming,* pp. 223–232, Paris, France, 1987.

[Nierstrasz 1987] O.M. Nierstrasz, "Active Objects in Hybrid," *Proceedings of the Second ACM Conference on Object-Oriented Programming Systems, Languages and Applications, SIGPLAN Notices,* vol. 22, no. 12, pp. 243–253, 1987.

[O'Brien et al. 1987] P.D. O'Brien, D.C. Halbert, and M.F. Kilian, "The Trellis Programming Environment," *Proceedings of the Second ACM Conference on Object-Oriented Programming Systems, Languages and Applications, SIGPLAN Notices,* vol. 22, no. 12, pp. 91–102, 1987.

[Purdy et al. 1987] A. Purdy, B. Schuchardt, and D. Maier, "Integrating an Object-Server with Other Worlds," *ACM Transactions on Office Information Systems,* vol. 5, no. 1, pp. 27–47, 1987.

[Russinoff 1988] D. Russinoff, "Proteus: A Frame-Based Nonmonotonic Inference System," in *Object-Oriented Concepts, Applications, and Databases,* ed. W. Kim and F. Lochovsky, Addison-Wesley, Reading, MA, 1988.

[Schaffert et al. 1986] C. Schaffert, T. Cooper, B. Bullis, M. Killian, and C. Wilpolt, "An Introduction to Trellis/Owl," *Proceedings of the First ACM Conference on Object-Oriented Programming Systems, Languages and Applications, SIGPLAN Notices,* vol. 21, no. 11, pp. 9–16, 1986.

[Skarra and Zdonik 1986] A.H. Skarra and S.B. Zdonik, "The Management of Changing Types in an Object-Oriented Database," *Proceedings of the First ACM Conference on Object-Oriented Programming Systems, Languages and Applications, SIGPLAN Notices,* vol. 21, no. 11, pp. 483–495, 1986.

[Snyder 1986a] A. Snyder, "CommonObjects: An Overview," *ACM SIGPLAN Notices,* vol. 21, no. 10, pp. 19–28, 1986.

[Snyder 1986b] A. Snyder, "Encapsulation and Inheritance in Object-Oriented Programming Languages," *Proceedings of the First ACM Conference on Object-Oriented Programming Systems, Languages and Applications, SIGPLAN Notices,* vol. 21, no. 11, pp. 38–45, 1986.

[Stroustrup 1986] B. Stroustrup, *The C++ Programming Language,* Addison-Wesley, Reading, MA, 1986.

[Swinehart et al. 1986] D. Swinehart, P. Zwellweger, and R. Beach, "A Structural View of the Cedar Programming Environment," *ACM Transactions on Programming Languages and Systems,* vol. 8, no. 4, pp. 419–490, 1986.

[Tomlinson and Scheevel 1988] C. Tomlinson and M. Scheevel, "Concurrent Object-Oriented Programming Languages," in *Object-Oriented Concepts, Databases, and Applications,* ed. W. Kim and F. Lochovsky, Addison-Wesley, Reading, MA, 1988.

[Tsichritzis et al. 1987] D.C. Tsichritzis, E. Fiume, S. Gibbs, and O.M. Nierstrasz, "KNOs: Knowledge Acquisition, Dissemination and Manipulation Objects," *ACM Transactions on Office Information Systems,* vol. 5, no. 1, pp. 96–112, 1987.

[Wirth 1983] N. Wirth, *Programming in Modula-2,* Springer-Verlag, Berlin, 1983.

[Yokote and Tokoro 1986] Y. Yokote and M. Tokoro, "The Design and Implementation of ConcurrentSmalltalk," *Proceedings of the First ACM Conference on Object-Oriented Programming Systems, Languages and Applications, SIGPLAN Notices,* vol. 21, no. 11, pp. 331–340, 1986.

[Yonezawa et al. 1986] A. Yonezawa, J.-P. Briot, and E. Shibayama, "Object-Oriented Concurrent Programming in ABCL/1," *Proceedings of the First ACM Conference on Object-Oriented Programming Systems, Languages and Applications, SIGPLAN Notices,* vol. 21, no. 11, pp. 258–268, 1986.

[Zimmerman et al. 1984] H. Zimmermann, M. Guillemont, G. Morisset, and J. Banino, "Chorus: A Communication and Processing Architecture for Distributed Systems," *Research Report No. 328, INRIA,* Rocquencourt, September 1984.

# 2

---

# My Cat Is Object-Oriented

Roger King

## INTRODUCTION

It's exciting to see religious fervor grip one's subdiscipline. It improves attendance at conferences, attracts consulting jobs, and increases the flow of research dollars. Indeed, object-oriented databases are a big thing. (At least they were when this was written.) And it couldn't have come at a better time. Just when we thought we'd all have to become AI people, database folks hit the big time.

It's interesting to note, however, that there is considerable disagreement concerning the definition of "object-oriented." We know it's a good thing, but not everyone agrees on what it is. In this chapter, we will not attempt to resolve this issue. We will simply provide a brief tutorial explaining the difference between object-oriented and so-called "semantic" data models. We will not try to define the two sorts of models thoroughly, but will provide references to the reader who might be unfamiliar with the literature.

This work was supported by ONR under contract number N00014-86-K-0054, and by Martin-Marietta under contract number 19X-CN981V (through DOE contract number DE-AC05-840R21400).

## 2.1 TRASH

I have a cat named Trash. In the current political climate, it would seem that if I were trying to sell him (at least to a Computer Scientist), I would not stress that he is gentle to humans and is self-sufficient, living mostly on field mice. Rather, I would argue that he is object-oriented.

What's interesting is that this sort of false advertising is currently common in the database research community. Obviously, it takes time to iron out common terms, and we shouldn't overreact to terminology differences. But the problem is that database researchers have recently begun to refine what they mean by object-oriented. As a result, certain research projects that have been advertised as being about object-oriented systems would fit more naturally in an existing, reasonably well defined category—semantic modeling. Indeed, after being asked to write a brief chapter on this topic, I have to admit that one example of this is [King 1986].

Here, in a nutshell, is the important distinction: Semantic models attempt to provide *structural abstractions* [Hull and King 1988; King and McLeod 1985] while object-oriented models are geared toward *behavioral abstractions* [Maier et al. 1986]. Semantic models grew out of the same sorts of concerns that drove researchers in AI Knowledge Representation [Atzeni and Parker 1986; Findler 1979; Israel and Brachman 1984; Mylopoulos 1980], and object-oriented models were inspired by advances in programming languages [Bobrow et al. 1986; Moon 1986]. In other words, semantic models are oriented toward the representation of data, while object-oriented languages are concerned with the manipulation of data.

A few prominent semantic models are the Binary model [Abrial 1974], the Entity-Relationship model [Chen 1976], the Semantic Data Model [Hammer and McLeod 1981], and the Functional model [Kerschberg and Pacheco 1976]. The database implementation described in [Maier et al. 1986] is adapted from what is perhaps the best known object-oriented programming language, Smalltalk [Goldberg and Robson 1983].

Essentially, semantic models provide constructors for creating complex types, while behavioral issues are often left undefined. In contrast, object-oriented models take an abstract data type approach of embedding operations (called "methods" in object-oriented languages) within types [Guttag 1977; Liskov et al. 1977]. In this way, an object is in control of its own behavior; it is sent "messages" to execute its methods, and may interpret these messages in any way it chooses. Some researchers do refer to semantic models as being "object-oriented," in order to stress that they provide mechanisms for structuring complex objects. So, the distinction between the two sorts of modeling is not always well defined. Further, a few experimental database systems attempt to provide both sorts of abstractions.

In fact, the synergy between these two points of view is impressive. Together they provide compatible ways of encapsulating both the structural and the behavioral aspects of complex objects. Consider, for example, software environments, an application that many feel is not properly supported by conventional DBMSs. This is due to the complex objects and behavioral capabilities that must be modeled [Bernstein 1987; Dittrich et al. 1986; Hudson and King 1988; Hudson and King in press; Penedo 1986]. A semantic model provides type constructors that may be used to represent software objects.

A small software environment schema is described in Fig. 2.1, using a graphical notation similar to that introduced for the IFO model [Abiteboul and Hull 1987]. A Source_Module might be a composite object, formed from three components with the names Name, Change_Date, and Text (representing the text of the source). This is typically called an *aggregation* [Smith and Smith 1977]. The text itself may be an aggregation made up of components called Variable_Declarations, Procedure_Declarations, and Sub_Modules (which are also of type Source_Module). The Change_Date may actually be a set of dates, representing the update history of the module. Such a set-valued property is called a *grouping* [Smith and Smith 1977]. (In the figure, a circled asterisk refers to grouping; a circled X refers to aggregation. The components of a grouping or an aggregation are shown with dotted arrows.)

An object of type Source_Module may also have a named property called Load, which associates it with its corresponding load module. This is typically called a *relationship* or an *attribute* (shown with a box in Fig. 2.1). We see that Change_Date of Source_Module could have been defined with a relationship that allowed multiple values, rather than with a grouping construct. Sometimes a fine distinction is made, and attributes are considered special sorts of relationships, ones in which the values are atomic and not themselves

**FIGURE 2.1** A SEMANTIC SCHEMA.

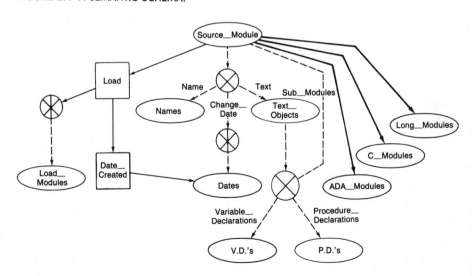

made up of parts. Also, some semantic models allow relationships (and not attributes) to have attributes of their own, just like objects. For example, the relationship Load may have an attribute called Date_Created, indicating the day the load module was created from the particular source module. (For the remainder of this chapter, the words attribute and relationship will be used interchangeably.)

Simply put, then, an aggregation defines the components that are required to make up an object, and a relationship defines a property of an object. If the identity of the objector objects which make up a piece of an aggregation is changed, the aggregate object changes identity, and it is now a different object. Thus, if different instances of Text_Objects are assigned to the aggregation component Text of a Source_Module object, the source module is no longer the same object. This is not true if only the value of a relationship changes. For example, the Load relationship of a Source_Module object can change (presumably by recreating and reloading the object module), and the source module does not change identity.

It is noteworthy that aggregation, grouping, and relationships/attribute connections may be used recursively. This provides a powerful capability for constructing types. For example, like components of aggregations, the values of attributes and relationships may be groupings. Also, the Load_Module object associated with a specific Source_Module might actually be a set of objects of type Load_Modules, each prepared with a different compiler and loader configuration. For more details on the recursive application of aggregation and grouping, see [Abiteboul and Hull 1987; Hull and King 1988].

An important distinction between semantic and object-oriented models is that although both support relationships (in object-oriented models these are called "instance variables"), only semantic models typically support an explicit aggregation construct. Thus, in an object-oriented model one must generally simulate an aggregation with a set of relationships. This means that the constraint that changing the identity component of an aggregation changes the identity of the aggregate object must be enforced externally.

It also means that we cannot distinguish relationships of aggregations from the aggregation components themselves. For example, in Fig. 2.1, the aggregation Source_Module has a relationship called Load. Presumably, the reason it is not part of the aggregation is that recreating the load module does not imply a change in the identity of the source module. If we were simulating the aggregation with relationships, we would not easily be able to group together the Name, Change_Date, and Text of a Source_Module, and differentiate them structurally from the Load relationship. A further complication is that certain constraints are difficult to represent, such as indicating that a given text object can participate in only one Source_Module aggregation.

It should also be noted that, unlike relationships of semantic models, instance variables in object-oriented languages are not always strongly typed. This is true in Smalltalk [Goldberg and Robson 1983], but strong typing exists in Emerald [Black et al. 1986; Jul et al. 1988] and Trellis/Owl [O'Brien et al. 1986]. Further, in some object-oriented models, the instance variables of an object may be referenced only by methods of that object [Stefik and Bobrow 1986], whereas the data languages of semantic models typically allow general access to the aggregation components and relationships of an object.

Now consider the fact that we always want a load module to be up to date. That means that if a source module changes, we want to recompile or relink. We might also want to do a recursive search of all submodules, and perform the update if any of them has changed. Software systems that perform this sort of task have been developed. A prominent one is called Make [Feldman 1979]. To provide this mechanism in an object-oriented paradigm, we could define a method called Update_Load within the type Load_Modules. If an instance of type Source_Module changes, or if the source of any of its submodules changes, the application could send a message to the source module, allowing it to respond using Update_Load. We see that semantic and object-oriented modeling together provide an elegant way of abstracting both the structural and behavioral complexity of software modules.

Besides the distinction between structural and behavioral capabilities, there is another central difference between object-oriented and semantic data models. This has to do with subtypes and the notion of inheritance. Most semantic and object-oriented models allow the user to break types into subtypes. (Often the association of a subtype with its parent type is called an ISA relationship.) There might be three kinds of modules: ADA_Modules, C_Modules, and Long_Modules (shown with heavy arrows in Fig. 2.1). Notice that the subtype containing long modules probably overlaps with both of the other subtypes. Thus, it is not necessarily true that subtypes must partition a parent type, although different semantic models have experimented with various rules concerning the overlapping of subtypes.

In a semantic model, aggregations and attributes/relationships are "inherited" down subtype trees. ADA modules would therefore be made up of the same components and would have the same attributes as modules in general. They might also have other, new attributes that define properties specific to ADA modules. In object-oriented models, properties are also inherited, but importantly, so are methods.

In some semantic and object-oriented models, a subtype may have more than one parent. The type that represents long ADA modules would be a subtype of both ADA_Modules and Long_Modules. (In fact, it would presumably be the intersection of the two types.) It would therefore inherit the structure (the aggregations) and properties (the relationships) of both parent types. This is called multiple inheritance [Snyder 1986], and it can cause some problems when both parents have aggregation components or attributes with the same names. It is also true that methods may be inherited from multiple types. An object of type Documents may inherit the Display_Me method from Source_Modules, as well as a method that formats it on the screen from a type called Formatted_Text.

## 2.2 SORRY, TRASH

We may not be able to agree on the exact definition of object-oriented modeling. But I hope that this brief tutorial has served to make one important distinction. So, semantic models and my cat will have to find another road to fame.

---

## SUMMARY

Semantic models focus on the recursive definition of complex objects, and on the inheritance of structural components (aggregations) and relationships. Object-oriented models focus on the definition and inheritance of behavioral capabilities, in the form of operations embedded within types, and also support simpler capabilities for structuring complex objects. But this distinction is not as sharp as it might seem. A few database research projects effectively encompass both sorts of models. A prominent example system is described in Chapter 11. Clearly, the trend is for database researchers to view object-oriented models as having both structural and behavioral encapsulation facilities.

## ACKNOWLEDGEMENTS

I would like to thank Charles McKay, Jonathon Bein, Dean Jacobs, Richard Hull, and in particular Jeff Haemer for a few very informative conversations. Won Kim's comments on an earlier draft of this chapter were particularly enlightening.

## REFERENCES

[Abiteboul and Hull 1987] S. Abiteboul and R. Hull, "IFO: A Formal Semantic Database Model," *ACM Transactions on Database Systems,* vol. 12, no. 4, pp. 525–565, 1987.

[Abrial 1974] J.R. Abrial, "Data Semantics," in *Data Base Management,* North-Holland, Amsterdam, pp. 1–59, 1974.

[Atzeni and Parker 1986] P. Atzeni and D.S. Parker, "Formal Properties of Net-Based Knowledge Representation Schemes," *Proceedings of the Second IEEE International Conference on Data Engineering,* pp. 700–706, February 1986.

[Bernstein 1987] P. Bernstein, "Database System Support for Software Engineering," *Wang Institute of Graduate Studies Technical Report, Tech. Rep.-87-01,* February 1987.

[Black et al. 1986] A. Black, N. Hutchinson, E. Jul, and H. Levy, "Object Structure in the Emerald System," *Proceedings of the First ACM Conference on Object-Oriented Programming Systems, Languages and Applications, SIGPLAN Notices,* vol. 21, no. 11, pp. 78–86, 1986.

[Bobrow et al. 1986] D. Bobrow, K. Kahn, G. Kiczales, L. Masinter, M. Stefik, and F. Zdybel, "CommonLoops: Merging Lisp and Object-Oriented Programming," *Proceedings of the First ACM Conference on Object-Oriented Programming Systems, Languages and Applications, SIGPLAN Notices,* vol. 21, no. 11, pp. 17–29, 1986.

[Chen 1976] P.P. Chen, "The Entity-Relationship Model—Toward a Unified View of Data," *ACM Transactions on Database Systems,* vol. 1, no. 1, pp. 9–36, 1976.

[Dittrich et al. 1986] K.R. Dittrich, W. Gotthard, and P.C. Lockemann, "DAMOKLES—A Database System for Software Engineering Environments," *Proceedings of the International Workshop on Advanced Programming Environments,* Trondheim, Norway, pp. 353–371, June 1986.

[Feldman 1979] S.I. Feldman, "Make—A Program for Maintaining Computer Programs," *Software—Practice and Experience,* vol. 9, pp. 255–265, 1979.

[Findler 1979] N. Findler, ed., *Associative Networks,* Academic Press, New York, 1979.

[Goldberg and Robson 1983] A. Goldberg and D. Robson, *Smalltalk-80: The Language and its Implementation,* Addison-Wesley, Reading, MA, 1983.

[Guttag 1977] J. Guttag, "Abstract Data Types and the Development of Data Structures," *Communications of the ACM,* vol. 20, no. 6, pp. 396–404, 1977.

[Hammer and McLeod 1981] M. Hammer and D. McLeod, "Database Description with SDM: A Semantic Database Model," *ACM Transactions on Database Systems,* vol. 6, no. 3, pp. 351–386, 1981.

[Hudson and King 1988] S. Hudson and R. King, "The Cactis Project: Database Support for Software Engineering," *IEEE Transactions on Software Engineering,* June 1988.

[Hudson and King] S. Hudson and R. King, "Cactis: A Self-Adaptive, Concurrent Implementation of an Object-Oriented Database Management System," *ACM Transactions on Database Systems,* in press.

[Hull and King 1988] R. Hull and R. King, "Semantic Database Modeling: Survey, Applications, and Research Issues," *ACM Computing Surveys,* June 1988.

[Israel and Brachman 1984] D.J. Israel and R.J. Brachman, "Some Remarks on the Semantics of Representation Languages," in *On Conceptual Modelling,* Springer-Verlag, New York, pp. 119–146, 1984.

[Jul et al. 1988] E. Jul, H. Levy, N. Hutchinson, and A. Black, "Fine-Grained Mobility in the Emerald System," *ACM Transactions on Computer Systems,* pp. 109–133, February 1988.

[Kerschberg and Pacheco 1976] L. Kerschberg and J.E.S. Pacheco, "A Functional Data Base Model," *Technical Report, Pontificia Universidade Catolica do Rio de Janeiro,* Rio de Janeiro, Brazil, February 1976.

[King 1986] R. King, "A Database Management System Based on an Object-Oriented Model," in *Expert Database Systems,* ed. L. Kerschberg, pp. 443–468, Benjamin/Cummings, Menlo Park, CA, 1986.

[King and McLeod 1985] R. King and D. McLeod, "Some Database Models," in *Database Design,* pp. 115–150, Springer-Verlag, New York, 1985.

[Liskov et al. 1977] B. Liskov, A. Snyder, R. Atkinson, and C. Schaffert, "Abstraction Mechanisms in CLU," *Communications of the ACM,* vol. 20, no. 8, pp. 564–576, 1977.

[Maier et al. 1986] D. Maier, J. Stein, A. Otis, and A. Purdy, "Development of an Object-Oriented DBMS," *Proceedings of the First ACM Conference on Object-Oriented Programming Systems, Languages and Applications, SIGPLAN Notices,* vol. 21, no. 11, pp. 472–482, 1986.

[Mylopoulos 1980] J. Mylopoulos, "An Overview of Knowledge Representation," *Workshop on Data Abstract, Databases, and Conceptual Modelling,* Pingree Park, CO, pp. 5–12, 1980.

[Moon 1986] D.A. Moon, "Object-Oriented Programming with Flavors," *Proceedings of the First ACM Conference on Object-Oriented Programming Systems, Languages and Applications, SIGPLAN Notices,* vol. 21, no. 11, pp. 1–8, 1986.

[O'Brien et al. 1986] P. O'Brien, B. Bullis, and C. Schaffert, "Persistent and Shared Objects in Trellis/Owl," *Proceedings of the Workshop on Object-Oriented Databases,* Pacific Grove, CA, pp. 113–123, 1986.

[Penedo 1986] M.H. Penedo, "Prototyping a Project Master Data Base for Software Engineering Environments," *Proceedings of the Second Symposium on Practical Software Environments,* December 1986.

[Smith and Smith 1977] J.M. Smith and D.C.P. Smith, "Database Abstractions: Aggregations and Generalization," *ACM Transactions on Database Systems,* vol. 2, no. 2, pp. 105–133, 1977.

[Snyder 1986] A. Snyder, "Encapsulation and Inheritance in Object-Oriented Programming Languages," *Proceedings of the First ACM Conference on Object-Oriented Programming Systems, Languages and Applications, SIGPLAN Notices,* vol. 21, no. 11, pp. 38–45, 1986.

[Stefik and Bobrow 1986] M. Stefik and D.G. Bobrow, "Object-Oriented Programming: Themes and Variations," *The AI Magazine,* pp. 40–62, 1986.

# 3

# A Shared View of Sharing:
## *The Treaty of Orlando*

Lynn Andrea Stein, Henry Lieberman, David Ungar

## INTRODUCTION

For the past few years, researchers have been debating the relative merits of object-oriented languages with classes and inheritance as opposed to those with prototypes and delegation. It has become clear that the object-oriented programming language design space is not a dichotomy. Instead, we have identified two fundamental mechanisms—*templates* and *empathy*—and several independent degrees of freedom for each. Templates create new objects in their own image, providing guarantees about the similarity of group members. Empathy allows an object to act as if it were some other object, thus providing sharing of state and behavior. The Smalltalk-80 language,[1] Actors, Lieber-

---

[1] In this chapter, the term "Smalltalk" will be used to refer to the Smalltalk-80™ programming language.

man's DELEGATION system, SELF, and HYBRID, each takes a different stand on the forms of templates and empathy.

Some varieties of template and empathy mechanisms are appropriate for building well-understood programs that must be extremely reliable, while others are better suited for the rapid prototyping of solutions to difficult problems. The differences between languages designed for these application domains can be recast as the differences between support for anticipated versus unanticipated sharing. One can even ascribe the ascent of object-oriented programming to its strong support for extension instead of modification. However, there are still many kinds of extension that remain difficult. The decomposition of an object-oriented language into template and empathy mechanisms, and the degree of support for extension provided by the forms of these mechanisms, comprise a solid framework for studying language design.

We begin this chapter with the text of our "Treaty," in which we outline the basis for our consensus. In Section 3.2, we discuss the differences between *anticipated* and *unanticipated* sharing. Section 3.3 defines more formally the fundamental terms and concepts we have identified. Several languages representing different paradigms are examined as examples of these mechanisms in Section 3.4. Finally, Section 3.5 describes the larger issues of software evolution that underly the issues raised here; in this context, our conclusions can be seen as a partial solution to the more general problems of sharing.

## 3.1 THE TREATY

Mechanisms for sharing knowledge and behavior between objects are among the most useful and also the most hotly debated features of object-oriented languages. The three authors of this chapter have previously published papers in which new sharing mechanisms for object-oriented languages were prominently featured. We met on the occasion of OOPSLA '87, in Orlando, Florida, and discovered through discussion that we shared a common outlook that both clarifies the reasons for design choices made in previous languages, and also points the way toward future research in this area. We call this consensus the *Treaty of Orlando*.[2]

WHEREAS the intent of object-oriented programming is to provide a natural and straightforward way to describe real-world concepts, allowing the flexibility of expression necessary to capture the variable nature of the world being modeled, and the dynamic ability to represent changing situations; and

WHEREAS a fundamental part of the naturalness of expression provided by object-oriented programming is the ability to share data, code, and definition, and to this end all object-oriented languages provide some way to define a

---

[2]The original treaty text appears in [Power and Weiss 1988].

new object in terms of an existing one, borrowing implementation as well as behavioral description from the previously defined object; and

WHEREAS many object-oriented languages—beginning with Simula-67, and including Smalltalk, Flavors, and Loops—have implemented this sharing through classes, which allow one group of objects to be defined in terms of another, and also provide guarantees about group members, or instances; and

WHEREAS these mechanisms—class, subclass, and instance—impose a rigid type hierarchy, needlessly restricting the flexibility of object-oriented systems, and in particular do not easily permit dynamic control over the patterns of sharing between objects; which dynamic control is particularly necessary in experimental programming situations, where the evolution of software can be expected to proceed rapidly; and

WHEREAS the signatories to this treaty have independently proposed seemingly disparate solutions to this problem, to wit:

[Lieberman 1986] proposed that traditional inheritance be replaced by delegation, which is the idea that sharing between objects can be accomplished through the forwarding of messages, allowing one object to decide at run time to forward a message to another, more capable object, and giving this new object the ability to answer this message on the first (delegating) object's behalf; in this scheme, prototypical objects—the "*typical* elephant," for example—replace abstract classes—e.g., the *class* elephant—as the repository for shared information;

[Ungar and Smith 1987] also proposed a prototype-based approach, using a drastic simplification of the Smalltalk model in which a single type of parent link replaces the more complex class/subclass/instance protocol; while this approach does not propose explicit delegation, through "dynamic inheritance" it shares the essential characteristics of allowing dynamic sharing patterns and idiosyncratic behavior of individual objects;

[Stein 1987] attempted a rapprochement between the delegation and inheritance views, pointing out that the class/subclass relationship is essentially this "delegation," or "dynamic inheritance," and that these new styles of sharing simply make a shift in representation, using what were previously considered "classes" to represent real-world entities rather than abstract groups; this approach gives a different way of providing idiosyncratic behavior and dynamic sharing, through extensions to the class-instance relationship;

WHEREAS the signatories to this treaty now recognize that their seemingly divergent approaches share a common underlying view on the issues of sharing in object-oriented systems, we now declare:

RESOLVED, that we recognize two fundamental mechanisms that sharing mechanisms for object-oriented languages must implement, and that can be used for analyzing and comparing the plethora of linguistic mechanisms for sharing provided by different object-oriented languages: The first is *empathy*, the ability of one object to share the behavior of another object without explicit redefinition; and the second is the ability to create a new object based on a *template*, a "cookie-cutter" that guarantees, at least in part, characteristics of the newly created object.

RESOLVED, that most significant differences between sharing mechanisms can be analyzed as making design choices that differ along the following three independent dimensions, to wit:

> *First,* whether *STATIC* or *DYNAMIC:* When does the system require that the patterns of sharing be fixed? Static systems require determining the sharing patterns by the time an object is created, while dynamic systems permit determination of sharing patterns when an object actually receives a message; and

> *Second,* whether *IMPLICIT* or *EXPLICIT:* Does the system have an operation that allows a programmer to explicitly direct the patterns of sharing between objects, or does the system do this automatically and uniformly? and

> *Third,* whether *PER OBJECT* or *PER GROUP:* Is behavior specified for an entire group of objects at once, as it is with traditional classes or types, or can idiosyncratic behavior be attached to an individual object? Conversely, can behavior be specified/guaranteed for a group?

RESOLVED, that no definitive answer as to what set of these choices is best can be reached. Rather, that different programming situations call for different combinations of these features: for more exploratory, experimental programming environments, it may be desirable to allow the flexibility of dynamic, explicit, per object sharing; while for large, relatively routine software production, restricting to the complementary set of choices—strictly static, implicit, and group-oriented—may be more appropriate.

RESOLVED, that as systems follow a natural evolution from dynamic and disorganized to static and more highly optimized, the object representation should also have a natural evolutionary path; and that the development environment should itself provide more flexible representations, together with tools—ideally automatic—for adding those structures (of class, of hierarchy, and of collection, for example) as the design (or portions thereof) stabilizes; and

RESOLVED, that this agreement shall henceforth be known as the TREATY OF ORLANDO.

## 3.2 ANTICIPATED VERSUS UNANTICIPATED SHARING

In this chapter, we distinguish between two kinds of sharing that arise in object-oriented systems; or rather, two kinds of motivations for introducing sharing into an object-oriented system. The distinction between these is an important determiner of preference among object-oriented language mechanisms. One is *anticipated* sharing. During the conceptual phase of system design, before actual coding starts, a designer can often foresee commonalities between different parts of the system, leading to a desire to share procedures and data between those similar parts. This is best accomplished by language mechanisms that provide a means for the designer to write down the anticipated structure to be shared by other components. In traditional Simula-like object-oriented languages, classes serve as the mechanism for encoding anticipated sharing of behavior, which may be utilized by a perhaps unanticipated number of instances.

In contrast, *unanticipated* sharing is less well served by traditional inheritance mechanisms. Unanticipated sharing arises when a designer would like to introduce new behavior into an object system that does not already provide for it, and may not have been foreseen when the original system was programmed. The designer may notice that new behavior can be accomplished, in part, by making use of already existing components, although procedures and data may have to be added or amended as well. Thus, a sharing relationship arises among components that are used in common for both their original, anticipated purposes and their new, unanticipated purposes. Obviously, since the new behavior has not been anticipated, being forced to state the sharing relationships in advance puts a restriction on the kinds of new behavior that can be introduced without modifying the previous system. The traditional class-subclass-instance mechanism requires textually distinguishing, in a static way, between those elements intended as common behavior, namely classes, and those expected to be idiosyncratic, the instances.

Supporting unanticipated sharing is important because software evolution often follows unpredictable paths. A language mechanism supports unanticipated sharing best if new behavior can be introduced simply by explaining to the system what the differences are between the desired new behavior and the existing behavior. Delegation, or dynamic inheritance, accomplishes this by allowing new objects to re-use the behavior of existing ones without requiring prior specification of this relationship.

The examples in [Lieberman 1986] stress the advantages of delegation in situations where reasonable behavioral extensions to a system are unlikely to be anticipated in the original design of a system. It is reasonable to want to define a "dribble stream" to record interaction on previously implemented I/O (input-output) streams (see Fig. 3.1), but it is unreasonable to require that the implementors of the original I/O streams have prepared in advance for the existence of dribble streams. On the other hand, it is reasonable to expect that a designer who first implements a stream to an interactive terminal will

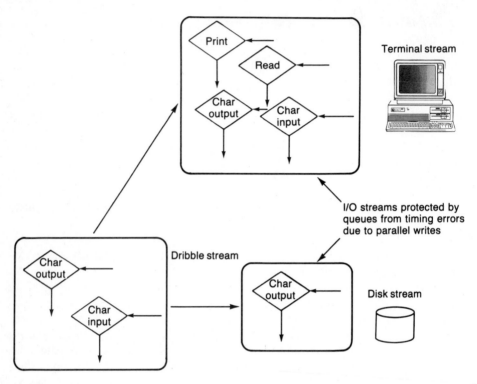

**FIGURE** 3.1 A DRIBBLE STREAM RECORDS INTERACTION ON A PREVIOUSLY IMPLEMENTED TERMINAL STREAM.

build it upon some object representing the abstract notion of "an I/O stream," anticipating that there will eventually be some other types of streams, such as disk or network streams. It would be silly to implement a disk stream by delegating to a terminal stream for common operations simply because the terminal stream happened to have been implemented first. This illustrates the difference between anticipated and unanticipated sharing. It is primarily an issue of software evolution and design aesthetics, and only indirectly a language issue.

The main result of [Stein 1987] can be rephrased in these terms: because a subclass is defined by stating the differences, in both procedures and data, between it and its superclass, the relation between subclass and superclass is better suited for unanticipated sharing than is the class-instance relation, which limits the differences between an instance and its class to the values of its variables.

## 3.3 Basic mechanisms

The arguments over what is fundamental in object-oriented programming have existed for as long as the field. Which features—classes, prototypes, inheritance, delegation, message passing, encapsulation, abstraction—are at the heart of object-oriented programming, and how these things relate to one another, are not issues that will soon be resolved. Rather than try to settle this debate, we present here two mechanisms that are used in most object-oriented languages: *empathy* and *templates*. We claim that they are fundamental in that they cannot be defined in terms of one another, and that most object-oriented languages can be described largely in terms of the ways in which they combine these mechanisms.

The first of these mechanisms underlies both inheritance and delegation. In all languages accepted as object-oriented there is some way in which one object can "borrow" an attribute—variable or method—from another. We propose to use the term *empathy* for this behavior:

We say that object A empathizes with object B for message M if A doesn't have its own protocol for responding to M, but instead responds to M as though it were borrowing B's response protocol. A borrows just the response protocol, but not the rest of B. That is, any time B's response protocol requires a message to be sent to **SELF** (or a variable to be looked up), it is sent to A, not to B; otherwise, A and B respond in the same way. For example, in Fig. 3.2, the **pen** at **(100,200)** *empathizes* with the **pen** at **(50,200)** for its Y variable, and for the **Draw** method.[3]

All incarnations of inheritance and delegation include empathy; they differ as to *when* and *how* the relationships are determined. Empathy may be explicit: "Execute **thisObject:thisRoutine** in my environment," as in the ability of CommonLoops to specialize method lookup. It may be by default: "Anything I can't handle locally, look up in **myParent** (and execute in my environment) with **SELF = me**," as in Smalltalk, SELF, and C++. It may be dynamic or static, per object or per group. These language choices are responsible for much of the variety of existing object oriented paradigms.

*Inheritance*, as found in Simula and Smalltalk, is the preprogrammed determination of default delegation paths, by group. It requires the generation of uniform groups of objects. It separates the delegatable (traditionally, methods only) from the nondelegatable (traditionally, the instance variables). The delegatable part is stored in the class; the nondelegatable is necessarily allocated independently for each instance.

But it is perhaps the interaction of delegation with the second fundamental mechanism, *templates*, that determines the most interesting and con-

---

[3] Formally, we say that object A *empathizes* with object B for M when the following holds: If B's behavior in response to M can be expressed as a function $\psi$ (B,M)—that is, B's method for M can be expressed as a function that takes **SELF** as an argument along with M—then A's response to M can be expressed using the same function $\psi$ as $\psi$(A,M)—A's behavior is derived by using A wherever B would have used itself. The symmetry in this behavioral definition of empathy may seem counterintuitive, but such symmetry is inherent in any behavioral definition. All a behavioral definition can do is say that the behaviors of two objects are similar according to some criterion; you can't tell "who did the implementing" unless you look into the code of the implementation.

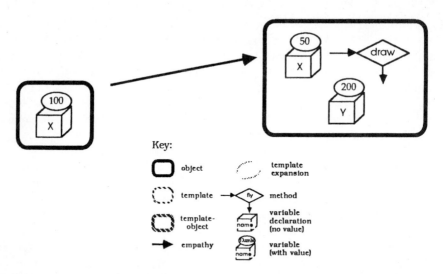

Key:

| ▢ object | ⌒ template expansion |
| ⌐⌐ template | →◇ fly method |
| ▢ template-object | name⌐ variable declaration (no value) |
| → empathy | name⌐ variable (with value) |

**FIGURE 3.2**　THE **PEN** AT (**100,200**) *EMPATHIZES* WITH THE **PEN** AT (**50,200**) FOR ITS **Y** VARI-ABLE, AND FOR THE **DRAW** METHOD.

troversial distinctions between types of object-oriented languages. A template is a kind of "cookie cutter" for objects: it contains all the method and variable definitions, parent pointers, etc., needed to define a new object of the same type. If the object may not gain or lose attributes once it is defined, we call the template *strict*.

In many languages, after the template is copied, or "instantiated," changes to this new object may be permissible, weakening the guarantee of uniform behavior by group. These variations on strict templates are discussed below. In addition, there are languages without templates; however, in these languages, such as Lieberman's DELEGATION, the system provides no inherent concept of "group," or "kind," of object.

In some languages, such as SELF and Actra, the template is itself an object. In others, it is embedded in another, generator object, usually called a *class*. A class is an object of one type that contains a template for objects of another type. Thus, **class elephant** is an object of type **Class**, but contains a template for objects of type **Elephant**. The objects cut from the template embedded in a class are known as its *instances*.

Traditionally, this class-instance relationship is strict: a *strict* (instance) *template* lists exactly those attributes that each object cut from that template must define, and no cookie-cut object can define attributes other than those in the template. Because the template is strict, each object cut from it will have a local copy of each attribute; these attributes cannot be redefined or removed, so they will never be delegated. A class thus guarantees the uniformity and independence of its "cookie-cut" instances.

However, this relationship can be relaxed in several ways. For example, a *minimal template* is a cookie cutter in the same sense, but once created, cookie-cut objects can define other attributes as well. An extended instance—one generated by a minimal template, then added to—does not, a priori, have a template for its type. Its descendants cannot be strict instances, since there is no template for their type. On the other hand, the extended instance can be *promoted*, transforming it into a class, of type **Class** but with a template for its original type. This class may then have instances.

Other relaxations in template enforcement create a variety of nonstrict templates. In languages where templates are themselves objects, templates are often entirely nonstrict. That is, an object may be created from a template, but subsequently go on to add or delete attributes, transforming it from a copy of its template into a new type of object, as in SELF.

## 3.4 SOME CASE STUDIES

In this section, we describe languages exemplifying three of the language paradigms we have identified. The first paradigm is the least constrained; Actors and DELEGATION are almost purely dynamic empathy systems, supporting the maximally flexible set of choices. SELF adds to this the concept of template, making grouping of objects possible. However, SELF does not have classes, and remains a fully dynamic and flexible language. The third paradigm is the "classical" style of object-oriented programming found in Simula and Smalltalk. While traditionally this paradigm has been used in a rigid and inflexible manner, we describe one language—HYBRID—that maintains the structure of a class-based system while allowing much of the flexibility of the previous two paradigms. A summary of language features is given in Table 3.1.

**TABLE 3.1** VARIOUS LANGUAGES AND THEIR ATTRIBUTES

| Language | Determination of Empathy | | | Template Mechanisms | |
|---|---|---|---|---|---|
| | **When** | **How** | **For** | **What** | **How** |
| Actors | runtime | explicit | per object | none | |
| DELEGATION | runtime | both | per object | none | |
| SELF | runtime | implicit* | per object | templates | nonstrict |
| Simula | compile time | implicit | per group | classes | strict |
| Smalltalk | object creation time | implicit | per group | classes | strict |
| HYBRID | runtime | both | both | any | nonstrict |

*However, mechanisms for explicit empathy exist in the language.

### 3.4.1 Actors and Lieberman's DELEGATION

The actor systems of Hewitt and his colleagues at MIT represent the most extreme orientation toward dynamic and flexible control. The basic actor model provides only for active objects and parallel message passing [Agha 1987] and so mandates no particular sharing mechanism. However, actual actor implementations [Lieberman 1987] have found it most natural to use delegation as the sharing mechanism, since the actor philosophy encourages using patterns of message passing to express what in other languages would require special-purpose mechanisms [Hewitt 1984].

Along the three dimensions of our treaty, actor systems can be classified as dynamic, explicit, and per-object. Sharing mechanisms in actors are dynamic, since message passing is a run-time operation, invoked without prior declaration. Delegation requires explicit designation of the recipient. Delegation is accomplished through a special message-passing protocol that includes the client (the equivalent of the **SELF** variable in Smalltalk-like languages) as part of the message. Since actor systems have no notion of type, sharing must be specified on a per-object basis. There are no template, class, or instantiation mechanisms defined in the kernels of actor languages. Of course, nothing precludes the use of delegation and object creation operations in actor systems to implement templates, or objects representing classes or sets.

The major conceptual difference between actors and the Simula family of languages arises in what is considered fundamental. In the traditional Simula-like languages, mechanisms of class, subclass, and instantiation are considered fundamental. The behavior of the message passing operation is explained in terms of them and their influence on variable and procedure lookup. In actor systems, the message-passing operation is considered fundamental. Even variable lookup must be explained in terms of sending messages to an object representing the environment. Thus, sharing mechanisms in actor systems are built on top of message passing.

**FIGURE 3.3** A DELEGATION HIERARCHY

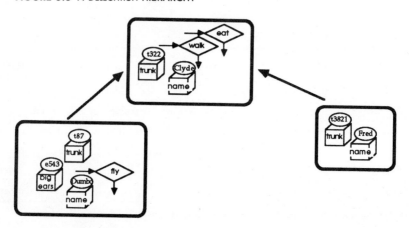

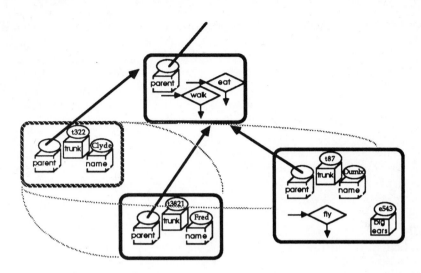

**FIGURE 3.4** A SELF HIERARCHY

DELEGATION [Lieberman 1986] is an outgrowth of the Actor languages. As such, it has no templates. Object creation is independent of the parent: a new object is created by making a new empty object that points to some other object (or doesn't, as is desired), and then filling in the details of what that object should contain. Thus, an object with no attributes but a **name** could be a child of (and therefore delegate to) an **elephant** or an **employee** or a **real**.

Since there are no "class defining objects," there are no "classes" or groups of objects of the same "type." Every object determines its own, unique "type." There is thus no distinction between creating a new object and creating a new "type" of object. In DELEGATION, everything is done on an object-by-object basis. DELEGATION is entirely dynamic; anything can change at any time. Empathy in DELEGATION can be either hierarchical (implicit) or explicit. Figure 3.3 shows a DELEGATION hierarchy.

### 3.4.2 SELF

SELF [Ungar and Smith 1987] was designed to aid in exploratory programming by optimizing expressiveness and malleability. It is essentially a template-based language; however, SELF templates are as much a matter of convention as of language design. New objects are created by cloning an existing one; the original object—called a prototype—behaves in much the same way as the standard template described above. In Fig. 3.4, a new **elephant** (Fred) has been created by copying an existing **elephant** (Clyde). Clyde is thereby functioning as a prototype, or template.

SELF templates are nonstrict, so the objects they create can extend or otherwise modify their template-defined properties. Some attributes in the child may simply be delegated to the parent object, while others may be handled locally or delegated elsewhere. The new object may also have additional attributes not defined for the template, creating a sort of "extended instance." New *kinds* of objects are created by making a new template—cloning and then modifying an existing object—so that it has the requisite properties. In this way, a sort of "subclass" behavioral inheritance can be created.[4] Thus, one can take an elephant and add big ears and the ability to fly. This elephant (Dumbo) is unique: there is no exact template for it.

The patterns of empathy in SELF are determined individually by each object. An object's **parent** slots list the objects it empathizes with. In the example, the **elephants** empathize with an object holding shared behavior—**walking, eating**, etc.—for **elephants**. Since an object may change the contents of its slots whenever it wishes, the patterns of empathy can change dynamically. Finally, since the **parent** attribute is part of a slot, the patterns of empathy are implicit in the attributes and contents of an object's slots, not explicitly in the code.[5] SELF's non-strict objectified templates and its individual, dynamic, and implicit patterns of empathy foster exploratory programming.

### 3.4.3 "Standard Inheritance" and HYBRID

Standard inheritance, exemplified by Smalltalk and all Simula-based languages, consists of class objects, which *contain* templates and therefore can generate instances, and the instances generated by these classes. New objects are simply cut from the template: every variable must be allocated individually for each object, while methods are shared through the template. New class, or generator, objects "inherit" the templates of their superclasses. This is operationally equivalent to delegating part of the template. These classes may themselves be instances. In this case, the metaclass contains a template for an object (the class) which *itself* contains a template.

In standard inheritance, all instances of a class fit exactly the template description. Once created, these objects retain their properties forever: each subclass must delegate to its specified superclass(es); each instance remains a member of its class for all time. The objects in Fig. 3.5 reflect this; in order to create Dumbo, the **flying elephant**, a new class—with a single instance—had to be created.

HYBRID [Mercado 1988] is a system that allows the traditionally static and strict relationships of standard inheritance to be dynamic and flexible. There is, after all, no inherent reason that all these relationships must be strict. A HYBRID template, although embedded in a class, behaves more like SELF's templates, allowing objects generated from this class-template to add

---

[4] It is worth noting that there is no distinction between the concepts of "extended instance" and "subclass" in this kind of language, since any extended instance is also a potential template for a new "type" of object.

[5] A limited form of explicit delegation is allowed but rarely used.

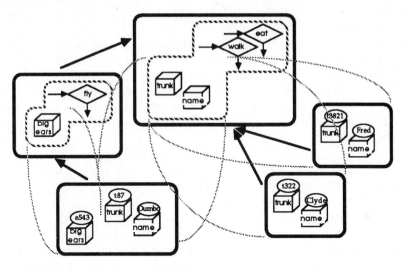

**FIGURE 3.5** A SMALLTALK HIERARCHY

or delete attributes. Thus, in Fig. 3.6, the unique **flying elephant** is just an extended instance of the **class elephant**. Of course, if **flying elephants** were common, HYBRID does not preclude the creation of a new class—in fact, the language will generate such a class *automatically* from a prototypical instance. In addition, HYBRID inheritance is dynamic, allowing run-time changes to the hierarchy, and instances are not distinguished from classes, allowing them to explicitly delegate—or share—attributes.

**FIGURE 3.6** A HYBRID HIERARCHY

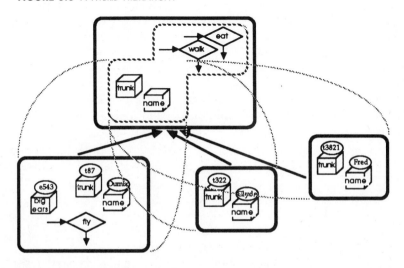

## 3.5 SHARING AND SOFTWARE EVOLUTION

The issue of what kind of behavioral extensions to a system can be accomplished without modifying previously existing code is of central importance. An important principle is that a conceptually small extension to the behavior of a system of objects should be achievable with a small extension to the code. The analysis of alternative mechanisms for sharing should proceed by considering their effects upon the necessity for future modifications of the code to accomplish behavioral extensions.

There are two kinds of changes that we perform in object systems. One is adding new code, or extending the system. The other is editing previously existing code, or modifying the system. These two kinds of changes have very different effects in the programming environment.

Adding new code to extend a system is good. It preserves the previous state of the system; at worst one can simply delete the extension to return to a previous state. Editing code is a much more problematic transformation. It is a destructive operation, both literally and figuratively. As an operation with side effects, editing code destroys irrecoverably the previous state of the system, unless careful backup/undo operations are performed. Perhaps worse is the propensity of editing operations to introduce inconsistencies in a system. Often, behavioral extensions are accomplished by editing several pieces of code in different places, and performing these operations manually leaves the possibility that not all the edits will be performed in a consistent manner.

In fact, one can recast the whole object-oriented enterprise in terms of the extension/modification dichotomy. The true value of object-oriented techniques as opposed to conventional programming techniques is not that they can do things the conventional techniques can't, but that they can often extend behavior by adding new code in cases where conventional techniques would require editing existing code instead. Objects are good because they allow new concepts to be added to a system without modifying previously existing code. Methods are good because they permit adding functionality to a system without modifying previously existing code. Classes are good because they enable using the behavior of one object as part of the behavior of another without modifying previously existing code.

In a conventional language, we might implement a data representation for a geometric shape as a list of points. A display procedure for this representation might dispatch on the kind of shape to more specialized procedures as follows:

To DISPLAY a SHAPE:
     * If the shape is a TRIANGLE, call DISPLAY-TRIANGLE.
     * If the shape is a RECTANGLE, call DISPLAY-RECTANGLE.

                 .

                 .

                 .

     * Otherwise, cause an UNRECOGNIZED-SHAPE error.
Define A-TRIANGLE to be the list of points (100, 100), (−50, 200), (150, −20).

The kind of shape could be recognized by appending a tag onto the list of points, or perhaps even by examining the length of the list.

We can now ask the question: What do we have to do to add a new shape to the display procedure? In the conventional system, this involves destructively editing the code to insert a new conditional clause:

```
To DISPLAY a SHAPE:
    * If the shape is a TRIANGLE, call DISPLAY-TRIANGLE.
    * If the shape is a PENTAGON, call DISPLAY-PENTAGON.
                            .
                            .
                            .

    * Otherwise. . .
```

The editing process leaves open the possibility for inconsistent edits, inadvertent deletion of old code, mismatch between protocols for using the data representation in the old and new clauses, and so forth.

In an object oriented language, by contrast, the representation modularizes the addition of each new object and message so that adding a new object or method can be done without any modification of previously existing code.

```
If I'm a SHAPE object, and I get a DISPLAY message,
    * I respond with an UNRECOGNIZED-SHAPE error.

Define a TRIANGLE to inherit from SHAPE.

If I'm a TRIANGLE and I get a DISPLAY message,
    * I respond with DISPLAY-TRIANGLE.

Define A-TRIANGLE to be an instance of SHAPE
    * With vertices (100, 100), (−50, 200), (150, −20).
```

Now, we can extend the system to know about pentagons simply by adding a new definition that extends the system.

```
Define a PENTAGON to inherit from SHAPE.

If I'm a PENTAGON and I get a DISPLAY message,
    * I respond with DISPLAY-PENTAGON.
```

One way of characterizing the themes common to our three original papers is that we observed that the implementation of unanticipated sharing between objects in Simula-style inheritance systems often required modification of existing code. We were searching for ways of implementing unanticipated behavioral extensions without modifying existing code, and concluded that the solution was to allow more dynamic forms of empathy. At the same time, we wish not to minimize the importance of language mechanisms for tradi-tional, anticipated sharing and believe future languages must seek a synthesis of the two.

The search for ways to accomplish interesting behavioral extensions of object-oriented systems by additive extensions to code is far from over. If we can find any situations in which a conceptually simple extension to the behavior of an object system seems to require gratuitous modification of existing code, it's the sign of a problem, and we ought to be looking for a solution. We give an example of one such situation as a guide for future research.

Occasions arise when we would like to specialize or extend not just a single object, but an entire hierarchy at once. No existing object-oriented language provides a mechanism for this that does not require the modification of previously existing code. Yet conceptually, we should be able to perform these changes by some sort of additive extension.

Suppose we would like to construct a hierarchy of geometrical objects, such as squares and triangles, that all respond to methods like **DISPLAY**. These would all be built on a common base object named **SHAPE**, which might contain variables for the common attributes like a **CENTER** point and perhaps a **BOUNDING-BOX**. Objects like **TRIANGLE** and **SQUARE** inherit from **SHAPE**. If we started out with black-and-white shapes, we could certainly add a **COLOR** attribute to **SHAPE** by simple extension. But this would leave us with the task of reproducing the entire hierarchy of subobjects emanating from **SHAPE** in new, colored versions. In most present systems, programmers would be tempted simply to add the **COLOR** attribute directly to **SHAPE** rather than creating a new **COLORED-SHAPE** object. This would automatically extend all the geometric objects to colored versions, but at the cost of a destructive editing operation. The previous black-and-white version would be lost, and the editing operation introduces the possibility of errors, such as accidentally sending a color command while running a previously existing black-and-white program, unless careful attention was paid to upward compatibility.

Some languages, like the Flavors object-oriented extension to Lisp, have addressed the issue of sharing of orthogonal features by using the approach of "mixins," using inheritance from multiple parents. This approach lets us create new objects possessing previously unanticipated combinations of behavior from previously existing abstractions. In this approach, a **COLOR-MIXIN** could be created independent of any shape properties, and a new type of object declared to inherit from **COLOR-MIXIN** as well as some specific shape property like **TRIANGLE**. However, this approach still involves all the steps of reproducing all elements of the shape hierarchy in their color versions, or modifications to the code to mix in the color feature retroactively. Thus the mixin feature does not provide true support for smoothly implementing unanticipated changes such as the black-and-white to color transition.

We don't have, at the moment, a solution to this problem; we state it merely to point out the direction in which we believe object-oriented systems must evolve.

## SUMMARY

We have described two sharing mechanisms, *templates* and *empathy*, which hide at the core of object-oriented programming languages. Templates allow two objects to share a common form. They may be embedded inside classes, or may be objects themselves. They may also vary in the degree of strictness they impose on system structure. Empathy allows two objects to share common state or behavior. The patterns of empathy may be determined statically or dynamically, per object or per group, implicitly or explicitly. The decomposition of object-oriented languages into template and empathy mechanisms can shed light on their similarities and differences, weaknesses and strengths.

## REFERENCES

[Agha 1987] G.A. Agha, *ACTORS: A Model of Concurrent Computation in Distributed Systems*, The MIT Press, Cambridge, MA, 1987.

[Birtwistle et al. 1973] G. Birtwistle, O. Dahl, B. Myhrtag, and K. Nygaard, *Simula Begin*, Auerbach Press, Philadelphia, 1973.

[Bobrow and Stefik 1981] D. Bobrow and M. Stefik, *The Loops Manual, Technical Report KB-VLSI-81-13,* Knowledge Systems Area, Xerox Palo Alto Research Center, 1981.

[Bobrow et al. 1986] D. Bobrow, K. Kahn, G. Kiczales, L. Masinter, M. Stefik, and F. Zdybel, "CommonLoops: Merging Lisp and Object-Oriented Programming," *Proceedings of the First ACM Conference on Object-Oriented Programming Systems, Languages and Applications, SIGPLAN Notices,* vol. 21, no. 11, pp. 17–29, 1986.

[Hewitt 1984] C. Hewitt, "Control Structures as Patterns of Passing Messages," in *Artificial Intelligence: An MIT Perspective,* ed. P. Winston, The MIT Press, Cambridge, MA, 1984.

[LaLonde 1986] W. LaLonde, "An Exemplar Based Smalltalk," *Proceedings of the First ACM Conference on Object-Oriented Programming Systems, Languages and Applications, SIGPLAN Notices,* vol. 21, no. 9, pp. 322–330, 1986.

[Lieberman 1986] H. Lieberman, "Using Prototypical Objects to Implement Shared Behavior in Object-Oriented Systems," *Proceedings of the First ACM Conference on Object-Oriented Programming Systems, Languages and Applications, SIGPLAN Notices*, vol. 21, no. 9, pp. 214–223, 1986.

[Lieberman 1987] H. Lieberman, "Concurrent Object-Oriented Programming in Act 1," in *Object-Oriented Concurrent Programming*, ed. A. Yonezawa and M. Tokoro, pp. 9–36, The MIT Press, Cambridge, MA, 1987.

[Mercado 1987] A. Mercado Jr., *Hybrid: Implementing Classes with Prototypes*, Master's Thesis, *Technical Report CS-88-12*, Brown University Department of Computer Science, Providence, RI, July 1988.

[Moon 1986] D.A. Moon, "Object-Oriented Programming with Flavors," *Proceedings of the First ACM Conference on Object-Oriented Programming Systems, Languages and Applications, SIGPLAN Notices*, vol. 21, no. 11, pp. 1–8, 1986.

[Power and Weiss 1988] L. Power and Z. Weiss, eds., *Addendum to the Proceedings of the Second ACM Conference on Object-Oriented Programming Systems, Languages and Applications, SIGPLAN Notices*, vol. 23, no. 5, 1988.

[SIG 1986] *ACM SIGPLAN Notices Special Edition on Object-Oriented Programming Languages*, vol. 21, no. 11, November 1986.

[Stein 1987] L.A. Stein, "Delegation Is Inheritance," *Proceedings of the Second ACM Conference on Object-Oriented Programming Systems, Languages and Applications, SIGPLAN Notices*, vol. 22, no. 10, pp. 138–146, 1987.

[Stroustrup 1986] B. Stroustrup, *The C++ Programming Language*, Addison-Wesley, Reading, MA, 1986.

[Ungar and Smith 1987] D. Ungar and R.B. Smith, "Self: The Power of Simplicity," *Proceedings of the Second ACM Conference on Object-Oriented Programming Systems, Languages and Applications, SIGPLAN Notices*, vol. 22, no. 10, pp. 227–242, 1987.

# 4

# The COMMON LISP Object-Oriented Programming Language Standard

David A. Moon

## INTRODUCTION

The COMMON LISP Object System is an object-oriented programming language embedded in COMMON LISP. This chapter describes the overall structure and philosophy of this language, offers a brief introduction to its major details, and discusses some of the design decisions behind the language. The chapter ends with comparisons of CLOS to two other object-oriented programming languages.

## 4.1 OVERVIEW

### 4.1.1 History and Philosophy of the COMMON LISP Object System

The COMMON LISP Object System (CLOS) is an object-oriented programming language embedded in COMMON LISP [Steele 1984]. CLOS is being developed by a working group under the X3J13 committee, which is charged with standardizing an "industrial quality" LISP in the United States. CLOS has been adopted as a standard, and it will be implemented on a wide variety of hardware platforms and operating systems sold by diverse vendors. Initially CLOS will be a *de facto* standard; later CLOS and COMMON LISP are expected to become official American National Standards.

The result of this standardization activity is that by 1989 it will be possible to write object-oriented LISP programs that are portable across the spectrum of personal computers, workstations, mainframes, and symbolic processing systems. In this way CLOS will follow the model of COMMON LISP, whose development and standardization began in 1982. By 1986, a *de facto* standard COMMON LISP was widely enough implemented that serious LISP programs could be written to be portable across many computer systems.

CLOS is firmly based on past experience with other LISP-based object-oriented programming languages, most notably Flavors [Moon 1986] and Common Loops [Bobrow et al. 1986]. However, rather than simply codifying existing practice, the designers of CLOS have made a substantial effort to produce an improved language that can be more broadly useful. In this way, too, CLOS's evolution resembles that of COMMON LISP. The designers have taken ideas about object-oriented programming from several sources and combined them. They have made an effort to simplify the language and removed some ideas that were tried in the past but not found especially useful. Compared to previous object-oriented extensions to LISP, CLOS should fit into COMMON LISP more smoothly and be more hardware-independent, and thus be accessible to more programmers [DeMichiel and Gabriel 1987].

CLOS aims to be powerful enough to support large, production-quality application programs in both the development and delivery phases—a goal requiring uncompromised efficiency. One approach would have been to adopt a very simple language that could easily be implemented efficiently. However, CLOS is more ambitious and provides more support for modular programming than would be possible in such a simple language. Thus CLOS does not overemphasize simplicity. Conceptual and expository simplicity are important, but simplicity of the internal implementation was not a goal. Much of the design effort was concerned with defining powerful features in such a way that they could be easily understood by users and could be implemented efficiently, even if the necessary implementation techniques are not obvious. In a way this resembles the philosophy of relational databases, in which a few powerful but easily understood concepts combine to produce a system that is quite powerful but would perform inefficiently in a naive implementation. In both cases, sophisticated implementation techniques are known that recover high efficiency without compromising the user-visible semantics.

CLOS is designed to fit smoothly into its host language, COMMON LISP, as an extension, rather than as a preprocessor or a completely separate language. CLOS programs are COMMON LISP programs that use a small set of additional language elements. To the existing concept of objects in COMMON

LISP, CLOS adds more powerful ways to control the structure and behavior of objects. CLOS extends the existing type system to incorporate classes, and extends the existing function-calling mechanism to incorporate methods.

CLOS is a sequential language that does not endorse any particular approach to concurrency. This allows CLOS to be embedded in all concurrent extensions of COMMON LISP.

### 4.1.2 The Overall Organization of CLOS

CLOS as a language can be characterized by a relatively sharp separation between structure and behavior, by multiple inheritance, and by an emphasis on generic functions. CLOS also contains facilities to make itself malleable and extensible, so that future ideas about object-oriented programming can be incorporated.

CLOS is structured into three layers of increasing sophistication. These are not three independent languages, but three aspects of a single language that coexist and are mutually consistent. The first layer is the basic language for everyday programming, providing a convenient syntax for defining the various parts of an object-oriented program. Most users will not need anything beyond this layer of CLOS and COMMON LISP itself.

The second layer reveals the primitives underlying the first layer. This layer includes functions to perform all the basic operations of developing and executing object-oriented programs. Where the first layer refers to entities by symbolic names, the second layer operates on them directly as objects. The second layer is used by programmers with special needs not satisfied by the first layer, as well as those writing tools to aid in program development.

The third layer describes CLOS itself in object-oriented, extensible terms. Users of the third layer can examine and modify the internal workings of CLOS and can implement entirely new object-oriented languages.

The following sections are an overview of the major features of CLOS. In the interest of brevity, the discussion omits many details and minor features. We concentrate on the underlying ideas, omitting syntactic details, and focus on the programming language rather than the program development environment. For complete detail, refer to the draft CLOS specification [X3J13 1988]. To learn to program in CLOS, refer to [Keene 1989].

## 4.2  BASIC CONCEPTS

### 4.2.1 The Structure of an Object

The term *structure* refers to the passive properties of an object, as distinguished from *behavior*, the active properties. Note that throughout this chapter the word *property* is used in an informal sense, not in its technical LISP sense. We will begin with the structural properties of objects.

Every object has *identity* as part of its structure. The identity of an object distinguishes this object from all other objects, while allowing all references to this object to be recognized as equivalent. The Common Lisp function EQL compares two object references and returns *true* if they refer to the same object. Objects are dynamically allocated whenever required. Each object is self-identifying, independent of any context or declarations. CLOS inherits these properties from Lisp; however, they are worth mentioning since they are necessary for a language to be considered fully object-oriented.

An object often refers to other objects. For example, each element of an array is another object. Objects created by CLOS refer to other objects through *slots*. Each slot contains one piece of data; more precisely, each slot refers to one object. A given object can be referred to by more than one slot: a slot does not contain an object in the way that an envelope contains a letter, it simply contains a reference to an object.

Each slot of an object is named by a symbol. In Lisp, symbols are the objects that are used for naming things; see [Steele 1984] for details. One way to access a slot is through the function SLOT-VALUE. The Lisp form (SLOT-VALUE *object symbol*) returns the contents of the slot of *object* that is named *symbol*. Similarly, the Lisp form (SETF(SLOT-VALUE *object symbol*)*value*) stores *value* into the slot.

### 4.2.2 Classes of Objects

Object-oriented programming involves classifying objects according to the similarities between them. CLOS organizes objects into *classes*. Every object *is an instance of* some class. The structure of an object consists of its identity, its class, and if it has slots, the contents of its slots.

Most classes have a name, which is a symbol that identifies the class in the printed representations of programs. CLOS provides anonymous classes in its second layer, but we will not discuss them in detail.

Most computer languages, including Common Lisp, have a concept of *type*. A type is a name for a (possibly infinite) set of objects. In Common Lisp an object can *be a member of* more than one type, because two sets can overlap and the sets can have subsets. Types are useful for organizing and classifying objects, and in some cases for compiler optimization. Classes are useful in the same way, so CLOS mandates that every class is a type. The members of a class are all the instances of that class plus all the instances of each subclass of that class. (We will see subclasses later.) The Common Lisp type operations work for classes as well as for the many other types defined by Common Lisp.

All instances of a particular class are similar in structure. They all have the same number of slots and the same set of slot names. Each object has its own slots, which have their own contents. (See Fig. 4.1.) A user-defined class in CLOS resembles a record type in a language like Pascal or Ada, as far as structure is concerned. The differences will become apparent when we discuss behavior and inheritance.

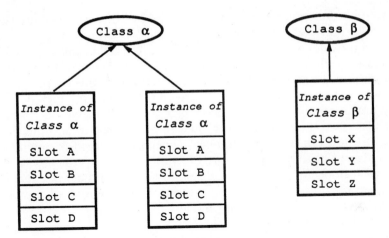

**FIGURE 4.1** THREE INSTANCES OF TWO CLASSES

Here is an example of a rather simple class definition:

```
(DEFCLASS ANIMAL ()
    ((COLOR)
     (DIET)
     (NUMBER-OF-LEGS :TYPE INTEGER)))
```

The class named ANIMAL defines three slots, named COLOR, DIET, and NUMBER-OF-LEGS. The contents of the NUMBER-OF-LEGS slot is restricted to integers, while the other two slots can refer to any type of object.

### 4.2.3 Behavior

The *behavior* of an object is the set of operations that the object can perform. The behavior comprises the active properties of an object, as distinguished from structure, the passive properties.

**Generic Functions and Methods** COMMON LISP expresses all computation in terms of functions. It operates on an object by calling a function and passing the object to the function as one of its arguments. Some COMMON LISP functions are *generic*, which means that they work for several different types of objects. For example, the + function adds numbers of any types: integer, floating-point, rational, or complex. The types of numbers involved do not have to be known in advance. Another example is the LENGTH function, which returns the number of elements in a sequence. The type of sequence (array, character string, or linked list) does not have to be known in advance.

A generic function can be implemented in COMMON LISP without CLOS, since the language allows functions to be called with varying types of arguments and provides ways to test the type of a value at run time. The body of the function would be a conditional form that tests the types of the arguments and performs code appropriate for the particular arguments supplied.

As an extension to COMMON LISP, CLOS formalizes the concept of generic functions and adds the concept of *methods*. A method defines what a particular generic function does when called with particular arguments. A generic function can have any number of methods. Instead of enumerating all possible cases in the body of one function, a CLOS programmer writes a separate method for each case. CLOS provides the framework that links the methods together to form a generic function. Selection of an appropriate method, based on the arguments, is automatic and does not have to be programmed explicitly.

We say that a method *specializes* a generic function. The generic function is called generic because it applies to many cases, while the method is called specialized because it applies to a single case. A method receives the same arguments that were supplied to the generic function. In general, some of these arguments are involved in determining what method to call, while the rest of the arguments are just parameters to the method.

The caller of a function never has to know whether or not the function is generic, because CLOS generic functions are called in the same way as ordinary LISP functions.

A generic function defines an interface, while a method is an implementation of that interface. CLOS checks that the number of arguments accepted by the method is consistent with the interface, but does not attempt to enforce any kind of semantic conformity that would require program understanding or a specification language. In CLOS, defining and enforcing the semantic contract of an interface remains the responsibility of the programmer rather than the language.

The advantage of using methods is their independence from each other, which means that the programmer does not have to think simultaneously about all the methods that exist. Each method has to deal with only a single case, so the programmer can concentrate on one thing at a time, which tends to improve the modularity of programs. The methods for a particular generic function need not all be written by the same programmer. New methods can be added at any time.

**Finding the Appropriate Methods**   How does CLOS decide what to do when a generic function is called? First it determines which of the generic function's methods are *applicable to* the arguments with which the generic function was called. Next it calls one or more of the applicable methods, passing the arguments along. If no methods are applicable, it calls an escape hatch, which typically reports an error. The values returned by the generic function are constructed from the values returned by the methods.

An object's repertoire of behavior consists of the set of generic functions that have methods applicable to the object. The behavior for a particular generic function depends on:

- which methods are applicable when the object is passed as an argument to that generic function.

- how CLOS arbitrates among multiple applicable methods.

Each method specifies its own applicability condition. CLOS allows several kinds of applicability; the most commonly used is a test of whether one particular argument is a member of a particular class. Thus all instances of a class have the same behavior, because the same methods are applicable to each of them.

In the simplest case, only one method is applicable; the generic function simply calls that method and returns whatever values the method returns. More complex cases involve the method inheritance and combination mechanisms discussed later.

**Defining Methods**   A method has five properties:

- the generic function that it specializes

- its applicability condition

- any qualifiers that identify the method's role

- a parameter list that receives the arguments

- the body executed when the method is called

The first layer of CLOS contains the DEFMETHOD macro for defining methods. Its syntax resembles COMMON LISP's DEFUN macro. A programmer using DEFMETHOD specifies the generic function by its name and specifies the method's body in the same way as for DEFUN. The body consists of an optional sequence of declarations followed by a sequence of LISP forms to be executed when the method is called. DEFMETHOD combines the applicability condition and the parameter list into a *specialized lambda list,* whose syntax extends COMMON LISP's standard lambda list syntax by allowing an applicability condition to be attached to a parameter specifier. The most common condition is the name of a class; the condition is satisfied when the value of the parameter is a member of the class. Qualifiers are objects, usually symbols, that identify a method's role within the framework for method inheritance. (See Section 4.4 for the details.) DEFMETHOD allows qualifiers to be inserted between the generic function name and the specialized lambda list.

For example:

```
(DEFMETHOD FEED :BEFORE ((ANI ANIMAL) FOOD)
   (UNLESS (MEMBER FOOD (SLOT-VALUE ANI 'DIET))
      (ERROR "~As don't eat ~A" ANI FOOD)))
```

This defines a method for the FEED generic function that is applicable when the first argument is a member of the class ANIMAL. FEED takes two arguments, the animal and the food, and the method receives these arguments into the parameters ANI and FOOD. The :BEFORE qualifier says that this method's role is not to implement the actual feeding, but just to run before the primary method in order to check the arguments. The body of the method signals an error such as "Tigers don't eat grass" if the food is not in the animal's diet.

**Accessors**   One very simple kind of behavior is reading or writing the contents of a slot. Earlier we saw how to access a slot by calling the SLOT-VALUE function. A more abstract way is to define a function whose body calls SLOT-VALUE, then call that function whenever we want to read the slot. We can define a similar function for writing the slot. Such functions are called *accessor functions*, because of the way they are used, not because they are fundamentally different from other functions.

Programmers must choose a naming convention for their accessor functions. Any name can be used, but the convention that is most consistent with COMMON LISP's built-in functions is to name the reader function with two words separated by a hyphen. The first word names the general category of objects to which this function applies; often this is a class name, but not always. The second word names the particular piece of information being read; often this is a slot name, but not always. The usual convention for writer functions is to use SETF with the reader function.

Accessor functions hide the representation of the information as a slot. We could change the accessor functions to read and write information represented in some other form without having to change their callers. An accessor function can be a generic function, so that different objects can implement it in different ways. The caller of the accessor function need not know or care which implementation a particular object uses. This abstraction allows such flexibility as:

- storing information in a slot in an internal representation, and converting it to a standard interface representation when it is read or written.

- a writer method that not only changes the contents of the slot, but also checks integrity constraints and propagates the new value to other places that depend on the same information.

■ a reader method that calculates the value as a function of other slots' values, rather than just fetching a precalculated value from a slot.

Calling a generic function that dispatches to a method that calls SLOT-VALUE might seem slower than calling SLOT-VALUE directly. However, in most CLOS implementations the speed difference is small. Some CLOS implementations have enough optimization of method lookup and SLOT-VALUE that when they can infer the class the more abstract technique is actually faster. CLOS's general goal of being efficient without compromising the user-visible semantics encourages this sort of implementation.

### 4.2.4 Object Creation

The function MAKE-INSTANCE creates a new object, given its class and some *initialization arguments* that describe its desired properties. Initialization arguments are keyword arguments [Steele 1984, pp. 61–63]. Each initialization argument has a name (a symbol) and a value (any object). The initialization arguments accepted by MAKE-INSTANCE vary, depending on the class.

The value of an initialization argument can be stored into a slot of the newly created object. The definition of a class specifies the names of such initialization arguments and the slots that they fill. For example,

```
(DEFCLASS ANIMAL ( )
    ((COLOR :INITARG :COLOR)
     (DIET :INITARG :DIET)
     (NUMBER-OF-LEGS :INITARG :LEGS
                     :TYPE INTEGER)))
```

This extension of the earlier DEFCLASS example adds an initialization argument to the definition of each slot. A sample object with all three slots filled could be created by:

```
(MAKE-INSTANCE 'ANIMAL :LEGS 4 :COLOR 'PURPLE :DIET ' (HAY
    CLOVER))
```

**Initialization Methods**  Simple filling of slots is not the only way to describe the properties of a new object. The programmer can also write *initialization methods*. After creating a new object, MAKE-INSTANCE calls the INITIALIZE-INSTANCE generic function. Methods for INITIALIZE-INSTANCE receive the initialization arguments and perform any required initializations. They can create subsidiary objects, enter the object into a registry of all instances of its class, extract some data from a database into slots, or implement additional initialization arguments. For example:

```
(DEFMETHOD INITIALIZE-INSTANCE :AFTER
        ((A ANIMAL) &KEY CARNIVORE HERBIVORE)
  (WHEN CARNIVORE
      (PUSH 'MEAT (SLOT-VALUE A 'DIET)))
  (WHEN HERBIVORE
      (PUSH 'LEAVES (SLOT-VALUE A 'DIET)))
  (PUSH A *ALL-ANIMALS*))
```

This initialization method accepts initialization arguments named :CARNIVORE and :HERBIVORE and adds additional items to the animal's diet. MAKE-INSTANCE accepts these initialization arguments and passes them along to the initialization method. This method also adds the newly created object to a list of all animals. The qualifier :AFTER ensures that this method runs after the DIET slot has been set from the :DIET initialization argument by the primary INITIALIZE-INSTANCE method.

A caterpillar could be created by:

```
(MAKE-INSTANCE 'ANIMAL :LEGS 36 :COLOR 'YELLOW :DIET' (BUDS)
    :HERBIVORE T)
```

which would initialize the DIET slot to (LEAVES BUDS).


**Default Values**   To make MAKE-INSTANCE easier to use, CLOS allows a class to define a default value form for each initialization argument. MAKE-INSTANCE evaluates this form when an initialization argument was not supplied by the caller of MAKE-INSTANCE. CLOS also allows a class to define a default value form for each slot. INITIALIZE-INSTANCE evaluates this form and stores the value into the slot when no initialization argument fills the slot.

Once an object has been created, there is no difference between values that were defaulted and values that were supplied as arguments to MAKE-INSTANCE. Slots are passive and simply remember a value, not where the value came from.


## 4.3 INHERITANCE

So far we have seen only individual classes in isolation from all other classes. This is worthy of the name object-oriented programming, as it allows programs to be organized around objects that correspond closely to the real-world or conceptual entities being modeled. However, such programs lack one of the most important aspects of the object-oriented style: explicit specification of relationships among classes. As a program-structuring technique, object-oriented programming should make large, complex programs more reliable, quicker to construct, and easier to modify. Object-oriented programming should encourage programmers to construct families of classes that are well-modularized, fit together smoothly, and can easily be extended with new family members. Through class relationships we can assemble both the structure and the behavior of an object from modular pieces supplied by different classes. Because relationships among classes are so important, most of CLOS is involved with specifying and controlling them.

A class can be a *subclass* of other classes. If A is a subclass of B, we call B a *superclass* of A. A class *inherits* characteristics from its superclasses and adds some characteristics of its own, which are inherited by its subclasses. The inherited characteristics are type, slots, methods, and initializations.

Superclass relationships are built up by inheritance. When defining a class, the programmer names just the *direct superclasses* of the class. The complete set of superclasses contains the direct superclasses, the superclasses of the direct superclasses, and some special classes that are implied without being named explicitly. (See Fig. 4.2.)

**FIGURE 4.2** CLASS 1 AND ITS SUPERCLASSES

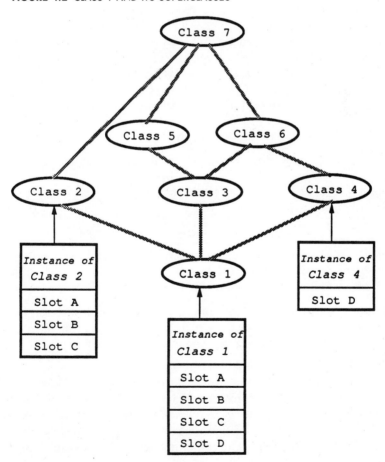

Through inheritance, a class's characteristics affect instances of its subclasses as well as the class's own instances. In fact, some classes exist only to supply characteristics to their subclasses, and do not have any instances of their own. A subclass can be regarded as a specialized or customized version of a superclass. Alternatively, superclasses can be regarded as building blocks from which a subclass is assembled. In the building-blocks model, a class will typically have several direct superclasses. Such a class is assembled by mixing and matching classes chosen from a family. Each member of the family is a class that contributes a single facet of behavior.

### 4.3.1 Inheritance Conflicts

Inherited characteristics can conflict. For example, two superclasses might both supply methods for the same generic function. A conflict can also occur between the class and one of its superclasses. CLOS resolves inheritance conflicts by defining an order of precedence that determines which class's characteristics dominate. Each class has a *class precedence list* that starts with the class itself and includes each superclass exactly once. Classes appearing earlier in this list are considered more specific than classes appearing later, and the characteristics of more specific classes dominate.

The class precedence list puts the class and its superclasses into a total ordering that is consistent with the following two local orderings:

- a subclass is more specific than a superclass.

- when defining a class, direct superclasses are listed in order of precedence.

Local orderings are easier to think about than a global ordering, so programmers usually work with these local orderings.

The class precedence list has several useful properties:

- If each class has only one direct superclass, the class procedure list is identical to the precedence used by single-inheritance languages such as Smalltalk [Goldberg and Robson 1983].

- When the direct superclasses are completely independent, that is, they have no common superclasses, all the superclasses of the first direct superclass precede all the superclasses of the second direct superclass.

- When the direct superclasses are independent except for a common ancestor class, a similar property holds, provided that the common ancestor appears only as the last element of a direct superclass list, never in the middle of one. The class precedence list consists of the noncommon superclasses of the first direct superclass, followed by the noncommon superclasses of the second direct superclass, and finally the common ancestor and its superclasses.

These properties allow building-block classes to be combined with predictable results, without detailed knowledge of whether those classes are monolithic or are themselves assembled from other classes. The class precedence list keeps the indirect superclasses in an order consistent with the order of the direct superclasses, whenever that does not violate the restriction that each superclass must appear in the class precedence list exactly once.

All CLOS implementations use exactly the same algorithm to compute this class precedence list, to ensure program portability. The details of the algorithm can be found in [X3J13 1988].

### 4.3.2 Type Inheritance

Every class is a type, whose members are all the instances of that class plus all the instances of each subclass of that class. This mapping of classes to types implies type inheritance: a member of a given class is also a member of each of its superclasses, so a class inherits the types of its superclasses. The mapping of classes to types also implies that a subclass is a subtype and a superclass is a supertype.

Note that the concepts of "instance of a class" and "member of a class" are not the same. An object is an instance of just one class. It is not an instance of any superclass of that class. However, it *is* a member of every superclass.

An object can be categorized according to its membership in classes. Inheritance of structure from superclasses, and method applicability based on class membership, mean that the type of an object controls the object's structure and behavior. Classes, considered as a system of types, are thus the fundamental organizing principle of CLOS programs.

### 4.3.3 Slot Inheritance

Each class defines some slots and inherits all the slot definitions of its superclasses. If no slot name is used twice, this is trivial. On the other hand, if there are two or more slot definitions with the same name, only one slot is created, with characteristics that are a combination of the slot definitions. The characteristics of a slot include:

- the name of the slot

- any restriction on the type of value that can be stored in the slot

- whether the slot is shared (we will see shared slots later)

- how the slot is initialized when a new object is created

Combining the type restrictions is simple. The contents of a slot must satisfy all the type restrictions; thus the effective type restriction is the greatest common subtype of the type restrictions.

A slot is either shared or local, so the most specific class that defines the slot controls this characteristic. The class precedence list determines which class is most specific.

### 4.3.4 Initialization Inheritance

Default values for initialization arguments and default values for initializing slots are inherited from superclasses. If there are conflicting default values, the one specified by the class that is most specific, according to the class precedence list, overrides the others.

The initialization arguments that can be used when making an instance of a given class are:

- initialization arguments for any slot defined by the class or one of its superclasses.

- initialization arguments accepted by any initialization method that is applicable to instances of that class.

Thus initialization arguments that fill slots are inherited through slot inheritance, while initialization arguments defined by initialization methods are inherited through method inheritance. MAKE-INSTANCE checks the arguments supplied to it against the inherited initialization argument names and reports an error if an initialization argument name is unrecognized.

### 4.3.5 Method Inheritance

Recall that the first thing CLOS does when a generic function is called is to determine which of the generic function's methods are applicable to the arguments. The usual method applicability condition checks that one argument is a member of a specified class. An instance of a subclass of the specified class satisfies this condition; thus the method is inherited by the subclass.

Method inheritance allows the building blocks from which a class is constructed to include behavior, in the form of methods, as well as structure. One particular method for a generic function can be shared by several classes if they all inherit the method from a common superclass. Designing programs to inherit shared behavior from a common source leads to better programs than the alternative practice of imitating an existing module by copying and modifying its code. Designing classes so that each one defines a single, independent module of behavior makes it easier to assemble a variety of programs from those classes. This kind of program organization is desirable because it makes programs easier to understand and maintain.

First consider the case where only one method is applicable. The generic function is then simply a way to call that method. Even when only one method is ever applicable to any particular set of arguments, a generic function might have several methods. This allows multiple implementations (methods) for a single interface (generic function). The relevant implementation is chosen at run time, according to the type of the arguments. In this case, each method must be a complete implementation.

## 4.4 METHOD COMBINATION

When more than one method is applicable, some form of conflict resolution is required. Conflict resolution for methods is more complicated than for slots, because methods themselves are more complicated than slots. Behavioral conflict resolution requires programming language concepts such as flow of control, which are not required for structural conflict resolution.

Rather than regarding multiple applicable methods as being in conflict, CLOS regards them as cooperating. The CLOS *method combination* mechanism controls and organizes the cooperation of several methods to form one implementation of a generic function. This mechanism helps keep the structure of large programs simple and comprehensible, by shielding programmers from the low-level programming details required for methods to cooperate. When a program is assembled from building-block modules, several modules can define methods for a particular generic function. Programmers can define modules that can be used separately or together in various combinations, with method combination providing the glue that connects them together. When a generic function has multiple implementations that are not totally different from one another, method inheritance allows the common parts of the implementations to be implemented only once and shared, while method combination connects the individual parts of the implementations to the shared parts. For some good examples of this, see [Keene 1989].

Method combination controls three decisions that CLOS must make when a generic function is called, after the set of applicable methods has been determined:

1. CLOS decides whether to call all of the applicable methods, just one of them, or a subset of them. If not all of the applicable methods are called, we say that the uncalled ones have been *shadowed*. Typically a method attached to a more specific (according to the class precedence list) class shadows a method attached to a less specific class. This suits the model of a subclass as a customized version of a superclass; desirable methods are inherited while other methods are replaced by shadowing them.

2. CLOS selects which method to call first, when more than one is called. The order of calling methods is important when methods have side effects that interact with each other.

3. CLOS handles the results returned by the methods. The simplest possibility is to choose one method and return its result, ignoring the results of any

other methods. Another common practice is to combine the results using a function such as arithmetic sum, or to collect the results into an array or a list.

The first and second decisions together determine flow of control. The third decision determines flow of data.

There are two approaches to the control of method combination: declarative and imperative. In the declarative approach, the programmer specifies for each generic function the name of a framework for method combination (see Section 4.4.2) and specifies for each method its role within that framework. The detailed flow of control and passing back of results are managed by the framework. In the imperative approach, the programmer uses ordinary LISP facilities to specify flow of control and data. CLOS supports both approaches; a programmer can choose the approach that is more comfortable for a particular application. The declarative form is useful when methods fit nicely into a framework, since it hides irrelevant detail. The imperative form is useful in complex situations, since it gives the programmer total control.

## 4.4.1 Standard Method Combination

The standard type of method combination in CLOS is a declarative framework, but also has an imperative aspect. There are four method roles: *Primary methods* define the main action of the generic function, while *auxiliary methods* fill three roles that modify the action.

In the absence of around methods (described later), the result returned by the most specific primary method is the result of the generic function. This method shadows any less specific primary methods. A common technique is to define a *default method*, which is a primary method applicable to a very general class. The default method implements a default behavior that is useful for most members of the class. When the default method is not useful, a primary method applicable to a subclass of the general class shadows it.

The first two auxiliary method roles are *before methods* and *after methods*, collectively called *daemon methods*. All before methods are called before the primary method, while all after methods are called after the primary method. Daemon methods are used for their side-effects, since any results they return are discarded. The most specific before method is called first. Less specific before methods follow in order. The most specific primary method is called after all the before methods. Following that, the least specific after method is called and more specific after methods follow in order. The most specific after method is called last. This order of execution of daemons provides a measure of encapsulation of superclasses: a class's before method is called before all methods of its superclasses; a class's after method is called after all methods of its superclasses.

The term "daemon" comes from the occasional use of daemon methods to watch for interesting situations without taking an active part in the behavior. A building-block class that implements behavior 1 and is aware of behavior 2 without actually implementing it would supply a primary method for behavior 1 and a daemon method for behavior 2. The primary method for behavior 2 supplied by some other class operates correctly without any awareness that a daemon method is "looking over its shoulder."

Daemon methods cannot change the control structure or the result returned by the generic function. This discipline imposed on the daemon methods limits the complexity of their interaction with the primary method, and thus makes programs easier to understand. Daemon methods are used for several purposes, for example:

- A before method can check preconditions that must be satisfied for the generic function to be performed correctly, and signal an error otherwise.

- A before method can cause side-effects that prepare for proper execution of the primary method. For example, a before method could make a window visible, expand an array, sort a table, or empty a buffer.

- A set of methods that all have to be executed, with each method handling aspects of the behavior pertinent to its own class, can be daemon methods. After methods for INITIALIZE-INSTANCE are an example.

- In a display-oriented program that gives computation priority over display update, a daemon can note a change in an object's state that requires it to be redisplayed later.

- When the primary method generates printed output, a daemon can print additional information before or after it.

The third auxiliary method role is the *around method*, which provides an imperative aspect. If any around methods are applicable, the most specific around method takes precedence over all other methods. The result of the generic function is the result returned by the most specific around method, instead of the result returned by the most specific primary method. The term "around" is based on the idea that an around method is wrapped around the other methods, controlling whether and when they are called. The most specific around method has complete control. It can shadow all other methods if it so chooses, but typically the body of this method invokes the function CALL-NEXT-METHOD, which calls the second most specific around method, if there is one. That method can use CALL-NEXT-METHOD in turn to pass control to the third most specific around method, if there is one. This continues until the least specific around method is reached. At that point, CALL-NEXT-METHOD calls the primary and daemon methods in the same way that CLOS would have called them had there been no applicable around methods.

Around methods can establish a dynamic environment for the execution of the other methods, for example locking a lock, establishing a CATCH to which a method can THROW in order to return immediately from the generic function, binding a SPECIAL variable, or establishing an UNWIND-PROTECT to clean up if execution of the generic function is aborted. Around methods can also be used for imperative control of method combination. A simple example is an around method that conditionally shadows the other methods. More complex control structures, even involving loops that invoke CALL-NEXT-METHOD multiple times, are possible; for example, an around method could keep trying the other methods repeatedly until some condition is satisfied. A third use for around methods is to modify the arguments to other methods or the results returned by them. If called with no arguments, CALL-NEXT-METHOD passes along the arguments that were supplied to the generic function, but if arguments are supplied to CALL-NEXT-METHOD, the method receives those arguments. In this way an around method can alter the arguments seen by other methods. For example, it could change the default for an optional argument, or it could convert the units in which a numerical argument is measured from inches to centimeters. Only alterations that do not change the set of applicable methods are permitted. CALL-NEXT-METHOD returns whatever result the method returns, but the caller of CALL-NEXT-METHOD is not required to return that as its own result. This result can be processed in any way. For example, this around method converts the units in which a numerical result is returned from centimeters to inches:

```
(DEFMETHOD WIDTH :AROUND ((W WINDOW))
   (/ (CALL-NEXT-METHOD) 2.54)
```

Primary methods can also combine imperatively. CALL-NEXT-METHOD in a primary method passes control to the next most specific primary method, which would otherwise be shadowed.

### 4.4.2 Other Types of Method Combination

Other declarative method combination frameworks are often useful. CLOS contains several built-in ones, which fall into four categories:

- PROGN simply calls all the methods, most-specific first.

- AND and OR call successive methods until one returns *false* (for AND) or *true* (for OR). This is used when several alternatives are to be tried until one succeeds.

- +, MAX, and MIN call all the methods and combine the results arithmetically.

- APPEND, NCONC, and LIST call all the methods and combine the results with list-structure operations.

Defining new declarative method combination frameworks is easy. A programmer can specify a LISP function that receives all methods' results as arguments, or a LISP special operator that defines a control structure. All of the frameworks listed above are defined in one of these two ways. If that is not powerful enough, a small program (similar to a LISP macro) can be written to specify the framework. The standard method combination framework is defined this way.

Programmers define new declarative method combination frameworks whenever necessary. Keeping the programming of method combination frameworks separate from programming of methods promotes modularity. When defining a method, the programmer can concentrate on just that method, ignoring the details of its interaction with other methods. When defining a method combination framework, only the interaction of the methods matters and their internal details can be ignored.

## 4.5 ADVANCED FEATURES OF CLOS

This section samples some of the more advanced features of CLOS. Many useful object-oriented programs can be written without using these features. CLOS could have been limited to just the basics needed for everyday programming, but the goal of supporting large, industrial-strength application programs dictates inclusion of the more advanced features that such programs can require.

### 4.5.1 Multi-Methods

Method applicability is more general than what we have seen so far. A method can test more than one argument; the method is applicable only if all arguments pass their tests. Such a method is called a *multi-method* because its applicability depends on multiple arguments. A multi-method defines joint behavior by two or more objects. For example, the following four methods (bodies omitted) define how to draw two types of graphical object on two different types of output device:

```
(DEFMETHOD DRAW ((OBJECT TRIANGLE) (DESTINATION SCREEN)) ... )
(DEFMETHOD DRAW ((OBJECT TRIANGLE) (DESTINATION PRINTER)) .. )
(DEFMETHOD DRAW ((OBJECT ELLIPSE) (DESTINATION SCREEN)) .... )
(DEFMETHOD DRAW ((OBJECT ELLIPSE) (DESTINATION PRINTER)) ... )
```

### 4.5.2 Individual Methods

A method can test the identity rather than the class of an argument. Such a method is called an *individual method* because it is applicable to only one individual object. This allows for differences in behavior between instances of a single class. For example, the following two methods define a general algorithm for drawing polygons and a more specific method that shadows the general algorithm in the case of a square:

```
(DEFMETHOD DRAW-POLYGON (INITIAL-EDGE (N-SIDES INTEGER)
      DESTINATION)
   ...)

(DEFMETHOD DRAW-POLYGON (INITIAL-EDGE (N-SIDES (EQL 4))
      DESTINATION)
   (DRAW-SQUARE INITIAL-EDGE DESTINATION))
```

### 4.5.3 Shared Slots

Earlier we stated that each object has its own slots with their own contents. In addition to these *local slots*, CLOS offers *shared slots*. Every member of a class sees the same contents of a shared slot; if one member modifies the slot, all see the new value. Shared slots provide a way for members of a class to communicate and cooperate. A shared slot resembles a global variable whose name is private to a portion of the program.

### 4.5.4 Everything is an Instance of a Class

Earlier we stated that in CLOS every object is an instance of some class. The full implications of this statement might not be immediately apparent. "Every object" includes not only the objects that the user defines, but all of COMMON LISP's built-in, primitive objects. For example, numbers are objects, and every number has a class, such as INTEGER, DOUBLE-FLOAT, or COMPLEX. The same is true of other LISP objects such as symbols, arrays, and character strings.

Since every object has a class, methods can be applicable to built-in objects. Generic functions thus can be used uniformly on all types of objects. The only important distinction between user-defined and built-in objects is representational: built-in objects do not have slots and cannot be created with MAKE-INSTANCE. Instead, COMMON LISP defines specific built-in functions for creating built-in objects and accessing their parts. For example, CONS, CAR, and CDR are the built-in functions for creating and accessing lists.

### 4.5.5 CLOS Models Itself with Meta Objects

A second implication of the statement that *everything* is an instance of some class is that several conceptual entities underlying the CLOS language are materialized as actual objects with well-defined behavior. These *meta objects* include classes, generic functions, and methods. CLOS provides a large suite of operations on meta objects and offers programmers the ability to define their own specialized meta objects, with their own methods for certain operations.

Meta objects constitute a working model of CLOS, represented within CLOS. This is not a pedagogical device or a simplified, scaled-down model of CLOS, but a direct interface to the actual underlying implementation. The CLOS implementation is itself implemented by methods operating on meta objects. This is analogous to relational database systems such as DB2 that store their schema in relational form and allow it to be manipulated by normal operations.

The meta object model can be used for *introspection*, in which an object-oriented program examines its own structure. This is especially useful in constructing tools for program development and optimization. Meta objects also provide abstract, machine-independent interfaces for controlling the machine-dependent optimizations that exist in most CLOS implementations.

The meta object model can also be used for *extension*, the implementation of new object-oriented languages within the CLOS framework. This extension technique allows for a measure of compatibility between the new language and CLOS itself, where the semantics of the two languages agree. It also makes implementation of new languages easier, because CLOS can be used as a toolkit of language components that are already implemented and optimized for each implementation's hardware and software environment. Thus CLOS serves as a vehicle for experimentation and will incubate the successor language that will one day replace it.

## 4.6 DESIGN ALTERNATIVES

In this section we discuss some alternate design choices that have been adopted by other object-oriented languages and briefly present the reasoning behind the CLOS design.

### 4.6.1 Generic Functions, Messages, or Overloading

Object-oriented programming languages have provided three different ways for a program to perform an operation on an object: generic functions, messages, and overloading.

A *generic function* looks to its caller like an ordinary function. However, it dispatches to methods based on the type of one or more of its arguments.

A *message* is a syntactic construct that singles out one object as the receiver of the message. The construct contains the name of the operation to be performed and some additional objects to be passed as arguments. A message dispatches to methods based on the type of the object that receives the message.

*Overloading* can be used in a language with compile-time type declarations. A program defines several functions with the same name, but different argument types. When a call to that name is compiled, the compiler uses compile-time type information to select which function to call. Many languages have overloading of built-in operators such as +, and several languages also allow programmers to define their own overloaded functions.

The syntax of an overloaded function call may appear identical to the syntax of a generic function call. However, overloading requires the types of the arguments to be known in advance. A particular overloaded function call will call the same function every time it is executed. On the other hand, a generic function call tests the types of the arguments at run time and can call a different method each time it is executed with different arguments.

An interesting fact about overloading is that it separates object-based algorithm selection from object-oriented data storage. Object-based algorithm selection allows the algorithm executed by a program to vary, depending on the types of the objects being manipulated, without visible changes to the program. All three of the language constructs discussed in this section provide object-based algorithm selection.

Object-oriented data storage makes type information available at run time. Generic functions and messages depend on object-oriented data storage. Overloading does not, because it is concerned only with the compile-time mapping of names to functions.

CLOS chose generic functions rather than overloading. Run-time method selection is important for CLOS, as it enables a program to be very flexible in the types of objects it can manipulate without having to be recompiled. In addition, CLOS is embedded in LISP; since LISP already supports object-oriented data storage and functions with run-time varying argument types, there is no reason for CLOS to avoid depending on those features.

CLOS chose generic functions rather than messages in order to minimize the number of new mechanisms added to COMMON LISP. Generic functions use the existing function call mechanism, while messages would require programmers to understand a new message-sending mechanism and to divide their programs into a function-based portion and a message-based portion. Early LISP-based object-oriented programming languages used messages, but CLOS recognizes that messages didn't do anything fundamentally different from functions. Using generic functions for object-oriented programming means that the caller of a program need not know whether the program is implemented with the object-oriented methodology or with some other methodology.

With generic functions multi-methods become possible, because a generic function doesn't single out one operand as the message receiver. Some have argued that multi-methods make the language less object-oriented, because a multi-method is the joint behavior of several objects and cannot be associated with one single object. The CLOS designers regard this as an unnecessarily narrow view of the meaning of object-orientedness. Expanding the concept of encapsulation of behavior to include joint encapsulation by several related objects is very different from having no concept of encapsulation.

## 4.6.2 Modularity and Extensibility

An object-oriented language provides:

- basic mechanisms for storing data in the form of objects and for letting behavior be determined by objects

- a set of conventions and tools for organizing large programs

One organizational aspect of CLOS concerns methods. Generic functions could have been implemented by the programmer writing a conditional form that tests the types of the arguments and performs code appropriate for the particular arguments supplied. Alternatively, an object's behavior could have been programmed as a single function, which receives the operation to be performed as an argument and uses it to select a piece of code to execute. Each of these approaches collects all behavior related in a certain way into a single place.

CLOS chooses instead to make each method a separate, independent piece of program text. This makes the program easier to modify and extend; a programmer can add new methods to a generic function without ever seeing the code of the existing methods. A program can be extended with new types of objects, new operations on existing objects, or both, without modifying the existing text of the program. Any collection of all related behavior into a single function or table is internal to the CLOS implementation, and is updated automatically by CLOS when a method is added or removed.

Formalizing the concepts of generic functions and methods makes it possible to write program development tools that assist the programmer in keeping track of these concepts. Both ways of aggregating behavior mentioned earlier can be presented simultaneously by these tools, showing all methods that implement a given generic function *and* all methods that are applicable to a given object. (See Fig. 4.3.)

Successful use of such a highly fragmented programming style requires programmers to define clear contracts for their generic functions. Each generic function actually needs two contracts: First, a contract between the generic function and its callers, to specify what behavior the callers can expect and what conditions they must satisfy. Second, a contract among the generic function's methods, to specify what a method must do, how the various method roles interact, and what inherited methods can be relied upon to do. Since a program is distributed among a set of textually separate method definitions, and since object-oriented programming speeds the modification of programs, the various parts of a program can easily become inconsistent with each other. The best way to prevent such a catastrophe is to define

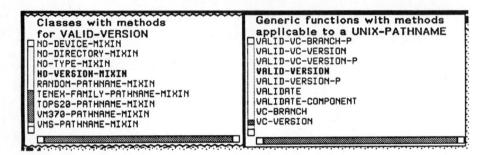

**FIGURE 4.3** TWO WAYS TO VIEW THE AVAILABLE METHODS

contracts: clear statements of how the parts should interact. Contracts can involve groups of related generic functions. CLOS provides tools to help with the bookkeeping involved in checking and changing contracts—for example, a function that finds all methods for a given generic function. However, CLOS does not directly implement the notion of contracts; this is a potentially fruitful area for future development.

### 4.6.3 Generic Classes

CLOS does not contain a built-in generic class facility, but a user can easily create his own. Many programmers use Lisp macros to create classes and methods from parameterized descriptions at compile time. In this fashion, CLOS inherits a generic class facility from Common Lisp's general ability for programs to create programs.

In addition, a CLOS user can use meta objects to implement a facility that creates new classes at run time. Such a facility is more general than the generic class facilities of other languages such as C++.

### 4.6.4 Protection and Name Hiding

When programming modularly, a programmer should not access or depend on private details of another module, but should program in terms of abstractions. This concept of *encapsulation* is especially important in object-oriented programming, which greatly increases the number of modules. Some programming languages include *protection* mechanisms that enforce modular programming style to some degree. Examples include opaque types in Modula-2 and private types in Ada. Protection of objects makes it impossible for an unauthorized module to access a particular object, or a particular part of an object, through any construct within the language.

The Lisp culture tends to oppose protection and enforcement, so CLOS does not contain a real protection mechanism. Instead it relies on informal conventions, such as "you should not call SLOT-VALUE outside of the module that owns the slot." All characteristics of a superclass are inherited; there is no way to ask to inherit some characteristics but not others. Similarly, there is no way to say that an instance of a subclass is not a member of a superclass. For these reasons, CLOS classes are not truly abstract data types. A careful programmer can achieve the effect of abstract data types by judiciously modularizing structure and behavior among classes, so that a superclass never has unwanted extra characteristics.

The fact that CLOS provides only encapsulation without protection has no effect on correct programs, which never assault the protection barriers. Adding protection to CLOS would prevent programmers from writing incorrect programs; unfortunately, it would also require either eliminating the introspection facilities or allowing introspective programs to bypass the protection in some way.

In addition to protection of objects, another form of protection is possible. With *hiding of names*, objects are unprotected but their names are hidden from unauthorized use. There might be a sneaky way to get to an object without using its name, and introspection facilities can be used to discover the name, but programs written in a "reasonable" style will avoid such tricks. Thus name hiding provides some of the benefits of protection without making it impossible for programmers to violate abstraction when they feel they must. CLOS provides three primitive forms of name hiding:

- COMMON LISP packages [Steele 1984] provide private name spaces for classes, generic functions, and slots.

- Generic function names can be lexically scoped. However, class and slot names always have global scope.

- A programmer can replace the first layer of CLOS, which provides names for objects, with a different naming scheme.

## 4.6.5 Multiple or Single Inheritance

In a single-inheritance language, each class can have only one direct superclass. The class precedence list of a class is then simply that class followed by the class precedence list of its direct superclass. The characteristics of a class are easy to compute because they are just the characteristics of the direct superclass with local modifications.

A multiple-inheritance language like CLOS allows more than one direct superclass. The class precedence list and inherited characteristics are more complex to compute. Structure and behavior can be a mixture of contributions from several superclasses. CLOS uses more complex inheritance mechanisms than a single-inheritance language to do this mixing in a manageable way. Multiple inheritance is required to handle orthogonal properties in a modular fashion [Cannon 1982] and to assemble programs from building blocks. In a single-inheritance language, it is impossible to create a pair of building block classes that can be used both alone and together. To combine two classes so that a third class inherits from both of them, one building block would have to have the other as a superclass. This building block then could not be used by itself. Multiple inheritance eliminates such restrictions.

A multiple-inheritance language includes single inheritance as a subset. This ensures that programs that are amenable to the simpler single-inheritance style can still be written in that style.

Single inheritance is used by languages with minimal run-time systems, for example C++ [Stroustrup 1986], because it is very easy to implement efficiently. By dispensing with any form of method combination, the implementation of methods can be very simple and require little run-time support. The storage representation of an instance of a class can consist of the storage representation of an instance of the direct superclass, with the slots added by that class appended to it. The position of a slot within an object is constant, regardless of the class. Access to a slot can be compiled as a constant offset from the beginning of the object, just like access to a field of an ordinary record.

In a multiple-inheritance language like CLOS the position of an inherited slot can vary among the classes that inherit it, depending on how many slots are defined by other superclasses. Slot references in CLOS require a more sophisticated implementation than in a single-inheritance language, but efficient implementation techniques have been demonstrated. Slot access can be compiled with one extra memory reference, to access a class-dependent table of slot positions (see Fig. 4.4). In practice, the positions of many slots do

**FIGURE 4.4** MULTIPLE INHERITANCE SLOT ACCESS IMPLEMENTATION

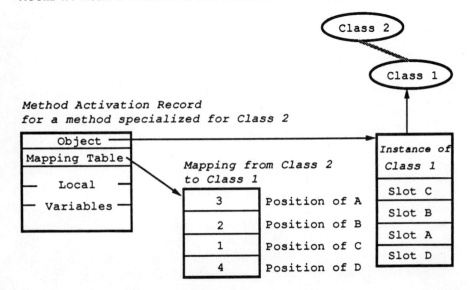

not actually vary. A compiler can take advantage of this and compile with single-inheritance techniques, if the programmer declares that no new subclasses will be defined later, or if the system automatically recompiles methods when new subclasses are defined.

## 4.7 COMPARISON WITH OTHER OBJECT-ORIENTED LANGUAGES

### 4.7.1 Comparison with Smalltalk

Smalltalk is an older object-oriented language, originally developed at Xerox Palo Alto Research Center in the early 1970s as a research vehicle for implementing interactive systems and for studying the learning of programming [Goldberg and Robson 1983]. Later Smalltalk evolved into a stable, *de facto* standard that has been implemented on a variety of hardware. It has been the inspiration for most LISP-based object-oriented programming languages and has been used for several real-world applications. However, it was not originally intended to be highly efficient or to support large programs.

Smalltalk is fully object-oriented: all objects have identity, a class, and slots. There is no form of data other than objects. Storage is object-oriented: all types are maintained at run time; storage allocation and deallocation are automatic. This is similar to CLOS, but in Smalltalk even program flow of control is implemented with objects, giving an extra level of flexibility to the programmer and an extra measure of efficiency challenges to the implementor.

Smalltalk uses messages for operating on objects. The syntax is based on the familiar algebraic infix notation. The operand to the left of the operator is the message receiver. For example, X + Y is a + message to the object that is the value of X, with Y as the single argument. A syntax extension allows multiple arguments; for example, PICTURE DRAW: SCREEN X: X Y: Y sends a DRAW:X:Y: message to the object that is the value of PICTURE, with SCREEN, X, and Y as arguments.

The principal dialect of Smalltalk uses single inheritance and contains no form of method combination other than shadowing and the equivalent of CALL-NEXT-METHOD. There have been a few experiments with multiple-inheritance extensions.

Unlike CLOS, Smalltalk is not embedded in another language. Smalltalk has fewer built-in classes than CLOS; in Smalltalk almost all object types are implemented in the normal way available to users, not in a special underlying language. Smalltalk has no mechanism other than messages for invoking behavior; CLOS would resemble Smalltalk in this way if all functions were generic. Where CLOS has COMMON LISP's primitive built-in functions that are understood specially by the compiler, Smalltalk has primitive methods that are understood specially by the compiler. Smalltalk allows programmers to define their own methods for the messages that have primitive methods. These features make the language very elegant and flexible, but a bit difficult to implement efficiently. CLOS probably would have made all functions generic if not for the practical difficulties of extending already existing COMMON LISP implementations.

Smalltalk has no significant protection or information hiding mechanisms. It has some introspection capabilities, but they are not as extensive or organized as CLOS meta objects. Smalltalk metaclasses serve an entirely different function from CLOS metaclasses.

### 4.7.2 Comparison with C++

C++ is an object-oriented variant of the well-known C language [Stroustrup 1986]. Like C, which has been called a machine-independent assembly language, C++ places a very strong emphasis on efficiency, even when it impairs abstraction. Thus C++ avoids language features that require more than minimal support at run time. By contrast, CLOS depends on a large run-time system.

C++ is not built on an object-oriented language like LISP, in which all data are in the form of objects, all objects have identity, and the type of any object can be determined at run time, independent of context. C++ provides both normal C data, which are not objects, and class instances, which are a special kind of record (or STRUCT). In either case storage management is not automatic and must be done by the programmer. C++ resolves all types at compile time, except that in certain limited circumstances a class instance can masquerade as an instance of a superclass. The behavior of a masquerading instance chooses methods based on the actual class.

C++ uses single inheritance. The principal reason for this seems to be to ensure that the storage representation of a class instance is identical to the storage representation of an instance of any superclass, considering only the slots that exist in the superclass. Each subclass (called a *derived class* in C++) simply appends more slots to the end of the storage representation. This makes possible the masquerade mentioned above. Single inheritance also allows positions of slots within instances to be compiled into methods as constants.

C++ uses messages (called *member functions*) to invoke behavior. The syntax OBJECT.MESSAGE(ARG1,ARG2) sends the MESSAGE message to the object that is the value of OBJECT, with arguments ARG1 and ARG2. MESSAGE cannot be a variable. Most messages have only one method, so the message-sending construct can be compiled as an ordinary function call with OBJECT as an extra argument. *Virtual functions* are messages that have more than one method and hence require a run-time indirection through a class slot to determine which method to call. There is no form of method combination other than shadowing. A program can get the same effect as CALL-NEXT-METHOD by calling the next method with a special qualified name. However, this forces the source program to include the name of the next method's class, making it difficult to reorganize program modularity.

C++ offers overloading of operators such as +. Operator overloading is a convenient alternate syntax for message sending; the first operand is the message receiver.

In addition to messages, C++ also has ordinary functions. Ordinary functions can be overloaded, but unlike operator overloading this has no connection with messages. Function overloading is a way to get behavior that depends on object type, but the type must be known at compile time. Somewhat confusingly, operator overloading can also be used as an alternate syntax for calling an ordinary function.

*Generic classes* in C++ are a simple macro-expansion mechanism for defining several derived classes that are similar to each other but vary in some parameter. This does not involve any run-time object typing. A generic class must always be instantiated to an actual class before a program can use it.

All of these language features are designed to require little or no support at run time; except for virtual functions they are entirely implemented by the compiler's resolution of names to addresses.

To help enforce abstraction, C++ has facilities for name hiding. Slots, functions, and messages can be declared private, making their names available only in methods and friend functions. A *friend function* is an ordinary function that has been declared to have the right to access the private names of a class.

C++ contains no facilities for introspection. The compiler and the run-time environment are completely separate, and only the compiler contains the meta information required for introspection.

## SUMMARY

CLOS is an object-oriented programming language, embedded in COMMON LISP, that will soon be implemented on a wide variety of hardware platforms and operating systems. CLOS is based on objects with named slots, classes with multiple inheritance, and generic functions with method combination. CLOS provides encapsulation but not protection. CLOS emphasizes power, efficiency, extensibility, and fitting smoothly into its host language. Providing support for a wide range of applications, including very large applications where tools for modularity are of paramount importance, takes precedence over simplicity. CLOS serves as a vehicle for experimentation and will incubate the successor language that will one day replace it.

## REFERENCES

[Bobrow et al. 1986] D. Bobrow, K. Kahn, G. Kiczales, L. Masinter, M. Stefik, and F. Zdybel, "CommonLoops: Merging Lisp and Object-Oriented Programming," *Proceedings of the First ACM Conference on Object-Oriented*

*Programming Systems, Languages and Applications, SIGPLAN Notices,* vol. 21, no. 11, pp. 17–29, 1986.

[Cannon 1982] H.I. Cannon, "Flavors: A Non-Hierarchical Approach to Object-Oriented Programming," Symbolics, Inc., 1982.

[DeMichiel and Gabriel 1987] L.G. DeMichiel and R.P. Gabriel, "The Common Lisp Object System: An Overview," *European Conference on Object-Oriented Programming, ECOOP '87,* Bigre, no. 54, pp. 201–220, June 1987.

[Goldberg and Robson 1983] A. Goldberg and D. Robson, *Smalltalk-80: The Language and its Implementation,* Addison-Wesley, Reading, MA, 1983.

[Keene 1989] S.E. Keene, *Object-Oriented Programming in COMMON LISP,* Addison-Wesley, Reading, MA, 1989.

[Moon 1986] D.A. Moon, "Object-Oriented Programming with Flavors," *Proceedings of the First ACM Conference on Object-Oriented Programming Systems, Languages and Applications, SIGPLAN Notices,* vol. 21, no. 11, pp. 1–8, 1986.

[Steele 1984] G.L. Steele, Jr., *Common Lisp: The Language,* Digital Press, 1984.

[Stroustrup 1986] B. Stroustrup, *The C++ Programming Language,* Addison-Wesley, Reading, MA, 1986.

[X3J13 1988] X3J13 Standards Committee documents 88-002R and 88-003.

# 5

# Concurrent Object-Oriented Programming Languages

Chris Tomlinson, Mark Scheevel

## Introduction

In this chapter we focus on concurrency in the context of object-oriented languages. We use the term *concurrency* to refer to multiple independent activities within a system, including control and communication; however, the topic of database concurrency control is not specifically addressed here. We do consider parallel and distributed forms of concurrency. This chapter is intended to be an introduction to current literature and issues in this area, but it is not intended to serve as an exhaustive survey. We will dwell mainly on language features and their implications while ignoring, for the most part, the implementation techniques involved.

It is important to distinguish between message passing as a metaphor for interaction among objects, popularized by [Kay 1980] and [Ingalls 1978], and "real" message passing as communication in the context of concurrent computational activity. There are a considerable number of design issues that arise when there is actual concurrency among computational activities. Most of these issues can be safely ignored when there is no real concurrency. These issues will be discussed in Section 5.2.

The message-passing metaphor treats objects as autonomous active entities that synchronize and exchange information with one another only by explicitly sending messages. This view is equivalent to stating that each object "completely encapsulates" some local state that may be accessed only by methods that are somehow associated with the object (usually via a "class" definition). Objects may access the local state of another object only by requesting that the recipient of a message execute some method.

This model has an advantage for concurrent programming over essentially shared-memory approaches that separate the universe into passive data structures and active processes. The shared-memory programming model introduces synchronization constructs such as semaphores that must be used with care in conjunction with data structure accessing. In contrast, message-passing combines information transfer (access to data) and synchronization into a single construct. This enhances the conceptual economy of the language. Additionally, a shared-memory model of concurrent programming does not lend itself to distributed implementations.

In practice, languages such as Smalltalk-80 [Goldberg and Robson 1983] and some LISP-based object-oriented extensions do not adhere to the model of complete encapsulation. This topic is discussed in considerable detail in [Snyder 1987]. The actual encapsulation semantics of objects becomes quite important in concurrent systems in two ways. First, incomplete encapsulation is relatively easy to support on shared memory architectures and somewhat more costly on message passing architectures. Second, incomplete encapsulation leads to concerns of interference.

There are at least three reasons to consider explicit features of concurrency in a programming language. First, the *real world* is concurrent (and distributed), and many information systems are intended to model aspects of the real world or to be embedded as significant components of a larger real-world system. Thus, it is appropriate to provide language support for expressing this concurrency and managing the distribution of computational resources. The task of the program designer will be eased if the means of expressing concurrency are closely matched to the concurrency to be modeled. Second, to the extent that a system is able to express and exploit the concurrency inherent in the solution to some problem, one can realize a performance gain over the typical sequential implementation. Third, in many cases requirements for fault tolerance or robustness of a system may be best met by replication of not only information but the means of processing. The design of such systems and their associated software can benefit from a well designed method of expressing concurrency.

We have discussed several reasons features for concurrency are of interest in programming languages in general. What benefits may concurrency provide for object-oriented languages in particular? One benefit is in the area of distributing single-user object-oriented environments to enhance their use in group settings. Perhaps the most obvious benefit is related, as mentioned above, to the fact that the object-oriented metaphor is built on the idea of describing things in terms of multiple independent and interacting entities. This is a natural consequence of the original intent that Simula-67 be used to describe simulations of real systems. Thus it is natural to extend object-oriented programming with concurrency features so that it may be used to perform more faithful simulations.

And how might object-oriented languages help to exploit concurrency? One important factor in the successful exploitation of concurrency is a high degree of reference locality—minimizing the amount of communication activity. Informally, there are two aspects to this factor: arranging for a program's most frequently accessed data to be its most easily accessed, and eliminating unnecessary sharing among relatively independent program parts. By nature of their structure, most traditional procedural languages blur these issues, making an already difficult situation worse. On the other hand, object-oriented languages explicitly identify those pieces of code and data that are intimately related, facilitating decisions about placement and separation. The construction of concurrent software is always a difficult task. It is to be expected that inheritance may play a role in reducing this difficulty by providing for the effective reuse of concurrent algorithms.

The remainder of this chapter is organized into four sections. The next section discusses issues that concurrency raises in the design of object-oriented language facilities. The next three sections discuss in turn the Actor model, systems derived from Smalltalk, and some other approaches that do not fall into the previous two categories.

## 5.1 CONCURRENCY ISSUES

There are several general issues in the design of concurrent programming languages and systems, including fairness of interaction primitives and formal semantic models of concurrency. We will not touch on these in this chapter. We will discuss briefly the choice of interaction primitives and resource management. See [Andrews and Schneider 1983] for an in-depth presentation. We then discuss two issues relevant to object-oriented languages: encapsulation and class consistency.

### 5.1.1 Interaction Primitives

An interaction between two objects involves at least one object *sending* a message to at least a second object that *receives* it (e.g., broadcasts may be received by multiple objects). There may be more than one construct provided to send or receive messages in a given language design. Another consideration for each of the constructs is whether the construct is *synchronous* or *asynchronous*. A synchronous construct is one that causes the object to *block* until some other message-related event occurs. An asynchronous construct is one that permits the object to continue processing once the construct is executed locally. These two dimensions give four possible choices: blocking send, nonblocking send, blocking receive, and nonblocking receive. All of these have been used in one way or another in various language designs.

The character of a concurrent language is determined by the set of sending and receiving constructs and the ways that these constructs interact. We will consider four possible sets of constructs that cover the major design approaches that have been taken. Later sections will identify how particular language designs extend these basic ideas.

The first set is a receive construct that blocks until a message is available to be processed and a send that simply hands the message over to the underlying system to be delivered without blocking the sender. We will call this interaction style *asynchronous message passing*. With this set of primitives the underlying system is responsible for buffering the messages that have been sent but not yet received. It is usual to assume that there is an unlimited buffering capacity. In practice, systems may impose a limit that when reached leads to the sender blocking until there is space available. This style of interaction is basic to the Actor model (Section 5.2) and Dally's Concurrent Smalltalk. Since we will be discussing a variety of approaches to interaction primitives, we will find it useful to have a graphical means of portraying the interactions. We will use event diagrams reminiscent of space-time diagrams in physics. Each object is represented by a vertical line with time flowing down. Dashed regions of an object's time-line indicate that the object is blocked—awaiting some external stimulus. Solid regions indicate that the object is active—performing computation steps that do not depend upon interactions. Figure 5.1 depicts a situation in which object **B** is blocked while waiting to receive a message. At some point object **A** uses a nonblocking send of a message **M** to **B** and contin-

**FIGURE 5.1** NONBLOCKING SEND/BLOCKING RECEIVE

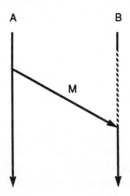

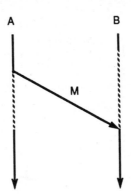

**FIGURE 5.2** SYNCHRONOUS MESSAGE PASSING:
MATCHING SEND AND RECEIVE

ues processing. Object **B** becomes unblocked when it receives **M**. At this point
**A** and **B** are concurrently active.

Another set of primitives is termed *synchronous message passing*. There
is a blocking send and a blocking receive. The send blocks until the receiver
accepts the message and the receive blocks until there is a message available.
This style of interaction is fundamental to the Concurrent Sequential Process
(CSP) family of languages [Hoare 1985]. This style of interaction is illustrated
in Fig. 5.2. One point that is often made regarding this interaction style is that
in principle there is no need for the underlying system to provide buffering
for messages. **M** can simply remain with **A** until it can be accepted by **B**, at
which point it may be transferred. In fact, with this interaction style objects
may be used to implement various buffering strategies so that asynchronous
message passing may be implemented using synchronous message passing.
Asynchronous message passing may also be used to implement synchronous
message passing.

The next set of primitives includes two sends, **call** and **reply**, and a
receive (Fig. 5.3). This basic form of interaction is supported, for example, by
the Thoth or V Kernel of [Cheriton 1982]. We will call this form of interaction
*nonblocking remote procedure call* (rpc). Here **A** remains blocked from the
point at which it issues the **call** until it receives the **reply**. On the other hand,
**B** is blocked only from the point at which it indicates that it is ready to receive
a **call** until it does receive a **call**. **B** is not blocked after it issues the **reply**, at
which point both **A** and **B** may proceed concurrently.

A related interaction style is the *future rpc* form, in which the caller may
proceed until the result is needed. If the result has been supplied via a **reply**,
then the caller is not blocked but simply continues; otherwise, the caller is
blocked until the **reply** becomes available. This style, illustrated in Fig. 5.4, is
supported in ABCL/1, for example (Section 5.2). The defining characteristic
of future rpc is that the caller is given a handle to a value to be supplied in

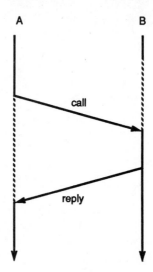

**FIGURE 5.3** NONBLOCKING REMOTE PROCEDURE CALL

the future. The reply primitive may be nonblocking as shown or a blocking form that can be characterized as a send followed immediately by a receive.

The discussion would not be complete without considering the pure *blocking rpc* style of interaction (Fig. 5.5). In this approach concurrency arises when **B** handles a call for some third object while **A** is performing other processing. This approach is typically used when the objective is *distributing* a

**FIGURE 5.4** FUTURE REMOTE PROCEDURE CALL

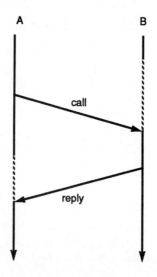

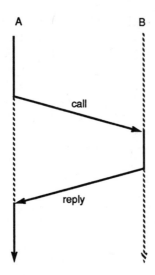

**FIGURE 5.5** BLOCKING REMOTE PROCEDURE CALL

serial language system so that multiple users can access objects that reside on different nodes of a networked computing facility. This leads to conventional serial code that in principle has the same functionality regardless of the placement of objects in the system. This approach is concurrent only to the extent that it supports relatively autonomous workstations that can concurrently share access to objects across a network. This approach really just implements serial procedural interfaces via a communication facility. Thus it preserves the familiar serial programming model. The future and nonblocking forms of rpc relax the strict procedural interface so as to provide some additional concurrency without a radical shift in the programming model. All of the rpc forms may be implemented as conventions in the use of either synchronous or asynchronous message passing.

Language designs usually include composite constructs that allow larger actions to specified in terms of the set of interaction primitives. For example, the CSP family provides a **choice** construct that permits an object (process) to nondeterministically engage in one of a set of send or receive actions. For example, an object at some point might indicate that it could either send to **A** or receive from **B**. The underlying system selects one of the alternatives nondeterministically if both are possible at some point. The Actor model permits an object to engage concurrently in a set of send actions.

### 5.1.2 Resource Management

We include under the heading of resource management the approaches the language adopts to deal with shared versus nonshared variables, object granularity, and location independence.

Object-oriented languages adopt a nonshared variable model in principle. That is, every variable is considered to be local to, or "owned" by, some object, and only that object has direct access to that variable. Other objects must request, via messages, that the "owning" object perform accesses on their behalf.[1] It is this facet of the object-oriented paradigm that makes it suitable for support on both local-area network based architectures and highly concurrent message-based architectures (e.g., [Dally 1987]). Although the model is particularly suited to nonshared memory architectures, it is possible to map the model onto shared memory architectures as effectively as languages that explicitly depend upon shared variables as the primary means of object interaction.

Object granularity refers to the bias that the language gives toward the *sizes* of objects that are intended to be cost-effective in an implementation of the language. For example, the Actor model expresses computations at an extremely fine grain of concurrency—so fine, in fact, that there are not any (native) serial data structures like lists or arrays. On the other hand, approaches that extend serial languages such as Smalltalk permit mixing serial data structures and algorithms within objects, with concurrent interactions among objects. These sorts of approaches tend to be biased towards larger granularity, in that the programmer has familiar serial idioms directly available and the implementation is likely to provide better performance over longer serial sections.

Transparency and location independence refer to the issue of whether the user of the language must be or can be aware of whether object interactions involve *remote* versus *local* interactions. The distinction of remote versus local tends to be of concern in distributed or loosely coupled systems. This follows from the wide disparity in cost of sending a message to an object on the same node as opposed to a different node. In some architectures the cost of sending messages is relatively insensitive to their respective locations, owing to the use of either shared memory multiprocessors or interconnection networks of very low latency (for example, two to three times a local memory reference). Message passing over local area networks is typically in the 10 millisecond range as opposed to local times on the order of 10 to 100 microseconds. While all approaches that will be discussed support location independence, the above considerations have led some (e.g., Emerald [Jul et al. 1987]) to provide additional facilities by which the user may specify relative placement of objects.

### 5.1.3 Encapsulation

In the ideal object-oriented model, each object maintains its own local state that is accessible only by its own local methods. All other (external) accesses

---

[1] In practice there are exceptions to this rule, such as Smalltalk-80 class variables. These exceptions raise problems of their own that will be discussed shortly.

are achieved via message passing. In practice, Smalltalk-like systems and many LISP-based object extensions violate this principle, giving rise to two kinds of problems in a concurrent setting.

The first problem is typified by class variables in Smalltalk-style systems. A class variable is accessible by an instance just as one of its local variables is, but in fact it is shared by all instances of the class and stored in the class object. In general, there are no provisions for mutual exclusion when accessing these class variables (Dally's Concurrent Smalltalk is an exception; see Section 5.3) and, consequently, there is a tremendous opportunity for interference in a truly concurrent system. Furthermore, acceptable performance for such a feature may make implementation on anything other than a shared-memory architecture difficult. The language model with class variables as a feature really presents two means of object interaction to the programmer, one via message passing and the other via variable access from one object to another. The issue is that these two different forms of interaction lead to competing architectural support requirements.

Further, since most class-based inheritance systems store the actual code for methods in a common structure in the class object, method lookup in these systems can also be viewed as a kind of class variable access, with potential for the same problems. On the other hand, the fact that method definitions can be treated effectively as read-only mitigates this problem somewhat. There are more general issues regarding the interaction of inheritance and encapsulation that are addressed by [Snyder 1987]. One approach to these issues is to replace inheritance, as a sharing mechanism, with a technique termed *delegation*. This will be discussed in the section on the Actor model. The section on Smalltalk derivatives will discuss other approaches that have been taken.

The second problem is similar, but arises from higher-order programming techniques that are manifested as block objects in Smalltalk-like systems (and dynamically created closures in LISP-based systems). Because of the scoping rules in these systems, a block object can retain references to the temporary variables of the method activation that created it and to the local variables of its parent instance. These blocks can then be sent to other objects and executed at arbitrary times. As with the class variable problem, there is generally no provision for mutual exclusion for variable references from blocks, and the same synchronization problems result.

## 5.1.4 Class Consistency

The issue of *class consistency* arises from the interaction of support for object migration and the potential for independent redefinition (or modification) of class definitions. *Object migration* is desirable in order to accomplish load balancing in a concurrent system and to bring objects together in a single location to minimize the cost of interaction. This latter purpose gives rise to the distinction between passing object names (or pointers) and migrating (moving) objects. This distinction does not really occur in the serial single processor setting.

If we assume that objects do not migrate and that creation of an object requires the existence of an appropriate class object at that same node, then objects are guaranteed to be consistent with their classes. On the other hand, if object migration is allowed, it is possible for an object to migrate to a node with an incompatible or missing class object.

This problem can arise, for example, in a federation of conventional, single-user Smalltalk systems. Since each user is typically free to alter the structure of existing classes or the class hierarchy at a node, one can expect inconsistencies to arise between nodes. It therefore seems that the proper approach is to work with a system-wide class hierarchy so that at any time there is a single definition of each class. While this kind of approach can go a long way toward solving the problems, attention must be paid to the design of the method lookup system, which is critical to performance (e.g., caching class objects at nodes). It can be argued that a system-wide hierarchy is not by itself an adequate solution if users are permitted to modify and augment the class hierarchy as they are currently allowed to in a single-user setting. It may be necessary to employ facilities that keep track of versions of class objects and the instances that correspond to these versions.

Having discussed a number of general issues in the design of concurrent object-oriented languages, we now turn to the Actor model.

## 5.2 ACTOR BASED APPROACHES

The actor model and associated languages are motivated by the perception that trends in Very Large Scale Integration (VLSI) will lead to the widespread availability of computers with very large numbers of relatively small processors. This will lead to the need for programming models and languages that can effectively harness the available computing power. Two objectives that have been identified in this context are *efficiency* and *expressiveness* [Agha 1986]. Efficiency is a question of how well the model matches the underlying physical architecture. In this sense the actor model represents one way in which VLSI trends may be expected to develop. Expressiveness characterizes how well the model matches the needs of the programmer in designing a concurrent piece of software.

The kinds of problems that actors are intended to support are large-scale concurrent symbolic computations. In contrast with so-called scientific computing, symbolic computations are very often dynamic, in that the structures over which the computation proceeds are constantly changing in shape and size. In scientific computing there is often a great deal of homogeneity to the problem; for example, there may be some well-defined algorithm that is to be applied at all locations in a spatial model. On the other hand, in symbolic computation there may be a variety of different algorithms that are to be used

at different places in the overall information structure. This latter characteristic leads naturally to an object-oriented view, in that each object may carry
with it the possibly unique means of computing that are appropriate to it.

The actor model of computation has been under development for more
than a decade. A classic paper on this model [Hewitt 1977] describes all
computation in terms of various patterns or idioms of message passing among
entities called *actors*. One hallmark of this model is that computation is viewed
as inherently concurrent and extremely fine-grained. In this sense the model
represents the least commitment to granularity in an underlying architecture.
Serial computation arises naturally as a consequence of the need to ensure that
*changes of state* are accomplished in a meaningful way. Another hallmark of
the model is that it provides for complete encapsulation of objects.

In this section we discuss the basic Actor model, the Cantor dialect developed at the California Institute of Technology, and the ABCL/1 language
developed by Yonezawa et al.

### 5.2.1 The Actor Model

A series of languages has been developed beginning with Act 1 [Lieberman
1987], continuing with Act 2 [Theriault 1983], and most recently including
Act 3 [Agha 1986; Agha and Hewitt 1987a; Agha and Hewitt 1987b]. These
languages reflect a succession of experiments in different aspects of expressing
and controlling object-oriented concurrency. A notable result of the work on
the Actor model is that there is a well developed formal semantics for this
approach to computation [Clinger 1981; Agha 1986].

**What Is an Actor?**    In this model, everything in a system is taken to be an
actor. In this respect the model is uniform in the same way that Smalltalk
takes everything to be an object. There are two important differences: (1) In the
Actor model, each actor is active in a manner that is completely independent
of all other actors. (2) All of the actions taken by an actor upon receipt of
a message are concurrent; that is, there is no implicit serial ordering of the
actions in a method (or script, as it is referred to in the Actor model). This
approach readily lends itself to descriptions of maximal concurrency. In the
rest of the discussion we will use the terms object and actor interchangeably.

All actors are characterized by an *identity* and a *current behavior*. Once
created, an actor's identity does not change even though the way that it behaves
over time may. The current behavior of an actor represents how the actor will
respond to the next message that it receives. An *unserialized* or immutable
actor is one that has the same behavior throughout its lifetime.

Actors may be partitioned into primitive and nonprimitive classes. Primitive actors are used in the model to avoid a conceptually infinite regress of
message passing. They correspond to the usual atomic types such as numbers and characters. An implementation will give direct treatment to passing

messages to a primitive actor. For example, an implementation will directly interpret passing the message [+ 4] to the actor 3 by identifying the operation and performing it. Primitive actors are sent directly in messages. Since primitive actors are unserialized, their identity may be represented by their state. That is, 3 is a sufficient identity for itself since its behavior is the same always and everywhere.

A nonprimitive actor has an identity that is represented by a *mail-address* and a current behavior that is composed of a set of *acquaintances* (the instance variables or local state) and a *script* that defines the actions that the actor will take upon receipt of the next message. The acquaintances of an actor are other actors to which messages may be sent or that may in turn be sent in messages. In a script, an acquaintance is accessed by simply mentioning the symbol to which it is bound. Additionally, **self** is always bound to the mail-address of the actor in whose behavior it appears. When a nonprimitive actor is sent in a message, it is actually the mail-address that is sent.

**Actions**   The current behavior of an actor can receive at most a single message—it is possible that no other actors have the mail-address for an actor, in which case it will never receive more messages and the underlying system can garbage-collect it. Upon receipt of a message, the current behavior may take a finite set of actions of the following four types: simple conditional, sending a message, creating a new actor, and specifying the replacement behavior. After the actions specified by the current behavior are performed, the current behavior terminates. If the replacement behavior has been explicitly specified, then it is the behavior that governs future processing of messages; otherwise, the replacement behavior is implicitly the current behavior. Thus actors are persistent but may be garbage-collected when the underlying system can verify that they are unreachable.

In the actor model there is no explicit construct for receiving. When a behavior is created it is ready to receive a message; however, in the following we may simply write **receive** to indicate where a reception would occur in an actor script. The reader is directed to [Agha 1986] in particular for a presentation of some syntaxes for expressing actor scripts. A consequence of this model is that the actions taken by the current behavior of an actor cannot depend upon any further receptions. In particular, performing a set of actions that depend upon some request-reply interactions with the acquaintances of an actor requires a sequence of behaviors.

Among the actions that may be specified in a script are simple conditionals. A conditional is a predicate, a set of actions to be evaluated if the predicate is true, and a set to be evaluated if the predicate is false. The adjective "simple" derives from the restriction that the predicate may depend only on the identity of actors and interactions with primitive actors. For example, in

(if (is? n 0) *then-part else-part*)

The predicate is simple because it just tests the identity of the actor **n** against the actor **0**. The predicate in a simple conditional is evaluated before either of the consequents is evaluated. Only the consequent that is enabled by the result of the predicate evaluation is itself evaluated.

Before discussing the primitive actions further, we will review the communication facilities that are presumed to be made available by the underlying system. Associated with the mail-address of an actor is a *mail-queue* that is used to buffer messages that have been sent to the actor but not yet received by some behavior. It is the responsibility of the *mail-system* to ensure that any message sent from one actor to another is eventually delivered to the mail-queue of the target actor as identified by the mail-address. The mail-system does not guarantee that the order in which messages are sent will be the order that they are received. This is a consequence of the fact that in the model all message sends are concurrent—there is no order of sending defined a priori on the set of message sends. The basic communication model is that of asynchronous message-passing discussed in Section 5.1.1.

The action of sending a message then is nonblocking. A target actor is designated along with some message, and the underlying system either directly executes the message if the target is a primitive actor or proceeds to ensure delivery of the message to the mail-queue designated by the target mail-address. In the following we will write:

(send *actor* [...])

to indicate sending a message to **actor**. The message consists of a list of other actors (some of which may serve as keywords).

The action of creating an actor requires specifying a script and the set of actors that are to be the initial acquaintances of the initial behavior of the new actor. Essentially the script is itself an actor that knows how to create a new actor when it receives a message with the initial acquaintances in it. The script actor plays a role similar to that of a class definition. In the following, actor creation will be written as:

(create *script* [...])

where the message is a list of the initial acquaintances of the actor that will be created according to **script**.

The action of specifying a replacement behavior is actually accomplished by identifying another actor that will control the processing of further messages. Thus in the actor model an actor is conceived as *becoming* another actor. This is quite similar to the *become* message in Smalltalk-80. It will be written:

(become *actor*) or (become *script*[...])

We hasten to point out that the above does not correspond to some approaches to actor syntax. It is often the case that the replacement actor is one that is newly created specifically as a replacement. In this case it is reasonable to speak of "the replacement behavior," as the identity of the new actor is not of interest. The next subsection will explore behavioral replacement in more detail.

To summarize to this point, with the exception of simple conditionals (which are necessarily serial), each behavior can be considered to be a set of primitive actions all of which occur concurrently when the behavior responds to a message. In general there may be any number of sends and creates but only one become. If there is no explicit become, then the implicit replacement behavior is the current behavior (i.e., no change in acquaintances or script). This may be depicted generically in the event diagram of Fig. 5.6.

**Behavioral Replacement**  It is by the mechanism of behavioral replacement that actors change state. In this section we will use an extended example, based on [Agha 1986], to illustrate this mechanism and some of the patterns of communication and conventions that arise with the actor model of computation. We hasten to point out that the example has been chosen to facilitate a concrete presentation of various aspects of the actor model, not as a particularly compelling application of concurrency. Initially, we define a simple checking account actor as follows:

```
(defBehavior simple-check-acc [balance]
    (script
        [[:deposit amount customer]
            (become check-acc [ (send balance [+ amount]) ])
            (send customer [:deposited amount])]
        [[:withdraw amount customer]
```

**FIGURE 5.6** PRIMITIVE ACTIONS FOR AN ACTOR BEHAVIOR

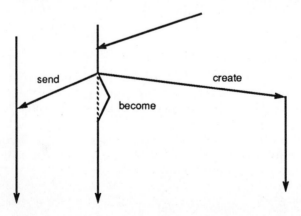

```
          (become check-acc [(send balance [- amount])])
          (send customer [:withdrew amount])]
      [[:balance customer]
          (send customer [:balance balance])]))
```

In this example we have used a more readable syntax for nested conditionals to select the method appropriate to the received message. An instance
of this actor can be created by **(create simple-check-acc [1000])**, for example.
The actor can respond to three different sorts of requests: **:deposit, :withdraw**,
and **:balance**. The **:deposit** message causes the actor to increment the **balance** acquaintance by the **amount** in the request. This is accomplished by
the (primitive) **send** of the **[+ amount]** message and then **becoming** a new
**simple-check-acc** with the **balance** that resulted from the primitive add. The
**:withdraw** request is handled similarly by a primitive subtraction. From now
on we will write expressions involving primitive actors in the more conventional form: **(balance + amount)**.

The **customer** is also sent a confirmation of the **:deposit**. In the actor
model, the use of **customers** is a convention that generalizes the idea of
a "continuation" in serial languages. In general, the **customer** is an actor
that is waiting for the result of some work, and will be able to continue
the overall computation when the result is received. This is the basis for
constructing behaviors that depend upon the results of other nonprimitive
actor computations, and will be illustrated later in this section. The **:balance**
request illustrates that it is not necessary to explicitly **become** another actor if
there is no change in the current behavior.

The dynamics of the preceding actor are illustrated in Fig. 5.7. This diagram depicts the mail-address for an instance of the **check-acc** actor as pointing to the mail-queue for the instance. All messages addressed to the actor
are delivered by the mail-system to the mail-queue. The figure shows what
happens when the s[th] message to be received is a request to **:withdraw 9** dollars from the account with a current **balance** of **307** dollars. The behavior is
shown as a circle with the script, **simple-check-acc**, and acquaintance **balance**
bound to the actor **307**. Since **307** minus **9** is **298**, the actor will **become** a new
**simple-check-acc** with its acquaintance **balance** bound to **298**.

The example has illustrated two cases of **become**, "no change of state"
and a state change effected by a "change of acquaintances." The next sort of
use of **become** involves a change of script as well as specifying new acquaintances. The **simple-check-acc** is particularly naive because it accepts **:withdraw**
requests when the **balance** is not positive. We will fix this by introducing an
**overdrawn-check-acc** actor that will not accept any further **:withdraw** requests
until some **:deposits** have been made to make the **balance** positive. The original **simple-check-acc** definition will be modified so that if a **:withdraw** makes
the **balance** nonpositive, then the account will **(become overdrawn-check-acc
[new-balance])**. Since it is a small town bank and trusts its customers, it per-

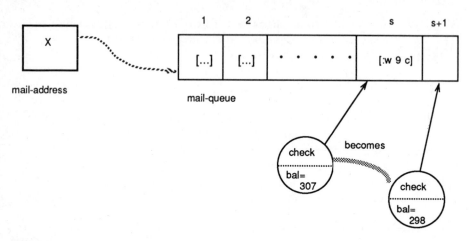

**FIGURE 5.7** BASIC ACTOR STRUCTURE

mits their accounts to run negative occasionally. The definition of the **:withdraw** request of the new **check-acc** actor is:

```
(defBehavior check-acc [balance]
    (script
        [[:deposit amount customer]...]
        [[:withdraw amount customer]
            (if  (gtr amount balance)
                (become overdrawn-check-acc [(balance − amount)])
                (become check-acc [(balance − amount)]))
            (send customer [:withdrew amount]))]
        [[:balance customer]...]))
```

The **:deposit** and **:balance** requests remain the same. The definition of the **overdrawn-check-acc** actor is:

```
(defBehavior overdrawn-check-acc [balance]
    (script
        [[:deposit amount customer]
            (if  (leq amount balance)
                (become overdrawn-check-acc [(balance + amount)])
                (become check-acc [(balance + amount)]))
            (send customer [:deposited amount]))]
        [[:withdraw amount customer]
            (send customer [:overdrawn])]
        [[:balance customer]...]))
```

These two behaviors alternate as the **balance** crosses zero dollars. This style of programming is similar to using **become** in Smalltalk-80 to switch an instance from one class to another. Certainly in this case it does not seem necessary to switch back and forth between behaviors. It would be equally reasonable to embed conditionals in the methods that would determine whether an **:over-drawn** response was warranted. In more general situations the conditionals would not be simple and would require techniques that we are about to illustrate. In all of the examples thus far it has been possible to determine the replacement behavior immediately while responding to the request. This is due to relying on numbers as primitive so that the + and − requests are directly interpreted and their results are available directly as the new acquaintances.

In general, the replacement behavior of a *serialized* or mutable actor cannot be determined so easily. If numbers were not primitive, then it would be necessary to arrange somehow that the result of the request to **balance** would be used to effect the replacement for the account. However, it is necessary when handling a request to indicate an appropriate replacement immediately. If the request is a **:deposit** or **:withdraw**, then it is certainly not correct to implicitly replace with **self**, as that would not reflect that there was an ongoing transaction with the **check-acc**. To explore how this sort of requirement is handled in the actor model, we postulate a modification to the **check-acc** behavior so that there is overdraft protection available via a backup **check-acc**. If a **:withdraw** request cannot be satisfied by funds in the **protected-check-acc**, then the associated **check-acc** is requested to supply the additional funds. We will define this new behavior as follows:

```
(defBehavior protected-check-acc [balance backup-acc]
    (script
        [[:deposit amount customer]...]
        [[:withdraw amount customer]
            (if (geq balance amount)
                {(become protected-check-acc [(balance −
                    amount) backup-acc])
                (send customer [:withdrew amount])}
                (let [[b (create empty-buffer [])]]
                    [p (create over-draft [self balance
                        backup-acc customer])]]
                    (become insensitive [b])
                    (send back-up acc [:withdraw (amount −
                        balance) p])))]
        [[:balance customer]...]))
```

where the **:deposit** and **:balance** requests are the same as in **check-acc**.

If there are enough funds in the account, then the **:withdraw** request behaves as in **check-acc**. On the other hand, if there are insufficient funds then it is necessary to give the **backup-acc** the opportunity to supply the necessary funds. The eventual state of the **protected-check-acc** depends upon the response from the **backup-acc**. While this state is being determined, an **insensitive** actor stands in for the **protected-check-acc**. The behavior of an **insensitive** actor is to buffer incoming requests until a **:become** request is received that specifies the actual replacement. The definition of an **insensitive** actor is:

```
(defBehavior insensitive [buffer]
    (script
        [[:become replacement]
            (become replacement)
            (send buffer [:release replacement])]
        [otherwise message
            (send buffer [:hold message])]))
```

When the **:become** request is received, the actor simply **becomes** the specified **replacement** and tells the buffer to **:release** its contents to the **replacement**. We will not detail the **buffer** here.

If the **backup-acc** has sufficient funds, then the **balance** of the **protected-check-acc** is to become **0** and the **:withdraw** request is honored. On the other hand, if the **backup-acc** does not have enough then the **balance** of the **protected-check-acc** is to remain unchanged and the **:withdraw** request is to be rejected. In the above, the **over-draft** actor that is bound to **p** serves to determine what the correct **balance** will be as well as the response to the **customer**. It is sent to the **backup-acc** as the **customer** of the :withdraw request. Thus when the **backup-acc** replies, it will be to the **over-draft** actor rather than to the original **customer** of the **:withdraw** request. The behavior of the **over-draft** actor is defined as:

```
(defBehavior over-draft [protected-acc balance backup-acc
        customer]
    (script
        [[:withdrew amount]
            (let [[new-acc (create protected-check-acc [0
                    backup-acc])]]
                (send protected-acc [:become new-acc])
                (send customer [:withdrew (balance +
                    amount)]))]
        [[:overdrawn]
            (let [[new-acc (create protected-check-acc
                    [balance backup-acc])]]
                (send protected-acc [:become new-acc])
                (send customer [:insufficient-funds]))]))
```

This **creates** a new actor to replace the **insensitive** actor that was established as the temporary replacement of the **protected-check-acc** while the **backup-acc** was processing the **:withdraw** request. This new actor is then sent in a :**become** request to the **insensitive** actor. It is the use of the **become** action in the **insensitive** actor that constitutes the most general case, namely, that in which the replacement is an actor that already exists. In this situation it is necessary for the mail-queue of the **insensitive** actor and that of the new **protected-check-acc** actor to become identified. This is illustrated in Fig. 5.8. Here **X** is the mail-address of the original account and $X_n$ is the behavior of the **insensitive** actor. The mail-address **Y** is that of the **protected-check-acc** actor that was created by the **overdraft** actor as the replacement behavior. Since in general there may be messages already enqueued for **Y** as well as for **X**, it is conceptually necessary to have a "forwarding" link from the old to the new.

The preceding discussion has used only basic constructs of the actor model. The pattern of communication that is used to delay further processing

**FIGURE 5.8** AN ACTOR BECOMES ANOTHER ACTOR

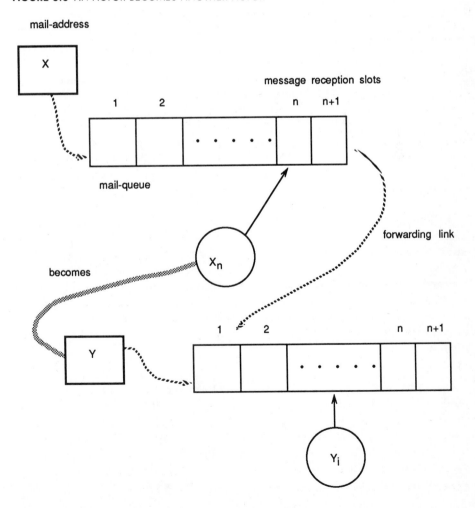

of requests until a previous request has been completed can be packaged via the **await** syntactic extension to make the process of programming with actors much less tedious and error-prone. Further, by convention the **customer** argument can be made implicit and access to the argument can be granted via a syntactic extension, **reply**. These concepts are explored in some detail in [Agha 1986]. We should point out that the **await** extension is not discussed there. We illustrate below how these extensions may be used to express the **protected-check-acc** definition. The extensions are highlighted in the definition.

```
(defBehavior protected-check-acc [balance backup-acc]
    (script
        [[:deposit amount]...]
        [[:withdraw amount]
            (if  (geq balance amount)
                {(become protected-check-acc [(balance —
                    amount) backup-acc])
                (reply [:withdrew amount])}
                (await backup-acc [:withdraw (amount —
                        balance)]
                    [[:withdrew amount]
                        (become protected-check-acc [0
                            backup-acc])
                        (reply [:withdrew amount])]
                    [[:overdrawn]
                        (reply [:insufficient-funds])])))]
        [[:balance]...]))
```

This definition combines the original **protected-check-acc** and the **over-draft** actor definitions in what should be a more understandable form. The **await** extension takes care of setting up the **over-draft**, **insensitive**, and **buffer** actors. The **await** expects an actor and a message to be sent by the actor, followed by the methods to be used in handling the reply from the actor. The methods are used to build the equivalent of the **over-draft** actor, and explicit **becomes** in a method are converted to **:become** requests to the **insensitive** actor along with the appropriate new actor. Implicit **becomes** are handled in the obvious manner.

**Issues**  The actor model does not define any form of code sharing as part of the model. It should be clear from the preceding examples that some approach to sharing definitions is appropriate. The various checking account actors have common specifications for some of their methods. The normal case of the **:withdraw** method of the **protected-check-acc** actor is the same as the **simple-check-acc** actor. This is a case in which "send to super" would be used in Smalltalk-80. Further, the **:deposit** method of **check-acc** is the same as that of **simple-check-acc**. In general, it is this kind of code reuse or sharing that inheritance is intended to support.

Delegation [Liebermann 1986; Liebermann 1987] is presented as an approach to sharing in the context of the actor model. Delegation is a set of conventions about how to use message passing among actors to get some of the effects of sharing that inheritance provides. The key idea is that any actor that *does not know how* to respond to a message should have one or more actors to which it can pass the request in order to get the work done. In this respect the idea is like chasing up the class hierarchy looking for the applicable method. These other actors are referred to as *proxies*. A proxy plays a role analogous to that of a superclass in inheritance-based schemes.

As with the convention that requests in actor languages include an actor to which the reply should be sent, the *delegation* convention involves sending along in every request an actor that plays the same role as the *self* pseudo-variable in inheritance-based languages. This actor is called the *client* in [Liebermann 1987]. In inheritance-based languages the self pseudo-variable is bound to the object that was the original recipient of a request so that methods activated in superclasses will be able to send to the original object and invoke appropriate methods according to the position of the original object's class in the hierarchy. Similarly, the client actor is passed along so that if the actor that eventually handles the request requires access to the original actor, then these messages may be sent to it and are subject to further delegation as in the case of inheritance-based systems.

We should point out that delegation as proposed differs in a significant operational way from the idea of inheritance. Namely, in delegation the request is executed by a method in the context of the proxy, not in the context of the client. In contrast, inheritance properly speaking involves executing the appropriate method in the context of the client, not that of the proxy. In this sense inheritance can be viewed as "copying" the code to be executed from the proxy to the client. No approach that would support this in the actor model has been discussed in the literature.

The intent of delegation is that it is a purely message-based way of getting the kinds of sharing that are achieved with inheritance. In principle, it solves the kinds of problems raised in Section 5.1.3 with respect to encapsulation and sharing via inheritance, since each actor just sends messages to the appropriate proxy actor in order to get the methods to run; similarly, the equivalent of class variables, namely acquaintances of a proxy, can be manipulated only by sending messages. It is not clear how well this intent is realized in practice, as none of the available references provide adequate treatment of the issues involved in delegating requests that involve changes of state.

Another issue with respect to the actor model is that of granularity. The actor model presents all computation in terms of extremely fine-grained concurrent activities. It is unclear to what extent this concurrency can be used in actual implementations to give an effective performance benefit. There is work under way (see [Dally 1987]) on architectures that are intended to support such very fine-grained message-passing languages. On more traditional architectures (including networks and multiprocessors) it would seem necessary to find ways of analyzing actor programs to "discover" significant serial sections that could be executed conventionally. This goes in the opposite direction from vectorizing compilers that try to discover opportunities for parallelism in a serial program.

The Cantor language [Athas and Seitz 1987], developed at California Institute of Technology as part of their ongoing program in massively concurrent architectures, is an actor-like language that has constructs to address the common cases of behavioral replacement. Such constructs provide some support for a compiler to implement common cases by simple branching and assignment rather than relying on a general mechanism for behavioral replacement.

Cantor differs from the pure actor model in that its primitive entities are treated nonuniformly with respect to the message-passing model, and actors may "self-destruct." In particular, it is not legitimate to **send** to *integer, real,* or *symbol* type objects. The issue of self-destructing actors is much the same as that of explicit deallocation of objects; namely, if there are outstanding references to such an actor, then erroneous behavior is almost assured. As with the pure actor model, aggregate structures such as arrays, matrices, queues, and stacks must be made out of collections of actors. Using these techniques, which support extremely fine-grained concurrency, a number of algorithms expressed in Cantor have been studied extensively in [Athas 1987].

## 5.2.2 ABCL/1

ABCL/1 [Shibayama and Yonezawa 1987; Yonezawa et al. 1986; Yonezawa et al. 1987] has evolved from the original Actor work by Hewitt, but it is more pragmatic. For example, whereas many object-oriented languages consider every entity in the system to be an object, ABCL/1 adopts the more eclectic point of view that objects coexist with other, more traditional types of data, such as numbers and lists. The important distinction is that objects communicate with one another by passing messages, whereas the more traditional pieces of data are manipulated by functions and operations as in, say, LISP. Another deviation is that common control constructs, such as if-then-else, are not necessarily viewed as instances of message-passing among objects, but as primitive concepts that do not imply a transfer of control among objects.

**Objects**   Like the Actor systems, ABCL/1 has no built-in system of inheritance for describing behavior. The behavior of an object is specified entirely by its *script*, which is a collection of message patterns and associated methods. An ABCL/1 object is created by executing an expression of the form:

```
[object object-name
    (state state-variable-names)
    (future future-variable-names)
    (script
            (=> message-pattern    action)
            ...
            (=> message-pattern    action))
    (private
            [(routine-name ... argument) = (routine routine-body)]
            ...
            [(routine-name ... argument) = (routine routine-body)])])]
```

The *object-name* is optional; it is useful if actions in the body of the object need to refer to the object. The optional **state** part declares a number of instance variables. These instance variables are fully encapsulated, in the sense that only the object in which they are defined can directly read and write their values. All other objects must send messages that request that the owner access the variables on the requester's behalf. The **future** part also declares instance variables, but indicates that these variables will be used in a special form of message passing described later; it, too, is optional. In reality, a **future** declaration creates another object that operates "behind the scenes" and instructs the compiler to expand references to the future variable into message-passing interactions with this extra object.

The **script** part is the heart of the object definition: it describes each message pattern to which the object is capable of responding and, for each message, the action or method to be executed in response. A message pattern consists of a tag (or selector), an optional formal parameter, and zero or more keyword/formal parameter pairs, all enclosed in square brackets. Optional reply destination and guard patterns may follow. The following are all valid message pattern expressions:

```
[:put aValue]
[:put aValue :at aLocation]
[:put aValue :at aLocation] @ reply-destination
[:put aValue :at aLocation] @ reply-destination where (< aValue 10)
```

The last two expressions illustrate the use of the optional reply destination: when a matching **:put:at** message is received, the variable **reply-destination** will be bound to the object to which reply messages should be sent. The fourth example also illustrates the use of a guard to further limit the messages that will match the message pattern: only those **:put:at** messages whose **aValue** argument is less than 10 will match this particular pattern. In the event that a message matches more than one message pattern in a script, the action associated with the top-most matching expression will be executed. If a message matches no message pattern, it is discarded without notification.

The **private** part of the object declaration defines a number of functions that can be used in the definitions of the object's methods but are invisible to other objects. Like the **state** and **future** parts, it is optional. The presence of these local functions obviates the need for the messages to **self** that most other languages require, and also sidesteps some issues of deadlock and message queue interference.

As in Actor systems, ABCL/1 objects are *serial*: only one of an object's methods will be executed at a time. In general, messages that arrive while one method is being executed are deferred for later execution. There is, however, provision for a class of high-priority messages whose arrival will interrupt the execution of ordinary methods. Message classes, and the interaction between them, will be discussed in more detail in a later section.

**Message Passing**   As in the Actor paradigm, ABCL/1 message passing is an asynchronous, point-to-point activity: an object is free to send a message to any other object that it "knows" about. There are three basic modes of message passing:

past   The sender issues the message and immediately resumes its activity without waiting for a response; this is identical to asynchronous message sending as defined in Section 5.1.1. This type of message sending is indicated by

   [*receiver* $\Leftarrow$ *message*]

or by

   [*receiver* $\Leftarrow$ *message* @ *reply-destination*]

when the reply destination differs from the sender. The second form is used when a receiver delegates, or forwards, a request to some third object but wants the third object to reply directly to the original sender. This form is available only in past-type message sending.

now   The sender issues the message and waits for a response (which, as mentioned above, does not necessarily have to come from the object to which the original message was sent). This type of message sending is indicated by

   [*receiver* $\Longleftarrow$ *message*]

and is equivalent to a blocking remote procedure call discussed in Section 5.1.1.

future   The sender issues the message and specifies the name of a future variable into which responses should be placed, and then immediately resumes its activity; it is equivalent to the future remote procedure call discussed in Section 5.1.1. This type of message sending is indicated by

[*receiver* $<=$ *message* $ *future-id*]

As alluded to before, **future-id** actually refers to another object to which responses to this message will be sent; its "value" will be obtained by sending it messages.

Yonezawa et al. point out that the now and future types of message passing can be reduced to past-type message passing by introducing auxiliary objects for synchronization purposes and using the forwarding form of past-type message sending, much as is done in Actor systems.

Finally, an object can send several messages in parallel through the use of a special construct. It is written like

{*message-sending-expr*$_1$ ... *message-sending-expr*$_n$}

This construct initiates all of the message-sending expressions at once, and does not terminate until all have terminated.

**Express-Mode Messages**  A significant difference from Actor systems is the introduction of a two-tiered priority system for messages: messages are sent in either the *ordinary* mode or the *express* mode. The type of mode is orthogonal to the type of message sending used: a future-type message may be sent in either mode, for example. The past, now, and future forms of express-mode message sending, respectively, are written as

[*receiver* $<<=$ *message*]
[*receiver* $<<==$ *message*]
[*receiver* $<<=$ *message* $ *future-id*]

The receipt of an express-mode message will cause the suspension of any computation underway due to an ordinary-mode message; when the computation caused by the express-mode message finishes, the ordinary-mode computation resumes, unless it was explicitly aborted by the express mode message. This facility allows a sort of "out-of-band" communication facility for interrupts and exceptional conditions that makes it easier to structure normal processing.

Object scripts must explicitly describe the handling of express-mode messages, just as they do ordinary-mode messages. In fact, the message mode should be considered part of the message pattern. Instead of the $=>$ symbol used to indicate an ordinary-mode message selector, express-mode message selectors use the $=>>$ symbol:

($=>>$ *pattern action*)

An express-mode message that otherwise satisfies an ordinary-mode message pattern and constraint will still not match, simply because it is an express-mode message. Similarly, an ordinary-mode message that otherwise satisfies an express-mode message pattern and constraint will also fail. As with ordinary-mode messages, an express-mode message that matches no message pattern is discarded without any notification to the sender.

**Message Queues and Object States**   Every object has two message queues associated with it: one for ordinary-mode messages and one for express-mode messages. An arriving message is either executed or queued depending upon its mode and the object's state at the time of arrival. An object can be in one of three states:

dormant   The object is not currently executing any method, and there are no messages in either message queue.

active   The object is currently executing a method.

waiting   The object is waiting for a specific response to a message issued while in the active mode. When an acceptable response arrives, the object will return to the active mode.

If the object is dormant, an arriving message will trigger the execution of its associated method, regardless of the message's mode. If the object is active and executing an ordinary-mode method, an arriving express-mode message will suspend the current method and begin execution of the express-mode method[2]; arriving ordinary-mode messages will be queued. If the object is executing an express-mode method, all incoming messages—regardless of mode—are queued.

An object enters the waiting state by executing a **select** expression within one of its methods, as in the following fragment:

```
[object
     (script
             ...
             (=> msg-pattern ...
                              (select
                                     (=> message-pattern action)
                                     ...
                                     (=> message-pattern action))
                     ...
            ...)]
```

---

[2] However, critical sections in ordinary-mode methods can be protected by enclosing the necessary code with (**atomic** ...). Express-mode messages will not interrupt such an ordinary-mode method until the critical section is completed.

Like an object's script, a **select** expression specifies a number of message patterns and associated actions. However, when the **select** is executed, the object begins selective message reception, during which it will act only on a message that matches one of the message patterns in the **select** expression. It does so by first scanning the ordinary-mode message queue for a message that matches one of the patterns. If one is found, it is removed from the queue (regardless of its position), and execution resumes with the associated action. If no matching message is found, the object waits, queueing incoming ordinary-mode messages until one arrives that matches one of the message patterns. The object then resumes execution with the appropriate action. Arriving express-mode messages interrupt the selective wait just as they would an active object.

Selective waiting is necessary for sequencing object interactions within a method. Like the concept of *insensitive actors* in Actor systems (see Section 5.2.1), it provides a means for objects to wait for responses to specific requests without interference from pending messages.

**An Example**  To make all of this more concrete, consider the example of a semaphore object that allows one process (object) exclusive access to some resource, adapted from [Yonezawa et al. 1987]. A consumer of a shared resource requests access to the resource by sending a **:P-op** message to the semaphore; when a response is received, the consumer is free to access the resource. When the consumer is finished with the resource, it sends a **:V-op** message to the semaphore, indicating its release. The consumer's definition, then, looks something like this:

```
[object theConsumer
    (script
        (=> some-message
            ...
            [theSemaphore <= [:P-op]]
            (select
                (=> [:go] where (= &sender theSemaphore)
                    ...access-resource...
                    [theSemaphore <= [:V-op])
                (=> any where (= &sender theSemaphore)
                    ...abort...))
            ...)
        ...))]
```

Notice the use of the **select** expression to limit the responses that will be accepted after sending the **:P-op** message to the semaphore. (Within an action body, the variable **&sender** is bound to the object that sent the corresponding message.)

The semaphore object, defined below, uses three instance variables to keep track of the state of the resource and those objects that have requested access to it. **Idle** is a boolean variable that records whether the resource is idle. **User** is a variable that holds the identity of the current user of the resource, if there is one; if there is no user, **user** is **nil**. Finally, **process-q** is a queue object that holds the identities of all requesters that have not yet been granted access to the resource. Although queue objects are not defined in this example, they are assumed to respond to the usual messages **:enqueue** and **:dequeue**. In the case of **:dequeue**, the queue object is assumed to return **:empty** if the queue is empty, or the identity of the first element in the queue if it is not.

```
[object theSemaphore
    (state [idle := t]
          [user := nil]
          [process-q := [CreateQ <== [:new]]])
    (script
          (=> [:P-op]
              (case idle
                    (is t        (grant-access &sender))
                    (otherwise [process-q <= [:enqueue &sender]]))))
          (=> [:V-op] where (= &sender user)
              (case [process-q <== [:dequeue]]
                    (is :empty      [idle := t]
                                    [user := nil])
                    (is aRequester (grant-access aRequester))))
    (private
          [(grant-access aRequester) = (routine
                                            [aRequester <= [:go]]
                                            [idle := f]
                                            [user := aRequester])])]
```

When a **:P-op** message arrives, the semaphore checks whether the resource is idle; if it is, access is granted to the requester. If the resource is not idle when the request arrives, the requester is enqueued without issuing a response. **:V-op** messages are accepted only from the current user; when one arrives (i.e., the resource is released), the semaphore checks whether any other requesters are waiting for the resource. If so, one is dequeued and granted access to the resource; if not, the instance variables are reset to the initial conditions. To grant access to a requester, the semaphore sends a **:go** message to the requester, flags the resource as not idle, and records the identity of the requester in **user**.

**Issues**   ABCL/1 programs employ lexical scoping as in Scheme and COMMON LISP, so objects that are created within the scripts of other objects can directly access the instance variables of their creators, thus leading to one of the forms of encapsulation violation described in Section 5.1.3. This will be manifested as nondeterministic behavior in a truly concurrent setting.

Although Yonezawa et al. repeatedly point out the superiority of ABCL/1 constructs over equivalent Actor formalisms, most of the constructs—such as **select**—appear to be straightforward primitive renderings of common Actor idioms that are usually provided as syntactic extensions anyway.[3] The two truly significant differences appear to be the provision for high-priority messages that can interrupt ordinary messages, and the lack of a general **become** facility by which an object can drastically alter its behavior.

## 5.3 SMALLTALK DERIVATIVES

This section discusses two approaches that have been taken to extending the Smalltalk language to support explicit concurrency. We do not discuss here approaches to distributing Smalltalk to provide for sharing of objects among conventional single-user systems. The interested reader may wish to pursue [Bennett 1987], [Decouchant 1986], and [McCullough 1987] as illustrative of work in this area.

### 5.3.1 ConcurrentSmalltalk

As its name suggests, ConcurrentSmalltalk[4] [Yokote and Tokoro 1986; Yokote and Tokoro 1987a; Yokote and Tokoro 1987b] arose as an evolutionary attempt to extend Smalltalk-80 with a concurrent semantics. While Smalltalk-80 possesses a notion of concurrency through process objects (created by sending a **fork** or **newProcess** message to a block object), the facility is relatively primitive, and synchronization is available only through semaphore objects. ConcurrentSmalltalk, on the other hand, uses the object as the basis of concurrent computation: all objects perform their computation in parallel, with synchronization achieved through various forms of message passing. However, one of the main goals of the ConcurrentSmalltalk project was to maintain source- and virtual-machine compatibility with Smalltalk-80, and this goal has significantly influenced the design.

**Asynchronous Message Passing**  In order to maintain compatibility with Smalltalk-80, ordinary message sending is treated as a remote procedure call: that is, the sending object is suspended until the receiving object returns a result. (This is also analogous to *now-type* message passing in ABCL/1.) Execution of an ordinary return expression—denoted by ⊺result—returns **result**

---

[3] For examples of the usual syntactic extensions, see [Agha 1986].

[4] In fact, Yokote and Tokoro have described two versions of ConcurrentSmalltalk. The version described in this chapter is their Version 2.

to the sender and terminates execution of the method. Such a paradigm will obviously not result in any parallel activity.

One method that ConcurrentSmalltalk adopts to introduce parallel computation is asynchronous message passing, in which the sender resumes computation immediately after sending the message. Syntactically, asynchronous message passing is indicated by suffixing a message passing expression with an &, as in

> anObject aMessage &.

The sender expects no reply to this form of message; should the receiver issue one, the underlying message delivery system will discard it silently.

**CBox Objects**   The future remote procedure call style of message passing is accomplished by introducing *CBox objects*. In effect, a CBox object is an intermediary that serves as a synchronization point for two asynchronously communicating objects. A CBox object is created by an expression similar to one for ordinary asynchronous message passing:

> aValue ← anObject aMessage &.

When an object **A** executes this expression, a new CBox object is created and its identifier is stored in the variable **aValue** while **aMessage** is sent on to **anObject**. However, **anObject** returns its result to the new CBox object, not to **A**. After sending the message, **A** resumes execution of its method; when it finally requires the result, it sends a **receive** message to the CBox object, as in

> aNum + aValue receive.

If the **receive** message arrives before the CBox object has received a response from **anObject**, the **receive** message is queued (and **A** is consequently blocked) until the result arrives. This style of interaction is nearly identical to future-type message passing in ABCL/1, except that futures in ABCL/1 behave as queues that can accept and return more than one result, while CBox objects appear to accept exactly one result.

Additional primitives provide synchronization with more than one CBox object, or one of a group of CBox objects. The **receiveAnd:** and **receiveAndAll:** messages specify that the receiving CBox object should not return a value to the sender until *all* of the other CBox objects provided as arguments also return. For example, the expression

> X ← C1 receiveAnd: C2 and: C3 and: C4

will not terminate until all of **C1, C2, C3,** and **C4** have received values. (The **receiveAndAll:** message, whose single argument is an array of CBox objects, is used when it is necessary to wait on more than four CBox objects.) Similarly, the **receiveOr:** message allows the sender to proceed after *any* of a group of CBox objects has received a value:

X ← C1 receiveOr: C2 or: C3 or: C4

will terminate as soon as one of **C1, C2, C3,** or **C4** receives a value. (The **receiveOrAll:** message is analogous to the **receiveAndAll:** message.)

**Nonblocking Reply (Acknowledgment)**   In addition to the usual return construct, which terminates execution of the enclosing method, Concurrent-Smalltalk also provides a nonblocking reply, or *acknowledgment,* that allows an object to reply to a sender *without* terminating the execution of the enclosing method. The syntax for acknowledgment is similar to the syntax for return:

↑↑result.

When such an expression is executed, the response is sent to the sender and the object immediately resumes execution with the expression following the acknowledgment. Any subsequent returns or acknowledgments will be ignored.

**Atomic Objects and Secretaries**   Like most Smalltalk extensions, Concurrent-Smalltalk suffers from interference problems arising from the concurrent execution of methods and blocks that contain references to shared variables. ConcurrentSmalltalk attacks these problems through the use of atomic objects and secretaries.

Whereas an ordinary object in ConcurrentSmalltalk will admit multiple concurrent activations of methods, an *atomic object* behaves as a serialized resource: it executes methods in the order in which it receives requests, queuing requests that arrive while it is executing, so that method executions cannot interfere with one another. However, this requires that messages sent to the pseudo-variables **self** and **super** be interpreted as local procedure calls rather than message passing in the usual sense. Without this special interpretation, these messages, like any others, will be enqueued until the current method completes; of course, the current method can't complete until these messages are handled, and so deadlock results. While this special treatment is not particularly troublesome from a practical standpoint, it does reduce the uniformity of the semantics.

*Secretaries* provide another mechanism for serializing execution. Conceptually, every object has an associated secretary, although the Concurrent-Smalltalk implementation does not actually construct an object's secretary until it is needed. An object's secretary maintains pools of ready-to-run and suspended method activations; it is also responsible for reactivating method activations when appropriate. A method activation can cause its suspension by sending a **relinquish:** message to the pseudo-variable **mySecretary**, as in

```
mySecretary relinquish: aBlock
```

The argument **aBlock** specifies the conditions under which the activation should be resumed: when **aBlock** yields **true** in response to the **value** message, the activation will be removed from the pool of suspended method activations and placed in the ready-to-run pool. When a method activation completes or is suspended, an object from the ready-to-run pool is selected and activated.

Conceptually, an object's secretary receives its messages and instantiates method activations for them. In the case of ordinary (nonatomic) objects, these activations may proceed in parallel, so the secretary does nothing special unless one of the activations issues a **relinquish:** message. Atomic objects, on the other hand, permit only one method activation to execute at a time, so if an atomic object is executing a method when a message arrives, its secretary will put the method activation for that message in the ready-to-run pool, where it will stay until the currently executing method completes or is suspended.

### 5.3.2 Dally's Concurrent Smalltalk

Dally [Dally 1986] uses Smalltalk-80 as the starting point for the development of a programming language designed to take advantage of highly parallel architectures that use message passing as the fundamental low-level interaction primitive. To pursue his goals, Dally made three significant extensions to the Smalltalk-80 model. First, he added an asynchronous form of message passing to the basic model; second, he added per-instance lock variables, much like instance variables, to control access conflicts among method activations; and third, he developed the notion of a distributed object as a fundamental system class. The following sections examine these extensions in turn.

**Asynchronous Message Passing**   To the traditional blocking remote procedure call style of message passing upon which Smalltalk-80 is based, Dally added a form of future remote procedure call that permits multiple requests to be sent. By terminating a statement with a comma, rather than a period, the programmer indicates that execution should immediately proceed with the next statement without waiting for a response to the just-issued message. For example,

```
anObject someMessage,
anotherObject someOtherMessage.
yetAnotherObject yetAnotherMessage.
```

sends the messages to **anObject** and **anotherObject** (more or less) in parallel. Execution will proceed at the third statement only after *both* of the first two statements have yielded responses.

**Lock Variables and Locking**   The semantics of Concurrent Smalltalk also allow more than one method, or multiple instances of the same method, of an object to be active at the same time. This is made possible by allocating a new context for each message that arrives at an object. This context becomes the locus of control for that method execution, while the original object is freed to receive other messages. Of course, since these multiple activations are free to proceed in parallel, and since they all have access to the instance variables of the object, the usual interference problems arise.

This problem is addressed by the introduction of lock variables and a primitive form of locking. Like instance variables, lock variables are defined on a per-class basis and instantiated on a per-instance basis. Each method specifies two (possibly empty) sets of locks: the set of locks that (in Dally's terminology) it *requires,* and the set of locks that it *excludes.* A method activation cannot begin until no currently executing activation requires any of the new activation's excluded locks or excludes any of the required locks. Thus, if a method requires *and* excludes a particular lock, it cannot execute until there are no other executing methods that require *or* exclude that lock; this is the case for a method that requires exclusive access to some resource. On the other hand, if a method simply excludes a lock (but doesn't require it), it can execute concurrently with any number of activations of the same method or other methods that only exclude the lock; this is the case for read-only access to a resource.

Although one lock variable per instance is sufficient to serialize an object's behavior, in many cases it is possible to achieve a finer degree of locking, and more potential concurrency, by defining more than one lock variable. For example, if a class defines two instance variables **a** and **b** that can be safely accessed and modified in parallel (i.e., they are independent), then each instance variable should be associated with its own lock variable. On the other hand, if **a** and **b** are related in such a way that it is unsafe to access one while modifying the other, they should both be associated with the same lock variable.

Consider the following example, adapted from [Dally 1986], of a class used to represent closed number intervals. Interval objects have two instance variables **lower** and **upper**, which record the lower and upper bounds of the interval, respectively. They have two lock variables, **lowerLock** and **upperLock**, for mediating access to those variables, and they respond to **contains:, adjustLowerBound:**, and **adjustUpperBound:** messages. The methods for those messages are given below.

**contains: aNUM**      *test for number in interval*
    exclude lowerLock upperLock.
    | lin uin|
    lin ← lower ≤ aNum,
    uin ← upper ≥ aNum.
    ↑(lin and: uin).

**adjustLowerBound: aNum**      *adjust the lower bound of the interval*
    require lowerLock exclude lowerLock.
    ||
    lower ← aNum.
    ↑self.

**adjustUpperBound: aNum**      *adjust the upper bound of the interval*
    require upperLock exclude upperLock.
    ||
    upper ← aNum.
    ↑self.

Because the method for the **contains:** message only excludes **lowerLock** and **upperLock,** any number of activations of the method can proceed in parallel. (Since none of these activations requires any locks, it is impossible for any of them to exclude another's required lock.) Since the **adjustLowerBound:** method both requires and excludes **lowerLock,** only one activation of that method can execute at a time; furthermore, there can be no concurrently executing activations of **contains:** when it is executing. A similar situation holds for **adjustUpperBound.** However, because the lock sets of **adjustLowerBound** and **adjustUpperBound** are disjoint, they may execute in parallel.

Dally also extends the definition of block objects to help increase concurrency. In Smalltalk-80, any temporary variables that a block uses are common to the method in which the block is created and, consequently, those temporary variables are subject to the same concurrent access problems as are instance variables. Dally addresses this problem by extending blocks to include their own temporary variables on a per-block-activation basis. For example, the statement

    someCollection do: [:each| :temp| ... *some actions* ...]

will allocate a unique temporary variable **:temp** for each activation of the block, just as it does for the argument **:each.** Blocks may also require and exclude locks, just as methods do, so that block activations can avoid interference with one another and with other method activations.

**Distributed Objects**  Dally's final extension is the notion of *distributed objects.* A distributed object consists of one or more *constituent objects,* all with the same behavior but, presumably, with different local data. To other objects in the system, a distributed object is a single entity, like any other object. However, an object that sends a message to a distributed object has no say in which of the constituents will field the message. Because there is usually more than one constituent, the distributed object is thus able to respond concurrently to multiple requests, even if each constituent can deal with only one message at a time.

Consider the simple example of a distributed collection (again adapted from [Dally 1986]) that responds to a **tally:** message by counting the number of objects in the collection that satisfy the block parameter.

**tally: aBlock**
    "count the number of objects that satisfy aBlock"
    ||
    (self neighbor) localTally: aBlock sum: 0 returnFrom: myId

**localTally: aBlock sum: anInt returnFrom: anId**
    | newSum|
    localData do: [:each| (aBlock value: each) ifTrue: [newSum ← newSum + 1]].
    (myId = anId)
        ifTrue: [requester reply: newSum]
        ifFalse: [(self neighbor) localTally: aKey sum: newSum returnFrom: anId].

**neighbor**
    ↑(myId \\ maxId).

When the **tally:** message arrives at a constituent, the constituent reacts by sending a **localTally:** message to its neighbor,[5] including with it the block to be used, the current count of objects that satisfy that block (initially 0), and the identifier of the constituent that originally received the **tally:** message. Notice that it does *not* reply immediately to the sender; the reply will be sent to the sender after the **localTally:** message has been seen by each constituent. When a constituent receives the **localTally:** message, it increments the current count by the number of objects in its **localData** that satisfy **aBlock**, and then checks to see whether it was in fact the constituent that initiated the round of **localTally:** messages. If so, it replies to the original requester (by sending a message to the **requester** pseudo-variable) and quits: if not, it forwards the updated information to the next constituent.

---

[5] In this example, the constituents are logically connected in a ring, and the neighbor is determined by a simple form of address arithmetic: for each constituent, the constant **myId** records that constituent's identifier relative to the entire distributed object, and the constant **maxId** records the total number of constituents in the distributed object. Thus, a ring can be embedded in the collection by simply associating each constituent with the constituent whose relative identifier is one greater (modulo **maxId**).

This example employs no "internal" concurrency: its utility lies in the fact that multiple constituents can field **tally:** messages simultaneously and establish a pipeline of **localTally:** messages in the distributed object. It is a straightforward exercise to rewrite this example so that the constituents also work in parallel in computing the tally (see [Dally 1986]), but we will not do so here. The strength of the distributed object notion is that it provides a concurrency abstraction more powerful and yet more modular and reusable than those usually provided to programmers. [Dally 1986] provides other examples of such structures.

**Issues**     Although locks seem to provide a workable solution for synchronization of instance variable access, there is still no analogous facility for class variables. Thus concurrently executing methods that access common class variables can still interfere with one another.

## 5.4 OTHER APPROACHES

In this section we cover several other concurrent object-oriented language proposals. Orient84/K combines a Smalltalk-like object-oriented model with a Prolog-style deductive execution mechanism. POOL-T is an example of a strongly typed concurrent object-oriented language.

### 5.4.1 Orient84/K

Orient84/K [Ishikawa and Tokoro 1986; Ishikawa and Tokoro 1987] has been designed as a tool for developing large, concurrent, knowledge-based systems, and as an experiment in integrating object-oriented, logic-oriented, and demon-oriented styles of programming. An Orient84/K system consists of many concurrently executing objects, called *knowledge objects*, each of which comprises three parts: a behavior part, which is similar to ConcurrentSmalltalk (see Section 5.3.1); a knowledge part, which is quite similar to Prolog; and a monitor part. The familiar metaclass/class/instance inheritance hierarchy from Smalltalk-80, augmented by a multiple inheritance scheme that is not discussed here, is used to organize and classify knowledge objects.

**The Behavior Part**     The behavior part of an Orient84/K knowledge object is very similar to an atomic object in ConcurrentSmalltalk, consisting of a collection of instance variables and a set of methods that describe the responses to messages that the object receives.

The message-passing primitives of Orient84/K are identical to those of ConcurrentSmalltalk: there are synchronous and asynchronous forms of message sending, and terminating and nonterminating forms of reply. Furthermore, the same syntax is used for the corresponding forms: asynchronous message sending is indicated by suffixing a synchronous message sending form with an ampersand; terminating replies are indicated by prefixing an expression with a single up-arrow (↑); and nonterminating replies are indicated by prefixing an expression with a double up-arrow (↑↑). However, synchronization with asynchronously invoked objects (the future remote procedure call style described in Section 5.1.1) is realized through **wait** and **orWait** primitives, rather than through a dereferencing message such as **receive** (i.e., the equivalents of ConcurrentSmalltalk's CBox objects are implicit). For example, the following fragment starts objects **object1** and **object2** on a task and then waits for both of them to finish:

```
p1 ← object1 foo &.
p2 ← object2 foo &.
wait (p1, p2).
... other actions ...
```

The other actions are not executed until both **p1** and **p2** are ready (i.e., until **object1** and **object2** have finished their tasks). In contrast,

```
p1 ← object1 foo &.
p2 ← object2 foo &.
orWait (p1: [... actions if p1 is ready first ...],
        p2: [... actions if p2 is ready first ...]).
... other actions ...
```

will also start **object1** and **object2** on their tasks, but will wait for only one of them to finish. Execution will proceed with the block associated with the first variable to become ready, and then with the other actions. The response from the object that finishes second will be ignored. Note that one object's execution is not automatically aborted when the other's execution finishes first; however, it is possible that the block associated with the "winner" could take some explicit action to halt the other.

Orient84/K objects are like ConcurrentSmalltalk's atomic objects in that only one method activation is allowed to execute at a time. However, messages and their corresponding methods have associated priorities (0 to 15, with 15 being highest), and an arriving message will interrupt the execution of any lower-priority method, suspending it until execution of the higher-priority message's method is completed or aborted. Message priorities are established by an object's monitor part at object creation time (as discussed later), but they can be dynamically altered by executing a **changePriority** statement, such as

```
changePriority(10, #foo).
```

which changes the priority of the **foo** method to 10.

Objects associate a *status* with each method. If a method is *active*, the arrival of a corresponding message will cause that method to be executed (or queued for execution if a higher-priority method is already executing). If the method is *inactive*, the message is queued but the method will not be scheduled for execution until its status is changed to active. Method status can be altered dynamically by the **activateMethod** and **deactivateMethod** requests, and tested by the **checkActivateMethod** request.

Methods also have associated access rights. An object can grant or exclude access to any of its methods to any combination of specific objects and classes, or to all objects. Like priorities, the initial access rights are established by the monitor part at object creation time, but they can be dynamically altered by **addPermission** and **deletePermission** requests. An unauthorized message is returned to its sender via a **messageNotAccepted** exception (see the discussion of the monitor part).

The combination of method status and access rights can be used to develop detailed schemes of exclusive access. Consider the following print server example, adapted from [Ishikawa and Tokoro 1986]:

```
behavior part fragment
open: aSender
        sender ← aSender.
        deactivateMethod(#open:)
        addPermission(specific(sender), #print:).
        addPermission(specific(sender), #close)!
close
        deletePermission(specific(sender), #close).
        deletePermission(specific(sender). #print:).
        activateMethod(#open:)!
print: anObject
        ...!
```

This code assumes that the print server starts out with unrestricted access rights for the **open:** message, and no external access rights for the **print:** or **close** messages. The first object to send an **open:** message to the print server causes the **open:** method to be deactivated, and it is granted permission to use the **print:** and **close** methods. When it relinquishes the print server by sending a **close** message, those permissions are revoked and the **open:** method is reactivated. Any **open:** requests that arrive while the **open:** method is inactive are queued until the print server is relinquished, at which point one will be selected and executed.

**The Knowledge Part**     The knowledge part of an Orient84/K knowledge object is a Prolog-like collection of first-order predicate logic relations that serves as something of a database for the knowledge object. Its contents can be examined and altered by methods in the behavior part through the use of five primitives: **forEachUnify, unify, addKb, appendKb**, and **deleteKb**. The primitives **forEachUnify** and **unify** are used to extract information from the knowledge part. The **forEachUnify** statement takes a goal expression and a block expression as arguments, and executes the block (in an appropriately extended environment) for each set of values that satisfies the goal. The **unify** statement accepts a goal and two blocks as arguments, one to execute in the event that the unification succeeds and the other to execute in the event that it fails.

In the following example, adapted from one in [Ishikawa and Tokoro 1987], the **dmail** relation in the knowledge part is used to select and print pairs of names and addresses.

*behavior part fragment*

```
forEachUnify(dmail(?name, ?address)                               1
    do: [printer name: name address: address &.                   2
        unify(mailCount(name, ?count))                            3
            ifTrue: [deleteKb(mailCount(name, count).             4
                count ← count + 1]                                5
            ifFalse: [count ← 1].                                 6
        addKb(mailCount(name, count))].                           7
```

*knowledge part fragment*

```
dmail(?name, ?address)                                            8
    | ?year ?month ?day ?m|                                       9
    sex(?name, #male),                                           10
    birthday(?name, ?year, ?month, ?day),                       11
    self(#checkAge, ?year),                                      12
    income(?name, ?m),                                           13
    self(#checkIncome, ?m),                                      14
    address(?name, ?address).                                    15
```

For each name and address pair that satisfies the **dmail** relation, the **forEachUnify** expression (line 1) binds the identifiers **name** and **address** to the appropriate values and executes the block in lines 2 through 7. An asynchronous printing request is issued for every name-address pair (line 2), and a count is maintained (in the **mailCount** relation) of how many times a particular name has been printed (lines 3 through 7). Line 3 checks whether there already is a count associated with **name:**. If so, the variable **count** is bound to that value, the fact is retracted from the knowledge part (line 4), and **count** is incremented (line 5). If there is no associated count, **count** is initialized to 1 (line 6). In either case, a new **mailCount** fact that relates **name** to the new value of **count** is asserted (line 7).

The **dmail** relation itself is defined in lines 8 through 15. For all practical purposes, it is a Prolog program with a slightly different syntax: logic variables are introduced by question marks, and all "temporary" logic variables (**?year, ?month, ?day**, and **?m**, in this example) are introduced in a list following the consequent. An interesting extension is the ability to invoke local methods of the behavior part through the **self** mechanism, as in lines 12 and 14. Any local method that returns a boolean value can be invoked in this manner, allowing access to procedural code when appropriate. Knowledge part relations can also refer to the knowledge object's instance variables, which are treated as constants in the knowledge part.

**The Monitor Part**   The monitor part of a knowledge object acts as its guardian, authorizing and scheduling incoming messages for the object, activating and deactivating its methods, and storing and launching its demons. For every method, the monitor part keeps an access list that describes which objects have access to that method. Permission may be granted to specific individuals and classes (i.e., any member of that class), or to all objects, as described for the behavior part.

At object creation time, the initial settings of method priorities and access permission are established according to assertions in the monitor part. For example, the monitor part assertion for access permission for the previous print server example would be

    accessibleFrom(*,#open:).

which asserts that the **open:** method is accessible by any object; by their absence from the assertion, the **close** and **print:** methods are assumed to be inaccessible. In the absence of any access permission assertion, all methods are assumed to be accessible by all objects. Any method whose initial priority is not explicitly given in a **priority** assertion is given an initial priority of 8.

The monitor part also serves as a repository for a number of demons that deal with method addition and deletion, relation addition and creation, variable access, and exception conditions, such as **messageNotAccepted**. When one of these demons is triggered, it invokes an associated method. Methods are associated with demons at class definition time, and there does not appear to be a way to alter these associations dynamically.

**Issues**   One significant difference between the Orient84/K behavior part and other Smalltalk-inspired languages is that it does *not* support the class **Block** per se, but instead defines the usual control structures as special syntactic forms recognized by the compiler and implemented primitively (not in terms of message-passing). An apparent consequence of this decision is that it is impossible to define new control structures without altering the compiler. Furthermore, many of the things that are ordinarily accomplished in Smalltalk-like systems by creating blocks and passing them to other objects seem to be forbidden. For example, in Smalltalk-80, it is straightforward to add a new subclass of **Collection** that provides its own method for **do:** that iterates over the elements of the collection; since the argument to **do:** is a block, it is not clear that the same thing can be accomplished in Orient84/K.

### 5.4.2 POOL-T

The POOL-T language [America et al. 1986; America 1987] has been developed in the context of the European ESPRIT project 415 on "Parallel Architectures and Languages for Advanced Information Processing." Programs in POOL-T are organized into *units*, which are collections of class definitions. A class definition defines the local state of its instances and the methods that are available for execution on instances of the class. Unlike Smalltalk-80, there is no inheritance of methods or instance variable specifications among classes. Further, classes are not objects; rather, they are static compile-time entities. POOL-T requires that all instance variables and method parameters be given a type corresponding to the class of object instances that are permitted to be bound to them. This strong typing supports static error detection.

Objects in POOL-T have, in addition to their local state and accessible methods, a *body* that is active on its own without the need for a message reception to activate it, in contrast with the actor model. Hence an object must indicate that it is ready to accept a message by using an **answer** statement that includes a list of the methods that the object is willing to accept for activation at that point in its execution. This is similar in function to the **select** construct of ABCL/1. The **answer** statement blocks the object execution until some other object performs a send of a message requesting activation of one of the methods that is accepted. POOL-T uses the nonblocking remote procedure call style as described in Section 5.1.1. Thus the sending object is itself blocked until the target executes an **answer** statement that accepts the message that is being sent, invokes the indicated method, and returns a result. The invoked method may specify additional post-processing after the **return** statement is executed.

All object interaction in POOL-T is accomplished via the send statement, which is notated as:

*target*! *method*($arg_1, \ldots, arg_n$).

Within an object, methods defined in the class of the object may be directly invoked as procedure calls, as with atomic objects in ConcurrentSmalltalk. This is necessary since the use of synchronous message passing would lead to immediate deadlock if an object tried to send to itself in order to activate one of its own methods.

The philosophy of POOL-T is similar to that of Ada [ANSI 1983] and CSP [Hoare 1985] with respect to its approach to object interaction. POOL-T differs from CSP in that objects (processes) may be created dynamically, and from Ada in that there is semantically a single queue of waiting requests rather than a queue per method. This latter distinction imparts a useful fairness property to the language—a waiting request cannot be indefinitely ignored.

## SUMMARY

There are a number of research activities that have not been discussed in this chapter and that present additional approaches to concurrent object-oriented systems design.

Emerald [Black et al. 1986a; Black et al. 1986b; Jul et al. 1987] is a strongly typed object-oriented language in which an object may have an optional process associated with it. Formes [Cointe et al. 1987] supports hierarchical processes and the class concept. Hybrid [Nierstrasz 1987] is a strongly typed language using a remote procedure call style of interaction and a concept of asynchronous delegation. OTM [Hogg and Weiser 1987] applies concurrency and an object model in a language intended for the expression of tasks in the office environment. Connection Machine C* [Rose and Steele 1987] uses a class structuring concept to organize highly data-parallel algorithms for the Connection Machine. Vulcan [Kahn et al. 1986; Kahn et al. 1987] provides a set of syntactic extensions to Concurrent Prolog that support an object-oriented style of programming including support for broadcasting, inheritance, and delegation.

In this chapter we have discussed the principal issues in design of concurrent object-oriented languages and several of the more prominent research projects in the area. A major issue in this area is the extension of inheritance concepts to the concurrent setting. Approaches that extend Smalltalk-80 with its inheritance features have had to cope with incomplete encapsulation by either accepting the potential for interference among concurrent activities or introducing locking to various degrees of granularity. The actor model has yet to settle upon an approach to code sharing. The relative youth of the field is reflected by the lack of reported experience with the use of concurrent object-oriented programming languages for significant applications.

## REFERENCES

[Agha 1986] G. Agha, *ACTORS: A Model of Concurrent Computation in Distributed Systems*. The MIT Press, Cambridge, MA, 1986.

[Agha and Hewitt 1987a] G. Agha and C. Hewitt, "Concurrent Programming Using Actors," in *Object-Oriented Concurrent Programming*, ed. A. Yonezawa and M. Tokoro, pp. 37-54, The MIT Press, Cambridge, MA, 1987.

[Agha and Hewitt 1987b] G. Agha and C. Hewitt, "Actors: A Conceptual Foundation for Concurrent Object-Oriented Programming," in *Research Directions in Object-Oriented Programming*, ed. B. Shriver and P. Wegner, pp. 49–74, The MIT Press, Cambridge, MA, 1987.

[America et al. 1986] P. America, J. de Bakker, J. Kok, and J. Rutten, "Operational Semantics of a Parallel Object-Oriented Language," *Proceedings of the Principles of Programming Languages*, vol. 13, pp. 194–208, 1987.

[America 1987] P. America, "POOL-T: A Parallel Object-Oriented Language," in *Object-Oriented Concurrent Programming*, ed. A. Yonezawa and M. Tokoro, pp. 199–220, The MIT Press, Cambridge, MA, 1987.

[Andrews and Schneider 1983] G. Andrews and F. Schneider, "Concepts and Notations for Concurrent Programming," *ACM Computing Surveys*, vol. 15, no. 1, pp. 3–43, March 1983.

[ANSI 1983] American National Standards Institute, *Reference Manual for the Ada Programming Language*, ANSI/MIL-STD 1815-A, United States Department of Defense, January 1983.

[Athas 1987] W. Athas, *Fine Grain Concurrent Computations, Technical Report 5242:TR:87*, Computer Science Department, California Institute of Technology, 1987.

[Athas and Seitz 1987] W. Athas and C. Seitz, *Cantor User Report Version 2.0 Technical Report 5232:TR:86*, Computer Science Department, California Institute of Technology, January 1987.

[Black et al. 1986a] A. Black, N. Hutchinson, E. Jul, and H. Levy, "Object Structure in the Emerald System," *Proceedings of the First ACM Conference on Object-Oriented Programming Systems, Languages and Applications, SIGPLAN Notices*, vol. 21, no. 11, pp. 78–86, 1986.

[Black et al. 1986b] A. Black, N. Hutchinson, E. Jul, H. Levy, and L. Carter, "Distribution and Abstract Types in Emerald," *IEEE Transactions on Software Engineering*, vol. 12, no. 12, December 1986.

[Cheriton 1982] D. Cheriton, *The Thoth System: Multi-process Structuring and Portability*, American Elsevier, 1982.

[Clinger 1981] W. Clinger, *Foundations of Actor Semantics*, MIT AI-TR-633, May 1981.

[Cointe et al. 1987] P. Cointe, J-P. Briot, and B. Serpette, "The Formes System: A Musical Application of Object-Oriented Concurrent Programming," in *Object-Oriented Concurrent Programming*, ed. A. Yonezawa and M. Tokoro, pp. 221–258, The MIT Press, Cambridge, MA, 1987.

[Dally 1986] W. J. Dally, *A VLSI Architecture for Concurrent Data Structures*, PhD. thesis, California Institute of Technology, 1986.

[Dally 1987] W. J. Dally, "Architecture of a Message-Driven Processor," *Proceedings of the 14th ACM/IEEE Symposium on Computer Architecture*, pp. 189–196, June 1987.

[Goldberg and Robson 1983] A. Goldberg and D. Robson, *Smalltalk-80: The Language and its Implementation*, Addison Wesley, Reading, MA, 1983.

[Hewitt 1977] C. Hewitt, "Viewing Control Structures as Patterns of Passing Messages," *Journal of Artificial Intelligence*, vol. 8, no. 3, pp. 323–364, June 1977.

[Hoare 1985] C. Hoare, *Communicating Sequential Processes*, Prentice-Hall, Englewood Cliffs, NJ, 1985.

[Hogg and Weiser 1987] J. Hogg and S. Weiser, "OTM: Applying Objects to Tasks," *Proceedings of the Second ACM Conference on Object-Oriented Programming Systems, Languages and Applications, SIGPLAN Notices*, vol. 22, no. 12, pp. 388–393, 1987.

[Ishikawa and Tokoro 1986] Y. Ishikawa and M. Tokoro, "A Concurrent Object-Oriented Knowledge Representation Language Orient84/K: Its Features and Implementation," *Proceedings of the First ACM Conference on Object-Oriented Programming Systems, Languages and Applications, SIGPLAN Notices*, vol. 21, no. 11, pp. 232–241, 1986.

[Ishikawa and Tokoro 1987] Y. Ishikawa and M. Tokoro, "Orient84/K: An Object-Oriented Concurrent Programming Language for Knowledge Representation," in *Object-Oriented Concurrent Programming*, ed. A. Yonezawa and M. Tokoro, pp. 159–198, The MIT Press, Cambridge, MA, 1987.

[Jul et al. 1987] E. Jul, H. Levy, N. Hutchinson, and A. Black, "Fine-Grained Mobility in the Emerald System," *Proceedings of the Symposium on Operating Systems Principles—1987*, pp. 62–74, October 1987.

[Kahn et al. 1986] K. Kahn, E. Tribble, M. Miller, and D. Bobrow, "Objects in Concurrent Logic Programming Languages," *Proceedings of the First ACM Conference on Object-Oriented Systems, Languages and Applications, SIGPLAN Notices*, vol. 21, no. 11, pp. 242–257, 1986.

[Kahn et al. 1987] K. Kahn, E. Tribble, M. Miller, and D. Bobrow, "Vulcan: Logical Concurrent Objects," in *Research Directions in Object-Oriented Programming*, ed. B. Shriver and P. Wegner, pp. 75–112, The MIT Press, Cambridge, MA, 1987.

[Kay 1980] A. Kay, "Smalltalk," in *Methodology of Interaction*, ed. Guedj, IFIP, North-Holland, 1980.

[Lieberman 1986] H. Lieberman, "Using Prototypical Objects to Implement Shared Behavior in Object-Oriented Systems," *Proceedings of the First ACM Conference on Object-Oriented Systems, Languages and Applications, SIGPLAN Notices*, vol. 21, no. 11, pp. 214–223, 1986.

[Lieberman 1987] H. Lieberman, "Concurrent Object-Oriented Programming in Act 1," in *Object-Oriented Concurrent Programming*, ed. A. Yonezawa and M. Tokoro, pp. 9–36, The MIT Press, Cambridge, MA, 1987.

[Meyrowitz 1986] N. Meyrowitz, ed., *Proceedings of the First ACM Conference on Object-Oriented Programming Systems, Languages and Applications, SIGPLAN Notices*, vol. 21, no. 11, November 1986.

[Meyrowitz 1987] N. Meyrowitz, ed., *Proceedings of the Second ACM Conference on Object-Oriented Programming Systems, Languages and Applications, SIGPLAN Notices*, vol. 22, no. 12, December 1987.

[Nierstrasz 1987] O. Nierstrasz, "Active Objects in Hybrid," *Proceedings of the Second ACM Conference on Object-Oriented Systems, Languages and Applications, SIGPLAN Notices*, vol. 22, no. 12, pp. 243–253, 1987.

[Rose and Steele 1987] J. Rose and G. Steele, Jr, "C*: An Extended C Language for Data Parallel Programming," *Proceedings of the Second International Conference on Supercomputing*, May 1987.

[Shibayama and Yonezawa 1987] E. Shibayama and A. Yonezawa, "Distributed Computing in ABCL/1," in *Object-Oriented Concurrent Programming*, A. Yonezawa and M. Tokoro, pp. 91–128, The MIT Press, Cambridge, MA, 1987.

[Shriver and Wegner 1987] B. Shriver and P. Wegner, eds., *Research Directions in Object-Oriented Programming*, The MIT Press, Cambridge, MA, 1987.

[Snyder 1987] A. Snyder, "Inheritance and the Development of Encapsulated Software Systems," in *Research Directions in Object-Oriented Programming*, The MIT Press, Cambridge, MA, 1987.

[Theriault 1983] D. Theriault, *Issues in the Design and Implementation of Act 2*, MIT AI-TR-728, June 1983.

[Wegner 1987a] P. Wegner, "Dimensions of Object-Based Language Design," *Proceedings of the Second ACM Conference on Object-Oriented Programming Systems, Languages and Applications, SIGPLAN Notices*, vol. 22, no. 12, pp. 168–182, 1987.

[Wegner 1987b] P. Wegner. "The Object-Oriented Classification Paradigm," *Research Directions in Object-Oriented Programming*, ed. B. Shriver and P. Wegner, pp. 479–560, The MIT Press, Cambridge, MA, 1987.

[Yokote and Tokoro 1986] Y. Yokote and M. Tokoro, "The Design and Implementation of ConcurrentSmalltalk," in *Proceedings of the First ACM Conference on Object-Oriented Systems, Languages and Applications, SIGPLAN Notices*, vol. 21, no. 11, pp. 331–340, 1986.

[Yokote and Tokoro 1987a] Y. Yokote and M. Tokoro, "Concurrent Programming in ConcurrentSmalltalk," in *Object-Oriented Concurrent Program-

*ming,* A. Yonezawa and M. Tokoro, pp. 129–158, The MIT Press, Cambridge, MA, 1987.

[Yokote and Tokoro 1987b] Y. Yokote and M. Tokoro, "Experience and Evolution of ConcurrentSmalltalk," *Proceedings of the Second ACM Conference on Object-Oriented Programming Systems, Languages and Applications, SIGPLAN Notices,* vol. 22, no. 12, pp. 406–415, 1987.

[Yonezawa et al. 1986] A. Yonezawa, J-P. Briot, and E. Shibayama, "Object-Oriented Concurrent Programming in ABCL/1," *Proceedings of the First ACM Conference on Object-Oriented Programming Systems, Languages and Applications, SIGPLAN Notices,* vol. 21, no. 11, pp. 258–268, 1986.

[Yonezawa et al. 1987] A. Yonezawa, E. Shibayama, T. Takada, and Y. Honda, "Modelling and Programming in an Object-Oriented Concurrent Language ABCL/1," in *Object-Oriented Concurrent Programming,* A. Yonezawa and M. Tokoro, pp. 55–90, The MIT Press, Cambridge, MA, 1987.

[Yonezawa and Tokoro 1987] A. Yonezawa and M. Tokoro, eds., *Object-Oriented Concurrent Programming,* The MIT Press, Cambridge, MA, 1987.

# 2 Object-Oriented Applications

# 6

## Proteus: A Frame-Based Nonmonotonic Inference System

David M. Russinoff

### INTRODUCTION

Early artificial intelligence systems relied on first-order predicate logic as a language for representing domain knowledge. While this scheme is completely general and semantically clear, it has been found to be inadequate for organizing large knowledge bases and encoding complex objects. As an alternative, various frame-based languages have been employed. These languages are designed to support the natural representation of structured objects and taxonomies. They have proved to be well suited for representing many useful relations, although they lack the general expressive power of the predicate calculus.

Knowledge-based systems may also be classified according to inference methods. Most deductive systems may be characterized as either goal-directed (backward chaining) or data-directed (forward chaining). In a goal-directed system, logical implications are encoded as rules that are used by the system to reduce goals to simpler subgoals. This allows knowledge to be represented implicitly, without using space in the knowledge base, until it becomes relevant to a current problem. In this framework, however, it is difficult for the knowledge base designer to build control into a system. Data-directed inference, on the other hand, is based on production rules, which the system uses to derive all logical consequences of new data automatically. While control of inference is more natural within this paradigm, it uses space less efficiently, representing all knowledge explicitly.

This chapter describes the knowledge representation and reasoning components of *Proteus* [Russinoff 1985b; Petrie 1987; Poltrock et al. 1986], a hybrid expert system tool written in COMMON LISP, under development at the Microelectronics and Computer Technology Corporation. Proteus is frame-based, but allows knowledge to be expressed in terms of arbitrary predicates. It also integrates goal-directed and data-directed inference, allowing the knowledge engineer the freedom to decide whether each logical implication is more suitably represented as a backward rule or a forward rule.

A central feature of Proteus is a nonmonotonic truth maintenance system (TMS), based on [Doyle 1979], which records logical inferences and dependencies among data. This allows efficient revision of a set of beliefs to accommodate new information, the retraction of a premise, or the discovery of a contradiction [Petrie 1987]. It also facilitates the generation of coherent explanations. Data dependencies and truth maintenance in Proteus are discussed in Section 6.2.

In Section 6.3, we introduce frames, along with classes, attributes, metaclasses, and types. Section 6.4 describes simple data, including attribute values that are attached to frames, as well as assertions associated with predicates. Here we discuss the use of the TMS in connection with single-valued slots and inheritance.

Finally, we describe the Proteus inference system and its integration with the TMS. Sections 6.5 and 6.6 deal with backward and forward chaining, respectively.

## 6.1 TRUTH MAINTENANCE

Each element of the Proteus database represents a potential belief. The status of this belief, which is subject to change, is reflected in the *support-status* of the datum, the value of which may be IN, indicating that it is currently believed, or OUT, indicating current disbelief. This value is assigned by the TMS in accordance with a list of *justifications* that have been attached to the datum.

Each justification consists of a pair of lists of data, the IN-list and the OUT-list of the justification. A justification is said to be *valid* and is considered to represent reason for belief in its associated datum if each element of its **IN**-list is **IN** and each element of its **OUT**-list is **OUT**. The justified datum is said to depend *monotonically* on each member of the justification's **IN**-list and *nonmonotonically* on each member of the **OUT**-list.

Also associated with each datum is a list of other data called its *supporters*. The supporters of a datum are considered to be responsible for its current support-status.

It is the function of the TMS to assign support-statuses and supporters to data in a manner that is consistent with their justifications, and to adjust these assignments continually as required by the addition of new justifications and the retraction of old ones. More precisely, the state of the database, as constructed by the TMS, must satisfy two requirements: *stability* and *well-foundedness*. A *stable* state is one that satisfies the following conditions:

1. A datum is IN if it has at least one valid justification. In this case its list of supporters is the result of appending the IN-list and OUT-list of one of its valid justifications. This justification is identified as the *supporting justification*.

2. A datum is OUT if it has no valid justification. Its supporters then include one representative of each of its invalid justifications: either an OUT member of the IN-list or an IN member of the OUT-list.

The requirement of well-foundedness is that no set of beliefs be mutually dependent, i.e., there may be no sequence of data $d_0,...,d_n$, all of which are IN, such that $d_0 = d_n$ and for $i = 1,...,n$, $d_{i-1}$ is a supporter of $d_i$.

An example of an admissible state is shown in Fig. 6.1. In this graph and those that follow, each circle corresponds to a justification, with an arrow pointing to the justified datum, positive arcs connected to the elements of the IN-list, and negative arcs to elements of the OUT-list. Thus, the datum representing a diagnosis of appendicitis has a valid justification with a two-element IN-list and a two-element OUT-list. The belief that the patient has a side pain is supported by a justification with an empty IN-list and an empty OUT-list and is said to be a *premise*. The datum representing the unreliability of the patient has an empty list of justifications and is therefore OUT. If this datum were to acquire a new valid justification, then its support-status as well as those of the data that depend on it (directly or indirectly) must be reevaluated, ultimately forcing the diagnosis OUT. This phenomenon, the development of a new belief resulting in the abandonment of an old one, characterizes *nonmonotonic reasoning*.

In the presence of nonmonotonic dependencies, the status-assignment problem may not have a unique solution. In the situation shown in Fig. 6.2, the TMS may succeed either by making P (and hence R) IN and Q (and hence S) OUT, or by giving the opposite assignments. This choice between alternative hypothetical assumptions can be made only arbitrarily, and may have to be revised later as new justifications are produced (e.g., if Q acquires a new valid justification while P is IN).

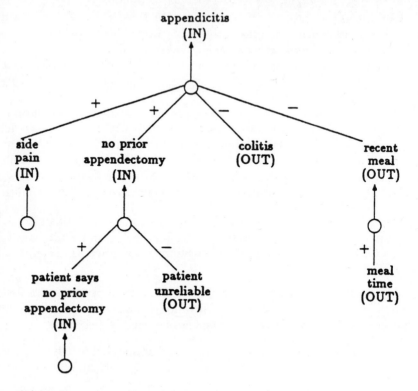

**FIGURE 6.1** A STABLE WELL-FOUNDED STATE

**FIGURE 6.2** ALTERNATIVE ASSUMPTIONS

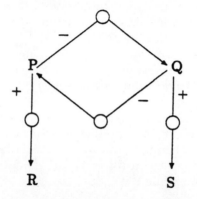

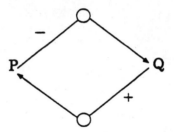

**FIGURE 6.3** UNSATISFIABLE DEPENDENCIES

Circularities involving nonmonotonic dependencies may also impose unsatisfiable constraints on the TMS, a situation that may be difficult to detect. Two simple examples of this are shown in Figs. 6.3 and 6.4. Note that the network of Fig. 6.4 does have a stable state (in which all data are IN), but this state is ill-founded and therefore inadmissable.

As described in [Russinoff 1985a], the Proteus TMS is *complete* in the sense that given any database with any set of justifications, it will achieve a stable well-founded state if such a state exists, and otherwise will recognize and report failure. This represents an improvement over the original TMS of Doyle [Doyle 1979], as well as other published procedures for truth maintenance [Charniak et al. 1980; Goodwin 1986]. These systems all fail (perhaps even fail to terminate) in the presence of certain circular dependencies that have been characterized as *odd loops*. An odd loop is a cycle of arcs with an odd number of minus signs, as in Figs. 6.3, 6.4, and 6.5. A dependency network containing such a loop may or may not be satisfiable. (The network in Fig. 6.5 does admit a solution.) While the presence of odd loops complicates the truth

**FIGURE 6.4** NO WELL-FOUNDED STABLE STATE

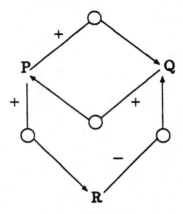

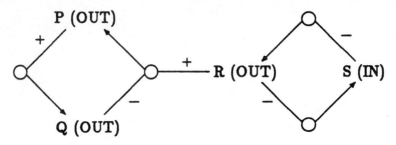

**FIGURE 6.5** A SOLVABLE ODD LOOP

maintenance task and is generally considered undesirable, they are sometimes unavoidable in practice, particularly in dependency networks that are based on input from several users.

In the sequel, we show how data dependency networks are created in Proteus by the user, by the frame system, and by both forward and backward inference.

## 6.2 FRAMES AND CLASSES

The data on which the TMS operates represent statements about objects. Before discussing the structure of these data, we shall describe the objects that they concern. These objects, called *frames*, are the subject of this section.

### 6.2.1 Classes, Subclasses, and Members

In the initial state of the system, there exist several frames. One of these, named **CLASS**, plays a special role as discussed below. The others are **LIST**, **CONS, NULL, SYMBOL, NUMBER, FIXNUM,** and **SINGLE-FLOAT**. The user may enlarge this set by creating new frames, one at a time.

There are two primitive relations defined on frames: *instance* and *child*. If a pair $(x,y)$ is an element of the instance relation, we say that *x is an instance of y*, or that *y is the type of x*. For a pair $(x,y)$ in the child relation, we say that *x is a child of y*, that *y is a parent of x*, or that *x is linked to y*. Figure 6.6 depicts these relations as they are defined in the initial state. Broken lines are drawn from instances to types, and solid lines from children to parents. Thus, **CLASS** is the type of every system-defined frame.

Two other important relations are defined in terms of these primitives: *subclass* and *member*. The subclass relation is defined as the reflexive transitive closure of the child relation. Thus, *x* is a subclass of *y* (equivalently, *y* is a *superclass* of *x*) if either *x* is identical to *y*, or *x* is a child of a subclass of *y*. The membership relation is defined as follows: *x* is a member of *y* if *x* is

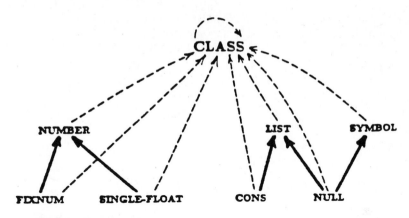

**FIGURE 6.6** BUILT-IN CLASSES

an instance of a subclass of $y$. In this case we may also say that $x$ *is a* $y$. In particular, a *class* is by definition a frame that is a member of **CLASS**. Note that every system-defined frame is a class, including **CLASS** itself.

As new frames are created by the user, he may also extend these relations by assigning types to instances and creating links (between user-defined classes only). This must be done in such a way, however, that at each stage of the development, the following properties are preserved:

1. The instance relation is a function; i.e., for each frame $x$ there exists a unique frame $y$ such that $x$ is an instance of $y$.

2. **CLASS** is the only frame that is an instance of itself. Thus, whenever a new frame is created, some preexisting frame must be specified as its type.

3. The subclass relation is a partial order. That is, if $x$ is a subclass of $y$ and $y$ is a subclass of $x$, then $x$ and $y$ are identical.

4. If $x$ is an instance of $y$, then $y$ must be a member of **CLASS**.

5. If $x$ is a child of $y$, then $x$ and $y$ must both be members of **CLASS**.

Thus, according to the last two of these properties, only classes may have instances, members, children, parents, subclasses, or superclasses. There is a further restriction on the classes that may be instantiated by the user: a user-defined frame may be an instance of **CLASS** or of any user-defined class, but it may not be an instance of **LIST, CONS, NULL, SYMBOL, NUMBER, FIXNUM,** or **SINGLE-FLOAT**. Instead, whenever the system encounters a COMMON LISP object whose datatype is the name of one of these system-defined classes, the object automatically becomes an instance of the named class. For example, if the number $3$ is read, it becomes an instance of

**FIXNUM** and thus a member of **NUMBER** (in other words, a number). When the symbol **NIL** is encountered, it is recognized as the unique instance of the class **NULL**, and hence both a list and a symbol.

An example of a user-defined system of frames is illustrated in Fig. 6.7. This example involves eight new classes, all of which are subclasses of the class **PERSON** and instances of the class **CLASS**. For clarity, classes are denoted in boldface and other user-defined frames in italics. *SHIRLEY*, for example, as an instance of **TA**, is not a class but is a TA, a graduate, a staff, a student, an employee, and a person.

### 6.2.2 Metaclasses

Of course, the existence of classes as frames provides the advantage of being able to reason about classes at the same level at which one reasons about the objects of which they are composed. It is often desirable to be able to reason

**FIGURE 6.7** USER-DEFINED CLASSES

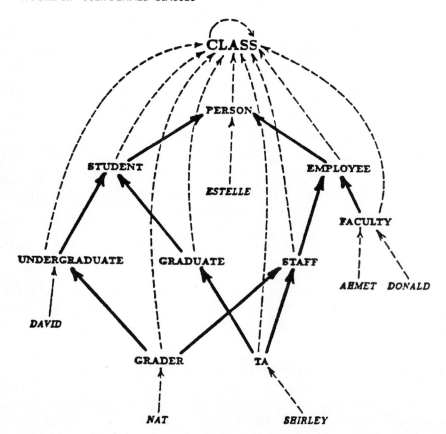

about classes of classes as well. The only class we have seen so far that has classes as members is **CLASS** itself. Any class that has a class as an instance must be a subclass of **CLASS**, in which case all of its members are classes. Such a class is called a *metaclass*. While **CLASS** is the only system-defined metaclass (and the only one in the example of Fig. 6.7), additional metaclasses may be created simply by linking any user-defined classes to **CLASS**.

The example of Fig. 6.8 includes several user-defined metaclasses (denoted in large bold print). This example is based on six classes of animals: **ANIMALIA** (the class of all animals) and five of its subclasses, which are related as indicated by the solid arrows connecting them. These classes could be constructed simply as instances of **CLASS**. But in order to represent and utilize the knowledge that these classes share more than mere classhood, we first define a metaclass called **BIOLOGICAL-CLASS**, intended to include the

**FIGURE 6.8** USER-DEFINED METACLASSES

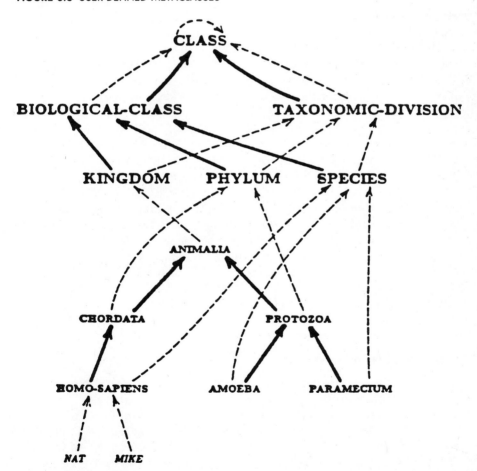

animal classes among its members. In fact, the animal classes are partitioned into smaller metaclasses by defining them as instances of **KINGDOM, PHYLUM**, and **SPECIES**, which are subclasses of **BIOLOGICAL-CLASS**. Note that **KINGDOM, PHYLUM**, and **SPECIES** are themselves not simply instances of **CLASS**, but are classes by virtue of being instances of the metaclass **TAXONOMIC-DIVISION**. Moreover, they are metaclasses by virtue of their links to the metaclass **BIOLOGICAL-CLASS**.

### 6.2.3 Attributes

Corresponding to each user-defined class is a (possibly empty) set of user-defined *attributes* associated with that class. Every attribute is defined for a unique class—the frames that may assume values for a given attribute are the members of the class for which it is defined. Thus, in the example of Fig. 6.7, if attributes called HOURLY-WAGE and TITLE are defined for the classes **EMPLOYEE** and **FACULTY**, respectively, then the frames that may have HOURLY-WAGE values are *NAT, SHIRLEY, AHMET,* and *DONALD*, while only *AHMET* and *DONALD* may assume TITLEs. These attribute values form a classification of data to be discussed in Section 6.4.

The manner in which attributes are inherited from their defining classes provides motivation for the construction of user-defined metaclasses, such as those of Fig. 6.8. If **ANIMALIA, CHORDATA**, etc. had simply been defined as instances of **CLASS**, there would have been no way for them to acquire attribute values. But as members of the user-defined class **BIOLOGICAL-CLASS**, they may assume values for any attributes defined for that class. Thus, if COMMON-NAME is among these attributes, then the statement "the COMMON-NAME of **PROTOZOA** is ONE-CELLED-ANIMAL" makes sense. The partitioning of **BIOLOGICAL-CLASS** into subclasses allows the definition of attributes that pertain to some biological-classes but not to all. For example, one might refer to the number of species of protozoa, but not the number of species of amoeba, while the number of species of animalia is not practically measurable. The attribute NUMBER-OF-SPECIES, therefore, should not be defined for the class **BIOLOGICAL-CLASS**, but rather for its subclass **PHYLUM**.

### 6.2.4 Variables and Types

Along with the objects that appear in Proteus data, there are also occurrences of variables. These are denoted as symbols with initial character "?". Variables, as usual, represent unspecified objects. The process of unification, which is central to the mechanisms of forward and backward chaining, is built on the basic operation of binding (i.e., assigning values to) variables. An unbound variable ?X may be bound either to an object or to another unbound variable

?Y. In the latter case, if ?Y is subsequently bound, its binding also becomes the binding of ?X,

Since objects in this system are classified by their types, it is natural and useful to classify variables in a similar way. Thus, following [Aït-kaci and Nasr 1985], a variable may be specified to be of a certain type. This is done by appending the name of a class to the variable name, using ":" as a separator, as in ?X:STUDENT. The consequence of assigning a type to a variable is that any binding of the variable is required to be a member of the variable's type.

In the presence of typed variables, the standard unification algorithm must be altered in several ways. First, before a variable is bound to an object, it must be verified that the object is a member of the variable's type. Second, before a variable is bound to another variable, it must be verified that the types of the two variables are compatible, so that it will be possible later to bind them to the same object. Thus, the two types must have a nontrivial common subtype. Finally, when a variable ?X is bound to a variable ?Y, the type of ?Y must be replaced in order to ensure that any later binding of ?Y is consistent with the type of ?X. The new type of ?Y should be the most general common subtype, or *greatest lower bound*, of the type of ?X and the old type of ?Y. For example (see Fig. 6.7), a variable ?X:UNDERGRADUATE could be bound to a variable ?Y:STAFF, with type of ?Y replaced by **GRADER**. ?Y could then be bound to *NAT*, but no longer to *SHIRLEY*, which would violate the type restriction on ?X.

Thus, the modified unification algorithm depends on the computability of the greatest lower bound (g.l.b.) of two variable types. Unfortunately, the partially ordered set of classes does not form a *lattice*; i.e., the g.l.b. of two classes may not exist. The classes **STUDENT** and **EMPLOYEE** of Fig. 6.7, for example, have two common subclasses, **GRADER** and **TA**. Since neither of these is a superclass of the other, neither can be said to be the g.l.b. of **STUDENT** and **EMPLOYEE**.

This problem is solved by generalizing the notion of *type*. A type is now defined to be a set of classes, none of which is a subclass of another. A type $t_1$ is a subtype of a type $t_2$ if each of the classes of $t_1$ is a subclass of at least one of the classes of $t_2$. An object is said to belong to a type if it is a member of at least one of its classes. It follows that an object belongs to a type if it belongs to any of its subtypes.

Under this ordering, the set of all types forms a lattice. The type of a variable may be any member of this lattice. The identification of each class $c$ with the type $\{c\}$ induces an embedding of the partially ordered set of classes into the lattice of types. In this context, the g.l.b. of two classes may always be computed. Thus, the g.l.b. of **STUDENT** and **EMPLOYEE** is the type **{GRADER,TA}**.

The empty set of classes, denoted *bottom*, is a subtype of every type. This type contains no objects and is not allowed as the type of a variable. If the g.l.b. of the types of two variables (e.g., ?X:STAFF and ?Y:FACULTY)

is *bottom*, then these variables cannot be unified; their types contain no common objects.

The set of all maximal classes is also a type, denoted *top*. It is a supertype of every type, and every object belongs to it. If no type is specified for a variable, then the variable's type is taken to be *top* as a default. There is no restriction on the binding of such a variable.

The cost of the expressive power of typed variables is the resulting complication of the unification algorithm. In order to minimize this cost, the g.l.b. operation must be a fast computation. This is accomplished by means of an encoding scheme that associates with each class $c$ a bit-string $B(c)$, in such a way that $c_1$ is a subclass of $c_2$ if and only if $B(c_1)$ is (bit-wise) less than or equal to $B(c_2)$. For a type $t = \{c_1,...,c_k\}$, $B(t)$ is constructed as the logical-or of the $B(c_i)$. The g.l.b. operation then reduces to logical-and. The details of this scheme are described in [Aït-kaci et al. 1985].


## 6.3 ASSERTIONS

There are two main classifications of data: *assertions* and *rules*. Assertions, as described in this section, represent simple statements. Rules, which are used by the system to derive assertions from other assertions, are further classified as *forward rules* and *backward rules*. These are the subjects of Sections 6.4 and 6.5.


### 6.3.1 Instance Slot Values

Recall that a frame may assume values for a given attribute if it is a member of the class for which the attribute is defined. In this case, an *instance slot* corresponding to the attribute is attached to the frame. One or more values may be stored in this instance slot. Thus, if an attribute DESCRIPTION is defined for the class **PERSON** of Fig. 6.7, then the frame *DONALD* may acquire DESCRIPTION values. An assertion such as

```
@assert (description donald tall)
```

results in the creation of a datum called an *instance slot value*, which is stored in *DONALD*'s DESCRIPTION slot. This datum is justified as a premise (i.e., with empty IN-list and OUT-list) and printed as

```
Instance Slot Value DESCRIPTION-1     (IN)
    (DESCRIPTION DONALD TALL)
```

When an attribute is initially defined, it is specified as either *single-valued* or *multiple-valued*. A frame may assume any number of coexisting

values for a multiple-valued attribute. If DESCRIPTION, for example, is
multiple-valued, then asserting a new DESCRIPTION for *DONALD* via

```
@assert (description donald young)
```

produces a new slot value, but has no effect on the old value. Thus, a query
for *DONALD*'s DESCRIPTION produces both values:

```
@?? (description donald ?X)
```

```
(DESCRIPTION DONALD TALL)
(DESCRIPTION DONALD YOUNG)
```

For a single-valued attribute, on the other hand, a frame may have
only one effective value at any time. Suppose the attribute NATIONALITY
is defined for class **PERSON** and declared to be single-valued, and that a
NATIONALITY is asserted for *NAT*:

```
@assert (nationality nat french)
```

```
Instance Slot Value NATIONALITY-1    (IN)
     (NATIONALITY NAT FRENCH)
```

If another value is later asserted for the NATIONALITY of *NAT*, then the
old value is overridden by the new one:

```
@assert (nationality nat swiss)
```

```
Instance Slot Value NATIONALITY-2    (IN)
     (NATIONALITY NAT SWISS)
```

```
@?? (nationality nat ?X)
```

```
(NATIONALITY NAT SWISS)
```

Actually, this restriction to a single value is enforced by the TMS:
whenever a value is asserted for a single-valued attribute, it is added to the
OUT-list of each justification of any preexisting conflicting value. Thus, the
old value remains in the database, but is ignored in answering the query
because it is now OUT. This method not only provides for the construction
of explanations, such as

```
@why NATIONALITY-1
```

```
Instance Slot Value NATIONALITY-1    (OUT)
     (NATIONALITY NAT FRENCH)
```

```
was replaced by

Instance Slot Value NATIONALITY-2      (IN)
     (NATIONALITY NAT SWISS)
```

but also allows an old value to be reinstated if the overriding value is removed:

```
@erase (nationality nat swiss)

@?? (nationality nat ?X)

(NATIONALITY NAT FRENCH)
```

In fact, it always ensures that the value that is IN is the one with the most recently created justification that is currently valid. Note that if several conflicting values for a slot are asserted in succession, then a reassertion of the original value will result in a complicated dependency network, including odd loops. This implementation, therefore, requires a complete TMS as discussed in Section 6.1.

### 6.3.2 Class Slot Values

Values for an attribute may be attached to subclasses of its defining class as well as to its members. Each of these subclasses contains a *class slot*, the values in which may be inherited by any member of the class to which it belongs. For example, the command

```
@assert (description ?X:person aerobic)
```

adds a value to the DESCRIPTION class slot of PERSON:

```
Class Slot Value DESCRIPTION-2      (IN)
     (DESCRIPTION ?X:PERSON AEROBIC)
```

This datum represents the belief that every member of **PERSON** is AEROBIC. Similarly, any subclass of **PERSON** may acquire class values for this attribute:

```
@assert (description ?X:faculty pompous)

Class Slot Value DESCRIPTION-3      (IN)
     (DESCRIPTION ?X:FACULTY POMPOUS)
```

The DESCRIPTION values associated with a member of **PERSON** are then the instance values assigned to it specifically, along with the class values assigned to the superclasses of its type. Hence,

```
@?? (description donald ?X)

(DESCRIPTION DONALD TALL)
(DESCRIPTION DONALD YOUNG)
(DESCRIPTION DONALD POMPOUS)
(DESCRIPTION DONALD AEROBIC)
```

For single-valued attributes, a more complicated mode of inheritance is used. A value for a single-valued class slot may be inherited by a member of the class only if no value has been assigned to that member's instance slot. Class slot values for these attributes are therefore called *default values.*

Default values assigned to a given class override each other in the same manner as instance values for a given frame, so that only one default value assigned to a class may be IN at any time. If an attribute value is sought for a given frame, the frame's instance slot is first examined for an IN value. If there is none, then each of the superclasses of the frame is examined (in depth-first order) until an IN default value is found.

Suppose that for the single-valued attribute NATIONALITY, the default values AMERICAN, CHINESE, and INDIAN are asserted for the classes **PERSON**, **STUDENT**, and **GRADUATE**, respectively. Suppose further that *NAT*'s NATIONALITY is asserted to be FRENCH and that *DONALD*'s is GERMAN. Then a query for the NATIONALITY values for all members of **PERSON** would produce the following:

```
?? (nationality ?X:person ?Y)

(NATIONALITY DONALD GERMAN)
(NATIONALITY AHMET AMERICAN)
(NATIONALITY SHIRLEY INDIAN)
(NATIONALITY NAT FRENCH)
(NATIONALITY DAVID CHINESE)
(NATIONALITY ESTELLE AMERICAN)
```

If a new default value were now asserted for **STUDENT**, only *DAVID*'s NATIONALITY would change:

```
@assert (nationality ?X:student texan)

?? (nationality ?X:student ?Y)

(NATIONALITY SHIRLEY INDIAN)
(NATIONALITY NAT FRENCH)
(NATIONALITY DAVID TEXAN)
```

If the default value for **GRADUATE** were retracted, then *SHIRLEY* would inherit from **STUDENT**:

```
@erase (nationality ?X:graduate indian)

?? (nationality ?X:student ?Y)

(NATIONALITY SHIRLEY TEXAN)
(NATIONALITY NAT FRENCH)
(NATIONALITY DAVID TEXAN)
```

### 6.3.3 Predicates and Assertions

Any attribute may be regarded as representing a binary relation whose domain is the set of members of some class. An instance slot value then corresponds to a pair of related objects, while a class slot value (at least for a multiple-valued attribute) corresponds to a set of such pairs. While this scheme is suitable for representing many kinds of information, it is somewhat restrictive.

One problem is that only relations of two arguments can be naturally represented in this way. Thus, the relation *x is in debt to y* may be realized as an attribute called IN-DEBT-TO defined for **PERSON**, and the statement *NAT is in debt to AHMET* is then asserted by assigning *AHMET* as a value to the frame *NAT*, i.e., by asserting (IN-DEBT-TO *NAT AHMET*). On the other hand, the unary relation *x is in debt* could not be represented so naturally as an attribute. Of course, we could define a Boolean-valued attribute IN-DEBT and represent *NAT is in debt* by asserting (IN-DEBT *NAT* T), but it would be preferable to be able to assert (IN-DEBT *NAT*). For a ternary relation, such as *x owes y dollars to z*, the representation problem is more difficult.

We are thus led to a generalization of the notion of *attribute*. As an alternative, a symbol may be declared to be a *predicate* and used to represent a relation of an unspecified number of arguments. Attributes and predicates are both called *relation symbols*. A *proposition* is a list whose members are a relation symbol followed by arguments. A proposition associated with an attribute must have exactly two arguments, but a predicate proposition may have any number of arguments. A proposition that resides in the database is called an *assertion*. Thus, a slot value is just an assertion pertaining to an attribute.

For example, if the symbol OWES is recognized as a predicate, then it may be used to represent the ternary relation mentioned above, and the statement *DAVID owes 15 dollars to DONALD* may be asserted by

```
@assert (owes david 15 donald)
```

to which the system responds by creating the new datum

```
Assertion OWES-1     (IN)
   (OWES DAVID 15 DONALD)
```

There is no restriction on the appearance of variables in the argument list of an assertion that is attached to a predicate. (In a slot value, a variable may appear only as the first argument, and then its type must be a subtype of the defining class of the attribute.) An assertion is classified as *general* or *particular* according to whether or not it contains any variables. The variables in a general assertion are understood to be universally quantified. Thus, the assertion

```
General Assertion OWES-2     (IN)
   (OWES ?U:UNDERGRADUATE 15 ?F:FACULTY)
```

represents the statement *each undergraduate owes 15 dollars to each faculty member.*


## 6.4 BACKWARD INFERENCE

An *instance* of a proposition is a second proposition that results from the first by performing some set of variable substitutions. When a proposition is presented to the Proteus theorem prover as a *goal*, it attempts to derive an instance of it from the knowledge in the database.

One way in which it might succeed is to unify the goal with an assertion. The process of unification amounts to finding the most general common instance of two propositions. If a goal is unifiable with an assertion that is IN, then the resulting instance of the goal is returned as the result of the proof. For example, if the database of Fig. 6.7 contains

```
Class Slot Value DESCRIPTION-5     (IN)
   (DESCRIPTION ?X:STUDENT IDEALISTIC)
```

then the goal (DESCRIPTION ?X:EMPLOYEE ?Y) could succeed by returning the instance (DESCRIPTION ?X:(GRADER TA) IDEALISTIC).

A goal may also be proved with the use of a *backward rule*. A backward rule is composed of a proposition, called its *consequent*, and one or more *antecedents*. A rule represents the belief that any instance of its consequent is true whenever any compatible instances of its antecedents are true. If a goal is unified with the consequent, then the corresponding instances of the antecedents become subgoals—recursively proving all of these subgoals completes the proof of the original goal. This process is known as *backward chaining* or *goal-directed inference*, and is the basis of Prolog [Clocksin and Mellish 1981] and other logic programming systems.

For example, in order to derive a value for *MICHAEL*'s UNCLE slot, the goal (UNCLE ?X MICHAEL) may be unified with the consequent of the rule

```
Backward Rule UNCLE-1      (IN)
   (UNCLE ?X ?Y)
    <--
   (PARENT ?X ?Z)
   (BROTHER ?Z ?Y)
```

creating the subgoals (PARENT MICHAEL ?Z) and (BROTHER ?Z ?Y). Suppose that the first of these is matched with the consequent of

```
Backward Rule PARENT-1      (IN)
   (PARENT ?X ?Y)
    <--
   (MOTHER ?X ?Y)
```

and is thus replaced by the subgoal (MOTHER MICHAEL ?Y), which is matched with

```
Instance Slot Value MOTHER-7      (IN)
   (MOTHER MICHAEL SUZY)
```

The second subgoal, which becomes (BROTHER SUZY ?Y), may then be derived from

```
Instance Slot Value BROTHER-23      (IN)
   (BROTHER SUZY DAVID)
```

The instance (UNCLE MICHAEL DAVID) of the original goal is thereby proved by backward chaining.

A Proteus predicate may alternatively be defined in LISP, rather than by rules and assertions. This provides the user the full power of LISP for knowledge representation and also allows access to COMMON LISP system functions, as in

```
Backward Rule POWER-OF-TWO-2      (IN)
   (POWER-OF-TWO ?X:FIXNUM)
    <--
   (<= 1 ?X)
   (EVENP ?X)
   (POWER-OF-TWO (/ ?X 2))
```

Here the predicate POWER-OF-TWO is defined in terms of the two predicates
<= and EVENP, both of which are defined by COMMON LISP. The first
subgoal produced by this rule succeeds if the function <= returns true for
the arguments 1 and the binding of ?X. Note that the interface between LISP
and the rule system also allows function calls to be embedded in antecedents,
as in the third antecedent above.

   An antecedent may also take the form of a proposition preceded by the
symbol UNLESS, as in

```
Backward Rule HAS-CHILD-1      (IN)
    (HAS-CHILD ?X)
    <--
    (MOTHER ?Y ?X)
    UNLESS (ADULT ?Y)
```

When an antecedent of this type is processed, the system attempts to prove the
proposition that follows the UNLESS (under the current variable bindings).
If this proof attempt fails, then the subgoal succeeds; if the proof succeeds,
then the subgoal fails.

   When a proposition proved by backward chaining is explicitly added to
the database as an assertion, it receives a justification that is constructed upon
examination of the proof. Thus, the proposition derived in the first example
of this section would result in

```
Instance Slot Value UNCLE-2
    (UNCLE MICHAEL DAVID)
```

which would acquire a justification with IN-list (UNCLE-1 PARENT-1
MOTHER-7 BROTHER-23), i.e., all the data involved in the proof, and
OUT-list ( ).

   Nonmonotonic dependencies are constructed from proofs that involve
UNLESS antecedents. For example, if the proposition (HAS-CHILD SUZY)
were derived from Backward Rule HAS-CHILD-1 and Assertion MOTHER-1
above, and

```
Assertion HAS-CHILD-5
    (HAS-CHILD-SUZY)
```

were created as a result, then the IN-list of its justification would be (HAS-
CHILD-1 MOTHER-7), but the justification would also reflect the dependency of the derivation on the failure to prove (ADULT MICHAEL). This is
done by making the OUT-list (ADULT-2), where

```
Assertion ADULT-2      (OUT)
    (ADULT MICHAEL)
```

is an unjustified assertion, created for the purpose of this justification (unless it already existed). If (ADULT MICHAEL) were to be asserted later, then Assertion ADULT-2 would become IN, and HAS-CHILD-5 would go OUT as it should.

The case of an UNLESS goal with unbound variables presents a new problem. Suppose, for example, that we have a predicate ORPHAN with an associated rule

```
Backward rule ORPHAN-1     (IN)
   (ORPHAN ?X)
   <--
   unless (PARENT ?X ?Z)
```

Then the goal (ORPHAN ANNIE) will succeed if (PARENT ANNIE ?Z) fails. In this case, the new justification for

```
Assertion ORPHAN-2:
   (ORPHAN ANNIE)
```

should contain only ORPHAN-1 in its IN-list, but there is no assertion, general or particular, that could be placed in the OUT-list to record the nonmonotonic dependency. This problem is solved by the introduction of a new datatype:

```
Failed Goal PARENT-2     (OUT)
   (PARENT ANNIE ?Z)
```

A *failed goal* is a datum that is created only in this situation. When a proof succeeds as a result of a failure to prove a proposition that follows UNLESS in an antecedent, the proposition that failed is inserted in the database without justification as a failed goal. It represents the belief that some instance of the proposition is true. That is, any variables in a failed goal are understood to be existentially quantified. The failed goal PARENT-2 above, which represents the belief that *ANNIE* has some parent, would appear in the OUT-list of the justification of ORPHAN-2.

If some instance of a failed goal is asserted at any time, the system automatically creates a monotonic dependency of the failed goal on the assertion. Thus, if the assertion ORPHAN-2 were justified as described above, and

```
Assertion PARENT-3:
   (PARENT ANNIE WARBUCKS)
```

were later to become IN, then the failed goal PARENT-2 would also be forced IN and hence ORPHAN-2 would go OUT.

## 6.5 FORWARD INFERENCE

A backward rule has effect only when it is relevant to a goal being processed
by the system. The insertion of a backward rule, therefore, affects only the
implicit informational content of the database, without causing new assertions
to be added explicitly. Consider, for example, the backward rule PARENT-1
of Section 6.4, which states that all mothers are parents. In the presence of

```
Instance Slot Value MOTHER-7     (IN)
    (MOTHER MICHAEL SUZY)
```

this rule enlarges the implicit database to include the proposition (PARENT
MICHAEL SUZY) without actually creating a new assertion.

The same logical implication expressed by PARENT-1 could alternatively be represented as a *forward rule*:

```
Forward Rule MOTHER-11
    (MOTHER ?X ?Y)
    -->
    (PARENT ?X ?Y)
```

While the two rules are logically equivalent, they are used quite differently.
The forward rule takes effect not when a goal matches its consequent (PAR-
ENT ?X ?Y), but rather when an assertion matches its antecedent (MOTHER
?X ?Y). In this event (assuming the new assertion is IN), another assertion,
representing the corresponding instance of (PARENT ?X ?Y), is automati-
cally added to the database. The PARENT assertion is then justified by the
MOTHER assertion and the rule. Thus, when the match between MOTHER-7
and MOTHER-11 is discovered, the result is a new datum

```
Instance Slot Value PARENT-4     (IN)
    (PARENT MICHAEL SUZY)
```

which is justified with an IN-list (MOTHER-7 MOTHER-11) and OUT-list
NIL. This process is known as *forward chaining* or *data-directed inference*.

A forward rule may have any number of antecedents and consequents.
Antecedents have the same form as those of backward rules. When a new assertion is unified with an antecedent of a forward rule, the set of remaining
antecedents is presented to the backward inference system as goals. For each
simultaneous proof of these goals, a *firing* of the rule occurs, i.e., its consequents are processed.

A consequent of a forward rule may be either a proposition or a LISP
form. When a rule is fired, an instance of each propositional consequent (corresponding to the derived instances of the antecedents) is asserted. The justifi-

cation for this assertion is constructed from the data involved in the derivation of the antecedents, as described in Section 6.4. Each LISP consequent is simply evaluated, with variables evaluating to their bindings.

Suppose, for example, that the database contains

```
Forward rule PATIENT-1     (IN)
    (PATIENT ?X)
    (SHOULD-TAKE ?X ?Y)
    -->
    (UNDER-TREATMENT ?X)
    (FORMAT T "Prescription for ~A: ~A" ?X ?Y)
```

when

```
Assertion PATIENT-2      (IN)
    (PATIENT BILL)
```

is added. The first antecedent of PATIENT-2 is matched with PATIENT-1, triggering an attempt to prove (SHOULD-TAKE BILL ?Y). Suppose that the instance (SHOULD-TAKE BILL ASPIRIN) is derived. Then after

```
Assertion SHOULD-TAKE-1      (IN)
    (SHOULD-TAKE BILL ASPIRIN)
```

is added to the database, the rule PATIENT-1 fires:

```
Assertion UNDER-TREATMENT-1      (IN)
    (UNDER-TREATMENT BILL)
```

is added, justified by PATIENT-1, PATIENT-2, and SHOULD-TAKE-1, and

```
Prescription for BILL: ASPIRIN
```

is printed.

Some thought is required in determining whether a given implication should be represented as a forward rule or a backward rule. A backward rule offers the advantage of increasing the inherent knowledge of a system without incurring the expense (in both time and space) of creating new assertions. It may be necessary, however, for this knowledge to be represented explicitly in order for it to take some desired effect.

Suppose, for example, that the assertion

```
Assertion ORPHAN-3      (IN)
    (ORPHAN GEORGE)
```

is added as a result of the rule ORPHAN-1 of Section 6.4. Then the OUT-list of its justification contains a datum corresponding to the last antecedent of the rule,

```
Failed Goal PARENT-5      (OUT)
     (PARENT GEORGE ?Z)
```

which was unprovable at the time ORPHAN-3 was created. Suppose that

```
Assertion MOTHER-12      (IN)
     (MOTHER GEORGE MARY)
```

were asserted later. It would then be desirable for PARENT-5 to come IN and for ORPHAN-3 to go OUT. The backward rule PARENT-1, however, could not cause this to occur. Although an instance of PARENT-5 would become provable, that instance would not be discovered. It would probably be preferable in this case to code the rule in the form of the forward rule MOTHER-11 instead. This would produce a new assertion

```
Assertion PARENT-6      (IN)
     (PARENT GEORGE MARY)
```

on which PARENT-5 would become monotonically dependent, and ORPHAN-3 would go OUT as desired.

## REFERENCES

[Aït-kaci et al. 1985] H. Aït-kaci, R. Boyer, and R. Nasr, *An Encoding Technique for the Efficient Implementation of Type Inheritance*, MCC Technical Report AI-109-85, 1985.

[Aït-kaci and Nasr 1985] H. Aït-kaci and R. Nasr, *LOGIN: A Logic Programming Language with Built-in Inheritance*, MCC Technical Report AI-109-85, 1985.

[Charniak et al. 1980] E. Charniak, C. K. Riesbeck, and D. V. McDermott, *Artificial Intelligence Programming*, Lawrence Erlbaum Associates, Hillsdale, NJ, 1980.

[Clocksin and Mellish 1981] W. F. Clocksin and C. S. Mellish, *Programming in Prolog*, Springer-Verlag, New York, 1981.

[Doyle 1979] J. Doyle, "A Truth Maintenance System," *Artificial Intelligence*, vol. 12, no. 3, 1979.

[Goodwin 1986] J. W. Goodwin, *WATSON: A Dependency Directed Inference System*, Research Report LiTH-IDA-R-84-10, Computer and Information Science Dept., Linköping University, 1986.

[Petrie 1987] C. Petrie, "Revised Dependency-Directed Backtracking for Default Reasoning," *Proceedings of AAAI-87*, Seattle, 1987.

[Poltrock 1986] S. Poltrock, D. Steiner, and N. Tarlton, "Graphic Interfaces for Knowledge-Based System Development," *Proceedings of ACM/SIGCHI*, Boston, MA, 1986.

[Russinoff 1985a] D. Russinoff, *An Algorithm for Truth Maintenance*, MCC Technical Report AI-062-85.

[Russinoff 1985b] D. Russinoff, *A Nonmonotonic Inference System*, MCC Technical Report AI-062-85.

# 7

---

# Pogo: A Declarative Representation System for Graphics

Mark A. Tarlton, P. Nong Tarlton

---

## INTRODUCTION

This chapter describes Pogo, an object-oriented graphics system for user interface construction developed in the Human Interface Laboratory at MCC. Its design is motivated by four major goals. First, we want to be able to support highly dynamic, interactive graphical interfaces, beyond those found in more conventional window/pop-up menu interfaces. Second, we want to support cooperative work applications, that is, applications where people are able to work closely together through a networked environment despite being in separate offices or buildings. Third, we want the system to be compatible with expert system tools and applications. We also want to be able to apply expert system technology to the graphics portion of user interfaces, during both design and execution. Finally, we want to avoid becoming too closely attached to a specific display technology or architecture. As we look toward future display systems, it is clear that advances will come on two fronts: through improvements in technology (e.g., faster chips and more memory) and through architectural advances, such as parallel processing and new rendering models. In designing Pogo, we wanted to be able to take advantage of both types of advances.

In Pogo, we have taken an approach to graphics that addresses all of these goals. In this approach we treat graphics as a two-stage process of representation and interpretation. The representation system is where the application or interface specifies what is to appear on the screen, while the display interpreters are responsible for performing the hardware-specific operations required to present an interpretation on the screen.

Pogo is an object-oriented system that combines both windows and graphics. The term "object-oriented" is used in two senses when describing graphics systems. It can refer to the programming language in which the system was implemented, or it can describe a style of graphics in which the scenes are constructed from simpler objects. In object-oriented programming systems (OOPS), programs are written by defining hierarchies of object classes, each of which may have variables and methods that are inherited by all of its subclasses. When an instance of the class is created, it acquires the properties of the class through an inheritance mechanism.

In object-oriented graphics systems, such as PHIGS [ANSI 1985], graphic objects are constructed by combining simpler graphic objects. For example, a graphic representation of an office could be constructed from objects such as a file cabinet and a desk, and these objects could be constructed from suitable arrangements of cubes and rectangles. Each new object is constructed by establishing a "component" relation with its constituents. In Pogo, these connections are defined by an aggregation relationship between the objects. The aggregation relationship defines compound objects as collections of simpler objects in specified spatial arrangements.

Pogo is an object-oriented graphics system implemented in an object-oriented programming language. Pogo defines a set of classes that correspond to the primitives of the graphics language and that support the object aggregation relations used in hierarchical graphics.

## 7.1 REPRESENTATION AND INTERPRETATION

In defining the Pogo representation system, the products of several efforts at MCC have been combined: GrafBag [Tarlton et al. 1986], an object-oriented hierarchical graphics system; Orion [Banerjee et al. 1987], an object-oriented database system; and Proteus [Russinoff 1988], an expert system tool implemented on top of Orion and providing both frames and rules for representing knowledge. Each of these systems assumes an object-oriented view of the world. The basic principle is that complex objects are constructed from simpler objects. Each object retains its own identity and exists within a hierarchical structure that reflects the composition relationships for the complex object. In trying to implement the kind of environment discussed earlier, each of these systems makes a unique contribution; the hierarchical graphic representation provides the structure, layout, and appearance of the graphic elements. Object-oriented programming provides a way of attaching behaviors to the objects seen on the screen, while the knowledge-base provides the means of representing knowledge about the objects in the interface, the relationships between the objects, and their semantics, enabling the system to reason about the objects on the screen. A user interface is constructed by defining additional classes that inherit from the Pogo classes. These additional classes specify how the Pogo classes must be specialized to serve the needs of the interface.

## 7.1.1 Example

The menu shown in Fig. 7.1 is an example of the integration of hierarchical graphics, object-oriented programming (OOP), and knowledge representation techniques. The graphical structure is represented as a hierarchical tree structure in Fig. 7.2. The root of the tree corresponds to the entire menu object. The menu has three components: the menu title, the menu border, and the menu choices. The menu choices component is itself composed of sub-components that are instances of menu items, and so on. In this example, the only nodes that have any direct graphical appearance are the leaves of the tree. The only graphical appearance the menu itself has is a result of its component parts. Each node in the tree defines a coordinate system for its descendants. For example, the top node, "menu," represents the entire menu object. When it is moved or sized, all of its components are moved or sized as well. However, the menu background represents only one part of the menu. If it is moved or sized, it does so relative to the rest of the menu, but does not affect any of the other menu components. This spatial information for each component is typically represented by a transformation matrix for each node.

**FIGURE 7.1** A MENU

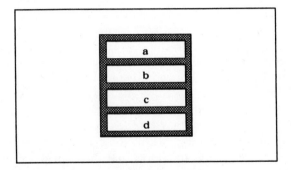

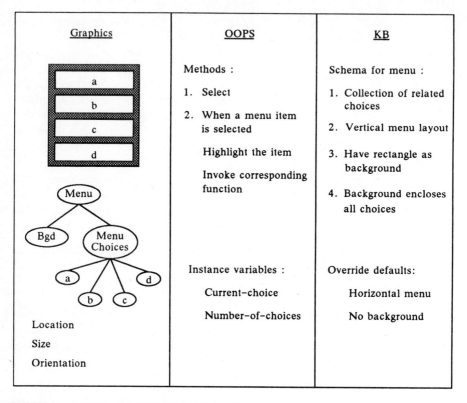

| Graphics | OOPS | KB |
|---|---|---|
| | Methods : | Schema for menu : |
| | 1.  Select | 1.  Collection of related choices |
| | 2.  When a menu item is selected | 2.  Vertical menu layout |
| | Highlight the item | 3.  Have rectangle as background |
| | Invoke corresponding function | 4.  Background encloses all choices |
| | Instance variables : | Override defaults: |
| | Current-choice | Horizontal menu |
| | Number-of-choices | No background |

**FIGURE 7.2** THE THREE VIEWS OF A MENU: GRAPHICS, OOPS, KB

By using object-oriented programming techniques, attributes such as the number of current choices, and methods such as the behavior for selection, can be defined for the menu object. These attributes and methods are in addition to those that are already defined for the graphical aspects of the menu components.

The knowledge base provides a schema or description of menus in general, such as how they are constructed and used, as well as a description of this menu in particular. For example, a menu is a collection of related choices, which are typically arranged vertically. The menu has a rectangle as a background, which encloses all of the choices. This description provides default attributes for the menu, but these attributes may be overridden. For example, the menu can be arranged horizontally or without a background, without affecting the basic properties of being a menu. There are two advantages to treating the graphical elements of an interface as elements in a knowledge base. First, expert system technology can be applied to the user interface, either through intelligent tools to assist in the design and implementation of user interfaces or by providing interfaces that themselves are intelligent and dynamically adapt to the user. Second, for the expert system developer, there is a seamless integration of the interface and application (the expert system) since the interface objects and the application objects have the same representational base.

### 7.1.2 Representation

Pogo is referred to as a "declarative representation system for graphics," which brings up three questions: What exactly are we trying to represent, what do we mean by "declarative," and why are we taking this approach?

The things we want to represent are the graphical objects that make up an interface to an application. Furthermore, we want to represent these objects at the same level of abstraction at which the user or the interface designer thinks of them—by the functions they perform or the concepts they represent. We do not want to represent interfaces at the level of pixels or drawing commands.

The word "declarative" refers to how the representation is constructed and manipulated, which in this case is through assertions or statements about *what* change is desired rather than *how* the change is to be made. Graphics are typically represented procedurally as a series of drawing commands or screen transformations, such as "bitblts," which manipulate pixel areas of a raster device. To make a change to the screen, either the procedure is modified and re-executed or some set of screen transformations is applied. With the first approach, it is difficult to make the desired change to a procedure, and the overhead of having to redraw everything when perhaps only a small change is made can be substantial. With the second approach, in the general case, it is extremely difficult to know exactly what transformations need to be applied to achieve the desired result without causing undesired side effects.

For example, consider a window that is displaying a rectangle and some text. With the procedural approach, this would be produced by roughly the following sequence of code:

```
(define-viewport :location
    (x y) :size (w h))          ; define clipping boundary
(set-color  :red)
(draw-rectangle x1 y1 x2 y2)    ; the lower left and upper right
                                ; corners
(set-color  :white )            ; for the text
(set-location x y)              ; location where the text should
                                ; start
(draw-text    "this is the
    text string")
```

In the declarative approach, the screen contents are described in terms of objects that are on the screen.

```
(create 'window "W" :location (x y) :size (w h))
(create 'rectangle "R" :location (x1 y1) :size (w1 h1) :color
    :red)
(create 'text "T" "this is the text string" :location (x y)
    :color :white)
(CONTAINS "W" ("R" "T")) ; this asserts that the window
                         ; "W" contains both the rectangle
                         ; "R" and the text "T"
```

At first glance, the differences between the two approaches are not that great. The differences become more apparent when we try to change the screen contents (e.g., change the location of the rectangle) or when we try to reason about the contents (e.g., what is in the window?). With the procedural model, the user must maintain an explicit description of what is on the screen so that changes can be made or questions answered. (Think about what is required to move the rectangle: the previous version must be erased and the new one drawn.) With the declarative approach, the user manipulates the *description* of the screen contents, rather than the screen itself. The representation system is then responsible for making sure that the screen reflects the current state of the representation.

With a declarative representation system, the emphasis is on stating what the desired effect is and not on how the change is to be achieved. If a window is to be moved from one part of the screen to another, the important fact is the assertion about its new location, not whether it is to be erased and redrawn, or bitblted to the new location. This "declarative" aspect of the representation system is not only convenient for the interface developer, but it is almost essential if we are going to reason effectively about the graphics.


## 7.1.3 Interpretation

The representation system is how we express what we want to see on the screen, and it is through the representation system that we describe the changes to the display. But, until now, we have not addressed *how* the abstract representation is transformed into pixels on a screen. The mechanism Pogo uses to do this is the display interpreter, which takes a structure representing the graphical objects and produces a visible interpretation of this structure on some piece of display hardware. In principle, the display interpreter is rather simple. It treats the representation structure as a directed graph, which is displayed by traversing the graph and drawing the nodes. To display a node, the display interpreter computes the current coordinate system by multiplying the node's local coordinate system by the parent's coordinate system. It then draws the geometric shape specified by the node's class and the current coordinate system. In practice, there is no obligation for a display interpreter to follow this simple strategy, but instead it may use whatever strategy makes optimal use of the specific capabilities and resources available to the particular display being supported. For example, a window may draw into a local bitmap instead of directly on the screen so that the next time the window needs to display itself, if there were no changes inside the window, the window simply copies the bitmap to the screen instead of redrawing its contents.

An important design goal in Pogo is to maintain a clear separation between the description of *what* is to appear on the screen and *how* a particular piece of hardware actually displays it. By choosing a sufficiently abstract set of primitives in the representation system and by defining a specific model of how the primitives are used, we allow the display the freedom to use the most efficient means of meeting the specification, which gives us a large measure of device independence without a correspondingly large performance penalty. As a result, this approach may be used on a variety of display devices or within other window systems.

## 7.2 THE POGO REPRESENTATION SYSTEM

Pogo adopts a model–world metaphor for describing graphics that was explored in GrafBag [Tarlton et al. 1986], Visage [Tarlton and Tarlton 1986], and The Visual Office [Lovgren and Poltrock 1987]. Complex objects are constructed by combining simpler objects, which may be further combined into even more complex objects. For example, an automobile engine is composed of many pieces; the total collection of the parts forms the engine. The engine can then be combined with other parts to form an automobile. This process of putting pieces together defines a hierarchical composition structure in which the spatial attributes of each part are defined relative to the rest of the assembly. Pistons move relative to the engine, the engine's location is relative to the car's frame, the location of the car is relative to the earth, and so on. Objects in the world have properties that define their appearance. This appearance, however, requires that something view the object. Cameras, such as video cameras, are objects capable of viewing other objects and projecting an image onto a display medium, such as a video monitor. In the real world, cameras and displays can also be considered as objects in the world they are viewing. That is, they can be attached to other objects in the world, and they can be viewed by other cameras as well. This intuitive notion of how cameras and displays work in the real world should help in understanding the fundamentals of Pogo.

In Pogo, all graphical objects inherit from the class "Form" (Fig. 7.3). A Form is an object with spatial attributes, such as size, location, and orientation. A Form is used to define a local coordinate system for its parts. Forms can be connected to other Forms by the Component relationship. The coordinate system of any subcomponent is defined relative to its parent's coordinate

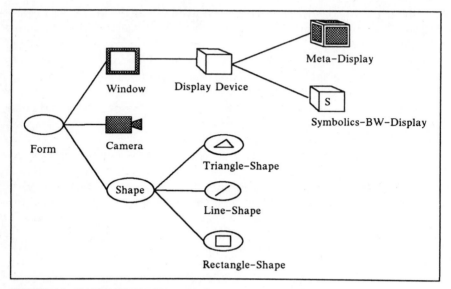

**FIGURE 7.3** CLASS INHERITANCE LATTICE

**FIGURE 7.4** OPERATIONS ON COORDINATE SYSTEM

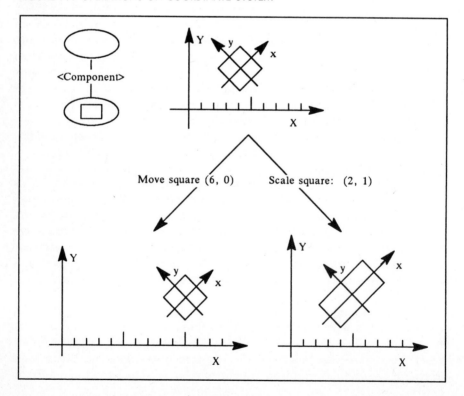

system. Operations on a Form, such as scale and move, modify the local coordinate system of the Form. This coordinate system information is contained in the Form's transformation matrix [Foley and Van Dam 1983]. A "move" operation changes the origin of the Form's local coordinate system relative to its parent's coordinate system, while the "scale" operation modifies the size of the Form's local coordinate system (see Fig. 7.4).

A Form by itself does not have any graphical appearance associated with it. Instead, the class Form is specialized into classes that do have a visible appearance. For example, a "rectangle" is a kind of Form that, in addition to all of the "Form" behaviors, has the added property of drawing four lines on the screen when it displays itself. A "Window" is also a kind of Form, but it has a quite different way of displaying itself. A Window displays itself by first defining a clipping region and then having all the Cameras that it "looks-at" draw into this region. Aside from this unique way of displaying itself, Windows can be treated like other Forms. For example, a Window can be scaled, moved, have Forms attached to it, or be attached to another Form. In Pogo, many objects normally not considered as "graphical objects," such as Windows or Cameras, are treated like any other graphical object.

A Display-Device object is a kind of Window that is able to interpret the Pogo structures it views in order to construct a presentation of the structure. A Pogo Display-Device object is often associated with a physical display device, which produces a visual interpretation of the Pogo structures on the physical display screen. Alternatively, a Display-Device could map the Pogo structures onto a hardcopy device, such as a laser printer, or produce other iconic or nongraphic interpretations such as a textual description of the structure. In each of these cases, the class "Display-Device" is specialized to meet the specific requirements of the physical display device or to produce the desired interpretation.

There are two primitive relations defined in Pogo; the "Component" relationship and the "Look-at" relationship. Component describes the relation between a complex object and its component parts, while Look-at defines a viewing relation. These relations are both directed; for example, Form X has a Component Y, or Y is a Component of X. By definition, Forms can be only the destination of a Look-at relation. In our notation, the Component relation will be indicated by a solid line between two nodes, while the Look- at relation will be denoted by a dashed line. In the next section, the rules for combining objects according to these relations will be presented together with examples that demonstrate the rules using this notation.

## 7.2.1 Component Relation Usage

1. A Form X can be a component of at most one superior Form. (See top of p. 160.)

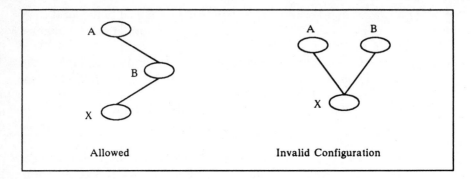

2. A Form can have any number of subcomponents. In the example below, form R is the superior Form with components Cl through Cn.

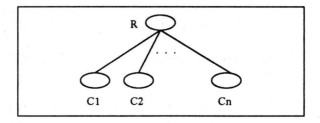

3. The component graph must not have cycles. Allowing cycles would violate our intuitive notion that an object cannot have itself as a subcomponent.

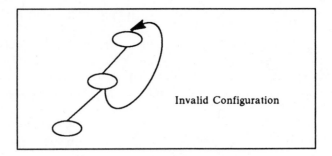

## 7.2.2 Look-At Relation Usage

1. Windows can Look-at Cameras only. This means that Cameras (or objects that inherit from Camera) are the only kind of object capable of projecting an image on a Window.

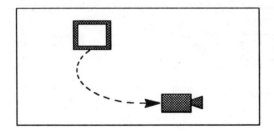

2. A Window can Look-at any number of Cameras. This allows images from several sources to be overlayed or mixed. This gives an effect similar to what is seen on television, where text is superimposed over an image, or where the weather person appears to be standing in front of a map. To get this effect, there is one video source (i.e., camera) for each type of data (one for the weather person and another for the map). The outputs of the various sources are then mixed into a single display.

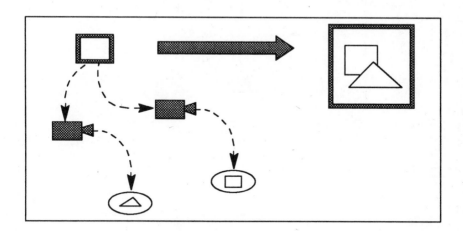

3. A Camera can be Looked-at by any number of Windows. This is identical to being able to connect more than one television set to a single television camera. Each Display gets the same picture to display. Depending on specific attributes of the Display, the final effect may be different. For example, televisions come in different sizes, some display in color while others are black and white, and they may have different display resolutions, allowing different degrees of detail to be apparent. (See top of p. 162.)

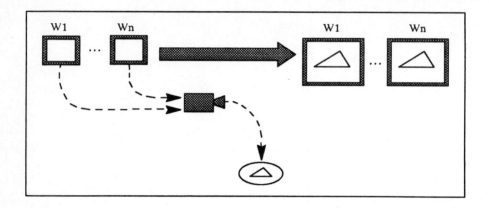

4. A Camera can Look-at any kind of Form, including Windows or other Cameras.

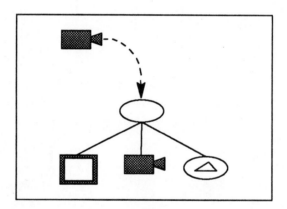

5. A Camera can Look-at any number of objects.

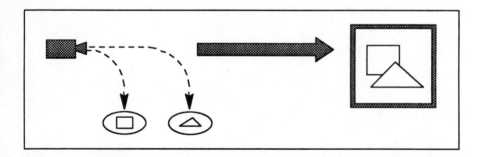

6. The Look-at graph may include cycles. This would allow a Window to display the image produced by a Camera looking at, among other things, the same Window.

NOTE: This should be used with caution because in cases where the apparent size of the Window does not decrease with each iteration, the display cycle will be infinite.

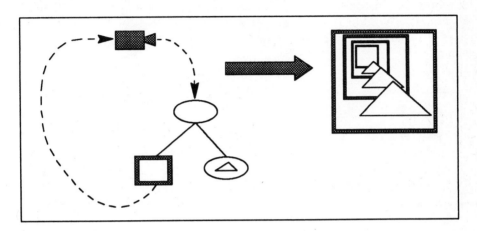

### 7.2.3 Examples

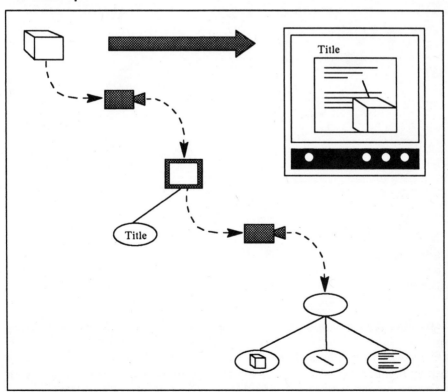

**Single Display, Single Window**   The example on the bottom of p. 163 shows a Display looking at a Window. The title of the Window is a component of the Window and as a result is not affected by the clipping region defined by the Window, but instead is projected by the Display's Camera into the Display's region. The Window is looking through a Camera at a Form (which does not have any shape of its own) with three subcomponents; a box shape, a line, and some text.

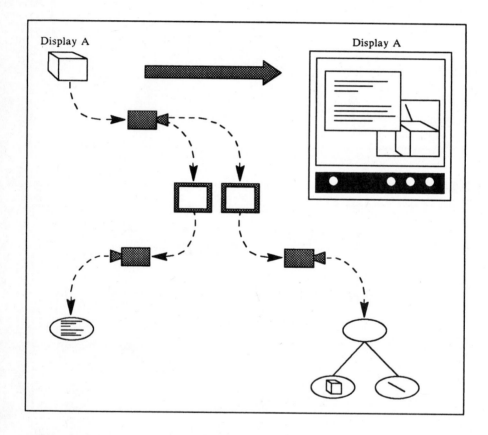

**Single Display, Two Windows**   In the example directly above, the Display's Camera is looking at two separate Windows, one of which is displaying text while the other is displaying some graphics.

**Cooperative Work Example**   In the example on the next page, one of the Windows of Display B is looking at Display A from the previous example. The result is that the entire contents of Display A is displayed within a single Window of Display B. This example shows how the Pogo representation system is able to support cooperative work with more than one display.

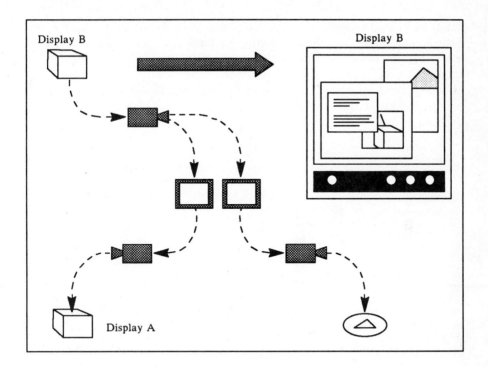

## 7.2.4 Communications

As we stated earlier, there is a shared vocabulary between the representation system and the display interpreter. This vocabulary is object-oriented, referring to *classes* and *instances* of objects along with their *attributes*. The messages from the representation system are declarative statements describing changes to the representation system, such as "Box-1 is an instance of class *BOX*," "the size of Box-1 is 3 by 5," and "Box-1 has a component Circle-1."

When any attribute of a Form is changed in the representation system, the Form sends a message about the change to all display devices that know about that Form. This is the mechanism that keeps all of the display interpreters informed about the current state of the representation system. If the change of attribute includes the addition of new Forms, as is the case when new components are attached to a Form, the subcomponents are instructed to describe themselves to all Displays that know about the parent Form but not about the subcomponents. In this way, the Display will know of the subcomponent objects before the message *"Parent* has a component *subcomponent"* is sent.

Recall that any object in the representation may appear on several displays at any one time. As a result, there is potentially a one-to-many mapping from representation object to display interpreter objects. We hope to maintain reasonable performance by keeping the length of the messages and the number of messages between the representation and displays down to a minimum. This is done by having the display device maintain its copy of the representation locally and by sending only the minimal description of the changes. In addition, we expect the messages to be "pipelined" so that no explicit acknowledgment is required between individual transfers. Figure 7.5 shows the separation between the representation and the various display interpreters. In this figure, the large arrows are intended to be assertional, highly abstract

**FIGURE 7.5** POGO REPRESENTATION–DISPLAY INTERPRETER COMMUNICATIONS

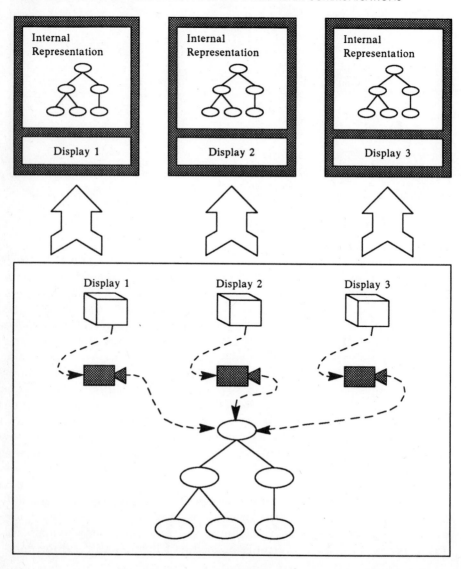

communication links conveying information about the changes to the representation system. It is the responsibility of the display interpreter to change its internal representation to match the Pogo Representation and to perform the necessary operations on the physical display to show the effects of the changes.

## 7.2.5 Meta-Displays

Up to this point, we have assumed that for each Display object in the Pogo representation system there is a physical display device and associated display

**FIGURE 7.6** DISPLAY AND META-DISPLAY

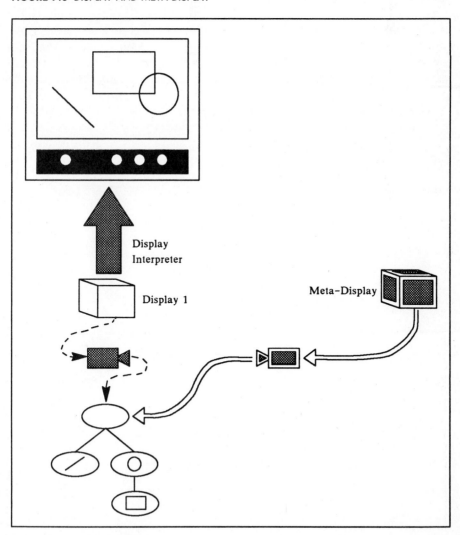

interpreter, and that the interpretation would in some sense be a literal interpretation of the representation (e.g., interpret an object of type *RECTANGLE* by drawing a rectangle on the screen). However, in Pogo there is no obligation for a Display to be associated directly with a piece of display hardware or to produce a literal interpretation of the specification. We have defined a kind of Display, the Meta-Display, that is not associated with a physical display device but instead constructs its interpretation from other Pogo objects. Figure 7.6 shows a Display, Display 1, viewing a simple scene composed of a Form and three geometric shapes. The Display's interpretation of this structure consists of the shapes being drawn on the screen of the display device. This same structure is also being viewed by a Meta-Display. In Fig. 7.7, we introduce several new classes of Pogo objects that will be used by the Meta-Display in producing its interpretation. These objects are types of aggregate objects, that is, objects formed by composing several simpler objects such as Forms, Lines, and Circles. Instead of showing all of the primitive components of the icons, we will simply use the high level icons of Fig. 7.7. Figure 7.8 shows that the interpretation produced by the Meta-Display is actually another Pogo structure consisting of Icons and Lines connecting the Icons. When the Meta-Display is viewed by a physical display, Display 2 in Fig. 7.9, we finally see the Meta-Display's interpretation, an iconic structure diagram.

By using the Meta-Display concept, we have constructed displays that produce schematic views of a Pogo structure rather than literal views. Since the Meta-Display produces its interpretation in terms of more Pogo objects rather than as display-specific drawing commands, the Meta-Display itself can be viewed on any physical display device for which there is a Pogo display interpreter. As changes are made to the initial structure, both the literal interpretation of Display 1 and the Meta interpretation will automatically be informed so that their appearances can be changed accordingly. Furthermore,

**FIGURE 7.7** CLASSES USED BY THE META-DISPLAY

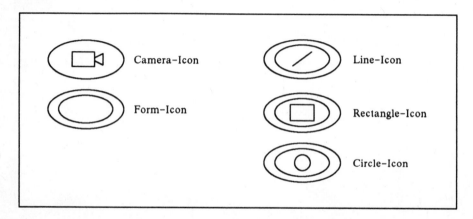

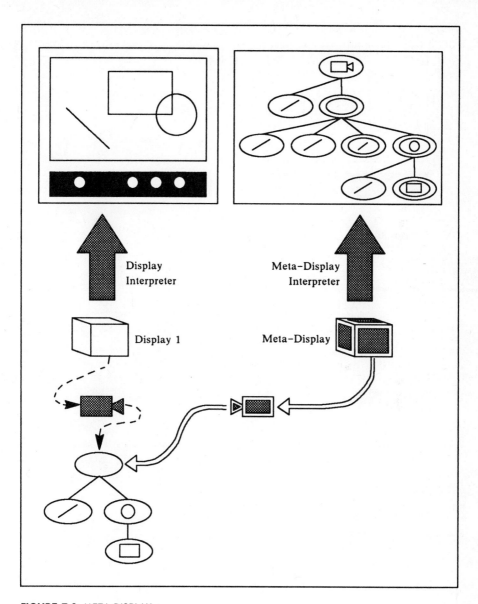

**FIGURE 7.8** META-DISPLAY

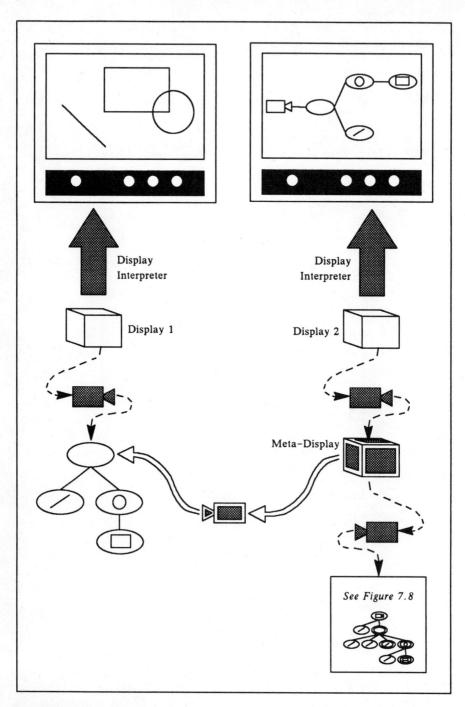

**FIGURE 7.9** META-DISPLAY

the Meta-Display is able to change its interpretation dynamically, providing a textual description of selected objects and their attributes.

## 7.3 Pogo display interpreter

Central to the approach taken in Pogo is the use of a *Display Interpreter* that constructs a visual presentation from the representation. The important features of this architecture are:

1. The *drawing* part of Pogo, the display interpreter, is separated from the *describing* part of Pogo, the representation system.

2. The screen contents are described in terms of *objects* that have *attributes*, and the *relationships* between these objects that allow complex, hierarchically structured objects to be described. The structuring mechanisms as well as the primitive classes of objects are an implicit part of Pogo.

3. The linkage between the representation system and the interpreter is through a declarative, assertion-based protocol, where the assertions refer to objects and their attributes.

4. *How* the interpretation is performed is device-specific, and the appearance of the interpretation can be modified for a device. For example, one display device may produce an interpretation using color, while a monochrome display may use textures or dithering in its interpretation, while yet another display might produce a textual description instead of a graphical interpretation. By allowing this freedom in interpretation, a large measure of device independence can be maintained without resorting to a "least common denominator" approach.

5. Because of the modularity between the representation system and the display interpreter, it is possible to have the representation system and interpreter on separate machines in a networked environment.

As a result of this architecture, we expect that Pogo will run well in distributed or networked environments with a heterogeneous assortment of display hardware and still support highly interactive, cooperative work applications.

### 7.3.1 Display Interpreter Overview

The purpose of a display interpreter is to produce a graphic interpretation of a Pogo representation structure. It is through this interpretation that the semantics of the representation are expressed. The purpose of the representation system is to provide an explicit description of what is on the screen so that the contents can be reasoned about or so that the contents can be changed in a simple, direct fashion. The purpose of the display interpreter is to take a representation structure as input and produce a screen image that meets this specification as closely as possible. The key to the Pogo approach is that the representation system and the display interpreters share a common vocabulary about the graphic objects and a common model of what the attributes and relationships "mean." Furthermore, the vocabulary and model are at a sufficiently high level of abstraction so that there is no commitment to a specific display device or even a display architecture. The goal is that display interpreters can be tailored to specific display devices, taking into account whatever functionality or limitations the device has in interpreting the representation structures. There is no obligation for the display interpreter to produce a "perfect" interpretation of the structure. For example, when displaying objects with a color attribute of RED on a black and white display, there is no way for the display to produce a red object. It may, however, try to map colors into gray scales or textures to convey the distinction of different colors. There is also no obligation for the display interpreter to produce a graphic image on a CRT display. It is reasonable to consider writing a display interpreter for a graphic hardcopy device such as a plotter, or even to produce a textual description of the objects and their attributes. In any case, as new primitives or attributes are added to this language, each display interpreter must be modified to handle the additions.

The default model of the display interpreter is that it acts much like a display-list interpreter of traditional hierarchical graphics [Foley and Van Dam 1983]. When the representation system asks a display to "redisplay itself," the display interpreter will create a root coordinate system and ask each of its immediate inferiors to "draw itself" relative to this coordinate system. Each object has a location, orientation, and size relative to its parent object's coordinate system. A new coordinate system is created by applying the local coordinates (location, orientation, and size) to the parent coordinate system. The object draws itself relative to this new coordinate system, which takes into account both the local and the inherited transformations. Part of the process of an object drawing itself is that all of the components of an object are recursively asked to draw themselves relative to the new coordinate system. The net result is that the display interpreter traverses the representation graph recursively, asking each node in the graph to apply its local coordinates and then draw itself.

As was mentioned earlier, Pogo is designed to support highly interactive and dynamic graphics in a networked environment. With interactive graphics, there are typically a large number of graphical objects, but only a few attributes or relationships change. As a result, much of the representation is unchanged between display cycles. In the current implementation of Pogo, the interpreter keeps its own copy of the represented objects, and changes are specified in terms of [object, attribute, value] triples. When a change is made, the interpreter must do two things: update its local representation and change the visual presentation of the objects to reflect the changes. Note that the message does not contain any information about *how* the display interpreter is to effect the change, but only describes what must be changed to keep the local representation consistent with the primary representation.

By having the display interpreter keep its own copy of the representation system locally, we can reduce the computational and network overhead for the things that do not change. Ideally, the display interpreter process will run on the display device, while the representation system will reside with the application code (Fig. 7.10). The form of the local representation depends on the requirements of the display device. This representation may contain other information about the actual device state or display primitives along with the Pogo attributes so that, as changes are made to the representation system, the display interpreter can map those changes into operations on the display. It is at this point that the display interpreter can be tailored to the specific capabilities of the display hardware in order to provide optimum performance.

### 7.3.2 Display Independence

What the display interpreter for a specific display must do when a change is made depends largely on the capabilities of the display device and the form of

**FIGURE 7.10** POGO DISPLAY INTERPRETER

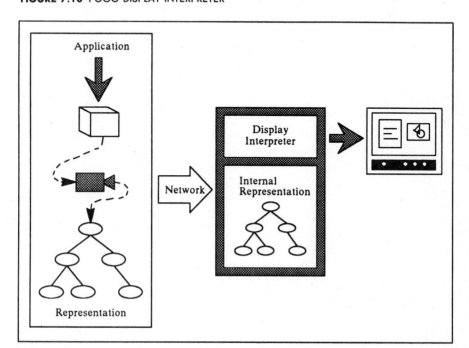

the local representation scheme. Although the primary Pogo representation system is intended to be generic and totally independent of any hardware architecture, the local representation at the display interpreter can be tailored to the specific capabilities and architecture of the display device and may contain additional information specific to the display device. The purpose of the local representation is to provide a common frame of reference for the communications between the Pogo representation system and the display device. When a message is received that the attribute for some object "X" has been changed, the interpreter must identify the local data structures corresponding to object "X," and perform whatever operations are required to make the specified change. For a display interpreter, making the change is more than just changing the value of some attribute. The display interpreter must also be concerned with changing the appearance of the screen to show the effect of the attribute change. In the simplest case, the display interpreter does nothing but change attribute values until it receives the message to "redisplay" itself, at which time it erases and then completely redraws the entire screen, a very expensive operation for most displays. In many cases, a better interpreter can be constructed that takes advantage of device-specific features to reduce the amount of redrawing that must be done. For example, if the location of a Window is changed, the display interpreter may perform a bitblt operation to physically move the Window from one area of the screen to another instead of redrawing the Window at the new location. The actual operation performed by a specific display interpreter will be determined by the capabilities of the display device and the sophistication of the display interpreter.

## Summary

We have given a brief introduction to Pogo, a declarative representation system for graphics that combines hierarchical graphics, object-oriented programming, and frame-based knowledge representation. We intend to use Pogo as a platform upon which research into knowledge-based graphical objects and interfaces can be more easily and more directly performed. The tools and applications using Pogo will view graphics as operations on a representation system that has, as a side effect, a visible presentation or interpretation. We are making a strong effort to make a distinction between *describing* what is to appear on the screen and actually *displaying* the graphics on some display hardware.

Key aspects of the declarative approach used by Pogo are:

1. The Pogo representation system fills the role of a knowledge representation system that allows AI techniques to be applied and that is compatible with AI or expert system applications.

2. The representation system supports hierarchical composition, so that graphic primitives can be grouped together to form more complex graphical objects, which can be further manipulated or combined.

3. The "semantics" of the object can be associated with its graphical appearance so that "behaviors" can be specified or associations made between a graphical object and the concept the graphic is intended to represent (as in the case of icons).

4. The representation can be interpreted for different purposes. For example, the obvious interpretation is to produce an image on a display screen. Another interpretation would be used by a "layout critic" application or to produce a schematic diagram of the graphic objects and the relationships between the objects.

5. The interpretation of the representation by a specific display device can be sensitive to the specific capabilities of the display device. For example, a bitblt display device can interpret the representation to specify graphics as bitblt regions, while a display-list device could interpret the representation to specify display-list segments and segment calls. This allows displays of radically different architectures to translate this representation into forms better suited to the capabilities of each specific device.

6. By sharing the representation rather than the specific graphic structures, cooperative work between several individuals on different displays can be effectively supported. Each display can keep an interpretation of the screen contents locally, and then only changes to the representation need to be sent to the displays. The display is free to effect the changes in the manner best suited to the capabilities of that specific display device and without interference from the other displays.

## REFERENCES

[ANSI 1985] *American National Standard Programmers Hierarchical Interactive Graphics System*, CBEMA, BSR X3.144-198X, Washington, D.C., 1985.

[Foley and Van Dam 1983] J.D. Foley and A. Van Dam, *Fundamentals of Interactive Computer Graphics*, Addison-Wesley Publishing Company, Reading, MA, 1983.

[Banerjee et al. 1987] J. Banerjee, H. Chou, J.F. Garza, W. Kim, D. Woelk, and N. Ballou, "Data Model Issues for Object-Oriented Applications," *ACM Transactions on Office Information Systems*, Vol. 5, No. 1, pp. 3-26, January 1987.

[Lovgren and Poltrock 1987] J.E. Lovgren and S.E. Poltrock, "The Visual Office: An Experiment in 3-D User Interface Development," MCC Technical Report Number HI-321-86-P, February 1987.

[Russinoff 1988] D.M. Russinoff, "Proteus: A Frame-Based Nonmonotonic Inference System," in *Object-Oriented Concepts, Databases, and Applications*, ed. W. Kim and F. Lochovsky, Addison-Wesley, Reading, MA, 1988.

[Tarlton et al. 1986] M.A. Tarlton, P.N. Tarlton, and S.E. Poltrock, "GrafBag: An Object-Oriented Graphics Package," MCC Technical Report Number HI-418-86-P, December 1986.

[Tarlton and Tarlton 1986] P.N. Tarlton and M.A. Tarlton, "Visage: A Dynamic 3-D Object-Oriented Graphical User Interface Editor," MCC Technical Report Number HI-405-86-P, December 1986.

# 8

## Objects, Messages, and Rules in Database Design

Jim Diederich, Jack Milton

---

### INTRODUCTION

ODDESSY (*O*bject-Oriented *D*atabase *D*esign *S*ystem) is a Computer Aided Database Design (CADD) system currently under development. ODDESSY is object-oriented in several respects. It is implemented in Smalltalk-80, which we believe to be the type of integrated language and environment that meets many requirements for the development of a flexible CADD system. In particular, Smalltalk promotes rapid prototyping, high productivity and low rewrite, and experimentation with new principles of design. For a discussion of experimental prototyping in Smalltalk see [Diederich and Milton 1987b], where it is characterized as "fearless programming." While Smalltalk does not support rules directly, ODDESSY is rule-based and treats rules as objects.

ODDESSY uses objects and messages as its database design language, as first reported in [Diederich and Milton 1987a]. In [Diederich and Milton 1987c] we demonstrated how it was possible to start with a few generic design objects and messages (ones not directly related to database design) and bootstrap (create) or extend either a database design language or a language for other design settings. We also demonstrated how rule conditions could be formulated using the same messages as those used in the design language.

Before discussing ODDESSY in detail, we briefly present a few basic notions about relational databases and relational design in Section 8.1. After the introduction to relational concepts, in Section 8.2 we briefly mention requirements for a flexible CADD system that can serve to test principles of design, a primary goal for the ODDESSY project. In Section 8.3 we discuss the ODDESSY prototype.

## 8.1 REVIEW OF RELATIONAL DATABASES

The relational model was developed in the early 1970s [Codd 1970] and spawned considerable theoretical as well as implementation activity. Several prototypes emerged in the mid to late 1970s, including Ingres [Stonebraker 1976] and System R [Astrahan et al. 1976]. A relational database consists of a collection of relations, or tables, and a specification of underlying domains for the entries in the table. The table entries are atomic values. Each table may be viewed as having a fixed number of columns and a variable number of rows in which order is unimportant (a table is a mathematical set of rows). Figure 8.1 depicts a relation representing a portion of a bicycle manufacturer's database. The column headers are the attribute names of the relation called **Bicycle_Models** and the rows are the tuples, each one representing a particular model in the database. There are four different models of bicycle manufactured by the company, represented as tuples in the example. This relation specifies the basic components of bicyles, and additional relations will be needed to specify the components of these components, customer orders, and so forth.

Data in several tables are related through matching column values, rather than through the specification of explicit links, as illustrated later in Section 8.1.3. A major contribution of the relational model is that it has a formal mathematical basis, whereas prior to its introduction the entire database field

**FIGURE 8.1** INITIAL RELATION FOR BICYCLE MODELS

**Bicycle_Models:**

| Model | Frame | Frm_Mtrl | Wheel_Set | Seat | Hbar_Set | Brk_Assy | Gear_Assy | Crnk_Assy |
|-------|-------|----------|-----------|------|----------|----------|-----------|-----------|
| Sprint | perf | alum | Pro | Italia | 854 | direct | 12 speed | Ace |
| Olympic | sup | carbon | Stratos | Stratos | 820 | direct | 18 speed | Corsa |
| Touring | std | steel | Dura | Saddle | 811 | side | 10 speed | Ace |
| Comp | perf | alum | Sol | Turbo | 850 | direct | 15 speed | Aero |

could be viewed as a large collection of ad hoc methodologies. In particular, the relational theory provided a formal basis on which to assess the quality of a specific database design. While explicit relational design methodologies are restricted to the relational model, some of the underlying principles carry over to database design in general.

### 8.1.1 Advantages and Disadvantages of Relational Systems

Perhaps the major advantages of relational databases are:

1. The basic forms in the model (tables) are very simple and understandable.

2. Data manipulation languages tend to be declarative, and effective techniques have been developed to optimize them, yielding reasonable performance for many applications.

3. A higher level of data independence, defined shortly, is achieved.

When queries become complex and when more exploratory access to a database through ad hoc queries is desired, it can be very advantageous to have declarative access to the database. Thus the user can specify what the basic structures of the relations are and what information is needed in any query. From this specification the relational database management system (DBMS) develops a procedure for retrieving that information, with the expectation that the procedure is near optimal, or at least reasonably fast.

It is also important to note that the simple record structure, where attributes are atomic, can also be considered a major disadvantage of relational systems because it is difficult to express the semantics of complex objects in this fashion. While this difficulty may not be a problem in many of the applications for which databases were originally developed, such as banking transactions and inventory management, it has proved to be significant in some of the more recent application areas in need of database management support, like Engineering Information Systems (EIS). Database researchers and developers are currently addressing the problems in several ways. Some precursors to these efforts can be found in [Hammer and McLeod 1981; King 1984]. Some current approaches preserve the relational model [Wiederhold 1986], some tamper with it by adding new features including user defined types [Stonebraker 1986], while others abandon it in favor of various approaches to object-orientation [Maier et al. 1986; Banerjee et al. 1987]. (A caveat: some interested parties say that a relational system can be made object-oriented, while others claim that object-orientation, including object identity and encapsulation, cannot live in the same world as declarative access to data and flexibility found in relational DBMS.)

## 8.1.2 Database Design

Current database design practice is typically divided into four main stages—requirements formulation and analysis, conceptual design, logical design, and physical design. In some cases other terminology is used for the last three stages. For example, some authors [Ullman 1988; Korth and Silberschatz 1986] denote the latter three levels as view level, conceptual level, and physical level, respectively.

Requirements formulation and analysis ". . . encompasses, among other things, an analysis of the organization's needs without any concern for constraints other than the manner in which the organization does its business" [Teorey and Fry 1982]. This level is thus highly organization-dependent and must be carried out by, or in conjunction with, people who are intimately familiar with how the organization functions. Because of the computer independence of this level, we assume that a careful job of analysis has been done and the results of the requirements level of design are available.

Physical design is primarily a precise specification of how data is to be physically stored on external media and what methods of access will be provided for the different data. Physical storage considerations include data encoding and compression, the partitioning of records into pieces and storage of the pieces in different places, and the physical clustering of records on disk in the hope of minimizing access time to subsequent records once a given record is accessed. Access methods include hashing, B-tree indexes, combinations of indexes and sequential access, and others. For a discussion of this level of design, see [Teorey and Fry 1982].

Logical design corresponds to constructing the database in terms of the underlying structures supported by the DBMS, which are relations in the case of a relational DBMS. The resulting logical records (or tuples) are defined in terms of their fields (or attributes) with no concern for physical considerations such as physical layout, record partitioning, and stored record size.

Conceptual database design came about with the perceived need to organize the semantics of the application prior to logical design. Higher level data models were developed to provide a framework for conceptual design. At this level we begin with the result of the organization-specific analysis and try to establish the appropriate building blocks of the given conceptual model. In the ER-Model [Chen 1976], for example, we would establish a set of entities and relationships between entities that model the organization, derived from the requirements formulation and analysis.

The design process typically starts at requirements analysis, then goes to the conceptual stage, then to the logical, and finally to the physical, with each step initially independent of the steps that follow. Of course, refinements at a given stage often dictate iterating through other stages to make adjustments, although ideally design tends to proceed in a top-down fashion. The ultimate purpose of the design is to create a database that meets necessary performance objectives, remains consistent at all times, provides data independence, and of course provides the data required in the operation of the organization. Data independence means essentially independence of applications from software and hardware systems. Since logical and physical structures change in response to performance needs and organizational changes, it is very important that application programs be as independent of these changes as possible.

With traditional DBMS the design phase results in the translation of the model into a form that lends itself to computer implementation. This form is called a schema, which is specified in the DBMS using a data definition language (DDL). Typically the construction of the schema has been under the control of one person (or group), the database administrator (DBA); and after it has been fine-tuned in the design process, it is compiled into machine-usable form. As users create applications and store data for the applications, the data must conform to "templates" specified in the schema. The schema is static in the sense that modifications often require a reorganization of the database, which can be very expensive for a large database. This large overhead effectively prevents the use of dynamic or interactive schema in traditional DBMS. For many new database applications there is a need to consider interactive systems with dynamic schemata [Cammarata 1986; Banerjee et al. 1987b; Kim et al. 1987].

## 8.1.3 Logical Design for Relational Databases

There are several approaches to relational design. One fundamental concern is that a relation $R$ may represent a "poor" design as illustrated below. This would require that it be decomposed into subrelations $R_1$, $R_2$, . . ., $R_n$ using techniques from relational theory to produce a "good" design. The sets of attributes $R_i$ are subsets of $R$. For example, $R(A,B,C,D,E)$ might be decomposed into $R_1(A,B,C)$ and $R_2(C,D,E)$.

**Functional Dependencies** Central to relational database theory and logical design is the concept of functional dependency. A key is a form of functional dependency. A *key* for a relation is a set of attributes whose values uniquely determine a tuple in the relation; that is, once the values of the key are known, the values of the remaining attributes are uniquely determined. In Fig. 8.1 **Model** serves as the key. The concept of key is generalized by the concept of functional dependency. The difference is that a functional dependency does not necessarily involve all of the attributes in a relation but can be between various subsets. In Fig. 8.1 we have assumed a semantic requirement (something specified in the requirements, independent of the current tuples in the relation) that a given frame type can be constructed out of only one type of material. In this case if we know the value of the **Frame** attribute in a given tuple, the value of the **Frm_Mtrl** attribute is uniquely determined. We write this functional dependency as **Frame → Frm_Mtrl**. If, on the other hand, the semantics allowed a particular frame to be made out of more than one type of material, then **Frm_Mtrl** would not be functionally dependent on **Frame**, even if the current contents of the relation seem to suggest a dependency. As another example, if **Frame** and **Wheel_Set** determine a single **Gear_Assy** (again this is a matter of semantics), then the functional dependency **Frame, Wheel_Set → Gear_Assy** holds.

The semantic specification of a database yields a collection of functional dependencies. Functional dependencies can be related in complex ways, and there can be redundancies of two types. First, a particular attribute in a given dependency may give no information, in which case it is said to be *extraneous*. For example, if a dependency **Frame, Wheel_Set, Crnk_Assy →** **Gear_Assy** is specified, the attribute **Crnk_Assy** is extraneous if **Frame** and **Wheel_Set** are sufficient to determine **Gear_Assy** uniquely. There are more subtle examples of extraneous attributes. Second, the information given by a particular dependency may be given by some or all of the others collectively, and it is said to be *redundant*. For example, if we have the dependencies **Model → Frame, Frame → Frm_Mtrl**, and **Model → Frm_Mtrl**, the latter is redundant, as it can be derived from the first two [Ullman 1988].

**Using Dependencies to Eliminate Anomalies**   Removal of extraneous attributes and redundant functional dependencies is an important early step in the part of the design process called normalization. Redundancies in the dependencies relate directly to poor logical design and can lead to various types of anomalies in the relation. For example, in the **Bicycle_Models** relation, the manufacturer might decide to change the type of material for **perf** frames to a new alloy, **alum_steel**. The first tuple would be updated accordingly by changing **alum** to **alum_steel**, but the current design of the relation means that the entire relation would have to be searched to find any other occurrences of that frame-material pair. If the same update were not made in the fourth tuple, we would have an instance of an update anomaly: an update was performed that left the database in an inconsistent state relative to the requirement that each frame have a single material type.

There is a conceptual problem that causes the anomaly. Presumably the primary purpose of the **Bicycle_Models** relation of Fig. 8.1 is to record information that is basic to different models. The **Frm_Mtrl** data that led to the update anomaly are more directly facts about frames than facts about models. This is reflected in the functional dependency mentioned above: **Frame → Frm_Mtrl**. A better way of avoiding the anomaly is to decompose the relation into two separate relations, as shown in Fig. 8.2, with relation schemes **Bicycle_Models (Model, Frame, Wheel_Set, Seat, Hbar_Set, Brk_Assy, Gear_Assy, Crnk_Assy)** and **Frames (Frame, Frm_Mtrl)**. Then any tuple in the new **Bicycle_Models** relation contains the name of the frame but no information about it. Frame information is stored in the **Frames** relation. Updates to the current material to be used in the construction of the frame type are therefore made in one place only, namely the **Frames** relation. Consequently, this update anomaly is avoided, thereby eliminating a database search.

**Bicycle_Models:**

| Model | Frame | Wheel_Set | Seat | Hbar_Set | Brk_Assy | Gear_Assy | Crnk_Assy |
|-------|-------|-----------|------|----------|----------|-----------|-----------|
| Sprint | perf | Pro | Italia | 854 | direct | 12 speed | Ace |
| Olympic | sup | Stratos | Stratos | 820 | direct | 18 speed | Corsa |
| Touring | std | Dura | Saddle | 811 | side | 10 speed | Ace |
| Comp | perf | Sol | Turbo | 850 | direct | 15 speed | Aero |

**Frames:**

| Frame | Frm_Mtrl |
|-------|----------|
| perf | alum |
| sup | carbon |
| std | steel |

**FIGURE 8.2** BICYCLE MODELS DECOMPOSITION

Once the **Bicycle_Models** relation is decomposed into two relations, it can be recovered by joining the two relations on common values of **Frame**. Relational theory helps determine those circumstances in which a relation can be recovered. There are other types of anomalies that can be eliminated through normalization. There are also additional types of dependencies, but further discussion is beyond the scope of this chapter. For a discussion of normalization theory, see [Ullman 1988, Chapter 7].

## 8.2 FUTURE CADD SYSTEM REQUIREMENTS

CADD tools have always lagged behind DBMS developments. Even today most tools handle only conceptual design, generally based on the ER-Model, and none fully integrates all stages of design. The game of catch-up is difficult to play. Advancing technology such as cheap memory, laser disks, and loosely and tightly coupled parallel distributed systems, as well as advancing concepts including temporal databases, knowledge bases, and abstract data types necessitate changes in the principles of design. CADD systems are typically bound to a fixed set of principles. In order to respond to this rapid technological change, what may be needed in addition are CADD tools for experimenting with new principles of design and for testing their utility.

For a CADD system to be flexible, it must be possible to incorporate new features rapidly and avoid significant rewrites of code for the system. To provide for this, it must be developed in a programming language that supports rapid prototyping, with a sophisticated environment for managing change. High-level graphics and interface development should be supported and integrated into the environment to allow enhancements and maintenance. A system built by hardwiring into the code the heuristics and methods for guiding and managing the design may be too inflexible to change. Therefore the system must be rule-based or support some other methodology for incorporating and changing heuristics. The next section will present our prototype system, in which we address many of these requirements.

# 8.3 ODDESSY

ODDESSY is a prototype CADD system. It currently supports relational design at the conceptual and logical levels. As mentioned in the introduction, it is implemented in Smalltalk-80 and is the first CADD system to use messages and objects for the design language. The language can be extended interactively, or a language for other design settings can be bootstrapped from a primitive set of constructs. One immediate advantage of using messages for the design language is that no underlying compiler is required for the design language. This makes it easy for the designers to define and extend the language in a manner analogous to having a dynamic schema. Naturally, the tradeoff is that rules and heuristics must be written to support language extensions. However, this seems more desirable than embedding design principles into the underlying system itself.

With regard to the requirement that a CADD system be rule-based for flexibility, ODDESSY supports rules as objects. The design language provides the foundations for a rule-based production system, as illustrated in our discussion of rules in Section 8.3.3. In particular, rule conditions can be formulated using the same messages as those used in the language.

ODDESSY is not tied to a single high-level conceptual model, but it will allow multiple approaches to data modeling. The data modeling process captures information found in many models as described in [Diederich and Milton 1987a], and rules can be written to extract implicitly defined information. Examples of this capability are given later.

## 8.3.1 Designing in ODDESSY

In the initial stages of the design process, objects in an application domain are often perceived in terms of their principal properties or attributes. For example, an employee may be viewed as an entity with attributes **number, name, department, manager, salary, title, dependents,** and so forth. As the design progresses, additional information will be captured. Facts such as "an employee can be identified by employee number," "an employee's manager is the same as the manager of the employee's department," and "every employee belongs to at most one department" represent just some of the information needed about entities in the course of designing a database. Each of these can be thought of as a layer (slice) of information about an employee entity.

**The Design Language via Messages and Objects**  Postponing momentarily a discussion of the message format and syntax, Fig. 8.3 shows several layers for specifying information about an entity named 'employee', as they appear in our display. Fig. 8.3a shows the entity's attributes, Fig. 8.3b shows which attributes serve as primary and alternate keys, and Fig. 8.3d specifies which attributes are single-valued and require a non-null value (**exactlyOne**) or may be null (**upToOne**). The layer in Fig. 8.3c equates an attribute in one entity with one in another entity. Other layers, not illustrated here, specify such things as which attributes are multivalued.

  The messages used to create various layers are restricted to two types. The first type is called a *vertical modifier*. These set the context for defining or refining the meaning of the design object in terms of other objects, aggregated

**FIGURE 8.3** SOME SPECIFICATION LAYERS

```
e ←   Entity named: 'employee'.
e hasAttributes.
e-'number'.
e-'name'.
e-'department'.
e-'manager'.
e-'salary'.
e-'title'.
e-'dependents'.
```

(a)

```
e ←   Entity named: 'employee'.
e hasIdentifiers.
e-'number'               ;isPrimary.
e-'name'                 ;isAnAlternate.
e-'department'.
e-'manager'.
e-'salary'.
e-'title'.
e-'dependents'.
```

(b)

```
e ←   Entity named: 'employee'.
e hasRelatedAttributes.
e-'number'.
e-'name'.
e-'department'.
e-'manager'        sameAs: 'manager';
                   ofEntity: 'department'.
e-'salary'.
e-'title'.
e-'dependents'.
```

(c)

```
e ←   Entity named: 'employee'.
e hasSingleValues.
e-'number'          ;exactlyOne.
e-'name'            ;exactlyOne.
e-'department'      ;upToOne.
e-'manager'         ;upToOne.
e-'salary'          ;exactlyOne.
e-'title'           ;upToOne.
e-'dependents'.
```

(d)

vertically below the object in question in our code layout. For example, **hasAttributes, hasIdentifiers, hasRelatedAttributes,** and **hasSingleValues** in Fig. 8.3 are vertical modifier messages, and set the context for refining the meaning of the design object named '**employee**'. The second type of message is called a *horizontal modifier*. These refine the meaning of the object in terms of the individual aggregated objects in the context of a vertical modifier. Thus, **isPrimary** and **isAnAlternate** in Fig. 8.3b are horizontal modifiers; so are **exactlyOne** and **upToOne** in Fig. 8.3d. Fig. 8.3c illustrates that horizontal modifiers can have arguments. Horizontal modifiers can be thought of as a means of attaching semantics, adjectives, to the attributes of a relation (or instance variables if working with objects in an object-oriented setting).

We call each vertical modifier and its associated horizontal modifiers a layer. To explain the syntax of layers, we consider Fig. 8.3b. In the first line, the temporary variable **e** is assigned (points at) a specific object named '**employee**' from the class **Entity**. In the next line, the object **e** is the receiver of the vertical modifier message **hasIdentifiers** to set the context (i.e., layer) for specifying additional semantics for its attributes. The '-', as in **e** - '**number**', is a binary message identifying the object whose name is '**number**' as the current attribute of interest for the object **e**. The horizontal modifier messages **isPrimary** and **isAnAlternate** refine the semantics of '**number**' and '**name**' in this context of specifying identifiers. Attributes, such as '**manager**', for which no modifier messages appear in this layer are displayed for esthetic reasons only (i.e., mainly for displaying all attributes in each layer). It should be kept in mind that the layers display the names of objects such as '**employee**' and '**number**', while the underlying system works with the objects they name, **employee** and **number**.

The general specification of a layer is a sequence of messages of the following form, where terms in [ ] are optional and may be repeated:

```
anObject ← aMetabaseName named: anObjectName.
anObject aVerticalModifierMessage.
    [anObject - anotherObjectName [aHorizontalModifierMessage]].
```

**Metatypes and Metabases**    The vertical modifiers, **hasAttributes, hasSingleValues, hasIdentifiers**, etc., are appropriate for specifying entities in a database design. Naturally, there are other kinds of objects in a database design, including queries, views, and data types, and each of these types requires a different set of layers to specify its relevant characteristics. For example, the vertical modifiers for queries could be **hasSelections** (for specifying selection criteria in the query), **hasMatches** (for matching attributes in an equi-join), and **hasOutput** (for specifying a projection). Figure 8.4a shows the source of the fields participating in a simple query to find all the names and numbers of employees with a salary of at least $100,000. Figure 8.4b shows an example of a layer for specifying a selection criterion in the query.

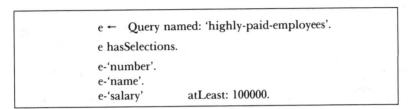

e ←     Query named: 'highly-paid-employees'.

e hasAttributes.

| e-'number' | ofEntity: | 'employee'. |
| e-'name' | ofEntity: | 'employee'. |
| e-'salary' | ofEntity: | 'employee'. |

(a)

e ←     Query named: 'highly-paid-employees'.

e hasSelections.

e-'number'.
e-'name'.
e-'salary'          atLeast: 100000.

(b)

**FIGURE 8.4** SOME LAYERS FOR A QUERY

We have seen two examples, an entity **employee** and a query **highly-paid-employees**, and some of the different layers needed to specify each. Since objects that are queries take one set of vertical and horizontal modifiers to specify them and entities take a different set, it is natural to define the concept of "type" in ODDESSY in terms of sets of modifiers. Consequently, we define a *metatype* as a collection of vertical and associated horizontal modifiers used in specifying objects of that kind. A *metabase* is a repository of objects of a particular metatype. Thus **Entity, Query, View**, and so forth are metatypes. In ODDESSY and in our discussion they also represent metabases of objects specified using their respective vertical and horizontal modifiers.

To expand a bit on the notion of metatype and to illustrate how we can extend our design language, we examine how we would proceed to define a metatype such as **Entity**. Since a metatype is defined by its vertical and horizontal modifiers, we can begin the definition of **Entity** by specifying the vertical modifiers, **hasAttributes, hasIdentifiers, hasRelatedAttributes**, etc., to be used with this metatype. Figure 8.5a illustrates that we do this by specifying these vertical modifiers as attributes of the object named **'Entity'**. The essential idea is that each metatype, in this example **Entity**, is also an object specified by layers, in the same fashion that design objects like **employee** and **department** are. Note that the object **Entity** belongs to a metabase called **MetabaseDef**. There are three predefined metabases called **MetabaseDef, VModifier**, and **HModifier** from which new metabases can be defined and extended.

Now, to continue the definition of **Entity**, we need to associate horizontal modifiers with each of its vertical modifiers. For example, Fig. 8.5b shows

| |
|---|
| e ←    MetabaseDef named: 'Entity'. |
| e hasAttributes. |
| e-'hasAttributes'. |
| e-'hasIdentifiers'. |
| e-'hasRelatedAttributes'. |
| e-'hasRelatedEntities'. |
| e-'hasSingleValues'. |

| |
|---|
| e ←    VModifier named: 'hasSingleValues'. |
| e hasAttributes. |
| e-'exactlyOne'. |
| e-'upToOne'. |

(a)                                                              (b)

**FIGURE 8.5** LAYERS FOR DEFINING A METATYPE

that this is done in part by specifying the horizontal modifiers as attributes of the vertical modifier of interest. Here, the vertical modifier **hasSingleValues**, which belongs to the metabase **VModifier**, has associated horizontal modifiers **exactlyOne** and **upToOne** as its attributes. Additional layers, not illustrated, in the **VModifier** metabase define how the horizontal modifiers are used with their respective vertical modifiers, such as what kind of argument to expect if the horizontal modifier has an argument. The interface, described in Section 8.3.2, then uses the metabase defining objects to display the layers for the design objects.

Now, to see how we can extend the design language, suppose we need to capture information about multivalued attributes of entities, such as **dependents** of **employee**. None of the layers in **Entity** provides for this. To overcome this problem, we extend the language by modifying the definition of **Entity**. This is done by adding a vertical modifier **hasMultipleValues**, whose name is of our own choosing, to the list of attributes in Fig. 8.5a. Then we would have to determine the appropriate horizontal modifiers to use with **hasMultipleValues** in a manner similar to the example in Fig. 8.5b. All of this can be done interactively during a design using the same interface discussed in Section 8.3.2. A fuller discussion can be found in [Diederich and Milton 1987c].

One special metatype is **Generic**. Objects that do not have attributes are typically found in this metabase. For example, **name, number**, and **salary** are members of the **Generic** metabase. Some objects will initially belong to **Generic**, but will migrate to another metabase when specified further. For instance, when an object first appears, as an attribute of another object, it is placed in the **Generic** metabase. One reason for maintaining separate metabases is for purposes of organization. Another is for use in rules for deducing implicit facts. As an example, knowing that **manager** is an **Entity** allows the system to deduce, subject to confirmation, that **e-'manager'** (i.e., **employee-manager**) is the same as **department-manager**. However, knowing that **number** is a **Generic** would not lead to the conclusion that **employee-number** has anything to do with **department-number**.

It should be noted that metatypes, and hence metabases, are defined by messages (vertical and horizontal modifiers) and not by structure. Contrast this with objects in Smalltalk where classes are initially, perhaps primarily, defined by their structure. Consequently, the definition of a metatype can be extended by defining more layers as they are needed and thereby capturing additional semantics of design objects. As a result, all objects have a uniform structure (layers) independent of the metabase to which they belong; that is, all layers have the same basic form. This simplifies working with rules, which are discussed in Section 8.3.3. Rules can therefore have a uniform structure and do not have to be tailored to individual object structure.

## 8.3.2 User Interface

Specifying and viewing layers, both for the design process and for defining new metabases and modifiers, takes place through the browser for the design system shown in Fig. 8.6. The browser has been implemented through the Smalltalk model-view-controller paradigm. Several alternative window layouts are available to the user. The one shown here is simply the best for reproduction on a page. Using a menu item, the design browser can be rapidly toggled between a configure state in which metatypes are created or modified

**FIGURE 8.6** AN ODDESSY BROWSER

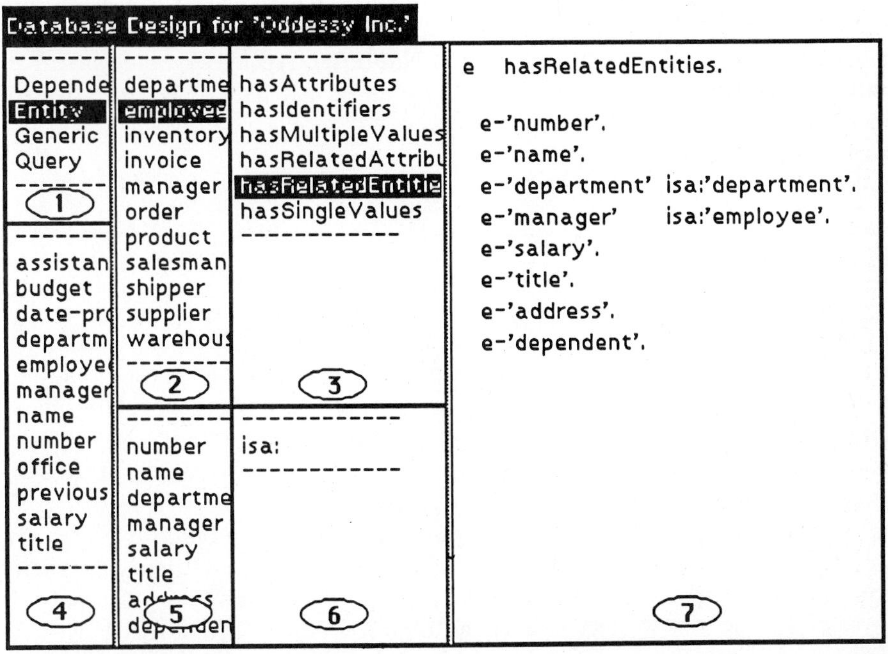

and a design state in which the existing metatypes are used to create and modify objects in the current design. Figure 8.6 shows the latter; the display in the configure state is similar. The upper left subview, subview 1, lists names of metabases, that is, repositories of design objects. Subview 2 is the list of objects in the selected metabase. Subview 3 displays vertical modifiers used in conjunction with the selected metabase. When a vertical modifier is selected, its associated horizontal modifiers are displayed in subview 6. In general, browsing consists of selecting objects and examining their layers. When selections are made in subviews 1 to 3, the layer for the object is displayed in the large subview 7. Several objects can be viewed simultaneously by opening multiple browsers. It is also possible to browse objects appearing in a layer in the same way that one can trace messages used in a Smalltalk method. The bottom left subview, 4, lists all design objects in all metabases, with similar tracing capability there.

Subview 5 of the browser lists the attributes of the object selected in subview 2. Subviews 5 and 6 are used principally for adding attributes to an object and for modifying them with horizontal modifiers. The basic interaction of specifying a design object consists of pointing at design objects with the cursor and selecting the appropriate action in a pop-up menu. For example, to specify additional information in a layer for an object, such as **employee** in Fig. 8.6, one can select the attribute to be modified in subview 5; specify the layer (i.e., choose modifiers in subviews 3 and 6 if they have not already been chosen); if the horizontal modifier requires an argument and the object already exists, select it in subview 4, or otherwise type the name of a new object in a fill-in-the-blank as part of the next step; and, finally, select a pop-up menu item that adds these choices to the layer. Deleting and modifying layers are carried out in a similar fashion. Naturally, typing at the keyboard is minimized since only new objects require entry. All new objects are treated as **Generic** metabase instances until they are moved to another metabase for further semantic refinement.

## 8.3.3 Rules

The information captured in the layers is exploited via rule-based protocols. By protocol we mean a specified subtask of the design system; for instance, creating or deducing functional dependencies, normalizing relations, doing logical record analysis for performance, structuring objects, deducing class hierarchies, and general assistance for the designer in evaluating the design are possible subtasks within a database design framework. As suggested earlier, it is likely that design systems will have to have some of the flexibility of rule-based systems to keep up with rapidly changing technology.

The rules test the facts stored in the layers and take actions if their conditions are met. The actions may be as simple as modifying an existing layer or adding a new layer to a design object. (Used in this way, the system acts like a production system, in which rules are used to change the current state of the knowledge base [McDermott 1982; van de Brug et al. 1986].)

The ability to extend the design language facilitates using rules. Rule conditions test existing layers, but rule actions sometimes require layers that have not been defined in the design language in order to save the results of their actions. For example, suppose we wish to use rules to deduce functional dependencies from layers specified for entities; an example of such a rule is given below. There are two approaches we can take to represent the functional dependencies produced by the rules:

1. We can define a new metatype called **FunctionalDependency** by creating appropriate vertical and horizontal modifiers to represent dependencies.

2. We can extend the definition of the metatype **Entity** by adding the vertical modifier **hasFunctionalDependencies** to the list of attributes in Fig. 8.5a and then adding some appropriate horizontal modifiers for **hasFunctionalDependencies**.

An example using alternative 2 is given in Fig. 8.11 near the end of Section 8.3.

**Rule Conditions via Messages**   Perhaps the key feature of rule formulation in ODDESSY is that the messages used for specifying the design are also used for formulating rule conditions. The syntax for simple rule conditions is shown in Fig. 8.7a. The only difference between the specification of a layer and the specification of a rule condition is the replacement of the binary operator '-' by the operator '@'. (In some implementations of Smalltalk '@' is reserved for point objects, so we use '-@' there.) Here **aVM** denotes a vertical modifier, **anHM** denotes a horizontal modifier without arguments, and **anHM:** denotes

**FIGURE 8.7** RULE CONDITION SYNTAX AND EXAMPLES

| | |
|---|---|
| (Ob1@Ob2) | aVM {isTrue, isFalse}. |
| (Ob1@Ob2) | aVM anHM        {isTrue, isFalse}. |
| (((Ob1@Ob2) | aVM anHM: #aValue) aCompOp {any value}) {isTrue, isFalse}. |
| | **(a)** |
| ('department'@'employee') | hasMultipleValues isTrue. |
| ('employee'@'number') | hasIdentifiers   isPrimary isTrue. |
| ((('ship'@'engine') | hasMultipleValues   atLeast: #aValue) $>=$ 2) is True. |
| | **(b)** |

a horizontal modifier with arguments. The symbol **#aValue** is a placeholder representing a dummy value (all keyword selectors require an argument). The symbol **aCompOp** is one of the standard comparison operators $>$, $<$, $>=$, $<=$, or $=$ (we actually use the symbol $*=$ for equality to avoid a conflict with another use of $=$). Some examples, using object names rather than objects, are given in Fig. 8.7b. The first line in Fig. 8.7b is a condition testing whether **employee** of **department** is a multivalued attribute. This will be true if the object named '**employee**' has been modified in the layer **hasMultipleValues** in the **Entity** '**department**'. The second line is a condition that tests whether '**number**' is a primary identifier of '**employee**'. The last line is a condition that tests whether '**ship**' has to have at least two engines. Also, more complex conditions can be expressed as conjunctions of the types shown.

Given the methods for formulating rule conditions already described, as the design language is extended the conditions can be written in terms of the extensions. For example, we have indicated how information about functional dependencies can be represented by extending the design language. Now, if we wish to write a set of rules to use the dependencies to create relational tables, we can use the messages **hasFunctionalDependencies** and its horizontal modifiers to formulate the rule conditions for doing this.

**Rule Example**   A rule for generating a functional dependency is shown in Fig. 8.8. We first examine the rule's structure, and then we discuss its meaning. The class **Rule** has the following instance variables:

| | |
|---|---|
| number | —an identifier |
| name | —a string |
| conditions | —an array of symbols of the conditions |
| conditionSelector | —a message selector for testing the conditions |
| actionSelector | —a message selector for executing the action |

The rule's conditions are stored as symbols in the instance variable **conditions**. This makes comparison of two rules' conditions possible. The conditions are compiled into code in a separate method whose message selector is stored in the **conditionSelector** of the rule. The method for the condition selector **conditionsFDRule2** in Fig. 8.8 is given in Fig. 8.9. (It can be generated directly from the rule's **conditions** and **conditionSelector** without intervention by the designer.) A rule's conditions are tested by sending it a message of the form **aRule perform: (aRule conditionSelector)**. Figure 8.9 shows the effects of testing the conditions: if some condition is not satisfied, it is returned; otherwise **true** is returned.

Finally, the message selector of the method that performs the rule's action is stored in the instance variable **actionSelector**. At this point in the

```
createFDRule2
    | rule |
rule <- Rule new.
rule
    number: 2;
    name: 'relatedAttributesRule';

    conditions: #(
                ((Ob1 @ Ob2) hasIdentifiers   isPrimary isFalse)
                ((Ob1 @ Ob2) hasIdentifiers   isPartOfPrimary isFalse)
                ((Ob1 @ Ob2) hasSingleValues isTrue)
                ((Ob1 @ Ob2) hasRelatedAttributes isTrue));

    conditionSelector: # conditionsFDRule2;
    actionSelector: #actionFDRule2.
(Rulebase at: #fdRules) at: rule number put: rule.
```

**FIGURE 8.8** A RULE TO CREATE FUNCTIONAL DEPENDENCIES

research, the actions are coded in a procedural manner; we are attempting to make them more declarative, as discussed below. The action occurs when the **actionSelector** is performed. No arguments are needed for rules since they are loaded into class variables **Ob1** and **Ob2** by the protocol using the rule.

Turning now to the meaning of the rule, the conditions test whether the attribute **Ob2** of **Ob1** is a single-valued attribute, is not part of a primary attribute, and is related to an attribute in another entity, as exemplified in the layer **hasRelatedAttributes** in Fig. 8.3c. If these conditions are satisfied, the action forms a pair of functional dependencies. For example, suppose that **Ob1** is the object represented by **'employee'** and **Ob2** is represented by **'manager'** in

**FIGURE 8.9** A CONDITION METHOD

```
conditionsFDRule2
((Ob1 @ Ob2) hasIdentifiers isPrimary isFalse) ifFalse:        [ ↑ conditions at: 1].

((Ob1 @ Ob2) hasIdentifiers isPartOfPrimary isFalse) ifFalse: [ ↑ conditions at: 2].

((Ob1 @ Ob2) hasSingleValues isTrue) ifFalse:                 [ ↑ conditions at: 3].

((Ob1 @ Ob2) hasRelatedAttributes isTrue) ifFalse:           [ ↑ conditions at: 4].

↑ true
```

the layers in Fig. 8.3. Then, since the rule conditions are satisfied, the action forms the dependencies, illustrated here using strings rather than objects:

  employee-manager → department-manager
  department-manager → employee-manager

Other rules, with the conditions that **Ob2** is a single-valued attribute of **Ob1** and that **Ob2** is not part the primary identifier of **Ob1**, create functional dependencies such as **employee-number → employee-manager** and **employee-number → employee-department**. After the various dependencies are deduced or specified, the routines for normalization determine which dependencies are redundant, as would be the case for **employee-number → employee-manager**, given a full specification of the 'department' entity.

  It appears possible to frame many actions in a declarative manner also. This is part of our continuing research and will be illustrated by an example. If the actions are more complex and involve highly algorithmic or heuristic procedures, then the full power of Smalltalk is available for carrying them out in methods. To illustrate how the actions of a rule can have a declarative form, suppose it is determined by a rule's conditions that **name** is a single-valued attribute of **employee**, which is not a primary identifier. Then we would want to create a functional dependency wherein the primary attributes of **employee** functionally determine **employee-name**. The action would have the form shown in Fig. 8.10.

  Note that the action in Fig. 8.10 examines each attribute (**anAttr**) of **Ob1**, which we can think of as representing **employee**. The conditions, just as in the rule conditions, test whether each attribute is the primary or part of the primary key. If so, the layer defined by **hasFunctionalDependencies** is specified in the same form as layers are specified by the designer, as seen in the block

**FIGURE 8.10** DECLARATIVE ACTIONS

```
actionRule1
Ob1  forAllItsAttributes:
  [:anAttr | ( (((Ob1 @ anAttr) hasIdentifiers isPrimary isTrue)
            | ((Ob1 @ anAttr) hasIdentifiers isPartOfPrimary isTrue))
       whenSatisfied:
         [Ob1 hasFunctionalDependencies.
           (Ob1-(Ob2 name)) impliedBy: (anAttr name);
                             of: (Ob1 name).]
  atEnd: [Ob1 - (Ob2 name)  standard; endGroup].
```

```
e <- Entity named: 'employee'.

e <- hasFunctionalDependencies.

e-'number'.
e-'name'              impliedBy: 'number';
                      of: 'employee';
                      standard;
                      endGroup.

e-'department'        impliedBy: 'number';
                      of: 'employee';
                      ... etc. ...
```

**FIGURE 8.11** A LAYER FOR **hasFunctionalDependencies**

of code following the message selector **whenSatisfied:**. The layer fragment is
shown in Fig. 8.11 to clarify this, since the code in Fig. 8.10 uses objects rather
than strings.

The code block following the selector **atEnd:** allows additional horizontal modifiers to be added to the layer after all primary key attributes have
been processed. In this case **endGroup** is used to mark the end of a group of
horizontal modifiers that constitute a meaningful collection of modifiers. For
example, if an attribute is the right side of more than one dependency, separate groups of modifiers are needed. If later this dependency were found to
be redundant, we could add the horizontal modifier redundant to the group.
The modifier **standard** is one of several currently used to distinguish types of
functional dependencies deduced by the system.

## SUMMARY

The small example of generating functional dependencies exemplifies the direction taken in ODDESSY: provide a simple, uniform, and even perhaps
natural way (layers) to specify the database requirements, and then provide
rule-based tools for assisting the activities of the design. ODDESSY's main
purpose is to support testing the utility of new principles of design. In this
regard, ODDESSY provides a simple and flexible framework for experimentation. The key is integration: Smalltalk, the ODDESSY implementation language, and the ODDESSY design language (modifiers, layers) have the same
standing—i.e., the design language is just an extension of the implementation language. While the initial intent of the project was to support relational
design, as principles emerge for object-oriented database design (see [Booch
1986] for a discussion of object-oriented development in general) it will be nat-

ural to use ODDESSY to experiment with these principles and to integrate it with a persistent object manager for Smalltalk. In the meantime, ODDESSY provides a tool for experimenting with relational design.

## REFERENCES

[Astrahan et al. 1976] M.M. Astrahan et al., "System R: A Relational Approach to Database Management," *ACM Transactions on Database Systems,* vol 1, no. 2, June 1976.

[Banerjee et al. 1987a] J. Banerjee et al., "Data Model Issues for Object-Oriented Applications," *ACM Transactions on Office Information Systems,* vol. 5, no. 1, pp. 3–26, January 1987.

[Banerjee et al. 1987b] J. Banerjee, W. Kim, H.-J. Kim, and H.F. Korth, "Semantics and Implemention of Schema Evolution in Object-Oriented Databases," *Proceedings of ACM SIGMOD,* San Francisco, CA, 1987.

[Batory 1986] D. Batory, "GENESIS: A Project to Develop an Extensible Database Management System," *Proceedings of the International Workshop on Object-Oriented Systems,* Computer Society Press, Rockville, MD, 1986.

[Booch 1986] G. Booch, "Object-Oriented Development," *IEEE Transactions on Software Engineering,* vol. SE-12, no. 2, pp. 211–221, February 1986.

[Cammarata and Melkanoff 1986] S.J. Cammarata and M.A. Melkanoff, "An Interactive Data Dictionary Facility," Expert Database Systems, Proceedings from the First International Workshop, ed. L. Kerschberg, Benjamin/Cummings, Menlo Park, CA, 1986.

[Carey et al. 1986] M. Carey et al., "The Architecture of the EXODUS Extensible DBMS," *Proceedings of the International Workshop on Object-Oriented Database Systems,* Pacific Grove, CA, 1986.

[Chen 1986] P. Chen, "The Entity-Relationship Model: Towards a Unified View of Data," *ACM Transactions on Database Systems,* vol. 1, no. 1, pp. 9–36, March 1976.

[Codd 1970] E. Codd, "A Relational Model for Large Shared Data Banks," *Communications of the ACM,* vol. 13, no. 6, pp. 377–387, June 1970.

[Diederich and Milton 1987a] J. Diederich and J. Milton, "ODDESSY: An Object-Oriented Database Design System," *Proceedings of the Third International Conference on Data Engineering,* Los Angeles, February 1987.

[Diederich and Milton 1987b] J. Diederich and J. Milton, "Experimental Prototyping in Smalltalk," *IEEE Software,* pp. 50–64, May 1987.

[Diederich and Milton 1987c] J. Diederich and J. Milton, "An Object-Oriented Design System Shell," *Proceedings of the Second ACM Conference on Object-Oriented Programming Systems, Languages, and Applications, SIGPLAN Notices,* vol. 22, no. 11, 1987.

[Diederich and Milton 1987d] J. Diederich and J. Milton, "New Methods and Fast Algorithms for Database Normalization," *ACM Transactions on Database Systems,* vol. 13, pp. 339–365, September 1988.

[Hammer and McLeod 1981] M. Hammer and D. McLeod, "Data Description with SDM: A Semantic Data Model," *ACM Transactions on Database Systems,* vol. 6, no. 3, pp. 351–386, September 1981.

[Kim et al. 1987] W. Kim, N. Ballou, J. Banerjee, H.-T. Chou, J. Garza, and D. Woelk, "Features of the Orion Object-Oriented Database System," *MCC Technical Report No. ACA-ST-308-87,* Austin, Texas, September 1987.

[King 1984] R. King, "Sembase: A Semantic DBMS," *Proceedings of the First International Workshop on Expert Database Systems,* Kiawah Island, SC, pp. 151–171, October 1984.

[Korth 1986] H. Korth and A. Silberschatz, *Database System Concepts,* McGraw-Hill, New York, 1986.

[Maier et al. 1986] D. Maier, J. Stein, A. Otis, and A. Purdy, "Development of an Object-Oriented DBMS," *Proceedings of the First ACM Conference on Object-Oriented Programming Systems, Languages and Applications, SIGPLAN Notices,* vol. 21, no. 12, pp. 472–482, 1986.

[McDermott 1982] J. McDermott, "R1: A Rule-based Configurer of Computer Systems," *Artificial Intelligence,* vol. 19, pp. 39–88, September 1982.

[Stonebraker 1976] M. Stonebraker, "The Design and Implementation of Ingres," *ACM Transactions on Database Systems,* September 1976.

[Stonebraker 1986] M. Stonebraker, "The Design of Postgres," *Proceedings of the International Conference on Management of Data, ACM-SIGMOD,* 1986.

[Teorey and Fry 1982] T.J. Teorey and J.P. Fry, "Design of Database Structures," Prentice-Hall, Englewood Cliffs, NJ, 1982.

[Ullman 1982] J.D. Ullman, *Database and Knowledge—Base Systems, vol. I,* Computer Science Press, Rockville, MD, 1988.

[van de Brug et al. 1986] A. van de Brug, J. Bachant, and J. McDermott, "The Taming of R1," *IEEE Expert,* pp. 33–39, Fall 1986.

[Wiederhold 1986] G. Wiederhold, "Views, Objects, and Databases," *Computer,* vol. 19, no. 12, pp. 37–44, December 1986.

# 9

# Integrated Office Systems

O.M. Nierstrasz, D.C. Tsichritzis

## INTRODUCTION

New techniques are sorely needed to aid in the development and maintenance of large application systems. The problem with traditional approaches to software engineering is amply evident in the field of office information systems: it is costly and difficult to extend existing applications, and to get unrelated applications to "talk" to each other. The object-oriented approach is already being tentatively applied in the modeling of "office objects" and in the presentation of these entities to users as such in "desktop" interfaces to office software. In order to fully exploit the approach to achieve integrated office systems, we need to use object-oriented programming languages, object-oriented run-time support, and object-oriented software engineering environments.

We can view the fundamental idea behind the object-oriented approach as that of *encapsulation:* object-oriented languages and systems exploit encapsulation in various ways in an attempt to enhance productivity through, for example, reusability mechanisms such as class inheritance. (See [Nierstrasz 1988] in this book for an elaboration of this view.) The importance of object-oriented techniques for software engineering has long been established: encapsulation has been successfully used by programmers ever since macros and subroutines were invented. Encapsulation is not only important for the purpose of decomposing large software problems into manageable pieces, but can also be exploited to achieve software maintainability, reusability, and even "rapid prototyping," as object-oriented systems like Smalltalk [Goldberg and Robson 1983] have demonstrated.

Commitments to existing software, languages, and operating systems have prevented application developers from taking full advantage of object-oriented techniques until now. The possibilities are especially evident in the domain of office information systems, since there is often a close and natural correspondence between the entities these systems manipulate and the real-world "objects" they refer to.

Office information systems are a paradigm of a new kind of application. For a long time the applications supported by computer systems were well-defined and reasonably well-structured. In such environments it was realistic to expect that we could define the "problem" inherent in the application, then do the requirements analysis, and follow on with implementation. In office information systems the "problem" often cannot be readily defined. Office procedures, being generally goal-oriented, are often ill-defined and exhibit large numbers of exceptions. Furthermore, they expand in scope and evolve in time, and thus suffer from constantly changing requirements and assumptions. We are therefore faced with an ill-structured application that is not clearly defined.

Object-oriented techniques are especially suited to deal with such applications. Each object is well-defined, but we are not expected to start with a definition of an overall object population behavior. We can change object behavior in time and we can add new objects. We have an environment where the whole is represented by the behavior of the parts. We claim that the object-oriented approach is well-suited for overall application development. In addition, traditional approaches, such as structured programming, cannot cope with applications like office information systems. Hence, for such applications, object-oriented techniques are not only important but necessary.

The particular needs of office information systems can be divided into the following main subtopics:

1. office modeling concepts

2. application development

3. application maintainability

4. user interface issues

The modeling issues are: identification, modeling and representation of "office objects," formulation of routine office procedures, encapsulation of (nonroutine or semiroutine) office tasks, and encapsulation of office knowledge.

Application development necessitates better languages, better run-time support, and better tools for developing applications (such as object design tools).

Application maintainability refers not only to routine maintenance but also to the ability to extend applications easily, to allow them to migrate to new environments (i.e., "porting"), and to allow different applications to communicate with one another.

The user interface issues are diverse, but some of the most important include the representation of system entities to the user, natural paradigms for interacting with and manipulating those entities, and "standard" interfaces across a range of applications on a per-user basis.

We shall focus on each of these issues and show how object-oriented techniques have contributed to software solutions. We shall argue that the adoption of object-oriented languages, systems, and tools is essential for developers of integrated office systems.

It is clearly possible to develop applications in an object-oriented fashion without using any object-oriented tools, programming constructs, or run-time support. However, the extent to which an application developer may exploit these techniques will be severely limited if these tools are not available, as we hope to demonstrate.

## 9.1 OFFICE MODELING CONCEPTS

The initial phase of application development involves modeling. Modeling is by definition a process of abstraction, since the point of a model is that one be able to concentrate on "important" properties and ignore the "unimportant" ones. Similarly, application development is a process of abstraction, except that the "important" properties are those that the user of the system will be aware of, and the "unimportant" ones are the implementations of the software components. Object-oriented approaches help us in this abstraction process by encouraging us to decompose problems into semi-independent objects.

There are various object models in use today, but the one that has the most relevance for applications programming is that which views objects as instances of abstract data types. In this model, the abstract interface to an object is a set of named operations that clients of that object may invoke. The static data (i.e., the *instance variables*) and the implementations of the operations (the *methods*) are hidden. The specification of the object's interface may include the invocation syntax of the operations, the argument and return types, and possibly other static properties of the object or its operations (for example, a formal or informal description of the semantics of an operation invocation).

This particular object model will support object-oriented techniques such as instantiation, parameterization, and class inheritance, to mention a few. There are also object models that are useful for capturing other aspects of office information systems (objects as part hierarchies; objects as sets of rules or facts), which we shall touch on in the discussion that follows. In one sense, however, the abstract data type object model is the most general, since we can always access the static properties of other object models through an operational interface.

### 9.1.1 Office Objects

It has been claimed that the best way to computerize the office is to *begin* by mimicking office functions in software [Ellis and Nutt 1980]. Not only does this provide application developers with a (relatively) well-defined initial goal, in terms of simulating the real objects of the office environment and their functionality in software, but it supposedly eases the cost of training office personnel to use the software, since they will be initially introduced to as few new concepts as necessary.

Furthermore, it can hardly be disputed that people are used to working in terms of manipulating and coordinating "objects." The objects we see in the office are mainly encapsulations of information: forms, letters, records, databases, reference manuals, and so on. The nature of the information they contain may vary a great deal, however. Many of the office "objects" encapsulate not only information but also methods for its manipulation.

Computerized office systems initially concentrated on encapsulating well-structured, routine entities, such as forms and records. Database management systems have proved invaluable for managing large numbers of similarly structured entities. Electronic forms systems exploit the regular structure of forms to provide forms-oriented interfaces to database systems [Tsichritzis et al. 1982; Tsichritzis 1982].

Traditional database models were typically not object-oriented, however, since they exposed database records as passive entities without any indication of their intended use. It was up to the application software to decide how the database was to be used. When new applications were built, there was no implicit guarantee that the database would continue to be used in a consistent fashion, since there was no mechanism for abstracting the proper usage of the database entities. This problem was remedied to some extent by the introduction of *database constraints* and *triggers*, which provided a way of discovering when things went wrong. They stopped short, however, of providing a way to specify what operations were valid to perform on objects. Current work on object-oriented databases attempts to remedy this shortcoming (see the subsequent chapters in this book).

Several object-oriented techniques are appropriate for the specification of electronic forms. The most obvious are classification and instantiation, since that is how paper forms are defined. Similarly, data abstraction is appropriate for parts of forms, since there are distinct categories of form fields that behave in very different ways [Gehani 1982]. Some examples are:

- optional, modifiable fields

- obligatory, nonmodifiable fields

- automatic fields

- "virtual" fields

An example of an obligatory, nonmodifiable field is an employee number. An automatic field (for example, the form creation date) is filled in by the system and stored with the rest of the form. Virtual fields, on the other hand, require no storage, being recomputed whenever they are displayed. Prices and totals on an order form might be handled in this way. Forms can be defined as conglomerations of fields of various field types, where the permissible set of field types is extendible.

Inheritance can play an important role in designing new forms, since many forms share common parts. For example, we can define a basic order form that provides certain standard fields required by, say, the accounting department. We may then define new order forms that inherit these standard fields, but may include extra information used only locally by certain departments. This kind of inheritance between form types is analogous to class inheritance in object-oriented languages such as Smalltalk, if we interpret the fields of a form as its public instance variables and methods.

Other kinds of office objects can also be defined using these techniques. Document types are now commonly viewed as *part hierarchies* [Horak 1985; ECMA 1983; Furuta et al. 1982]. As with forms, one may define new types of document parts as need arises. Furthermore, these parts may be made up of other parts; for example, chapters are made up of sections and paragraphs, and diagrams are made up of graphical entities. Documents themselves are not normally made up of a static combination of these parts. Certain document types may exhibit some common structure; for example, standard business letters must contain certain parts in fixed positions, but the body of a document is frequently quite flexible. We can further draw an analogy between document types and object classes, and correspondingly define forms of inheritance that permit document types to share part structures. The document structure can be defined either by using a formal grammar, or equivalently by defining for each part how it may be expanded in terms of permissible subparts. New document types may be defined by inheriting and refining the structure of existing types.

*Part inheritance* is concerned with the sharing of parts or values between object instances. (Notice that class inheritance can be viewed as part inheritance applied to class objects.) We make use of part inheritance when, for example, we create new document instances that inherit (copy) text from existing documents. More interesting is the case in which document types are determined implicitly by the contents of the documents, as is the case with text-formatting languages in which contents and formatting statements are freely mixed: here we can dynamically change the "type" of a document by copying parts of existing documents to the one we are editing. This kind of activity is supported by WYSIWYG document editors that allow copying of parts between different documents, or reuse of an existing document as a template for a new one. The danger is that undisciplined use of part inheritance leads to a profusion of document types and a loss of regularity.

A third kind of inheritance that is very important for documents is what we shall call *scope inheritance*. With class inheritance, all future instances will have the properties inherited by their class. With part inheritance, only the current instance inherits parts from another object. With scope inheritance, certain properties of an object are determined by its current scope, or environment. When that scope changes, those properties of that object will implicitly change. For example, if a piece of text is moved from the body of a section into a quotation, its display characteristics (text width, point size, etc.) may change, although it is still the same object. The difference between these different kinds of inheritance is in the nature of the properties inherited, and when the inheritance occurs (see also Chapter 1 of this book).

Documents can be seen as a generalization of the concept of a form, since their structure is more flexible. At some point the paradigm of a document takes over that of an object, because any object can be seen as a document if there is a way of presenting it and a way of "editing" it (i.e., interacting with it). This phenomenon is already apparent in the work done on "electronic books" and "hypertext" [Cook 1984; Meyrowitz 1986; Weyer and Borning 1985]. (A "document," it would seem, is anything that has words in it, and doesn't change too often, even if there are many different ways of looking at it!)

Finally, there is a set of office objects that are more dynamic than forms or documents, and can be classified as "office tools." These are objects that can be used to manipulate other objects. Some common examples are mailboxes, spreadsheets, and editors. Here too is the potential for exploiting class inheritance. Tools depend on the fact that the objects they manipulate have certain common properties. A mailbox can hold anything, as long as it is a message. A generic editor can be used to edit any object that can be displayed and that understands the edit operations. The properties required by a tool can be encapsulated in the operations of an object class, and inherited by any class that is to be compatible with that tool. The implementation of those operations may vary, since objects may have different internal structure, but this should be transparent to a generic tool.

### 9.1.2 Office Procedures

Thus far we have concentrated on passive office objects that have counterparts in the physical office. The operations that are valid for manipulating these objects may be encoded as part of their object classes, if an object-oriented approach is used. By *office procedures* we mean the routine sequences of operations that are used to manipulate office objects [Hogg et al. 1985].

Office procedures are also objects that office workers should be able to manipulate, since "routine" procedures may have a life span lasting anywhere from a few minutes to the lifetime of the office, and may be routine only for a single worker or for everybody in the company. Office workers should not, however, be expected to learn how to program in order to specify or use computerized office procedures.

Attempts to provide users with the ability to automate routine functions have mostly concentrated on "programming-by-example" techniques for encoding office procedures [Zloof 1982; Halbert 1984]. With this approach, one first builds a system containing electronic representations of office objects and functions. Such a system is then enhanced by permitting users to "teach" the system to perform routine functions by stepping through the procedures using examples. For instance, an office worker who uses an electronic forms system to coordinate order forms and inventory forms can teach the system to notify him or her when matching forms appear by stepping through the procedure to find matching forms, and indicating the action to be taken. The advantage of this approach is that the user specifies procedures using the same interaction mechanisms as are used to manipulate the office objects manually. It is not necessary to learn a completely new language.

Tools for specifying office procedures have also focused on the event-driven behavior of office work. Office procedures are typically *triggered* upon completion of some awaited event: the arrival of a message, the completion of a form, the modification of a document. The by-example approach can be used to specify triggers by allowing the user to give an example of a situation that will trigger the procedure. Alternatively, it is possible to describe the conditions using a language that models information flow by *augmented Petri nets* [Zisman 1978; Barron 1982] or other formalisms that decompose procedures into triggered steps, for example, finite automata or production rule systems.

Event-driven behavior lends itself well to graphical representations (such as those commonly used to depict Petri nets and finite automata). This suggests that graphical programming may be a promising approach for enabling office workers to specify certain kinds of office procedures; for example, users could specify trigger conditions and actions, and see the local or global effects in terms of a graphical display of the resulting event-triggering behavior. Semiautomatic processing and routing of forms in a large community of users could be depicted as a flow diagram induced by users' local office procedures. Users could then use the graphical representation to navigate through the network of interacting procedures and either modify the graph directly to establish different triggering scenarios, or use the graph to access the procedures in a different form. The graph would be dynamically updated by analyzing the interaction between procedures, using techniques such as those described in [Nierstrasz 1985].

### 9.1.3 Office Tasks and Office Knowledge

Whereas routine office procedures are triggered under well-defined circumstances and result in specific actions to be taken, *office tasks* are goal-oriented and cannot necessarily be encoded according to a precise procedure to be followed. Examples of tasks as opposed to procedures are managing a meeting and developing a new product.

The execution of an office task typically consists of many phases during which office objects are manipulated according to routine, mechanizable procedures or according to nonroutine, knowledge-intensive procedures. Either kind of procedure is event-driven, but only the former may be fully automated. The latter, while not mechanizable, can benefit from triggering (e.g., by notifying office workers what work is ready to be done next), and can benefit from decision support tools [Bui and Jarke 1986] and from knowledge-based approaches [Croft and Lefkowitz 1988].

Encapsulation techniques are important for decomposing office knowledge. Conceptual modeling techniques have traditionally decomposed knowledge into object-like entities, and have found it useful to apply such notions as instantiation, classification, structuring (aggregation), and inheritance [Mylopoulos and Levesque 1983]. Similarly, rule-based approaches for encoding knowledge in languages like Prolog have benefited from the object-oriented paradigm by encapsulating knowledge or beliefs inside objects (see [Russinoff 1988] in this book). Conflicting theories can thus be tolerated as long as knowledge objects do not interfere with one another.

"KNOs" are a programming paradigm for encapsulating knowledge and goals as knowledge objects [Tsichritzis et al. 1987]. The principal idea is that KNOs are mobile, active entities that can gather information from their environment, and can exchange rules and knowledge with other KNOs. A system for defining KNOs [Casais 1988] has been implemented using the LISP flavors package [Moon 1986]. In this system, KNOs belong to one or more KNO classes, and are able to inherit parts dynamically while they execute. The operations of a KNO are encoded as production rules, each consisting of a name, a trigger condition, and a series of actions. The actions may be used to modify a KNO's state, to communicate with other KNOs via an intermediate *blackboard* object, create new KNOs, move to another environment, learn and "unlearn" rules, and create and communicate with *limbs* (subordinate KNOs that may be distributed to other environments).

## 9.2 APPLICATION DEVELOPMENT

Object-oriented techniques and languages help to cut down the cost of developing software in many ways. The most significant way in which they do so is by providing the possibility of a large software base of well-designed, prepackaged, reusable objects. (For a survey on software reusability, see either [Biggerstaff and Perliss 1984] or [Biggerstaff and Richter 1987].) Object-oriented languages not only adopt the old idea of reusable libraries of subroutines, but they extend the ways in which software can be made reusable by supporting mechanisms such as object instantiation, operator overloading (i.e., "tailoring" of object classes), run-time binding (when appropriate), class inheritance, and parameterization.

A programmer who is familiar with the reusable object base can, in principle, configure a "prototype" application in a fraction of the time it would take to program from scratch, with a minimum of programming effort. Furthermore, it has been shown that object-oriented techniques and mechanisms are in no way inconsistent with strong (static) typing, or with efficient compilation (rather than interpretation). Thus the commonly-held view that objects are "only" good for prototyping is misleading, since these prototypes certainly do not have to exhibit poor performance.

Despite the clear advantages that object-oriented programming offers the application developer, there are several important issues to be addressed before one can start programming with objects. Fundamentally, of course, we must have an object-oriented programming language available for our use.

This immediately introduces an integration problem. We would like to be able to reuse existing software and applications that were developed without the benefit of an object-oriented methodology, and integrate them with newly-developed applications. We rarely have the luxury of being able to choose our environment when we have to build an application. Fortunately, there are several possible solutions to this problem, all of which have to do with encapsulation: since the implementation of an object is hidden from us, there is no reason the internal environment of an object must be the same as the environment in which it is used. Encapsulation may therefore be used to hide the implementation language. The practical alternatives are:

1. Use an object-oriented extension of an existing programming language (such as C++ [Stroustrup 1986], Objective C [Cox 1986], or LISP flavors [Moon 1986]).

2. Use an object-oriented language that is translated into the target programming language (such as Eiffel, which is translated into C [Meyer 1986]).

3. Use an object-oriented language augmented with a package for interfacing to other languages within the programming environment (e.g., calling Fortran libraries from C++, or whatever).

The other fundamental issue is that of run-time support for the object environment. This may entail support for:

■ object naming

■ persistence

■ distribution (e.g., remote communication)

- concurrency

- transaction management

- version management (for objects and object classes)

- security

An environment that provides basic run-time support for objects at this level allows the application developer to concentrate on the configuration of the objects in the intended application, and permits standard solutions to these low-level problems to be adopted across a range of applications.

These fundamental issues aside, the application developer has to solve two difficult problems posed by the object-oriented paradigm:

1. What are the objects of my application?

2. What objects will help me to implement it?

The first is the traditional "decomposition" problem: How can I break my problem down into manageable pieces? The second is the composition problem: What tools are available to me to solve my subproblems? In addition, we have the traditional problems of managing large pieces of software: version management and software distribution management.

Obviously, there is a certain amount of "black magic" involved in properly decomposing a problem into objects. Even though we may intuitively know what objects we have to deal with, it is often difficult to decide what should be a "property," a "part," or an "acquaintance," just as it is difficult to decide what should be visible and what should be hidden. We call this the *object design problem.*

Techniques for designing "objects" in other areas, such as database schema design and computer-aided design, do not have to deal with the full range of techniques and mechanisms offered by object-oriented languages.

The composition problem is currently answered only through "browsers" that help the programmer to browse through the base of object classes, and through programmer familiarity with the set of reusable object classes that are available. Both of these solutions are inadequate for dealing with extremely large collections of object classes, say in the tens of thousands. The obvious approach of putting the object classes in a database fails because the data are highly dissimilar. What kind of queries would one pose to such a database?

Simply grouping object classes according to subject matter to aid browsing is also inadequate, since there are many possible groupings. This is comparable to the problem of browsing through an encyclopedia to find the answer to a loosely-defined question. An "electronic encyclopedia" approach can work only if we know where to *start* browsing, and we can also be sure that the appropriate links exist for us to follow. Knowing which object classes may be useful for solving a particular problem is a good example of "expert" knowledge that can be acquired only through experience. Even the original implementor may not be able to anticipate all the uses to which the objects may reasonably be put. This suggests that knowledge about object usage should be incrementally added to the "object class encyclopedia," based on the experience of programmers who have actually used those classes to build applications. Furthermore, we expect that an expert system interface would be the most natural way to pose queries that can be used to direct the browsing task.

There is a final bit of "magic" we have avoided up to now, namely, how do objects become reusable? It should be obvious that one can hardly sit down and design a new object class that will be instantly useful to a host of applications. Rather, we expect that application developers will discover that certain objects that have been tailored for particular applications can, with some careful redesign, be generalized and made useful to other problem domains. Object classes that evolve in this way gradually become more generic and enter the software base of reusable objects. This suggests that our object encyclopedia should not only manage tried and proven object classes, but that it should keep track of evolving classes, and help us to detect and forge software generality.

## 9.3 APPLICATION MAINTAINABILITY

Unfortunately, once we have developed software, the job is far from done. Aside from the tedious work of testing and debugging, we must maintain software because the conditions and requirements for its use change. The application may need to be extended, or ported to a new machine, or modified to solve a slightly different problem, or integrated with somebody else's software, or even hacked apart so that certain parts can be reused. In the field of office information systems the issue of constantly changing requirements is ever more pressing, as software is being used to address more complex and ill-defined problems.

Object-oriented techniques provide solutions to some, but not all, of these problems. Provided that objects' specifications do not change, modification of their internal behavior should not affect the context in which they are used. For example, porting an application to a new environment should entail only re-implementation of the "machine-dependent" objects.

Encapsulation also provides the possibility of reusability of objects: since objects are "self-contained," it is in principle possible to take them out of one environment and reuse them in another. As we have pointed out, however, it is rarely true that objects designed for one application will be automatically useful for another. Such objects typically evolve through several iterations before they stabilize and acquire a level of generic usefulness. Nevertheless, we believe that encapsulation makes it easier to isolate and evolve generic software.

Adding functionality to an application is often possible through the mechanism of class inheritance. This works only if one can capture this increased functionality by strictly adding on to the objects that already exist in an application. Parts of the application that knew instances of the old parent class will continue to work with the instances of the subclass, and it is even possible to allow instances of both classes to co-exist. For example, a forms system may be upgraded to deal with multimedia forms. The old interface will be able to cope with both kinds of forms, although it will not be able to make use of the new functionality. New operations may, if necessary, violate encapsulation, and have direct access to the static data of the originally defined object, but this may cause difficulties if we later decide to evolve the old class independently, or change its implementation.

Object encapsulation can also be extremely important for integrating applications, if we realize that the object specification language need not be the same as the implementation language. That is, one could conceivably use an object-oriented language to describe encapsulations (the interfaces to objects), and feel free to use other languages in their implementations. There are two important reasons for doing this. First, we may have already invested a great deal in software that is not written in a particular object-oriented language. Repackaging software in terms of objects is an exercise in defining its valid external interfaces, and in identifying its reusable components. Second, we may find that different languages are more appropriate for implementing different kinds of objects. If we believe that a carpenter should use the best tool for a given task, then it is reasonable to allow a programmer to use the best language for solving a problem. For example, we can imagine an object-oriented interface to a "knowledge object" programmed internally in Prolog.

## 9.4 User interfaces

As computer software is used to accomplish more abstract and complex tasks, the user interfaces to these systems must become correspondingly more sophisticated. The problem is how to provide the user with the most reasonable presentation of the state of the system and its functionalities. Fortunately, as more cycles become available for more complicated computer systems, we can skim off more cycles for more sophisticated interfaces.

Objects not only provide us with a useful paradigm for organizing software, but they also suggest a corresponding interface paradigm: for every software object in the system that we wish to represent or interact with, there can be a corresponding "presentation object" that will be visible to the user on a display. Furthermore, the paradigm of *direct manipulation* will allow the user to interact "directly" with objects by issuing commands to one or more "current" presentation objects that can provide visual feedback regarding resultant side-effects. We see these ideas work not only in document editor-formatters, but also in interfaces with virtual sliders, buttons, levers, and so on.

Task switching in a direct-manipulation environment is possible just as it is in the real world: we simply shift our attention from one set of objects to another by, for example, moving between windows. With command-style interfaces the current "mode" is often implicit. We must remember whether we are in *insert* or *delete* mode, or which directory we are in. By contrast, the current context is always explicitly presented in a direct-manipulation interface.

The main difficulty with this approach is that it requires a fair bit of creativity to decide on good paradigms for presentation and for manipulation. How should we represent a mailbox? What feedback should we get when incoming mail is received, or when outgoing mail is delivered? What interaction paradigm is appropriate for performing a database query? (Are command-style interaction paradigms inevitably best for some kinds of tasks, or do we just lack the intuition and insight we need to package them in terms of direct manipulation?)

Another important difficulty is that we must decide between richness and uniformity. A rich user interface is pleasant if it allows us to perform a large number of complex tasks with minimal effort, but it may be more of a nuisance if it takes a long time to learn, and if it is inconsistent with interfaces to other applications we regularly use. A powerful tool is severely undermined if we can apply it only with a users' manual constantly open on our desk.

Can we use object-oriented techniques to help us build user interfaces to object-oriented applications? If it is truly possible to separate an application from its user interface, then it should be possible to configure an interface for an application after the fact by selecting reusable presentation and interaction objects from a library [Myers 1987]. In this way, applications could be tailored by user interface designers to apply a consistent set of rules across an environment of users. It remains to be seen whether the idea of user interface management systems [Buxton et al. 1983; Foley 1986] can be given new life in the context of object-oriented programming.

## SUMMARY

There are very good traditional reasons for exploiting object-oriented approaches in the development of office information systems. Software reusability, maintainability, and reliability are the main contributions in the domain of software engineering. Furthermore, the notion of software objects is quite close to that of modeling of office objects. Languages that permit us to directly describe the properties of the objects manipulated by our applications can help us build our software more quickly and reliably. Certain object models can also make it easier for us to deal with other issues that are important for office information systems, such as concurrency, distribution, and persistence. Objects' well-defined boundaries help us to understand exactly *what* must be concurrent or distributed or persistent, and therefore help us to build systems with low-level support for objects that have these properties.

Object-oriented techniques, however, are not only important for developing office system applications, they are *essential* for the success of integrated office systems, as they are for any open, evolving, distributed application domain. Encapsulation is necessary for evolution since it is the fundamental mechanism for software reusability. All other object-oriented mechanisms depend on it (such as inheritance, parameterization, and polymorphism). Incremental development, changing requirements, and integration of disparate applications may be difficult to handle in an object-oriented world, but they are next to impossible without it.

We are discovering that the traditional software cycle of requirements analysis, application specification, programming and debugging, and installation is not appropriate for today's vaguely defined, ill-structured, rapidly changing applications. Office workers are known for their ability to adapt to day-to-day alterations in loosely defined office procedures. If we believe that office information systems will be able to provide office workers with meaningful support, then our application systems should be similarly flexible, adaptable, reusable, and amenable to evolution.

Objects encapsulate a locally well-defined behavior, but make few assumptions about their global context. Object applications can evolve because their behavior is determined implicitly by the object populations that implement them. When objects are added, modified, or combined, the global behavior of the system will change as a matter of course.

If these techniques are to pay off, then we must be prepared to evolve our old programming languages, software environments, and operating systems. Just as one may employ structured programming techniques when programming in assembler, one may apply object-oriented techniques in antiquated software environments. On the other hand, it should be clear that we will not be able to take full advantage of objects until our software environments are themselves object-oriented from top to bottom.

## References

[Barron 1982] J.L. Barron, "Dialogue and Process Design for Interactive Information Systems using Taxis," *Proceedings ACM SIGOA*, pp. 12–20, June 1982.

[Biggerstaff and Perliss 1984] T.J. Biggerstaff and A.J. Perliss, ed., "Special Issue on Reusability," *IEEE Transactions on Software Engineering*, vol. SE-10, no. 5, September 1984.

[Biggerstaff and Richter 1987] T.J. Biggerstaff and C. Richter, "Reusability Framework, Assessment, and Directions," *IEEE Software*, vol. 4, no. 2, pp. 41–49, March 1987.

[Bui and Jarke 1986] T.X. Bui and M. Jarke, "Communications Design for Co-oP: A Group Decision Support System," *ACM Transactions on Office Information Systems*, vol. 4, no. 2, pp. 81–103, April 1986.

[Buxton, et al. 1983] W. Buxton, M.R. Lamb, D. Sherman, and K.C. Smith, "Towards a Comprehensive User Interface Management System," *Computer Graphics*, vol. 17, no. 3, pp. 35–42, July 1983.

[Casais 1988] E. Casais, "An Object-Oriented System Implementing KNOs," *Proceedings of the Conference on Office Information Systems (COIS)*, pp. 284–290, March 1988.

[Cook 1984] P.R. Cook, "Electronic Encyclopedias," *Byte*, pp. 151–167, July 1984.

[Cox 1986] B.J. Cox, *Object Oriented Programming—An Evolutionary Approach*, Addison-Wesley, Reading, MA, 1986.

[Croft and Lefkowitz 1988] W.B. Croft and L.S. Lefkowitz, "Using a Planner to Support Office Work," *Proceedings of the Conference on Office Information Systems (COIS)*, pp. 55–62, 1988.

[ECMA 1983] ECMA, "Office Document Architecture," TC 29/83/56, Fourth Working Draft, 1983.

[Ellis and Nutt 1980] C.A. Ellis and G. Nutt, "Computer Science and Office Information Systems," *ACM Computing Surveys*, vol. 12, no. 1, pp. 27–60, March 1980.

[Foley 1986] J. Foley, ed., "Special Issues on User Interface Software," *ACM Transactions on Graphics*, vol. 5, no. 2–4, 1986.

[Furuta et al. 1982] R. Furuta, J. Scofield, and A. Shaw, "Document Formatting Systems: Survey, Concepts and Issues," *ACM Computing Surveys*, vol. 14, no. 3, pp. 417–472, September 1982.

[Gehani 1982] N. Gehani, "The Potential of Forms in Office Automation," *IEEE Transactions on Communications*, vol. Com-30, no. 1, pp. 120–125, Jan 1982.

[Goldberg and Robson 1983] A. Goldberg and D. Robson, *Smalltalk 80: the Language and its Implementation*, Addison-Wesley, Reading, MA, 1983.

[Halbert 1984] D.C. Halbert, "Programming by Example," Ph.D. Thesis, Department of Electrical Engineering and Computer Science, University of California, Berkeley, CA, 1984.

[Hogg et al. 1985] J. Hogg, O.M. Nierstrasz, and D.C. Tsichritzis, "Office Procedures," in *Office Automation: Concepts and Tools*, ed. D.C. Tsichritzis, pp. 137–166, Springer-Verlag, Heidelberg, 1985.

[Horak 1985] W. Horak, "Office Document Architecture and Office Document Interchange Formats: Current Status of International Standardization," *IEEE Computer*, vol. 18, no. 10, pp. 50–60, October 1985.

[Meyer 1986] B. Meyer, "Genericity versus Inheritance," *Proceedings of the First ACM Conference on Object-Oriented Programming Systems, Languages and Applications, SIGPLAN Notices*, vol. 21, no. 11, pp. 391–405, 1986.

[Meyrowitz 1986] N. Meyrowitz, "Intermedia: The Architecture and Construction of an Object-Oriented Hypermedia System and Applications Framework," *Proceedings of the First ACM Conference on Object-Oriented Programming Systems, Languages and Applications, SIGPLAN Notices*, vol. 21, no. 11, pp. 186–201, 1986.

[Moon 1986] D.A. Moon, "Object-Oriented Programming with Flavors," *Proceedings of the First ACM Conference on Object-Oriented Programming Systems, Languages and Applications, SIGPLAN Notices*, vol. 21, no. 11, pp. 1–8, 1986.

[Myers 1987] B.A. Myers, "Creating User Interfaces by Demonstration," Ph.D. Thesis, CSRI Technical Report #196, Department of Computer Science, University of Toronto, May 1987.

[Mylopoulos and Levesque 1983] J. Mylopoulos and H. Levesque, "An Overview of Knowledge Representation," in *On Conceptual Modelling: Perspectives from Artificial Intelligence, Databases and Programming Languages*, ed. M. Brodie and J. Mylopoulos, pp. 3–17, Springer-Verlag, New York, 1983.

[Nierstrasz 1985] O.M. Nierstrasz, "Message Flow Analysis," in *Office Automation: Concepts and Tools*, ed. D.C. Tsichritzis, pp. 283–314, Springer-Verlag, Heidelberg, 1985.

[Nierstrasz 1988] O.M. Nierstrasz, "A Survey of Object-Oriented Concepts," in *Object-Oriented Concepts, Databases, and Applications*, ed. W. Kim and F. Lochovsky, Addison-Wesley, Reading, MA, 1988.

[Russinoff 1988] D. Russinoff, "Proteus: a Frame-Based Nonmonotonic Inference System," in *Object-Oriented Concepts, Applications, and Databases*, ed. W. Kim and F. Lochovsky, Addison-Wesley, Reading, MA, 1988.

[Stroustrup 1986] B. Stroustrup, *The C++ Programming Language*, Addison-Wesley, Reading, MA, 1986.

[Tsichritzis et al. 1982] D.C. Tsichritzis, F. Rabitti, S.J. Gibbs, O.M. Nierstrasz, and J. Hogg, "A System for Managing Structured Messages," *IEEE Transactions on Communications*, vol. Com-30, no. 1, pp. 66–73, January 1982.

[Tsichritzis 1982] D.C. Tsichritzis, "Form Management," *Communications of the ACM*, vol. 25, no. 7, pp. 453–478, July 1982.

[Tsichritzis et al. 1987] D.C. Tsichritzis, E. Fiume, S. Gibbs, and O.M. Nierstrasz, "KNOs: KNowledge Acquisition, Dissemination and Manipulation Objects," *ACM Transactions on Office Information Systems*, vol. 5, no. 1, pp. 96–112, January 1987.

[Weyer and Borning 1985] S.A. Weyer and A.H. Borning, "A Prototype Electronic Encyclopedia," *ACM Transactions on Office Information Systems*, vol. 3, no. 1, pp. 63–88, January 1985.

[Zisman 1978] M. Zisman, "Use of Production Systems for Modelling Asynchronous Concurrent Processes," in *Pattern-Directed Inference Systems*, pp. 53–68, Academic Press, New York, 1978.

[Zloof 1982] M.M. Zloof, "Office-by-Example: A Business Language that Unifies Data and Word Processing and Electronic Mail," *IBM System Journal*, vol. 21, no. 3, pp. 272–304, 1982.

# 3 Object-Oriented Database Systems

# 10

# Overview of the Iris DBMS

D.H. Fishman, J. Annevelink, D. Beech, E. Chow, T. Connors,
J.W. Davis, W. Hasan, C.G. Hoch, W. Kent, S. Leichner,
P. Lyngbaek, B. Mahbod, M.A. Neimat, T. Risch, M.C. Shan,
W.K. Wilkinson

## INTRODUCTION

The Iris database management system is a research prototype of a next-generation DBMS being developed at Hewlett-Packard Laboratories. We are exploring new database features and functionality through a series of increasingly capable prototypes. In this chapter, we present a snapshot of the current system and discuss its capabilities and those we are exploring for future implementations.

Iris is intended to meet the needs of new and emerging database applications [Fishman et al. 1987] such as office information and knowledge-based systems, engineering test and measurement, and hardware and software design. These applications require a rich set of capabilities that are not supported by the current generation (i.e., relational) DBMSs. In addition to the usual requirement for permanence of data, controlled sharing, backup, and recovery, the new capabilities that are needed include: rich data modeling constructs, direct database support for inference, novel data types (graphic images, voice, text, vectors, matrices), lengthy interactions with the database spanning minutes to many days, and multiple versions of data. Data sharing must be provided at the object level in the sense of both concurrent and serial sharing, allowing a given object to be accessed by applications that may be written in different object-oriented programming languages. The Iris DBMS is being designed to meet these needs.

Figure 10.1 shows the layered architecture of Iris. Central to this architecture is the Iris Object Manager [Lyngbaek et al. 1987], the query and update processor of the DBMS. The Object Manager implements the Iris Data Model [Derrett et al. 1985; Derrett et al. 1986], which falls into the general category of object-oriented models that support high-level structural abstractions such as classification, generalization/specialization, and aggregation [Hammer and McLeod 1981; Smith and Smith 1977; Abrial 1974; Chen 1976; Shipman 1981] as well as behavioral abstractions [Brodie 1981; Mylopoulos et al. 1980; King

**FIGURE 10.1** IRIS SYSTEM STRUCTURE

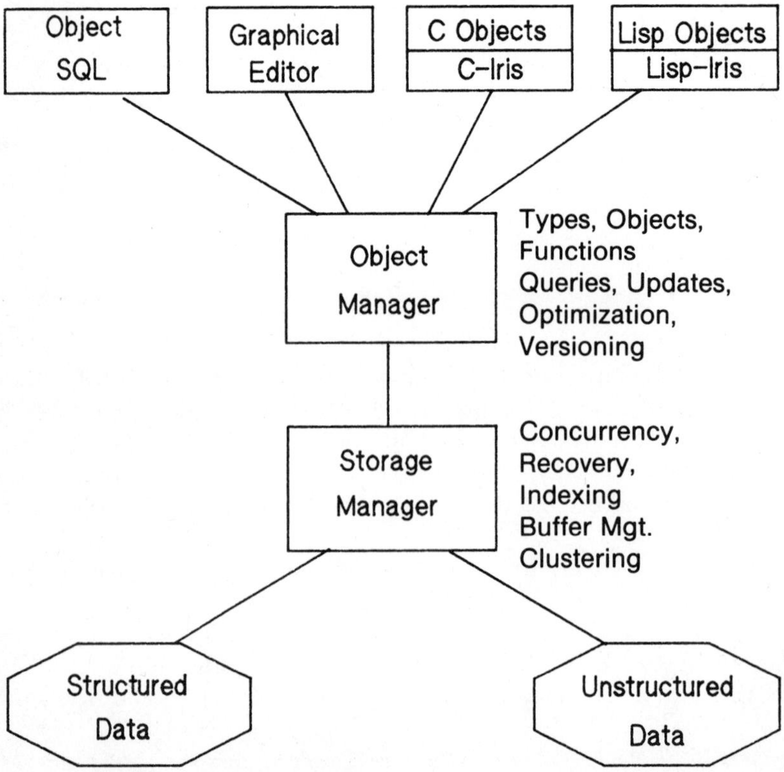

and McLeod 1982]. The query processor translates Iris queries and functions into an extended relational algebra format that is optimized and then interpreted against the stored database. Rather than inventing a totally new formalism upon which to base the correct behavior of our system, we rely on the relational algebra as our theory of computation [Lyngbaek and Vianu 1987]. This has proved very convenient in terms of coexisting with, and migrating from, existing database applications.

The Iris Storage Manager is (currently) a conventional relational storage subsystem. It provides associative access and update capabilities to a single relation at a time and includes transaction support.

Like most other database systems, Iris is accessible via stand-alone interactive interfaces or through interface modules embedded in programming languages. Interface modules, such as those labeled C-Iris and Lisp-Iris in Fig. 10.1, facilitate access to persistent objects from various programming languages. Construction of interfaces is made possible by a set of C language subroutines that defines, indeed *is*, the Object Manager interface.

Currently, three interactive interfaces are supported. One is simply a driver for the Object Manager interface. Another interactive interface, Object SQL (OSQL), is an object-oriented extension to SQL. We have chosen to extend SQL rather than invent a totally new language because of the prominence of SQL in the database community, and because, as we explored the possibility, the extensions seemed natural. A third interactive interface, the Graphical Editor, allows the user to interactively explore the Iris metadata (type) structures as well as the interobject relationship structures defined on a given Iris database. It is written in Objective-C and supports updates to schema and data.

We are also exploring three kinds of programmatic interfaces. The first kind is a straightforward embedding of OSQL into various host languages. The second kind is an encapsulation of the Iris DBMS as a programming language *object* [Cox 1986; Stroustrup 1986; Snyder 1986] whose methods correspond to the functions in the C subroutine interface to the Iris Object Manager. The third kind of programmatic interface we are exploring is part of a longer-term investigation into *persistent objects*, the intent of which is to make programming language objects transparently persistent and sharable across applications and languages.

The capabilities of the Object Manager are discussed in Section 10.1. The various Iris interfaces are discussed in Section 10.2. Our plans to modify and extend the Storage Manager are discussed in Section 10.3.

## 10.1 IRIS OBJECT MANAGER

The Iris Object Manager implements the Iris data model by providing support for schema definition, data manipulation, and query processing. The data model is based on three constructs—*objects, types,* and *functions*—and it supports inheritance and generic properties, constraints, complex or non-normalized data, user-defined functions, version control, inference, and extensible data types. The roots of the model can be found in previous work on DAPLEX [Shipman 1981], the Integrated Data Model [Beech and Feldman 1983], the DAPLEX extension [Kulkarni 1983], and the Taxis language [Mylopoulos et al. 1980].

### 10.1.1 Objects

Objects represent entities and concepts from the application domain being modeled. They are unique entities in the database with their own identity and existence, and they can be referred to regardless of their attribute values. For example, each object has an assigned, system-wide, unique object identifier, or OID. This supports referential integrity [Date 1981], and is a major advantage over record-oriented data models in which the objects, represented as records, can be referred to only in terms of their attribute values [Kent 1979].

Objects are described by their behavior, and can be accessed and manipulated only by means of functions. As long as the semantics of the functions remain the same, the database can be physically as well as logically reorganized without affecting application programs. This provides a high degree of data abstraction and data independence.

Objects are classified by type. Objects that belong to the same type share common functions. Types are organized into a type hierarchy with inherited functions. Consequently, an object may have multiple types. Objects serve as arguments to functions and may be returned as results of functions. A function may be applied to an object only if the function is defined on a type to which the object belongs.

By a *property* of an object we mean a function of one argument that returns a value when applied to the object. Thus, we model properties of Iris objects with functions. Functions that can be defined include predicates and functions of multiple arguments, providing direct support of binary or *n*-ary relationships.

The Iris data model distinguishes between *literal objects,* such as character-strings and numbers, and *nonliteral objects* such as persons and departments. Nonliteral objects are represented internally in the database by object identifiers. Literal objects have no user-accessible object identifier and are directly representable. As such, they cannot be created, destroyed, or updated by users. The Object Manager provides primitives for explicitly creating and deleting nonliteral objects, and for assigning and updating values to their functions. Referential integrity is supported: when a given object is deleted, all references to the object are deleted as well.

## 10.1.2 Types and Type Hierarchies

Types are named collections of objects. Objects belonging to the same type share common functions. For example, all the objects belonging to the Person type have a Name and an Age function. Functions are computations defined on types (see Section 10.1.3); they are applicable to the instances of the types. In effect, therefore, types are constraints; that is, a type constrains the permissible functions that can be applied to an object of that type.

Types are organized in a type structure that supports generalization and specialization. A type may be declared to be a subtype of another type. In that case, *all* instances of the subtype are also instances of the supertype. It follows that functions defined on the supertype are also defined on the subtype. We say that the functions are *inherited* by the subtype. In Iris, a subtype inherits all functions defined on its supertypes. This is different from other object systems in which the functions of a supertype may *optionally* be inherited by a subtype. Of course, an Iris supertype may have instances that do not belong to any of its subtypes.

The Iris type structure is a directed acyclic graph. A given type may have multiple subtypes and multiple supertypes. Figure 10.2 illustrates a type graph with five types, each having a number of properties. The Employee type is a direct subtype of the Person and Taxpayer types, and the Employee type itself has two direct subtypes, Manager and Engineer.

Instances of type Employee also belong to the Taxpayer and Person types. The functions defined on Person and on Taxpayer are inherited by Employee. Thus, Employee objects have all six functions: Salary, Withholdings, Name, Age, Social-Security-Number, and Dependents. We may create a new type, Consultant, as follows.[1] All supertypes of the new type are listed in such a declaration.

**Create type** Consultant **subtype of** Person, Taxpayer;

Functions do not actually "belong" to types. For display purposes, as in Fig. 10.2, functions defined on a single argument are grouped with that argument type. A function of multiple arguments would not be so grouped (e.g., a function between Manager and Consultant that returns a consultant's date-of-hire).

Function names may be *overloaded,* that is, functions defined on different types may have identical names even though their definitions may differ. Thus, a database designer can introduce a function in its most general form by defining it on a general type and later refine the function definition for the more specialized subtypes. For example, the Employee type may have a general Salary function whereas the Manager and Engineer types have Salary functions that are specific to the two job categories. This approach to design is called stepwise refinement by specialization [Mylopoulos et al. 1980].

---

[1] The examples in this section are presented in OSQL (see Section 10.2.1).

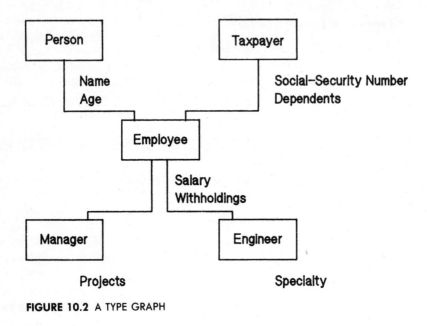

**FIGURE 10.2** A TYPE GRAPH

When an overloaded function is applied to a given object, a single specific function must be selected at the time of application. The specific function is determined by the type of the object to which it is applied. If the object belongs to several types that all have specific functions of the given name, the function of the most specific type is selected. If a single most-specific type cannot be found, user-specified rules for function selection will apply. These rules are specified for families of functions that share the same names. These concepts also apply to functions taking several arguments.

The type Object is the supertype of all other types and therefore contains every object. Types are objects themselves, and their relationships to subtypes, supertypes, and instances are expressed as functions in the system [Lyngbaek and Kent 1986].

In order to support graceful database evolution, the Object Manager allows the type graph to be changed dynamically. For example, new types may be created, existing types may be deleted, and objects may gain or lose types throughout their lifetime. For example, an existing consultant object (bound to the variable "mohammed") may become an employee.

**Add type** Employee **to** mohammed;

However, new subtype/supertype relationships among existing types currently cannot be created. Thus, we could not make the type Consultant a subtype of the Employee type. Such operations will be supported in the future.

## 10.1.3 Functions and Rules

An Iris function is a computation that may or may not return a result. Functions are defined on types and are applicable to the instances of the types. Iris distinguishes retrieval functions from update functions. Thus, a retrieval function may not have side-effects. Updates are discussed in Section 10.1.4. Iris supports user-defined functions that are compiled, stored, and executed under the control of the database management system. The specification of an Iris function, logically, consists of two parts: a *declaration* and an *implementation*, as discussed below. Note that OSQL also allows both specifications to be combined into a single **create function** statement.

**Function Declaration**    A function declaration specifies the name of the function and the number and types of its parameters and results. For example:

> **Create function** Marriage(Person p) $->$ <Person spouse,
>     Charstring date> **forward**;

creates a function called Marriage. The **forward** clause declares that the function implementation will be specified later. As a convenience, if **forward** is omitted, by default the function is given a *stored* implementation as described later.

A function may return a compound result, as in the above example, where the result of the function contains both the spouse and the date of the marriage. Given an implementation, the Marriage function can be invoked as follows (assume "bob" is a variable bound to a Person object):

> **Select** s,d **for each** Person s, Charstring d
>     **where** <s, d> = Marriage(bob);

This statement may be abbreviated as:

> **Select each** Person s, Charstring d
>     **where** <s, d> = Marriage(bob);

or more simply:

> **Select** Marriage(bob);

The function declaration is also used to specify participation constraints on the number of occurrences of each parameter and result value. For example, the interface has mechanisms for declaring function results to be *required* or *unique*. A required result means that a result value must exist for each possible parameter value in the database. A unique result means that distinct parameter values will be mapped onto distinct result values. We also distinguish between *single-valued* functions and *multi-valued* functions. Single-valued functions are functions that return only one result value for each invocation. In contrast, multi-valued functions may return many result values. For example, a function that returns all the children of a person would be a multi-valued function. A function that returns the mother of a person would be a single-valued function.

A database designer may wish to group database functions conceptually in either of two ways:

1. Grouping according to argument types; for example, collecting all of the functions on persons. This gives the sense of defining the properties of objects. This is the traditional object-oriented approach. We note that functions of multiple arguments do not fit into such a grouping.

2. Grouping by relationships; for example, collecting functions and their inverses. This gives the sense of defining families of semantically related functions.

Either of these ways of grouping functions together is valid in its context, and the Iris data model does not insist on one or the other.

Information about objects is modeled in Iris using (Boolean) *predicate functions*. For example, the fact that a person has a name is represented as a predicate connecting the person object and the name object. This approach is different from that of the Entity-Relationship (E-R) Model [Chen 1976], which allows objects to have attributes. The attribute concept is modeled in Iris by using functions whose values are derived from the predicates. Thus, a predicate, Person_Age, that connects persons and their ages could be defined as follows:

**Create function** Person_Age(Person p, Integer a)**forward**;

where Person_Age(john, 31) is true if the person specified has the age specified. Once Person_age has been implemented, we may then derive the functions

```
Age(Person) = Integer;
Person_with_Age(Integer) = Person;
```

which are inverses of each other. The Age function can be regarded as a property of Person. In this way, most simple functions are easily invertible since they are derived from predicates.

Relationships can be *n*-ary; for example, a relationship between mother, father, and child can be represented as a predicate function with three parameters. An *n*-ary predicate can be used to derive a family of related functions; for example,

```
Father(Person) = Person;
Child(Person) = Person;
Parents(Person) = (Person mom, Person pop);
```

and so on. In general, an $n$-ary predicate has $2^n$ related functions. The related functions may be derived by using the **create function** operation described below.

**Function Implementation**   Iris functions may be implemented in any of several ways. These methods are outlined next. Separating the function declaration from its implementation supports data abstraction, allowing users to change the implementation dynamically without affecting application programs.

**Stored Functions**   One way to implement a function is to store it as a table mapping input values to their corresponding result values. Such a table may be implemented and accessed by standard relational database techniques. The **cluster** operation allows the user to specify that a function is to be implemented in this way. Thus:

```
Create function Marriage(Person p) -> <Person spouse,
    Charstring date>forward;
Cluster Marriage;
```

causes the creation of a table with, in the case of the preceding declaration, three columns for person, spouse, and date. The table can then be populated by applying an update operation to the Marriage function as described later. As mentioned earlier, the default implementation is to store all functions. Thus, removing the **forward** clause would make the cluster statement unnecessary.

The mappings of several functions may be stored together in a single table. For example, given Name and Address functions defined on Person:

```
Cluster Name on Person, Address on Person;
```

would create a table containing person OIDs with their names and addresses. Restrictions have been introduced to ensure that such a table is in first normal form.

**Derived Functions**   The definition of a function may be specified in terms of other functions. For example:

```
Create function Emp_Manager(Employee e) -> Manager as
    select m for each Manager m
        where m = Department_Manager(Emp_Department(e))
```

This simple definition specifies how the manager of an employee may be derived from other functions using a **select** statement. Section 10.2.1 contains more examples of the use of the **select** statement.

In general, function definitions may contain arbitrary queries and include calls to any implemented function. In the following example, function Important_Manager calls a derived function, Emp_Manager, two stored functions, BirthDate and Salary, and a foreign function, DateCompare (described later).

```
Create function Important_Manager ( ) —> Manager as
    select m for each Manager m, Employee e
        where Salary(e) > 10000 and m = Emp_Manager(e) and
            DateCompare(BirthDate(e),BirthDate(m)) > 0;
```

Note that the BirthDate function may be applied to both Employee and Manager types, since they are subtypes of Person (assuming BirthDate is defined on Person). The definition for the derived function is compiled by the Object Manager into an internal relational algebra representation. The relational algebra expressions for the called functions are merged into this relational algebra expression, with selections and joins added where appropriate. The complete expression is optimized and then interpreted at execution time. Derived functions may be arbitrarily complex.

As a performance enhancement, Iris supports *materialized derived functions*. This is similar to the notion of materialized views in relational systems. Iris can precompute a derived function and store the results in a table. Subsequent invocations of the function are satisfied from the table. Updates invalidate the table. Currently, the table is not regenerated automatically.

**Foreign Functions**   A third method is to implement the function in some general-purpose programming language, such as C. We call these *foreign* functions because they are written in a language that Iris does not understand, and hence cannot optimize. For the class of applications Iris intends to support, it is desirable to be able to extend Iris's capabilities easily in unanticipated ways (e.g., to allow access to specialized storage managers, or to permit specialized operations as may be associated with new, user-defined data types such as vector and matrix operations). We have explored this capability by providing foreign functions in Iris for access to non-Iris databases. As an example, the foreign function DateCompare, mentioned earlier, may be defined as follows.

```
Create function DateCompare (Charstring date1, Charstring
    date2) —> Integer as link 'date_cmp';
```

The file 'date_cmp' should contain the machine object code for implementing DateCompare. Typically, it is produced by the language compiler for whatever language is used to write the foreign function. 'Date_cmp' is presumed to contain certain subroutine entry points for implementing the function (e.g., *open, get_next*). At execution time, when DateCompare is invoked, Iris transfers control to those entry points to evaluate and return results for the function call.

We emphasize that, although Iris cannot optimize the *implementation* of a foreign function, it can optimize the *usage* of a foreign function. Since the query optimizer is rule-based, one need only add rules appropriate to the particular foreign function of interest. For example, given a foreign function that adds two integers, one might add an identity rule to eliminate the addition function call whenever one operand is a zero constant. In fact, the Iris Storage Manager, itself, might be viewed as a foreign function given the rules for table and index selection and join ordering. Of course, the system is not implemented in this way since performance dictates a tight coupling between the modules.

The invocation of foreign functions is facilitated by the simple, well-defined interface between the query processing system and the storage subsystem. Each foreign function appears to the query processor as a virtual data set in the storage subsystem. Parameters (where required) are passed as if they were the key to an indexed lookup in a traditional data set. The query processor retrieves information by making a procedure call to the storage subsystem. If the referenced data set is a foreign function, a dynamic loader is invoked to retrieve the foreign function from the file system; control actually transfers to the body of the foreign function (in the future, foreign function bodies will be stored in the database). Foreign functions return data in the same format used by the storage subsystem for traditional data sets. Any language can be used to write a foreign function so long as the object code can be linked with the query processor. The query optimizer knows which functions are stored in the storage subsystem as traditional data sets so that standard optimizing techniques may be applied.

As previously mentioned, complete optimization of queries involving foreign functions is impossible without a characterization of the function's behavior. Optimization "hooks" are a very interesting research topic. Currently, Iris is vulnerable to bugs in the body of a foreign function. Thus, at the very least, the implementation of foreign functions should be a privileged operation.

**Rules**   In Iris, rules are simply modeled as functions. For example, given a *Parent* function, we can define a *Grandparent* function as follows:

```
Create function Grandparent(Person p) -> Person as
    select gp for each Person gp
        where gp = Parent(Parent(p));
```

A more complex rule may be defined as follows:

```
Create function Older_Cousin(Person p) -> Person as
    select c for each Person c
        where c = Child(Sibling(Parent(p))) and Age(c) >
            Age(p);
```

We note that the nested-functions notation used in Iris' functional notation dispenses with the variables needed in logic programming languages, such as Prolog [Clocksin and Mellish 1981], to carry results from one function call to the next. Variables can, however, be used in Iris function bodies, if required.

An important difference between C functions and Prolog rules (taking C and Prolog as examples of a traditional programming language and a rule-based language) is that a C function returns a single result, whereas a rule returns a stream of results. Iris functions can return multiple results, and a nested function call returns the concatenation of all the results obtained from calling the inner function. For example, the function call:

```
Children(Member(sales_dept))
```

returns all of the children of all of the members of the Sales Department.

Like Prolog, Iris makes the closed-world assumption—any fact that is not deducible from the data in the database is assumed to be false. The current Iris prototype supports only conjunctive, disjunctive, and nonrecursive rules, but negation and recursion are being studied.

**Bags and Aggregate Functions**   The previous sections described functions defined on individual objects. There is also a need for functions over bags[2] of objects, such as *Average*. Bags in Iris are defined via nested **select** statements. This is similar to the use of nested queries in SQL. For example, the following query computes the average salary of all employees.

```
Select y for each Real y
    where y = Average (select Salary(x) for each Employee x);
```

The nested **select** statement returns a bag of values that are then used as input to the Average function. Iris semantics are such that nested **select** statements and function calls are equivalent in retrievals. Thus, given a function, EmpSal(), that returns the salaries of all employees, the above query could be rewritten by replacing the nested **select** statement by a call to EmpSal.

A nested **select** statement may refer to variables defined outside its scope. Such variables are known as *correlated* variables. In effect, they link the results

---

[2] Bags are multi-sets (i.e., sets that may contain duplicates).

of the nested **select** statement to the outer query. For example, the following query computes the average salary of each department:

```
Select Dept_Name(d), y for each Real y, Department d
    where y = Average (select Salary(x) for each Employee x
        where Emp_Department(x)=d );
```

We point out that bags are not Iris objects. They may not be stored directly in the database. If a bag must be preserved, the correct solution is to define a function and store the bag's elements as the results of the function. Also, note that Iris supports multiple bag definitions at any level in the query. SQL restricts users to, at most, one subquery per level.

Aggregate functions in Iris are implemented as foreign functions with bag operands. For example, Average might be created as follows:

```
Create function Average (bag of Real) -> Real
    as link 'avg_r';
```

where the file 'avg_r' contains the machine object code to implement Average. The **bag of** clause declares the argument to be a bag.

This approach of implementing aggregates as foreign functions simplifies query translation and query execution by reducing the number of possible operators. It also allows the user to implement new aggregate operations as needed. For example, by using a **distinct** clause to eliminate duplicates (Section 10.2.1), true set operations such as union, intersection, and difference could be implemented if an Iris application required them.

### 10.1.4 Update Operations

An update operation changes the future behavior of a stored or derived Iris function. For example, the operation:

```
Set Department_Manager(sales_dept) = john;
```

will cause future invocations of the Department_Manager function with the parameter sales_dept to return the object currently bound to the variable john. Iris also supports updates to multivalued functions. The **add** operation can be used to add additional values. For example,

```
Add Member(sales_dept) = barbara;
```

adds barbara to the set of members of the Sales Department. More powerful updates may be accomplished, by operations of the form

> **Add** Member(sales_dept) = p **for each** Person p
>     **where** p = Member(toy_dept);

This causes all members of the Toy Department also to become members of the Sales Department. Values can be removed from single- and multivalued functions using the **remove** operation. For example,

> **Remove** Member(sales_dept) = sue;

removes the employee bound to variable sue from the Sales Department. More powerfully:

> **Remove** Member(sales_dept) = e **for each** Employee e
>     **where** e = Member(sales_dept) **and** Age(e) > 70;

removes from the Sales Department all employees older than 70, and

> **Remove** Member(sales_dept);

drops all employees from the Sales Department.

Each function in Iris may have up to four compiled representations: one each for **select**, **set**, **add**, and **remove**. If the **select** operation is a simple derived function,[3] the implementation of the update operations can be deduced by the system. But for more complex **select** operations, say one involving a join, it will be necessary for the function definer to specify the update implementations. Currently, Iris does not support these update specifications.

**Delete Operations**  The **delete** operation can delete any user-defined object, type or function. The effect of a **delete** is propagated to all related information. For example, the operation:

> **Delete type** Engineer;

will cause the type Engineer to be deleted. In addition, all functions with Engineer as an argument or result type are deleted. However, instances of the Engineer type are not deleted. Instead, those objects simply "lose" the Engineer type.

**Procedures**  Update operations may be collected into a single parameterized function, known as a procedure. For example, the first two updates of this subsection may be collected into a single, general-purpose procedure.

---

[3] A simple derived function is a **select** statement over a single predicate function.

```
Create function Update_Dept (Department dept, Manager mgr,
       Employee emp) as
begin
       Set Department_Manager(dept) = mgr;
       Add Member(dept) = emp;
end;
```

Currently, update procedures have no return values.

## 10.1.5 Version Control

One of the goals of Iris is to support application areas that are not well supported by existing database managers, such as computer-aided design, computer-aided software engineering, and office automation. A common requirement of these applications is the desire to preserve alternative states for a particular entity. This requires the existence of an object versioning mechanism in order to provide controlled access to these values [Lorie and Plouffe 1983; Katz 1985; Katz et al. 1986; Landis 1986; Chou and Kim 1986]. A version control mechanism has been implemented as an integral part of the Iris Object Manager [Beech and Mahbod 1988].

In Iris, as in other object systems, an object retains its identity throughout its existence although its state may change (i.e., its function values may be modified by **set**, **add**, or **remove**). Versions are like snapshots of an object in certain states, and are modeled by distinct objects. Thus, in Iris, separate objects correspond to each version and to the entity of which they are versions.

**Generic Instance, Specific and Generic References**   One crucial aspect of version control in Iris is that it offers a form of indirect addressing, whereby objects can make *generic* references to other objects. The generic instance is an abstraction of the entity that may, itself, have properties (properties whose values are uniform over all versions). There is one generic instance per each *version set*, that is, the set of all versions of an object. Information about the version set and the predecessor- successor relationships that hold between members of the set are maintained by functions on the generic instance and version objects.

Any reference to a versioned object can be either a *specific reference* to a particular version of the object, or a *generic reference* to the entity's generic instance. A generic reference can at any time be coerced to refer to a specific version of an object.

**Transformation of Unversioned Objects**   Iris provides the ability to create versions of what were originally unversioned objects. We feel this is important because it is not always possible to know beforehand which parts of a design to place under version control. The alternative is to treat all objects as versioned, and this may impose undue overhead.

As an example, the following converts the unversioned object, "mod1", to a versioned object:

```
oreate version from mod1 instance modlvl;
```

The result is that a new object, modlvl, will be created with the same user types as the original, unversioned object. In addition, it will acquire the system type Version and it will be the first version of the version set. The original object, mod1, will lose its system type Unversioned and acquire the system type Generic. Retaining its original OID, it will act as the generic instance of the newly created version set. Thus, the generic instance serves as a placeholder for existing references to the original, unversioned object.

**Version Control Operations**   Versions of an object are created explicitly by the user. A number of Iris commands, such as **checkin, checkout, lock**, and **unlock**, allow for creation and manipulation of versions and for controlled sharing of versions among users. For example, the following command creates a successor version of modlvl:

```
oheokout modlvl as modlv2;
```

This creates a new version, modlv2, that can be modified and later checked back into the database with the request:

```
oheokin modlv2;
```

Since versions are objects, destruction of versions and schema modifications such as adding new types or removing existing types from version objects are performed with existing Iris operations. However, these operations on versioned objects are subject to additional constraints. For example, a type cannot be removed from a version unless it is removed from the entire version set.

Controlled sharing of versions among users is achieved through *version locks*, which are user-settable, long-term locks. As in RCS [Tichy 1982], objects may be locked at **checkout** and unlocked at **checkin**:

```
oheokout modlvl key modkeyl as modlv2;
```

The lock key is returned in variable modkeyl. The lock prevents other users from deriving a successor of modlvl. Given the key, the version may be unlocked at **checkin**:

```
oheokin modlv2 key modkeyl;
```

## 10.1.6 Query Processing

Iris queries are expressed in terms of functions and objects. The Storage Manager deals with relational algebra and tables. The task of query processing in Iris is shared by two modules. The Query Translator compiles queries from their object representation to a relational algebra representation. The Query Interpreter evaluates the transformed query, invoking the Storage Manager to access the database and foreign functions to access other data sources. In this section, we provide a brief overview of the Query Translator and Query Interpreter modules.

**Query Translator**  The Object Manager interface requires queries to be expressed in a tree structure, known as an *F-Tree*. The nodes of an F-Tree include function calls, comparison operators ($=, \neq, <, >, \leq, \geq$), the logical operators (**and, or, not**: negation is currently not supported), and variables and constants.

The query translation process consists of three main steps. First, the F-Tree is converted to a canonical form. This involves a series of tree transformations that are done to simplify subsequent transformations. For example, nested function calls are unnested by introducing auxiliary variables. The second step converts the canonical F-Tree to an extended relational algebra tree known as *B-Tree*. This is a mechanical process in which function calls are replaced by their stored implementations (which are themselves B-Trees) and comparison and logical operators are converted to relational algebra selection and cross-product operators.

The resulting B-Tree consists of projection, selection, cross-product, and table nodes. The semantics of the tree are that results of a child node are sent to the parent node for subsequent processing. For example, a projection node above a table node would filter out columns of the table.

The final, and most complex, step is to optimize the B-Tree. The optimizer is rule-based. Each rule consists of a test predicate and a transformation routine. The test predicate takes a B-Tree node as an argument; if the predicate evaluates to true, the transformation routine is invoked. The predicate might test the relative position of a node (e.g., selection node above a projection node) or the state of a node (e.g., cross-product node has only one input). The possible transformations include deleting the node, moving it above or below another node, or replacing the node with a new B-Tree fragment. As in [Graefe and DeWitt 1987], the system must be recompiled whenever the rules are modified.

Rules are organized into rule-sets that, together, accomplish a specific task. For example, one rule-set contains all rules concerned with simplifying expressions (e.g., constant propagation and folding). Optimization is accomplished by traversing the entire B-Tree for each rule-set. During the traversal, at a given node, any rule in the current rule set may be fired if its test predicate is true.

The optimization steps (i.e., rule-sets) can be roughly described as follows. There is an initial rule set that converts the B-Tree to a canonical form. The canonical form consists of a collection of query blocks. Each query block contains a projection node, a selection node, and a cross-product node. A second rule-set eliminates redundant joins, which has the effect of reducing the number of tables in a cross-product. A third rule set is concerned with simplifying expressions. A fourth rule set chooses a join order. A fifth rule set handles Storage Manager-specific optimizations, such as finding projection and selection operations that can be done in the Storage Manager.

The final (optimized) B-Tree is then sent to the Query Interpreter, which processes the query and returns the result to the user. However, the B-Tree may not represent a query but may, instead, be the newly defined body of a derived function. In this case, the B-Tree is simply stored in the database system catalog for later retrieval when compiling queries that reference the derived function.

The Query Translator is quite flexible and can accommodate any optimization that can be expressed in terms of a predicate test on a node and a tree transformation. We expect to take advantage of this to optimize queries that call foreign functions.

**Query Interpreter**   The Query Interpreter module evaluates a B-Tree and produces a set of tuples that may be returned to the user or stored back into the database (for example, to update the results of a function). The Query Interpreter treats each node in the B-Tree as a *scan object*. Each node in the B-Tree has three associated operations: *open-scan*, *get-next*, and *close-scan*. When the Query Interpreter is passed a B-Tree, it simply calls the open-scan operation for the root of the B-Tree, and then calls get-next until no more tuples are returned. Then close-scan is called. An open-scan operation may call the Query Interpreter recursively to retrieve results from a subtree. For example, given a projection node, the portion of the B-Tree below the projection node represents the source of the tuples for the projection operation. Thus, an open-scan on a projection node must recursively open a scan on the subtree in order to get the tuples.

The get-next operation returns the next tuple in the scan. For example, get-next on a table node will request the Storage Manager to return the next stored tuple in the previously opened scan.

The Query Interpreter is fully re-entrant. It can handle B-Trees of arbitrary complexity, not just the simple project–select–cross-product trees mentioned earlier. In particular, nested queries can easily be processed.

## 10.2 IRIS INTERFACES

The Iris DBMS may be accessed via both interactive and programmatic interfaces. These interfaces are implemented using the library of C subroutines that define the Iris Object Manager interface. The library is intended to be

a platform upon which stand-alone interfaces and interfaces to various programming languages are built. In addition, programmers may use this library
directly. The following subsections discuss the design and functional capabilities of the existing interactive and programmatic interfaces to Iris.

### 10.2.1 Object SQL Interface

The initial Iris interfaces stayed quite close to the atomic level of the operations supported by the Object Manager. However, for more general use, it
was decided to develop a higher-level interface that would take the primitive
notion of an atomic object and combine it with the set of property (single-
argument) functions that the user considered to be intrinsic to the nature of the
object. This is much like the treatment of entities and their attributes in the
E-R model, or like one use of the tables in the relational model [Codd 1970],
where a row represents an object and each column represents a property. It
is also close to the concept of an abstract type or class in an object-oriented
programming language.

Given the definitions of two types of objects such as Person and Document, simple means are needed to create instances of these types, and to
introduce relationships such as "is author of" or "has approval rights over"
between persons and documents. This corresponds to the relationship-sets in
the E-R model, and to the other usage of relational tables to relate objects
(row in other tables) by referring to their key values. Programming languages
tend to lack high-level support for relationship-sets of this kind.

The functional emphasis in Iris suggests the use of a functional style of
interface for expressing the relationships among interconnected objects. We
therefore examined such languages as DAPLEX [Shipman 1981], GORDAS
[Elmasri and Wiederhold 1981], and IDM [Beech and Feldman 1983]. However,
because of the strong similarities of these languages to a relational language
such as SQL [Date 1984], we also explored possible extensions to SQL to
accommodate the object model and a more functional style. As a result of the
study, we concluded that an Object SQL (OSQL) interface would be feasible
and attractive.

The three main extensions we have made beyond SQL to adapt it to the
object and function model are:

- Users manipulate types and functions rather than tables.

- Objects may be referenced directly rather than indirectly, through their keys.
  Interface variables may be bound to objects on creation or retrieval and ma,
  then be used to refer to the objects in subsequent statements. For example,
  see the variables "Jones," "Smith," and "d1" later in this section.

- User-defined functions and Iris system functions may appear in **where** and
  **select** clauses to give concise and powerful retrieval.

A few keyword alternatives were also introduced into existing SQL. It is possible to mechanically reinterpret all existing keywords, but for human users some of the keywords would be found very misleading when applied to the object model.

A few examples should illustrate both the general similarity of OSQL to SQL, and the advantages of an object-based query language. Supposing that we wish to automate some office procedures for obtaining approvals for documents, some of the actions and corresponding OSQL statements could be as follows.

We need a type, Person, with property functions name, address, and phone. Each Person object must have a value for the name function:

```
Create type Person
    (name Charstring required,
     address Charstring,
     phone Charstring);
```

Such creation of a type with properties is a syntactic shorthand for separately creating a type and each of the functions. Additional functions taking this type as an argument may be separately created and are semantically equivalent to properties created with the type. We also note that, since such properties can be multivalued, a type may not correspond directly to a relational table.

To represent people with approval rights, we create a new type, Approver, as a subtype of Person. The type has a single property function, expertise (we assume Topic has already been created as a type), in addition to the three properties inherited from Person. The new property function is multivalued:

```
Create type Approver subtype of Person
    (expertise Topic many);
```

Some people will be authors of documents, and we also need a document type:

```
Create type Author subtype of Person;
Create type Document
    (title Charstring required unique,
     authorOf Author required many,
     subject Topic,
     status Charstring required,
     approverOf Approver many);
```

Note that the document title is declared as unique so that duplicate titles are disallowed. Next, we need a stored function, grade, that, for a given document and approver, returns the grade assigned to the document by the approver:

```
Create function grade (Document, Approver) -> Integer;
```

Now, create three instances of the type Approver and assign values to the property functions name (inherited from the type Person) and expertise. Bind the interface variables Smith, Jones, and Robinson to the objects created:

```
Create Approver (name, expertise) instances
    Smith ('Albert Smith', software),
    Jones ('Isaac Jones', (finance, marketing)),
    Robinson ('Alan Robinson', (hardware, marketing,
        manufacturing));
```

The expertise values (software, finance, etc.) are interface variables bound to Topic objects. Add the type Author to the two objects bound to interface variables Jones and Robinson. This shows objects being given multiple types:

```
Add type Author to
    Jones,
    Robinson;
```

Enter a document written by Jones:

```
Create Document (title, authorOf, status) instance
    d1 ('The Flight from Relational', Jones, 'Received');
```

Assign approvers to the document d1, and assign a grade to it:

```
Set approverOf(d1) = (Smith, Robinson);
Set grade(d1,Smith) = 3;
```

Make a type for approved documents, and approve d1:

```
Create type ApprovedDocument subtype of Document;
Add type ApprovedDocument to d1;
```

Get the title of document d1, the titles of all approved documents, and the titles of all documents of which Smith is an approver:

```
Select title(d1);
Select title(ad)
    for each ApprovedDocument ad;
Select title
    for each Document d
    where Smith = approverOf(d);
```

A **distinct** clause may be used in the result list to eliminate duplicate results. Find the names of all authors with some document awaiting approval:

```
Select distinct authorOf(d)
    for each Document d
    where status(d) = 'Received';
```

It is interesting to consider OSQL as a potential evolutionary growth path for SQL. Some of the new features of OSQL could be supported in a straightforward way on a relational system, while others would require a more ambitious object manager. Migration is never easy, but the OSQL approach could smooth the path for migration of both users and programs from SQL to the object world [Beech 1988].

### 10.2.2 Iris Graphical Editor

The Iris Graphical Editor provides a graphical interface that enables a user to browse and update an Iris database. The type hierarchy is displayed as a directed, acyclic graph. For each type, one may display the functions defined on that type or the instances of that type. Each such type or instance may, in turn, be *inspected* to examine its properties (i.e., functions of one argument defined on that type).

A given Iris object may have multiple supertypes through its immediate and transitive supertype relationships. The Graphical Editor produces property sublists for each type of an object. If the property function is single-valued, the Graphical Editor simply displays the result of the property function applied to the object. For multivalued functions, an Iris query is generated and "<IRIS-SCAN>" is displayed. In this case, the user may request that the scan be evaluated, either in the same or a new window. The Graphical Editor supports both an indented textual view and a tree view. Function values may be updated using the Graphical Editor.

Schema updates, such as type and function creation and deletion, are supported in the Graphical Editor. Also supported are session control operations, such as commit and rollback. For schema update operations, users supply required information via mouse selections.

An Iris type tree is illustrated in Fig. 10.3. Since the entire tree does not fit on the display, the subtree containing the user-defined types was placed in a separate window. Instances of type Programmer were selected, and the Editor found and applied the *name* property to the Programmer instances.

Figure 10.4 illustrates a type creation window. In the display, note that *expertise* and *programmer_owns* are multivalued functions represented by scans. The user has asked (via menu selection) for the values of *expertise*, but the values for *programmer_owns* have not yet been retrieved. In the New Type window, the type *Developer* is being created, which is to be a subtype of *Programmer*. One new function on *Developer* has been specified: *Responsibility*, which will return, possibly many, instances of *Program*.

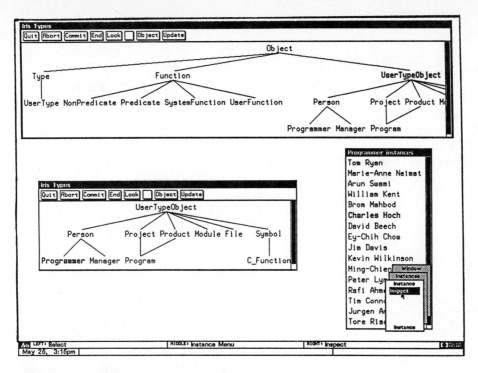

**FIGURE 10.3** GRAPHICAL EDITOR—TYPE TREE

**FIGURE 10.4** GRAPHICAL EDITOR—TYPE CREATION

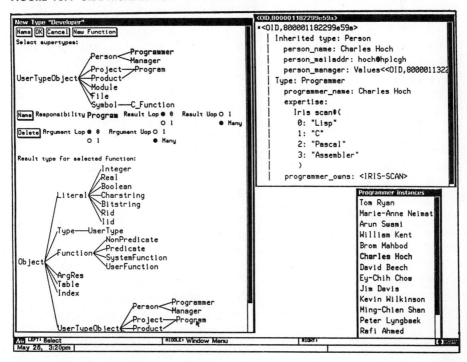

### 10.2.3 Iris Programming Language Interfaces

In this section we will discuss the various Iris programming language interfaces, all based on the functionality provided by the Object Manager C subroutine library.

**Embedded OSQL Interface**   OSQL has been implemented both as a stand-alone interactive interface and as a language extension. OSQL is currently embedded in COMMON LISP [Steele 1984] via macro extension. A more general embedded interface is being provided for C that is based on the existing ANSI standard for SQL embedding. The traditional arguments for embedding query languages also apply to OSQL. In addition, the user-defined types provided by the object model should prove helpful in overcoming the "impedance mismatch" in passing information between host and embedded languages.

**Loosely Integrated Object-Oriented Interface**   Based on the functionality provided by the Object Manager library, we can define a layer of abstraction that exposes the Iris data model to a programmer. Following the object-oriented paradigm, this interface may be represented as a collection of object types (classes) and their associated operations. Instances of these classes represent the entities required to access and manipulate an Iris database. Typical classes might include DataBase, Function, Type, Scan, and Object.

For example, the class DataBase might support operations to start a new database, connect to an existing database, commit or abort a transaction, etc. Instances of the Function class might provide operations to create and/or update functions. A variety of programming languages may be used for such an interface and, depending on the constructs offered by the language, more or less of the implementation details may be hidden from programmers. A loosely coupled interface to Iris has been implemented in LISP.

**Tightly Integrated Object-Oriented Interface**   In order to support persistent object extensions, it is necessary to tightly integrate object-oriented programming languages with Iris. This requires a mechanism for object activation; that is, objects should be retrieved automatically when needed by an application program. An object-activation mechanism needs a schema or mapping that specifies how programming language objects are to be represented in the database and vice-versa. One advantage of an explicit schema is that there can be many such mappings: one for every application interface. This simplifies the sharing of objects between otherwise heterogeneous applications.

By retrieving an object from the database, an application program effectively caches the object. Subsequent changes to the state of the object are not automatically propagated back to the database. A tightly coupled interface must ensure consistency between the cached object and the database object. Conventional transaction-oriented mechanisms do not appear suitable. Instead, we are investigating the use of both a versioning and a monitoring mechanism.

The versioning mechanism will be an interface to the versioning facilities described in Section 10.1.5. The monitor mechanism will allow an application to request that an Iris function be monitored for some specified argument objects. Iris will notify the application whenever the monitored function value changes. The application may then retrieve the new function value.

Persistent-CLOS (PCLOS [Paepcke 1988]) is one attempt at building a tightly integrated interface between Iris and an object language. It interfaces object-oriented programs to Iris by transparently mapping CLOS objects onto the database. CLOS is an object layer on top of COMMON LISP that is evolving into a standard [Bobrow 1987]. PCLOS allows programmers to make objects transient or persistent by sending messages to them. Transient and persistent objects are semantically and syntactically equivalent, except for the effects of concurrency control and, of course, life span. State accesses to persistent objects are transparently intercepted and appropriate commands are sent to Iris for information update and retrieval. Transient objects are not known to Iris and cannot be accessed by other users.

The implementation of PCLOS is quite natural in that CLOS classes, instances, and slots map into Iris types, objects, and functions, respectively. The system automatically generates the appropriate Iris schemata from CLOS class hierarchies. Special care is needed when data of LISP-specific types are stored in slots and therefore in the database. A CLOS converter object manages all mappings of such data items to formats storable in Iris or databases accessed through Iris. Whenever possible, PCLOS uses database literals. If there are no such appropriate primitives, the information is encoded in ASCII.

The system stores information about CLOS classes in the database to permit the reconstruction of in-memory class hierarchies at run-time before instances are accessed. This includes mainly slot specifications that are not reflected in the database type hierarchy. We use this for consistency checks and expect to use the information to access our object bases from other object-oriented languages.

The default behavior of PCLOS is to leave all persistent data in the database, except when it is needed for processing. Modifications are immediately written back and committed to Iris. This mode of operation has the advantage of maximizing opportunities for concurrency. The disadvantage is very heavy database traffic and subsequent performance problems. All persistent objects respond to messages instructing them to cache or uncache themselves or to perform other functions needed for cache management. We are experimenting with the proper balance of caching in the database client versus server memory spaces.

## 10.3 IRIS STORAGE MANAGER

The Iris Object Manager is built on top of a conventional relational storage manager, namely that of HP-SQL [HP SQL]. HP-SQL's Storage Manager is very similar to System R's RSS [Blasgen et al. 1979]. Tables can be created and dropped at any time. The system supports transactions with savepoints and restores to savepoints, concurrency control, logging and recovery, archiving, indexing, and buffer management. It provides tuple-at-a-time processing with commands to retrieve, update, insert, and delete tuples. Indexes and threads (links between tuples in the same table) allow users to access the tuples of a table in a predefined order. Additionally, a predicate over column values can be defined to qualify tuples during retrieval.

We plan to extend and modify this storage subsystem to support the Iris data model better and to provide capabilities needed to support our diverse set of intended applications. In this section, we discuss two planned extensions: support for foreign operators and long fields.

### 10.3.1 Operators

As discussed in Section 10.1, Iris functions can be implemented as stored tables, derived functions, or foreign functions. Derived functions are defined in terms of other functions that, in turn, may be implemented as stored, derived, or foreign functions. The initial step of the Iris Query Translator module is to (recursively) retrieve the definitions of all derived functions in the query. It is then left with an expression tree consisting of tables, relational algebra operators, and calls to foreign functions. This tree is subsequently simplified and optimized. Part of the query optimization strategy is to delegate to the Storage Manager as much of the execution tree as possible. This reduces the number of calls to the Storage Manager as well as the amount of data passed between the Storage Manager and the Query Interpreter module of the Object Manager. Currently, operations involving multiple tables (joins), complex operations over a single table (aggregation), and foreign functions are all evaluated by the Query Interpreter, outside the Storage Manager.

One of the basic functions of the Storage Manager is the retrieval of tuples from tables. A retrieval request includes a table identifier and may include a selection predicate, a projection list, and a preferred access method. The Storage Manager begins by opening a scan on the table. The scan specifies any projection list, a selection predicate, and whether the scan should be sequential or via an access method. The selection predicate is composed of conjunctions and disjunctions of operators applied to constants and column values. For example:

```
(Column6 eq "Smith") and ((Column3 neq 5) or (Column2 gt
    Column 1))
```

All operators known to the Storage Manager are binary and return a single boolean value.

Associated with each scan is a finite state machine that evaluates the selection predicate. The Storage Manager iterates through the scan by retrieving the next tuple and invoking the finite state machine to evaluate the predicate. If the output of the finite state machine is **true**, the tuple is returned. Otherwise, the tuple is dropped. Note that part of the predicate may be evaluated by an access method. For instance, in the example above, if an index exists on Column6, the open scan command may specify that the index should be used to retrieve tuples from the table. In this case, the term (Column6 **eq** "Smith") in the predicate is evaluated by the access method, while the term ((Column3 **neq** 5) **or** (Column2 **gt** Column1)) is evaluated by the finite state machine. Thus, prior to opening the scan, the Storage Manager may split the selection predicate into a subexpression for the access method and a subexpression for the finite state machine.

In the current version of Iris, the limited form of selection predicates recognized by the Storage Manager limits the portion of the query tree that the Query Translator may delegate to the Storage Manager. In particular, it may delegate only certain binary operators, and the operands of those operators must be either a column and a constant or two columns of the same table.

As discussed in Section 10.1, we plan to support operator extensibility by implementing new operators as foreign functions. Thus, in its internal implementation, Iris will not understand the semantics of "factorial," for example, beyond the fact that it takes one operand of type integer and returns one value of type integer. To evaluate the function, the Query Interpreter will invoke the body of the foreign function.

The obvious next step is to delegate evaluation of foreign functions to the Storage Manager whenever possible. Thus, we plan to extend the Storage Manager so that it can evaluate any operator or foreign function so long as all column input parameters belong to the same table. This requires relaxing the Storage Manager assumption that all operators are binary and return boolean values. Even more interestingly, it implies that columns returned from the Storage Manager may not even be stored in the database (e.g., the result of an arithmetic operation). Note that a long-term goal will be to support operators over sets of tuples, such as aggregate operators. Just as the operator '=' can be executed directly by the finite state machine or indirectly by retrieval via a hashing access method or B-tree access method, foreign operators will be allowed to have several implementations; depending on their presence and estimated cost, the optimizer will decide which implementation to choose.

### 10.3.2 Long Fields

The Storage Manager is also being extended to support field lengths that exceed its maximum page size of 4K bytes. Each long field will be assigned a unique identifier by the Storage Manager. Tuples may use this identifier to reference the entire long field or some subset identified by a list of offsets and lengths. Long fields will be stored in a data structure similar to that used by EXODUS [Carey et al. 1986]. The basic operations on long fields will be retrieval and update. Retrieval of a long field will be allowed by reference (i.e., its unique identifier) or by value (i.e., the actual content of the long field) and may include a length. A retrieval request returns the requested bytes as a single byte stream. An update request similarly may be by reference or value and, essentially, replaces one byte sequence with another. This may cause the long field to expand or contract.

With each long field will be maintained a list of tuples that reference it. This list is needed to maintain some integrity in the management of long fields. For instance the addition or deletion of bytes to a long field may invalidate a reference to a subset of it. Types, such as "voice," "text," and "bitmap," will be associated with long fields. Foreign functions and operators will be allowed on long fields as on any other fields. Space efficient versioning facilities, similar to those in [Woelk and Kim 1987] and [Carey et al. 1986], will be available for long fields to avoid nearly identical copies of large amounts of data.

## SUMMARY

The Iris prototype is implemented in C on HP-9000/350 UNIX workstations. These are MC68020-based computers. A port to HP's reduced instruction set (RISC) architecture computers is being contemplated. The Storage Manager is the (still essentially unmodified) storage manager of HP's HP-SQL DBMS product. This is an RSS-like storage subsystem, augmented with parent-child links, to support both a relational and a network query processor.

The Object Manager is entirely new code. It consists of an implementation of the model discussed in Section 10.1, and its associated query processor. All features described in this chapter have been implemented except recursive functions, negation, OSQL embedding in C, and the extensions discussed in Section 10.3. All of these are in various stages of design and development.

The interfaces that have, thus far, been implemented for Iris include OSQL and the Graphical Editor, OSQL embedded in LISP, and the PCLOS interface. An Objective-C–Iris integration has been prototyped and is being extended to provide a basis for integrating other object-oriented programming languages, including C++. Of course, there is also the C subroutine library that *is* the Object Manager interface, the use of which is required to implement all Iris interfaces.

**Acknowledgments**   Nigel Derrett was one of the initial investigators on the Iris project. He made many significant contributions, including the design and implementation of the query translator module. Henry Cate adapted the HP-SQL Storage Manager for use in Iris. Andreas Paepcke designed and implemented the PCLOS interface and was an early and persistent Iris user.

## REFERENCES

[Abrial 1974] J.R. Abrial, "Data Semantics," in *Data Base Management,* J.W. Klimbie and K.L. Koffman, eds., pp. 1–59, North-Holland, Amsterdam, 1974.

[Beech 1988] D. Beech, "A Foundation for Evolution from Relational to Object Databases," in *Advances in Database Technology—EDBT 1988,* Lecture Notes in Computer Science 303, J.W. Schmidt, S. Ceri and M. Missikoff, eds., Springer-Verlag, 1988.

[Beech and Feldman 1983] D. Beech and J.S. Feldman, "The Integrated Data Model—A Database Perspective," *Proceedings of the 9th International Conference on Very Large Databases,* Florence, 1983.

[Beech and Mahbod 1988] D. Beech and B. Mahbod, "Generalized Version Control in an Object-Oriented Database," *IEEE 4th International Conference on Data Engineering,* February 1988.

[Blasgen et al. 1979] M.W. Blasgen et al., "Architectural Updates to System R," IBM Research Report RJ2654, June 1979.

[Bobrow 1987] D.G. Bobrow et al., "Common Lisp Object System Specification," ANSI Report 87-001, September 1987.

[Brodie 1981] M.L. Brodie, "On Modeling Behavioral Semantics of Data," *Proceedings of the 7th International Conference on Very Large Data Bases,* Cannes, France, September 1981.

[Carey et al. 1986] M. Carey, D.J. DeWitt, J.E. Richardson and E.J. Shekita, "Object and File Management in the EXODUS Extensible Database System," *Proceedings of the 12th International Conference on Very Large Data Bases,* Kyoto, Japan, August 1986.

[Chen 1976] P.P. Chen, "The Entity-Relationship Model: Toward a Unified View of Data," *ACM Transactions on Database Systems,* vol. 1, no. 1, pp. 9–36, 1976.

[Chou and Kim 1986] H. Chou and W. Kim, "A Unifying Framework for Version Control in a CAD Environment," *Proceedings of the 12th International Conference on Very Large Data Bases,* Kyoto, Japan, August 1986.

[Clocksin and Mellish 1981] W.F. Clocksin and C.S. Mellish, *Programming in Prolog,* Springer-Verlag, New York, 1981.

[Codd 1970] E.F. Codd, "A Relational Model of Data for Large Shared Data Banks," *Communications of the ACM,* vol. 13, no. 6, June 1970.

[Cox 1986] B.J. Cox, *Object Oriented Programming: An Evolutionary Approach*, Addison-Wesley, Reading, MA, 1986.

[Date 1981] C.J. Date, "Referential Integrity," *Proceedings of the 7th International Conference on Very Large Data Bases*, Cannes, France, September 1981.

[Date 1984] C.J. Date, *A Guide to DB2*, Addison-Wesley, Reading, MA, 1984.

[Derrett et al. 1985] N. Derrett, W. Kent and P. Lyngbaek, "Some Aspects of Operations in an Object-Oriented Database," *Database Engineering*, vol. 8, no. 4, IEEE Computer Society, December 1985.

[Derrett et al. 1986] N. Derrett, D.H. Fishman, W. Kent, P. Lyngbaek and T.A. Ryan, "An Object-Oriented Approach to Data Management," *Proceedings of Compcon 31st IEEE Computer Society International Conference*, San Francisco, March 1986.

[Elmasri and Wiederhold 1981] R. Elmasri and G. Wiederhold, "GORDAS: A Formal High-Level Query Language for the Entity-Relationship Model," in *Entity-Relationship Approach to Information Modeling and Analysis*, P.P. Chen, ed., ER Institute, 1981.

[Fishman et al. 1987] D.H. Fishman, D. Beech, H.P. Cate, E.C. Chow, T. Connors, J.D. Davis, N. Derrett, C.G. Hoch, W. Kent, P. Lyngbaek, B. Mahbod, M.A. Neimat, T.A. Ryan and M.C. Shan, "Iris: An Object-Oriented Database Management System," *ACM Transactions on Office Information Systems*, vol. 5, no. 1, pp. 48–69, January 1987.

[Graefe and DeWitt 1987] G. Graefe and D.J. DeWitt, "The EXODUS Optimizer Generator," *SIGMOD Conference Proceedings*, San Francisco, May 1987.

[Hammer and McLeod 1981] M. Hammer and D. McLeod, "Database Description with SDM: A Semantic Database Model." *ACM Transactions on Database Systems*, vol. 6, no. 3, pp. 351–386, September 1981.

[HP SQL] HPSQL Reference Manual, Part Number 36217-90001, Hewlett-Packard.

[Katz 1985] R.H. Katz, *Information Management for Engineering Design*, Springer-Verlag, New York, 1985.

[Katz et al. 1986] R.H. Katz, E. Chang and R. Bhateja, "Version Modeling Concepts for Computer-Aided Design Databases," *SIGMOD Conference Proceedings*, Washington, D.C., May, 1986.

[Kent 1979] W. Kent, "Limitations of Record-Based Information Models," *ACM Transactions on Database Systems*, vol. 4, no. 1, pp. 107–131, March 1979.

[King and McLeod 1982] R. King and D. McLeod, "The Event Database Specification Model," *Proceedings of the International Conference on Improving Database Usability and Responsiveness*, Jerusalem, Israel, 1982.

[Kulkarni 1983] K.G. Kulkarni, *Evaluation of Functional Data Models for Database Design and Use*, Ph.D. Thesis, University of Edinburgh, 1983.

[Landis 1986] G.S. Landis, "Design Evolution and History in an Object-Oriented CAD/CAM Database, "*Proceedings of Compcon 31st IEEE Computer Society International Conference*, San Francisco, March 1986.

[Lorie and Plouffe 1983] R. Lorie and W. Plouffe, "Complex Objects and Their Use in Design Transactions," *Proceedings of Databases for Engineering Applications*, Database Week 1983 (ACM), May 1983.

[Lyngbaek and Kent, 1986] P. Lyngbaek and W. Kent, "A Data Modeling Methodology for the Design and Implementation of Information Systems," *Proceedings of the International Workshop on Object-Oriented Database Systems*, Pacific Grove, CA, September 1986.

[Lyngbaek and Vianu 1987] P. Lyngbaek and V. Vianu, "Mapping a Semantic Database Model to the Relational Model," *SIGMOD Conference Proceedings*, San Francisco, May 1987.

[Lyngbaek et al. 1987] P. Lyngbaek, N. Derrett, D.H. Fishman, W. Kent and T.A. Ryan, "Design and Implementation of the Iris Object Manager," *Proceedings of a Workshop on Persistent Object Systems: Their Design, Implementation and Use*, Scotland, August 1987. Also available as HP Labs Technical Report STL-86-17, December 1986.

[Mylopoulos et al. 1980] J. Mylopoulos, P.A. Bernstein and H.K.T. Wong, "A Language Facility for Designing Database-Intensive Applications," *ACM Transactions on Database Systems*, vol. 5, no. 2, pp. 185–207, June 1980.

[Paepcke 1988] A. Paepcke, "PCLOS: A Flexible Implementation of CLOS Persistence," in *European Conference on Object-Oriented Programming*, S. Gjessing and K. Nygaard, eds., pp. 374–389. Lecture Notes in Computer Science, Springer-Verlag, Berlin.

[Shipman 1981] D. Shipman, "The Functional Data Model and the Data Language DAPLEX," *ACM Transactions on Database Systems*, vol. 6, no. 1, pp. 140–173, March 1981.

[Smith and Smith 1977] J.M. Smith and D.C.P. Smith, "Database Abstractions: Aggregation and Generalization," *ACM Transactions on Database Systems*, vol. 2, no. 2, pp. 105–133, June 1977.

[Snyder 1986] A. Snyder, "CommonObjects: An Overview," *SIGPLAN Notices*, vol. 21, no. 10, pp. 19–28, October 1986.

[Steele 1984] G.L. Steele, *Common Lisp: The Language*, Digital Press, 1984.

[Stroustrup 1986] B. Stroustrup, *The C++ Programming Language,* Addison-Wesley, Reading, MA, 1986.

[Tichy 1982] W.F. Tichy, "Revision Control System," *Proceedings of the IEEE 6th International Conference on Software Engineering,* September 1982.

[Woelk and Kim 1987] D. Woelk and W. King, "Multimedia Information Management in an Object-Oriented Database System," *Proceedings of the 13th International Conference on Very Large Data Bases,* Brighton, England, September 1987.

# 11

# Features of the ORION Object-Oriented Database System

Won Kim, Nat Ballou, Hong-Tai Chou, Jorge F. Garza, Darrell Woelk

## INTRODUCTION

In the Advanced Computer Architecture Program at MCC, we have built a prototype object-oriented database system, called ORION. It is being used to support the data management needs of Proteus, an expert system shell prototyped in the same program. In ORION we have directly implemented the object-oriented paradigm [Goldberg 1981; Goldberg and Robson 1983; Bobrow and Stefik 1983; Symbolics 1984; Bobrow et al. 1985], added persistence and shareability to objects through transaction support, and provided various advanced functions required by applications from the CAD/CAM, artificial intelligence, and office information systems domains. Advanced functions supported in ORION include versions and change notification [Chou and Kim 1986; Chou and Kim 1988], composite objects [Kim et al. 1987b], dynamic schema evolution [Banerjee et al. 1987a; Banerjee et al. 1987b], transaction

management [Garza and Kim 1988], queries [Banerjee et al. 1988], and multimedia data management [Woelk et al. 1986; Woelk and Kim 1987].

ORION is a single-user, multitask database system that runs in a workstation environment, and is intended for applications in AI [Stefik and Bobrow 1986], multimedia documents [Ahlsen et al. 1984; IEEE 1985; Woelk et al.
1986], and computer-aided design [Afsarmanesh et al. 1986], implemented in
the object-oriented programming paradigm. ORION has been implemented
in COMMON LISP [Steele 1984] on a Symbolics 3600 LISP machine [Symbolics
1985], and has also been ported to the Sun workstation under the UNIX operating system. The Symbolics version of ORION will directly support data
management needs of a number of data-intensive application systems under
development at MCC.

In Section 11.1 we present a high-level overview of the architecture of
ORION. Sections 11.2 through 11.7 highlight six of the major features of
ORION, namely, dynamic schema evolution, version control and change notification, composite objects, associative queries, transaction management, and
multimedia information management. In these sections, we borrow liberally
from [Banerjee et al. 1987b; Chou and Kim 1986; Chou and Kim 1988; Kim
et al. 1987; Banerjee et al. 1988; Garza and Kim 1988; Woelk and Kim 1987].

## 11.1 OVERVIEW OF THE ORION ARCHITECTURE

Figure 11.1 shows a high-level block diagram of the ORION architecture. The
message handler receives all messages sent to the ORION system. These include messages for user-defined methods, access messages, and system-defined
functions. A *user-defined method* is a method that the user defines and stores
in ORION. An *access message* is one that retrieves or updates the value of an
attribute of a class. *System-defined functions* include all ORION functions

FIGURE 11.1 ORION-1 ARCHITECTURE

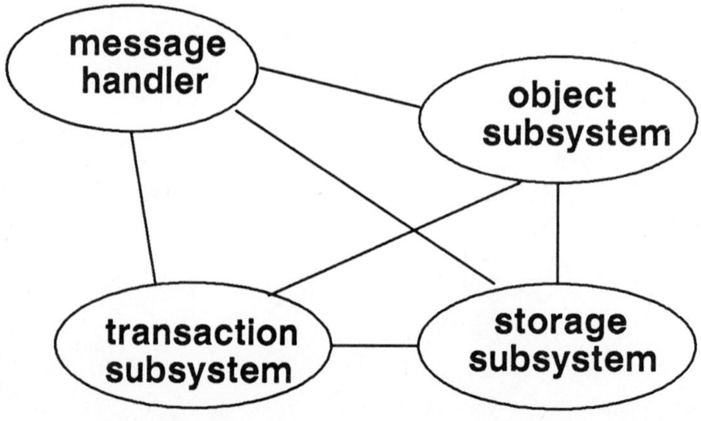

for schema definition, creation and deletion of instances, transaction management, and so on.

The object subsystem of ORION provides high-level functions, such as schema evolution, version control, query optimization, and multimedia information management.

The storage subsystem provides access to objects on disk. It manages the allocation and deallocation of segments of pages on disk, finds and places objects on the pages, and moves pages to and from the disk. It also manages indexes on attributes of a class to speed up the evaluation of associative queries.

The transaction subsystem provides a concurrency control and recovery mechanism to protect database integrity while allowing the interleaved execution of multiple concurrent transactions. Concurrency control uses a locking protocol, and a logging mechanism is used for recovery from system crashes and user-initiated aborts.

## 11.2 SCHEMA EVOLUTION

ORION applications require considerable flexibility in dynamically defining and modifying the database schema, that is, the class definitions and the inheritance structure of the class lattice [Woelk et al. 1986]. Existing object-oriented systems support only a few types of changes to the schema without requiring system shutdown, because they are programming language systems. Even existing conventional database systems allow only a few types of schema changes: for example, SQL/DS allows only dynamic creation and deletion of relations (classes) and addition of new columns (instance variables) in a relation [IBM 1981]. This is because the applications they support (conventional record-oriented business applications) do not require more than a few types of schema changes, and also the data models they support are not as rich as object-oriented data models.

We have developed a taxonomy of schema change operations that are useful and that can be supported in a database system without causing either system shutdown or database reorganization. We have also developed a framework for understanding and enforcing the semantics of each schema change operation. Our formal framework consists of a set of properties of the schema called *invariants*, and a set of *rules* for preserving the invariants. The invariants hold at every quiescent state of the schema, that is, before and after a schema change operation. They provide a basis for the definition of the semantics of every meaningful schema change, by ensuring that the change does not leave the schema in an inconsistent state (one that violates any invariant). However, for some schema changes, the schema invariants can be preserved in more than one way. The rules guide the selection of one most meaningful way.

In this section, we provide a taxonomy of schema changes that we support in ORION, and summarize the set of invariants and rules. Refer to [Banerjee et al. 1987b] for a detailed discussion of schema evolution in ORION.

### 11.2.1 Schema Evolution Taxonomy

ORION supports two types of schema changes to the contents and structure of a class lattice: changes to the definitions of a class (contents of a node) on a class lattice, and changes to the structure (edges and nodes) of a class latice. Changes to the class definitions include adding and deleting attributes and methods. Changes to the class lattice structure include creation and deletion of a class, and alteration of the IS-A relationship between classes. The taxonomy of schema changes given here is an abbreviated version of that given in [Banerjee et al. 1987b].

1. Changes to the contents of a node (a class)
   1.1 Changes to an attribute
       1.1.1 Add a new attribute to a class
       1.1.2 Drop an existing attribute from a class
       1.1.3 Change the name of an attribute of a class
       1.1.4 Change the domain of an attribute of a class
       1.1.5 Change the inheritance (parent) of an attribute (inherit another attribute with the same name)
   1.2 Changes to a method
       1.2.1 Add a new method to a class
       1.2.2 Drop an existing method from a class
       1.2.3 Change the name of a method of a class
       1.2.4 Change the code of a method of a class
       1.2.5 Change the inheritance (parent) of a method (inherit another method with the same name)

2. Changes to an edge
   2.1 Make a class $S$ a superclass of a class $C$
   2.2 Remove a class $S$ from the superclass list of a class $C$

3. Changes to a node
   3.1 Add a new class
   3.2 Drop an existing class
   3.3 Change the name of a class

We review the semantics of four of the schema change operations: 1.1.2, 2.1, 2.2, and 3.2.

**1.1.2 Drop an Instance Variable *V* from a Class *C***   If $V$ is dropped from $C$, it must also be dropped recursively from the subclasses that inherited it. If $C$ or any of its subclasses has other superclasses that have instance variables of the same name as that of $V$, it inherits one of those instance variables. In case $V$ must be dropped from $C$ or any of its subclasses without a replacement, existing instances of these classes lose their values for $V$.

**2.1 Make a Class *S* a Superclass of a Class *C***   The addition of a new edge from $S$ to $C$ must not introduce a cycle in the class lattice. $C$ and its subclasses inherit instance variables and methods from $S$, provided that no name conflicts arise. Instances of $C$ and its subclasses receive the null value for the newly inherited instance variables. Operations 1.1.1 and 1.2.1 are applied, respectively, to add instance variables and methods of $S$ to $C$.

**2.2 Remove a Class *S* from the Superclass List of a Class *C***   The deletion of an edge from $S$ to $C$ must not cause the class lattice to become disconnected. In case $S$ is the only superclass of $C$, the immediate superclasses of $S$ now become the immediate superclasses of $C$ as well, while the ordering of these superclasses with respect to $S$ remains the same for $C$. Thus, $C$ does not lose any instance variables or methods that were inherited from the superclasses of $S$. $C$ only loses those instance variables and methods that were defined in $S$. If the deletion of the edge from $S$ to $C$ does not leave the class lattice disconnected, $C$ is left with one fewer superclasses, and it must drop the instances variables and methods it had inherited from $S$. The operations for dropping an instance variable (Operation 1.1.2) and a method (Operation 1.2.2) are applied, respectively, for each instance variable and method to be dropped from $C$.

**3.2 Drop an Existing Class *C***   All edges from $C$ to its subclasses are dropped, using Operation 2.2. Next, all edges from the superclasses of $C$ into $C$ are removed. Finally, the definition of $C$ is dropped, and $C$ is removed from the lattice. The subclasses of $C$ continue to exist. If the class $C$ was the domain of an instance variable $V1$ of another class $C1$, then $V1$ is assigned a new domain, namely the first superclass of the dropped class $C$.

## 11.2.2 Invariants of Schema Evolution

We have identified five invariants of the object-oriented schema from the ORION data model. They are summarized here.

**Class Lattice Invariant**   The class lattice is a *rooted* and *connected directed acyclic graph* (DAG) with named nodes and labeled edges. The DAG has only one root, a system-defined class called OBJECT. The DAG is connected, that is, there are no isolated nodes. Every node is reachable from the root. Nodes are named, and each node in the DAG has a unique name. Edges are labeled such that all edges directed to any given node have distinct labels.

**Distinct Name Invariant**   All instance variables of a class, whether defined or inherited, have distinct names. Similarly, all methods of a class, whether defined or inherited, must have distinct names.

**Distinct Identity (Origin) Invariant**   All instance variables, and methods, of a class have distinct identity (origin). For example, in Fig. 11.2, the class Submarine can inherit the instance variable Weight from either the class WaterVehicle or the class NuclearPoweredVehicle. However, in both these superclasses, Weight has the same origin, namely, the instance variable Weight of the class Vehicle, where Weight was originally defined. Therefore, the class Submarine must have only one occurrence of the instance variable Weight.

**Full Inheritance Invariant**   A class inherits all instance variables and methods from each of its superclasses, except when full inheritance causes a violation of the distinct name and distinct identity invariants. In other words, if two instance variables have distinct origin but the same name in two different superclasses, at least one of them must be inherited. If two instance variables have the same origin in two different superclasses, only one of them must be

**FIGURE 11.2** RESOLUTION OF NAME CONFLICTS

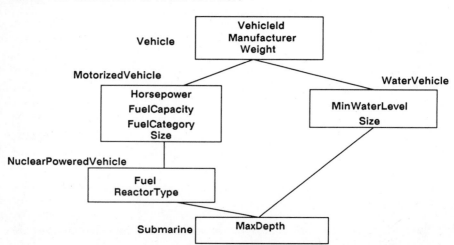

inherited. For example, in Fig. 11.2, Submarine must inherit Size, whether it is from NuclearPoweredVehicle or from WaterVehicle, or even from both (by assigning new names, in order to maintain the distinct name invariant). Further, Submarine must inherit Weight only once, from either NuclearPoweredVehicle or WaterVehicle.

**Domain Compatibility Invariant**  If an instance variable $V2$ of a class $C$ is inherited from an instance variable $V1$ of a superclass of $C$, then the domain of $V2$ is either the same as that of $V1$, or a subclass of $V1$. For example, if the domain of the instance variable Manufacturer in the Vehicle class is the Company class, then the domain of Manufacturer in the MotorizedVehicle class (a subclass of Vehicle) can be Company or a subclass of Company, say, MotorizedVehicleCompany.

Another aspect of the domain compatibility invariant is that the shared value or default value of an instance variable must be an instance of the class that is the domain of that instance variable.

### 11.2.3 Rules of Schema Evolution

A class lattice in a quiescent state must preserve all the invariants. For some of the schema changes, however, there is more than one way to preserve the invariants. For example, if there is a name conflict among instance variables to be inherited from superclasses, the full inheritance invariant requires that at least one of the instance variables be inherited, but it does not say which. In order to guide the selection of one option among many in an algorithmic and meaningful way, we have established twelve essential rules, including some that we have adopted from existing object-oriented systems. These rules are discussed in [Banerjee et al. 1987b], and will not be presented here.

The rules fall into four categories: default conflict resolution rules, property propagation rules, DAG manipulation rules, and composite object rules. The *default conflict resolution rules* permit the selection of a single inheritance option whenever there is a name or identity conflict. They ensure that the distinct name and distinct identity invariants are satisfied in a deterministic way. The ORION user may, however, override these rules by explicit requests to resolve conflicts differently.

The properties of an instance variable, once defined or inherited into a class, can be modified in a number of ways. In particular, its name, domain, default value, shared value, or the composite link property may be changed. Also, an instance variable that is not shared-valued can be made shared-valued, or vice versa. Further, the properties of a method belonging to a class may be modified by changing its name or code. The *property propagation rules* provide guidelines for supporting all changes to the properties of instance variables and methods.

The *DAG manipulation rules* govern the addition and deletion of nodes and edges from the class latice. These rules ensure that drastic changes are avoided when an edge or a node is added to or removed from a class lattice.

The *composite object rules* are used to enforce the semantics of composite objects, as we will show in Section 11.4.

## 11.3 VERSIONS AND CHANGE NOTIFICATION

There is a general consensus that version control is one of the most important functions in various data-intensive application domains, such as integrated CAD/CAM systems [Katz and Lehman 1984; Katz et al. 1986; Chou and Kim 1986] and office information systems dealing with compound documents [Woelk et al. 1986]. Users in such environments often need to generate and experiment with multiple versions of an object, before selecting one that satisfies their requirements.

An object in general recursively references other "lower level" objects. An object may be referenced (shared) by any number of objects, and may in turn reference any number of other objects. When an object is updated or deleted, or a new version of the object is created, some or all of the objects that have referenced it may become invalid, and thus need to be notified of the change [Neumann and Hornung 1982].

This section provides a summary of ORION support for versions and change notification. We refer the interested reader to [Chou and Kim 1986; Chou and Kim 1988] for additional details.

### 11.3.1 Versions

We distinguish two types of versions on the basis of the types of operations that are allowed on them. They are transient and working versions.

A *transient version* has the following properties.

1. It can be updated by the user who created it.

2. It can be deleted by the user who created it.

3. A new transient version may be derived from an existing transient version. The existing transient version then is "promoted" to a working version.

A *working version* has the following properties.

1. It is considered stable and cannot be updated.

2. It can be deleted by its owner.

3. A transient version can be derived from a working version.

4. A transient version can be "promoted" to a working version. Promotion may be explicit (user-specified) or implicit (system-determined).

The reason we impose the update restriction on working versions is that it is considered stable and thus transient versions can be derived from it. If a working version is to be directly updated after one or more transient versions have been derived from it, we need a set of careful update algorithms (for insert, delete, and update) that will ensure that the derived versions will not see the updates in the working version.

There are two ways to *bind* an object with another versioned object: static and dynamic. In *static binding*, the reference to an object includes the full name of the object, the object identifier, and the version number. In *dynamic binding* [Katz and Lehman 1984; Atwood 1985], the reference needs to specify only the object identifier, and may leave the version number unspecified. The system selects the default version number. Clearly, dynamic binding is useful, since transient or working versions that are referenced may be deleted, and new versions created.

**Implementation**   Because of the performance and storage overhead in supporting versions, we require the application to indicate whether a class is *versionable*. When an instance of a versionable class is created, a *generic object* for that instance is created, along with the first version of that instance. A generic object is essentially a data structure for the version-derivation hierarchy of an instance of a versionable class. It is deleted when the version-derivation hierarchy for its instance contains no versioned object. A generic object consists of the following system-defined instance variables:

1. default version number

2. a next-version number

3. a version count

4. a set of version descriptors, one for each existing version on the version-derivation hierarchy of the object

The default version number determines which existing version on the version-derivation hierarchy should be chosen when a partially specified reference is dynamically bound. The next-version number is the version number to be assigned to the next version of the object that will be created. It is incremented after being assigned to the new version.

A version descriptor contains control information for each version on a version-derivation hierarchy. It includes

1. the version number of the version

2. the identifier of the versioned object

3. a list of references to the descriptors of child versions

Each version instance of a versionable object contains three system-defined attributes, in addition to all user-defined attributes. We allow the application to read, but not to update, any of these attributes:

1. version number

2. version type

3. object identifier of its generic object

The version number is needed simply to distinguish a version instance of a versionable object from other version instances of the same versionable object. The version type indicates whether the version instance is a transient version or working version. This information is maintained so that the system may easily reject an attempt to update a working version. The generic object identifier is required so that, given a version instance, any other version instances of the versionable object may be found efficiently.

**Messages**   A versioned object is created initially by the *create* command, which creates the generic-object data structure for the object. The *derive* command is used to derive a new transient version and allocate a new version number for it. If the parent was a transient version, it is automatically promoted to a working version. The *replace* operation causes the contents of a transient version to be replaced by a workspace copy the user specifies. A transient version is explicitly promoted to a working version, making the version non-updatable, through the *promote* command. The user may delete a version or an entire version-derivation hierarchy by using the *delete* command. If a generic object is deleted, all versions of the instance for which the generic object was created are deleted. If a working version is deleted from which other versions have been derived, the version is deleted, but the fact that the version existed is not deleted from the generic object. The user uses the *set_default* command to specify the default version on a version-derivation hierarchy of an object. A specific version number or the keyword "most-recent" may be specified as the default.

## 11.3.2 Change Notification

In a distributed environment, change notification involves both sending mail messages from the server to the workstations, and recording timestamps in data structures associated with the objects. In ORION, only the version time-stamping technique has been implemented. Each object that participates in change notification has two distinct timestamps. One timestamp, called the *change-notification timestamp*, indicates the time the object was created or the last time it was updated. The other, called the *change-approval timestamp*, indicates the last time at which the owner of the object approved all changes to the objects it references.

Let V.CA and V.CN denote the change-approval and change-notification timestamps of an object V. Let R be the set of objects that are referenced by object V. If no object in R has a change-notification timestamp that exceeds the change-approval timestamp of V (i.e., for all X in R, $X.CN <= V.CA$), then V is *reference-consistent*. V is *reference-inconsistent* if there are one or more objects in R that have been updated, but the effects of these updates on V have not been determined.

To make V reference-consistent, the effects of the updated objects in R must be determined, and, if necessary, V must be updated. If the updates to objects in R have no effect on V, only V.CA needs to be changed to the current time. Otherwise, V.CN (and possibly V.CA if the changes are approved) must be set to the current time.

**Implementation** ORION supports change notification as an option on user-specified attributes of a class. The user may specify attributes to be *notification-sensitive*; if a change occurs on the value of any of these attributes of an instance of the class, the instance is notified of the change.

ORION provides three system-defined attributes for a class for which the notify option is on:

1. change-notification timestamp

2. change-approval timestamp

3. a set of change-notification events

The change-notification timestamp associated with an object indicates the last time at which a change has been made to the object. The change-approval timestamp indicates the last time the user approved changes to all objects referenced through all notification-sensitive attributes. Changes are notified either on an update or on a delete operation, or both. "Delete" is the default, and "update" subsumes "delete."

If the class $D$ is the domain of a notification-sensitive attribute of a class $C$, then each instance of $D$, as well as $D$'s subclasses, contains a change-notification timestamp. Whenever a new instance $d$ of $D$ (or a subclass of $D$) is created, or an existing instance is changed, its change-notification timestamp captures the time of that event. At a later time, when an instance $c$ of $C$ makes a reference to the instance $d$ through a notification-sensitive attribute, the user or application can compare the change-approval timestamp of $c$ with the change-notification timestamp of $d$, and decide whether the change to $d$ needs approval. When an instance $d$ of the class $D$ is deleted, an instance $c$ of $C$ will have a dangling reference. The dangling reference is itself an indication of reference-inconsistency, if the reference is made through a notification-sensitive attribute. The system maintains the information necessary to determine whether an instance is reference-consistent. However, it is the user's or application's responsibility to determine reference-consistency, and then take measures to make the instance reference-consistent, if necessary.

## 11.4 COMPOSITE OBJECTS

The notions of instance variables, domains, and object identifier, although powerful, cannot represent the IS-PART-OF relationship between objects. The IS-PART-OF relationship captures the notion that an object *is a part of* another object; and, along with the IS-A relationship, it is one of the fundamental data modeling concepts. A composite object is that part of a conventional nested object on which we impose the IS-PART-OF relationship.

Many applications require the ability to define and manipulate a set of objects as a single logical entity for the purposes of semantic integrity, and efficient storage and retrieval [Lorie and Plouffe 1983; IEEE 1985; Kim et al. 1987a]. We define a *composite object* as an object with a hierarchy of exclusive component objects, and refer to the hierarchy of classes to which the objects belong as a *composite object hierarchy*. A non-root class on a composite object hierarchy is called a *component class*. Each non-leaf class on a composite object hierarchy has one or more instance variables whose domains are the component classes. We call such instance variables *composite instance variables*. A constituent object of a composite object references an instance of its component class through a composite instance variable. We call such a reference a *composite reference* or *composite link* between an object and its dependent object (or between a class and its component class).

In this section, we summarize the semantics of composite objects, and two ways in which we make use of them to enhance performance of retrieving composite objects. The interested reader will find more details in [Kim et al. 1987b].

### 11.4.1 Semantics

**Dependent Objects**   Composite objects augment the semantic integrity of an object-oriented data model through the notion of dependent objects. A *dependent object* is one whose existence depends on the existence of another object, and is owned by exactly one object. For example, we show the schema for a class Vehicle in Fig. 11.3. The body of a vehicle is owned by one specific vehicle, and cannot exist without the vehicle that contains it. As such, a dependent object cannot be created if its owner does not already exist. This means that a constituent object (except the root) of a composite object cannot be created unless its parent exists. Further, when a constituent object of a composite object is deleted, all its dependent objects must also be deleted.

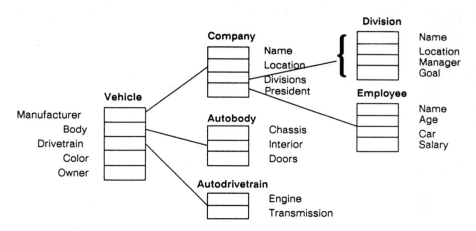

**FIGURE 11.3** SCHEMA FOR CLASS VEHICLE

In a composite object, no dependent object can be referenced more than once. Thus, a composite object is a hierarchy of objects (and not a general digraph). However, any object within a composite object can be referenced by objects that do not belong to the composite object through a noncomposite link. These references can have the complete generality of a digraph, including cycles. For example, an instance of the class Vehicle can have a composite link to an instance of the class Autobody through the instance variable Body. No other instance of Vehicle can reference this instance of Autobody through the instance variable Body. Further, if an instance of some other class, say Inventory, has a reference to this instance of Autobody, the reference must be through a noncomposite instance variable.

Further, a class may be the domain of more than one composite instance variable. However, again only one object may have a composite reference to any instance of the class as a dependent object. For example, two classes called Car and Truck may both have a composite instance variable Body whose domain is the class Autobody. However, no instance of Autobody can simultaneously be a part of a Car and a Truck.

**Schema Evolution on a Composite Object Hierarchy** The composite link property of an instance variable of a class is inherited by all subclasses of that class. For example, if the class Automobile is a subclass of Vehicle, it inherits the instance variable Body from Vehicle. Further, because Body is a composite instance variable in the Vehicle class, it will also be a composite instance variable in the Automobile class.

A composite instance variable may be changed to a noncomposite instance variable, that is, it may lose the composite link property. However, we do not allow a noncomposite instance variable to later acquire the composite link property. The reason is that an object may be referenced by any number of instances of a class through a noncomposite instance variable, but a dependent object of a composite object may be referenced by only one instance of a class through a composite instance variable. To change a noncomposite instance variable to a composite instance variable, it is necessary to verify that existing instances are not referenced by more than one instance through the instance variable. This in turn makes it necessary to maintain a list of reference counts with each object, one reference count for each instance variable through which the object may be referenced. We avoid this complexity in ORION by not permitting a noncomposite instance variable to be changed to a composite instance variable.

The integrity of a composite object lies in the fact that all dependent objects owe their existence to their parents. In particular, if a parent object is deleted, all its dependent objects are deleted; and if a parent object loses a composite instance variable, the dependent object referenced is deleted. However, we allow objects to *disown* their dependents, if their composite instance variables are changed to noncomposite. Disowned objects are not deleted when their previous parents are deleted, since they are no longer dependent on the existence of their previous parents.

The composite link property impacts the semantics of only Operations 1.1.2, 1.1.5, 2.1, 2.2, 2.3, and 3.2 (see Section 1.2.1). Its impact on Operation 1.1.2 is as follows. The instance variable must of course be dropped from all subclasses of the class. All instances of these classes are affected as well. They lose their values for the dropped instance variable. Further, to preserve integrity, all objects that are recursively dependent on the dropped instances must also be dropped. For example, when the instance variable Body is dropped from the class Vehicle, all objects dependent on instances of Vehicle and its subclasses through the instance variable Body will have to be deleted from the database. Many instances of Autobody may thus be deleted. However, not all instances of Autobody need be deleted. Those that are not a part of composite objects rooted at instances of Vehicle or its subclasses will continue to exist.

### 11.4.2 Performance Enhancement Using Composite Objects

We now discuss two important ways in which we use the semantics of composite objects in ORION to improve the performance of the system. One is to use the composite object as a unit of clustering in the database, so that a large collection of related objects may be retrieved efficiently from the database. Another is to use it as the unit of locking, so that the number of locks that must be set may be minimized in retrieving a composite object from the database.

**Clustering Composite Objects**  The notion of a composite object also offers an opportunity to improve the performance of a database system. A composite object may be used as a unit for clustering related objects in the database. This is because, when an application accesses the root object, it is often likely to access all (or most) dependent objects as well. Thus, it is advantageous to store all constituents of a composite object as close to one another as possible on secondary storage.

In ORION all instances of the same class are placed in the same storage segment on disk. Thus, a class is associated with a single segment, and all its instances reside in that segment. The user does not have to be aware of segments; ORION automatically allocates a separate segment for each class. For clustering composite objects, however, it is often advantageous to store instances of multiple classes in the same segment. User assistance is required to determine which classes should share the same segment.

The user may issue a Cluster message as a hint for ORION to cluster instances of a class with instances of other classes. A Cluster message specifies a list of class names. Instances of classes specified in the list are to be placed in a single segment. The user may sometimes need to cluster a new class $C$ with some existing classes that have already been allocated a segment. In that case, the user needs to issue a Cluster message, in which the list of class names is a pair, namely, the class $C$ and any one of the existing classes with which $C$ should share a segment. Instances of $C$ will then share the same segment with the existing classes.

**Locking Composite Objects**  The fundamental motivation of the *granularity locking protocol* in today's commercial database systems is to minimize the number of locks to be set in accessing the database [Gray 1978]. For example, when most of the instances of a class are to be accessed, it makes sense to set one lock for the entire class, rather than one lock for each instance. A lock on a class will imply a lock on each instance of the class. However, when only a few instances of a class need to be accessed, it is better to lock the instances individually, so that other concurrent transactions may access any other instances. The shortcoming of the granularity locking protocol is that it does not recognize a composite object as a single lockable granule, like a class or an instance of a class. To lock a composite object using the granularity locking protocol will mean either locking all component classes on a composite object hierarchy, or locking all constituent objects within a composite object. Neither option is satisfactory: the first option will result in the locking of all composite objects that belong to the composite object hierarchy; and the second option can result in a large number of locks.

In an environment where multiple applications may concurrently access a shared database, a composite object may be used as a unit of locking to reduce the system overhead associated with concurrency control; that is, a composite object should be locked as a unit, rather than requiring a lock for each component of a composite object. The locking protocol is given in [Kim et al. 1987b], and will not be repeated here.

## 11.5 QUERIES AND QUERY OPTIMIZATION

In this section, we provide the model of queries that has been implemented in ORION, and indicate a broad strategy for processing a given query. Further details are found in [Banerjee et al. 1988].

### 11.5.1 Query Model

The object-oriented data model, in its conventional form, allows one to represent an arbitrarily complex object as a recursively nested object. An object may be defined with a set of attributes. A class may be specified as the *domain* of an attribute; and the domain class, unless it is a *primitive class* (such as the String, Integer, or Boolean class), in turn consists of a set of attributes, and so on. The internal state of an object consists of the values of all its attributes. The value of an attribute is an instance of its domain, if the domain is a primitive class; and a reference to (*object identifier of*) an instance of the domain, otherwise. If the domain of an attribute is a set of a class, the value of that attribute for any instance will be a set of object identifiers. If an attribute of a class may take on a single instance of the domain, we will call it a *scalar attribute*; otherwise, we will call it a *set attribute*.

For example, in Fig. 11.3, we show the schema of a Vehicle class in terms of the attributes Manufacturer, Body, Drivetrain, Color, and Owner. The domain of the Color attribute is the primitive String class. The domain of the Manufacturer attribute is the class Company, the attribute Body has Autobody as its domain, and the domain of Drivetrain is the Autodrivetrain class. Each of the classes Company, Autobody, and Autodrivetrain consists of its own set of attributes, which in turn have associated domains. The domain of the President attribute of the class Company is the class Employee. The attribute Divisions of the class Company is a set attribute whose domain is the class Division. (This is represented by the brace in Fig. 11.3.)

The nesting of an object through the domains of its attributes immediately suggests that to fully fetch an instance, the instance and all objects it references through its attributes must be recursively fetched. This means that to fetch one or more instances of a class, the class and all classes specified as nonprimitive domains of the attributes of the class must be recursively traversed. For example, to fetch instances of the class Vehicle in Fig. 11.3, the classes that need to be traversed include not only Vehicle, but also the domains of nonprimitive attributes of Vehicle, namely, Company, Autobody, and Autodrivetrain, as well as the domains of nonprimitive attributes of these classes.

A query may be formulated against an object-oriented schema, which will fetch instances of a class that satisfy certain search criteria. A query may restrict the instances of a class to be fetched by specifying predicates against any attributes of the class. In [Banerjee et al. 1988] we show that the predicates on the attributes, and attributes themselves, may be expressed by a message-based syntax. An attribute may be one of two types: simple and complex. A *simple attribute* is one whose domain is a primitive class. A *complex attribute* is one whose domain is a class with one or more attributes, including other complex attributes. A predicate (a relational operator message, such as $>$, $<$, or $=$) on a simple attribute is called a *simple predicate*; one on a complex attribute is called a *complex predicate*. Further, a query that involves only simple predicates is called a *simple query*, and one that involves one or more complex predicates is called a *complex query*.

We may represent a class and the domains of all its complex attributes involved in a query in the form of a directed graph, which we will call a *query graph*. Each node on a query graph represents a class, and an edge from a node $A$ to a node $B$ means that the class $B$ is the domain of a complex attribute of a class $A$. A query graph has only one root, the class whose instances are to be fetched. Each leaf node of a query graph has only simple attributes. A query graph may contain cycles.

## 11.5.2 Query Processing

A query with one complex predicate on a class requires the traversal of two classes: the class on which the predicate is applied, and the class that is the domain of the complex instance variable. A complex query, as it involves a number of classes, brings out many of the same issues that complicate joins of relations in relational databases [Selinger et al. 1979]. It is important to consider all meaningful permutations of classes in the query graph representation of a query in object-oriented databases. However, the semantics of queries in object-oriented databases make it possible to eliminate many of the permutations of classes that may not be eliminated in evaluating relational queries [Banerjee et al. 1988].

Given any permutation of $n$ classes, there are two fundamental ways of traversing the classes in the permutation: forward and reverse traversal. In the *forward traversal*, the classes on a query graph are traversed in a depth-first order starting from the root of the query graph, and following through the successive domains of each complex instance variable. In the *reverse traversal*, the leaf classes of a query graph are visited first, and then their parents, working toward the root class. The following illustrates the two traversal techniques.

**Forward Traversal**  As an example, let us consider the following query based on the schema of Fig. 11.3. (As the semantics of the query is relatively clear from the syntax, we will not explain it here.)

```
Q1.  (select 'Vehicle '(equal Manufacturer Name ''Ford''))
```

A forward traversal for the query will start with the set of all instances of the class Vehicle. For each of these instances, the value of its attribute Manufacturer is traversed next. That value is an instance of the class Company, and has an attribute Name. The value of the attribute Name is traversed next. It has a simple value (an instance of the primitive class String). If the value is the string "Ford", the Company instance qualifies. In turn, the Vehicle instance that has that Company instance as its manufacturer also qualifies.

A query containing Boolean operators may also be evaluated via forward traversal. Consider the following query:

```
Q2.  (select 'Vehicle '(and   (equal Manufacturer name ''Ford'')
                              (< Owner Age 20)))
```

A forward traversal will again start with the set of all instances of Vehicle. Each instance of Vehicle qualifies if the forward traversal is successful along both the logical paths (Manufacturer Name) and (Owner Age).

**Reverse Traversal**   Consider once again the query Q1. Instead of starting with the set of all instances of Vehicle, reverse traversal starts the Name attribute of the class Company (and its subclasses). All instances of Company are identified that have the name "Ford". The identifiers of these instances are now looked up in the Manufacturer attribute of the instances of the class Vehicle.

Reverse traversal is usually mixed with forward traversal when Boolean operators are present. As an example, consider the query Q2. After reverse traversal is performed along the path (Manufacturer Name), the result is a set of Vehicle instances. Instances of this set are now traversed forward along the path (Owner Age), and only those instances are retained for which the owner's age is less than 20.

## 11.6 Transaction Management

ORION satisfies the concurrency control requirements of the rich object-oriented data model it supports, in particular, operations on a class lattice and composite objects. ORION incorporates important enhancements to the performance of transactions, including the concepts of sessions and hypothetical transactions. A *session* is a sequence of transactions, and the active transaction of a session may exist simultaneously in multiple windows on a workstation to alleviate the problem of long-duration waits in long-duration transactions in interactive application environments. A *hypothetical transaction* is a transaction that always aborts, and is important in application environments in which the users often experiment with "what-if" changes to the database. A hypothetical transaction allows the database system to avoid much of the overhead involved in concurrency control and recovery of normal transactions.

In this section, we summarize our implementation of sessions and hypothetical transactions, and summarize our approach to concurrency control and recovery. [Garza and Kim 1987] describes transaction management in ORION in greater detail.

### 11.6.1 Sessions

A *session* encapsulates a sequence of transactions. Since the transactions within a session are strictly serial, that is, one transaction ends before the next one starts, there is only one active transaction per session. Hence, the same workspace can be serially used to keep track of properties of all transactions within the session. Thus, the concept of session is useful for improving system performance.

A user can use ORION by first creating a session or by using the default session the system provides. A *default session* is created immediately upon the initialization or restart of ORION. The user may open and close any number of sessions, and multiple windows (or multiple UNIX shells) for the same session (including the default session). All windows of the session run the same transaction, the currently active transaction of the session. Any active transaction of a session will compete for resources (via locking) with those of all other sessions (including the default session).

ORION allows a session to have multiple windows primarily as a short-term solution to the long-duration wait problem that arises in long-duration interactive transactions [Haskin and Lorie 1982; Kim et al. 1984; Katz and Lehman 1984]. In a future version of ORION, we plan to implement the long-transaction model that we have proposed earlier [Bancilhon et al. 1985; Korth et al. 1988]. When multiple sessions are concurrently active, the active transaction of a particular session $S$ may be blocked if it cannot obtain a lock. In such an event, no more requests will be processed from the blocked window until either (1) a certain installation-determined timeout period expires, or (2) the requested lock is obtained. If the user wishes to continue with session $S$ even while waiting for the lock, the user may do so by creating another window for $S$. Since all windows of a session run the same transaction, they share the same locks; thus a user may create two windows with the same session name, update an object in one window, and examine (or even update) the same object in another window.

The user may close the windows of a session one at a time. If the closed window happens to be the only window of the session, the session itself is closed. If the currently active transaction of that session has not been committed or aborted, ORION automatically aborts that transaction, and then closes the session. Once a window is closed, the most recently deactivated session of that window is reactivated. In other words, on a single window, sessions are activated and deactivated in a stack-like fashion. The user cannot close the default session; it remains open until an ORION shutdown.

ORION supports two types of transactions: normal and hypothetical. A session may contain any sequence of normal and hypothetical transactions. When a *normal transaction* commits, all its updates are permanently recorded in the database; and when it aborts, all its changes are undone, and irretrievably lost. A *hypothetical transaction*, in contrast, is a transaction that always aborts. No matter how such a transaction is ended, its changes are never reflected in the database. Thus, hypothetical transactions provide a mechanism for experimenting with the effects of "what-if" changes to the database. Since the changes are never recorded permanently, the user has the freedom of examining the impact of complex changes to the database, and yet does not have to worry that the database will become corrupted or unavailable due to conflicting concurrent transactions. The concept of a hypothetical transaction is related to that of a hypothetical database proposed in [Stonebraker and Keller 1980; Stonebraker 1981].

Of course, the conventional transaction mechanism, with its abort option, can be used to provide the desired effect of a hypothetical transaction. However, the conventional transaction mechanism incurs significant overhead to make it possible for a transaction to be recoverable and to shield a transaction from the effects of other concurrently executing transactions. Within a hypothetical transaction, the first time an object is updated, a copy of the object is made for all subsequent updates within the transaction. The initial object is never updated. We call the initial object the *shadow copy*, and the new copy that gets updated the *current copy*. The current copy is discarded when the transaction terminates, regardless of whether the transaction commits or aborts. Further, each hypothetical transaction has its own current copy of an object for updates, so that multiple hypothetical transactions may concurrently update the same object.

Since a hypothetical transaction makes updates only to the current copy of an object, and each hypothetical transaction has its own current copy of the object, only a Share (S) lock needs to be set on the single shadow copy of an object, both for read and for update. An S lock is needed to prevent some concurrently executing nonhypothetical transaction from directly updating the shadow copy of the object, thereby causing the hypothetical transaction to read *dirty data*, data that are subject to a backout by the nonhypothetical transaction.

## 11.6.2 Concurrency Control

The ORION transaction subsystem provides a concurrency control mechanism to protect the database integrity while allowing the interleaved execution of multiple concurrent transactions. We have chosen the locking technique for our concurrency control mechanism. One reason is that locking is a well-understood technique, having been used in most commercial database systems. Another reason is that the current theory of locking provides a sound basis for the incorporation of the sophisticated concurrency control requirements.

Transactions in ORION are *serializable transactions*, which means that ORION completely isolates a transaction from the effects of all other concurrently executing transactions. A serializable transaction acquires a read lock before reading an object, and a write lock before updating an object [Gray 1978]. This corresponds to the notion of level-3 consistency in SQL/DS, and protects a transaction from such consistency anomalies as lost updates, dirty read, and unrepeatable read [IBM 1981].

Object-oriented databases require three types of hierarchy locking. One is the conventional granularity-hierarchy locking, to minimize the number of locks to be set. To support granularity locking, a database is modeled as a hierarchy (in general, a directed acyclic graph) of successively smaller entities (commonly called *locking granules*), and an explicit lock on any given node of the hierarchy implies locking of all its descendant nodes. As shown in Fig. 11.4, a database may consist of a number of classes (relations) and indexes on the classes; a class consists of instances, and an index on a class has pointers to instances of the class. For example, when a write (W) lock is set on a class, all instances of the class are implicitly locked in W mode.

[Gray 1978] presents the locking protocol used in SQL/DS for granularity locking. Briefly, to set an R or W lock on a node of the lock-granularity hierarchy, all ancestors of the node are first locked in *intention mode*, either intention read (IR) or intention write (IW), respectively, in a root-to-leaf order. When an explicit lock on a node is released, the intention-mode locks on the ancestors of the node are released in a leaf-to-root order or in any order when the transaction terminates.

The other two types of locking requirements for ORION applications require significant extensions to the current theory of locking. One is the class lattice. In object-oriented systems, a class inherits attributes and methods from its superclasses, which in turn inherit these properties from their superclasses. Therefore, while a class and its instances are being accessed, ORION must

**FIGURE 11.4** HIERARCHY OF LOCK GRANULES

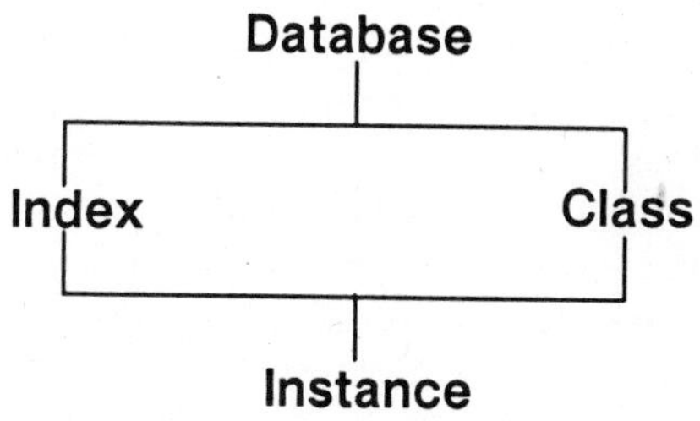

ensure that the definitions of the class's superclasses (and their superclasses) will not be modified.

A second extension to the current theory of locking concerns the composite objects. A composite object is a collection of logically related objects, for example, an assembly of parts, which ORION will treat as a unit of physical clustering, integrity, and locking. Ideally, we should set one lock for the entire composite object, rather than one on each of the component objects.

We have developed and implemented lock modes and locking protocols that satisfy all three types of locking requirements. Further details are given in [Garza and Kim 1988; Kim et al. 1987b]. The current commercial database systems support only one of the three requirements, namely the granularity locking.

### 11.6.3 Recovery

Transaction recovery means preservation of the atomicity property of a transaction. This means that, ideally, despite all possible failures of the computer system, all updates of a committed transaction will be reflected in the database, and all updates of an aborted transaction will be purged from the database. Of course, no database system can support transaction recovery against all possible failures of the computer system, which may include simultaneous failures of the processor, main memory, secondary memory, and communication medium between processors.

Most commercial database systems support database recovery from soft crashes (which leave the contents of disk intact) and hard crashes (which destroy the contents of disk). ORION supports transaction recovery only from soft crashes and user-initiated transaction abort. In other words, ORION does not support archival dumping of the database to recover from disk head crashes. The need to support multiple concurrent transactions led us to select the logging scheme over the shadow-page scheme [Gray et al. 1981]. There are three options in a log-based transaction recovery scheme: maintain only the UNDO log, only the REDO log, or both the UNDO and REDO logs. We have implemented the UNDO logging option, after weighing the advantages and disadvantages of each option.

UNDO logging means that only the "before" values of the attributes of an object will be recorded in the log. If a transaction aborts, the log is read backward to back out all updates. When a transaction commits, the log is first forced to disk, and then all pages updated by the transaction are forced to disk, consistent with the Write Ahead Log protocol [Gray 1978]. Note that the pages containing updated objects are forced to disk: this is necessary because, if the updates remain only in the database buffer and the system crashes, there is no way to re-do them using the UNDO log. This is one drawback of UNDO logging. The other two logging options require only the log pages to be forced to disk.

**Multimedia Data Logging**   [Haskin and Lorie 1982] pointed out that naive use of the logging techniques can cause some serious problems for the long, multimedia data that ORION must support. A strict log-based recovery will keep UNDO and/or REDO logs of very long data. As shown in Fig. 11.5, we distinguish a multimedia datum from its descriptor. The descriptor references, via an object identifier, the multimedia datum. The storage subsystem maintains a list of free storage blocks that may be allocated for storing multimedia data. The long data manager in the object subsystem logs the changes in the descriptors and the free list, but not the multimedia data. In this way, if a transaction that created a multimedia datum aborts, the descriptor will be returned to referencing nil, and the entry in the free list that points to the storage block allocated to the multimedia datum will be reset as available for allocation. Similarly, if a transaction that deleted a multimedia datum aborts, the reference in the descriptor will be returned to its initial value and the free-list entry will be deleted. This technique, proposed in [Haskin and Lorie 1982], achieves the shadowing effect without the complexity associated with the conventional shadowing mechanism [Lorie 1977; Gray et al. 1981].

## 11.7 MULTIMEDIA INFORMATION MANAGEMENT

In ORION we have attempted to satisfy three major design objectives for supporting the capture, storage, and presentation of many types of multimedia information: extensibility, flexibility, and efficiency. The requirement for extensibility (generalizability and modifiability) is the ability of the system developers and end users to extend the system, by adding new types of devices and protocols for the capture, storage, and presentation of multimedia information.

Flexibility refers to fine control over the capture and presentation of multimedia objects. It is important to be able to store and retrieve both one- and two-dimensional multimedia objects, and to transfer multimedia objects into the application workspace or the presentation devices. Further, it is useful

**FIGURE 11.5** LOGGING OF MULTIMEDIA DATA

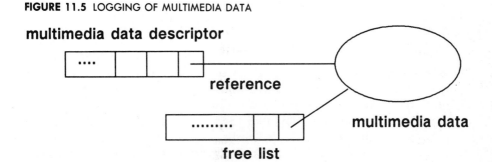

to allow control (such as pause, resume, and rewind) of both the capture and the presentation of multimedia objects.

Efficiency is important in both storage utilization and data transfer performance. Multimedia objects are in general very large, and keeping multiple copies of large objects such as images and audio can lead to a serious waste of secondary storage media. Multimedia applications require the transfer of large amounts of data between capture devices, storage devices, and presentation devices. In some cases, this information will be transferred from a storage device to a presentation device without ever being written to the system memory. In many cases, however, the digitized multimedia object will be buffered in the system memory.

In this section, we further elaborate on these requirements and summarize the approach we have used in ORION to satisfy them. The interested reader will find details in [Woelk and Kim 1987].

### 11.7.1 Extensibility

Extensibility is required to support new multimedia devices and new functions on multimedia information. For example, a color display device may be added to a system with relative ease, if at a high level of abstraction the color display can be viewed as a specialized instance of a general display device that is already supported in the system. The color display device may be further specialized by adding windowing software, and the windows can in turn be specialized to create new display and input functionality. It is also important to be able to add new multimedia storage devices, or to change the operating characteristics of storage devices. For example, read-only CD ROM [CD ROM 1986] disks and write-once digital optical disks [Christodoulakis and Faloutsos 1986] are both storage devices having desirable characteristics for the storage of certain types of multimedia information.

We have implemented the multimedia information manager (MIM) component of ORION as an extensible framework explicitly using object-oriented concepts. The framework consists of definitions of class hierarchies and a message passing protocol not only for the multimedia capture, storage, and presentation devices, but also for the captured and stored multimedia objects. Both the class hierarchies and the protocol may be easily extended and/or modified by system developers and end users as they see fit.

**Class Lattices**    Multimedia information is captured, stored, and presented in ORION using lattices of classes, which represent capture devices, storage devices, captured objects, and presentation devices. However, each instance of one of the device classes represents more than just the identity of a physical device, as we will describe in the following paragraphs. The class lattices for the presentation and storage of multimedia information are described in this section. The class lattice for capture device classes is not described here due to space limitations. The capture device class lattice is described in [Woelk and Kim 1987].

The class lattice for the presentation of multimedia information is described below. The predefined presentation-device instances can be stored in the database and used for presenting the same multimedia object using different presentation formats. Methods associated with a class are used to initialize parameters of a presentation device and initiate the presentation process. The class lattice for the presentation devices as shown in Fig. 11.6. The shaded classes are provided with ORION. Other classes in the lattice are shown to indicate potential specializations for other media types by specific installations.

Every multimedia object stored in ORION is represented by an instance of the class captured-object or one of its subclasses. Figure 11.7 illustrates the class lattice for captured objects. The captured-object class defines an attribute named storage-object, which has as its domain the class storage-device. The class lattices for storage devices and for disk streams are also shown in Fig. 11.7. Transfer of data to and from storage-device instances is controlled through disk-stream instances. An instance of the read-disk-stream class is created whenever a multimedia object is read from disk. The read-disk-stream instance has a storage-object attribute that references the mag-disk-storage-device instance for the multimedia object. It also has a read-block-list attribute, which maintains a cursor indicating the next block of the multimedia object to be read from disk. Similarly, an instance of the write-disk-stream class is created whenever data is written to a multimedia object. The shaded classes in Fig. 11.7 are provided with ORION. Other classes in the lattice indicate potential specializations.

**Message Passing Protocol**   ORION supports presentation of multimedia information using a message-passing protocol between instances of the presentation device, storage device, and stored object classes. The protocol is fully

**FIGURE 11.6** PRESENTATION DEVICE CLASS LATTICE

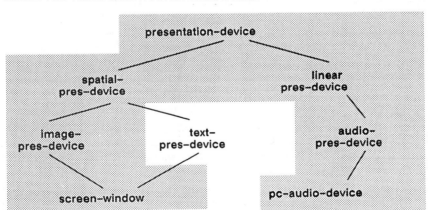

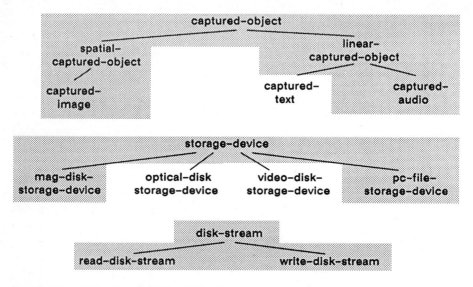

**FIGURE 11.7** CAPTURED-OBJECT, STORAGE-DEVICE, AND DISK STREAM CLASS LATTICES

described in [Woelk and Kim 1987]. In this section we outline the protocol for the presentation of multimedia information. We will present the example of a bit-mapped image; however, the protocol is similar for many types of multimedia information.

Figure 11.8 shows an instance of the vehicle class, which has been defined by an application program. It also shows instances of the image-pres-device, captured-image, read-disk-stream, and mag-disk-storage-device classes described earlier. The arrows represent messages sent from one instance to another instance. The vehicle instance has the image attribute that specifies the identity of a captured-image instance that represents a picture of the vehicle. It also has the display-dev attribute that specifies the identity of an image-pres-device instance. This image-pres-device instance has attributes predefined by the user that specify where the image is to be displayed on the screen and what part of the image should be displayed. When the vehicle instance receives the picture message, the picture method defined for the class vehicle will send a present message to the specified image-pres-device instance.

The present method of the image-pres-device class transfers image data from the captured-image instance and displays the image on a display device. The image-pres-device instance has attributes that specify the rectangular portion of the image to be displayed. It translates these rectangular coordinates into linear coordinates to be used for reading the image data from disk. It then initiates the reading of data by sending the open-for-read message to the captured-image instance.

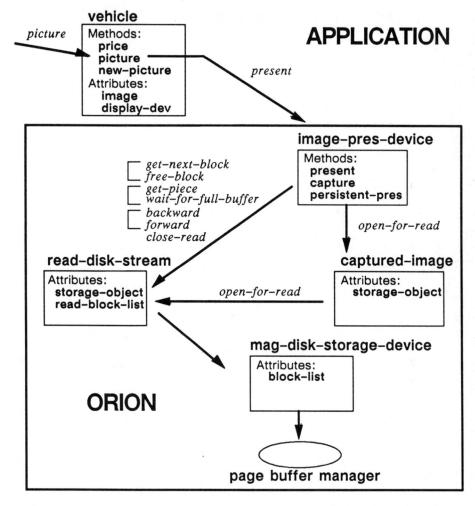

**FIGURE 11.8** MESSAGE PASSING PROTOCOL FOR PRESENTATION OF MULTIMEDIA INFORMATION

The captured-image instance then creates a read-disk-stream instance and returns its identity to the image-pres-device instance. The image-pres-device will then send a get-next-block message to the read-disk-stream.

The read-disk-stream instance calls the ORION page buffer manager to retrieve a block of data from disk. The address of the ORION page buffer containing the block is returned. The image-pres-device instance will transfer the data from the page buffer to a physical presentation device, and then send a free-block message to the read-disk-stream to free the page buffer.

A cursor will also be automatically incremented so that the next get-next-block message will read the next block of the multimedia object. When the data transfer is complete, the image-pres-device sends a close-read message to the read-disk-stream instance.

## 11.7.2 Flexibility

For the purposes of capture, storage and presentation, the MIM supports both one- and two-dimensional multimedia objects. One-dimensional multimedia objects are those with a sequential internal format, such as text or audio. A specific audio passage can be presented by specifying an offset and a length in logical units, such as seconds. Two-dimensional multimedia objects are those with a two-dimensional internal format, for example, a bit-mapped image. The application may identify a specific rectangular portion of an image for presentation by specifying the upper-left corner, height, and width of a rectangle. The MIM translates these values into physical offsets in the disk storage. Some multimedia objects, such as an animated bit-mapped image, can be categorized as both spatial and linear.

The MIM supports two types of transfer of multimedia objects from the database: persistent and nonpersistent, depending on whether the multimedia object remains in the system memory for manipulation by an application after its transfer. An example of nonpersistent presentation is the playing of audio data; the audio information is transferred from the database directly to the audio hardware. The MIM handles the buffering and movement of data. An example of persistent presentation is the display of a bit-mapped image in a window on the screen of the workstation. When the application requests that a selected image be displayed in a specific window, the image is transferred from the database to a specific area in the memory space of the application. Following any modifications made to this area of memory during a transaction, the application can transfer the object back to the database.

Once the transfer of data has begun, the MIM allows the application to control the presentation or capture of multimedia data in a variety of ways. For example, during the playback of audio, the application should be able to cause the playback to pause, continue, fast-forward, fast-backward, play faster, play slower, rewind, and stop.

To allow the application to identify a portion of a multimedia object in logical units (such as seconds), we have defined the captured-object class with attributes that describe the general translation from the storage representation to the presentation representation. They include logical-measure and physical-to-logical-ratio. The logical-measure attribute contains the definition of the logical unit of measurement (such as seconds or frames). The physical-to-logical-ratio attribute indicates the ratio of the physical length to the logical length (such as bytes of digitized audio per second).

The persistent presentation option on a presentation device is set by sending a message. After an image has been displayed and modifications made to the image, the image-pres-device instance can be sent a capture message to write the copy of the image to a captured-image instance.

To provide explicit control over the direction of presentation of multimedia information, our implementation has the presentation-device instance explicitly control the cursor that is maintained by the read-disk-stream.

### 11.7.3 Efficiency

In ORION, a multimedia object is stored in a number of physical storage blocks, such that versions of the multimedia object will share those storage blocks that contain common information, and new storage blocks are allocated only for those portions of the multimedia object that hold different information. As versions of the multimedia object are updated or deleted, storage blocks that are no longer needed are automatically returned to free space for re-allocation to other multimedia objects.

We have optimized data transfer efficiency in ORION by eliminating unnecessary copying of multimedia data as it is transferred between magnetic disk storage and presentation devices in the system. We accomplish this by giving presentation-device instances and capture-device instances the capability to directly manipulate data in the ORION page buffers, thus eliminating the need to copy the data from the page buffers. Further, rather than logging the before or after image of a multimedia object (which is potentially very large), we log only the mag-disk-storage-device instance that has an attribute describing the disk blocks containing the multimedia object. All disk blocks allocated by a mag-disk-storage-device instance during a transaction are automatically deallocated if the transaction aborts. All disk blocks deallocated by a mag-disk-storage-device instance during a transaction are not actually deallocated until the transaction commits.

## SUMMARY

In this chapter, we provided a high-level description of some of the most prominent features of ORION. ORION is a workstation-based prototype object-oriented database system that we have designed and implemented. ORION will of course be a concrete vehicle for evaluating the performance consequences of directly implementing object-oriented concepts in a database system. We expect that ORION will also be a useful vehicle for experimenting with and evaluating various concepts we have developed.

## REFERENCES

[Afsarmanesh et al. 1986] H. Afsarmanesh, D. Knapp, D. McLeod and A. Parker, "An Object-Oriented Approach to VLSI/CAD," *Proceedings of the International Conference on Very Large Data Bases,* August 1985.

[Ahlsen et al. 1984] M. Ahlsen, A. Bjornerstedt, S. Britts, C. Hulten and L. Soderlund, "An Architecture for Object Management in OIS," *ACM Transactions on Office Information Systems,* vol. 2, no. 3, pp. 173–196, July 1984.

[Atwood 1985] T. Atwood, "An Object-Oriented DBMS for Design Support Applications," *Proceedings of the IEEE COMPINT 85,* pp. 299–307, September 1985.

[Bancilhon et al. 1985] F. Bancilhon, W. Kim and H. Korth, "A Model of CAD Transactions," *Proceedings of the International Conference on Very Large Data Bases,* August 1985.

[Banerjee et al. 1987a] J. Banerjee et al., "Data Model Issues for Object-Oriented Applications," *ACM Transactions on Office Information Systems,* January 1987.

[Banerjee et al. 1987b] J. Banerjee, W. Kim, H.J. Kim and H.F. Korth, "Semantics and Implementation of Schema Evolution in Object-Oriented Databases," *Proceedings of the ACM SIGMOD Conference,* 1987.

[Banerjee et al. 1988] J. Banerjee, W. Kim and K.C. Kim, "Queries in Object-Oriented Databases," *Proceedings of the 4th International Conference on Data Engineering,* Los Angeles, CA, February 1988.

[Bobrow and Stefik 1983] D.G. Bobrow and M. Stefik, *The LOOPS Manual,* Xerox PARC, Palo Alto, CA, 1983.

[Bobrow et al. 1985] D.G. Bobrow, et al., *CommonLoops: Merging Common Lisp and Object-Oriented Programming,* Intelligent Systems Laboratory Series ISL-85-8, Xerox PARC, Palo Alto, CA, 1985.

[CD ROM 1986] *CD ROM, The New Papyrus,* S. Lambert and S. Ropiequet, ed., Microsoft Press, Redmond, WA, 1986.

[Chou and Kim 1986] H.T. Chou and W. Kim, "A Unifying Framework for Versions in a CAD Environment," *Proceedings of the International Conference on Very Large Data Bases,* August 1986.

[Chou and Kim 1988] H.T. Chou and W. Kim, "Versions and Change Notification in an Object-Oriented Database System," *Proceedings of the Design Automation Conference,* June 1988.

[Christodoulakis and Faloutsos 1986] S. Christodoulakis and C. Faloutsos, "Design and Performance Considerations for an Optical Disk-Based, Multimedia Object Server," *IEEE Computer,* pp. 45–56, December 1986.

[Garza and Kim 1988] J.F. Garza and W. Kim, "Transaction Management in an Object-Oriented Database System," *Proceedings of the ACM SIGMOD Conference,* 1988.

[Goldberg 1981] A. Goldberg, "Introducing the Smalltalk-80 System," *Byte*, vol. 6, no. 8, pp. 14–26, August 1981.

[Goldberg and Robson 1983] A. Goldberg and D. Robson, *Smalltalk-80: The Language and its Implementation*, Addison-Wesley, Reading, MA, 1983.

[Gray 1978] J.N. Gray, *Notes on Data Base Operating Systems*, IBM Research Report RJ2188, IBM Research, San Jose, CA, 1978.

[Gray et al. 1981] J.N. Gray et al., "The Recovery Manager of a Data Management System," *ACM Computing Surveys*, vol. 13, no. 2, pp. 223–242, June 1981.

[Haskin and Lorie 1982] R. Haskin and R. Lorie, "On Extending the Functions of a Relational Database System," *Proceedings of the ACM SIGMOD Conference*, pp. 207–212, June 1982.

[IBM 1981] *SQL/Data System: Concepts and Facilities*, GH24-5013-0, File No. S370-50, IBM Corporation, January 1981.

[IEEE 1985] *Database Engineering*, IEEE Computer Society, vol. 8, no. 4, December 1985 special issue on Object-Oriented Systems (edited by F. Lochovsky).

[Katz and Lehman 1984] R. Katz and T. Lehman, "Database Support for Versions and Alternatives of Large Design Files," *IEEE Transactions on Software Engineering*, vol. SE-10, no. 2, pp. 191–200, March 1984.

[Katz et al. 1986] R. Katz, E. Chang and R. Bhateja, "Version Modeling Concepts for Computer-Aided Design Databases," *Proceedings of the ACM SIGMOD International Conference on Management of Data*, Washington, D.C., May 1986.

[Kim et al. 1984] W. Kim, D. McNabb, R. Lorie and W. Plouffe, "A Transaction Mechanism for Engineering Design Databases," *Proceedings of the International Conference on Very Large Databases*, Singapore, 1984.

[Kim et al. 1987a] W. Kim, H.T. Chou and J. Banerjee, "Operations and Implementation of Complex Objects," *Proceedings of the Data Engineering Conference*, Los Angeles, CA, 1987.

[Kim et al. 1987b] W. Kim et al., "Composite Object Support in an Object-Oriented Database System," *Proceedings of the Second International Conference on Object-Oriented Programming Systems, Languages, and Applications*, Orlando, FL, October 1987.

[Korth et al. 1988] H. Korth, W. Kim and F. Bancilhon, "On Long-Duration CAD Transactions," *Information Science*, October 1988.

[Lorie 1977] R. Lorie, "Physical Integrity in a Large Segmented Database," *ACM Transactions on Database Systems*, vol. 2, no. 1, pp. 91–104, March 1977.

[Lorie et al. 1983] R. Lorie and W. Plouffe, "Complex Objects and Their Use in Design Transactions," *Databases for Engineering Applications, Database Week 1983 (ACM),* pp. 115–121, May 1983.

[Neumann and Hornung 1982] T. Neumann and C. Hornung, "Consistency and Transactions in CAD Databases," *Proceedings of the International Conference on Very Large Data Bases,* Mexico City, Mexico, September 1982.

[Selinger et al. 1979] P.G. Selinger et al., "Access Path Selection in a Relational Database Management System," *Proceedings of the ACM SIGMOD Conference,* Boston, MA, pp. 23–34, 1979.

[Steele et al. 1984] Guy L. Steele Jr., Scott E. Fahlman, Richard P. Gabriel, David A. Moon and Daniel L. Weinreb, *Common Lisp,* Digital Press, 1984.

[Stefik and Bobrow 1986] M. Stefik and D.G. Bobrow, "Object-Oriented Programming: Themes and Variations," *The AI Magazine,* pp. 40–62, January 1986.

[Stonebraker and Keller 1980] M. Stonebraker and K. Keller, "Embedding Expert Knowledge and Hypothetical Data Bases into a Data Base System," *Proceedings of the ACM SIGMOD Conference on Management of Data,* Santa Monica, CA, pp. 58–66, 1980.

[Stonebraker 1981] M. Stonebraker, "Hypothetical Data Bases as Views," *Proceedings of the ACM SIGMOD Conference on Management of Data,* pp. 224–229, 1981.

[Symbolics 1984] *FLAV Objects, Message Passing, and Flavors,* Symbolics, Inc., Cambridge, MA, 1984.

[Symbolics 1985] *User's Guide to Symbolics Computers,* Symbolics Manual 996015, March 1985.

[Woelk et al. 1986] D. Woelk, W. Kim and W. Luther, "An Object-Oriented Approach to Multimedia Databases," *Proceedings of the ACM SIGMOD Conference on Management of Data,* Washington D.C., May 1986.

[Woelk and Kim 1987] D. Woelk and W. Kim, "Multimedia Information Management in an Object-Oriented Database System," *Proceedings of the International Conference on Very Large Data Bases,* Brighton, England, September 1987.

# 12

# The GemStone Data Management System

Robert Bretl, David Maier, Allen Otis,
Jason Penney, Bruce Schuchardt, Jacob Stein,
E. Harold Williams, Monty Williams

## INTRODUCTION

Servio Logic Corporation has been involved in research and development of object-oriented data management systems since 1983 [Copeland and Maier 1984; Maier et al. 1985; Maier and Stein 1986; Maier et al. 1986]. Our first product, GemStone, merges object-oriented language concepts with those of database management technology [Purdy et al. 1987; Penney et al. 1987; Penney and Stein 1987].

After briefly considering object-oriented extensions to traditional programming languages, our efforts focused on examining Smalltalk's language and data model [Goldberg and Robson 1983]. While there is much to like in Smalltalk, it is lacking in support for database applications, and oriented toward a single user. In addition, we found the language to be geared toward small objects, and thought that many of the previous implementation techniques would not scale up in a disk-based environment. Therefore, we decided to develop a disk-based storage manager and an object-oriented database language called OPAL, which rectifies these deficiencies in Smalltalk and is used for data definition, data manipulation, and general computation.

Section 1 discusses the advantages of the Smalltalk paradigm. In Section 2, its deficiencies and the functional extensions needed for a data management system are examined. The manner in which GemStone addresses these deficiences and provides data management extensions is presented in Section 3. Section 4 discusses associative access. Finally, in Section 5, we present our approach to schema modification.

## 12.1 LANGUAGE

Initially we developed a mostly declarative query language; however, it was deficient in procedural capabilities needed to model the update behavior of real-world entities. Thereafter, object-oriented extensions to traditional programming languages, such as C and Pascal, were briefly considered. However, compiling and linking does not lend itself to rapid and flexible prototyping. Furthermore, while we acknowledge the potential performance benefits of such extensions, we note three countervailing arguments. First, there is the potential for wild stores into portions of virtual memory used for object space. While compilation-time type checking can catch most unintended stores into these portions of virtual memory, the free use of pointers in languages such as C makes it impossible to prevent wild stores, even in mature code. Wild stores are much more destructive in persistent languages than they are in nonpersistent ones: their effects persist beyond the execution of the program and may not show up until long after the program has completed. Second, the potential performance benefits are not needed for many application areas, particularly those where development and maintenance costs have traditionally been high. Third, we believe that Smalltalk systems as well as GemStone will improve their runtime performance as they mature.

Given the problems with providing object-oriented extensions and educating users to a completely new language, we chose to follow the Smalltalk paradigm in developing OPAL. Other object-oriented languages support many of the features of Smalltalk such as identity, inheritance hierarchies, modeling of complex objects, and behavior encapsulation. Two of the main reasons for choosing Smalltalk over the alternatives are discussed here.

### 12.1.1 Intensional Semantics

While Smalltalk provides an **allInstances** message to enumerate the elements of a class, the semantics of classes are not extensional. A class describes the intended use of its instances by describing their structure and behavior, and is in this sense *intensional*. A class does not serve to denote the collection of all its instances, its *extension*.

The intensional nature of Smalltalk classes is witnessed by its deletion semantics. Smalltalk has no explicit deletion mechanism. The space for an object is subject to reclamation only if the object is no longer reachable through references from other objects starting from a special root collection of objects. Thus, once a reference exists, it will continue to be valid. The **allInstances** message can return instances that are no longer reachable but whose space has not been reclaimed. The primary usefulness of **allInstances** is in performing schema modification (as we will discuss later).

In the relational world, where there is rarely more than one relation on a given schema, relation schemata may be considered extensional. In an object-oriented environment, the semantics and usefulness of extensional schemata are not as clear. For example, should a class's extension include instances of its subclasses? We expect there to be multiple explicit collections of instances of a given class. The expectation is even greater in a shared environment where several users or independent applications may maintain separate, possibly disjoint, collections of instances. It is these collections over which users will enumerate, not all instances of a class.

Relational systems have difficulty in managing dangling tuples and supporting referential integrity. This difficulty stems in no small part from the extensional semantics of relational schemata. Referential integrity comes "for free" in Smalltalk. One object refers directly to another object, not to a name for that object. The reference cannot be created if the other object does not exist, and the referenced object will exist as long as the reference to it is maintained.

The alternative of allowing objects to be explicitly deleted makes the enforcement of referential integrity extremely difficult. Systems that do not support referential integrity can attempt to "fix" dangling references by removing them or taking some other corrective action. Such corrective actions almost always involve locating those objects containing dangling references or maintaining a record of all references to an object.

From a semantic point of view, explicit deletion can be dangerous, especially in the shared environment of GemStone. For example, developing a consistent authorization mechanism would be problematic: cleaning up references to deleted objects would effectively require writing all referring objects in order to remove the reference. From a performance point of view, we see no inherent advantage of fixing dangling references over garbage collection. Lastly, note that most, if not all, of the advantages of extensional classes can be achieved by controlling the propagation of references to instances of a class.

## 12.1.2 Associating Types with Objects

Unlike most programming languages that support abstract data types, Smalltalk associates types with values, not the slots holding the values. We now consider some of the advantages of such typing.

We want to help database designers to model application domains they previously may have shied away from because of complexity or lack of regular structure. However, modeling an enterprise for the first time is a much different undertaking than building a database application for an area that has already been modeled but has not yet been computerized. The basic modeling for financial record keeping was done long before computers, and the structure of the information involved readily fits into standard record-based data models. A development schedule based on schema definition, application writing, database population, and debugging is reasonable. Not so with a CAD task being modeled for the first time, or a database to support an expert system. The application area has not been modeled before, and there will be many iterations of the database schema before the application is mature [Albano et al. 1985; Albano and Orsini 1984; Maier and Price 1984]. Being able to start writing database routines without completely specifying the structure and behavior of every class of entities can be of great advantage. By associating types with values, expressions can still be type-checked (at run time), and the designer still retains flexibility in object structure. Typing objects also supports polymorphism, as a procedure need not assume anything about the structure of the value of a variable, only that it responds to a certain message.

## 12.2 Deficiencies and Extensions

Smalltalk is generally implemented as a single-user, memory-based, single-processor system. It does not meet the requirements of a database system. While Smalltalk provides a powerful user interface and many tools for application development, it is oriented to a single-user workstation. To meet the requirements of a database system, the following enhancements are needed.

### 12.2.1 Name Spaces

Smalltalk assumes a single user per image and so provides a single global name space. It is unreasonable to expect either that users share a single global name space, or that user name spaces are disjoint. An effective mechanism for the controlled sharing of multiple name spaces must be provided.

### 12.2.2 Concurrency Control

A data management system must provide concurrent access. We want each user to see a uniform and consistent version of the database, even with other users running simultaneously. By *uniform* we mean that there is no distinction in the language between temporary and persistent objects, unlike a conventional database application environment with a hard division between structures in the programming language and structures in the database. In GemStone, any object is potentially persistent, dependent only on reachability from a database root. By *consistent* we mean that the programmer operates on a snapshot of the database in which only that programmer's changes to objects are visible; the actions of others cannot affect the progress of his program. Of course, in a shared system, this ideal of privacy can only be approximated because other programs are changing the database.

Control of visibility is not the only additional requirement in a shared system. The changes that individual programs make may conflict, so some mechanism is required either to *prevent* conflicting actions during transaction execution (pessimistic concurrency control) or to *discard* conflicting updates when a transaction attempts to commit (optimistic concurrency control).

Depending on the degree of contention on an object, either pessimistic or optimistic concurrency control can be appropriate. When contention is high, pessimistic concurrency control reduces wasted effort in aborting transactions at the expense of managing locks. When contention is low, optimistic concurrency control maximizes concurrency, and the control mechanism is transparent to programs in the absence of conflict. In addition, read-only transactions should not cause conflict.

Objects in GemStone may be viewed as spanning a continuum from objects that correspond to values of variables in traditional programming languages to those that correspond to design objects as may be found in VLSI databases. Contention is unlikely on objects that correspond to program variables. Imposing pessimistic concurrency control on objects at this end of the continuum is an unnecessary burden. Contention is more likely on objects at the other end of the continuum. In the case of design objects, the amount of work that must be undone when contention is detected may be unacceptable. For such objects, pessimistic concurrency control is more desirable.

We note an alternative solution to the problem of transactions losing work in an optimistic system. This solution is to allow all transactions to commit and to create multiple versions of objects when conflicts arise [Ecklund et al. 1987]. This approach defers the difficulty in resolving between nonserializable updates of the database. Nonserializable versions must explicitly be merged to get back to a single "current" version.

## 12.2.3 Data Integrity

Various kinds of failures (program, processor, media) and violations (consistency, access, typing) can compromise the validity and integrity of a database. A database system must be able to cope with failure by restoring the database to a consistent state, and should prevent violations from occurring.

By *program failure* we mean that an application program may fail to complete, say, because of a run-time error. By *processor failure*, we mean that the processor handling GemStone storage management fails. For such failures, the database must be kept intact. By *media failure* we mean that disk flaws may cause committed data to be lost. Protecting against the first two kinds of failure requires that copies of objects on disk be kept consistent and updated carefully, while the third type of failure requires replication of objects on disk.

The integrity of a database can be violated if a user accesses data that he or she should not be permitted to see. In Smalltalk, all objects are available to the user. A data management system must provide means for assigning ownership and access privileges to objects. Integrity constraints, such as uniqueness of keys and referential integrity, are assertions that a priori exclude certain states of the database. At a minimum, the database should support constraints that require fields of an object or the elements of a collection to be of a certain class.

## 12.2.4 Large Object Space

A data management system must store both large numbers of objects and objects that are large in size. In most Smalltalk implementations the number and size of objects are limited by the size of main or virtual memory. (LOOM [Kaehler and Krasner 1983] relaxes this limitation on the number, but not the size, of objects.) Large disk-based objects require new storage techniques. Some objects will be too large to fit in main memory, and must be paged in. While virtual-memory implementations page large objects, we saw the need for more sophisticated disk formats for large objects to avoid fragmentation of storage and expensive update operations.

In Smalltalk, to "grow" an object, such as an array, a new, larger object is created and the contents of the smaller object are copied into it. If the object to be grown is a **Set**, or subclass thereof, then a rehashing of every element of the set may be required. The time required to update or extend an object should be proportional to the size of the update or extension, *not* to the size of the object being updated. Simple hashing does not scale up to handle sets of the size that a database management system must be able to represent efficiently. The basic operations of union, intersection, and difference become prohibitively expensive. Additionally, Smalltalk hashes set elements by value, not identity, and provides no trigger mechanism to rehash an object in the set(s) to which it belongs when the object's value changes. For these reasons, Smalltalk's repertoire of basic storage representations was inadequate for supporting large collections.

Most Smalltalk implementations include a **become:** message, which interchanges the identity of two objects. For example, after executing **A become: B**, all references to **A** refer to **B** and vice versa. Its primary use is in growing objects, changing the class of an object, and atomic update. For example, to cause an instantaneous update of a displayed object **C**, a Smalltalk method would make a copy **D** of **C**, perform changes on **D**, then execute **C become: D**. Its side effects are difficult to anticipate and control, in particular with regard to maintaining constraints such as instance variable typing. The use of the **become:** message is not desirable in a disk-based environment. Rather, other mechanisms can support, in a more efficient and tractable manner, the features that **become:** is used to implement.

Searching a long collection by a sequential scan will give unacceptable performance with a disk-based object. Thus, a data management system should support associative access on elements of large collections: It should supply storage representations and auxiliary structures to support locating an element by its internal state. Searching for elements should be at most logarithmic in the size of the collection, rather than linear. This requirement reinforces the need for typing on collections and instance variables. To index a collection **E** of employees on the value of the **salary** instance variable, the system needs assurances that every element in **E** has a **salary** entry. Furthermore, if that index is to support range queries on **salary**, the system needs a declaration that all **salary** values will be comparable according to some total order. Along with storage-level support for associative access, language constructs that allow associative access must be introduced.

### 12.2.5 Physical Storage Management

A disk-based system must provide features for managing the physical placement of objects on disk. Smalltalk is a memory-resident system, and so there is no need to say where an object goes. The database administrator, or an application programmer, should be able to specify that certain objects are often used together and so should be clustered on the disk. The administrator should be able to take objects offline, say for archiving, and bring them back online later.

## 12.3 OUR APPROACH

This section describes how we addressed the deficiencies of Smalltalk in the design of GemStone.

### 12.3.1 Name Spaces

Multiple name spaces are managed by GemStone. Instances of class **UserProfile** are used to represent properties of each user, including a list of dictionaries (identifier-object mappings) that are used to resolve symbols when compiling OPAL code for that user. When an identifier is encountered in OPAL code, and that identifier is neither an instance variable nor a class variable, the dictionaries are searched in order to find an object corresponding to that identifier. There may be any number of dictionaries for a user, to accommodate various degrees of sharing. For example, a programmer's first dictionary may contain objects and classes for his or her portion of a project, the second may be for objects shared with other programmers working on the same project, and the third could contain system objects.

## 12.3.2 Workspaces

GemStone supports multiple concurrent users by providing each user session with a workspace. Whenever a session modifies an object, a shadow copy of that object is created. The shadow copy is inaccessible to other sessions until the transaction is committed. One of the advantages of shadowing over logging is that different consistent versions of the database may be accessed by different transactions. An alternative approach to shadowing in an object-oriented database system is given by Thatte [Thatte 1986].

## 12.3.3 Transactions and Recovery

Aborting a transaction means throwing away objects shadowed in the workspace, and committing means replacing shared objects with their shadow. The only major requirement is that the operation be atomic—that the changes of a transaction are made, seemingly, all at once.

Our unit of recovery is a transaction. Changes made by committed transactions are kept, and changes not yet committed are lost. Because the shared version of the database is never overwritten, logs are not needed to bring the database to a consistent state, since it never leaves one. The real work on recovery is garbage collection: removing detritus of the transactions that had not committed before the crash.

To guard against media failure, we have introduced a structure called a *repository*. Every object resides in some repository. (Currently, all objects reside in a single repository.) A repository is the unit of replication. A repository may be taken offline, which means all its objects become inaccessible. **Repository** is an OPAL class providing an internal representation for repositories. A **Repository** instance can respond to a message **replicate**, which means that two (or more, if desired) copies of the repository will be maintained on-line (at increased cost in time and space). The copies know about each other, and if the medium for one fails, the other is still available.

## 12.3.4 Concurrency Control

GemStone provides both optimistic and pessimistic concurrency control. In this manner a session may operate optimistically on objects that are unlikely to produce conflict, thus avoiding the overhead of locking, and pessimistically on objects that are likely to produce conflict. For our initial implementation, optimistic concurrency control was chosen because it is transparent to programs in the absence of conflict and it favors readers over writers. It is our belief that it is easier to implement a pessimistic scheme on top of an optimistic one than vice-versa. In addition, we believe that pessimistic concurrency control alone is not sufficient for an object-oriented system.

We first describe the optimistic aspect of GemStone's concurrency control, which takes advantage of the shadows supported by our resiliency mechanism. For each transaction, GemStone keeps track of which objects the transaction has read or written. At commit time, GemStone checks for read-write and write-write conflicts with transactions that have committed since the time the transaction began. If there are none, the transaction commits by merging its changes with those of other transactions that have committed since the transaction began.

This optimistic scheme is transparent to the application, and ensures that read-only transactions never conflict with other transactions. Such a transaction gets a consistent copy of the database state, does its reading, and has no changes to make to shared objects on commit. This scheme never deadlocks, as a session experiences no contention with other sessions before a commit point.

GemStone's pessimistic concurrency control merges seamlessly with its optimistic concurrency control. Transactions that run optimistically do not have to contend with locks, and a transaction can access some objects pessimistically while accessing others optimistically. The abstraction for atomically merging updates into the shared database remains the mechanism for transaction commit.

The equivalent serial ordering of transactions that have successfully committed is the same as the order in which the commits were processed. Although there may be other orderings that allow greater concurrency (more successful commits), reordering is not attempted.

Under our optimistic methodology, a transaction can fail to commit because of two types of contention.

1. Read-Write Conflict: A transaction $A$ that reads an object $O$ and writes another object will conflict on $O$ if another transaction has written $O$ and committed since $A$ began.

2. Write-Write Conflict: A transaction $A$ that writes an object $O$ will conflict on $O$ if another transaction has written $O$ and committed since $A$ began.

Locking an object assures that neither of the above conflicts will occur. Read locks prevent conflict of the first type. Write locks prevent conflict of the second type. A transaction that holds either a read or write lock on an object is guaranteed that the object will not be written. From the viewpoint of a transaction that is running optimistically on the object, neither lock will affect its ability to access the object and commit prior to the locking transaction if the transaction does not write the object. Multiple transactions may hold a read lock on an object. Only a single transaction may hold a write lock on an object. An object may not be simultaneously read locked and write locked.

To an optimistic transaction, a read or write lock is indistinguishable from an actual read or write. Locks do not change the view of the world given to optimistic transactions. New objects are always created optimistically, as there can be no conflict on the object. However, storing references to newly created objects may cause concurrency conflict on the referencing object.

Note that our write locks differ from traditional write locks in that the locked object may be read optimistically. In addition to allowing greater concurrency and making the lock transparent to an optimistic transaction, this interpretation is consistent with our optimistic concurrency control. Also note that a transaction that uses locks is still governed by the optimistic control mechanisms. The locks are simply a means to guarantee that, with regard to the locked objects, the transaction will pass the criteria for commit under GemStone's optimistic mechanism.

In addition to supporting long transactions, pessimistic concurrency control is also useful for class modification. A class object describes the structure and behavior of all of its instances. Changes to the behavior require no modification of instances, but there is an interobject constraint that the structure of any object match the template set forth in its class. It is not sufficient that a tool for class modification update all the instances visible in its session; concurrent sessions may be creating new instances of the class using the template in the old class definition.

Enforcing such a constraint is easy in a system where locking is the only means of concurrency control. In such a system, a write lock on the class would not allow another transaction to create an instance of the class. However, our write-locks allow concurrent reads, which are all that a transaction needs to create an instance of the class. *Exclusive* locks handle this scenario. If an exclusive lock on an object is held by a transaction, the only other transactions that can access the object and successfully commit are read-only transactions. If a transaction holds an exclusive lock on an object, then no other transaction may hold any locks on the object. In particular, if a class object is exclusive-locked, no other transaction may create an instance of it, since the class object must be examined in order to create the instance.

## 12.3.5 Authorization

*Segments* are the logical units of ownership and authorization. Every user has at least one segment, and when he or she creates new objects, they go in an owned segment. Segments have no upper bound on the number of objects they can contain, other than the number of objects in the system. A user may grant read or write permission on a segment to other users. Such grants must always come from the original owner. Read or write permission on a segment implies the same permission on all objects assigned to the segment.

There are some subtleties of read and write permission in an object model. First, having the identity of an object (its OOP) is not the same as reading the object. Second, having permission on an object does not imply having permission on all its subobjects. So, for example, an **Employee** object, along with the values for instance variables **empName**, **ssNo**, and **address**, could reside in one segment. By putting a **SalaryHistory** object in another segment, authorization can be granted to just a portion of an employee's personnel information.

## 12.3.6 Path Expressions and Typing in OPAL

In order to facilitate associative access, OPAL supports instance variable typing and paths.

**Typing**   In OPAL, constraints on the values of named instance variables may be specified when creating classes. Each named instance variable may be constrained by declaring a *class-kind*, which is a class, for the variable. In an instance of class *C*, each named instance variable, for which a class-kind is specified in *C*, may only have a value that is either **nil** or a kind of[1] the class-kind specified.

Class-kind constraints are inherited through the class hierarchy, and can be made more restrictive in a subclass. Consider a class, **Employee**. Suppose instance variable **name**'s class-kind is **PersonName**. If **TitledPerson** were a subclass of **Employee**, then the class-kind of **name** could be a subclass of **PersonName**, say, **TitledPersonName**.

A class-kind constraint may be specified for subclasses of **Bag** or **Set**. A **Bag** or **Set** instance may contain only members that are **nil** or match the specified class-kind. Such a constraint is declared in the class of the collection, which means that a subclass of **Bag** or **Set** must be created to support instances with typed elements. Consider class **Employee** discussed above. By creating a subclass **EmpSet** of **Set** whose class-kind is **Employee**, sets can be created that contain only **nil** and objects that are a kind of **Employee**. Class-kind constraints for collections are inherited by subclasses. In the same manner as for named instance variables, class-kind constrains can be made more restrictive in subclasses. For example, a class **SetOfEmployee** whose class-kind is **Employee** can have a subclass **SetOfManager**, whose class-kind is **Manager**, since **Manager** is a subclass of **Employee**.

**Path Expressions**   A *path expression* (or simply a *path*) is a variable name followed by a sequence of zero or more instance variable names called *links*. The variable name appearing in a path is called the *path prefix*; the sequence

---

[1] An object *O* is a *kind of* its class and its class's superclasses.

of links, the *path suffix*. The value of a path expression $A.L_1.L_2.\cdots.L_n$ is defined as follows:

1. If $n = 0$, then the value of the path expression is the value of $A$.

2. If $n > 0$, then the value of the path expression is the value of instance variable $L_n$ within the value of $A.L_1.L_2.\cdots.L_{n-1}$ if $A.L_1.L_2.\cdots.L_{n-1}$ is defined and $L_n$ is an instance variable in the value of $A.L_1.L_2.\cdots.L_{n-1}$. Otherwise, the value of the path expression is undefined.

A path suffix $S$ is *defined with respect to* a path prefix $P$ if the value of $P.S$ is defined.

Consider a variable **anEmp** whose value is an instance of **Employee**. The value of the path **anEmp.name** is defined if **name** is an instance variable defined in **Employee**. Its value would be the value of **anEmp**'s **name** instance variable. The value of **anEmp.name.first** is defined if the value of **anEmp.name** is defined and **first** is an instance variable in the value of **anEmp.name**. Its value would be the value of instance variable **first** in the value of **anEmp.name**.

Path expressions may be used anywhere in OPAL that an expression is allowed, but normally appear only in associative selection queries.

## 12.3.7 Large Object Space

In designing GemStone, we have tried always to set limits on object numbers and sizes so that physical storage limits will be encountered first. A GemStone system can support $2^{31}$ objects ($2^{32}$ counting instances of **SmallInteger**) and an object can have up to $2^{31}$ instance variables.

When an object is larger than a page, the object is broken into pieces and organized as a tree spanning several pages. A large object can be accessed and updated without bringing all the pages of an object into a workspace. The tree structure for large objects makes it possible to update pieces of them without rewriting the whole object, much as for the object table. Since pages of a large object need not be contiguous in secondary storage, such objects can grow and shrink with no need to recopy the entire object. A similar means for storing large objects is used in EXODUS [Carey et al. 1986].

GemStone supports five basic storage formats for objects: *self identifying* (e.g., **SmallInt, Character, Boolean**), *byte* (e.g., **String, Float**), *named, indexed,* and *nonsequenceable collections*. The byte format is used for classes whose instances may be considered unstructured (structure is imposed by the methods that operate on the objects). The named format supports access to the components of an object by unique identifiers, instance variable names. The indexed format supports access to the components of an object by number, as in instances of class **Array**. This format supports, without copying, both insertions of components into the middle of an object and growth to accommodate more components. The nonsequenceable collection (NSC) format is used for collection classes, such as **Bag** and **Set**, in which instance variables are *anonymous*: members of such collections are not identified by name or index, but a collection can be queried for membership, and have members added, removed or enumerated.

We feel that main- and virtual-memory-based Smalltalk systems could benefit from the extensions GemStone has made to the basic object storage model. Smalltalk implementations with increased numbers of OOPs already exist. Supporting objects that can grow or shrink dynamically avoids a great deal of the copying that current Smalltalk implementations do. In applications that require large objects, the overhead for copying is more onerous.

The basic data formats that an object management system provides should support reasonably direct and efficient implementations of user-defined data types. We feel that at least three types of basic data structuring mechanisms are required: *sequencing* (records), *iteration* (arrays), and *collections* (sets). Our thesis is that no two of these structuring primitives can efficiently simulate the third. Relational database systems support only sequencing and collections, and must encode arrays. Smalltalk supports sequencing and iterations, and encodes sets. GemStone supports all three.

### 12.3.8 GemStone Architecture

A GemStone system consists of a database monitor, GemStone sessions, and application interfaces. The database monitor allocates OOP and disk pages, and serves as a critical region monitor for commits and aborts. For each client application, there is one GemStone session. Each GemStone session provides the full functionality of GemStone. Application interfaces exist for C, Parc Place Smalltalk-80, and Smalltalk/V. In addition, there is a command line interface called Topaz that provides direct access to the full functionality of the system.

Figure 12.1 shows a possible configuration of a GemStone system. Currently, a VAX, SUN3, or SUN4 may serve as the host. Supported workstations include IBM-PCs and compatibles, Apple Macintosh IIs, SUN3s, SUN4s, Tektronix 4300 series workstations, and Tektronix 4400 series workstations. When using SUN3s or SUN4s as workstations, GemStone sessions may be run on either the host computer or the client workstation. Location transparency is provided in that the client need not be aware of whether the GemStone session is resident or running on the host. The ability to run GemStone sessions on client workstations or the host in a mixed SUN environment is our first step toward full heterogeneous network support.

## 12.4 ASSOCIATIVE ACCESS IN GEMSTONE

The basic problem in associative access is to efficiently select from a collection those members meeting a selection criterion. For example, one may want to

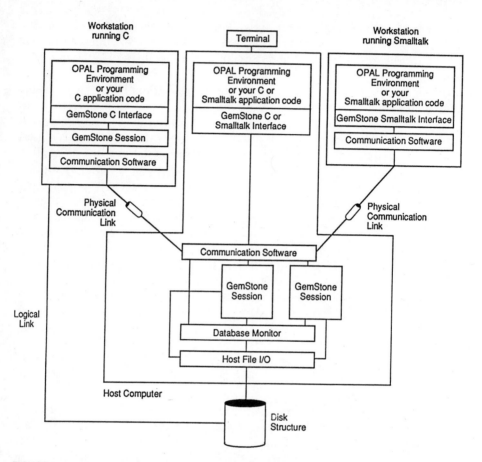

**FIGURE 12.1** CONFIGURATION OF A GEMSTONE SYSTEM

find all objects that contain a given object as the value of a particular instance variable. One can index on instance variables that are nested several levels deep in an object to be indexed, such as the **manager** variable of the **Department** object that fills an **Employee**'s **worksIn** variable. The **manager** of a **Department** object can change with no change being apparent in an **Employee** object that references that **Department** object. This localization of change influences the complexity of index maintenance.

In GemStone, a class defines the structure of its instances, but rarely keeps track of all those instances. Instead, collection objects—**Arrays**, **Bags**, **Sets**—serve to group those instances. An object may belong to more than one collection, unlike relational, hierarchical, or network models, where a record belongs to a single relation, parent, or set. Such multiple membership is allowed in the hybrid relational-network model [Haynie 1981].

## 12.4.1 Issues

In this section, the issues the GemStone model presents with respect to associative access and indexing are elaborated.

**Structure Versus Behavior**   A major issue is whether indexes are based on the structure (the instance variables) of objects, or the behavior (the responses to messages). If indexes are based on message notation, GemStone must know which structural changes in an object can influence the result of a message, so that it knows when to update the appropriate indexes. Indexing based on structure has the advantage that it can be supported without accessing the execution model, while message-based indexing requires access to the methods used in responding to messages. Indexing on structure violates the privacy of objects, as it bypasses an object's behavior.

**Index Structure**   If we want to index objects on their internal structure, one concern is how deep to index. Are only the immediate instance variables of an object indexed, or are indexes on instance variables of instance variables allowed?

Should an index be based on identities of key objects or their values? An identity index is immune to changes in the key object's state. However, an identity index on **Strings** will not support range queries. On the other hand, in an index on **String** objects that is sorted by their contents, changes to the characters of one of the **String** objects must be detected by GemStone and reflected in the index. If the programmer supplies a method for the comparison, how do we know it is transitive?

If we do index on paths with multiple links, there is the choice of a single index for the whole path, or several indexes, one for each link. For **anEMP.worksIn.manager**, there could be one index on **worksIn.manager** mapping managers directly to the employees they manage, or one index on **worksIn** mapping departments to employees, and another on **manager**, mapping managers to departments.

**Indexing on Classes versus Collections**   Another decision to be made in designing associative access is what to index, classes or collections. Several applications can use instances of the same class, and store them in different collections. For example, if an application wants to index **Employee** objects on their last names, should it build one index on all instances of **Employee**, or an individual index on each collection of **Employee**s it uses? If an application that uses only a subset of the **Employee** objects builds an index on the whole **Employee** class, then any other application that uses **Employee** objects pays the overhead of maintaining the index on updates.

Indexing a collection allows the possibility that instances of subclasses be included in a collection that is indexed. For example, a last name index could be built on a collection of instances of **Person** and its subclasses, such as **Employee, StockHolder**, and **Manager**. Indexing on a class basis makes it easier to trace changes to the state of an object that could cause the object to be positioned differently within an index. The implementation of a class-based index could include triggers on methods that update instance variables relevant to the index.

Another consideration with class-based indexing is whether the index includes subclasses. For example, should a last-name index on **Person** include all **Employee** and **StockHolder** objects? Having a separate index for each class would complicate access when a user wanted to query over the combined classes. A single combined index may impose performance overhead on a query against instances of a single class.

### 12.4.2 Indexing in OPAL

In OPAL, only nonsequenceable collections (NSCs) support indexes, and only when proper typing exists for the path being indexed [Maier and Stein 1986]. By so requiring type information, the access path that an index represents can be determined at the time of index creation, using only class objects; there is no need to recompute the access path represented by a path expression for each element of an NSC. GemStone's indexing mechanism supports indexes into collections that contain instances of subclasses, such as an index on last names into an NSC constrained to hold **Persons** that also contain **StockHolders** and **Employees.**

OPAL supports two kinds of indexes: identity and equality. Since the identity of an object is independent of its class, identity indexes support only the search operators $==$ (identical to) and $\sim\sim$ (not identical to). Equality indexes support the search operators $=$, $\sim=$, $<$, $<=$, $>$, and $>=$. Not every class supports these operators, which means constraints on paths for equality indexes are stricter than those for identity indexes. Consider class **Employee** discussed earlier. In addition to instance variable **name**, let **address** be an instance variable defined in **Employee** that is constrained to **Address**. Further, in **Address** let **state** be an instance variable constrained to **String** and let **zip** be an instance variable constrained to **SmallInteger**. In **SetOfEmployee** objects, either identity or equality indexes can be created on the suffixes **name.first**, **address.state**, and **address.zip**. Identity indexes can be created on **address, name**, the empty path, and possibly other paths.

Indexes on paths are implemented by a sequence of index components, one for each link in the path suffix. For an index into a **SetOfEmployee** object on **name.last**, there would be an index component from **name** values of elements of the **SetOfEmployee** object to those elements, and a component from **last** values of **PersonName** objects to those **PersonNames** that are the **name** value of some element of the **SetOfEmployee** object.

All data structures used in implementing indexes are stored in object space, and so are managed by GemStone. In this manner, OPAL's concurrency control mechanism handles concurrency conflicts on index structures. Currently, index components are implemented using B$^+$-trees ordered on the type of the corresponding link.

The component for the last link in an identity index is ordered on OOP. In the component for the last link in an equality index, the ordering of key values is determined by the class-kind of the key values. If the path suffixes of two indexes have a common prefix, then the indexes will share index components. For example, **address.state** and **address.zip** on the same collection can share the **address** component.

Objects in GemStone may be tagged by the system with a *dependency list*. Objects that participate in an index component have that component in their dependency list. Dependency lists aid in maintaining indexes when objects are updated.

**The Query Language**   We have chosen to provide associative access through a limited calculus sublanguage. However, we have been careful in constructing the language so that associative queries can be viewed as procedural OPAL code. GemStone supports selection on collections with NSC implementations—subclasses of **Set** and **Bag**. Selection conditions are conjunctions of comparisons, where the comparisons are between path expressions and other path expressions or literals. While simple conjunctive selections might seem limited, in an object-oriented model there is no need for many of the joins used in relational systems, as these joins often serve to recompose entities that were decomposed for data normalization. Most joins are replaced by path-tracing, which GemStone supports.

An associative query is a variation on a **select** expression. Suppose an **Employee** object also has a **worksIn** instance variable whose class-kind is **Department**. The following query, where **Emps** is a collection of employees, will make use of all indexes available on the paths in the terms of the query.

```
Emps select:
    {anEmp | anEmp.name.last = 'Jones' &
    anEmp.salary > anEmp.worksIn.manager.salary}
```

We have extended all of OPAL to allow path expressions. The meaning of the previous query is the same as for the corresponding OPAL expression within a regular **block**:

```
Emps select:
    [anEmp | anEmp.name.last = 'Jones' &
    anEmp.salary > anEmp.worksIn.manager.salary]
```

In comparison with conventional DBMSs, where a declarative query language is often embedded in a procedural programming language, there is little impedance mismatch between OPAL and its query sublanguage.

## 12.5 SCHEMA MODIFICATION

A major consideration in designing a schema modification methodology is how to bring existing objects in line with a modified class. One approach, screening, is to defer (possibly indefinitely) modifying the persistent store; values are either filtered or corrected before they are used. Skarra and Zdonik [Skarra and Zdonik 1987] explore an approach in which filters are placed between instances of an older version of a class and methods that expect instances of a newer version of the class. The ORION system [Banerjee et al. 1987] employs persistent screening on objects presented to an application; the representations of objects are corrected as they are used.

The other approach, conversion, changes all instances of the class to the new class definition, ensuring that auxiliary definitions (such as a class's methods) agree with the new definition. The two approaches offer the choice of "pay me now or pay me later." In the screening approach, execution speed is compromised by screening. In the conversion approach, much time can be consumed at the time a class is modified.

As the ORION mechanism exploits screening, we have focused our research efforts on conversion. Our goal is to develop a flexible mechanism in which either screening or conversion may be used as appropriate. Furthermore, we would like to provide a hybrid mechanism in which screening is used until garbage collection is performed. At that time, the remaining instances of modified classes would be converted.

What follows is an exploration of a conversion-only mechanism for GemStone that we hope to integrate later with screening to achieve our goal. A more detailed discussion of our work may be found elsewhere [Penney and Stein 1987].

### 12.5.1 Invariants of Schema Modification

In this section, we discuss those invariants of GemStone that must be preserved across schema modifications. The *Full Inheritance* and *Class-Kind* invariants are similar to invariants specified for ORION [Banerjee et al. 1987].

**Representation Invariant**    The representation of an object is determined by its class. An object's storage format, size, variables, and constraints upon those variables must be as specified by the object's class.

**Class Hierarchy Invariant**    Classes and the subclass relation form a hierarchy (a tree). By the definition of a tree, there are no disconnected components, and each class, with the exception of the root, has a unique superclass. Class **Object** is the root of the hierarchy.

**Full Inheritance Invariant** The representation of instances determined by a class is inherited by all of its subclasses. For example, all subclasses of an indexable class are indexable (e.g., class **String** is indexable; hence, its subclass **Symbol** is also indexable). Additionally, with the exception of class **Bag**, the superclass of every NSC class is an NSC class. Every class inherits every instance variable defined in its superclass.

**Class-Kind Constraint** The constraint on an inherited variable (named, indexed or anonymous) must be consistent with the constraint in the superclass. The constraint on an inherited variable must be the same as, or a subclass of, the constraint in the superclass.

**Dangling Reference Constraint** There are no dangling references in GemStone. The value of a variable is a reference to an object. There are no references to nonexistent objects. Therefore, the value of an object must be maintained as long as the object is reachable from the persistent database.

**Information Loss Constraint** Information is preserved. When a user holds a reference to an object, then both the reference and the object itself are retained for the user.

The information loss constraint bears additional discussion. GemStone does not allow explicit deletion. The system guarantees that both the values of variables and the objects referenced by the values are retained, unless a user with adequate authorization either removes the reference or otherwise makes it unreachable by the user. Note that this is stronger than the dangling reference constraint, which does not prohibit removing references.

It is possible for a schema modification to affect objects to which the user may have no rights. For example, a user may drop an instance variable from a class while one of its instances is owned by another user. By receiving a complete report to the initiator of the schema modification and owners of modified objects, each user retains all information about his or her objects that would otherwise be lost by the schema modification. The report must be sufficient for the user to reconstruct those modified objects that he or she owns. For example, the owner of an object is informed when the object's class has an instance variable removed, and is given the value of the removed variable.

## 12.5.2 Class-Modifying Primitives

GemStone allows a class to be added as a leaf of the class hierarchy. The list of additional schema modifications given here is not complete in a graph-theoretic sense. Our primary motivation is to provide modifications that are useful, well understood, and have a reasonable implementation. For example, GemStone does not provide operations to arbitrarily change the superclass of a class.

**Renaming a Named Instance Variable**   The name of an existing instance variable may be changed. For example, to reduce ambiguity, the **weight** attribute of class **Vehicle** may be changed to **grossWeight** when adding the instance variable **curbWeight**. In order to preserve the representation invariant, renaming is not allowed if the new name is already defined in the class. To preserve the full inheritance invariant, renaming is not allowed if the named instance variable is inherited from the superclass. The renaming is propagated to all subclasses. Further, if the renaming would fail in any subclass (if the new name is already defined), then the operation is not allowed.

**Making a Class Indexable**   Existing objects may be made indexable to extend their semantics. For example, class **Automobile** may be extended so that its instances directly list their service visits. To maintain the class-kind invariant, the operation is not allowed if a subclass is already indexable and the constraint on its indexable component would cause a violation of the class-kind invariant.

**Adding a Named Instance Variable**   All instances of a class may have an additional instance variable defined. In order to preserve the representation invariant, adding a named instance variable is not allowed if another instance variable already has the name. This condition is checked in each subclass, as well. If, in any subclass of the modified class, the named instance variable is already present and its constraint would cause a violation of the class-kind invariant, then the operation is disallowed. If the named instance variable is not defined in a subclass, then the modification is propagated to that subclass. This condition preserves the full inheritance constraint. All instances of the class to which the instance variable has been added gain a value of **nil** for the new instance variable in order to maintain the representation invariant.

**Making an Indexable Class Nonindexable**   All instances of a class may have their indexable portion removed. The indexable components of instances of the class are removed to preserve the representation invariant. The modification is not propagated to subclasses of the modified class. The operation may be applied individually to all these subclasses to achieve the same effect. In order to preserve the full inheritance invariant, a class may not be made nonindexable if its superclass is indexable.

**Removing a Named Instance Variable**   All instances of a class may have an existing instance variable removed. To preserve the full inheritance invariant, an instance variable may not be removed if it is inherited from a superclass. The modification is not propagated to subclasses of the modified class. The same effect may be achieved by repeatedly applying the operation to the modified class's subclasses.

**Modifying the Constraint on a Variable** A given instance variable may have its constraint changed. A constraint is *specialized* when the new constraint is a subclass of the old constraint. A constraint is *generalized* when the new constraint is a superclass of the old constraint. Modifications for which the constraint is neither specialized nor generalized may be achieved by removing and then re-adding the named instance variable with the new constraint.

The constraint on an instance variable may not be generalized if the instance variable is inherited and the new constraint is not a subclass of the inherited constraint. This preserves the class-kind invariant. Instances of the class need not be modified to preserve the representation invariant, as all objects that satisfied the old constraint will satisfy the new one. The modification is not propagated to subclasses of the modified class.

The constraint on an instance variable may not be specialized if, in any subclass of the modified class, the constraint on the instance variable is not a subclass of the new constraint. This preserves the class-kind invariant. In order to preserve the representation invariant, instances in which the value of the variable does not satisfy the new constraint have that value replaced by **nil**. The modification is not propagated to subclasses of the modified class.

**Removing a Class** A class may not be removed if it has any instances. Gem-Stone has a message by which an object can change its class to a subclass of its current class; this message can be used to remove all instances of a given class. Without loss of generality, we can assume that the class defines no additional instance variables to those in its superclass. This can be achieved by a series of named instance variable removals.

The superclass of all instances of the removed class is changed to the superclass of the removed class. The removed class may be referred to as a constraint from another class. To maintain the dangling reference constraint, these constraints are changed to the removed class's superclass. Other references to the class may exist; the class is marked as obsolete, so that new instances may not be created. To preserve the class hierarchy invariant, class **Object** may not be removed.

**Adding a Class** GemStone currently allows the addition of new leaves to the class hierarchy. All invariants are preserved through the addition. To add an interior node to the hierarchy, the new class's name, its superclass, and its subclasses are specified. The subclasses must currently be immediate subclasses of the given superclass to preserve the class hierarchy invariant. The representation specified by the new class will be the same as that specified by the superclass to preserve the representation invariant. To satisfy the full inheritance invariant, no new variables are introduced into the class and the constraints on inherited variables remain unchanged. Note that new instance variables can be added subsequently.

### 12.5.3 Other Considerations

Our treatment of class modification has so far addressed only the issue of structural integrity. Interaction with authorization mechanisms, concurrency control, object's behavior, and binding conventions must also be considered.

**Authorization**   Modifying a class may require rewriting the class and all of its instances. The change may have to be propagated transitively to subclasses (e.g., adding a named instance variable requires that all subclasses have the instance variable as well). If the owner of a class does not own all of its instances, it is possible that a schema modification will attempt an unauthorized write. It is unreasonable to require complete authorization to all affected objects in order to change a class; thus, write authorization to a class is deemed sufficient to permit modifying the class and writing all objects necessary to the task.

Despite the possibility of violating authorization, a schema modification will not allow its initiator to infer the existence of objects and values for which he or she does not have read permission. Both the initiator of a modification and the affected users must receive reports, as described in Section 12.5.1. The initiator's report describes all modified objects for which he or she has read or write permission. An affected user's report describes all modified objects owned by that user. In particular, the initiator's report will not contain objects for which he or she does not have read permission.

**Concurrency**   Modifying a class in a shared environment can cause a violation of the representation invariant. Consider two users, one of whom is modifying a class. If the first user creates and commits an instance of the class before the second user finishes modifying the class, the transaction performing the schema modification will not be aware of the new instance. The representation of the instance committed by the first user will not be in agreement with the modified class, thus violating the representation invariant. A class must be exclusive-locked before it can be modified. As explained in Section 12.3.4, exclusive-locking a class prevents the creation of instances of the class and the sending of messages to instances.

Many schema modifications require enumerating all instances of an affected class. Maintaining a list of all instances can increase concurrency conflict; two transactions attempting to create instances of a given class will be in conflict on the list.

A **TransparentBag** allows simultaneous insertions and removals without transaction conflict. Updates (insertions and removals) to a **TransparentBag** are reapplied to the most recent value of the **TransparentBag** at transaction commit. A list of all instances of a class can be safely maintained using a **TransparentBag**: if two sessions create an instance of a class and add it to a class's list of all instances, the system will correctly merge both additions to the **TransparentBag**. In a similar manner, a list of all subclasses of a class can be safely maintained using a **TransparentBag**.

**Behavior**   Our presentation has focused on preserving structural consistency. Our invariants are expressed in terms of the representations of objects and the allowed values of objects. While our invariants assure that the structure of every object is consistent with the class hierarchy, they do not guarantee that the structure assumed by the methods is present. For example, when an instance variable is removed, there may be methods that rely on the presence of the removed variable. The behavior of objects is of importance. When behavior is shared, a seemingly minor modification can have unexpected global ramifications.

Consider modifying a class's method. One may wish to verify that senders of the message to instances of the class will still behave properly. In most Smalltalk-like systems, locating the senders of a message to instances of a particular class is extremely difficult. In short, one cannot assume that "messages completely define the semantics of an object" [Banerjee et al. 1987]. This is a form of behavioral consistency that is of extreme importance, but, for the moment, it remains only a design objective in object-oriented systems.

The methodology of Skarra and Zdonik [Skarra and Zdonik 1987] goes a long way toward preserving behavior. The problems they address go beyond class modification to versioning of classes, objects, and methods. In effect, their methodology implements schema modification by the use of versions. Our current interest is confined to solutions that do not require versioning.

**Binding**   Every software system has some notion of binding in the objects it manipulates. For example, object-oriented systems bind variables to values, objects to classes, and messages to methods. In traditional programming languages, variables, temporaries, code, and attributes are all bound. Generally, conventional languages perform every binding. For example, code is bound to a name at compilation, and names are bound to addresses at link time. Late binding provides flexibility at the expense of efficiency. Early binding provides efficiency at the expense of flexibility. A general rule of thumb is to apply early binding in a stable environment; that is, an environment where the bindings will not change. Late binding is applied in an unstable environment.

In GemStone, message lookups are performed by the interpreter, not the compiler. Thus, messages are bound to methods late. Not only may the results of a message lookup vary frequently (from one lookup to the next), but the lookup itself cannot be performed until the class of the receiver is known. Instance variable binding, on the other hand, is done by the compiler. An intermediate binding is also available by using literal variables [Goldberg and Robson 1983].

Altering an environment may invalidate bindings. Modifying a class is an environmental modification. Late binding will attempt to adapt to the new environment. Early bindings will reflect the old environment and may not be correct. After a change in the environment, early bindings that may be affected must be detected and corrected. If it is not possible to correct these early bindings, it is immediately known. Detecting problems with late bindings caused by an environmental change is extremely difficult. For example, if a message is removed from a class, the binding that occurs when the message is sent to an instance will fail. These attempts to send the message to an instance of the class cannot be statically anticipated. In a conventional language the removal of a procedure can be validated through compiling and linking.

The rebindings required by a schema modification are unavoidable. However, managing schema modification by binding everything at the last possible moment seriously degrades performance and makes it impossible to anticipate bindings that will fail.

Philosophically, we believe that schema modification should be used appropriately. It is appropriate as both the modeled world and our understanding of it change; however, it is not a panacea for poor design practices.

## CONCLUSION

Among the areas under consideration for future research and development are: increased heterogeneous network support; extensions to the associative access query language; additional indexing mechanisms; additional schema modification operations; extending the segment concept to provide a hierarchy of shareable libraries; additional support for interoperability; and extending the repertoire of concurrency control mechanisms.

## REFERENCES

[Albano et al. 1985] A. Albano, L. Cardelli and R. Orsini, "Galileo: A Strongly-Typed Interactive Conceptual Language," *ACM Transactions on Database Systems*, vol. 10, no. 2, June 1985.

[Albano and Orsini 1984] A. Albano and R. Orsini, "A Prototyping Approach to Database Applications Development," *Database Engineering*, vol. 7, no. 4, December 1984.

[Banerjee et al. 1987] J. Banerjee, W. Kim, H. Kim and H. Korth, "Semantics and Implementation of Schema Evolution in Object-Oriented Databases,"

*Proceedings of the ACM/SIGMOD Annual Conference on Management of Data*, 1987.

[Carey et al. 1986] M.J. Carey, D.J. DeWitt, J.E. Richardson, E.J. Shekita, "Object and File Management in the EXODUS Extensible Database System," *Proceedings of the Conference on Very Large Databases*, Kyoto, Japan, 1986.

[Cattell 1983] R.G. Cattell, "Design and Implementation of a Relationship-Entity-Datum Model," Xerox CSL 83-4, May 1983.

[Chan et al. 1981] A. Chan, S.A. Fox, W.-T.K. Lin and D. Ries, "Design of an ADA Compatible Local Database Manager (LDM)," TR CCA 81-09, Computer Corporation of America, November 1981.

[Copeland and Maier 1984] G. Copeland and D. Maier, "Making Smalltalk a Database System," *Proceedings of the ACM/SIGMOD International Conference on the Management of Data*, 1984.

[Ecklund et al. 1987] D.J. Ecklund, E.F. Ecklund, B.O. Eifrig and F.M. Tonge, "DVSS: A Distributed Version Storage Server for CAD Applications," *Proceedings of the Conference on Very Large Databases*, Brighton, Britain, September 1987.

[Goldberg 1984] A. Goldberg, *Smalltalk-80: The Interactive Programming Environment*, Addison-Wesley, Reading, MA, 1984.

[Goldberg and Robson 1983] A. Goldberg and D. Robson, *Smalltalk-80: The Language and Its Implementation*, Addison-Wesley, Reading, MA, 1983.

[Gray 1984] M. Gray, "Databases for Computer-Aided Design," in *New Applications of Databases*, G. Garadarin and E. Gelenbe, eds., Academic Press, New York, 1984.

[Haynie 1981] M.N. Haynie, "The Relational/Network Hybrid Data Model for Design Automation Databases," *Proceedings of the IEEE 18th Design Automation Conference*, 1981.

[Kaehler and Krasner 1983] T. Kaehler and G. Krasner, "LOOM—Large Object-Oriented Memory for Smalltalk-80 Systems," in *Smalltalk-80: Bits of History, Words of Advice*, Addison-Wesley, Reading, MA, 1983.

[Maier et al. 1985] D. Maier, A. Otis and A. Purdy, "Object-Oriented Database Development at Servio Logic," *Database Engineering*, vol. 18, no. 4, December 1985.

[Maier and Price 1984] D. Maier and D. Price, "Data Model Requirements for Engineering Applications," *Proceedings of the International Workshop on Expert Database Systems*, 1984.

[Maier and Stein 1986] D. Maier and J. Stein, "Indexing in an Object-Oriented DBMS," *Proceedings of the International Workshop on Object-Oriented Database Systems,* September 1986.

[Maier et al. 1986] D. Maier, J. Stein, A. Otis and A. Purdy, "Development of an Object-Oriented DBMS," *Proceedings of the ACM Conference on Object-Oriented Programming Systems, Languages, and Applications,* September 1986.

[Penney et al. 1987] D.J. Penney, J. Stein and D. Maier, "Is the Disk Half Full or Half Empty?: Combining Optimistic and Pessimistic Concurrency Mechanisms in a Shared, Persistent Object Base," *Proceedings of the Workshop on Persistent Object Stores,* Appin, Scotland, August 1987.

[Penney and Stein 1987] D.J. Penney and J. Stein, "Class Modification in the GemStone Object-Oriented DBMS," *Proceedings of the ACM Conference on Object-Oriented Programming Systems, Languages, and Applications,* September 1987.

[Purdy et al. 1987] A. Purdy, D. Maier and B. Schuchardt, "Integrating an Object Server with Other Worlds," *ACM Transactions on Office Information Systems,* vol. 5, no. 1, January 1987.

[Skarra and Zdonik 1987] A.H. Skarra and S.B. Zdonik, "Type Evolution in an Object-Oriented Database," in *Research Directions in Object-Oriented Programming,* B. Shriver and P. Wegner, eds., MIT Press, Cambridge, MA, 1987.

[Thatte 1986] S.M. Thatte, "Persistent Memory: A Storage Architecture for Object-Oriented Database," *Proceedings of the International Workshop on Object-Oriented Database Systems,* September 1986.

# 13

# OZ+: An Object-Oriented Database System

Stephen P. Weiser, Frederick H. Lochovsky

## Introduction

The original goal motivating the development of OZ+ was to merge object-oriented language concepts with those of database systems and produce a programming environment that would be well-suited to the needs of office information system (OIS) implementors. From the object "world," OZ+ acquired techniques for the natural representation of the real-world entities and tasks associated with an office. From the database "world," OZ+ acquired efficient methods for the storage and retrieval of persistent data in a multiuser environment.

The current state of OZ+ reflects its origin and its development environment. OZ+ evolved from an earlier object-oriented system, named OZ, to which it consequently bears some resemblance. During the course of the development of OZ+, a decision was made to use it as the underlying layer of the Office Task Manager (OTM), another project being developed at the University of Toronto [Hogg and Weiser 1987; Lochovsky 1987]. The requirements of this project influenced the choice of features in OZ+, such as support for object execution concurrency, although OZ+ stands on its own merits as an object-oriented OIS programming environment.

The rest of this chapter is organized as follows. In Section 1 we discuss the features and limitations of OZ, our initial attempt at designing an object-oriented OIS programming environment. This discussion sets the stage for Section 2, where the OZ+ object model and language are discussed. The representation of OZ+ objects in memory is the subject of Section 3. OZ+ object persistence and related issues are considered in Section 4.

## 13.1 OZ

OZ was developed at the University of Toronto as a prototype system to demonstrate the appropriateness of objects for modeling office activities [Mooney 1984; Nierstrasz et al. 1983; Twaites 1984]. The OZ object model owes much of its inspiration to concepts that have become familiar through the published literature on Smalltalk [Goldberg and Robson 1983], Actors [Hewitt 1977], abstract data types [Guttag 1977], and modules with persistent data. It is worthwhile to offer a brief synopsis of OZ, as the terminology that we present will be relevant to the examination of OZ+ that forms the bulk of this chapter.

An OZ *object* is a discrete entity that encapsulates both data and an allowable set of operations on that data. The data is concealed by the object; it can be accessed and manipulated only by the object's own operations. In turn, each operation's implementation, or the *way* in which it does something, is hidden to the outside world. An object's public interface is constituted only by its name (which allows the object to be uniquely identified in a given population of objects) and instructions on how its operations may be invoked. These instructions typically provide a specification of an operation's name, parameter list, and the results it can be expected to return.

An object's data, referred to as its *contents*, are described by a set of *instance variables*. These variables are of simple types integer, character string, or object identifier. An OZ object is said to be *flat*[1] because it aggregates scalar data values rather than other objects. This is analogous to speaking of first normal form (1NF) relations as flattened forms of more generalized relations whose attributes may themselves be relations [Codd 1970].

An OZ object's operations are referred to as its *rules*, or collectively as its *behavior*. A rule may be invoked by a message sent to it from a rule in another object. A message specifies a particular object (each OZ object has a unique system-generated object identifier or *oid*), a rule name, and a

---

[1] Even though an OZ object can store the object identifier of another OZ object, the user views these two objects as independent objects (i.e., an object identifier variable can be thought of as a foreign key of another object).

possible set of parameter values to be passed to that rule. A rule thus invoked may return a value to the message-sending object. Note that OZ employs a *blocking-send/receive/reply* message protocol. That is, the sending object is blocked (i.e., it does not continue executing) until its message is both received and replied to.

An OZ object is an *instance* of some given object *class* (or *type*). Object instances of the same class share the same description of their instance variables and rules. They are distinguished by their unique oids and potentially differing instance variable values. Classes are organized as nodes in an *m-ary tree* structure,[2] and inherit instance variables and rules from all ancestor nodes.[3]

OZ objects are dynamically created and destroyed. The first event in the *life-span* of an object is the execution of its *alpha* rule and the last is the execution of its *omega* rule. These rules ensure that an OZ object has some autonomy in matters concerning its birth and death.

The set of all object instances is referred to collectively as the *object universe*. The object universe can be partitioned on the basis of class—all objects belong to exactly one class. The majority of these classes are user-defined and vary across user applications. There also exist a small number of predefined classes, which are invariant across all applications, such as the **user** class, which contains a set of rules that facilitate the interaction of users with the system.

The OZ *object manager* is responsible for the management of the object universe. It is conveniently thought of as itself being composed of a number of managers. The *classDefinition manager* accepts new class definitions passed to it by users and translates them into an internal interpretable code (called OZ−). The *inheritance manager* determines the variables and rules that are inherited by each object of a new class. The *memory manager* provides space in memory for new objects, locates existing objects, and performs garbage collection of unneeded objects. The *rule manager* interprets OZ code and thereby executes rules in given objects. The *message manager* passes the messages generated during rule execution to their destination objects. Finally, the *event manager* coordinates rule executions and synchronizes state changes in objects.

### 13.1.1 Distinctive Features of OZ

Office activities have been described as largely event-driven and semistructured, with a high level of parallelism requiring synchronization and coordination [Hammer and Sirbu 1980; Morgan 1980; Sirbu et al. 1981]. OZ was designed specifically to model office activities, and consequently it contains

---

[2] A tree structure whose nodes may have any number of children.

[3] This is a single inheritance scheme. A class inherits only one superclass directly, but this class in turn has inherited its own superclass, which has inherited its own superclass, . . . ending with a specially predefined *root* class that itself has no superclass.

features that reflect its application domain. These features, which distinguish OZ from general-purpose object-oriented systems such as Smalltalk, are:

1. OZ rules (or operations) consist of *conditions* and *actions*. Conditions can test the state of the object containing the rule (i.e., the value set of its variables) and the state of other objects (indirectly obtained through sending messages and receiving responses). It is necessary for all conditions to be true before any actions can be taken. Thus conditions assist in coordinating the actions among communicating objects. They also allow great flexibility in restricting the messages which a rule will act upon.

2. Rules have specified *acquaintances*, which are classes of objects from which the rule will accept messages.[4] This facilitates object independence. Objects "choose" what other types of objects they are willing to let invoke their rules.

3. Rules may be *self-triggering*. If a rule has no specified acquaintances, the rule will invoke itself and perform its actions when its conditions all become true. The object containing a self-triggering rule appears to act spontaneously—it will perform an action or actions without having received a message telling it to do so. Thus OZ objects may exhibit a kind of autonomy not found in other object-oriented systems.

4. State-changing rule actions are synchronized by *events*. The state-changing actions of a rule do not occur independently but rather in concert with those in other objects. A group of communicating objects that "reach an agreement" to perform their state-changing actions together are said to participate in an event. Events enlarge upon the notion of actions being performed in a particular rule only when its conditions are true. An event will be performed only when the conditions of *all* participating rules are true. An event can be viewed as an atomic change of state within the object universe.

5. Interaction between human users and OZ is facilitated by a predefined class of *user* objects. Each user is represented internally by a member of this class, that user's own user object instance, which acts as the liaison between the user and other OZ objects. (Thus, while the user *class* is predefined and invariant, its member objects will vary with the user population.) A user object is responsible for converting user input into OZ messages and also for translating OZ messages into a language that the user can understand and respond to appropriately. In general, we may say that the user object presents the user with an environment, or user interface, through which the user may interact with other objects.

---

[4] A rule will accept messages from any instance of its acquaintances.

### 13.1.2 Limitations of OZ

Let us enumerate some of the limitations of OZ, as the correction of these limitations provided the original incentive for the development of OZ+.

1. The OZ object model imposes a *flat* structure on object contents. An object model should provide for natural representation; that is, a simple, direct mapping from real-world entities into their object model counterparts.

2. OZ events are executed in a strictly *sequential* manner. This introduces a severe modeling restriction: any two real-world events cannot be *accurately* modeled in a natural fashion as two corresponding OZ events unless one is guaranteed to end before the other begins.

3. OZ objects exist exclusively in memory. As memory is volatile, the *persistence* of objects cannot be guaranteed. In the event of a system crash, the information content of all OZ objects is irrecoverably lost.

## 13.2 OZ+

A data model may be viewed as a specification language for representing real-world entities relevant to a particular application domain [Gibbs and Tsichritzis 1983]. The data models associated with conventional database systems are generally restrictive in their ability to model the data-intensive aspects of real-world entities. They are limited by a finite number of data types and, particularly in the case of the relational data model, the need to normalize data. Object-oriented data models in general, and the OZ+ object model in particular, are extensible. The OZ+ object model also provides for a more natural representation of real-world entities and their activities. In this section we highlight those aspects of the OZ+ object model that enhance the facilities of the OZ object model.

### 13.2.1 Hierarchical Structure of OZ+ Objects

OZ+ objects are not as constrained in their structure as OZ objects. They may themselves be composed of other OZ+ objects. This provides OZ+ objects with a potentially hierarchical structure that is well-suited for the natural representation of office objects [Weiser 1985]. OZ+ objects are allowed to contain any number of *simple* objects. A simple object is an abstraction of the notion of *variable*—both are responsible for holding data values such as strings or integers. In addition, OZ+ objects can aggregate any number of non-simple or *complex* objects as well [Kim et al. 1987a; Kim et al. 1987b; Lorie and Plouffe 1983]. Each complex object may itself, in turn, aggregate simple and complex objects. Complex objects may also have set occurrences.

A complex object may be thought of as an abstraction of the notion of a structure or a record in programming languages. In terms of a record, a complex object allows such desirable features as repeating groups and record nesting. A complex object may also be profitably viewed as a tree. The object itself is the root node, and the objects that it aggregates are the children of this node. Each of the child node objects, which are simple, is a leaf node. Each of those that is complex is itself a parent node. The nodes of a set occurrence are siblings. The OZ+ type definition code fragment below illustrates the hierarchical structure of an example **student** object's contents:

```
student : (
    student_no : int ;
    student_name : string ;
    grades : set  (
        course : string ;
        marks : (
            first_term : int ;
            second_term : int ;
            )
        )
    )
        .
        .
        .
```

The **student_no**, **student_name**, and **grades** objects are aggregated by the complex parent **student** object. The **grades** object is complex; the other two are simple. The **grades** object is parent to a set of identically structured complex objects, composed of the simple **course** object and the complex **marks** object. The **marks** object is itself composed of simple objects.

A discussion of the ramifications of hierarchical structuring on *rules* in OZ+ is deferred until Section 13.2.4. For now, our focus will continue to be centered on the data-intensive aspects of OZ+ objects.

### 13.2.2 Simple Objects

In the OZ+ object model, a variable type is abstracted into a simple object class, a variable declaration into instance creation of a class, and a type operation into a rule associated with the class. The most important consequence of this abstraction is the "purity" of OZ+ in terms of its object orientation. Variables and their operators are of dubious desirability precisely because of their non-object status. Their removal adds substantially to the simplicity and elegance of the OZ+ language.

The basic language construct involving simple object types is the *message statement*, or simply the *statement*. Statements are responsible for instigating the basic activity of objects: the sending and receiving of *messages*. A statement has the syntax:

```
<result name>:<object name><rule name><rule parameter list>
```

where **<rule parameter list>** is defined as a list of object names having the form:

```
(<object name>₁;<object name>₂;...;<object name>ₙ;)
```

A list of one element may be left unbracketed. The final semicolon may be omitted from any list.

If **a** and **b** are the names of existing integer objects, then **t : a + b** is a statement. The statement's *execution* causes a *message* to be sent to **a**, invoking its + rule with the parameter list **b**. A message returns a *result*, which is itself an object. In the case of the message statement **t : a + b**, the result would be an integer object, named by **t**, holding the additive value of the integers held by **a** and **b**. We note that the only language construct used here is the message statement. The symbol + is not part of the language; it is only the name of a rule.[5]

With this basic construct, the message statement, we can represent all operations involving data types and their operators. It gives the OZ+ language three desirable properties:[6]

1. *homogeneity*—OZ+ is purely object-oriented. The traditional notions of "variable" and "operator" are dispensed with.

2. *uniformity*—Types and their operators are all identically "packaged" in objects. In other words, any operation is invoked with the same message-statement syntax.

3. *extensibility*—To add a new type to OZ+ requires no change in the language, only the acceptance of a new user-defined object type or the addition to the system of a new predefined simple type.

Some syntactic shorthand has been introduced into the OZ+ grammar to make it somewhat less baroque. The introduction of syntactic shorthand into OZ+ allows the formation of rather conventional looking statements (i.e., the kind of assignment statement that might be found in a traditional programming language). What is notable, however, is that we give such statements

---

[5] This is a *conceptual* interpretation and does not necessarily reflect the underlying method of statement execution. Simple objects, such as integers, are implemented in the execution environment as variables (along with their type operators) rather than as objects to improve time and space efficiency.

[6] We think these properties *should* be common to all object-oriented languages, but they are not.

a *pure* object-orientation and base them on a *single* language construct (the message statement). For example, **a := 2 ∗ (d − e)** is decomposable into **tl : d − e ; a := 2 ∗ tl**, which is further decomposable into the formal message statements: **tl : d − e ; t2 : 2 ∗ tl ; t3 : a := t2.**[7]

OZ+ provides a wide range of simple object types suitable for the representation of office data. These include object oid, character, string, integer, float, boolean, decimal, date and time, as well as bulk and text types. Each simple object type possesses an appropriate set of rules for manipulation of the data type that it holds. While the integer type contains such expected rules as **+** and **−**, the text type contains rules such as **edit** and **match** (search for a given character pattern in a text value).

The choice of simple types and rules in OZ+ is meant to be regarded as provisional rather than absolute. Our intention is to give users a good set of "building blocks" out of which they might construct more complex types (e.g., a multimedia document type). It may be appropriate to include some of these complex types as simple types in OZ+ at a future date.[8] It is also likely that new rules may be added to existing types if they are deemed desirable (e.g., a compression rule for text).

### 13.2.3 Complex Objects

A complex object may structure the objects it contains in a number of ways. The most basic is as a simple aggregate where the complex object is the parent of a set of named siblings, each of which may have a different type. The sibling objects contained in a complex object may themselves be simple or complex. Complex objects that are simple aggregates of other objects are said to have a **list** type. Complex objects may be specified in a number of other ways to allow the convenient representation of *unordered set* occurrences of objects (**set** type), *ordered set* or *array* occurrences of objects (**array** type), and *m-ary tree structure* ordering of objects (**tree** type).

### 13.2.4 Rules

In the same manner that OZ+ abstracts instance variables into simple objects, it abstracts rules into *rule* objects. A rule object is considered to be a **list** type complex object in OZ+. The child objects that it aggregates are referred to as the statements of the rule. They are strictly ordered by their appearance in the

---

[7] Note that **2** is a constant integer object whose ∗ rule is invoked. The set of constant object instances associated with a given simple type may be thought of as predefined objects.

[8] A complex type "becomes" a simple type when the system is coerced into regarding it as *atomic*, i.e., not built up from other types. The fact that it is possible to express one simple type in terms of others is irrelevant. For example, if a "bit" type exists, should we stop thinking of the integer type as simple because it can be constructed in terms of this bit type?

rule declaration (ordering of statements is obviously of critical importance for rule execution). All rule statements are message statements. A rule is redeclared each time it is invoked and destroyed immediately after returning the message sent to it. It thus has no existence when it is not executing.

The statement messages of an object are executed in a top-to-bottom fashion when an object is executed. When a statement fails, execution of the rule ends and the rule returns the predefined **FAIL** object as its result.

For referring to any of the siblings of a complex object from a rule within the object that contains this complex object, we adopt the chain naming convention **<complex object name>.<name$_x$>**. We generalize this convention so that within the context of an object instance, any of its object descendants can be named unambiguously. Consider the sketch of an example object instance **a** that follows:

```
a : (
   b : (
      c : (
         d :
         e :
         )
      )
   )
```

**b, b.c, b.c.d**, and **b.c.e** are examples of unambiguous name chains within the context of **a**. Within the context of **c**, one could unambiguously refer to **d** or **e** without chaining; within the context of **b**, one can unambiguously refer to **c** without chaining; and so on.

### 13.2.5 User-Defined Object Types

All system-supplied object types, both simple (**int, string, float,** ...) and complex (**list, set, array, tree**) can be used in the formation of user-defined object types. Once a user-defined type has been accepted by the object manager, it may be used indistinguishably from system-supplied types in the formation of further user-defined object types.

In the sense that any complex object is an aggregate of other objects, any complex object type is an aggregate of other types. Thus the **student** type is the aggregate of the **student_no, student_name,** and **grades** types. Note that the "top-level" type definition (i.e., the one that is not given as the child of any other type, such as the **student** type) is the user-defined type that is made available for use in later user-supplied type definitions; its constituent object types are not. This is not an arbitrary decision. The top-level object type defines *independent* objects; their existence is independent of the existence of any other object (as they are not contained in any other object). The lower-level object types define *dependent* objects; their existence is dependent on their containment in some other object. As a dependent object type "depends" on the independent object type that is its ancestor for its existence, it makes sense not to allow it the status of a global type (which would then, somewhat contradictorily, allow it a separate existence as an independent type as well).

When a user defines a new type $X$, he may make use of a previously defined independent type $X_i$, which may itself be an aggregate of dependent child types $X_{i,1}$ through $X_{i,n}$. Thus, $X$ has access to all the variables and rules of each $X_i$ as well as its dependent children $X_{i,1}$ through $X_{i,n}$. In the event of name conflicts, the simple objects of $X$ "cancel out" the complex ones. In addition, a strict ordering of the complex object types is applied so that the child objects of those complex objects defined first "cancel out" the child objects of those complex objects defined later if a conflict occurs.

When a user defines a new type, its children are partitioned into *permanent* and *temporary* object types. Permanent types specify dependent objects that are created when their parent is created and are destroyed when it is destroyed. The primary examples of such objects are the data-holding child objects associated with a particular independent object instance. Temporary types specify dependent objects that come into existence when they are referenced and that are destroyed when they cease to be referenced. The primary examples of such objects are rules, which exist only from the time they are invoked until the end of their execution. Data-holding objects declared within the scope of a rule are also temporary objects.

Other burdens on the user when defining a new type are the specification of the child types, which are *rules*, and of these, those that are *self-triggering rules*. Rules must be some subset of the temporary types.

A *user object* acts as the liaison between a user and the system, allowing among other functions the submission of user-defined object types. Although user interface issues are an important aspect of OZ+ (as of any programming environment), we do not focus on them in this chapter.

### 13.2.6 Message Sending

When a statement is executed, a message is sent to an object. This message is itself an OZ+ object that has the form:

```
msg: (
    msgOid: objID          /*message identifier*/
    senderOid: objID       /*object instance identifier of
                             sender*/
    senderType: objType    /*object instance type of sender*/
    receiverOid: objID     /*object instance identifier of
                             receiver*/
    receiverRule: ruleType /*rule name of receiver*/
    params: anyObj         /*parameter objects*/
    result: anyObj         /*result object*/
)
```

The message, being a complex object, has its own unique oid. **anyObj** is a "generic" type (i.e., the object referred to has a temporarily unknown type).

The message is directed by the *message manager* from the sender object to the specified rule in the receiver object. The message becomes accessible to this rule as a child of the rule (with the name **msg**). The following code fragment illustrates how the receiving rule interprets **msg**:

```
balance : int
    .
    .
    .
addDepositToAccount : (
    msg.senderType in (bankTeller ; supervisor) /*Is sender
        type є acquaintances?*/
    deposit<—msg.params.1     /*<— is generic renaming rule*/
    deposit : : int           /*generic typing rule*/
    tellerName<—msg.params.2
       .
       .
       .

    balance := balance + deposit
       .
       .
       .

    msg.result := balance
        )
```

The **addDepositToAccount** rule specifies its *acquaintances* (the object types from which it will accept messages) by using the generic **in** rule. This statement will fail, causing the rule as a whole to fail, whenever the sender object is not among the rule's acquaintances. If rule execution succeeds, the message manager will return the message result to the sender. If rule execution fails, the result will contain the **FAIL** object.

### 13.2.7 Control of Flow of Execution in Rules

The **for** and **if** rules, which are inherited by all object instances, allow a simulation of two kinds of flow of execution that are common in traditional programming languages. A **for** statement has the form:

```
for(<set name>;<for body name>)
```

where **<for body name>** names a rule *within* the rule containing the **for** message.[9] This rule, which has the parameter **<element name>**, is sent a message by the **for** rule for each element of **<set name>**. In this way, the **for** rule iterates through **<set name>**, sending an element of **<set name>** in each message to the **<for body rule>**. The following code fragment is self-explanatory:

```
totalSales:(sales::set(int))
    (boss;president)
    (
    salesTotal:int
    salesTotal:= 0
        .
        .
        .

    calculateTotal:()()(salesTotal:= salesTotal+ sale)()
        .
        .
        .

    for(sales;calculateTotal)
        .
        .
        .

    )(salesTotal)
```

In a very similar fashion, the **if** rule allows a choice to be made regarding which of two rules will be invoked. The **if** rule has the form:

```
if(<if clause name>;<else clause name>)
```

where the **<if clause name>** and **<else clause name>** are rules contained in the rule in which the **if** rule is invoked. The **if** rule calls the **<if clause name>** rule; only if it fails is the **<else clause name>** rule called.[10] Embedding of rules within rules allows arbitrary levels of nesting of this "if-then-else" construct.

### 13.2.8 Self-Triggering Rules and Events

Self-triggering rules in OZ+ are parameterless rules that execute whenever all their statements are executable (i.e., no statement returns a **FAIL** object result).

---

[9] Rules are complex objects that may therefore contain other complex objects. These contained complex objects may themselves be rules. A rule within a rule is referred to as a *subrule*.

[10] If both fail, the **if** statement is considered to have failed, which will cause rule failure.

The object manager continuously tests all self-triggering rules in all objects to determine whether any of them are executable.[11]

Before defining OZ+ *events*, let us recap the salient features of OZ+ rule execution. A rule **R** is defined as a list of statements $S_1S_2 \cdots S_n$.[12] The execution of **R** is defined as the sequential execution of $S_1$ through $S_n$. **R** is said to execute successfully if $S_1$ through $S_n$ execute successfully. **R** is said to fail execution if any $S_i$ fails execution.

A statement execution causes a statement (the *sender*) to send a message to another rule (the *receiver*), which may reside in the same or a different object. The receiver executes before returning a message reply. Note that each message issued from a sender in an object results in a pyramid (or tree) of message sending in the following manner. The issued message invokes the execution of the receiver rule. The execution of the receiver rule proceeds by the sequential execution of its statements. The execution of each of its statements results in the sending of a message to still other receiver rules. The process continues recursively, ending in the rules of simple objects, which do not originate messages during their execution. (The building blocks of simple rules must by definition lie outside the OZ+ language; they are not composed of OZ+ statements themselves.)

If a message reply holds a **FAIL** object, the sender statement fails, causing the rule that contains it to fail. Recursively, this will cause a chain of **FAIL** objects to be passed backward to the rule that *originated* the pyramid of message sending. A little thought will show that this rule can be only a self-triggering rule. If it were not, it would itself pass a **FAIL** object back to the object that invoked it. Self-triggering objects, though, are not invoked by other objects. In consequence, any rule failure will induce rule failures in a pyramid (or tree) of communicating rules whose apex (or root) is a self-triggering rule.

An OZ+ *event* is the successful execution of a self-triggering rule. This implies that all rule executions generated from the originating self-triggering rule are successful. The failure of any one of these will induce a failure in the self-triggering rule (by the passing upward of **FAIL** objects) and consequently a failure of the event. However, this is not the whole story concerning events. Events are the atomic unit of state change in the OZ+ object universe. That is, when an event is successful, all the objects that participated in the event change state together as a unit. Conceptually, these state changes occur at the same moment. If the event is unsuccessful, no state changes occur in any of the participating objects. Thus events in OZ+ are an important mechanism for coordinating state changes in communicating objects.

---

[11] The object manager does not actually *continuously* test these rules. In rough terms, the object manager keeps track of the object states that have caused rule conditions to fail in the past. Whenever any of these states change, a test is made to see whether this will affect the executability of the rule.

[12] We are assuming no statement composition, as all statement compositions can be rewritten as a set of statements without composition.

It should be obvious that in the course of formation of an event, statements in rules in participating objects may seem to induce state changes before the event is completed (and confirmed successful). For example, a statement such as $a := a + 1$ would seem to increment the simple integer object $a$ immediately upon its execution. However, what actually occurs is the following. The event manager (the submanager of the object manager responsible for handling event formation) working in tandem with the execution manager (the submanager responsible for rule code interpretation) records any potential state changes in objects associated with a successful event in an *event tree*. The actual object states are not disturbed. If the event completes successfully, the event tree is used to update the states of the participating objects. If it fails, the event tree is discarded and the participating objects remain intact.

The OZ+ messaging paradigm is a form of Remote Procedure Call (RPC). Execution is blocked after sending a message until a message is returned from the receiver. This paradigm is implicitly sequential; execution blocking does not allow more than one statement of a rule to be active concurrently.

In contrast, OZ+ events are implicitly parallel. Event formation begins when a self-triggering rule attempts to execute. Event formation begins *independently* of the formation of other events; the event manager may be actively attempting the formation of any number of events at any point in time.

A particular object **O** may be a participant in the formation of any number of events $E_1 \cdots E_n$. Each event $E_i$ "sees" its own virtual version $O_i$ of object **O**, which is effectively the current working state of **O** as a participant in the formation of $E_i$. Each of these events is said to *compete* for the opportunity of permanently altering the state of object **O**. The first event $E_x$ to *complete* is given the right to replace the contents of **O** with $O_x$. All the other competing events must at this point backtrack in their event formation to account for the new state of **O**.

The logic of this procedure should be quite clear. An event is an atomic phenomenon, occurring all at once at some discrete time; it has no effective existence while it is forming. Thus when $E_x$ completes, competing events must behave as if this event was completed *before* they began formation. Any object states altered by the completion of $E_x$, which the competing events reference, must be accounted for.

The following example code fragment indicates how one event may be used to spawn two parallel events. Here, **fireAlarm**, **sprinkler**, and **smokeDetector** are all self-triggering rules in the same object.

```
smoke := FALSE;
startFireAlarm := FALSE;
startSprinkler := FALSE;
        .
        .
        .
```

```
fireAlarm:(
    startFireAlarm==TRUE;/*Execute rule when this
             statement succeeds*/
        .
        .
        .

sprinkler:(
    startSprinkler==TRUE; /* Execute rule when this
             statement succeeds */
        .
        .

smokeDetector:(
    smoke==TRUE;          /*Execute rule when this statement
             succeeds*/
        .
        .

    startFireAlarm:= TRUE;
    startSprinkler:= TRUE;
        .
        .
        .
```

**smokeDetector** starts **fireAlarm** and **sprinkler** in parallel events by a flag-setting technique. Note that the event manager will allow a given self-triggering rule in a given object to instigate only one event at a time. In other words, the same rule in the same object cannot instigate competing events. For example, only one **fireAlarm** event is induced to form by the setting of the **startFireAlarm** flag. However, once the event completes, it will be reinstigated unless the flag's status has been reset.

## 13.3 INTERNAL REPRESENTATION OF OBJECTS IN MEMORY

In this section we shall provide the reader with some insight into the manner in which OZ+ objects are represented in memory.

### 13.3.1 The OZ+ Object Universe

OZ+ is a system designed specifically for the implementation of office information systems (OISs). A particular OIS is implemented in OZ+ as a set of objects known collectively as an *object universe*. The object universe is the object-oriented equivalent of "program + data" in traditional programming environments. That is, it is composed of both information to be manipulated (data) and the methods necessary for manipulating it (program).

An OZ+ object universe is formally defined as the set of all *independent* OZ+ objects associated with a particular OIS implementation. An independent object, which is a complex object with no parent, is defined as the set of its child *dependent* objects. Each of these child objects is either a complex object, in which case it is itself a set of dependent objects, or a simple object.

The *state* of the object universe is given by the value set of its independent objects. The value of an independent object is given by the value set of its *permanent* child objects. The value of a complex (dependent) object is defined in the same way. The value of a simple (dependent) object is an ordered set of bytes. The interpretation of the byte set associated with a given simple object is the responsibility of the simple object type's rules. (Thus an integer object would manipulate this byte set as an integer, a text object as a string of characters, etc.)

For each object type there exists a special **type** object. A **type** object, being an independent object, is defined as the set of its child dependent objects. These objects include the *temporary* objects of the type that names the **type** object. In the context of the **type** object, these objects are permanent. Hence, the value of a **type** object includes the value set of the temporary objects of its associated type. In consequence, from the object universe state can be derived the value of any permanent object *and* any temporary object. The object universe state is therefore sufficient to characterize the total information content at any point in time of any particular OIS implemented in OZ+.

### 13.3.2 Memory Representation of Object Value

An independent object's value[13] is represented in memory as an ordered set of pointers. The $i$th pointer points to the object's $i$th child. These pointers point to locations in memory (where its child objects reside). The ordering of the object's children is determined by a well-defined procedure when the object's type definition is first accepted by the object manager. This procedure yields the object's unique identifier (held by the simple **oid** object associated with every complex object) as the first object pointed to, followed by the simple objects (ordered by their order of appearance in the type definition), which in turn are followed by the complex objects. Thus, an independent object **X** is represented as:

$$X = (X_{oid}, X_1, \ldots, X_j, X_{j+1}, \ldots, X_n)$$

where $X_{oid}$ points to the **oid** object, $x_1$ through $x_j$ point to simple objects, and $x_{j+1}$ through $x_n$ point to complex objects.

---

[13] In the rest of the chapter, the term "object" will often be used instead of "the object value memory representation." Context should always make it clear that this is what is meant.

The internal name of an object is its index into this set, beginning with the "0th" element of the set ($\mathbf{x}_{oid}$, whose internal name is consequently 0). The $i$th child object of the **type** object associated with **X** names the type of the $i$th child of **X** and contains the structural information necessary for the interpretation of this type (or at least a pointer to where that information can be found in some other **type** object). Thus, structural information, which is invariant across instances of a type, is recorded only once for each type.

The internal representation of a **student** object, for example, would consist of an ordered set of pointers to the object's children (**oid, student_no, student_name, grades**). The associated **type** object would name object identifier, string, integer, and set of grades, respectively, as the types of the **student** object's children. Consultation of the **type** object associated with **grades** would yield further information on its structure.[14]

A non-set-occurring complex dependent object is represented in memory in the same manner as independent objects. The set-occurring complex object is represented by an unordered set of pointers, each of which points to a complex object value of the same type. (For example, the **grades** element of the **student** value pointer set itself points to a set of pointers, each element of which points to a complex object value of type **grades**.) Note that the non-set-occurring complex object has a fixed number of ordered elements in its pointer set, whereas the set-occurring complex object has a variable number of unordered elements. These suggest the data structures used to store these pointer sets in C (the underlying programming language in which the OZ+ system is implemented): an array of pointers and a linked list of pointers, respectively. A simple object is represented in memory as an ordered set of bytes.

### 13.3.3 Locating Objects in Memory

Given the address of a parent object **X**, the $i$th child's address will be available at **X(i)**, where we regard **X** as a pointer array. The time required to locate a child, given the parent, is therefore **O**(1). If the parent object has a set occurrence of length $n$, a child may be located in **O**($n$) by movement through the linked list of set elements. An independent object that has no parent can be found by consultation of the lookup table managed by the *location manager*. This table maps independent object oids into the memory locations of the objects. The oids are indexed so that search time is at worst **O**($\log(n)$), $n$ being

---

[14] We are ignoring or glossing over certain implementation details. For example, the **type** object does not need to keep type information on the 0th element of its associated type, as it is known to always point to the object identifier. Also, consider that a **type** object is itself an independent object and will actually be represented as a set of pointers. (For example, the element associated with **student_name** would be a pointer to the **type** object named by **string**. The element associated with the **grades** set would point to a child object responsible for specifying pointers to the **type** objects of both **set** and **grades**.)

the number of independent objects of a given type in memory (the algorithm makes use of object type).

A message can be sent only to an independent object of a known type. The independent object value can be located in no worse than $O(\log(n))$ time. The temporary objects of this object (which include the rule being invoked) are located in its **type** object, which can be located in $O(\log(N))$ time, $N$ being the total number of types. Hence a message can be sent in at worst $O(\log(\max(n,N)))$ time. Generally, the number of types $N$ will be smaller than the number of instances of a particular independent type, which itself may be rather small, yielding very fast message sending.

Within the context of a given object, message sending is much faster. Consider the addition of two simple integer objects $\mathbf{a} + \mathbf{b}$ with the same parent $\mathbf{X}$. The objects $\mathbf{a}$ and $\mathbf{b}$ will have internal names given by their index into $\mathbf{X}$, say $\mathbf{i}$ and $\mathbf{j}$ respectively. In order to do the addition, we will have previously located the **type** object of $\mathbf{X}$ (to find the rule in which the addition is located). Addition therefore requires the following:

1. Location of the type of $\mathbf{X(i)}$ in its **type** object, which is $O(1)$ since we already know the address of the **type** object of $\mathbf{X}$.

2. Location of the $+$ rule in the **type** object named by **int**, which is $O(\log(N))$.

3. The execution of the $+$ rule with parameters pointed to by $\mathbf{X(i)}$ and $\mathbf{X(j)}$, which is $O(1)$.

Now this is overall $O(\log(N))$, but we can do much better. At system startup time, we can hash the names of all the simple types by using standard algorithms, so that location of a simple type's **type** object is $O(1)$. This produces an overall execution time of $O(1)$ for rules whose parameters are simple objects in the same parent.

## 13.4 OBJECT PERSISTENCY

Up until this point, we have considered an OZ+ object universe whose constituent objects are memory-resident. As memory is volatile, we cannot guarantee the persistence of such objects. Therefore, features generally associated with data base management systems (DBMSs) have been incorporated into the OZ+ system so that we may provide for object persistence.

### 13.4.1 Overview

Memory is highly volatile because it is susceptible to processor failure (i.e., the failure of the processor or its operating system—what we usually speak of as a system crash). Our first inclination might therefore be to maintain the OZ+

object universe exclusively on disk rather than in memory. If we adopted such a scheme, rule execution would proceed at a significantly slower pace than with a memory-based object universe. The disk read and/or write operations associated with the access of object state would be far more time-consuming than the corresponding operations in memory. This in itself is not necessarily objectionable. The only requirement of interest is that the OZ+ system be capable of meeting the "worst case" modeling demands placed upon it within its intended application domain, the office.

The first solution that suggests itself is the maintenance of the object universe in memory with periodic backups to disk. This is a less than ideal solution for many reasons. If there is no virtual memory support, an object universe maintained in memory has a severe upper constraint on size (available memory is usually much smaller than disk space). If a virtual memory facility does exist, we have the problem of highly inefficient swapping between memory and disk of object-oriented programs by traditional virtual memory facilities.[15]

Finally, we note that the backing up of the entire object universe from memory to disk all at once would be a time-consuming operation for a universe of even moderate size. Such an operation could be performed only at some "slow" period in the model of any real-world office (e.g., 2:00 a.m.). We are forced to make an a priori assumption about our model that may not hold (that there will be such slow periods when we can perform backups). In addition, a processor failure between backups would still cause the nonrecoverable loss of all changes of state since the last backup. Worse yet, a direct copy of the object universe from memory to disk that was interrupted by a processor failure could produce irremediable inconsistencies in the disk object universe state.

As a compromise to the extremes of maintaining the object universe state exclusively in memory or on disk, we adopt the following scheme. At any point in time, the existence of a consistent (although not necessarily up-to-date) version of the object universe state on disk is guaranteed. When a particular rule has a high likelihood of being executed in the near future, a copy of each of the objects that it will need to access is brought into memory, unless such copies already exist there. When the rule executes, it will access only memory-based objects and not their disk-based counterparts. Changes of state are induced on the "active" memory-based objects by the rules that access

---

[15] It is well-known that most virtual memory facilities rely on the "locality of reference" principle, which generally holds well for traditional programming languages but may not for object-oriented ones. The locality of reference principle essentially predicts that if one item on a page of information swapped into memory is accessed, then other items on that page have a high probability of also being accessed in the near future. As object-oriented programs are not executed "linearly" like traditional languages, but rather as a complex pattern of messages flowing among a multitude of objects, this principle may not properly apply to them. Traditional virtual memory techniques could inefficiently swap pages containing only a very small percentage of needed program and data between memory and disk.

them. Disk is periodically updated to reflect these changes in a manner that guarantees the consistency of the disk-based object universe. The rest of this section provides more detail on how this is accomplished.

### 13.4.2 Managing Objects in Memory

Let us envision a point in time when a consistent version of an OZ+ object universe resides on disk and there are no objects in memory. The *event manager* will immediately attempt to form events.[16] In the process of trying to form an event, the event manager will determine the oids of objects that might participate in the event as well as the particular rules within objects that it will attempt to execute. The location of the state of an object with a given oid and the location of the rule code of a particular rule are found by consulting the *location manager*.

The OZ+ location manager keeps track of the locations of all objects in memory. Given an oid, it will return a pointer to the object, if it exists in memory. The location manager maintains a hash table so that it can locate a pointer to an object in constant time. This is an important consideration, as event-completion time is a function of message-passing time, which is directly proportional to the time spent locating an object. If the location manager determines that the object is not in memory, it will ask the *disk manager* to bring it in. (This manager will be discussed in detail shortly.) Once the object is in memory, the location manager will then return the pointer to the object. Note that a request to the location manager for an object's pointer is fulfilled in the same manner whether or not the object was originally in memory. Given a rule name, the location manager works in the same manner to locate its code. This is of course to be expected, as we have shown previously that in OZ+ a rule is a complex object and may be handled like any other object. A rule's name, or more precisely its internal name, is given uniquely by its complex object oid. A rule's code is given by its complex object state.

Once in memory, an object tends to remain there if it is periodically active. Each object is given an activity rating, which characterizes the frequency with which an object is accessed by rule executions. Objects that are virtually inactive (i.e., those that have not been accessed over a long period of time) are deleted from memory (after making sure that their disk-based counterparts are up to date). In consequence, the more active an object, the more likely it is to remain in memory indefinitely. In this way, we minimize the traffic from disk to memory. Again we should note that this scheme does not distinguish between objects and rules. Rules are treated as complex objects and given an activity rating as such. However, in general, a particular rule has a much higher probability of being accessed than a particular object state (since there may be many thousands of differentiable object instances associated with any

---

[16] To form events, the event manager consults its database of self-triggering rules within objects.

given object type, but only one set of rules). Thus, at any given time, memory will likely contain all those rules that are invoked with any frequency. In particular, all self-triggering rules (whose firing conditions are continually tested by the event manager) are likely to remain in memory permanently once they have been brought in.

### 13.4.3 Managing Objects on Disk

As we have pointed out, memory is volatile. Therefore, when objects in memory are updated, their corresponding disk-based images should also be updated to ensure a consistent and up-to-date object universe state. This function is performed by the OZ+ disk manager, which must provide for the following:

1. The storage of sufficient information on disk to recapture the state associated with each object instance in memory (the object's "data" part).

2. The storage of sufficient information to recapture the structure and rules common to all object instances of the same type in memory (the object's "program" part).

3. The storage of sufficient information to recapture the various relationships that exist among object types.

4. The ability to quickly locate and bring into memory any or all of the information given in 1, 2, and 3.

5. The ability to update the information in 1, 2, and 3 in a manner that guarantees consistency.

6. The standard housekeeping functions associated with the management of disk space (garbage collection of discarded objects, handling fragmentation problems, etc.)

Functions 1, 2, and 3 can be collapsed into one. As we have seen previously, OZ+ associates a special object instance (of type **type**) with each type that holds, as part of its own state, the structural and behavioral information associated with that type. Thus the information in 2 is found in 1. The information in 3 is similarly coerced into 1. Hence, we need not consider 2 and 3.

We are left with functions 1, 4, 5, and 6. Numerous questions are associated with the design of a disk manager to carry out these functions. Consider just a few of these. How is the data content of each object to be represented on disk? How is the object universe to be organized on disk? How can a particular object be efficiently located? How should disk paging be taken advantage of? How can fragmentation effects caused by additions, updates, and deletions of variable size objects be avoided?

Most of these questions are the object-oriented analogs of those that are necessarily asked and answered in the design of any DBMS. We might therefore profitably make use of some existing technology, such as a relational DBMS (rDBMS), to help in answering them. In fact, in OZ+ the disk manager is built "on top of" an available rDBMS. In the rest of this section, the design of this disk manager is outlined. The relative performance of the OZ+ disk manager to relational disk managers is measured by a comparison of various storage management functions involving objects and relations, respectively. We contend that the OZ+ disk manager is in most respects as efficient (in terms of time and space usage) as one that we might have built from the ground up.

In order to make use of an rDBMS, data must be organized in relations. By implication, an algorithm must exist to translate OZ+ objects into relational representations. Here we discuss only the translation of OZ+ complex objects into relations. For a discussion of class hierarchy translation into relations, the reader is referred to [Kim et al. 1987a; Lyngbaek and Vianu 1987].

An algorithm to translate OZ+ complex objects into relations becomes immediately apparent if we examine an arbitrary complex object. Every such object aggregates a set of other OZ+ objects. Each of the objects that it aggregates is itself either complex or simple. If simple, then its state is given by a scalar data value of some simple type (integer, string, float, text, etc.). We can map the name, type, and value of each simple object aggregated into a relational attribute with the same name, type, and value. We can map the name and oid of each complex object into a relational attribute with the same name, a type appropriate for holding oid values such as long integer, and a value given by the oid. Now, we can form a relational tuple out of these attributes with the same name as the complex object. If this process is recursively continued for each aggregated complex object, it will ultimately produce a set of relational tuples with the same information content as the original complex object. It is not difficult to see how this process can be generalized so that complex object types are mapped into relations in such a manner that all OZ+ objects can be represented as tuples in this relational schema. Let us formalize the general outline of this *object to relation translation* (ORT) algorithm.

Each complex OZ+ object $\mathbf{X}$ is an aggregate of its child OZ+ objects $\mathbf{X}_i$:

$$\mathbf{X} : \mathbf{X}_{oid} \ \mathbf{X}_1 \ \mathbf{X}_2 \ \mathbf{X}_3 \ldots \mathbf{X}_n \tag{1}$$

where $\mathbf{X}_{oid}$ names the (simple) child object that holds the object oid. From (1) we form the relations:

$$\mathbf{X}(\mathbf{X}_{oid}, \mathbf{X}_i, \mathbf{X}_j, \ \ldots \ , \mathbf{X}_k) \tag{2}$$

where the $\mathbf{X}_i$'s name the simple child objects in (1), and:

$$\mathbf{X\_X}_i \ (\mathbf{X}_{oid}, \mathbf{X}_{i\_oid}) \tag{3}$$

where the $\mathbf{X}_i$'s name the complex child objects in (1), $\mathbf{X\_X}_i$ is a relation name formed out of the names of the parent and child complex objects, and $\mathbf{X}_{i\_oid}$ is a renaming of the oid of the child complex object.

To illustrate with a concrete example, consider the OZ+ object:

```
a : (
    oid : objID;
    b : int;
    c : set (
        oid : objID;
        x : int;
        y : (
          oid : objID;
          z : char;
          b : float;
          )
        )
    d : int;
    )
```

Using the form of (1), **a** is specified as **a : oid b c d**. From (2) we obtain the relation **a** ($\mathbf{a}_{oid}$, **b**, **d**) where $\mathbf{a}_{oid}$ is a renaming of **oid**. From (3) we obtain the relation **a\_c** ($\mathbf{a}_{oid}$, $\mathbf{c}_{oid}$) where the oids are renamed as before. This relation will link a particular parent object **a** with a set of child objects **c**. Continuing recursively on **c**, we end up with the following set of relations:

```
A1 :  a(a_oid, b, d)
A2 :  a_c(a_oid, c_oid)
A3 :  c(c_oid, x)
A4 :  c_y(c_oid, y_oid)
A5 :  y(y_oid, z, b)
```

When a new object type definition is received by the OZ+ object manager, this algorithm is used to translate the complex object names into relational names (**A1, A3, A5**), relationships between parent and child complex objects into linking relations (**A2, A4**), and simple type names into attribute names (**A1, A3, A5**). Relation names are formed in such a manner as to guarantee uniqueness, given that the internal complex object names from which they are formed are guaranteed to be unique.[17]

For the majority of simple object types, there exists a direct mapping of type into attribute domain (integer into integer, float into float, etc.). We also make use of an rDBMS that includes structured attribute domains (such as text or bulk) so that these simple types also have an obvious mapping into the rDBMS. The base set of simple types in OZ+ includes one type corresponding to each attribute domain of its underlying rDBMS (EMPRESS [EMPRESS 1986]).

For simple types in which such a direct correspondence is not provided by the underlying rDBMS, OZ+ by necessity includes algorithms for mapping values of such a type into existing attribute domains in its rDBMS and back again. Suppose, for example, OZ+ supported complex numbers as a simple type and there was no rDBMS attribute domain directly corresponding to this type. The complex number type can be mapped into simple types that already exist (e.g., an ordered pair of float types) and, with a small extension to the ORT algorithm, be represented in two successive attribute domains. In general, for each simple OZ+ type, the ORT algorithm provides an appropriate mapping onto the available set of attribute domains.

After using the ORT algorithm to encode a complex object type definition into a relational scheme, it is a straightforward matter to encode the state of any object of that type as a set of relational tuples. For each complex object, the states of its simple object children are stored as attribute values of a tuple in the relation corresponding to the complex object's type definition. The correspondence between complex object and tuple is uniquely determined by the tuple's oid attribute value. (Every complex object has an oid that is encoded as the *key* of a tuple so that it can always be uniquely identified.)

All the OZ+ ORT algorithm transformations are 1-1 and onto. Thus, a unique *relation to object translation* (ROT) algorithm may be found for the relations formed by the ORT algorithm to decode them back into their original object form.

The ORT algorithm demonstrates the simple nature of the object to relation encoding process. The algorithm allows us to utilize an rDBMS to provide function 1, and consequently functions 2 and 3, described at the beginning of this section.

Function 4 is also easily provided. Given a complex object type name, the unique relation that corresponds to it can be found in $O(1)$ time. The object's oid value, the "high level" tuple that corresponds to the object, can be found uniquely by using the relation's oid attribute as a key.

A retrieved tuple will be translated into a complex object whose child objects are either simple objects containing data values or simple objects

---

[17] Complex objects' internal names have integer values which are unique in the name set of all complex objects. The corresponding relation name is the character-string representation of this integer value prefixed with a letter, for example, 10 -> "r10".

containing pointers (oids) to complex child objects. While it is advantageous to swap the contents of the child complex objects into memory, it is *not* so for the child complex objects' siblings *until* they themselves are specifically referenced by a rule. We offer some reasons for believing this to be so:

1. If a rule accesses one simple data object contained in a complex object, say an integer, there is no reason to bring the simple object's sibling, say a complex object holding 50,000 bytes of data, in along with it unless we know it will be accessed as well. This would involve the needless movement of a large amount of data into memory.

2. As simple objects tend to be much smaller than complex objects, reason 1 is not as powerful for simple objects. In addition, for reasons related to the manner in which object-oriented programs are written by programmers, there is a substantial degree of "locality of reference" among simple object siblings[18] (i.e., if a simple object is referenced, the probability that one of its simple object siblings will be referenced in the near future increases).

3. A simple object's simple siblings are all likely to be brought into memory on one disk page as (a) the collective length of the elements of a tuple will usually be small relative to disk page size, and (b) the elements of a tuple are generally stored contiguously on disk, and (c) a good rDBMS may very well attempt to store the elements of a tuple on the same disk page. Hence there is no advantage (in terms of swapping traffic savings) in bringing in the sibling complex objects, which are themselves represented by other tuples, until they are specifically referenced.

Provision must be made for the possibility of failure during the process of updating the object universe state on disk. Such an occurrence could lead to irremediable inconsistencies in disk state. A simple illustration of this is the recording of a change in time (recorded as separate hour and minute values) from 11:59 to 12:00. If 11 is updated to 12 and a crash occurs before 59 can be updated to 00, the time recorded on disk will be 12:59. This situation is easily remedied by adopting a write ahead log policy [Gray 1978] (i.e., writing the changes first to a (nonvolatile) buffer on disk, and then from the buffer to the database).

Change of state in the OZ+ object universe is induced by means of events, which are analogous to transactions in traditional database systems. An event consists of the change in state of a number of objects in a conceptually atomic manner (i.e., all at the same instance in time). In practice, however, an atomic

---

[18] Rule statements are the simple object children of a rule, their complex object parent. Such simple objects have a relatively high degree of locality of reference because rule statements are executed sequentially. The scalar data items corresponding to a particular "calculation" are also likely to be grouped together as simple object siblings in a single container (a complex object) by an OZ+ programmer.

change of state must be simulated by a consecutive series of updates over a finite period of time, performed immediately after an event has been formed. The update policy that we adopt must therefore guarantee the successful writing of the complete set of updates associated with an event to disk before changes are made to the disk object universe state.

In case of a crash, recovery begins with a message to the disk manager informing it that the system has just "restarted." The disk object universe may at this point be inconsistent, as the crash may have occurred during its update. Fortunately, the update policy guarantees that there is sufficient information available to bring it back into a consistent state. At this point, the event manager can begin forming new events. A final kind of failure with which traditional DBMSs must concern themselves is program failure—the failure of an application program leading to database inconsistencies. The method by which events are utilized to update object universe state on disk implicitly guards against such a failure. Program failure, in the OZ+ context, is the failure of an application process that accesses the object universe, because of an exception condition or run-time error. As all object universe "access" is mediated by the event manager, it is the only process with which we must concern ourselves (if any other process fails, the event manager will simply cause the event in which it participates to fail). If the event manager itself fails, all partially completed events, which have not as yet been permanently recorded on disk, are simply discarded.

## SUMMARY

In this chapter we discussed the design and implementation of OZ+, an object-oriented database system. OZ+ incorporates concepts derived from research in object-oriented systems and data base systems into a programming environment for implementing office information systems.

From the object-oriented systems perspective, OZ+ provides support for complex objects that seem to be a natural means of representing many office objects. It also supports true concurrency of object execution. Self-triggering rules and the event paradigm also serve to give OZ+ a different character from other object-oriented languages, and one that should be useful in the domain of office modeling. Our strict adherence to the object paradigm gives the OZ+ object model and language a conceptual simplicity that we hope will prove useful in providing insights into the nature of object-oriented programming.

From the database systems perspective, OZ+ utilizes an existing rDBMS to manage objects in secondary (disk) memory. Algorithms have been developed to encode an OZ+ object class definition into a set of relations and similarly to encode an OZ+ object into a set of relational tuples, as well as to perform the inverse operation. These algorithms are fast and do not contribute significantly to the overhead of swapping objects back and forth between memory and disk. Furthermore, we can utilize the search methods associated with the rDBMS for rapid location of particular objects. In general, the time taken to find a particular object instance in a set of objects of the same type is the same as the time taken to locate a particular tuple in a relation using a primary search key. (With any good rDBMS, this time will be at most logarithmic in the size of the collection.) The only real negative aspect to this approach is that it does not give us the flexibility to take advantage of disk paging—that is, we would like to be able to group objects likely to be accessed together on one page so that they could be swapped in and out of memory together.

OZ+ is being prototyped on a set of Sun-3/50 clients supported by a Sun-3/280 file server [Sun 1986]. It is written in C [Kernighan and Ritchie 1978] and Turing Plus [Hold and Penny 1987] under version 4.2bsd of the UNIX operating system [Thompson and Ritchie 1978]. The EMPRESS relational data base management system [EMPRESS 1986] is used as the underlying disk storage and access mechanism.

## ACKNOWLEDGMENT

This research was supported by the Natural Sciences and Engineering Research Council of Canada under grants A3356 and G1360.

## REFERENCES

[Codd 1970] E.F. Codd, "A Relational Model of Data for Large Shared Data Banks," *Communications of the ACM,* vol. 13, no. 6, pp. 377–387, 1970.

[EMPRESS 1986] *EMPRESS/32: Relational Data Base Management System,* EMPRESS Software, Inc., 1986.

[Gibbs and Tsichritzis 1983] S.J. Gibbs and D.C. Tsichritzis, "A Data Modelling Approach for Office Information Systems," *ACM Transactions on Office Information Systems,* vol. 1, no. 4, pp. 299–319, 1983.

[Goldberg and Robson 1983] A. Goldberg and D. Robson, *Smalltalk 80: The Language and Its Implementation,* Addison-Wesley, Reading, MA, 1983.

[Gray 1978] J.N. Gray, *Notes on Data Base Operating Systems,* IBM Research Report RJ2188, IBM Research Lab, San Jose, CA, 1978.

[Guttag 1977] J. Guttag, "Abstract Data Types and the Development of Data Structures," *Communications of the ACM,* vol. 20, no. 6, pp. 396–404, 1977.

[Hammer and Sirbu 1980] M. Hammer and M. Sirbu, "What Is Office Automation?," *Proceedings of the 1980 Office Automation Conference,* pp. 37–49, 1980.

[Hewitt 1977] C. Hewitt, "Viewing Control Structures as Patterns of Passing Messages," *Artificial Intelligence,* vol. 8, no. 3, pp. 323–364, 1977.

[Hogg and Weiser 1987] J.S. Hogg and S.P. Weiser, "OTM: Applying Objects to Tasks," *Proceedings of the ACM Conference on Object-Oriented Programming Systems, Languages and Applications,* pp. 388–393, 1987.

[Holt and Penny 1987] R.C. Holt and D.A. Penny, *Notes on Turing Plus,* Department of Computer Science, University of Toronto, Toronto, Canada, 1987.

[Kernighan and Ritchie 1978] B.W. Kernighan and D.M. Ritchie, *The C Programming Language,* Prentice-Hall, Englewood Cliffs, NJ, 1978.

[Kim et al. 1987a] W. Kim, H.T. Chou and J. Banerjee, "Operations and Implementation of Complex Objects," *Proceedings of the Data Engineering Conference,* 1987.

[Kim et al. 1987b] W. Kim, J. Banerjee, H.T. Chou, J.F. Garza and D. Woelk, "Composite Object Support in an Object-Oriented Database System," *Proceedings of the ACM Conference on Object-Oriented Programming Systems, Languages and Applications,* pp. 118–125, 1987.

[Lochovsky 1987] F.H. Lochovsky, "Managing Office Tasks," *Proceedings of the IEEE Office Automation Symposium,* pp. 247–249, 1987.

[Lorie and Plouffe 1983] R. Lorie and W. Plouffe, "Complex Objects and Their Use in Design Transactions," *Proceedings of the ACM SIGMOD Databases for Engineering Applications Conference,* pp. 115–121, 1983.

[Lyngbaek and Vianu] P. Lyngbaek and V. Vianu, "Mapping a Semantic Data Model to the Relational Model," *Proceedings of the ACM SIGMOD Conference,* pp. 132–142, 1987.

[Mooney 1984] J. Mooney, *Oz: An Object-based System for Implementing Office Information Systems,* M.Sc. Thesis, Department of Computer Science, University of Toronto, 1984.

[Morgan 1980] H.L. Morgan, "Research and Practice in Office Automation," *Proceedings of the IFIP Congress,* pp. 783–789, 1980.

[Nierstrasz et al. 1983] O.M. Nierstrasz, J. Mooney and K.J. Twaites, "Using Objects to Implement Office Procedures," *Proceedings of the CIPS Conference,* pp. 65–73, 1983.

[Sirbu et al. 1981] M. Sirbu, J. Schoichet, J. Kunin and M. Hammer, *OAM: An Office Analysis Methodology,* Memo OAM-16, Office Automation Group, MIT, Cambridge, MA, 1981.

[Sun 1986] *The Sun Workstation Architecture,* Sun Microsystems Inc., Mountain View, CA, 1986.

[Thompson and Ritchie 1978] K. Thompson and D. Ritchie, "The UNIX Time-Sharing System," *Bell Technical Journal,* vol. 57, no. 6, pp. 1905–1929, 1978.

[Twaites 1984] K.J. Twaites, *An Object-based Programming Environment for Office Information Systems,* M.Sc. Thesis, Department of Computer Science, University of Toronto, 1984.

[Weiser 1985] S.P. Weiser, "An Object-Oriented Protocol for Managing Data," *IEEE Database Engineering,* vol. 8, no. 4, pp. 41–48, 1985.

# 4 Architectural Issues in Object-Oriented Systems

# 14

Storage Management for
Objects in EXODUS

Michael J. Carey, David J. DeWitt, Joel E. Richardson,
Eugene J. Shekita

## INTRODUCTION

In the 1970s, the relational data model was the focus of much of the research
in the database area. At this point, relational database technology is well understood, a number of relational systems are commercially available, and they
support the majority of business applications relatively well. One of the fore-
most database problems of the 1980s is how to support classes of applications
that are not well served by relational systems. For example, computer-aided
design systems, scientific and statistical applications, image and voice applications, and large, data-intensive artificial intelligence applications all place
demands on database systems that exceed the capabilities of relational systems.
Such application classes differ from business applications in a variety of ways,
including their data modeling needs, the types of operations of interest, and
the storage structures and access methods required for their operations to be
efficient.

After Carey et al., "Object and File Management in the EXODUS Estensible Database System,"
*Proceedings of the 12th International Conference on Very Large Databases,* 1986.

A number of database research efforts have recently begun to address the problem of building database systems to accommodate a wide range of potential applications via some form of extensibility. Such projects include EXODUS at the University of Wisconsin [Carey and DeWitt 1985; Carey et al. 1986b; Carey and DeWitt 1987], PROBE at CCA [Dayal and Smith 1985; Manola and Dayal 1986], POSTGRES at Berkeley [Stonebraker and Rowe 1986; Rowe and Stonebraker 1987], STARBURST at IBM Almaden [Schwarz et al. 1986; Lindsay et al. 1987], and GENESIS at UT-Austin [Batory et al. 1986]. Although the goals of these projects are similar, and each uses some of the same mechanisms to provide extensibility, the overall approach of each project is quite different. STARBURST, POSTGRES, and PROBE are complete database systems, each with a (different) well-defined data model and query language. Each system aims to provide the capability for users to add extensions such as new abstract data types and access methods within the framework provided by their data model. STARBURST is based on the relational model; POSTGRES extends the relational model with the notion of a procedure data type, triggers and inferencing capabilities, and a type hierarchy; PROBE is based on an extension of the DAPLEX functional data model, and includes support for spatial data and a class of recursive queries.

The EXODUS project is distinguished from all but GENESIS by virtue of being a "database generator" effort as opposed to an attempt to build a single (although extensible) DBMS for use by all applications. The EXODUS and GENESIS efforts differ significantly in philosophy and in the technical details of their approaches to DBMS software generation. GENESIS has a stricter framework (being based on a "building block" plus "pluggable module" approach), whereas EXODUS has certain powerful fixed components plus a collection of tools for a database implementor (DBI) to use in building the desired system based around these components.

The EXODUS group is addressing the challenges posed by emerging database applications by developing facilities to enable the rapid implementation of high-performance, application-specific database systems. EXODUS provides a set of kernel facilities for use across all applications, such as a versatile storage manager (the focus of this chapter) and a general-purpose manager for type-related dependency information. In addition, EXODUS provides a set of tools to help the DBI to develop new database system software. The implementation of some DBMS components is supported by tools that actually generate the components from specifications; for example, tools are provided to generate a query optimizer from a rule-based description of a data model, its operators, and their implementations [Graefe and DeWitt 1987]. Other components, such as new abstract data types, access methods, and database operations, must be explicitly coded by the DBI because of their more widely varying and highly algorithmic nature.[1] EXODUS attempts to sim-

---

[1] Actually, EXODUS will provide a library of generally useful components, such as widely applicable access methods including B+ trees and some form of dynamic hashing, but the DBI must implement components that are not available in the library.

plify this aspect of the DBI's job by providing a programming language with constructs designed specifically for use in writing code for the components of a DBMS [Richardson and Carey 1987]. Finally, we are currently developing a data model and an associated query language to serve as starting points for subsequent EXODUS DBMS implementation efforts.

In this chapter we describe the object and file management facilities of EXODUS. The initial design of the EXODUS storage manager was outlined in [Carey et al. 1986a]; this is an updated description, reflecting changes in the design that occurred as we developed the (now operational) first version of the system. The chapter is broken down as follows: The next section describes related work on "next generation" storage systems. In Section 14.2, an overview of the EXODUS storage system is presented and the key characteristics of the EXODUS storage manager are described. Section 14.3 describes the interface that is provided by the EXODUS storage manager to the higher levels of EXODUS. In Section 14.4, which makes up the majority of the chapter, we present a detailed description of our data structures for object storage and summarize results from an early performance evaluation of the algorithms that operate on large storage objects. Section 14.4 also describes the techniques employed for versioning, concurrency control, recovery, and buffer management for such objects. Section 14.5 sketches the techniques used to implement files of storage objects.

## 14.1 RELATED WORK

There have been a number of other projects to construct file and object management services related to those provided by EXODUS. In [Kaehler and Krasner 1983], LOOM, a Large Object-Oriented Memory for Smalltalk-80, is described. LOOM extended the object storage capabilities of Smalltalk-80 to allow the manipulation of up to $2^{31}$ objects instead of $2^{15}$ objects. Problems associated with large objects were not addressed, and the system provided no facilities for sharing (e.g., shared buffers, concurrency control or recovery).

Another related system is the file system for the iMAX-432 [Pollack et al. 1981]. This file system provided support for system-wide surrogates to name objects and for atomic actions on objects using a modification of Reed's versioning scheme [Reed 1983]. The design was based on the premise that most objects are small (less than 500 bytes); special consideration was given to clustering related objects together and to garbage-collecting deleted objects to minimize wasted file space.

The GemStone database system [Maier et al. 1986] (also see Chap. 12) is an object-oriented DBMS based on a Smalltalk-like data model and interface. In terms of storage management, GemStone objects are decomposed into collections of small elements (à la Smalltalk objects); the system's object manager is responsible for clustering related elements together on disk via segments. The Gemstone architects have investigated indexing issues that arise in an object-oriented DBMS environment. Large objects and collections of objects are represented on disk via mechanisms similar to those employed in EXODUS (and described in this chapter).

The Darmstadt Database Kernel System [Deppisch 1986; Paul et al. 1987] is also related to our work, having been motivated by similar application-related considerations. However, the emphasis of their kernel architecture is on support for complex records (i.e., nested relations), and in particular on clustering their components and providing an efficient means to relocate entire complex objects (e.g., from a host to a workstation). Components of complex objects are viewed as records with bytestring attributes. Objects are passed between the kernel and its clients by copying data between a page-oriented kernel buffer and a client-provided object buffer.

The storage system of POSTGRES [Stonebraker and Rowe 1986; Stonebraker 1987] is based on the use of tuples and relations. Each tuple is identified by a unique 64-bit surrogate that never changes. Tuples are not updated in place. Instead, new versions of modified tuples are inserted elsewhere into the database. A "vacuuming" process moves old data to an archival disk for long-term storage. Since complex objects are implemented through the use of POSTQUEL as a data type, no explicit mechanisms are provided for the storage or manipulation of large complex objects.

Finally, the object server developed at Brown University [Skarra et al. 1986] is also relevant. The object server provides a notion of objects and files similar to that of EXODUS. However, the main focus of their work has been on issues arising from a workstation/server environment; for example, they provide a set of "notify" lock modes to support efficient object sharing in such an environment.

## 14.2 OVERVIEW OF THE EXODUS STORAGE SYSTEM

The following paragraphs highlight the key characteristics of the EXODUS storage system that will be expanded upon in the remainder of the chapter.

**Storage Objects**   The basic unit of stored data in the EXODUS storage system is the *storage object*, which is an uninterpreted byte sequence of virtually unlimited size. By providing capabilities for storing and manipulating storage objects without regard for their size, we gain significant generality. For example, an access method such as a B+ tree can be written without any knowledge of the size of the storage objects it is manipulating. Not providing this generality has severely limited the applicability of WiSS [Chou et al. 1985], another storage system that was developed at the University of Wisconsin. While WiSS provides a notion of long records, one cannot build a B+ tree on a file of long records because of the way the system's implementation differentiates between long and short records.

**Concurrency Control and Recovery**   To further simply the user's[2] task of extending the functionality of the database system, both concurrency control and recovery mechanisms are provided in EXODUS for operations on shared storage objects. Locking is used for concurrency control, and recovery is accomplished via a combination of shadowing and logging.

**Versions**   As discussed in [Dayal and Smith 1985], many new database applications require support for multiple versions of objects. In keeping with the spirit of minimizing the amount of semantics encapsulated in the storage system of EXODUS, a generalized mechanism is provided that can be used to implement a variety of versioning schemes.

**Performance**   An important performance issue is the amount of copying that goes on between the buffer pool and application programs. If an application is given direct access into the buffer pool, security may become a problem. On the other hand, in a database system supporting a VLSI design system, or many other new applications, the application may require direct access to the storage objects in the buffer pool in order to obtain reasonable performance—copying large (multi-megabyte) complex objects between the database system and the application may be unacceptable. EXODUS storage system clients are thus given the option of directly accessing data in the buffer pool; clients that will almost certainly take advantage of this option are the application-specific access methods and operations layers. For applications in which direct access poses a security problem, a layer that copies data from database system space to user space can easily be provided.

**Minimal Semantics**   One of our goals is to minimize the amount of information that the storage system must have in order to manipulate storage objects. In particular, in order to keep the system extensible it seems infeasible for the storage system to know anything about the conceptual schema. (By conceptual schema, we mean the way in which data is interpreted by higher levels of the system.) On the other hand, semantics can sometimes be useful for performance reasons. For example, it was shown in [Chou and DeWitt 1985] that buffer management performance can be improved by allowing the buffer manager to capture some semantics of the operations being performed. Our solution is to keep schema information out of the storage system, but then to allow *hints* to be provided that can help in making decisions that influence performance in important ways. For example, the buffer manager accepts

---

[2] Internally, we speak of such "users" as "database implementors" (or DBI's for short). We do not intend to imply that EXODUS can be extended by the naive user, as we expect EXODUS to be extended for a given application domain once, by a DBI, and then modified only occasionally (if at all) for applications within that domain.

hints guiding its choice of replacement policies, and the storage manager also supports clustering hints that guide its placement of objects on disk.

## 14.3 THE STORAGE MANAGER INTERFACE

Before describing the details of how large storage objects and file objects (collections of storage objects) are represented in the EXODUS storage system, we briefly outline the nature of the interface provided for use by higher levels of EXODUS. In most cases, we expect the next level to be the layer that provides the access methods (and perhaps version support) for a given EXODUS application. This layer is likely to change from one application to another, although we expect to provide a library of standard access methods and version management code that can be used or extended by the authors of an application-specific DBMS. The intended implementation language for such a layer is E [Richardson and Carey 1987], which shields clients from some of the details of the storage manager interface, although we also expect to support some clients who wish to use only the storage manager of EXODUS.

The EXODUS storage system provides a procedural interface. This interface includes procedures to create and destroy file objects and to scan through the objects that they contain. For scanning purposes, the storage system provides a call to get the object identifier of the next storage object within a file object. It also provides procedures for creating and destroying storage objects within a file; all storage objects must reside in some file object. For reading storage objects, the EXODUS storage system provides a call to get a pointer to a range of bytes within a given storage object; the desired byte range is read into the buffers, and a pointer to the bytes is returned to the caller. Another call is provided to inform EXODUS that these bytes are no longer needed, so EXODUS "unpins" them in the buffer pool. For writing storage objects, a call is provided to tell EXODUS that a subrange of the bytes that were read is to be replaced with an indicated new bytestring of the same size. For shrinking or growing storage objects, calls to insert bytes into and delete bytes from a specified offset in a storage object are provided, as is a call to append bytes to the end of an object (a special case of insert). Finally, for transaction management, the EXODUS storage system provides begin, commit, and abort transaction calls. We also anticipate the inclusion of transaction-related hooks, such as a call to release certain locks early, to aid in the efficient implementation of concurrent and recoverable operations on new access methods.

In addition to the functionality just outlined, the EXODUS storage system accepts a number of performance-related hints. For example, the object creation routine accepts hints about where to place a new object (e.g., "place the new object near the object with id $X$"); such hints can be used to achieve clustering for related or complex objects. It is also possible to request that an object be alone on a disk page and the same size as the page, which is very useful when implementing access methods. In regard to buffer management, information about how many buffer page frames to use and what replacement policy to employ are accepted by the buffer manager. This is supported by allowing a *buffer group* to be specified with each object access; the buffer manager accepts this information on a per-buffer-group basis, which allows variable-partition buffer management policies such as DBMIN [Chou and DeWitt 1985] to be easily supported.

## 14.4 STORAGE OBJECTS

As described earlier, *storage objects* are the basic unit of data in the EXODUS storage system. Storage objects can grow and shrink in size, and their growth and shrinkage is not constrained to occur at the end of an object, as the EXODUS storage system supports insertion and deletion anywhere within a storage object. This section of the chapter describes the data structures and algorithms that are used for efficient support of storage objects, particularly large dynamic storage objects.

Storage objects can be either small or large, although this distinction is hidden from clients of the EXODUS storage system. Small storage objects reside on a single disk page, whereas large storage objects occupy multiple disk pages. In either case, the object identifier (OID) of a storage object is of the form (*page #, slot #*). Pages containing small storage objects are slotted pages, as in INGRES, System R, and WiSS [Astrahan et al. 1976; Stonebraker et al. 1976; Chou et al. 1985]; as such, the OID of a small storage object is a pointer to the object on disk. For large storage objects, the OID points to a *large object header*. This header resides on a slotted page with other large object headers and small storage objects, and it contains pointers to other pages involved in the representation of the large object. All other pages in a large storage object are private to the object rather than being shared with other small or large storage objects (except that pages may be shared between versions of the same object, as we will see later). When a small storage object grows to the point where it can no longer be accommodated on a single page, the EXODUS storage system automatically converts it into a large storage object, leaving its object header in place of the original small object.[3] We considered the alternative of using surrogates for OIDs rather than physical addresses, as in other recent proposals [Pollack et al. 1981; Copeland and Maier 1984; Skarra et al. 1986; Stonebraker and Rowe 1986; Stonebraker 1987], but we rejected this alternative because of what we anticipated would be its high cost—with surrogates, it would always be necessary to access objects via a surrogate index. (Besides, a surrogate index can be implemented above the storage manager level for applications where surrogate support is required.)

---

[3] Note that for performance reasons the inverse operation is not done; once a small object is converted to a large object, it is never converted back to a small object.

### 14.4.1 Large Storage Objects

The data structure used to represent large objects was inspired by the ordered relation data structure proposed for use in INGRES [Stonebraker et al. 1983], although there are a number of significant differences between our insertion and deletion algorithms and those of Stonebraker's proposal. Figure 14.1 shows an example of our large object data structure. Conceptually, a large object is an uninterpreted sequence of bytes; physically, it is represented on disk as a B+ tree index on byte position within the object, plus a collection of leaf (data) blocks. The root of the tree (the large object header) contains a number of (*count, page #*) pairs, one for each child of the root. The count value associated with each child pointer gives the maximum byte number stored in the subtree rooted at that child; the count for the rightmost child pointer is therefore also the size of the object. Internal nodes are similar, being recursively defined as the root of another object contained within its parent node; thus, an absolute byte offset within a child translates to a relative offset within its parent node. The left child of the root in Fig. 14.1 contains bytes 1–421, and the right child contains the rest of the object (bytes 422–786). The rightmost leaf node in the figure contains 173 bytes of data. Byte 100 within this leaf node is byte $192 + 100 = 292$ within the right child of the root, and it is byte $421 + 292 = 713$ within the object as a whole.

The leaf blocks in a large storage object contain pure data—no control information is required since the parent of a leaf contains the byte counts for each of its children. The size of a leaf block is a parameter of the data structure, and it is an integral number of contiguous disk pages. For often-updated objects, leaf blocks can be made one page in length so as to minimize the amount of I/O and byte-shuffling that must be done on updates; for more static objects, leaf blocks can consist of several contiguous pages to lower the I/O cost of scanning long sequences of bytes within such objects. (The leaf block size can be set on a per-volume basis.) As in B+ trees, leaf blocks are allowed to vary from half full to completely full.

**FIGURE 14.1** AN EXAMPLE OF A LARGE STORAGE OBJECT

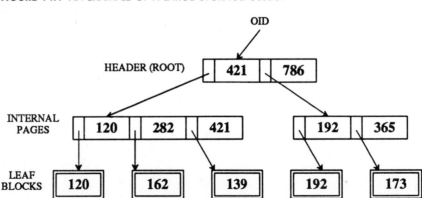

Each internal node of a large storage object corresponds to one disk page, and contains between $n_e$ and $2n_e + 1$ (count, pointer) pairs. We allow a maximum of $2n_e + 1$ pairs because our deletion algorithm works in a top-down manner and the nature of its top-down operation requires that it be possible to merge a half-full node of $n_e$ entries and a node with $n_e + 1$ entries into a single full node (as we will see shortly). Finally, the root node corresponds to at most one disk page, or possibly just a portion of a shared page, and contains between 2 and $2n_e + 1$ (count, pointer) pairs.

Table 14.1 shows examples of the approximate object size ranges that can be supported by trees of height two and three, assuming two different leaf block sizes. The table assumes 4K-byte disk pages, 4-byte pointers, and 4-byte counts, so the internal pages contain between 255 and 511 (count, pointer) pairs. It should be obvious from the table that two or three levels will suffice for most large objects.

Associated with the large storage object data structure are algorithms to *search* for a range of bytes, to *insert* a sequence of bytes at a given point in the object, to *append* a sequence of bytes to the end of the object, and to *delete* a sequence of bytes from a given point in the object. The insert, append, and delete operations are quite different from those in the proposal of Stonebraker et al. [Stonebraker et al. 1983], as the insertion or deletion of an arbitrary number of bytes into a large storage object poses some unique problems compared to inserting or deleting a single record from an ordered relation. Inserting or deleting one byte is the analogy in our case to the usual single-record operations, and single-byte operations would be far too inefficient for bulk inserts and deletes. The append operation is a special case of insert that we treat differently in order to achieve best-case storage utilizations for large objects that are constructed via successive appends. We consider each of these algorithms in turn.

**Search** The search operation supports the retrieval of a sequence of $N$ bytes starting at byte position $S$ in a large storage object. (It can also be used to retrieve a sequence of bytes that are to be modified and rewritten, of course.) Referring to the (count, pointer) pairs using the notation $c[i]$ and $p[i]$, where

**TABLE 14.1** SOME EXAMPLES OF OBJECT SIZES

| No. of Tree Levels | Leaf Block Size | Object Size Range |
|---|---|---|
| | 1 | 8KB–2MB |
| 2 | 4 | 32KB–8MB |
| | 1 | 2MB–1GB |
| 3 | 4 | 8MB–4GB |

$1 \leq i \leq 2n_e + 1$, and letting $c[0] = 0$ by convention, the search algorithm can be described as follows:

1. Let *start* = S, and read the root page and call it page P.

2. While P is not a leaf page, do the following: Save P's address on the stack, and binary search P to find the smallest count $c[i]$ such that *start* $\leq c[i]$. Set *start* = *start* $- c[i-1]$, and read the page associated with $p[i]$ as the new page P.

3. Once at a leaf, the first desired byte is on page P at location *start*.

4. To obtain the rest of the N bytes, walk the tree using the stack of pointers maintained in step 2.

Considering Fig. 14-1 again, suppose we wish to find bytes 250–300. We set *start* = 250, binary search the root, and find that $c[1] = 421$ is the count that we want. We set *start* = *start* $- c[0] = 250$ (since $c[0] = 0$ by convention), and then we follow $p[1]$ to the left child of the root node. We binary search this node, and we find that $c[2] = 282$ is the count that equals or exceeds *start*; thus, we set *start* = *start* $- c[1] = 130$ and follow $p[2]$ to the leaf page with 162 bytes in it. Bytes 130–162 of this node and bytes 1–18 of its right neighbor (which is reachable by walking the stack) are the desired bytes.

**Insert**    The insert operation supports the insertion of a sequence of N bytes after the byte at position S. Since N can be arbitrarily large, an algorithm that efficiently handles bulk insertions is required; as mentioned before, the standard B-tree insertion algorithm works only for inserting a single byte, which would be too inefficient for large insertions. Our insert algorithm can be described as follows:

1. Traverse the large object tree until the leaf containing byte S is reached, as in the search algorithm. As the tree is traversed, update the counts in the nodes to reflect the number of bytes to be inserted, and save the search path on the stack.

2. Call the leaf into which bytes are being inserted L. When L is reached, try to insert the N bytes there. If no overflow occurs, then the insert is done, as the internal node counts will have been updated in step 1.

3. If an overflow occurs, proceed as follows: Let M be the left or right neighbor of L with the most free space (which can be determined by examining the count information in L's parent node), and let B be the number of bytes per leaf block. If L and M together have a sufficient amount of free space to accommodate N *modulo* B bytes of data (i.e., the overflow that would remain after filling as many leaves with new data as possible), then evenly distribute the new data plus the old contents of L

and $M$ evenly between these two nodes and $[N/B]$ newly allocated nodes. Otherwise, simply allocate as many leaves as necessary to hold the overflow from $L$, and evenly distribute $L$'s bytes and the bytes being inserted among $L$ and the newly allocated leaves.

4. Propagate the counts and pointers for the new leaves upward in the tree, using the stack built in step 1. If an internal node overflows, handle it in the same way that leaf overflows are handled (but without the neighbor check).

The motivation for the neighbor checking portion of step 3 is to avoid allocating an additional leaf node in cases where the overflow can instead be accommodated by a neighboring node. This adds only a small cost to the overall expense of insertion, as it is unnecessary to access a neighboring leaf unless it is determined (based on examining the parent's count values) that the redistribution of data between $L$ and $M$ will indeed succeed, whereas the neighbors would have to be read from disk before this could be known in the case of a standard B+ tree. Note that this modification does increase the I/O cost for insertion in cases where such redistribution is possible—instead of reading $L$ and then writing back $L$ and a new node created by splitting $L$ (along with $[N/B]$ other new nodes), $L$ and $M$ are both read and written. However, the I/O cost increase is worth it in this case, as the modification leads to a significant improvement in storage utilization [Carey et al. 1986a]. Also, it might be argued that the additional cost for reading $M$ is not the whole picture—by redistributing the data in this way, we avoid having the system go through the process of allocating an additional node from the free list to handle the overflow.

**Append**   The append operation supports the addition of $N$ bytes to the end of a large object. Appending $N$ bytes differs from inserting $N$ bytes in the way that data is redistributed among leaf pages when an overflow occurs. The append algorithm is as follows:

1. Make a rightmost traversal of the large object tree. As the tree is being traversed, update the counts in the internal nodes to reflect the effect of the append. As always, save the search path on the stack.

2. Call the rightmost leaf $R$. If $R$ has enough free space to hold the new bytes, then append the bytes to $R$. The append operation is now complete in this case.

3. Otherwise, call $R$'s left neighbor (if it exists) $L$. Allocate as many leaves as necessary to hold $L$'s bytes, $R$'s bytes, plus the new bytes being appended to the object. Fill $L$, $R$, and the newly allocated leaves in such a way that all but the two rightmost leaves of the tree are completely full. Balance

the remaining data between the two rightmost leaves, leaving each leaf at least half full. (If $L$ has no free space, we can ignore $L$ during this step.)

4. Propagate the counts and pointers for the new leaves upward in the tree, using the stack built in step 1, and handle internal node overflow as in the insertion algorithm.

The key point of this algorithm is that it guarantees that a large object which is constructed via successive append operations will have maximal leaf utilization (i.e., all but the last two leaves will be completely full). This is particularly useful because it allows large objects to be created in steps, something that may be necessary if the object being created is extremely large. While this algorithm could be improved to yield higher internal node utilization by treating the internal nodes in the same way that leaves are treated, we decided not to do this; doing so would increase the I/O cost of the algorithm, and internal node utilization is not as critical as leaf node utilization because of the large fanout of internal nodes.

**Delete**   The delete operation supports the deletion of $N$ bytes starting at a specified byte position. In a B+ tree, the analogous problem would be that of range deletion, that is, deleting all keys between some lower and upper bounds. Again, since the traditional B+ tree deletion algorithm removes only one record at a time, it would be unacceptably slow for large deletions. Instead, our bulk delete algorithm proceeds in two phases. In the first phase, it deletes the specified range of bytes, possibly leaving the tree in an unbalanced state. The second phase makes one pass down the tree structure to rebalance the tree. (Note that the second phase is less expensive than it may sound, as most of the relevant nodes will be buffer-resident after the first phase.)

Deletion of an arbitrary range of bytes from the leaves of a large object will, in general, imply the deletion of a number of entire subtrees, leaving a "raw edge" of damaged nodes. These nodes form the *cut-path* of the deletion. In general, the *left* and *right cut-paths* will start at the root, include some number of common nodes, and then split off and proceed down the tree to two different leaves. The node at which the left and right cut-paths diverge is called the *lowest common ancestor* or *lca* for the delete. Figure 14.2 illustrates the relationship between the deleted portion of the tree, the left and right cut-paths, and their *lca*. Note that if any of the nodes remaining in the tree have underflowed, they must necessarily occur along the cut-path. The rebalancing algorithm therefore traces the cut-path in a top-down fashion, attempting to "zipper up" the split in the tree.

In order to minimize the I/O cost of the deletion algorithm, we use a small data structure in memory, *path*, which describes the cut-path. The *path* data structure is built during the delete phase of the algorithm, and it stores the disk address of each cut-path node plus the number of children that it has (including nodes from both the left and right cut-paths). The

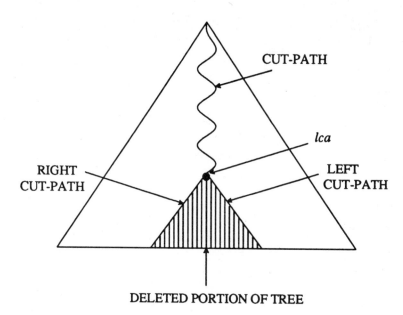

**FIGURE 14.2** TERMINOLOGY FOR DELETION ALGORITHM

information stored in *path* is sufficient to determine whether a node is *in danger* of underflowing (as defined shortly). The rebalancing algorithm then examines *path* in a top-down fashion—for each *path* node, if it is in danger of underflowing, its corresponding tree node is merged or reshuffled with a neighboring node until it is safe.

The notion of a node being in danger of underflowing (possibly without actually having underflowed) is what allows the rebalancing algorithm to operate in one downward pass through the tree. A node is in this situation if it cannot afford to have a pair of its child nodes merged into a single child node, as this would cause the node itself to underflow. To prevent this possibility, all potential underflows are instead handled on the way down the tree by merging endangered nodes with neighboring nodes, or else by borrowing entries from neighboring nodes if such merging is impossible (i.e., if both neighbors have more than $n_e$ entries). A node is said to have *underflowed* if either of the following conditions holds for the node:

1. The node is a leaf and it is less than half full.

2. The node is an internal node and it has fewer than $n_e$ entries (or fewer than two entries if it is the root node).

We say that a node is *in danger* of underflowing if any of the following three conditions holds:

1. The node has actually underflowed.

2. The node is an internal node with exactly $n_e$ entries (two entries if it is the root), and one of its children along the cut path is in danger.

3. The node is the *lca*, and it has exactly $n_e + 1$ entries (three entries if it is the root), and both of its children along the cut path are in danger.

Given this background and our definitions of underflowed and endangered nodes, we can now describe each phase of the deletion algorithm as follows:

**Deletion Phase**

1. Traverse the object to the left and right limits of the deletion. All subtrees completely enclosed by the traversal are deleted, and the counts in all nodes along the cut-path are updated to show the results of the deletion. Also, for each node along the cut-path (as the tree is traversed), create a representative node in the main-memory data structure *path* that records the address of the node and the number of children that it has left.

2. Traverse the *path* data structure bottom-up, marking each node that is in danger (as defined above).

**Rebalancing Phase**

1. If the root is not in danger, go to step 2. If the root has only one child, make this child the new root and go to step 1. Otherwise, merge/reshuffle[4] those children of the root that are in danger and go to step 1.

2. Go down to the next node along the cut-path. If no nodes remain, then the tree is now rebalanced.

3. While the current node is in danger, merge/reshuffle it with a sibling. (For a given node along the cut-path, this will require either 0, 1, or 2 iterations of the while loop.)

4. Go to step 2.

One additional note is in order with regard to the I/O cost of the deletion phase of the algorithm—in this phase, only one leaf block ever has to be touched. Entirely deleted nodes can simply be handed back to the free space manager directly, as their addresses are available in their parent node; furthermore, deletion can be accomplished for the partially deleted leaf block on the left cut-path by simply decrementing the byte count in its parent node.

---

[4] The merge/reshuffle step decides whether nodes can be merged or whether bytes must be reshuffled with a neighbor, does it, and then updates *path* to maintain a consistent view of the cut-path.

Thus, only the partially deleted leaf block on the right cut-path needs to be read and rewritten during the deletion phase.

**Performance Characteristics**  Before we actually implemented our large object data structure and algorithms, we constructed a main-memory prototype in order to investigate various design alternatives and performance tradeoffs. In our study, we assumed a 4K-byte page size, and we tried using both 1-page and 4-page leaf blocks. Our experiments consisted of using the append operation to construct objects of several different initial sizes (with an initial storage utilization of approximately 100%), and then running a mix of randomly generated read (search), insert, and delete operations on the objects. We experimented with 10-MB and 100-MB objects, and we ran tests with 1-byte, 100-byte, and 10K-byte search, insert, and delete operations. The details of this study are described in [Carey et al. 1986a]. We summarize the major results here, and refer the interested reader to the original paper for further details.

Basically, we found that the EXODUS large storage object mechanism can operate on very large dynamic objects at relatively low cost, and at a very reasonable level of storage utilization. In particular, with the insert algorithm described in this chapter, which avoids allocating new leaf pages unless both neighbors are unable to accommodate the overflow, we obtained average storage utilizations in the range from 80 to 85 percent. These results were obtained in the presence of random byte insertions and deletions; for large static objects, utilizations of close to 100 percent would be the norm, and utilizations in the 90 to 100 percent range would be expected for objects where updates are more localized. With respect to the choice of leaf block size, our experiments highlighted the expected tradeoffs: 4-page leaf blocks were definitely advantageous for large, multipage reads, leading to a 30 to 35 percent performance improvement compared to 1-page leaf blocks. However, they increased the cost somewhat for updates, and led to a 5 to 10 percent decrease in storage utilization in the presence of random insertions and deletions. Multipage leaf blocks thus offer the greatest advantages for large, relatively static objects (e.g., raster images), where storage utilization will be close to 100 percent (because such objects are built via appends and are not subjected to frequent, random updates).

## 14.4.2 Versions of Storage Objects

As described earlier, the EXODUS storage system also provides support for versions of storage objects. The support provided is quite primitive, with updates to a versioned object leading to the creation of a new version of the object. An object is designated as being either a versioned or nonversioned object when it is first created. When a versioned storage object is updated, its object header (or the entire object, in the case of a small storage object) is copied to a new location on disk and updated there as a new version of the object. The OID of the new version is returned to the updater, and the OID of the old version remains the same (i.e., it is the OID that was originally passed to the update routine, since OIDs are physical addresses). To ensure that the cost of copying the new version elsewhere is not as prohibitive as it might otherwise be [Carey and Muhanna 1986], the new version is placed on the same page of the file object, or else on a nearby page, if possible. (Note that we do not use versions as our recovery mechanism, or this would be unreasonable.)

The reason for such a primitive level of version support is that different EXODUS applications may have widely different notions of how versions should be supported, as evidenced by the wide range of version-related proposals in the recent literature [Stonebraker 1981; Dadam et al. 1984; Katz and Lehman 1984; Batory and Kim 1985; Clifford and Tansel 1985; Klahold et al. 1985; Snodgrass and Ahn 1985; Katz et al. 1986]. Therefore, we leave the maintenance of data structures such as graphs of the versions and alternatives of objects to a higher level of the system, a level that will vary from application to application (unlike the storage system). The reason that we do not leave version management out of the EXODUS storage system altogether is one of efficiency—it could be prohibitively expensive, in terms of both storage space and I/O cost, to maintain versions of very large objects by maintaining entire copies of objects.

Versions of large storage objects are maintained by copying and updating the pages that differ from version to version. Figure 14.3 illustrates this by an example. The figure shows two versions of the large storage object of Fig. 14.1, the original version, $V_1$, and a newer version, $V_2$. In this example, $V_2$ was created by deleting the last 36 bytes from $V_1$. Note that $V_2$ shares all nodes of $V_1$ that are unchanged, and it has its own copies of each modified node. A new version of a large storage object will always contain a new copy of the path from the root to the new leaf (or leaves); it may also contain copies of other internal nodes if the change affects a very large fraction of the object. Since

**FIGURE 14.3** TWO VERSIONS OF A LARGE STORAGE OBJECT

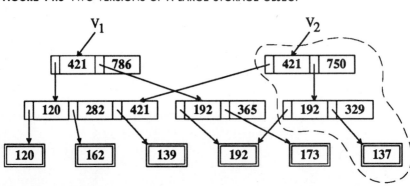

the length of the path will usually be two or three, however, and the number of internal pages is small relative to the number of pages of actual data (due to high fanout for internal nodes), the overhead for versioning large objects in this scheme is small—for a given tree height, it is basically proportional to the difference between adjacent versions, and not to the size of the objects.

Besides allowing for the creation of new versions of large storage objects, the EXODUS storage system also supports the deletion of versions. Again, this is necessary from an efficiency standpoint; it is also necessary if the storage system is to successfully hide the physical representation of storage objects from its clients. The problem is that, when deleting a version of a large object, we must avoid discarding any of the object's pages that are shared (and thus needed) by other versions of the same object. In general, we will have a situation like the one pictured in Fig. 14.4, where we wish to delete a version $V$ that has a direct ancestor $V_a$ (from which $V$ was derived) and descendants $V_{d_1}$ through $V_{d_n}$ (which were derived from $V$).

A naive way to ensure that no shared pages are discarded would be to traverse all other versions of $V$, marking each page as having been visited, and then traverse $V$, discarding each unmarked page. The problem with this approach is that there may be many versions of $V$, and consequently the number of pages visited could be quite large. One way to cut down on the number of pages visited is to observe that, if an ancestor of version $V_a$ shares a page with a page with $V$, then $V_a$ itself must also share that same page with $V$. Likewise, if a descendant of $V_{d_1}$ shares a page with $V$, then $V_{d_1}$ itself must also share that page with $V$. Thus, it suffices to visit just the pages of the direct ancestor and the direct descendants of an object, that is, the *adjacent* versions of an object (the version from which the object was directly derived, or versions that were themselves directly derived from the object).

We can further reduce the number of pages visited by observing two things. First, if a page is shared by two versions of a large object, then the

**FIGURE 14.4** AN EXAMPLE VERSION HISTORY

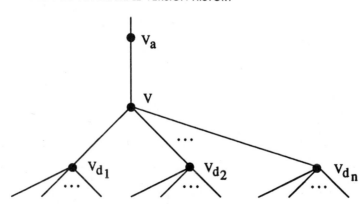

entire subtree rooted at that page must be shared by the two versions. (An example is the leftmost child of the two version root pages in Fig. 14.3.) Second, if a subtree is shared by two versions, then the root of that subtree must have the same height (i.e., distance above the leaf level) in both versions of the object. (Again, see Fig. 14.3.) The first observation means that we need only to visit a shared subtree's root; there is no need to visit its descendant pages since they are necessarily shared. The second observation means that if we scan versions of equal height level by level, then we can detect the roots of shared subtrees as the level is scanned; further, for versions of unequal height, we need not check for shared pages until we get down to the appropriate level in the taller of the two versions.

Suppose for the moment that we wish to delete version $V$ of an object, and that $V$ has just one direct descendant, $V_d$. Further, suppose that $V$ and $V_d$ are the same height. Then, based on these two observations, the deletion algorithm can be described as follows:

1. For each internal level $l$ of $V$, do the following (working top-down from the root level, where $l = 0$):

   a. Scan the index nodes at level $l$ in $V$, tentatively marking all of the page numbers encountered in the nodes at this level for deletion. (Note that these page numbers are for pages at level $l+1$.)

   b. Now scan level $l$ in $V_d$. If a marked page number is encountered, unmark it and avoid scanning that page (and the subtree rooted at that page) in subsequent iterations.

   c. Discard the pages from level $l+1$ of $V$ that are still marked for deletion after step b.

2. Finish by discarding the root of $V$ as well.

This algorithm is easily generalized to handle the case where the heights of versions $V$ and $V_d$ are unequal. If the height of $V$ is greater, then we delay scanning $V_d$ until we are scanning the level in $V$ with the same height as the root of $V_d$; the case where the height of $V_d$ is greater is handled similarly. It should also be clear that the algorithm can be generalized for the case where there are several versions adjacent to $V$ (i.e., an ancestor and several descendant versions). In this latter case, step b must be performed for level $l$ of each adjacent version, as a page of $V$ cannot be discarded unless no adjacent version shares that page with $V$. As input, then, the version deletion operation takes the OID of the version to be deleted and the set of OIDs of its adjacent versions; it deletes the specified version while leaving intact all of the pages that it shares with adjacent versions. As described earlier, we leave the problem of maintaining information about adjacent versions, like those in the example of Fig. 14.4, to a higher level of the system.

To implement this algorithm efficiently, one can use a breadth-first search to scan the objects and a main-memory hash table to store the page numbers of the marked pages. Note that it is *never* necessary to read any leaf pages from the disk with this algorithm—in the worst case, where there is no sharing of pages between versions, the algorithm simply ends up visiting every nonleaf page of every version, which is much better than also visiting the leaves. (Leaf blocks make up the vast majority of each version—with internal node fanouts of several hundred, nonleaf pages represent less than 1 percent of the storage requirements for very large objects.) In typical cases, however, the algorithm will visit relatively few pages, as adjacent versions are likely to share the bulk of their pages. Thus, despite its apparent complexity, this approach is likely to be cheaper in terms of I/O cost than an approach based on reference counts, as a reference counting scheme would almost certainly require reference counts to be inspected on all deleted leaf pages (requiring these pages to be read).

### 14.4.3 Concurrency Control and Recovery

The EXODUS storage system provides concurrency control and recovery services for storage objects. Initially, concurrency control is being provided via hierarchical two-phase locking [Gray 1979] at the levels of file objects and storage objects. Our eventual plans involve locking byte ranges of storage objects, with a "lock entire object" option being provided for cases where object level locking is sufficient. While we expect object level locking to be the norm for small storage objects, byte range locking may be useful for large storage objects in some applications: For updates that change the contents of a byte range without changing the size of the range (i.e., updates that read and then rewrite bytes in some range), concurrent searches and updates in disjoint regions of the object will be permitted. However, updates that insert, append, or delete bytes will lock the byte range from where the operation begins to the end of the object, as the offsets of the remaining bytes are indeterminate until the updater either commits or aborts.

To ensure the integrity of the internal pages of large storage objects while insert, append, and delete operations are operating on them (e.g., changing their counts and pointers), non-two-phase B+ tree locking protocols [Bayer and Scholnick 1977] will be employed. Searches and byte range updates will descend the tree structure by chaining their way down with read locks, read-locking a node at level $i+1$ and then immediately releasing the level $i$ read-lock, holding only byte range read or write locks in a two-phase manner. Since inserts, appends, and deletes will normally affect an entire root-to-leaf path,[5] the root and internal pages along the path for this type of update

---

[5] Recall that inserting, appending, or deleting bytes causes counts to change all the way up to the root. We may decide to treat write operations similarly to simplify the recovery code.

will be write-locked for the duration of the operation (e.g., the insert, delete, or append); again, though, only byte range write locks will be held in a two-phase manner once the operation has completed. We have opted to use locking techniques because they are likely to perform at least as well as other concurrency control techniques in most environments [Agrawal et al. 1987].

For recovery, small storage objects are being handled via classical logging techniques and in-place updating of objects [Gray 1979; Lindsay et al. 1979]. Log entries are operation-oriented, recording byte-range update operations and their arguments. Recovery for large storage objects is handled using a combination of shadows and operation logging—updated internal pages and leaf blocks are shadowed up to the root level, with updates being installed atomically by overwriting the old object header with the new header [Verhofstad 1978]. Prior to the installation of the update at the root, the other updated pages must be written to disk; also, the name and parameters of the update operation will be logged, with the log sequence number [Gray 1979; Lindsay et al. 1979] of the update log record being placed on the root page of the object. This ensures that operations on large storage objects can be undone (by performing the inverse operation) or redone (by re-performing the operation) as necessary in an idempotent manner. The same recovery scheme will be employed for versioned objects as well.

### 14.4.4 Buffer Management for Storage Objects

As described earlier, one objective of the EXODUS storage system design was to minimize the amount of copying that takes place between higher-level software and the system buffer. A second (related) objective is to allow sizable portions of large storage objects to be scanned directly in the buffer pool. To accommodate these needs, we allocate buffer space in either single-page units or variable-length *chunks*, where each chunk consists of an integral number of contiguous pages. Single-page units are used for data structures that occupy one page or less of disk space, such as small objects. Requests for single-page units are handled separately to improve system performance, as we expect the majority of buffer requests to be associated with small objects. Chunks are used exclusively for buffering the data of large storage objects. The ability to allocate variable-length chunks simplifies higher-level software by making it possible to read and then scan a multipage sequence of bytes in a large storage object without concern for page boundaries.

Figure 14.5 sketches the key aspects of the EXODUS buffering scheme for large storage objects. Suppose an EXODUS client requests that a sequence of $B_r$ bytes be read from object $O$. If these bytes are not already resident in the buffer pool, the non-empty portions of the leaf blocks of $O$ containing the desired range of bytes (leaf blocks $P_1$, $P_2$, and $P_3$ in Fig. 14.5) are read into one contiguous chunk $C$ of buffer pages. Leaf blocks are supported by our I/O routines as a unit of transfer between the disk and the buffers, so this can

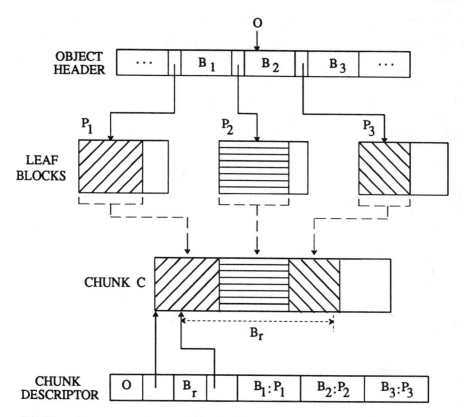

**FIGURE 14.5** CONTIGUOUS BUFFERING IN EXODUS

be accomplished by obtaining a chunk of the appropriate size from the buffer space manager and then reading $P_1$, $P_2$, and lastly $P_3$ into the block—in that order, and so that $P_2$ begins right after the end of the non-empty portion of $P_1$, with $P_3$ being placed similarly. (While this constrains the order in which the leaf blocks of a large object can be read into the buffer pool, we do not view this as a serious limitation. Also, chained I/O could potentially be used to advantage here, as in [Paul et al. 1987].) A *chunk descriptor* is maintained by the buffer manager for the current region of $O$ being scanned, including information such as the OID of $O$, a pointer to its first page frame in the buffer pool, the length of the portion of the chunk containing the bytes requested by clients, a pointer to the first such byte, and information about where the contents of the chunk came from (for buffer replacement purposes). In the rare event that another client has already read a portion of $B_r$ into some other chunk $C'$, then $C$ is still allocated. This time, however, only the portion of $B_r$ that does not appear in $C'$ is read from disk; the remaining portion of $B_r$ that appears in $C'$ is then replicated in $C$ via a memory-to-memory copy. To avoid inconsistencies, measures are taken to ensure that replicated data are never updated. In particular, any replicated portions of a chunk are deleted from the buffer pool before the chunk is updated. (Concurrency control ensures that this is always possible, as a write lock must be obtained prior to the update.)

Since chunks can be variable-length runs of page frames, the EXODUS buffer manager employs more sophisticated free space management techniques than other buffer managers that we have encountered. To satisfy requests for various sizes of chunks, we employ a data structure that maintains lists of free chunks for each currently available size. When a new chunk is requested, the data structure is examined to find the "best" free chunk that satisfies the request. The notion of "best" that we currently use favors chunks of the size requested, breaking up larger free chunks only when necessary; within a given free chunk size, the chunk with the fewest dirty pages is taken. When there is no free chunk large enough to satisfy the request, an attempt is made to coalesce free chunks that are adjacent to each other. If coalescing fails to construct a large enough chunk, then the request is rejected. Although this sounds expensive, preliminary test results have shown that most chunk requests can be satisfied without coalescing.

Finally, as mentioned in the previous section, buffer space allocation and replacement are performed using the notion of a *buffer group*. When a client opens a buffer group, it specifies the number of page frames for the group (*group-size*) and the replacement policy (*group-policy*) that should be employed when replacing its pages. A buffer group descriptor is returned to the client, and it is passed to the storage manager by the client with requests for subsequent operations on storage objects. These operations are then performed with respect to the group, meaning that if the client has *group-size* pages in use, replacement is performed from within the group's pages using *group-policy* as the replacement strategy. A client is permitted to have multiple buffer groups open at once, so buffering schemes such as DBMIN [Chou and DeWitt 1985], which allocates a buffer partition to each active index and relation instance in a relational query, can be supported. Simple schemes such as global LRU are also easily supported via the buffer group mechanism.

## 14.5 FILE OBJECTS

*File objects* in the EXODUS storage system are collections of storage objects (i.e., sets of storage objects, with the restriction that an object resides in exactly one set). File objects are useful for grouping objects together for several purposes. First, the EXODUS storage system provides a mechanism for sequencing through all of the objects in a file, so related objects can be placed in a common file for sequential scanning purposes. Second, objects within a given file are placed on disk pages allocated to the file, so file objects provide support for objects that need to be located together on disk.

### 14.5.1 File Representation

The representation of file objects in EXODUS is similar in some respects to the representation of large storage objects. A file object is identified by its OID, which is a pointer to the root page (i.e., the header) of the file object. Storage objects and file objects are distinguished by a bit in their object headers. Like large storage objects, file objects are represented by an index structure similar to a B+ tree, but the key for the index is different in this case—a file object index uses *disk page number* as its key. Each leaf page of the file object index contains a collection of page numbers of slotted pages contained in the file; the actual slotted pages themselves are managed separately, using standard techniques for page allocation and free space management. (Figure 14.6 shows a file object and how its index relates to the slotted pages on which its objects reside.) The file object index thus serves as a mechanism to gather the pages of a file together, but it also has several additional properties of interest: It facilitates the scanning of all of the objects within a given file object *in physical order* for efficiency, and it supports the fast deletion of an object with a given OID from a file object (as we will see in a moment). We considered several other file designs before settling on this one, including the possibility of representing files as large storage objects containing a sequence of OIDs,

**FIGURE 14.6** EXODUS FILE OBJECT EXAMPLE

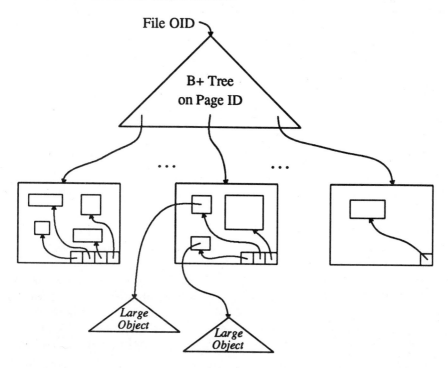

but none supported fast object deletion as well as this scheme does. Note also that since all of the objects in a file are directly accessible via their OIDs, file objects are *not* to be confused with surrogate indices—external references to an object within a given file object are OID values, and these point *directly* to the object.

Creation of a file object allocates the file object header. Later, when an object is to be created within the file object, the object creation routine can be called with an optional hint of the form "place the new object near $X$," where $X$ is the OID of an existing object within the file. When this hint is present, the new object is inserted on the same slotted page as $X$ if possible. (Recall that $X$'s OID identifies the desired page.) If there is not enough space on $X$'s page, then the new object is inserted on a neighboring page of the file if possible. If a neighboring page is inspected and it is also found to be full, then a new slotted page near $X$'s page is allocated for the newly inserted object and its page number is inserted into the file object B+ tree; the OID of the file object is recorded on the newly allocated page. If no location hint is present, $X$ is simply appended to the file by placing it on the last page listed in the file object index, with overflows being handled in the manner just described. To speed the location of a neighboring page for overflow handling, each slotted page has a "neighbor hint" field containing the page number of the most recent neighboring page on which one of its overflows was placed.

Deletion of an object within a file is accomplished by simply removing the object from the page where it resides. If the page becomes empty as a result, its page number must be deleted from the file object index, and the page itself must be returned to the free space manager. Lastly, the deletion of an entire file object must lead to the deletion of all of the objects residing on slotted pages listed in the file object index, the return of those pages to the free list, and then the removal of the index itself. If a slotted page contains one or more large object headers or file object headers, then these must of course be recursively deleted; otherwise, the page can be freed immediately. Each leaf page entry in a file object index has a bit that indicates whether the corresponding slotted page contains any large object headers (or file object headers), permitting the necessary check to be performed when the file is deleted without reading slotted pages that contain only small objects.

### 14.5.2 Other File Object Issues

Concurrency control and recovery for file objects are handled through mechanisms similar to those used for large storage objects. Concurrency control (for page number insertions and deletions) is provided using B+ tree locking protocols. Recovery is accomplished by shadowing changes up to the highest affected level of the file object index, logging the insert or delete operation, and finally overwriting the highest affected node to atomically install the update. Note that these concurrency control and recovery protocols are exercised only when the file index is modified by the insertion or deletion of page number entries, which occurs only when a slotted page is added or removed from the file object; the storage object concurrency control and recovery mechanisms handle slotted page changes that do not involve updates to the file object index.

The final nontrivial issue related to file objects is how one might sort a file object, given that it is not a sequential file. In particular, since schema information has carefully been kept out of the EXODUS storage system, the storage system does not have sufficient information to do this on its own—it has no idea what fields the storage objects in a given file object might have, nor does it know what the data types for the fields are. Such sorting can be accomplished at the client level by exchanging the contents of storage objects according to the client's notion of how the objects should be reordered. Note that sorting necessarily moves the contents of objects from page to page, so their OIDs are no longer valid when sorting has been performed. (This is the main way in which OIDs differ from surrogates, as all other storage system operations preserve the integrity of OIDs by leaving a forwarding address at an object's original location when the object must be relocated.)

## SUMMARY

In this chapter, we described the design and implementation of the storage management component of EXODUS, an extensible database management system under development at the University of Wisconsin. The basic abstraction in the EXODUS storage system is the storage object, an uninterpreted variable-length record of arbitrary size. File objects are used for grouping and sequencing collections of storage objects. The data structures and algorithms used to support large storage objects were described, and the results of a study of their performance were summarized; they support large dynamic storage objects efficiently, both in terms of storage utilization and in terms of access and update performance. An approach was described for maintaining versions of large objects by sharing common pages between versions, and an efficient version deletion algorithm was presented. Also described in this chapter were the EXODUS notion of file objects and our novel approach to buffer management. Concurrency control and recovery mechanisms were briefly covered as well.

As of this writing, the design of the EXODUS storage system is complete, and an initial version of the system (based on the ideas presented in this chapter) is fully operational. Included in this version of the system are support for small and large objects, file objects, buffering of variable-length portions of objects, and shadow-based atomic updates for large objects and file objects. With the exception of concurrency control, most multiuser aspects of the design have been accounted for in this implementation. We are now actively building the next version of the system, which will include support for versions and full multiuser transaction management (including concurrency control and operation logging).

## Acknowledgments

This research was partially supported by the Defense Advanced Research Projects Agency under contract N00014-85-K-0788, by the National Science Foundation under grant DCR-8402818, by IBM through a Fellowship and a Faculty Development Award, by DEC through its Initiatives for Excellence program, and by a grant from the Microelectronics and Computer Technology Corporation (MCC). Also, the authors wish to acknowledge the contributions of several other people affiliated with the EXODUS project, including Goetz Graefe, Mohamed Isa Hashim, Dan Frank, M. Muralikrishna, and David Haight.

## References

[Agrawal et al. 1987] R. Agrawal, M. Carey, and M. Livny, "Concurrency Control Performance Modeling: Alternatives and Implications," *ACM Transactions on Database Systems*, vol. 12, no. 4, December 1987.

[Astrahan et al. 1976] M. Astrahan et al., "System R: Relational Approach to Database Management," *ACM Transactions on Data Systems*, vol. 1, no. 2, June 1976.

[Batory and Kim 1985] D. Batory and W. Kim, *Support for Versions of VLSI CAD Objects*, MCC Working Paper, March 1985.

[Batory et al. 1986] D. Batory et al., "GENESIS: A Reconfigurable Database Management System," Technical Report No. TR-86-07, Department of Computer Sciences, University of Texas at Austin, March 1986.

[Bayer and Scholnick 1977] R. Bayer and M. Scholnick, "Concurrency of Operations on B-trees," *Acta Informatica*, vol. 9, 1977.

[Carey and DeWitt 1985] M. Carey and D. DeWitt, "Extensible Database Systems," *Proceedings of the Islamorada Workshop on Large Scale Knowledge Base and Reasoning Systems*, February 1985.

[Carey et al. 1986a] M. Carey et al., "Object and File Management in the EXODUS Extensible Database System," *Proceedings of the 1986 VLDB Conference*, Kyoto, Japan, August 1986.

[Carey et al. 1986b] M. Carey et al., "The Architecture of the EXODUS Extensible DBMS," *Proceedings of the International Workshop on Object-Oriented Database Systems*, Asilomar, CA, September 1986.

[Carey and Muhanna 1986] M. Carey and W. Muhanna, "The Performance of Multiversion Concurrency Control Algorithms," *ACM Transactions on Computer Systems,* vol. 4, no. 4, November 1986.

[Carey and DeWitt 1987] M. Carey and D. DeWitt, "An Overview of the EXODUS Project," *Database Engineering,* vol. 10, no. 2, June 1987.

[Chou and DeWitt 1985] H-T. Chou and D. DeWitt, "An Evaluation of Buffer Management Strategies for Relational Database Systems," *Proceedings of the 1985 VLDB Conference,* Stockholm, Sweden, August 1985.

[Chou et al. 1985] H-T. Chou, D. DeWitt, R. Katz, and A. Klug, "Design and Implementation of the Wisconsin Storage System," *Software Practice and Experience,* vol. 15, no. 10, October 1985.

[Clifford and Tansel 1985]. J. Clifford and A. Tansel, "On an Algebra for Historical Relational Databases: Two Views," *Proceedings of the 1985 SIG-MOD Conference,* Austin, Texas, May 1985.

[Copeland and Maier 1984] G. Copeland and D. Maier, "Making Smalltalk a Database System," *Proceedings of the 1984 SIGMOD Conference,* Boston, MA, May 1984.

[Dadam et al. 1984] P. Dadam, V. Lum, and H-D. Werner, "Integration of Time Versions into a Relational Database System," *Proceedings of the 1984 VLDB Conference,* Singapore, August 1984.

[Dayal and Smith 1985] U. Dayal and J. Smith, "PROBE: A Knowledge-Oriented Database Management System," *Proceedings of the Islamorada Workshop on Large Scale Knowledge Base and Reasoning Systems,* February 1985.

[Deppisch et al. 1986] U. Deppisch, H-B. Paul, and H-J. Schek, "A Storage System for Complex Objects," *Proceedings of the International Workshop on Object-Oriented Database Systems,* Pacific Grove, CA, September 1986.

[Graefe and DeWitt 1987] G. Graefe and D. DeWitt, "The EXODUS Optimizer Generator," *Proceedings of the 1987 SIGMOD Conference,* San Francisco, CA, May 1987.

[Gray 1979] J. Gray, "Notes On Database Operating Systems," in *Operating Systems: An Advanced Course,* R. Bayer, R. Graham, and G. Seegmuller, eds., Springer-Verlag, 1979.

[Kaehler and Krasner 1983] T. Kaehler and G. Krasner, "LOOM—Large Object-Oriented Memory for Smalltalk-80 Systems," in *Smalltalk-80: Bits of History, Words of Advice,* G. Krasner, ed., Addison-Wesley, Reading, MA, 1983.

[Katz and Lehman 1984] R. Katz and T. Lehman, "Database Support for Versions and Alternatives of Large Design Files," *IEEE Transactions on Software Engineering,* vol. SE-10, no. 2, March 1984.

[Katz et al. 1986] R. Katz, E. Chang, and R. Bhateja, "Version Modeling Concepts for Computer-Aided Design Databases," *Proceedings of the 1986 SIGMOD Conference*, Washington, DC, May 1986.

[Klahold et al. 1985] P. Klahold, G. Schlageter, R. Unland, and W. Wilkes, "A Transaction Model Supporting Complex Applications in Integrated Information Systems," *Proceedings of the 1985 SIGMOD Conference*, Austin, TX, May 1985.

[Lindsay et al. 1979] B. Lindsay et al., *Notes on Distributed Databases*, IBM Research Report No. RJ2571, IBM San Jose Research Center, July 1979.

[Lindsay et al. 1987] B. Lindsay et al., "A Data Management Extension Architecture," *Proceedings of the ACM-SIGMOD International Conference on Management of Data*, San Francisco, CA, 1987.

[Maier et al. 1986] D. Maier et al., "Development of an Object-Oriented DBMS," *Proceedings of the First Annual ACM Conference on Object-Oriented Programming Systems, Languages, and Applications*, Portland, OR, 1986.

[Manola and Dayal 1986] F. Manola and U. Dayal, "PDM: An Object-Oriented Data Model," *Proceedings of the International Workshop on Object-Oriented Database Systems*, Pacific Grove, CA, September 1986.

[Paul et al. 1987] H.-B. Paul et al., "Architecture and Implementation of the Darmstadt Database Kernel System," *Proceedings of the ACM-SIGMOD International Conference on Management of Data*, San Francisco, CA, 1987.

[Pollack et al. 1981] F. Pollack, K. Kahn, and R. Wilkinson, "The iMAX-432 Object Filing System," *Proceedings of the Eighth Symposium on Operating Systems Principles*, Pacific Grove, CA, December 1981.

[Reed 1983] D. Reed, "Implementing Atomic Actions on Decentralized Data," *ACM Transactions on Computer Systems*, vol. 1, no. 1, March 1983.

[Richardson and Carey 1987] J. Richardson and M. Carey, "Programming Constructs for Database System Implementation in EXODUS," *Proceedings of the 1987 SIGMOD Conference*, San Francisco, CA, May 1987.

[Rowe and Stonebraker 1987] L. Rowe and M. Stonebraker, "The POSTGRES Data Model," *Proceedings of the 13th International Conference on Very Large Data Bases*, Brighton, England, 1987.

[Schwarz et al. 1986] P. Schwarz et al., "Extensibility in the Starburst Database System," *Proceedings of the International Workshop on Object-Oriented Database Systems*, Pacific Grove, CA, September 1986.

[Skarra et al. 1986] A. Skarra, S. Zdonik, and S. Reiss, "An Object Server for an Object-Oriented Database System," *Proceedings of the International Workshop on Object-Oriented Database Systems*, Pacific Grove, CA, September 1986.

[Snodgrass and Ahn 1985] R. Snodgrass and I. Ahn, "A Taxonomy of Time in Databases," *Proceedings of the 1985 SIGMOD Conference*, Austin, TX, May 1985.

[Stonebraker et al. 1976] M. Stonebraker, G. Wong, P. Kreps, and G. Held, "The Design and Implementation of INGRES," *ACM Transactions on Database Systems*, vol. 1, no. 3, September 1976.

[Stonebraker 1981] M. Stonebraker, "Hypothetical Data Bases as Views," *Proceedings of the 1981 SIGMOD Conference*, Boston, MA, May 1981.

[Stonebraker et al. 1983] M. Stonebraker, H. Stettner, N. Lynn, J. Kalash, and A. Guttman, "Document Processing in a Relational Database System," *ACM Transactions on Office Information Systems*, vol. 1, no. 2, April 1983.

[Stonebraker and Rowe 1986] M. Stonebraker and L. Rowe, "The Design of POSTGRES," *Proceedings of the 1986 SIGMOD Conference*, Washington, DC, May 1986.

[Stonebraker 1987] M. Stonebraker, "The POSTGRES Storage Manager," *Proceedings of the 13th International Conference on Very Large Data Bases*, Brighton, England, 1987.

[Verhofstad 1978] J. Verhofstad, "Recovery Techniques for Database Systems," *ACM Computing Surveys*, vol. 10, no. 2, June 1978.

# 15

---

# Indexing Techniques for Object-Oriented Databases

Won Kim, Kyung-Chang Kim, Alfred Dale

---

## INTRODUCTION

ORION, like most conventional database systems, supports secondary indexes on user-specified attributes (columns) of specified classes (relations). Such indexes speed up associative searches of the database for queries with search criteria. While the scope of access of a query against a single relation R in a relational database is just R, that of a query against a class C in an object-oriented database is in general the class C and all subclasses of C, and their subclasses, etc. Since an attribute of a class C is inherited into all its descendant classes, it may make sense to maintain an index on an attribute for all classes on a class hierarchy rooted at class C, rather than maintaining a separate index on the attribute for each of the classes in the class hierarchy.

We will refer to an index that is maintained on an attribute of a single class as a *single-class index*, and an index on an attribute of all classes on a class hierarchy rooted at a particular class as a *class-hierarchy index*. ORION currently supports only single-class indexing. We have decided to quantify the tradeoffs between class-hierarchy indexing and single-class indexing, by formulating a reasonably simple cost model for the size (number of nodes) and height of a B-tree index. We have used the cost model for two extensive sets of experiments. One set of experiments was conducted to compare the size of a class-hierarchy index and the sum of the sizes of the corresponding set of single-class indexes. The other set of experiments compared the height of a class-hierarchy index and the sum of the heights of single-class indexes on the corresponding class hierarchy. The height of an index is a direct measure of performance of an index in evaluating a query that includes a predicate on an indexed attribute. Our experiments led us to conclude that a class-hierarchy index outperforms single-class indexing when the scope of a query exceeds two classes. The results on the size of an index were inconclusive; sometimes a class hierarchy requires more storage space, and other times the corresponding set of single-class indexes takes up more space.

In this chapter, we make two original contributions. First, we provide a formal model of a query under an object-oriented data model, and identify the utility of a class-hierarchy index. To our knowledge, the concept of a class-hierarchy index has not been discussed before in the literature. Second, we present the preliminary results of simulation experiments we have conducted on the size and performance tradeoffs between a class-hierarchy index and a corresponding set of single-class indexes.

The remainder of this chapter is organized as follows. In Section 15.1, we describe a formal model of an object-oriented query, and identify the utility of a class-hierarchy index in evaluating an object-oriented query. We present our model of a B-tree index in Section 15.2. Then in Section 15.3 we discuss the assumptions we have made in the cost model of an index we have formulated, and organization of the simulation experiments we have conducted based on the cost model. In Sections 15.4 and 15.5, we formulate the cost model for the size and performance of an index, respectively, and present the experimental results.

## 15.1 Evaluation of an Object-Oriented Query

The object-oriented data model, in its conventional form, is powerful enough to represent a complex object as a recursively nested object. An object may be defined with a set of instance variables. A class may be specified as the *domain* (type) of an instance variable, and the domain class, unless it is a *primitive* class (such as the string, integer, or boolean class), in turn consists of a set of instance variables, and so on. The internal state of an object consists of the values of all its instance variables. The value of an instance variable is an instance of its domain, if the domain is a primitive class; and a reference to (*object identifier* of) an instance of the domain, otherwise. For example, in Fig. 15.1, we show the schema of a Vehicle class in terms of the instance variables Manufacturer, Body, Drivetrain, and Color. The domain of the Color instance variable is the primitive String class. The domain of the Manufacturer instance

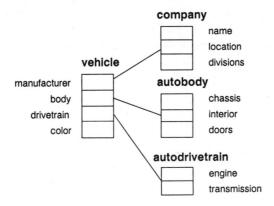

**FIGURE 15.1** NESTED ATTRIBUTES OF THE VEHICLE CLASS

variable is the class Company, the instance variable Body has Autobody as its domain, and the domain of Drivetrain is the AutoDrivetrain class. Each of the classes Company, AutoBody, and AutoDrivetrain consists of its own set of instance variables, which in turn have associated domains (which for simplicity we do not show).

The nesting of an object through the domains of its attributes immediately suggests that to fully fetch an instance, the instance and all instances that the instance references through its attributes must be recursively fetched. This means that to fetch one or more instances of a class, the class and all classes specified as nonprimitive domains of the attributes of the class must be recursively traversed. For example, to fetch instances of the class Vehicle in Fig. 15.1, the classes that need to be traversed include not only Vehicle but also the nonprimitive domains of Vehicle, namely, Company, AutoBody, AutoDrivetrain, as well as nonprimitive domains of these classes.

In general, a query may be formulated against an object-oriented schema, which will fetch instances of a class that satisfy certain search criteria and output only specified attributes of the instances fetched. A query may restrict the instances of a class to be fetched by specifying predicates against any instance variables of the class. An example of a query against the schema of Fig. 15.1 is the following:

**Q1.** Find all blue vehicles manufactured by Ford Motor Company

In an object-oriented database, an attribute may be one of two types: simple or complex. A *simple attribute* is one whose domain is a primitive class. A *complex attribute* is one whose domain is a class with one or more attributes, including complex attributes. A predicate on a simple attribute will be called a *simple predicate*, while one on a complex attribute will be called a *complex predicate*. Further, a query that involves only simple predicates will be called a *simple query*, and one that involves one or more complex predicates will be called a *complex query*.

We may represent a class and the domains of all its complex attributes in the form of a directed graph, which we will call the *query graph*. Each node on a query graph represents a class, and an edge from a node A to a node B means that class B is the domain of a complex attribute of class A. A query graph has only one root, the class whose instances are to be fetched. Each leaf node of a query graph has only simple attributes. A query graph may contain cycles.

The process of fetching nested objects, which we will call *object instantiation*, is similar to relational query evaluation. We may view a class as a relation and an attribute of a class as a column of a relation. A relation is augmented with a system-defined *unique identifier* (UID) column for the identifier of the tuples. Then the retrieval of an instance of the domain class D of an attribute A of a class C is similar to the relational join of a tuple of a relation C with a tuple of a relation D, where the join columns are column A of relation C and the UID column of relation D. We hasten to remark that, despite these similarities, there are a few significant differences between relational query evaluation and object instantiation. We will present a detailed discussion of these issues in a forthcoming report.

There is in general more than one way (often called a query-evaluation plan [Selinger et al. 1979]) for evaluating a query that will yield the correct result. However, each plan incurs a different cost. There are two fundamental options in plans for traversing the nested classes for object instantiation: forward and reverse traversal. The *query optimizer* of a database system is to consider a number of reasonable plans based on these options (and their combinations) for evaluating any given query, and to select one with the minimum expected cost.

In *forward traversal*, the classes on a query graph are traversed in a depth-first order starting from the root of the query graph, and following through the successive domains of each complex instance variable. As an example, let us consider query Q1. A forward traversal of the query graph starts with the set of all instances of the class Vehicle in which the Color attribute has a value "blue." For each of these instances, the value of its attribute Manufacturer is extracted; that value is an instance of the class Company. The value of the attribute Name in the Company instance is then examined. If the value is the string "Ford", the Company instance qualifies, and in turn, the Vehicle instance which has that Company instance as its manufacturer satisfies the query.

Another way to perform object instantiation is *reverse traversal*, in which the leaf classes of a query graph are visited first, and then their parents, working toward the root class. As an example, consider once again query Q1. Instead of starting with the set of all instances of Vehicle, query evaluation starts with the class Company. All instances of Company are identified that have the string "Ford" in the Name attribute. The UIDs of these instances are then looked up in the Manufacturer attribute of the class Vehicle. The result of the query is the set of instances of Vehicle that have the string "blue" in the Color attribute and that contain in the Manufacturer attribute a UID that is in the list of UIDs for Ford Motor Company instances.

To support efficient retrieval of tuples that satisfy search predicates, the storage subsystem of a relational database system usually supports secondary indexes on user-specified columns of relations [Stonebraker et al. 1976; IBM 1981]. Similarly, object-oriented database systems may maintain an index on an attribute of a class. For example, if an index is maintained on the primitive attribute Name of the class Company, it can be used to advantage in a reverse traversal of the query graph for our example query Q1. On the other hand, if there is an index on the Color attribute of the class Vehicle, it may be used in a forward traversal of the query graph. In either case, the use of an index can significantly reduce the I/O cost of traversing the query graph for object instantiation.

One of the major differences between a relational database and an object-oriented database is that in an object-oriented database a class may be specialized into a number of subclasses. For example, in Fig. 15.2 we show a database class hierarchy that includes the class Vehicle and the domain classes of the attributes of the class Vehicle. The class Vehicle is shown to have been specialized into the class Automobile and the class Truck. Similarly, the class Company has subclasses VehicleCompany and ComputerCompany. In general, a class may have any number of subclasses and/or superclasses. The root of a class hierarchy is a system-defined class OBJECT, and any class the user defines without a superclass is by default a subclass of the class OBJECT [Banerjee et al. 1987b].

The fact that an object-oriented database schema explicitly captures the IS-A relationship between a pair of classes has two major impacts on the semantics of object instantiation. One is that the access scope of a query

**FIGURE 15.2** A CLASS HIERARCHY

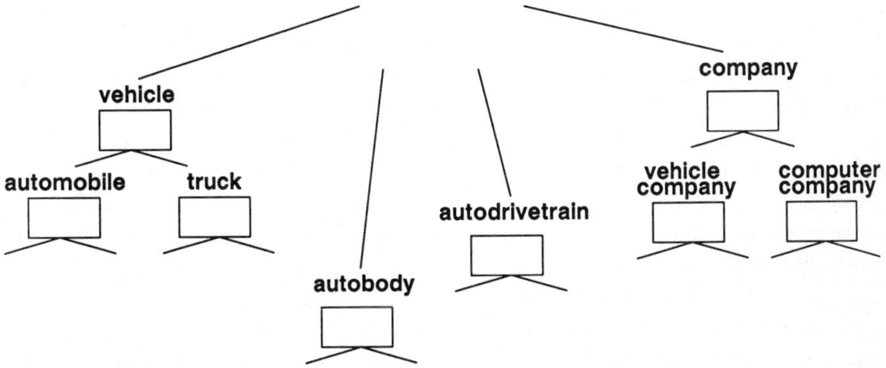

against a class may be only the instances of the class, or it may also include the instances of all subclasses of the class. For example, the user may issue a query against the class Vehicle to fetch only the instances of the class Vehicle, or may issue a single query against the class Vehicle to fetch all qualified instances of the class Vehicle and subclasses of Vehicle.

Another major impact is that the domain D of an attribute of a class C is really the class D and all subclasses of D. For example, the Manufacturer attribute of the class Vehicle may take as its value an instance of the class Company or an instance of any subclass of Company. This means that in the reverse traversal of the query graph for Q1, the class Company and all its subclasses must be traversed.

These semantics of object instantiation force major changes in the way a database system can use indexes. Traditionally, an index has been maintained on an attribute of a single class (or a relation). This means that to support the evaluation of a query whose access scope is a class hierarchy, the system must maintain one index on the attribute for each of the classes in the class hierarchy. However, it is clear that often it may make sense to maintain one index on the attribute for a class hierarchy, and use it to evaluate queries against any single class in the class hierarchy or any sub-hierarchy of the class hierarchy. We will call the traditional approach of maintaining one index per class *single-class indexing*, and refer to the alternative approach of maintaining one index on an attribute for a hierarchy of classes *class-hierarchy indexing*.

Intuitively, it appears that a class-hierarchy index may in general be more effective in evaluating a query whose access scope spans a major subset of the classes in the indexed class hierarchy, while a single-class index should be more appropriate for a query against a single class. In the remainder of this chapter, we quantify the tradeoffs between these two indexing techniques in an object-oriented database in terms of storage requirements and I/O performance in object instantiation.

## 15.2 INDEX STRUCTURE

In this section we describe the formats of the nodes of the B-tree index that we will model. These formats are based on the single-class B-tree index we have implemented in ORION. It is also similar to that used in IBM's relational database system SQL/DS [IBM 1981]. In a relational database, the columns have primitive data types; thus, the key values in an index are primitive data such as integers or strings. In an object-oriented database, the domain of an attribute may be either a primitive class or some user-defined class. Therefore, the key values in an index can be either the UIDs of the instances of the domain class or some primitive values.

Figure 15.3 shows the format of a nonleaf node. The node consists of $f$ records, where each record is a pair (key, pointer), and key in turn is a

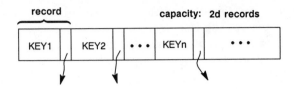

**FIGURE 15.3** A NONLEAF NODE

pair (key-length, key-value), where key-length is the length in bytes of the key-value. The fanout, $f$, is between $d$ and $2d$, where $d$ is the *order* of a B-tree. The fanout of the root node can be between 2 and $2d$ records. The pointer in each record contains the physical address of the next-level index node. If a record needs to be inserted into a node that contains $2d$ records, the node is split and the $2d+1$ records are distributed to two nodes.

A leaf node of an index has a format different from that of a nonleaf node. Further, the format of a leaf node of a single-class index is different from that of a class-hierarchy index, as shown in Fig. 15.4a and 15.4b. An index record in a leaf node of a single-class index consists of the record-length, key-length, key-value, overflow-page pointer, the number of elements in the list of UIDs of the objects that hold the key-value in the indexed attribute, and the list of UIDs.

An index record in a leaf node of a class-hierarchy index consists of the record-length, key-length, key-value, overflow-page pointer, key-directory, and, for each class in the class hierarchy, the number of elements in the list of UIDs for the objects that hold the key-value in the indexed attribute, and the list of UIDs. The key-directory consists of the number of classes that contain objects with the key-value in the indexed attribute, and, for each such class,

**FIGURE 15.4** (a) A LEAF NODE OF A SINGLE-CLASS INDEX. (b) A LEAF NODE OF A CLASS-HIERARCHY INDEX.

(a)

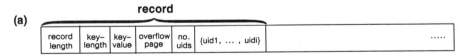

(b)

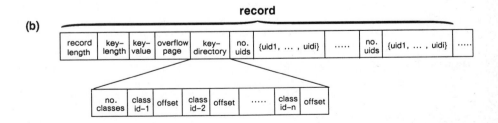

the class identifier and the offset in the index record at which to find the list of UIDs of the objects. The leaf node of a class-hierarchy index groups the list of UIDs for a key-value in terms of the classes to which they belong.

The rationale for this organization is that a class-hierarchy index is maintained on an attribute for a class hierarchy consisting of $n$ classes rooted at a class C, and that the index may often need to be used for a query that is directed to a subclass of the class C. If the leaf node is organized as in a single-class index, an exhaustive scan of the entire list of UIDs for a key-value is necessary to screen the UIDs that do not belong to the classes relevant to a query. Further, if a class in the class hierarchy is dropped, the UIDs of instances for the class must be deleted from the class-hierarchy index; the organization shown in Fig. 15.4b facilitates deletion of a list of UIDs for any class on a class hierarchy.

A leaf-node index record may be *small* (not larger than the size of an index page) or *large* (larger than the index-page size). A small index record can grow to a large index record or simply grow out of bounds of its current index page. There are a number of ways to deal with these *leaf-node overflow* situations. The approach we have adopted is as follows. On one hand, if a small index record grows out of bounds of its index page, but remains a small record, the index page is split. On the other hand, if an index record becomes a large record, an entire leaf node is assigned to it, and the part of the record that still does not fit in the node is stored in overflow page(s). This is the use of the overflow-page pointer field in a leaf-node index record; if the value of this field is zero, the index record can be presumed to be fully contained in the current index page.

## 15.3 SIMULATION EXPERIMENTS

The cost model we developed for our simulation experiments uses a number of parameters. The following set of parameters captures the characteristics of the database.

$D_i$    number of distinct keys for an attribute of a class $C_i$

$N_i$    cardinality of a class $C_i$ (number of instances of $C_i$)

$K_i$    average number of UIDs per key in an attribute of a class $C_i$ ($K_i = \lceil N_i / D_i \rceil$)

The next set of parameters represents the characteristics of the index nodes. We note that the first four parameters apply to both a single-class index and a class-hierarchy index.

$d$    order of a nonleaf node (minimum number of nonleaf node index records)

$f$     average fanout from a nonleaf index node
($d <= f <= 2d$, for any nonleaf node other than the root node)
($2 <= f <= 2d$, for the root node)

$P$     size of an index page in bytes

$kl$     average length of a key value for an indexed attribute

$L$     average length of a nonleaf-node index record in bytes

$XS$     average length of a leaf-node index record in bytes for a single-class index

$XC$     average length of a leaf-node index record in bytes for a class-hierarchy index

$c$     average number of classes for a key in a leaf-node index record for a class-hierarchy index

$cn$     total number of classes indexed by a class-hierarchy index

Most of the parameters in our cost model can affect in varying degrees the size and performance of an index. To keep the cost model and our experiments tractable and to allow a fair comparison of the two types of indexing techniques, we have made the following assumptions.

1. All key values have the same length. This implies that all nonleaf node index records in both a single-class index and a class-hierarchy index have the same length.

2. In a class-hierarchy index, the number of classes containing instances with the indexed key value is the same for each key value; that is, the number-of-classes field has the same value in each leaf-node index record in a class-hierarchy index.

3. The key values of an attribute are uniformly distributed among instances of a class. This, along with assumption 1, implies that all leaf-node index records in a given single-class index have the same length. Further, this assumption, along with assumptions 1 and 2, implies that all leaf-node index records in a given class-hierarchy index have the same length. In particular, in any given index, leaf-node index records are either all *small* (not larger than the size of an index page) or all *large* (larger than the index-page size).

   Without this assumption, we have the unenviable task of having to incorporate into the cost model the fact that each leaf-node index record has a different size. This assumption may not be realistic; however, most of the simulation studies of the performance of database systems have made the same assumption, and the results of such studies nonetheless have proved to be useful.

In the next sections we provide separate cost formulations for the two sizes of leaf-node index records. The separate treatment was deemed necessary to account for the overflow pages for the large index records.

4. The root class C of a class hierarchy for which a class-hierarchy index is maintained is also the class against which a query is directed. This assumption is necessary to allow a fair comparison between single-class indexing and class-hierarchy indexing. In general, a query may be directed against a descendant class of C, and the class-hierarchy index on C may have to be used to evaluate the query. Then only a part of the index contains entries that correspond to the classes relevant to the query. The choice of a class for which a class-hierarchy index is maintained must be carefully made, possibly with computerized physical database design tools.

5. Each nonleaf (and nonroot) index node has the same fanout $f$, in both a single-class index and a class-hierarchy index. This assumption is also necessary to allow a truly fair comparison of the two types of indexing techniques.

6. The cardinality of a class in a class hierarchy is independent of the cardinality of any of its superclasses or subclasses; that is, there is no correlation between the number of instances of a class and that of any other class on the same class hierarchy. When a class S is created as a subclass of a class C, a subset of the instances of C may migrate to S. If the class C has not been partitioned into a sufficient number of subclasses, C may have more instances than any of its subclasses. However, a class C may sometimes be an abstract class and have no instances associated with it, while its subclass S may have many instances.

The distribution of the key values across the classes of a class hierarchy has significant impact on the tradeoffs between single-class indexing and class-hierarchy indexing. For example, if the key value of an indexed attribute is confined to instances of only one class C, a class-hierarchy index may be less efficient than a single-class index on the class C. However, if the key value is contained in instances of all the classes in the class hierarchy, traversing a class-hierarchy index may be more efficient than traversing a single-class index on each of the classes in the class hierarchy.

In general, each class of a class hierarchy may contain a unique value for the key. There are two extreme cases for the distribution of key values: disjoint distribution and inclusive distribution. In a *disjoint distribution*, each key value of an indexed attribute is found in only one class; that is, all values of the attribute are unique to each class of the class hierarchy. In a disjoint distribution, each class in a class hierarchy has unique values on the indexed attribute. The total number of unique key values is

SUM OF $(D1, D2, ..., Di)$ for classes $C1, C2, ..., Ci$

In an *inclusive distribution,* one class of the class hierarchy has all key values for an indexed attribute. The total number of unique key values in an inclusive distribution is

MAX $(D1, D2, ..., Di)$ for classes $C1, C2, ..., Ci$

Obviously, these distributions represent two extreme cases. Nevertheless, they represent the best or worst cases for the indexing techniques with which we are concerned. Further, a realistic distribution of key values will be somewhere between these extremes. Therefore, we have made some efforts to analyze the behavior of these two extreme distributions of key values.

To simplify the presentation of our cost model, we have used explicit figures in the expression of some of the parameters, as follows. These figures are based largely on the B+-tree index implementation in ORION.

1. For the key-length and next-level-page pointer fields in a nonleaf node index record, we use 2 and 4 bytes, respectively. The record-length, number of UIDs, and overflow-page pointer fields in a leaf-node index record take up 2, 2, and 4 bytes, respectively. The number-of-classes field in the key-directory in a leaf-node record of a class-hierarchy index needs 2 bytes, and each offset field takes up 2 bytes. The class id requires 4 bytes.

2. The index page size used was 4096 bytes. Further, we will assume that the average length of a key value is equal to the size of a UID. The length of a UID is 8 bytes. This in turn means that $L = 14$, $XS = Ki * 8 + 18$, and $XC = Ki * 8 + c * 10 + 16$ bytes.

3. For the value of $f$ we used 218, assuming a UID size of 8 bytes and the block size of 4K bytes. The order $d$ of a B-tree is $P / L = 146$.

The following summarize the organization of the simulation experiments we have conducted.

1. We constructed nine experiments. Within each experiment, we made 20 simulation runs by varying the parameters $Ni$ and $Di$, as well as $cn$. The total number of simulation runs we made was thus 180.

2. The number of classes in the class hierarchy was varied between 2 and 6.

3. In the first five experiments, we used values for $Ni$ between 20,000 and 200,000; and in the last four experiments, $Ni$ was varied between 50,000 and 255,000.

4. For the nine experiments, $Di$ ranged from 100 to 400 (so that $Ki$ was varied from 200 to 500), from 40 to 1000 (for $Ki$ between 500 and 200), from 100 to 1000 (for $Ki$ about 200), from 40 to 400 (for $Ki$ about 500), from 60 to 575 (for $Ki$ about 350), from 350 to 600 (for $Ki$ between 150 and 500), from 500 to 1300 (for $Ki$ around 200), from 100 to 600 (for $Ki$ about 500), and from 150 to 750 (for $Ki$ about 350).

## 15.4 INDEX SIZES

To compare the secondary storage requirements of a class-hierarchy index and a corresponding set of single-class indexes, we have formulated a cost model for the size of an index. The size of an index is the total number of index nodes, where each node occupies a physical page on secondary storage. In this section, we will present our cost model for the size of both a single-class index and a class-hierarchy index, and then present the results of our simulation experiments.

### 15.4.1 Cost Model for the Size of an Index

[Knuth 1973] derives bounds for the height of a B-tree and the number of nodes in each level of the B-tree, given the order and the number of keys. [Comer 1979] also provides asymptotic bounds for the height and number of nodes in each level of a B-tree, using a slightly different definition. We have derived our own formulas largely to reflect the implementation details of a B-tree index in a database system. Further, the variation of the B-tree we are considering is somewhat different from that used in [Knuth 1973] and [Comer 1979].

The cost model formulated here uses the parameters we defined in Section 15.3. We provide separate sets of formulas for a single-class index and a class-hierarchy index. Further, for each type index, we provide separate formulas for small and large leaf-node index records. We also introduce the following additional symbols:

$L0$    number of leaf-level index pages, including overflow pages

$L1$    number of leaf-level index pages, excluding overflow pages

$NL$   number of nonleaf level index pages

### 1. Single-Class Index

**Small Leaf-Node Index Records ($XS <= P$)**

F1: number of leaf pages, $L0 = \lceil Di / \lfloor P / XS \rfloor \rceil$

F2: number of nonleaf pages, $NL = \lfloor L0/f \rfloor + \lfloor \lfloor L0/f \rfloor / f \rfloor + .... + X$, where each term is successively divided by $f$ until the last term $X$ is less than $f$. If the last term $X$ is not 1, then 1 is added to the total (for the root node).

**Example 1**   Let $Di = 100$, $Ni = 20000$, and $f = 5$. Then $Ki = 20000/100 = 200$. The number of records in a leaf page is 2. Thus $L0 = 100/2 = 50$, and $NL = 50/5 + (50/5)/5 + 1 = 13$.

### Large Leaf-Node Index Records ($XS > P$)

F3: number of leaf pages, excluding the overflow pages, $L1 = Di$

F4: number of nonleaf pages, $NL = \lfloor L1/f \rfloor + \lfloor \lfloor L1/f \rfloor / f \rfloor + .... + X$, where F4 is defined similarly to F2

F5: number of leaf pages, including the overflow pages, $L0 = L1 * \lceil XS/P \rceil$

**Example 2**   Let $Di = 50$, $Ni = 30000$, and $f = 5$. Then $Ki = 30000/50 = 600$, $L1 = 50$, $NL = 50/5 + (50/5)/5 + 1 = 13$, and $L0 = 50 * 2 = 100$.

F6: total number of index pages for a class $Ci = L0 + NL$

### 2. Class-Hierarchy Index

### Small Leaf-Node Index Records ($XC <= P$)

F7: number of leaf pages, $L0 = \lceil Di / \lfloor P/XC \rfloor \rceil$

F8: number of nonleaf pages, $NL = \lfloor L0/f \rfloor + \lfloor \lfloor L0/f \rfloor / f \rfloor + .... + X$, where each term is successively divided by $f$ until the last term $X$ is less than $f$. If the last term $X$ is not 1, then 1 is added to the total, as in F2.

**Example 3**   Let $Di = 220$, $Ni = 50000$, $c = 3$, and $f = 5$. Then $Ki = 50000/220 = 228$. The number of records in a leaf page is 2. Thus $L0 = 220/2 = 110$, and $NL = 110/5 + (110/5)/5 + 1 = 27$.

### Large Leaf-Node Index Records ($XC > P$)

F9: number of leaf pages, excluding the overflow pages, $L1 = Di$

F10: number of nonleaf pages, $NL = \lfloor L1/f \rfloor + \lfloor \lfloor L1/f \rfloor / f \rfloor + .... + X$, where F10 is defined similarly to F8

F11: number of leaf pages including overflow, $L0 = L1 * \lceil XC/P \rceil$

**Example 4**    Let $Di = 200$, $Ni = 110000$, $c = 3$, and $f = 5$. Then $Ki = 110000/200 = 550$, $L1 = 200$, $NL = 200/5 + (200/5)/5 + ((200/5)/5)/5 = 49$, and $L0 = 200$.

F12: total number of class-hierarchy index pages $= L0 + NL$

## 15.4.2 Results of Experiments

In this section we present and analyze the results of our experiments with the cost model presented in Section 15.4.1. We implemented a simulation program and made a large number of simulation runs by varying the parameters of the cost model.

Figure 15.5 shows the results of one of our nine experiments, in which $Ni$ varied between 50,000 and 255,000, $Di$ varied between 500 and 1300, and $Ki$ was about 200. The figure shows the number of index pages created for a class-hierarchy index and for single-class indexes. For class-hierarchy indexing, we show the results for three different distributions of key values: inclusive, disjoint, and mixed. The index size of a class-hierarchy index, for any distribution, is sometimes larger and sometimes smaller than the sum of the sizes of the corresponding set of single-class indexes. For different distributions of key values, the size of a class-hierarchy index may be larger than the sum of the sizes of corresponding single-class indexes, largely because of overflow pages created as the leaf-node index records become large.

**FIGURE 15.5** COMPARISON OF INDEX SIZES

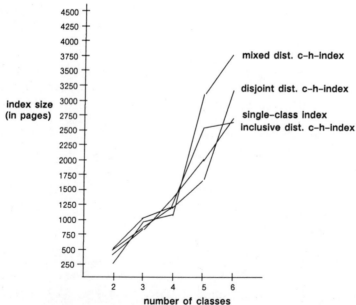

The change in the number of index pages created for a class-hierarchy index ranges from a 37% decrease to a 50% increase with respect to single-class indexing. With an inclusive distribution, the range is from a 27% decrease to a 48% increase. With a disjoint distribution, the range is from a 16% decrease to a 15% increase.

## 15.5 PERFORMANCE

In this section, we first formulate a cost model for the performance of a single-class index and a class-hierarchy index. We then present the results of a performance comparison between the two types of indexes. The performance comparison was conducted for two types of queries: single-key queries and range queries. For either type of query, we computed the number of index pages that need to be fetched to evaluate a given query. A *single-key query* is one in which the search condition consists of a single predicate of the form (key = value). A *range query* is one in which the predicate is of the form (key < value), (key > value), or (key between value-1 and value-2). Since our results for a query with a single predicate readily generalize to a query involving a conjunction (predicate AND predicate AND ...) or a disjunction (predicate OR predicate OR ...) of single predicates, we do not consider the latter explicitly.

### 15.5.1 Single-Key Query Evaluation

**Cost Model**   The number of index pages fetched to evaluate a query is precisely the height of the index used. To compute the height of an index, we can use a formula similar to F2 or F4 used to calculate the number of nonleaf pages.

F13: height of an index = number of terms in $(L0 + \lfloor L0/f \rfloor + \lfloor \lfloor L0/f \rfloor / f \rfloor + \ldots + X$, where a previous term is successively divided by $f$. $L0$ is the number of leaf pages. The division by $f$ stops when the value of the last term $X$ is less than $f$. If $X$ is not 1, add 1 to the height. If the index contains overflow pages, the average number of overflow pages per leaf page must be added to the height. The formula is used for both single-class indexes and a class-hierarchy index.

**Example 5**   Let $Di = 100$, $Ni = 20000$, and $f = 5$. Then $Ki = 20000/100 = 200$. Using Fl, $L0 = 100/2 = 50$. The number of terms in $(50 + 50/5 + (50/5)/5)$ is 3. Since the last term is not 1, and there are no overflow pages, the height of the index is 4.

**Simulation Experiments**   In Fig. 15.6 we observe that, irrespective of key distributions and the number of classes in the class-hierarchy, the number of index pages fetched with a class-hierarchy index is always equal to or smaller than

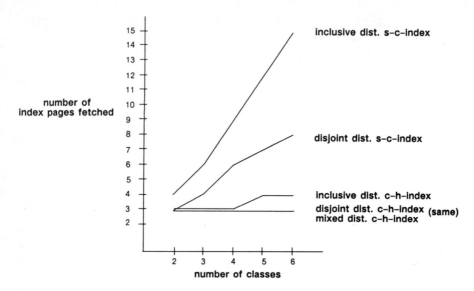

**FIGURE 15.6** COMPARISON OF SINGLE-KEY QUERY PERFORMANCE

in single-class index if there are at least two classes in a class-hierarchy. Figure 15.6 summarizes the results of our experiment.

In the case of single-class indexing, with an inclusive distribution of the key values among all classes in the indexed class hierarchy, the height of a single-class index must be traversed for each of the classes. With a disjoint distribution, only those single-class indexes must be traversed that contain the desired key value. In all other indexes, only the root page needs to be accessed.

In the case of class-hierarchy indexing, the number of index pages that must be accessed for a single-key query is equal to the height of the index, regardless of how the key values are distributed. However, the values of parameters $Di$, $Ni$, $Ki$, and $XC$ cause the heights of the indexes to be different for inclusive and disjoint distributions.

For a class-hierarchy index with an inclusive distribution of key values, the reduction in the number of index pages fetched is between 25% and 73% with respect to single-class indexing. The reduction is between 0% and 63% for a disjoint distribution. For a mixed distribution, the reduction is between 25% and 80% with respect to single-class indexing with an inclusive distribution, and between 0% and 63% with respect to single-class indexing with a disjoint distribution.

## 15.5.2 Range Query Evaluation

**Cost Model** An important consideration in range query evaluation is the distribution of the key values in the range among the classes in a class hierarchy. In the case of an inclusive distribution, the range of key values is obviously confined to one class. This means that, in the case of single-class indexing, we must fully traverse an index for each class on a class hierarchy. With a disjoint distribution, the range values are scattered among all classes of a class hierarchy. In the case of single-class indexing, only the indexes for those classes in the class hierarchy that contain a value in the range must be fully traversed; only the root pages must be accessed for all other indexes on the classes.

Before we derive the formula for the number of index pages fetched, we need to introduce symbols $UKi$ and $NRQ$, as follows.

$UKi$     number of unique keys in a leaf-level index node

$NRQ$    number of key values in the range specified for a given query

In a single-class index,

$$UKi = \lfloor P\ /\ XS \rfloor$$

for small leaf-node index records ($XS <= P$), and

$$UKi = 1$$

for large leaf-node index records ($XS > P$).
In a class-hierarchy index,

$$UKi = \lfloor P\ /\ XC \rfloor$$

for small leaf-node index records ($XC <= P$), and

$$UKi = 1$$

for large leaf-node index records ($XC > P$).
We now derive formulas for the number of index pages to be fetched. We need the following additional symbols:

$RL$     number of leaf pages fetched, excluding overflow pages

$nRL$    sum of leaf pages fetched, excluding overflow pages, from $n$ single-class indexes

$SRL$    sum of leaf pages fetched, including overflow pages, from $n$ single-class indexes

$SRN$    sum of nonleaf pages fetched from $n$ single-class indexes

$IP1$     total number of index pages fetched, excluding overflow nodes

$IP2$     total number of index pages fetched, including overflow nodes

## 1. Range Values in One Class

First, we consider the case in which all range values are in one class. As mentioned earlier, indexes on the attribute for all classes in a class hierarchy must be searched for an inclusive distribution of the key values; for a disjoint distribution, only those indexes of the classes that contain any value in the range must be fully traversed.

If $NRQ=1$, that is, in the limiting case where the range consists of only one key value, $RL=1$.

F14: If $UKi=1$, $RL=NRQ$

**Example 6**   For a single-class index, let $Di=50$, $Ni=30000$, and $f=5$. Then $Ki=30000/50=600$. Since $Ki*8+18>4096$, $UKi=1$. If we have $NRQ=20$, $RL$ is 20. Since $UKi$, the number of different keys in a leaf page, is 1, the number of leaf pages that must be fetched is $NRQ$.

F15: If $UKi>1$,

$$RL=\lfloor NRQ/UKi \rfloor + 1, \text{ if } n \text{ is 0 or 1}$$
$$RL=\lfloor NRQ/UKi \rfloor + 2, \text{ if } n > 1$$

where $n = \mod (NRQ, UKi)$

**Example 7**   For a class-hierarchy index, let $Di=220$, $Ni=50000$, $c=3$, and $f=5$. Then $Ki=50000/220=228$. Since $Ki*8+46<4096$, $UKi=4096/(228*8+42)=2$. If $NRQ=15$, $n=1$ and thus $RL=15/2+1=8$ pages.

F16: If $XS<=P$ for a single-class index, or if $XC<=P$ for a class-hierarchy index, then the maximum number of index pages fetched is

$$IP1=RL + (\lfloor RL/f \rfloor + X) + (\lfloor \lfloor RL/f \rfloor + X/f \rfloor + X) + \ldots + 1$$

where the number of terms in the formula is equal to the height of the index for the class. $X$ is 1 if the remainder of division by $f$ in the term is either 0 or 1; otherwise $X$ is 2.

**Example 8**   For a single-class index, let $Di=100$, $Ni=20000$, and $f=5$. Then $Ki=200$. Since $Ki*8+18<4096$, $UKi=4096/(200*8+18)=2$. If $NRQ=10$, $RL=6$. The height of the index with these parameter values is 4. Thus $IP1=6 + (6/5+1) + ((6/5+1)/5+2) + 1 = 6 + 2 + 2 + 1 = 11$.

F17: For large leaf-node index records ($XS>P$) in a single-class index,

$$IP2 = IP1 + RL * \lfloor XS / P \rfloor$$

where $RL$ and $IP1$ have been defined in F14 (or F15) and F16, respectively.

F18:  For large leaf-node index records $(XC > P)$ in a class-hierarchy index,

$$IP2 = IP1 + RL * \lfloor XC / P \rfloor$$

where $RL$ and $IP1$ have been defined in F14 (or F15) and F16, respectively.

**Example 9**  For a class-hierarchy index, let $Di = 200$, $Ni = 110000$, $c = 5$, and $f = 5$. Then $Ki = 550$. Since $Ki*8 + 66 > 4096$, $UKi = 1$. If $NRQ = 10$, $RL = 10$. Since the height of the index is 4, $IP1 = 10 + (10/5 + 1) + (3/5 + 2) + 1 = 16$ pages. Then $IP2 = 16 + (10*((550*8 + 66)/4096)) = 26$ pages.

## 2. Range Values Scattered Among More Than One Class

For single-class indexing, if the key values in a given range are scattered among more than one class, each of the indexes of the classes whose instances contain any of the values in the range must be fully traversed. $SRL$, the number of leaf pages to be fetched, is the sum of the $RLs$, including overflow pages, for all indexes that must be fully searched. To compute $SRL$, we can make use of the formulas for $RL$, namely, F14 and F15.

F19:  $SRL = $ sum of $RL * \lceil XS / P \rceil$ of each index.

In computing $SRN$, the $nRL$ used is the sum of the $RLs$ for all indexes that must be fully traversed.

F20:  $SRN = (\lfloor nRL / f \rfloor + X + ... + Vi + Vj + ... + Wi + Wj + ... + Xi$

Each term (except the first) is successively divided by $f$, and then 1 or 2 is added to the result as in F16, except for any term whose position in the formula is the same as the height of its respective index (such as $Vj$ and $Wj$). Let $Vi$ be the term produced when the number of additions of terms is equal to (height$-1$) of one index. $Vj$ is then $(((Vi-1)/f) + X)$. The next term to be added after $Vj$ is then $((Vj/f) + X)$. The addition of terms continues until the number of terms in the formula is next equal to (height$-1$) of another index involved. Let that term be $Wi$. The value of $Wj$ is then $(((Wi-1)/f) + X)$. The addition of terms again continues until the number of terms equals (height$-1$) of the largest index. Hence $Xi$ is the last term added when (height$-1$) of the largest index is reached. If two indexes have the same height and both are the largest index, the terms are added until the number of additions is equal to (height$-1$) of any one of them.

F21: maximum number of index pages fetched $= SRL + SRN$

**Example 10**   For a single-class index, let $Di = 50$, $Ni = 10000$, and $f = 5$. Then $Ki = 200$. Also, $RL = 6$ if $NRQ = 10$. The height of this index is 3. Assume that there is another index with $Di = 120$, $Ni = 30000$, and $f = 5$. The $Ki$ for the second index is 250, and $RL = 6$ if $NRQ = 10$. The height of this index is 4. Now $SRL = 12$. The $nRL = 6 + 6 = 12$, so $SRN = (12/5+2) + (4/5+2) + ((2-1)/5+1) = 4 + 2 + 1 = 7$ pages. Thus if the range values are scattered over two classes as defined above, the total number of index pages is $12 + 7 = 19$.

When comparing the number of index pages fetched between single-class indexing and class-hierarchy indexing for a range query, the following observations can be made. In single-class indexing, with an inclusive distribution of key values, indexes for all classes in the class hierarchy must be searched. For each class, the number of index pages that must be fetched is given in formula F16 or F17. With a disjoint distribution, indexes for only those classes containing instances with one of the values in the range are searched. When the key values in the range are all in one class, the number of index pages to be fetched is given in formula F16 or F17. When the values are scattered over several classes, the maximum number of index pages fetched is given in formula F21.

In class-hierarchy indexing, since we have a single index, the situation is identical to the case where all range values are in one class. The number of index pages to be fetched, given in formula F16 or F18, is not affected by the type of key-value distribution. It is affected only by the values of the parameters $Di$, $Ni$, $Ki$, and $UKi$.

**Simulation Experiments**   We studied two different cases, both for the same set of range values that we varied for each experiment. In one case, all the values are assumed to be in any one of the classes in the class hierarchy. Figure 15.7 summarizes the results of our experiment. It shows that, when the number of values in the range is 20, class-hierarchy indexing requires fewer index pages to be fetched than does single-class indexing for the same key-value distribution, if there are at least two classes in the class hierarchy. In class-hierarchy indexing, disjoint distribution generally requires fewer index pages to be fetched than is the case with an inclusive key distribution. One reason for this is that overflow nodes are created in an inclusive distribution. Another reason is that the value of $UKi$ is normally greater in a disjoint distribution than in an inclusive distribution; this results in more keys being packed per leaf page, so that fewer leaf pages are fetched for a fixed number of range values.

In the other case, the range key values are scattered evenly in two classes, that is, each class contains half the key values. Figure 15.8 shows that the result is similar to the first case, for 20 key values in the range. We consider only a

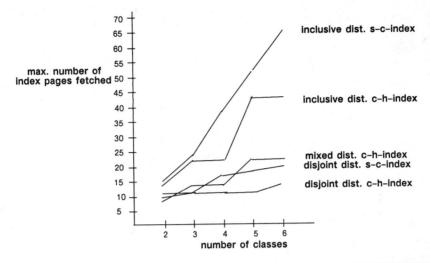

**FIGURE 15.7** COMPARISON OF RANGE-QUERY EVALUATION (KEY VALUES DISTRIBUTED IN ONE CLASS)

**FIGURE 15.8** COMPARISON OF RANGE-QUERY EVALUATION (KEY VALUES SPLIT BETWEEN TWO CLASSES)

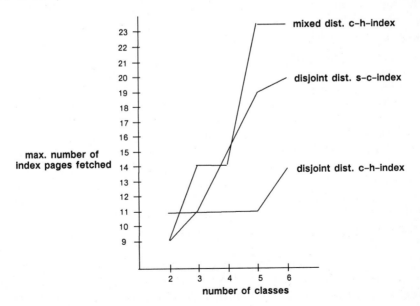

disjoint distribution, since inclusive distribution is meaningless. Sometimes, single-class indexing requires fewer index pages to be fetched than does class-hierarchy indexing. This is because, in a disjoint distribution of key values, only the indexes for the classes containing the range values need to be searched, and the individual single-class index is smaller than the class-hierarchy index.

We have also compared the maximum numbers of index pages fetched for class-hierarchy indexing and for single-class indexing. Class-hierarchy indexing results in a reduction of between 5% and 39% in the number of index pages fetched compared to single-class indexing, in the case of an inclusive distribution. For a disjoint distribution, the range is from a reduction of 38% to an increase of 10%. In the case of a mixed distribution, the range is from a reduction of 20% to an increase of 28% over single-class indexing with a disjoint distribution. The reduction is between 40% and 65% compared to single-class indexing with an inclusive distribution of key values among classes in the class hierarchy.

For a range query in which the key values are scattered over two classes, we consider only disjoint and mixed key distribution because inclusive key distribution is not meaningful for this scenario. For disjoint key distribution, the maximum number of index pages fetched ranges from a reduction of 42% to an increase of 20% for class-hierarchy indexing compared to single-class indexing. For a mixed key distribution class-hierarchy index, the range is from a reduction of 8% to an increase of 27% compared to a disjoint key distribution single-class index.

We note that a disjoint distribution represents the best case for single-class indexing, in terms of the number of index pages that must be fetched, for both single-key query and range-query evaluation. Only indexes for the classes containing the key values need to be traversed, and thus only the single-class indexes for the classes need to be fetched.

## Summary

In an object-oriented database, the scope of a query is often a class hierarchy rooted at a particular class. This means that to support the evaluation of a query whose access scope is a class hierarchy, the system must maintain one index for each of the classes involved in the query. A single-class index is the traditional index that is maintained on an attribute of a single class. A class-hierarchy index is one that may be maintained on an attribute of all classes on a class hierarchy.

In this chapter, we formulated the cost model for the size and performance of a single-class index and a class-hierarchy index. We then presented the results of simulation experiments we have conducted to quantify the trade-offs between the two types of index. The preliminary results show that a class-hierarchy index tends to be more efficient than a single-class index in terms of the number of index pages that must be fetched for a given query, as long as there are at least two classes in a class hierarchy. As for the index size, a class-hierarchy index may be smaller or larger than the sum of the corresponding single-class indexes. For the index structure that we modeled, the index size depends on how many overflow nodes are created and how efficiently each leaf-level node is utilized.

## Acknowledgments

We are grateful to Jorge Garza for a discussion of the implementation details of an index in a database system, and to Hong-Tai Chou for comments on the assumptions we have made for our cost formulation and simulation experiments.

## References

[Banerjee et al. 1987a] J. Banerjee et al., "Data Model Issues for Object-Oriented Applications," *ACM Transactions on Office Information Systems,* January 1987.

[Banerjee et al. 1987b] J. Banerjee, W. Kim, H.J. Kim, and H.F. Korth, "Semantics and Implementation of Schema Evolution in Object-Oriented Databases," *Proceedings of the ACM SIGMOD Conference on the Management of Data,* San Francisco, CA, May 1987.

[Blasgen and Eswaran 1977] M.W. Blasgen and K.P. Eswaran, "Storage and Access in Relational Data Bases," *IBM System Journal,* No. 4, 1977.

[Bobrow et al. 1985] D.G. Bobrow, K. Kahn, G. Kiczales, L. Masinter, M. Stefik and F. Zdybel, *CommonLoops: Merging Common Lisp and Object-Oriented Programming,* Intelligent Systems Laboratory Series ISL-85-8, Xerox PARC, Palo Alto, CA, 1985.

[Chan et al. 1982] A. Chan et al., "Storage and Access Structures to Support a Semantic Data Model," *Proceedings of the International Conference on Very Large Databases,* September 1982.

[Comer 1979] D. Comer, "The Ubiquitous B-Tree," *Computing Surveys,* vol. 11, no. 2, June 1979.

[Date 1983] C.J. Date, *An Introduction to Database Systems,* vol. 2, Addison-Wesley, Reading, MA, 1983.

[IBM 1981] *SQL/Data System: Concepts and Facilities.* GH24-5013-0, File No. S370-50, IBM Corporation, January 1981.

[Knuth 1973] D. Knuth, *The Art of Computer Programming,* vol. 3, Addison-Wesley, Reading, MA, 1973.

[Maier and Stein 1986] D. Maier and J. Stein, "Indexing in an Object-Oriented DBMS," Oregon Graduate Center, Technical Report: CS/E-86-006, May 1986.

[Selinger et al. 1979] P.G. Selinger et al., "Access Path Selection in a Relational Database Management System," *Proceedings of the ACM SIGMOD Conference,* Boston, MA, pp. 23–34, 1979.

[Steele 1984] G.L. Steele, *Common Lisp: The Language,* Digital Press, 1984.

[Stonebraker et al. 1976] M. Stonebraker, E. Wong, P. Kreps, and G. Held, "The Design and Implementation of INGRES," *ACM Transactions on Database Systems,* vol. 1, no. 3, pp. 189–222, September 1976.

[Ullman 1982] J. Ullman, *Principles of Database Systems,* Computer Science Press, 1982.

[Woelk et al. 1986] D. Woelk, W. Kim, and W. Luther, "An Object-Oriented Approach to Multimedia Databases," *Proceedings of the ACM SIGMOD Conference on the Management of Data,* Washington, D.C., May 1986.

# 16

## Concurrency Control and Object-Oriented Databases

Andrea H. Skarra, Stanley B. Zdonik

## INTRODUCTION

Transaction processing is concerned with controlling the way in which programs share a common database. A transaction is normally viewed as both the unit of concurrency and the unit of recovery for database applications. As a unit of concurrency, the steps of several transactions can be interleaved so that they will not interfere with each other. As a unit of recovery, a transaction either succeeds totally or it has no effect on the database. The system can always recover to the boundaries of a transaction, such that results of partially completed transactions will not be visible.

Sharing is important for object-oriented databases as well. This chapter describes several ways in which the view of sharing in an object-oriented database might be different from the traditional view. Some of this work is very young and as yet does not have the same level of agreement or theory that exists for traditional transaction processing. Nevertheless, it is an important new direction in database system research. We do not intend this survey to be complete, but rather we intend it to be representative of the area.

Section 16.1 introduces the traditional concepts of transaction processing, and Section 16.2 discusses how they might be different for object-oriented databases. Section 16.3 details the notion of type-specific concurrency control, and Section 16.4 describes a new model of concurrency control for cooperative environments.

## 16.1 TRANSACTION PROCESSING

Transactions are programs that are typically developed independently of each other. For reasons of efficiency, it is desirable to allow the database system to interleave the steps of concurrently executing transactions. However, since they are written without knowledge of each other, it is possible to get interleavings that produce unexpected results [Bernstein et al. 1987]. Interleaving cannot, therefore, be done indiscriminately. There must be some criterion that will allow us to reject some interleavings while accepting others. On the basis of this criterion, a transaction processing system will synchronize transaction executions so that the incorrect interleavings cannot occur.

The transaction concept, as it appears in many database systems, often combines several important notions including:

- visibility

- recovery

- consistency

Visibility refers to the ability of one transaction to see the results of another transaction while it is executing. Recovery is the ability of the system, in the face of failure, to regain some state that is considered to be correct. Consistency refers to the correctness of the state of the database that a committed transaction produces.

Atomicity is also discussed as a characteristic of transactions. By atomicity we mean that, as viewed from the perspective of other transactions in the system, any given transaction either happens in its entirety, or it does not happen at all. In reexamining the transaction concept for advanced applications, such as design environments, we will need to consider each of the above three dimensions and decide whether they should all be addressed uniformly by a single mechanism.

If we choose to enforce atomicity for all transaction execution histories allowed by the system, then we are constrained in the ways in which we can approach visibility, recovery, and consistency. If we expect atomic transactions, then intermediate results of one transaction cannot be made visible to other transactions. Also, atomicity requires that, in the face of failure, it must be possible to roll back any partially completed transactions. The common view of consistency requires that any integrity constraint $C$ on a database $d$ is satisfied at the transaction boundaries. $C(d)$ is satisfied before a transaction begins executing as well as after it completes. Inside the transaction $C(d)$ may be violated, but the constraint must be reestablished by the time the transaction completes.

The measure of correctness for interleaved schedules of concurrent transactions that is used throughout the literature on transaction processing is serializability. Serializability follows naturally from the atomicity requirement of transactions. Conceptually, atomic entities have no divisible substructure. Therefore, it only makes sense to define correctness in terms of results that are obtained by executing transactions without interleaving (i.e., serially). An execution of a set of transactions, $T = \{T1, \ldots, Tn\}$, is expressed as a history $H(T)$. $H(T)$ is *serial* when, for any two transactions $Ti$ and $Tj$ in $T$, all operations of $Ti$ appear before those of $Tj$ or all the operations of $Tj$ appear before those of $Ti$. $H(T)$ is said to be *serializable* if the result of the interleaved transactions is equivalent to the result of some serial execution of $T$. That is, the concurrent, interleaved execution is correct if it can be shown to be equivalent to a truly serial execution.

Serializability defines correctness in terms of the results that would be obtained if there were no interleaving. It is important to understand that one of the benefits of this definition is that if a database can guarantee that this property will hold, then the creators of the transaction code need not concern themselves about the interference of other transactions. This simplifies the problem of reasoning about the correctness of programs. Program units that are correct in isolation will remain correct when they are executed in a concurrent environment.

An extension to the traditional theory of transactions allows the otherwise flat model of transactions to include transactions within transactions. This kind of transaction model has become known as nested transactions [Moss 1986]. A nested transaction structure consists of a set of child transactions that execute atomically with respect to their parent and their siblings. Nested transaction schemes require that the results that a parent sees from its nested children be as though the children execute serially. That is, a parent transaction does not see any internal structure of its children. If a child transaction fails or aborts, its results are eliminated just as in a nonnested scheme.

The motivation for a nested transaction scheme is to allow transactions to exploit parallelism that might naturally occur within themselves. The benefits of being able to safely specify parallel execution of transaction pieces include performance improvements and better control over recovery. The performance benefits are essentially the same as those we had with single-level transactions, but here the benefit can be extended through arbitrarily many levels of procedural abstraction. The benefit to recovery occurs when a part of a transaction fails. With a nested scheme, we need only roll back a part of the work. This part can be ignored or restarted independently of the other parts.

## 16.2 OBJECT-ORIENTED SYSTEMS

On the surface, concurrency control in object-oriented databases resembles that of traditional databases. Transactions are programs that make requests of the database, and at least for some applications, serializability seems appropriate as a correctness criterion. We can imagine an object-oriented database in which an object is the unit of granularity for the locking scheme. Transactions lock objects in a two-phase manner, and produce serializable results. Yet, there are at least two areas in which the nature of object-oriented databases or the ways in which they can be used might influence the approach to concurrency control. They are:

- using type-level semantics to achieve greater concurrency

- using type-level semantics to allow nonserializable behavior

The rest of this section will discuss each of these possibilities. This chapter will focus primarily on the first issue since solutions are more well-developed; however, we will mention an approach that is relevant to the second point at the end.

Object-oriented databases can be distinguished from their predecessors in that they incorporate an extensible type system [Maier and Stein 1987; Zdonik and Wegner 1986]. Users can extend the system's types to include new types that are indistinguishable from the built-in types. The extension is possible because the system implements the notion of data abstraction. An abstract data type is characterized by a set of operations that can be used to access and manipulate its instances. The operations are the only ways in which other programs can interact with instances of the type.

The strict operational interface defined by the abstract data types is important, since in previous database systems it was possible to interact with instances of a type in terms of arbitrary combinations of operations on that type's representation. The representations that were typically available included basic structuring types like Records, Arrays, and Files. With this level of abstraction, the most that we could talk about was reading and writing of objects or components of objects.

We will illustrate this distinction with an example. Suppose that we have an employee database. We might represent a set of employees by a relation type called Employees that contains employee records with the fields emp#, name, and salary. Programs that interact with Employees can read or write the fields of these relations in arbitrary ways. This means that, as far as the database system is concerned, read and write operations are the level of abstraction at which external applications will interact. Therefore, serializability theory has produced algorithms that are cast in terms of the semantics of reading and writing. That is, locking protocols involve special locks for reading and writing based on the way in which these two operations interfere with each other.

On the other hand, object-oriented systems provide new types with operations that are typically at a higher level than reading and writing. The operations might interact in ways that are quite different from standard reading and writing. In fact, by using the semantics of the operations that are provided for a type, we might be able to achieve more concurrency than by simply looking at the operations as reads and writes. This leads us to a crucial difference in what is possible for concurrency control techniques in object-oriented databases. Examples of this type of concurrency control are contained in Section 16.3.

A second way in which concurrency control might differ for object-oriented databases derives from the kinds of applications that appear to be driving their development. At present one of the most promising areas of application for object-oriented databases is design environments, including programming environments, electrical and mechanical CAD tools, and office information systems. In all of these areas, we find requirements for cooperative work. That is, we must be able to support programs that assist multiple people in achieving a common goal. They work together to reach this end, and the computer must make the sharing of information throughout this process as natural as possible.

Collaborative design argues for a mechanism that relaxes some of the constraints of a strictly serial world. We can relax serializability by allowing arbitrary communication between transactions; however, we lose our previous ability to conveniently argue about the correctness of transactions. If transactions can interact in unpredictable ways, it becomes difficult to understand how a concurrent mix of transactions might affect the database. An important question is then: how can we allow for the kind of sharing that we need and still preserve some notion of correctness? One approach that seems promising involves extending the type-specific concurrency control work to allow for application-specific correctness criteria that are cast in terms of allowable sequences of operations. This point of view will be discussed briefly at the end of this document.

## 16.3 SEMANTIC CONCURRENCY CONTROL

Models of semantic concurrency control use data semantics and application semantics to schedule transactions. They use the relationship between operations defined on a data type or between operations invoked by a transaction type to optimize concurrency. Object-oriented databases are well suited for semantic concurrency control, since they contain abstract types. The types define data semantics. Moreover, typical applications, such as design environments, are characterized by long and collaborative transactions in which concurrency must be optimized for adequate overall performance.

Concurrency is optimized by an approach based on data semantics in two ways. First, equivalence of histories is decided semantically. A history is equivalent to another (e.g., a serial history) when a difference between their results cannot be detected by data operations. The histories are semantically indistinguishable, even though objects may be in slightly different states. Second, operations are characterized in finer detail than as only Read or Write actions. Greater concurrency is possible because fewer operations have to be scheduled as though they conflict. Conflicting operations cannot execute concurrently since the result depends on the order of their completion. Indeed, conflicting operations in a serializable history must appear in the same relative order as in the equivalent serial one [Bernstein et al. 1987].

For example, traditional methods exploit the semantics of Read and Write operations in managing concurrent accesses to data. However, they ignore the semantics of the data items themselves. All data are viewed as simple types, such as Record or File, on which the only valid operations are the relatively low level Read and Write. In contrast, the use of data and operation semantics in managing accesses to a type such as Directory can result in a greater degree of concurrency than would be allowed by the use of only Read/Write semantics. Consider the Enter and List operations defined on directories. Under Read/Write semantics, Enter is a Write operation and conflicts with other Enter operations. List is a Read operation and also conflicts with Enter. Under Directory semantics, however, two transactions that perform only entries into a directory can be arbitrarily interleaved. The directory may be implemented as a linked list whose order depends on the interleaving sequence, while List returns entries in alphabetic order. The state of the directory object itself depends on the interleaving, but differences in its state are not distinguishable by List. Thus, Enter operations do not conflict with each other, and concurrency is improved over that realized with only Read/Write semantics.

Semantic approaches can be broadly divided into two groups. Models of the *data approach* define concurrency properties on abstract data types according to the semantics of the type and its operations. Models of the *transaction approach* define concurrency properties on transactions according to the semantics of the transactions and the data they manipulate. The interleaving of concurrent transactions is implicitly constrained in the data approach by operation conflicts defined on abstract data types. In the transaction approach, interleavings are explicitly constrained by specifications on transactions.

In the data approach, an object offers a uniform, concurrent behavior, regardless of the semantics of applications using it. It is a more modular approach, and it allows decentralized concurrency control. In contrast, the transaction approach requires control that is centralized with respect to each group of concurrent transactions, and operation semantics have to be reconsidered in the context of each new transaction. An advantage of the transaction approach is the ease with which application semantics can be added to the concurrency control. In the data approach, semantics contributed by applications are added as new operations on data types. Addition of application semantics to types may be viewed as a violation of modularity, and the addition of operations to a type may be complicated by problems associated with schema changes [Skarra and Zdonik 1987]. We consider models of the data approach in this chapter. Examples of the transaction approach can be found in [Garcia-Molina 1983], [Garcia-Molina and Salem 1987], and [Lynch 1983].

In the following subsections, we describe several transaction management models that use semantic information about data and operations to improve concurrency in distributed systems. Distributed systems and design environments alike can exhibit processing delays that significantly impede throughput of transactions under traditional concurrency control. Delays in design environments are due to the length of transactions, while delays in distributed systems are due to the rate and fragility of network communication. Each model views transactions as atomic units of work (i.e., transactions are indivisible), and it synchronizes concurrent transactions under serializability. Each defines a conflict relation over the operations of a type, such that conflicting operations appear in a serializable history in the same relative order as in the equivalent serial one.

In the first approach (intertype synchronization), objects manage their own concurrency control, but synchronization between objects of different types occurs outside of the objects. In the second approach (local concurrency control), concurrency control algorithms are strictly local to objects, but nevertheless guarantee global atomicity. Local concurrency control is relevant to domains, such as design, in which tasks and data are commonly distributed among different machines. Also, the second approach demonstrates the subtle interactions between recovery and synchronization.

## 16.3.1 Intertype Synchronization

[Schwarz 1984] extends the traditional transaction model by redefining a transaction as a sequence of typed operations on objects that are instances of shared abstract types. Semantic knowledge about individual types is used in the model to develop synchronization and recovery strategies that allow more concurrency. Some of the strategies produce nonserializable results. The semantics include information about the typed operations, as well as the arguments and the results of operations. For purposes of recovery, the model assumes that an undo operation is defined for every operation of a given type.

The synchronization protocol is made up of several components. First, the execution of a group of concurrent transactions is characterized by an ordering property. The property may be serializability, or it may be a weaker correctness condition. Next, concurrency specifications are defined on each abstract data type that satisfy particular ordering properties of transactions that access instances of the type. Concurrency control is determined locally by a type for its instances. Finally, the system provides atomicity of transactions. Hence, types cooperate so that the prevailing ordering property is globally satisfied across transactions and types. In particular, the synchronization protocol embodies the following requirements for operations on shared abstract types:

- An operation cannot be permitted to observe or manipulate the state of an object during the invocation of another operation on the object. This requirement prevents the propagation of inconsistent data.

- The ordering property of a group of transactions must be preserved in interleaving the transactions' operations at each object. Moreover, the property must be preserved consistently across all objects shared by the transactions. This requires local synchronization of an object to cooperate with that of other objects to preserve the ordering property.

- Transactions cannot view data that might change if another transaction were to abort. This requirement prevents cascading aborts.

**Dependencies**  Concurrency control in the model uses the notion of dependencies between transactions. A dependency forms between two transactions when they both access the same object. For example, assume T1 and T2 are two concurrently executing transactions. T2 is dependent on T1 if an only if T1 performs an operation on an object and then T2 performs an operation on the same object. A schedule resulting from the interleaving of T1 and T2 is serializable when the dependencies that form during its execution are acyclic. A cycle in the dependency graph would mean, for example, that some operation in T2 occurs after some operation in T1 that occurs after some other operation in T2. Thus, the interleaved schedule could not be serialized such that either T1 preceded T2 or vice versa.

   The dependencies described in the last paragraph assume no semantic information about the operations or the object. No matter what operations are invoked, edges are added to the dependency graph when transactions touch the same object. However, the use of semantics may allow some dependencies to be ignored (i.e., we need not add an edge to the graph), without violating the correctness of the interleaved history. For example, if a cycle in the graph results from T1 and T2 both reading the same object, the schedule is still serializable. The dependency resulting from two transactions reading the same data is *insignificant* with regard to serializability.

   The concurrency semantics for an object are defined as a dependency specification with the object's abstract data type. A specification indicates, for all possible pairs of operations defined on the type, which of the resulting dependencies between transactions are significant with regard to a given correctness criterion (e.g., serializability). If a specification is not given with a type, dependencies form between transactions whenever they access the same instance of the type, regardless of the operations invoked.

As an example, consider the type Book on which the operations Read and Write are defined. The following is the complete set of dependencies that form when transactions read or write books, with the notation

$$D_i.\ T_j:\ X < T_k:\ Y$$

signifying that the $i$th kind of dependency forms when transaction $T_j$ invokes the operation X, and then $T_k$ invokes Y on the same book; $T_K$ becomes dependent on $T_j$.

D1.  $T_j$: Read $<$ $T_k$: Read
D2.  $T_j$: Read $<$ $T_k$: Write
D3.  $T_j$: Write $<$ $T_k$: Read
D4.  $T_j$: Write $<$ $T_k$: Write

In this example, there are four kinds of dependencies that can form when transactions access books. However, only the last three are significant in a concurrency control mechanism that provides serializability. D1 dependencies can be ignored because of the semantics of the Read operation. Thus, the dependency specification for Book that provides serializability is composed of D2, D3, and D4 dependencies. The concurrency control mechanism need only keep track of those dependencies in the dependency specification (i.e., the graph contains edges only for D2, D3, and D4 dependencies).

**Cooperative Types**   The synchronization protocol generates histories whose correctness is determined by the ordering property of the concurrent transactions. The sequence of operations in a global, interleaved history that satisfies the property, however, is determined by concurrency specifications defined with the abstract data types whose instances are manipulated by the transactions. That is, the operation sequence allowed at a given object is determined *locally* by its type, rather than by a global specification. Hence, the global history, as the aggregate of the objects' local histories, is determined by local specifications. For example, assume that the correctness criterion for a history of concurrent transactions is serializability, and the types manipulated by the transactions define specifications that satisfy serializability. Operations invoked at each object will be scheduled according to the specification of its type, and the resulting local sequence will be serializable within the context of the object.

When the transactions touch objects of different types, however, the equivalent serial ordering(s) of the local schedules must be mutually consistent in order for global serializability to be satisfied. If transactions T1 and T2 are both modifying a Queue object and a Directory object, then in *both* objects either T1 precedes T2 or T2 precedes T1. Any other ordering is not globally serializable, even though the schedule at each object may be locally serializable. The model accommodates synchronization across types, such as Queue and Directory, by designating them as *cooperative types*. The dependency specification for a group of cooperative types consists of the combined specifications of the individual types in the group. The same mechanism then applies uniformly to objects of the same or of a different type. Dependencies that form between transactions accessing one of the cooperative types are added to those between transactions accessing another of the types. An absence of cycles in the resulting group of dependencies indicates a serializable schedule when each of the participating types defines a dependency specification that guarantees serializability.

**Concurrency Control**   The implementation of the concurrency control scheme just described does not actually allow dependencies to form. Assume a transaction, T2, is allowed to read data written by an uncompleted transaction, T1. T1 could write to the data again before committing, or it could abort. Thus, T2 may receive data that are inconsistent or at least different from the committed data. Moreover, the data may be passed to other transactions that are dependent on T2. Cascading aborts can result. Instead, the implementation includes a locking algorithm that suspends T2 rather than allowing a dependency on T1 to form.

The locking algorithm uses the dependency specification of a type as the definition of conflict between the operations of the type. Two operations of a type conflict with each other if a significant dependency would form between transactions invoking them. In the Book example, Read and Write operations both conflict with Write because of D2, D3, and D4 dependencies. Read operations do not conflict because a D1 dependency is not significant. The locking algorithm uses the operation conflicts to introduce delays in transaction processing. If transaction T2 invokes an operation O on an object that conflicts with an operation previously invoked by T1, the execution of O is delayed and T2 is suspended until T1 commits. The delays induce a serialization order on the schedule; in particular, the resulting order of the equivalent serial schedule is consistent with the commit order of the transactions.

**FIFO Queue Semantics**   The viewing of operations as simply Reads or Writes, rather than exploiting more detailed semantic information, may result in concurrency limitations that are too strict for a given type. Instead, the type designer can make use of operation semantics, including operation arguments and results, in the dependency specification to further increase concurrency. [Schwarz 1984] describes the FIFO Queue as an example; it has two operations.

1. QEnter($q$, $p$): Adds an entry $p$ to the end of the Queue object $q$. The undo operation for QEnter removes the entry.

2. QRemove($q$): Removes the entry at the head of $q$ and returns the value of $p$ contained therein. If $q$ is empty, the operation blocks and waits until $q$ becomes nonempty. The undo operation for QRemove restores the entry to the head of $q$.

In addition, queues have numerous restrictions that must be maintained by the transaction scheduler. For instance, entries made by the same transaction must appear in the queue as a contiguous block. Also, entries made by a transaction cannot be observed by other transactions until the entering transaction commits.

The dependency specification for the Queue type makes use of the arguments passed to the operations and the results that they can return. It is assumed that each entry in the queue can be uniquely identified; for the purposes of the following specification, p$j$ is considered to be a different queue entry from p$k$. The complete set of dependencies that form when transactions access queues is as follows, with the notation E(p$j$) signifying that the transaction entered p$j$ in the queue and R(p$k$) signifying that the transaction removed p$k$ from the queue:

D1. T$m$: E(p$j$)$<$T$n$: E(p$k$)
D2. T$m$: E(p$j$)$<$T$n$: R(p$k$)
D3. T$m$: E(p$j$)$<$T$n$: R(p$j$)
D4. T$m$: R(p$j$)$<$T$n$: E(p$k$)
D5. T$m$: R(p$j$)$<$T$n$: R(p$k$)

The dependency specification for queues that guarantees serializability consists of D1, D3, and D5 dependencies. D2 dependencies are insignificant, since the ordering of concurrent transactions performing the operations cannot be detected by the transactions themselves or by any future transactions. Similarly, D4 as the inverse of D2 is insignificant. Casting the operations as Reads and Writes would unnecessarily limit concurrency. QEnter would be cast as a Write operation, and QRemove would be cast as a Read followed by a Write. Consequently, both D2 and D4 dependencies would have to be included in the specification in order to guarantee serializability.

**Weakly-FIFO Queue Semantics**  For some abstract data types, serializability may be too restrictive as a correctness criterion. In these cases, a weaker ordering property may be more appropriate by virtue of the higher levels of concurrency achieved without a sacrifice in type-specific consistency. A weaker ordering property is obtained by including fewer of the complete set of dependencies that can form between transactions in the type's dependency specification.

For example, queues are frequently used as producer/consumer buffers. The exact ordering of entries on the queue is not particularly important, provided an entry reaches the head of the queue at approximately the same time as other entries of the same vintage; an entry should not languish in the queue forever. Queues of this nature are *weakly-FIFO*. The complete set of dependencies is the same as that defined for the FIFO Queue type; however, the dependency specification for the weakly-FIFO Queue type includes only D3 dependencies. Entry order is not strictly serializable, but cascading aborts are avoided, since an entry is not visible to other transactions until it has committed. Moreover, the semantics of the data type are supported by the concurrency protocol, so that weakly-FIFO queues are guaranteed to be semantically consistent.

### 16.3.2 Local Concurrency Control

The concurrency control and recovery schemes in [Fekete et al. 1987; Herlihy and Weihl 1988; Weihl 1983; Weihl 1988] represent a departure from traditional transaction processing in several ways. First, the approach is data dependent. The definitions of atomicity and serializability rely on the explicit specification of the data and operation semantics by the data types. Second, the approach supports modular design. Global atomicity of the system is achieved by satisfying properties that are local to individual data objects. Finally, the approach analyzes serializability and recovery together, rather than treating them separately, because of the subtle interactions between the two.

**Atomicity** Global atomicity (i.e., the atomic execution of concurrent transactions) is defined in this approach by the semantics of data types and their operations. A history of a system (i.e., a schedule) is serializable if the committed transactions in the history can be executed in some serial order and have the same *semantic effect*. The schedule is said to be *equieffective* with the serial schedule, since the effect of the serializable schedule is indistinguishable from that of the serial one. Global atomicity is preserved in this model by concurrency control algorithms that are localized to the individual objects manipulated by the transactions, rather than by a single global algorithm that applies uniformly to all objects regardless of type. The algorithms ensure *local atomicity properties* of the manipulated objects.

A local atomicity property is a property P of specifications of objects such that the following is true: if the specification of every object in a system satisfies P, then every history in the system's behavior is atomic. That is, each object manages its own concurrency control, and generates serializable schedules that are based solely on its local context. In addition, if the concurrency algorithm at each object satisfies the local atomicity property designated for the system, then the behavior of the system as a whole (i.e., the history involving all the objects) will be serializable as well. As a result, a single system can use a different concurrency control algorithm at each object if needed, provided every algorithm satisfies the same local atomicity property. The flexibility is particularly important for systems whose components perform most efficiently under different algorithms or for loosely coupled distributed systems.

Any local atomicity property must be such that in satisfying the property the objects agree on at least one serialization order for the committed transactions; otherwise, the system history is not serializable. However, each object has purely local information; no object has complete information of the global computation of the system on which to base its local history. Thus, a local atomicity property describes the way that objects agree on a serialization order for committed transactions. Two examples of local atomicity properties are *dynamic atomicity* and *hybrid atomicity*. Both are *optimal* local atomicity properties; no strictly weaker local property suffices to ensure global atomicity. A detailed description of dynamic atomicity and hybrid atomicity can be found in papers cited earlier.

**Two Models**    Two models are described for the design of a type-specific concurrency control and recovery system based on local atomicity properties. One model supports dynamic atomicity and defines a *conflict relation* over each type's operations for concurrency control that is determined by commutativity of the operations. The other supports hybrid atomicity and defines operation conflicts by means of serial dependency relations. Both models allow the arguments and results of operations to be used in determining conflicts.

Conflict relations are (generally binary) relations over a type's operations, such that an operation pair (O1,O2) is in the relation when O1 cannot execute concurrently with O2. Generally, operations conflict when their effect is order-dependent. Consequently, conflict relations are the means by which an interleaved schedule is decided for equieffectiveness with a serial one. Two schedules cannot have conflicting operations in arbitrary orders and still be guaranteed to have the same effect. In particular, conflicting operations in a serializable schedule must appear in the same relative order as in the equivalent serial one [Bernstein et al. 1987].

Recall that [Schwarz 1984] defines a conflict relation over the operations of each type, such that two operations conflict if a *significant* dependency forms between transactions invoking them. However, the reason for labeling a particular dependency as significant is not explicitly uniform across types. The set of all possible dependencies for a type is considered as a whole, and a group of them is chosen as significant in order to satisfy an ordering property such as serializability. The criteria for dependency significance (and hence operation conflict) may have less to do with individual operations and rather more to do with the overall semantics of types. In contrast, the models described in this section make the definition of conflict explicit. That is, conflict between operations is defined on the basis of commutativity or serial dependencies, which are discussed in detail later.

The conflict relations defined on types are used by a locking protocol in each model to manage concurrent access to objects. Each conflict-based protocol generates schedules that are serializable in the transaction commit order. A lock is associated with each operation defined on a type; two locks conflict when the corresponding operation pair is an element of the type's conflict relation. The execution of conflicting operations induces a serialization order on a schedule, since their relative ordering must be the same as that in the equivalent serial schedule. Consequently, locking schemes delay the execution of an operation (and generally the transaction that invokes it) until active transactions that have invoked conflicting operations have terminated. Locking dynamically influences both the schedule (by delaying operation execution) and the commit order (by delaying transaction execution).

The concurrency and recovery schemes in the models support different local atomicity properties and use different criteria to define conflict relations on types. The systems demonstrate that there are subtle interactions between the algorithms chosen for concurrency control and recovery. Moreover, the level of concurrency allowed by a protocol depends not only on data type and operation semantics, but also on the definition of conflict used by the concurrency control mechanism. The locking protocol satisfying hybrid atomicity that defines operation conflicts in terms of serial dependency relations permits more concurrency than existing commutativity-based protocols.

**Commutativity** [Fekete et al. 1987; Weihl 1988] describe models for concurrency control and recovery systems that are based on dynamic atomicity; [Fekete et al. 1987] describes a nested transaction model, and the [Weihl 1988] model is nonnested. In both cases, commutativity is used as the basis for a type's conflict relation, and concurrency and recovery are treated together because the definition of commutativity used depends on the recovery algorithm chosen. A conflict relation based on commutativity means that two operations conflict if they do not commute (i.e., if the result of a sequence containing the two operations depends on the order of their execution).

[Weihl 1988] defines commutativity in terms of a state machine as *forward commutativity* and *backward commutativity*. If M is a state machine, R and S are two sequences of transitions of M, and R(s) is the state reached by traversing R from state s, then we say that R and S commute forward if, for every s in which R and S are both defined, $R(S(s)) = S(R(s))$ and $R(S(s))$ is not the null state. That is, R and S are defined in s, R is defined in S(s), S is defined in R(s), and the final states are the same whether R S or S R is traversed from s. We can *push R forward over S* (and vice versa).

Given the same machine and sequences, we say that R and S commute backward if $R(S(s)) = S(R(s))$ for *every* state s. If one execution order starts in state s1 and results in s2, then the reverse execution order will also result in s2 when started from s1. That is, if we know that we can execute R and then S, then we know that we can execute S and then R; one order implies the other. We can *push R backward over S* (and vice versa). Examples in the paper illustrate cases in which the forward commutativity relation is strictly larger than the backward commutativity relation (i.e., more operations commute forward than commute backward). In other cases, the two relations are incomparable.

For example, assume Deposit and Withdraw operations are defined on the Account type. Withdrawals return successfully if accounts have sufficient funds; otherwise, they return an error. We consider Deposit and Withdraw operations that return successfully after modifying the state of an account (i.e., its balance). Deposits commute forward with withdrawals but not backward. When a successful Deposit and Withdraw are both defined in some state s1, the same state s2 is reached whether Deposit precedes Withdraw in a sequence that executes from s1 or vice versa. Thus, they forward commute; one can be pushed forward over the other. However, the successful execution of a Deposit followed by a Withdraw does not imply that the reverse order would complete successfully. Thus, they do not backward commute.

In contrast, withdrawls commute backward with each other but not forward. The successful completion of two Withdraw operations in a sequence implies that the same state would be reached by the sequence even if the operations were in the reverse order. Thus, Withdraw operations backward commute; one can be pushed backward over the other. However, from a state s1 in which two Withdraw operations are defined (i.e., each would individually return successfully), it is not necessarily the case that a sequence containing both would result in the same s2 regardless of the order of the operations. Both operations are defined in s1 because each withdraws an amount less than the balance in s1. However, if the total amount withdrawn by the operations exceeds the balance in s1, then s2 depends on which Withdraw executes first. The second Withdraw fails in either order and does not affect the balance. Hence, they do not forward commute. Deposits, on the other hand, both forward and backward commute with each other.

The definition of commutativity chosen for the conflict relation in a concurrency control scheme depends on the recovery algorithm used. The nonnested transaction model described in [Weihl 1988] describes two recovery algorithms. Each algorithm requires a different definition of commutativity for the conflict relation used in concurrency control, and only one of the definitions is correct for each. An intentions list algorithm is used with a conflict relation based on forward commutativity, while an undo log algorithm is used with backward commutativity. The nested transaction model described in [Fekete et al. 1987] uses an intentions list recovery scheme and, therefore, forward commutativity as a conflict relation.

In both recovery algorithms, a log is kept at an object for each active transaction. In the intentions list algorithm, however, only the *permanent* state of the object (i.e., the state resulting from only committed transactions) is visible to active transactions. Hence, an object's visible state is not changed by a transaction until it commits; the operation sequence in the transaction's log is then applied to the object. However, operations return results to transactions at the time of invocation. Each result is obtained by executing the operation in the state that is derived by applying the prior operations in the transaction's log to the permanent state of the object. Only the forward commutativity definition can be used as a conflict relation when the intentions list recovery algorithm is chosen.

For example, assume an intentions list recovery algorithm is used for an account whose balance is $10 (i.e., the permanent state is $10). Two transactions, T1 and T2, withdraw $8 and $6 respectively. Each withdrawal is legal within the view of the invoking transactions, which is just the permanent state of the object in both cases. If backward commutativity were used to define the conflict relation, the withdrawals would be allowed to proceed concurrently because they do not conflict. However, if both transactions then commit, the resulting execution does not satisfy dynamic atomicity. In fact, the execution is not even atomic, since there is no order in which the transactions can be serialized without violating consistency constraints (e.g., the balance must be nonnegative).

In contrast, the undo log algorithm maintains the *current* state of the object (i.e., the state resulting from committed and active transactions). When a transaction invokes an operation, the result is generated in the context of the current state of the object. The operation is recorded in the transaction's log, and the current state of the object is updated to reflect the effect of the operation. Hence, the state in which each operation executes includes the effects of other active transactions, unlike the intentions list algorithm. Only the backward commutativity definition can be used as a conflict relation when the undo log recovery algorithm is chosen.

For example, assume undo log recovery is used for an account whose initial balance is $10. Transactions T1 and T2 deposit $5 and withdraw $15, respectively. If forward commutativity were used to define the conflict relation, then the operations would not conflict, and the transactions would be allowed to proceed concurrently. Each operation is legal within the view of the appropriate transaction, which is the current state of the object. The balance goes from $10 to $15 in the view of T1 and from $15 to $0 within the view of T2. However, the history is not correct unless both transactions commit in T1 T2 order. If T1 aborts and T2 commits, the history is not atomic. If they commit in T2 T1 order, then the history is not serializable in commit order, and the resulting balance may be inconsistent with other objects in the system.

**Serial Dependency**   [Herlihy 1987; Herlihy and Weihl 1987] describe a model for concurrency control and recovery that satisfies hybrid atomicity and uses a serial dependency relation as the basis for defining operation conflicts. Informally, conflict is defined in terms of invalidation. Two concurrent transactions execute no conflicting operations and can be serialized in either order when neither transaction invalidates the other. The notion of invalidation as a basis for conflict is weaker than commutativity, which requires that both serializations define equivalent states.

A dependency relation can be defined over the operations of each type, such that an operation, O1, *depends on* any other operation, O2, that can invalidate it by appearing earlier in a sequence. That is, if there exist operation sequences H1 and H2 such that H1 O2 H2 and H1 H2 O1 are legal sequences, but H1 O2 H2 O1 is not, then O2 *invalidates* O1, and O1 *depends on* O2. For example, the Account type has Deposit and Withdraw operations. Withdrawals return successfully if accounts have sufficient funds; otherwise, they return an error. An unsuccessful Withdraw can be invalidated by prior Deposit operations, but successful Withdraws cannot. Thus, unsuccessful Withdraw operations depend on (i.e., conflict with) Deposits, but successful ones do not.

The protocol described in [Herlihy and Weihl 1987] manages concurrent access to an object with a timestamping and locking scheme that is based on the dependency-based conflict relation defined by the object's type. The protocol maintains several components for each object.

- An intentions list for each transaction consisting of the sequence of operations that are to be applied to the object if the transaction commits.

- The object's committed state, which reflects the effects of committed transactions. The committed state may be thought of as the intentions lists for the committed transactions, arranged in timestamp order.

- A set of locks that associates each operation with the set of active transactions that have executed that operation. Locks are related by a symmetric conflict relation that can take arguments and results into account.

The result of an operation invoked by transaction T on an object is obtained by executing the operation in the state that is derived by appending the intentions list of T to the committed state of the object. The result is computed before the new operation is actually appended to T's intentions list, since T must first obtain a lock for the operation, and the model allows operation arguments and results to be used in defining conflict relations. If a conflict exists, the lock request is refused and the result is discarded. The invocation is later retried (and may at that time return a different result). If the lock is granted, the operation is appended to the intentions list and the result is returned. When a transaction commits, its intentions list is merged into the committed state in timestamp order.

[Herlihy and Weihl 1988] shows that their protocol is less restrictive and can achieve at least as much concurrency as commutativity-based protocols. Further, lock conflict relations induced by dependency may be weaker than or incomparable to those defined by commutativity. The concurrency advantage is especially apparent for operations that do not return the state of the object as part of their result. The definition of commutativity used in the comparison is forward commutativity.

For example, the Account type has Deposit, Withdraw, and Post operations. Post posts interest to accounts (e.g., Post(5) multiplies the account balance by 1.05) and returns a result of *OK*. The conflict relation over Deposits and successful Withdraws is the same whether induced by dependency or forward commutativity. However, Post conflicts with both Deposit and successful Withdraw in the forward commutativity case, and with neither in the dependency case. Post operations are not invalidated by previous Deposit and Withdraw operations. A transaction T always receives the result *OK* when it invokes Post. Moreover, the Post operation does not actually change the account balance until T commits, when its intentions list is applied to the account.

In contrast, the definition of forward commutativity requires Post to conflict with both Deposit and successful Withdraw. Recall that operations O1 and O2 conflict if they are individually defined in a state s1, and if the state s2 reached by a sequence containing O1 and O2 depends on the order of their execution. That is, a sequence in which O1 precedes O2 must result in the same account balance as one in which O2 precedes O1, where the initial balance is the same in both cases. Otherwise, O1 conflicts with O2. Clearly, the effect of a sequence containing Post and Deposit or containing Post and successful Withdraw depends on the order of the operations.

### 16.3.3 Comparison of the Data Approaches

All models of the data approach synchronize transactions under semantic serializability. A conflict relation is defined over the operations on each abstract data type, such that two operations conflict when either the semantic effect or the validity of a history is dependent on the order of their execution. A history is semantically equivalent to a serial history when conflicting operations appear in the same relative order in both. Synchronization algorithms use conflict-based locking schemes to generate histories that are serializable in the commit order of the concurrent transactions. Conflict-based locking is a generalization of traditional locking protocols that are based on Read/Write semantics.

The models use different definitions of conflict. In some cases, operations conflict if they do not commute (i.e., forward or backward commutativity). In others, operations conflict when dependencies form between transactions that invoke them. Dependency-based conflict may occur as a result of information flow between transactions (e.g., one transaction reads data written, but not yet committed, by another), inconsistencies between transactions in their view of the data (e.g., two transactions' queue entries are interleaved and the resulting nonserializable ordering is visible to future transactions), or invalidation (e.g., one operation preceding another invalidates a history). Moreover, some models allow arguments and results to be considered in defining conflict. In others, nonconflicting operations must be compatible over all parameters and object states. The definition of conflict used in a system may depend on the recovery algorithm. For example, forward commutativity is used with intentions list recovery, and backward commutativity is used with undo logs.

The definition of concurrency semantics individually on abstract data types allows decentralized concurrency control by objects. The advantages of a distributed approach include modularity and the avoidance of a central bottleneck (i.e., there is more concurrency in the concurrency control mechanism itself). Objects themselves schedule their operations so as to generate locally serializable histories. Thus, the global system history is the result of local control, and it is serializable only when the local histories of objects touched by the same concurrent transactions agree on at least one equivalent serial schedule.

Each model supports decentralized control to some degree. In the most general case, a system defines a local atomicity property that allows strictly local control (e.g., dynamic atomicity, hybrid atomicity). Different concurrency algorithms that satisfy the property can be used in different parts of the system. The model described in [Allchin 1983; Allchin and McKendry 1983] supports strictly local control, but uses only pessimistic synchronization algorithms. Objects described in [Schwarz 1984] control concurrency locally, but synchronization between different types touched by the same transaction occurs outside of individual objects.

## 16.4 A TRANSACTION MODEL FOR DESIGN APPLICATIONS

Our current research represents a response to the need of design transactions for flexibility in concurrency control [Bancilhon et al. 1985; Katz and Weiss 1984; Kim et al. 1984; Skarra et al. 1986]. We propose a transaction model for computer-supported, cooperative environments that more completely captures the design process. The model acknowledges and exploits the special requirements and characteristics of design activities and design data, and it maintains database consistency by adherence to semantic correctness criteria during concurrent processing. The context for the model is an object-oriented database system that supports a data abstraction facility [Zdonik and Wegner 1986]. Abstraction is an effective method for modeling design data and for managing its complexity. Moreover, the semantics embodied by abstract data types provide a definition medium for correctness of concurrent histories. We define a specification and control paradigm that allows a database system to make guarantees about the semantic integrity and resiliency of concurrent, cooperative transactions. We address the following issues in developing the model.

- **Cooperation:** The cooperation among tasks required by a design application is supported in the model by a specification method and a control structure for task and data sharing. Sharing protocols are explicitly and uniformly defined on both transactions and abstract data types by application and type designers. The model integrates cooperating transactions with independent transactions. An object simultaneously allows collaboration among some transactions and prevents interference between others.

- **Data and transaction semantics:** The model exploits both transaction and data semantics in a consistent framework to improve concurrency and to decide the correctness of histories.

- **Correctness:** Concurrency correctness criteria disallow histories that produce anomalous effects on the database. Thus, application designers can reason about transactions independently of the concurrency context in which they execute. The model synchronizes both atomic and cooperating transactions under semantic correctness criteria. That is, the correctness of a history is defined and decided semantically. The criteria for cooperating transactions are based on operation sequences rather than constraints. Consequently, correctness requirements such as design verification protocols can be specified.

- **Hierarchical, interdependent transactions:** Complex design transactions are divided into smaller, manageable subtransactions. Typically, subtransactions are spanned by constraints and are incompletely specified. Moreover, constraints may be added dynamically. As a result, subtransactions are interdependent, collaborative, and inherently parallel. The model uses a nested framework to localize data visibility and constraint satisfaction hierarchically and to support incremental definition of concurrency protocols. Task and data sharing among siblings in the framework is defined by their parent. Nonserializable behavior is confined to subtrees.

- **Long, interactive, dynamically constructed transactions:** The model describes conflict resolution strategies appropriate for design transactions. Transactions are not suspended or aborted in the service of concurrency control. Communication is based on asynchronous protocols. Checkpoint recovery reinstates partial execution of independent and cooperating transactions following system failures.

### 16.4.1 Transactions

A *transaction* is a sequence of operations that represents a logical unit of work. Each operation is defined by an abstract type and executes atomically on database objects; at least one of the objects is an instance of the type. An *atomic transaction* is an indivisible operation sequence that preserves data consistency. We model a design task as a nested structure of transactions. The root is an atomic transaction, and nodes are either atomic transactions or *transaction groups* (TGs). A TG has members called *cooperating transactions*, and it supports a controlled form of task and data sharing among its members. The key elements of the model consist of the following:

- Transaction groups (TGs) within a nested framework
- Semantic correctness criteria for concurrency control
- Local control at TGs for cooperating transactions
- Local control at objects for atomic transactions

### 16.4.2 Transaction Groups

Informally, a TG is an explicitly defined, active entity that coordinates its members and provides an interface between them and the database at large. In particular, a TG manages the tasks and objects that are shared by its members and serves as a locus of control for concurrency (and recovery). A TG produces an operation sequence, S, by dynamically interleaving the sequences of its members. S satisfies semantic correctness criteria that the TG defines over objects it manipulates; semantic correctness criteria are based on operation sequences.

The interleaving of two nodes within the nested framework is defined by their lowest common ancestor. Atomic transactions define serializability for their descendents. In contrast, a TG, G, defines semantic protocols for (non-serializably) interleaving its members and subgroups. G typically defines a subgroup, G', to synchronize subtransactions of a transaction in G. Alternatively, G may delegate to G' the control of specific cooperating transactions in G that execute under distinct interleaving protocols. G' is a member of G as well as a subgroup. As a member, its operation sequence (produced by interleaving its members) is interleaved with other members of G according to G's protocols. As a subgroup, it defines its own protocols and control measures for its members.

Synchronization of transactions is decentralized and is controlled at two levels. That is, synchronization is controlled by TGs and by objects. A TG schedules its members (and subgroups) locally, and an object schedules atomic transactions locally. A TG whose parent is an atomic transaction is interleaved with its siblings at the object level, and it is interleaved as though it were an atomic transaction. Object level synchronization does not distinguish cooperating transactions and subgroups within a TG subtree. In both TGs and objects, concurrent operations are scheduled by conflict relations defined over abstract data types. Conflicts can be redefined by TGs to reflect application-specific semantics.

### 16.4.3 Concurrency Control within Objects

Synchronization at an object prevents interference and information flow between concurrent transactions. Objects maintain local serializability with algorithms that also guarantee global serializability. We implement object-level concurrency control with a refinement of the [Weihl 1988] type-specific, conflict-based algorithm. In particular, we compare operation sequences under forward commutativity rather than just operations. The method improves concurrency by allowing a conflict between two operations to be reversed by other operations, so that suspended transactions may proceed sooner. In this chapter, we detail only the synchronization within TGs.

### 16.4.4 Concurrency Control with Transaction Groups

The objective of synchronization in objects and TGs alike is consistency in concurrent histories. However, the functions that synchronization performs in objects and in TGs are different. An object synchronizes transactions that are individually consistent (i.e., atomic transactions). It protects the consistency in each transaction against violation by another (i.e., serializability). In contrast, cooperating transactions may or may not be individually consistent. Rather, correctness is defined for the history as a whole. Consequently, a TG protects consistency in the emerging history against violation by one of the group members.

We define new correctness criteria for concurrent transactions, namely *semantic patterns*. A pattern is an operation sequence that represents a semantic action and preserves consistency within or between objects. Patterns are defined by abstract data types and TGs, and each includes operations of one or more types. A consistent history of cooperating transactions satisfies the semantic patterns that apply to the group. A pattern can be an arbitrary, partially ordered collection of operations, provided a recognizer and a conflict detector can be constructed for it. TGs must simultaneously recognize pattern matches and synchronize pattern interleaving in order to produce consistent histories of their members. Our examples illustrate the use of patterns in cooperative settings.[1]

A correct history, H, satisfies the patterns in its *consistency set*. A pattern is *active* until it is satisfied. The consistency set contains *required* and *requested* patterns that initiate during H. Pattern P is required by operation O when O is part of P, and any H that contains O must satisfy P for consistency. For example, the type Airplane defines a pattern, P1: Board_Passengers() Deplane_Passengers(), which is required by both operations. A pattern may be required by only some of the operations it contains. For example, flight service on airplanes might include a pattern, P2: Board_Passengers() followed by Serve_Meal(). P2 is not required by Board_Passengers(); passengers don't always get a meal on a flight. However, P2 is required by Serve_Meal(); meals are served only on flights with passengers. Patterns can be explicitly requested by group members. In particular, patterns that are not required by any operations must be requested in order to appear in a consistency set. Requested

---

[1] For simplicity, we exclude operation arguments from the examples.

patterns are analogous to agreements or contracts among the participants as to the form of their collaboration. The patterns include cooperative tasks defined at the group or type level. For example, food and beverage service protocols may be cast as requested patterns, since they vary between airlines and may vary between flights.

A TG, G, dynamically produces a correct history, H, through conflict avoidance strategies. For each operation, O, G adds patterns to the consistency set of H that are required by O. G then tests O against active patterns in the set. O conflicts with pattern P under the following circumstances, where Po is another active pattern containing O:

C1: The effect of O disrupts a condition within P (i.e., O reverses the effect of preceding operations in P), and P requires the condition for upcoming operations.

C2: The effect of an upcoming operation in P, Op, disrupts a condition within some Po (i.e., Op reverses the effect of O), and Po requires the condition for its upcoming operations.

Operation specifications are required to decide C1 and C2 conflicts. Tables that capture the specifications are defined on abstract types and may be redefined by TGs. The conflicts indicate only impending inconsistency. It may be possible in both cases to allow O to proceed, provided the reversed conditions are reinstated. We do not discuss conflict management and resolution here.

For example, assume that patterns P2, P3, and P4 are active for history H. P2 is the food service pattern described earlier. P3 is a seat assignment pattern, P3: Board_Passengers() followed by Bump_Passengers() or Assign_Standby(). P4 includes Read_Passenger_List(). A TG member invokes Board_Passengers(). The operation does not conflict with any active patterns, and it matches an operation in P2 and P3. The TG appends the operation to H and adds P1 (defined by type Airplane) to the consistency set of H. P1 is required by the operation. If Deplane_Passengers() or Read_Passenger_List() is next invoked, P1 or P4 is matched. However, Deplane_Passengers() conflicts under C1 with both P2 and P3, and Read_Passenger_List() conflicts under C2 with P3. Notice that the effect of an operation includes its return value(s).

A conflict table on type T has a row and column for each of T's operations. A blank entry in a C1 table indicates that the (row, column) operations are compatible under backward commutativity, and a blank entry in a C2 table indicates compatibility under forward commutativity (cf. Section 16.3.2). A nonblank entry at (O1, O2) consists of operations whose effect, when preceded by O1, depends on whether O2 executes after O1. A TG can redefine table entries if necessary to reflect application semantics. For example, the C2 conflict between Read_Passenger_List() and operations that change the list might be eliminated by a group to allow reads during simultaneous updates.

The approach represents an alternative method for defining and deciding correctness of concurrent histories. It readily supports parallel and cooperative tasks under specifiable correctness criteria. Concurrency is improved over defining patterns as large (atomic) operations on types, since patterns specify breakpoints where interleaving can occur. Moreover, patterns are not required to execute serializably. A pattern P1 may begin before and end after a P2. The form of specification is declarative, so that complex, parallel tasks do not have to be sequenced within transactions. Moreover, the model allows the incorporation of application semantics with a uniform specification method for types and transactions.

Patterns also support facilitation (i.e., a single Board_Passengers() suffices for more than one pattern). Facilitation improves efficiency among cooperating transactions, and it allows the specification of correctness criteria such as validation operations on a design. Validation is required to prove individual components correct, but the operation executes on the entire design. All components must commit in order to validate any. Serializability does not support validation specifications as criteria for correctness of histories, because under serializability, only correct components can commit. A circular situation exists in which a component must commit to be validated, and it must be validated before it can commit.

## SUMMARY

Although many of the techniques from traditional transaction processing can be carried over to object-oriented databases, some aspects of concurrency control might also be handled differently. For example, the additional semantics in object-oriented databases can be used to improve concurrency and to express correctness criteria other than serializability.

We have shown how several proposals have successfully increased the amount of concurrency that is obtainable by making use of type-level semantics. Several schemes improve concurrency by exploiting semantics at the data level. This line of research suggests the specification of recovery mechanisms at the type-level as a direction for future research.

We concluded with a short description of how object-oriented semantics might be used to allow nonserializable interactions between cooperating transactions. This work builds on some of the ideas of type-specific concurrency control and uses a variation of nesting as its conceptual framework.

## REFERENCES

[Allchin 1983] J.E. Allchin, "An Architecture for Reliable Decentralized Systems," Ph.D. Dissertation, Technical Report GIT-ICS-83/23, School of Information and Computer Science, Georgia Institute of Technology, September 1983.

[Allchin and McKendry 1983] J.E. Allchin and M.S. McKendry, "Synchronization and Recovery of Actions," *Proceedings of the Second Annual ACM Symposium on Principles of Distributed Computing*, 1983.

[Bancilhon et al. 1985] F. Bancilhon, W. Kim, and H.F. Korth, "A Model of CAD Transactions," *Proceedings of the Eleventh International Conference on Very Large Data Bases*, 1985.

[Bernstein and Goodman 1982] P.A. Bernstein and N. Goodman, "A Sophisticate's Introduction to Distributed Concurrency Control," *Proceedings of the Eighth International Conference on Very Large Data Bases*, 1982.

[Bernstein and Goodman 1983] P.A. Bernstein and N. Goodman, "Multiversion Concurrency Control—Theory and Algorithms," *ACM Transactions on Database Systems*, vol. 8, no. 4, December 1983.

[Bernstein et al. 1987] P.A. Bernstein, V. Hadzilacos, and N. Goodman, *Concurrency Control and Recovery in Database Systems*, Addison-Wesley, Reading, MA, 1987.

[Bloom 1979] T. Bloom, "Synchronization Mechanisms for Modular Programming Languages," M.S. Dissertation, Technical Report MIT/LCS/TR-211, Laboratory for Computer Science, Massachusetts Institute of Technology, January 1979.

[Fekete et al. 1987] A. Fekete, N.A. Lynch, M. Merritt, and W.E. Weihl, "Nested Transactions, Conflict-Based Locking, and Dynamic Atomicity," Technical Report MIT/LCS/TM-340, Laboratory for Computer Science, Massachusetts Institute of Technology, September 1987.

[Garcia-Molina 1983] H. Garcia-Molina, "Using Semantic Knowledge for Transaction Processing in a Distributed Database," *ACM Transactions on Database Systems*, vol. 8, no. 2, June 1983.

[Garcia-Molina and Salem 1987] H. Garcia-Molina and K. Salem, "Sagas," Technical Report CS-TR-070-87, Department of Computer Science, Princeton University, January 1987.

[Garza and Kim 1987] J.F. Garza and W. Kim, "Transaction Management in an Object-Oriented Database System," Technical Report ACA-ST-292-87, Microelectronics and Computer Technology Corporation, September 1987.

[Gray 1981] J. Gray, "The Transaction Concept: Virtues and Limitations," *Proceedings of the Seventh International Conference on Very Large Data Bases*, 1981.

[Herlihy 1987] M.P. Herlihy, "Optimistic Concurrency Control for Abstract Data Types," *Operating Systems Review*, vol. 21, no. 2, April 1987.

[Herlihy and Weihl 1988] M.P. Herlihy and W.E. Weihl, "Hybrid Concurrency Control for Abstract Data Types," *Proceedings of the ACM Symposium on Principles of Database Systems*, 1988.

[Hornick and Zdonik 1987] M.F. Hornick and S.B. Zdonik, "A Shared, Segmented Memory System for an Object-Oriented Database," *ACM Transactions on Office Information Systems*, vol. 5, no. 1, January 1987.

[Katz and Weiss 1984] R.H. Katz and S. Weiss, "Design Transaction Management," *Proceedings of the 21st Design Automation Conference*, 1984.

[Kim et al. 1984] W. Kim, R. Lorie, D. McNabb, and W. Plouffe, "A Transaction Mechanism for Engineering Design Databases," *Proceedings of the Tenth International Conference on Very Large Data Bases*, 1984.

[Kung and Papadimitriou 1979] H.T. Kung and C.H. Papadimitriou, "An Optimality Theory of Concurrency Control for Databases," *Proceedings of ACM-SIGMOD International Conference on Management of Data*, 1979.

[Korth 1983] H.F. Korth, "Locking Primitives in a Database System," *Journal of the Association for Computing Machinery*, vol. 30, no. 1, January 1983.

[Korth and Kim 1985] H.F. Korth and W. Kim, "A Concurrency Control Scheme for CAD Transactions," Technical Report TR-85-34, Department of Computer Science, University of Texas at Austin, December 1985.

[Lamport 1978] L. Lamport, "Time, Clocks, and the Ordering of Events in a Distributed System," *Communications of the ACM*, vol. 21, no. 7, July 1978.

[Liskov and Weihl 1986] B. Liskov and W.E. Weihl, "Specifications of Distributed Programs," *Distributed Computing*, vol. 1, pp. 102–118, 1986.

[Lynch 1983] N.A. Lynch, "Multilevel Atomicity—A New Correctness Criterion for Database Concurrency Control," *ACM Transactions on Database Systems*, vol. 8, no. 4, December 1983.

[Maier and Stein 1987] D. Maier and J. Stein, "Development and Implementation of an Object-Oriented DBMS," in B. Shriver and P. Wegner, eds., *Research Directions in Object-Oriented Programming*, MIT Press, Cambridge, MA, 1987.

[Moss 1986] J.E.B. Moss, "An Introduction to Nested Transactions," COINS Technical Report 86-41, Department of Computer and Information Science, University of Massachusetts at Amherst, September 1986.

[Papadimitriou and Kanellakis 1984] C.H. Papadimitriou and P.C. Kanellakis. "On Concurrency Control by Multiple Versions," *ACM Transactions on Database Systems*, vol. 9, no. 1, March 1984.

[Reed 1983] D.P. Reed, "Implementing Atomic Actions on Decentralized Data," *ACM Transactions on Computer Systems*, vol. 1, no. 1, February 1983.

[Reiss 1987] S.P. Reiss, "Working in the Garden Environment for Conceptual Programming," *IEEE Software*, vol. 4, no. 6, November 1987.

[Schwarz 1984] P.M. Schwarz, "Transactions on Typed Objects," Ph.D. Dissertation, Technical Report CMU-CS-84-166, Department of Computer Science, Carnegie Mellon University, December 1984.

[Skarra et al. 1986] A.H. Skarra, S.B. Zdonik, and S.P. Reiss, "An Object Server for an Object-Oriented Database," *Proceedings of the International Workshop on Object-Oriented Database Systems*, ACM/IEEE, 1986. *Revised in* A.H. Skarra, S.B. Zdonik and S.P. Reiss. "ObServer: An Object Server for an Object-Oriented Database," Technical Report CS-88-08, Department of Computer Science, Brown University, July 1987.

[Skarra and Zdonik 1987] A.H. Skarra and S.B. Zdonik, "Type Evolution in an Object-Oriented Database," in B. Shriver and P. Wegner, eds., *Research Directions in Object-Oriented Programming*, MIT Press, Cambridge, MA, 1987.

[Spector et al. 1987] A.Z. Spector, D. Thompson, R.F. Pausch, J.L. Eppinger, D. Duchamp, R. Draves, D.S. Daniels, and J.J. Bloch, "Camelot: A Distributed Transaction Facility for Mach and the Internet—An Interim Report," Technical Report CMU-CS-87-129, Department of Computer Science, Carnegie Mellon University, June 1987.

[Weihl 1983] W.E. Weihl, "Data-dependent Concurrency Control and Recovery," *Proceedings of the Second Annual ACM Symposium on Principles of Distributed Computing*, 1983.

[Weihl 1988] W.E. Weihl, "Commutativity-Based Concurrency Control for Abstract Data Types," *IEEE Proceedings of the 21st Annual Hawaii International Conference on System Sciences*, 1988.

[Weihl and Liskov 1985] W.E. Weihl and B. Liskov, "Implementation of Resilient, Atomic Data Types," *ACM Transactions on Programming Languages and Systems*, vol. 7, no. 2, April 1985.

[Zdonik and Wegner 1986] S.B. Zdonik and P. Wegner, "Language and Methodology for Object-Oriented Database Environments," *IEEE Proceedings of the 19th Annual Hawaii International Conference on System Sciences*, 1986.

# 17

## Optimizing Smalltalk Message Performance

Fred Mellender, Steve Riegel, Andrew Straw

## INTRODUCTION

The main goal of the Alltalk project is to provide transparent database support to the Smalltalk programmer. We have provided permanence to Smalltalk objects without adding any new language syntax, classes, or methods to the "standard" image. An additional goal is to understand the architecture required for efficient implementation of image and document processing applications.

Our system is written entirely in C and runs under UNIX on Sun workstations.

Various techniques for optimizing Smalltalk are available, but some reduce the portability of the implementation. Unlike the system in [Deutsch and Schiffman 1984], we do not create machine code at runtime, and we do not hand-tune the assembly code output of the C compiler as in [Miranda 1987]. These self-imposed restrictions achieve portability but have required us to search for new techniques for optimization. In this chapter, we offer three ideas that, to our knowledge, have not been mentioned elsewhere.

The organization of this chapter is as follows: Section 17.1 contains an overview of Alltalk and an introduction to Smalltalk message passing and terminology. An example that is used in the rest of the chapter is presented. Section 17.2 reviews some known techniques for optimizing Smalltalk message execution. Section 17.2.1 presents our design for five new instructions for integer arithmetic. Section 17.2.2 describes a method for dynamic replacement of message-sends with code that can be executed in the context of the invoking method. We call this technique *message flattening*. Section 17.2.3 quantifies the performance improvement of these techniques. Section 17.3 introduces Smalltalk storage management by discussing a garbage collection technique called *generation scavenging*, which is used in some high-performance Smalltalk implementations. The Alltalk garbage collector and buffer management system are discussed in Sections 17.3.1 and 17.3.2 respectively. Section 17.4 presents our plans for future work.

## 17.1 Overview of the Alltalk implementation and Smalltalk terminology

The Alltalk system has the following major components (see Fig. 17.1).

1. A *compiler* processes Smalltalk source code and builds the object code and other objects that are required by the interpreter. All objects are placed in the database.

2. The Alltalk runtime system is separate from the compiler, and consists of the following subcomponents.

   A. *Interpreter.* This subsystem executes the object code generated by the compiler. The interpreter calls many of the other components in our system.

   B. *Method fetcher.* The interpreter calls the method fetcher to obtain the object code of the Smalltalk method that is required to process a message-send.

   C. *Object manager.* This subsystem accepts calls from the interpreter and the method fetcher to fetch and create objects. It returns a memory pointer to the object.

   D. *Buffer manager.* This subsystem is called upon by the object manager when space is needed for a new object, or when an existing object must be accessed. It returns a pointer to the spot in memory that is to be used for the object.

   E. *Collector.* This is the Alltalk garbage collector, which is invoked periodically by the interpreter in order to delete unreachable objects.

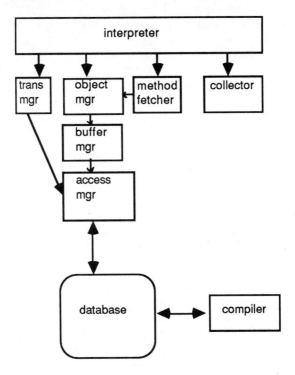

**FIGURE 17.1** ALLTALK ARCHITECTURE

The other subsystems are not discussed in this chapter, but are briefly described here for completeness. The *access manager* is called by the buffer manager to fetch an object from the database and place it into a buffer. It is also called by the *transaction manager* at commit time to flush the appropriate data from the buffers to the database. In addition to a "commit" call, the transaction manager can accept an "abort" call, which invalidates any data in the buffers that has been updated by the transaction.

Smalltalk is an object-oriented programming language (described fully in [Goldberg and Robson 1983]). We illustrate Smalltalk message passing logic with an example, defining terminology as we go. Figure 17.2 contains the Smalltalk source code for a (contrived) book processing application, and Fig. 17.3 contains the corresponding pseudo-assembly code generated by the Alltalk compiler.

Beginning at line 34 of Fig. 17.2 we see the definition of the *class* Book, whose *superclass* is class Document. All *instances* of class Book will contain *instance variables* "editor" and "listOfChapters," as well as any instance variables that are inherited from the superclass (Document) of Book. The content of an instance variable is always the identifier of an object. These identifiers are called *oops* in Smalltalk (for "object oriented pointers"). In Alltalk, oops

```
1
2          Class Chapter :Document
3          | authors numberOfAuthors |
4          [
5
6          !Chapter methodsFor: 'accessing'
7
8          |
9          authors
10               ↑ authors
11
12         !Chapter methodsFor: 'updating'
13
14         |
15         addAuthor: anAuthor
16
17              numberOfAuthors <− numberOfAuthors + 1.
18              authors at: numberOfAuthors put: anAuthor.
19
20         ]
21
22         Class AuthorArray :Array
23         [
24
25         !AuthorArray methodsFor: 'updating'
26
27         |
28         at: anIndex   put: anAuthor
29              ↑ <primitive 100 self anIndex anAuthor>
30         ]
31
32
33
34         Class Book :Document
35         | editor listOfChapter |
36         [
37
38         !Book methodsFor: 'updating'
39
40         |
41         addAuthor: anAuthor   to: aChapterTitle
42
43              | aChapter |
44              aChapter <− listOfChapters
45                   findTitle: aChapterTitle.
46              aChapter addAuthor: anAuthor.
47              aChapter authors print.
48         ]
```

**FIGURE 17.2** SMALLTALK SOURCE CODE FOR A BOOK APPLICATION

```
.class Chapter Document

.imethod authors
.mattr 6

.line 10
      mov   tl,i6[authors]
.line 12
      mret tl

.mend 2 0

.imethod addAuthor:

.line 17
      mov   t3,i7[numberOfAuthors]
      mov   t4,1
      saddl t3,0,t2,2,#+
      mov   i7[numberOfAuthors],t2
.line 18
      mov   t3,i6[authors]
      mov   t4,i7[numberOfAuthors]
      mov   t5,tl[anAuthor]
      send  t3,0,t2,3,#at:put:
.line20
      mret t0[self]

.mend 6 0

.class AuthorArray Array

.imethod at:put:
.mprim 100

.line 29
      prim t3,100,t0[self],3
.line 30
      mret t3

.mend 4 0

.class Book Document
.supervar 6
.ivar editor listOfChapters

.imethod addAuthor:to:
.mparam anAuthor aChapterTitle
.mtemp aChapter

.line 44
      mov t4,i7[listOfChapters]
.line 45
      mov t5,t2[aChapterTitle]
      send t4,0,t3[aChapter],2,#findTitle:
```

**FIGURE 17.3** ALLTALK ASSEMBLY CODE FOR BOOK APPLICATION

```
.line 46
     mov t5,t3[aChapter]
     mov t6,tl[anAuthor]
     send t5,0,t4,2,#addAuthor:
.line 47
     send t3[aChapter],0,t5,1,#authors
     send t5,0,t4,1,#print
.line 48
     mret t0[self]

.mend 7 0
```

**FIGURE 17.3** (CONTINUED)

are signed 32-bit integers. Negative oops are used to represent positive integers. Thus an oop of −15 represents the positive integer 15. Since positive integers are very common in most programs, this encoding technique (used in all Smalltalk implementations that we know of) saves space (no objects are set up for positive integers) as well as time (there is no overhead to "fetch" a positive integer object). All other oops must be "dereferenced" to find the object and its associated data store (i.e., its instance variables). This dereferencing in Alltalk is an access to the *object manager*, which can create new objects and fetch existing objects from the database.

Beginning at line 40 of Fig. 17.2 we can see the definition of the *method* for adding an author to a chapter of a book, given the chapter title. The *selector* of this method is "addAuthor:to:". We also see that this method has one *method temporary* used to hold intermediate results, "aChapter." There are two parameters to this method, named "anAuthor" and "aChapterTitle."

The Alltalk compiler generates instructions, each of which consists of an *operation code* followed by some parameters, the number and value of which depend on the operation code. In traditional Smalltalk implementations, the operation code is called a *bytecode* because it is only one byte long. These bytecodes and their semantics are defined in [Goldberg and Robson 1983]. In the Alltalk system, however, the operation codes are two-byte integers and do not correspond to those in "by-the-book" implementations.

Most methods are written entirely in Smalltalk, employing message-sends, assignment statements, and return statements. Some methods also employ calls to *primitives*. These primitive calls invoke C language procedures and are used to do the most basic operations in the system, such as arithmetic and array update, as well as to provide access to the underlying hardware (e.g., cursor position and mouse signals). We see in Fig. 17.2, line 28 that the method with selector "at:put:" just invokes primitive 100, with parameters "self" (i.e., the oop of the receiver of the current message, which in this case is an array of authors), and (the oops of) an index and a new array element (anAuthor). Primitive 100 will actually update the array object ("self") at the index specified by "anIndex," with the parameter specified by "anAuthor." In standard Smalltalk, primitives do not return to the calling method unless they "fail," but instead return to the method that invoked the one that called the primitive. "Failure" of a primitive causes control to return to the method that invoked the primitive. Smalltalk code following the primitive invocation is thus executed to handle the "failure." Alltalk has defined primitive invocation and error processing in a nonstandard way, as will be explained later.

Let us now follow how a message-send is processed in Alltalk, using the method defined in Fig. 17.2 at line 40, and referring to the assembly code in Fig. 17.3. We focus our attention on the processing required to execute the message-send in line 46 ("addAuthor:").

In the first place, the compiler assures that the receiver and any parameters to the message-send are lined up in a contiguous set of temporaries (temporaries are explained below). This is the purpose of the two *mov* instructions ahead of the *send* instruction for line 46, in Fig. 17.3: the receiver of the message is placed in temporary 5 and the parameter in temporary 6. The actual *send* instruction is processed as follows (see Fig. 17.4):

1. Establish a *context* to process the message-send (addAuthor) and link it back to the current context (for addAuthor:to:). The new context will contain space to hold any method temporaries (in our example, method "addAuthor:" has none), as well as other *compiler temporaries* used to hold (the oops of) the receiver of the message (aChapter), the parameters to the message-send ("anAuthor"), as well as any space needed for intermediate values generated by the compiler (in our example, four additional temporaries, t2 through t5, are required). The context uses an array to hold all of these context temporaries. In assembly instructions, temporaries are referred to via an index into this array. For example, the first *mov* instruction generated for line 17 (in Fig. 17.3) says to move the contents of instance variable 7 into temporary 3.

2. Copy the receiver and the parameters of the message-send into the new context's temporaries, beginning at temporary 0. The number of temporaries to copy is indicated by the fourth parameter in the *send* instruction (2 in our example). The index of the first temporary to copy from the calling context (which the compiler has assured has been set to the receiver of the new message) is indicated by the first parameter in the *send* instruction. This is temporary 5 in our example. Thus the reader will see that the oop of the receiver of the current message can always be found in temporary 0 of the current context, and the $n$ parameters to the message follow in temporaries 1 through $n$.

3. Ask the object manager to fetch the receiver (aChapter, in our example). The object manager returns a memory pointer to the object, and this pointer

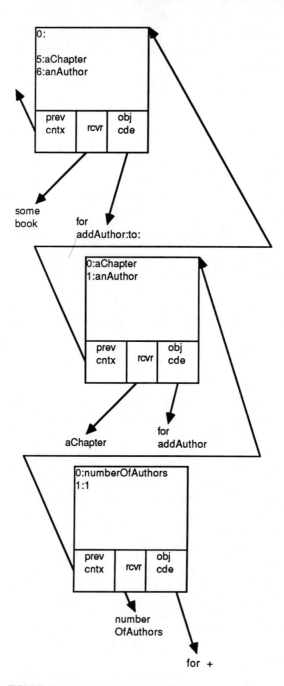

**FIGURE 17.4** CONTEXT MANAGEMENT

is cached in the new context. The interpreter uses this pointer to address the instance variables of the receiver. These are referred to in the assembly code with an index. Hence we see, in the assembly code for line 17 (Fig. 17.3), the instruction to move instance variable 7 of the receiver into temporary 3 of the context.[1]

4. Ask the method fetcher to fetch the object code (which is also an object in the database) that is required to process the send-message. The selector (i.e., the oop of the symbol whose value is "addAuthor:") and the class of the receiver are passed as parameters to the method fetcher. The method fetcher goes to the class of the receiver to find the *class dictionary* that contains a cross-reference between (oops of) selectors of methods defined in the class, and the corresponding (oop of the) object code. If the selector is not found here, the superclass of the class is searched, and so forth. The method fetcher calls the object manager to retrieve the object code, and then returns a memory pointer to this object. This pointer is cached in the new context by the interpreter.

5. The interpreter's *current instruction pointer* is set to point to the first instruction in the newly fetched object code, and the instructions for the method that processes the method-send are then interpreted and executed one at a time. Some of these instructions will very likely be message-sends, and the process will be repeated.

The method "addAuthor:" consists of two message-sends. The assembly code in Fig. 17.3 is tagged with line numbers 17 and 18 for easy reference back to the source code. The method terminates with a return statement (operation code of *mret*) at line 20 in Fig. 17.3. By default, methods return "self" (i.e., the receiver of the current message) if no other indication is given by the programmer. The messages "addAuthor" and "+" and the contexts that are required to process them are diagramed in Fig. 17.4. Note that the instruction to process the message-send for the "+" selector has a special operation code generated by the compiler, *sadd1*. This will be discussed later.

When a return instruction is encountered, the interpreter reacts by placing the oop of the object that is to be returned into the appropriate temporary in the calling context. The index of the temporary in which to place it is indicated as the third parameter in the original *send* instruction (for line 46, this indicates that the answer from "addAuthor:" should be placed in temporary 4). Upon return, the current instruction pointer is set to the instruction in the calling context that follows the message-send just processed.

---

[1] The reader may be puzzled as to why "numberOfAuthors" is instance variable 7. The reason is that 6 instance variables are inherited from Chapter's superclass, Document. Also, the first instance variable is indexed with 0.

## 17.2 TECHNIQUES FOR OPTIMIZING SMALLTALK MESSAGE EXECUTION

An examination of the performance of a typical Smalltalk system reveals that much CPU time is spent in processing message-sends. For each message-send, the system must set up a new context, fetch the class of the receiver, fetch the object code of the method to be executed, then interpret and execute the method's object code. When the method terminates, space for the context can often be released to the system for reuse later. Various techniques exist to optimize parts of this message-sending logic, and we now review some of these.

The first technique is to put contexts on a stack and bypass the normal Smalltalk storage allocation/garbage collection logic. This approach is complicated by the fact that contexts are considered objects in Smalltalk, and can be assigned to instance variables, passed as parameters, and so forth. A stack-based system must detect when a context needs to be "objectified" (e.g., when it is assigned to an instance variable or returned from a method) and make it into a "real" object. An additional complication (in Alltalk) is that the data cached in the context via memory pointers (i.e., the receiver and the object code pointers) must be replaced with "oops," since the context object can be written to the database and the memory pointers would then have no meaning. This "dual representation" of contexts increases the complexity of the logic in the interpreter. Nevertheless, the vast majority of context allocation/deallocation does behave like a stack ([Deutsch and Schiffman 1983] concludes that more than 85% of the contexts can be treated as stack entries). Alltalk uses a stack technique similar to that in [Moss 1987].

Another technique to speed up message-sends is to reduce the look-up logic required for finding the oop of the object code that corresponds to a selector. One way is simply to cache the results of the look-ups in a table. Entry into the table is the combination of the class of the receiver and the selector. In this slot in the table we place the oop of the object code for the required method. The table can be accessed with a hash function and the object code oop thus retrieved without going through the superclass chain. Such a method cache is described in [Ballard and Shirron 1983].

A greater improvement in finding the object code oop is described in [Deutsch and Schiffman 1984]. Here, each occurrence of the send-message instruction (in the object code of methods) has a cache that serves the same function as a table entry in the preceding technique. When the message-send is first interpreted, normal look-up in the class (and possibly superclass) dictionaries is executed. The *send* instruction cache is then modified to contain the class of the (current) receiver as well as the results of the selector look-up (i.e., the oop of the object code). The next time the same *send* instruction is interpreted, the class of the (new) receiver is compared to that cached in the *send* instruction being executed. If they are the same, the object code oop can be obtained from the cache in this *send* instruction. Deutsch and Schiffman measured that this cache is effective 95% of the time, indicating that a subsequent execution of a specific instance of a message-send in a method is very likely to have a receiver whose class is the same as for its previous execution.

## 17.2.1 Integer Arithmetic Instructions

The Alltalk implementation improves on the Deutsch/Schiffman instruction cache by avoiding some message-sends altogether. To determine the best candidates for elimination, we measured the frequency of message-sends in a "typical" application (described later). We discovered that the majority were invoking methods that did nothing more than execute a primitive and then return. Of these, most messages were sent to do integer arithmetic, mainly additions and subtractions. Of these, "plus 1" and "minus 1" occurred frequently. Another common message is one that does nothing more than return the value of an instance variable of the receiver. Thus it seemed that eliminating these kinds of message-sends would be a "big win" (statistics presented later confirm this). We now describe how this is accomplished in the Alltalk system.

As mentioned earlier, Alltalk has a different instruction set than that of traditional Smalltalk. Among the new instructions are those for the following integer options: "=", "+", "−", "+1", and "−1". The compiler will generate special instructions for each of these upon encountering a message-send with the indicated selector. For example, for the message-send of line 17 of Fig. 17.2, we see that the operation of *sadd1* was generated (in Fig. 17.3), indicating that a constant 1 is to be added to the receiver. The format for each of these new integer arithmetic instructions is the same as that of the *send* instruction, except that the operation code is different for each.

The interpreter handles the integer arithmetic operation codes thus:

1. Determine whether the receiver is a positive integer (i.e., has a negative oop). Recall that as in the *send* instruction, the index of the temporary that contains the receiver is found in the first parameter to the instruction (this is temporary 3 in our example of Fig. 17.2, line 17, *sadd1* operation code). If the receiver is not a positive integer, we cannot determine its class without fetching it via a call to the object manager, so we will process the instruction as a normal *send* operation. Since the instruction format is the same as for a *send* except for the operation code value, all we need do is branch to the *send* instruction handler in the interpreter.

2. The operations "+1" and "−1" have no variable parameters in the instruction: the "1" is implied by the operation code itself. The others ("=", "+", "−") require that the parameter be examined by the interpreter at execution time. The location of the parameter (as in the *send* instruction) can be found in the next contiguous temporary after the receiver (in the example of Fig. 17.3, line 17, this is temporary 4). Since our example is *sadd1*, the

"+1" operation, this parameter need not be checked: the compiler has determined it. If the parameter needs to be checked, the interpreter performs the audit (oop of parameter must be negative). If it fails, we again default to normal *send* instruction processing.

3. If the receiver and parameter pass the positive integer test, the interpreter executes the action implied by the operation code "in- line," without setting up any context and without fetching any method. This can be done because all the needed information is contained in the instruction. In our example of line 17, the interpreter would put the oop of the result of adding 1 to the receiver into temporary 2.

Use of these integer arithmetic instructions avoids creation of contexts to process the addition, subtraction, and test-equal messages sent to Integers. The disadvantage of this technique is that it removes the ability of the programmer to redefine the selectors '+', '−' and '=' for class Integer. (These are now considered reserved words for class Integer.) They can be redefined in any other class, however.

## 17.2.2 Message Flattening

Message flattening is another, more general, technique to allow invoked methods to be executed in the context of the calling method. Like integer arithmetic instructions, it saves the overhead for creating a new context and reclaiming it when control returns to the calling context. Message flattening can be regarded as an extension to the instruction cache described earlier [Deutsch and Schiffman 1984]. The basic idea is to cache enough information about the called method in the *send* instruction itself, and then to execute the appropriate logic in the context of the calling method.

We first discuss message flattening for "primitive only" methods. We define a "primitive only" method as one that has the following characteristics:

1. The only statement in the method is the return of the results of a primitive call.

2. The first parameter to the primitive must be "self".

3. The subsequent parameters to the primitive must be identical in number and order to those passed to the method itself.

An example of a "primitive only" method can be found in Fig. 17.2 at line 28. Let us examine the assembly code that is generated for such a "primitive only" method (Fig. 17.3, for line 29). As in the send-message code generation, the compiler will place the parameters to the primitive in a contiguous set of temporaries. Since the first parameter is self, and since the other parameters are in the same order as those in the method parameter list, the compiler knows that the runtime send-message logic will have copied the receiver and the $n$ parameters to temporaries 0 through $n$ in the (now) "current" context (recall the send-message logic described earlier). Thus the compiler recognizes that the parameters are already "lined up" and does not need to generate any *mov* instructions ahead of the primitive invocation. Next, the compiler generates the execute primitive instruction, *prim*. Note that in the Alltalk system, *the actual operation code of the instruction to execute a primitive is the primitive number itself* (100 in our example), although the assembly instruction uses *prim* to indicate all primitive operations, and shows the primitive number as a parameter. The other parameters in the assembly instruction for primitive execution are:

1. the index of the temporary in which to place the answer (temporary 3 in our example)

2. the index of the temporary that contains the first parameter (temporary 0 in our "primitive only" case, since the first parameter is "self")

3. the total number of parameters (3 in our example)

The last assembly instruction generated for the method is *mret*, which returns the answer from the primitive to the calling method.

Now look at the *send* instruction generated as a result of a message-send to a "primitive only" method (line 18 in Fig. 17.2 and Fig. 17.3). This *send* instruction contains all of the information required to invoke the primitive directly (without processing the message-send), except for the primitive number itself. We have the parameters to the primitive "lined up," starting in temporary 3, the number of parameters to the primitive is the same as that to the message-send (the fourth parameter to the *send* instruction: 3, in our example), and we know where to put the answer (the same place we would put the answer to the message-send itself, temporary 2).

Now we are ready to discuss how the "primitive only" methods are flattened at runtime. The actual format of the *send* instruction in the object code, as a C language structure, is similar to that in Fig. 17.5. The C language structure for the *execute primitive* operation is similar to Fig. 17.6.

The likely_class field is the same as the Deutsch/Schiffman cache: we put the class of the last receiver here. For methods that are not flattened, the likely_meth_or_islot is the same as the Deutsch/Schiffman object code oop cache: it contains the oop of the object code. When the method is fetched, if it is a "primitive only" method, we put the primitive number in the likely_prim_or_bcode, and mark the likely_meth_or_islot cache as invalid. (The compiler tags the object code of "primitive only" methods so that it is easy to identify them at runtime, and to find the primitive number). When the *send* instruction is executed, if the class of the receiver of the instruction is the same as that in the cache likely_class, and if likely_prim_or_bcode is a valid primitive number, we set the current operation pointer to the field

```
struct send_message
{
        short bytecode; /*0x'100'*/
        long  selector;     /*entry into class's selector dictionary*/
        long  likely_class;  /*class of last receiver of this bytecode*/

        long  likely_meth_or_islot;
        short likely_prim_or_bcode;
        unsigned short    num_args;

        unsigned short    arg_start_slot;/*temp slot where args start. 'Self'
                                (i.e. the receiver) is always in this
                                spot, followed by the other parms*/

        unsigned short    put_answ_slot; /*where to put obj returned by this msg.*/
};
```

**FIGURE 17.5** OBJECT CODE FORMAT OF THE *SEND* INSTRUCTION

likely_prim_or_bcode. This will cause the interpreter to decode this field as if
it were an operation code (recall that the operation code to execute primitive
"xxx" is "xxx"). Since the remaining fields in the *send* operation structure
have exactly the same meaning and position as those in the *prim* operation
structure (following the operation code), we cause the primitive to be invoked
with the correct parameters and the answer placed in the correct temporary.

It will be observed later that "primitive only" methods lie at the heart of
the system and do much of the work in any application. In order to increase
the applicability of method flattening, Alltalk follows the syntax of Little
Smalltalk [Budd 1987] for primitives. A primitive expression can be used
wherever objects are permitted, and they never "fail" in the sense of traditional
Smalltalk. (To "fail" a primitive, we return a distinguished object from the
primitive, like "nil," and test this in Smalltalk code following the primitive.)
We have written most of our heavily used primitives so that error conditions
are handled in the primitive itself, rather than in Smalltalk code. Thus the
example at line 29 in Fig. 17.2 will do all error detection in the C language

**FIGURE 17.6** OBJECT CODE FORMAT OF THE *PRIM* INSTRUCTION

```
    struct execute_primitive
    {
            short bytecode; /*value is the primitive number itself*/
            unsigned short   num_args;
            unsigned short   arg_start_slot;
            unsigned short   put_answ_slot; /*temp in which to place
                                        obj returned by primitive*/
    };
```

routine that implements primitive 100. If we had put the error detection in Smalltalk code, following the primitive invocation, we would no longer have a "primitive only" method, and we could not flatten the message-send at runtime. We have been careful to code only the most heavily used, basic methods as "primitive only." Table 17.1 contains a partial list.

Note that when integer arithmetic instructions fail the test of whether the receiver and parameter are positive integers, they will likely result in a "primitive only" method execution, since the selectors for Float as well as those for Integer are listed in Table 17.1. It should also be noted that we have in no way "hard-coded" the meaning of any of the selectors. Any of the methods can be rewritten, in Smalltalk, at any time. The only effect is that the compiler will no longer tag them as "primitive only," and they will be executed normally.

The other kind of message-send that is flattened is less ubiquitous than "primitive only" but is still fairly common. This is the "return instance variable" method, an example of which is in Fig. 17.2 and Fig. 17.3 at line 8. Here we are merely returning (the value of) an instance variable of the receiver (in our example, "authors", the sixth instance variable in the object). Note that such a method requires no additional storage for temporaries and can be easily executed in the calling context. Again, the compiler marks the object code as a "return instance variable" method, and tags it with the index of the instance variable to be returned. Processing of the *send* instruction is similar to that described earlier. This time, we place the index of the instance variable of the receiver in the likely_meth_or_islot of the *send* operation structure, and put an indicator in likely_prim_or_bcode to indicate that this is a "return

**TABLE 17.1** "PRIMITIVE ONLY" METHODS

| | |
|---|---|
| Array | size |
| Behavior | basicNew, basicNew:, new, new: |
| BitBlt | copyBits, drawLoopX:Y: |
| ByteArray | size, at:, at:put:, replaceFrom:to:with:, new: |
| Character | $<, =, >$, value |
| Cursor | beCursor, cursorLink: |
| Float | $*, +, -, /, <, <=, =, >, >=, \mathtt{\sim}=$ |
| Integer | $*, +, -, /, <, <=, =, >, >=, \mathtt{\sim}=$ |
| Object | at:, at:put:, basicAt:, basicAt:put:, =, == |
| String | =, at:, at:put: |
| WordArray | size, at:, at:put: |

instance variable" method. If the cached likely_class matches the class of the receiver, and if the method is a "return instance variable" kind, the interpreter branches to a routine that:

1. asks the object manager to fetch the receiver of the (to be flattened) message-send, and

2. places the correct instance variable value (as indicated in likely_meth_or_islot) in the correct temporary (as indicated in put_answ_slot, the same place that the answer to the now flattened message would have been placed).

It can be seen that by flattening "primitive only" and "return instance variable" methods, and by converting some message-sends to integer arithmetic instructions at compile time, we save the construction and destruction of a new context, the overhead of parameter copying (to the new context), and the processing of the *mret* (method return) instruction that would be interpreted in the called method. We also save a call to the object manager to fetch the object code of the method. In our example of Fig. 17.2, line 40, we see that the message-send at line 46 would invoke the addAuthor method at line 14 with a normal send-message. AddAuthor, however, executes its entire method without message-sends, since the message-send at line 17 is replaced with an integer arithmetic operation (*saddl*), and that at line 18 is "primitive only." The first message-send at line 47 (which returns the authors of aChapter) is also flattened since it is a "return instance variable" method.

## 17.2.3 Performance Results of Message Flattening and Integer Arithmetic Instructions

To quantify the performance improvements, we have written an application typical of those we are targeting for the Alltalk system. This application reads a document from a Unix file, converts it to the Office Document Architecture (ODA) standard for document interchange [Horak 1985], and loads it in the database. The application then formats it (justifies and breaks lines and pages) and places the formatted object in the database along with links to the unformatted object. Then the document is displayed on the screen. The document contains text, vector graphics, and a bitmap picture.

Table 17.2 presents the total cpu time, counts of (non-flattened) message-sends, counts for the flattened messages of type "return instance variable" and "primitive only," and counts of the integer arithmetic instructions executed for three experiments: 1) no optimizations, 2) message flattening only, and 3) message flattening plus integer arithmetic instructions. The application was run on a Sun 3/160, with 8 megabytes of memory.

The arithmetic instruction counts in experiment 3 are broken down in Table 17.3. Some of these (35,226) failed the positive integer test and were re-executed as flattened primitives.

**TABLE 17.2** PERFORMANCE OF NEW BYTECODES AND
MESSAGE FLATTENING

|           | exp1      | exp2     | exp3    |
|-----------|-----------|----------|---------|
| cpu time  | 110 sec   | 70 sec   | 64 sec  |
| msg sends | 499,158   | 87,913   | 87,913  |
| flat-inst | 0         | 20,910   | 20,910  |
| flat-prim | 0         | 390,335  | 255,567 |
| int-arith | 0         | 0        | 134,768 |

In summary, about 82% of the total messages were flattened or transformed to integer arithmetic instructions, saving about 42% of the CPU time.

## 17.3 STORAGE MANAGEMENT IN SMALLTALK

One of the strengths of Smalltalk is automatic garbage collection. This relieves the programmer of having to explicitly delete objects that are no longer "reachable" (i.e., no longer referenced directly or indirectly through the instance variables of some reachable object; in Smalltalk, the root of all reachable objects is the Smalltalk dictionary). Since many objects are created to hold temporary results and other transient data, automatic garbage collection is a system necessity as well as an application convenience.

The precise method for garbage collection is not specified in the formal Smalltalk definition, and various schemes have been tried. (A good survey of garbage collectors appears in [Cohen 1981]; papers in [Krasner 1983] discuss the impact of garbage collection on Smalltalk performance.) The system that appears to have the best performance is "generation scavenging" [Ungar 1987], which we now review.

Generation scavenging uses four areas of memory, called OldSpace, NewSpace, OldSurvivorSpace, and NewSurvivorSpace, to hold objects.

**TABLE 17.3** BREAKDOWN OF ARITHMETIC BYTECODES

|     |        |
|-----|--------|
| +   | 14,504 |
| −   | 10,821 |
| +1  | 97,335 |
| =   | 41,703 |
| −1  | 5,631  |

OldSpace objects are considered permanent—they are never examined by the collector for deletion. Also, OldSpace objects never move out of OldSpace. New objects are allocated in NewSpace when they are created. OldSurvivorSpace contains objects that have survived the previous round of "scavenging," defined later. NewSurvivorSpace is used to hold reachable objects during the scavenging process, as they are moved out of OldSurvivorSpace and NewSpace.

Whenever a reference is made from an OldSpace object to one in either NewSpace or OldSurvivorSpace, the oop of the OldSpace object is placed in a list, the "rememberedSet." Such references occur whenever the oop of a "young" object (one in either NewSpace or OldSurvivorSpace) is placed into the instance variable of an object in OldSpace.

Scavenging consists of looking at the following objects.

1. Those referenced by the "virtual machine registers." For Alltalk, these would be objects whose oops are in context temporaries and those pointed to by the contexts' object code pointers and receiver pointers.

2. Those referenced by instance variables of objects in the rememberedSet.

Any such object that is in either NewSpace or OldSurvivorSpace is moved to NewSurvivorSpace. If an object in the rememberedSet no longer references any "young" object, its oop is now removed from the rememberedSet.

After all of these objects have been examined, the "transitive closure" of all objects in NewSurvivorSpace is examined. The "transitive closure" of an object $O$ is the set of all objects that are referenced directly or indirectly by $O$'s instance variables. Any object in this set that is still in NewSpace or OldSurvivorSpace is also moved into NewSurvivorSpace. When all of the objects have been "scavenged," the following statements hold:

1. No object left in NewSpace can be reached from any object outside of NewSpace.

2. No object left in OldSurvivorSpace can be reached by an object in OldSpace or in NewSurvivorSpace (all such objects were moved into NewSurvivorSpace).

Thus at this point, we can completely empty all of the area in NewSpace and in OldSurvivorSpace, and we can "flip" OldSurvivorSpace and NewSurvivorSpace (i.e., we begin to use OldSurvivorSpace as the NewSurvivorSpace, with the previous NewSurvivorSpace now having the role of an OldSurvivorSpace).

Figure 17.7 presents an example of generation scavenging. The rememberedSet indicates that only the old objects 23, 25, and 27 can (potentially) contain references to objects that are not in OldSpace. Object 23 is examined, and it is determined that it has an instance variable that points to an object

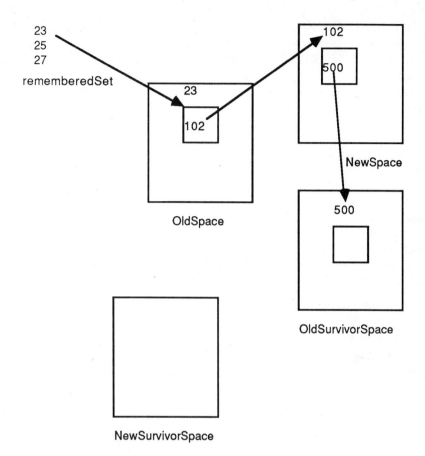

**FIGURE 17.7** GENERATION SCAVENGING

in NewSpace (object 102). Object 102 is moved to NewSurvivorSpace. When NewSurvivorSpace is scanned it will be discovered that object 102 has an instance variable that points to an object in OldSurvivorSpace (object 500), so object 500 is also moved to NewSurvivorSpace. In Fig. 17.7, the only objects reachable from OldSpace are precisely the ones we moved: 102 and 500.

The objects in OldSpace are collected by an off-line mark/sweep collector, after they have been moved to disk, when Smalltalk has been shut down.

Scavenging can introduce noticeable pauses in the operation of the Smalltalk system unless the number of reachable objects in the OldSurvivorSpace is kept small. This is insured by "tenuring" long-lived objects that persist in the OldSurvivorSpace. Tenuring consists of moving objects into OldSpace if they have survived a sufficient number of "flips." On the other hand, to move an object into OldSpace too soon is to waste space in OldSpace if this object becomes "dead" (no longer reachable). Since OldSpace storage is not reclaimed when the system is running, choosing when to tenure an object is a rather important decision. The problem can be alleviated by setting up (a fixed number of) "generations" of storage. An object moves from generation to generation as it "ages," ultimately moving to OldSpace if it survives long enough. Ungar gives a thorough analysis in [Ungar 1987].

### 17.3.1 The Alltalk Garbage Collector

The Alltalk collector has the following properties that differ from generation scavenging.

1. It never physically moves any object from one spot in memory to another. This feature simplifies our system, since we are not thereby required to update the cached real memory pointers in the contexts (for object code and receiver objects).

2. It is incremental in that a little bit of the work that needs to be done is executed upon each assignment statement into an instance variable and upon Smalltalk return statements, rather than all of the logic being executed at once.

3. It is coordinated with our interpreter and database buffer manager in order to:

   a. Determine when an object is no longer pinned by a real memory pointer. This permits timely reuse of the object's memory space.

   b. Ensure that no object is written to the database unless it is reachable from some object already in the database. This prevents us from writing "garbage" objects.

In the Alltalk system, each context is associated with a *region*. The identifier of a region is an integer, and when we start up Alltalk the first context will be assigned to region 0. Every object created by (the Smalltalk method associated with) a context is assigned to the region number of that context. Each object fetched from the database is assigned to the region associated with the context from which the fetch was made, unless the object is already assigned to a lower region number (i.e., it has been fetched by a context earlier in the calling chain). If a fetched object is already assigned to a higher region number than the fetching context, the object is reassigned to the (lower) region number of the fetching context.

Region numbers are attributes of an object, associated with the object while it is in memory. It has nothing to do with where the object is stored. Nevertheless, we say that the object is "in" the region. When we speak of "moving" an object to another region we mean that its region attribute is altered, not that we change its storage address. The region number has no meaning for an object that is in the database and that has not been fetched by some context.

When a sufficient number of objects occupy a region (we have set this limit to 100), we assure that the next context to be created will be associated with a region number whose identifier is one higher than the previous one. Thus we can assert the following statements:

1. Region numbers increase by one or stay the same for contexts as we traverse the calling chain.

2. The region number of a context never changes.

3. The region number associated with an object can be lowered (see below), but it is never raised. An object is assigned to only one region at a time.

In the following discussion we will speak again of the transitive closure of an object, $X$. For Alltalk, this is the set of all objects *that are in main memory*, and referred to directly or indirectly by $X$'s instance variables. The purpose of processing the transitive closure of a reachable object is to mark newly created objects (in order to prevent their deletion). Although in-memory, updated, database objects must be examined, it is never necessary for Alltalk to access the database in processing the transitive closure of an object. The reason is that the commit logic ensures that whenever an object is written to the database, so is that part of its in-memory transitive closure that is inconsistent with the current state of the database. Thus a database object that has not been updated since the last commit need not be examined since its transitive closure is guaranteed to be already in the database.

Whenever an assignment into one of an object's instance variables is made, the interpreter calls a routine to determine whether the object being updated has a region number that has a lower identifier than that of the new reference. If it has, the referenced object (i.e., the new value of the instance variable) is "moved to" the lower region. Then the transitive closure of the "moved" object is processed. An object in the closure is also moved to the lower region unless it is already associated with the region of the updated object, or with a lower region. This means that if $X < Y$, no object whose region identifier is $X$ can reference an object whose region identifier is $Y$. That is, *there are never any references from lower regions into higher ones.*

Similarly, when a method ends, the region number of the object being returned from the method is compared to that of the context being returned to. If the former is larger than the latter, the returned object (and its transitive closure) are all moved to the region of the returned-to context, as required. This means that *all objects referenced by a context belong to the region of the context, or to a region with a lower identifier.*

Thus, whenever Smalltalk returns from a context associated with (say) region 5 to one in region 2, all of the objects that were created in regions 5, 4, and 3 and that are still associated with region 5, 4, or 3 can now be safely discarded (if they were referenced by an object in a lower region, they would have been moved to some region lower than or equal to 2). It is also the case that any object that was fetched from the database and that is still in region 5, 4, or 3 no longer has a memory pointer to it from any context; any such context has since returned, and will no longer be using the pointer(s).

Upon every Smalltalk method return, the interpreter compares the region number that will be assigned to the next context to be created, to the region number of the context being return to. If the former is a least two larger than the latter, we call the collector to collect all regions whose identifiers are higher than that of the context being return to. Then the interpreter adjusts the identifier of the region that is to be associated with the next context created. This is set to be one larger than the identifier of the region of the context that is being returned to. Thus we reuse region numbers.

The collector is called with a region number. It assumes that the specified region, and all regions with a higher identifier, are to be collected. It scans all of the objects that belong to the requested regions (objects are chained together by their region number at the time they were fetched from the database, created, or "moved"). During the scan, each object is examined as follows:

1. If the object is already present in the database, and has been updated since the last transaction commit point, we cannot reuse its buffer space until the current transaction ends, since it must be restored to the database upon commit. Thus we "move" it to a region that has an identifier that is one lower than that of the lowest region being collected. Objects in the transitive closure of the object are also moved to this region, as required. Region 0 is never collected until the last context in a Smalltalk process terminates. When this happens, we force a transaction commit, which causes all regions to be "cleaned" (see below).

2. Any other object in the region can have its space marked (logically) "deleted" if it is not in the database, or "reusable" if it is in the database. Either marking has the effect of allowing our buffer manager to reuse the object's memory space as needed (see below).

An example of the collector's operation is given in Fig. 17.8. Contexts C1 and C2 executed in region 1. C1 created object 1.1 and C2 created object 2.1. C2 then called a method whose context was C3. Since region 1 had more than 50 objects in it at this time, a new region (region 2) was created for C3. Object 2.1 was passed as a parameter to C3, which invoked a method whose context is C4. C4 was set up in region 3. The receiver to C4 was object 2.1 (the parameter that was passed to C3). C4 made a new object (4.2) and assigned it into an instance variable of object 2.1. Since 2.1 is at a lower region than 4.2, we move 4.2 to 2.1's region, region 1. C4 made object 4.3 and 4.1, and returned 4.1 to context C3. The returned object 4.1 is moved to the region of the invoking context, region 2. C3 returns object 3.1 to context C2, and this

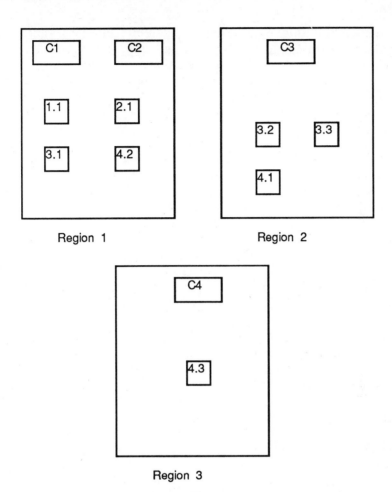

**FIGURE 17.8** ALLTALK GARBAGE COLLECTION

is also moved to region 1. Since the next context to be created would go in region 3, and since we have returned to region 1, we can call the collector to examine regions 2 and 3. All objects left in regions 2 and 3 (3.2, 3.3, 4.1, and 4.3) are discarded. The next context to be created will go in (the new, empty) region 2.

It is possible, but rare, for a region to accumulate many "garbage" objects before a context at a lower region is returned to. For example, method A can call method B, which creates a new object and returns it to method A. Method A can examine the object, find it wanting, and ask method B to try again. All of the objects created by method B are associated with the region of method A, and A is not returning to a context of a lower region number. To deal with this possibility, Alltalk looks at the number of objects in each region whenever any new object is created. If required, the collector is called to *clean* regions that have accumulated an "excessive" number of objects since the last "cleaning" (we have set the limit to 250).

The cleaner is a subsystem of the collector. It removes all unreachable objects from the region passed to it, and from all regions with a higher identifier. A standard mark/sweep on the union of these regions is employed. The following is the criteria for "marking" an object:

1. An object is marked if it is referenced by a context in the regions being cleaned. The reference could be through a context temporary, a receiver pointer, or an object code pointer.

2. An object in a region being cleaned is marked if it is a database object, in-memory, and has been updated since the last commit.

3. An object is marked if it is in the transitive closure of a marked object, and either is not already in the database or has been updated since the last commit. No object is marked (nor is its transitive closure examined for marking) unless it is in one of the regions being cleaned.

The "sweep" phase justs consists of processing the unmarked objects in the regions that were cleaned. Any such object that is not in the database has its space marked "deleted." Any object that is in the database has its space marked "reusable."

We complete the discussion of the Alltalk collector by mentioning the following details, without elaboration.

1. Objects can be shared across Smalltalk processes, which complicates our scheme somewhat. Region numbers are unique within a process, but the object can really be "in" different regions, one for each process that has accessed it. The collector assures that no object will be deleted until each process has invoked the collector for the region (within that process) that contains the object.

2. Commit logic guarantees that objects are never written to the database unless they are reachable by some object already in the database. At a later time, however, this reference can be deleted and the object can be made unreachable. We have an off-line mark/sweep to remove such "database garbage."

### 17.3.2 Alltalk Buffer Management

It remains to discuss how Alltalk is able to reuse space without actually moving objects around in memory. We use a simplification of the "buddy system" [Aho et al. 1983]. The use of "buddy systems" in Smalltalk storage management is discussed in [Decouchant 1986].

It is a function of our in-memory buffer manager to manage space for new objects as well as for those that are fetched from the database. All objects are placed into some "slot" in some "buffer." A "slot" is a fixed amount of space that contains room for some (in-memory only) control data and exactly one object. Since the slot is of fixed length, some space will be wasted if the object is smaller than the slot size. A "buffer" is simply a fixed number of slots that occupy contiguous storage. Most buffers have slots that are all of the same size.

We keep a total of seven buffers: small slot, medium slot, and large slot buffers for (the object code of) compiled methods, another set of three for non-method objects, and one "huge" buffer for oversize objects. Both methods and non-methods can go in "huge." Except for the "huge" buffer, all buffers have fixed-size slots. Memory for the buffers is preallocated, except for "huge," which is maintained using the UNIX storage allocation routines ("malloc" and "free"). The buffer layout is diagramed in Fig. 17.9. The purpose in having different buffer sets for method and non-method objects is to allow the system to be tuned for method management independently of the requirements for other database objects.

When a new object must be allocated, or an existing object must be fetched from the database, it is the responsibility of the buffer manager to do the following:

1. Select the appropriate buffer based on type of object (method or non-method) and the size of the object. We will choose the buffer with the smallest slot size whose slots are large enough to contain the object.

2. Find a slot in the selected buffer to hold the object. The selected slot will be one that the collector has marked either "deleted" or "reuseable." Recall that an object's slot is "reusable" if the object is in the database, but does not have any real memory pointer to it (from the contexts' object code pointers or receiver pointers), and also has not been updated since the last commit. The following algorithm, a modified LRU (Least Recently Used), is currently employed.

   a. Every time an object is fetched upon request by the interpreter, we increment a usage count in the control data in the slot that holds the object.

   b. The buffer manager sweeps the selected buffer, beginning from where it stopped on the previous sweep, and wrapping to the beginning when necessary. For each slot that is swept, the usage counter is decremented.

   c. Any slot that was marked "deleted" by the collector will be chosen for reuse. Any slot that is marked "reusable" will be reused, provided the usage count is 0 (after having been decremented by the logic in b.).

   d. If no such slot can be found, a second sweep is made, ignoring the usage counter.

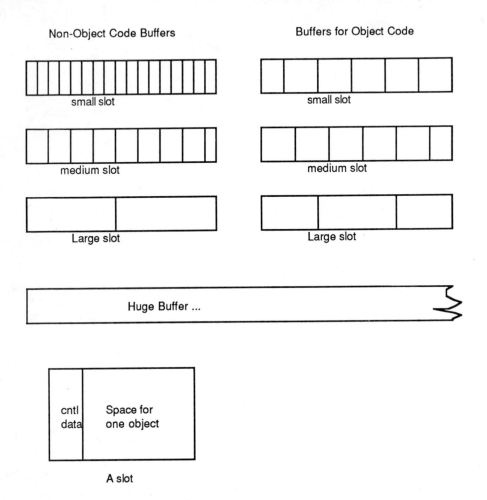

**FIGURE 17.9** ALLTALK BUFFER LAYOUT

The Alltalk buffer manager design differs from "buddy systems" in that the "slots" are never split or recombined. If we run out of space in any of our buffers, the system stops. It can be seen that the use of fixed slot-size buffers eliminates the need for storage compaction. This results in a somewhat faster and simpler garbage collection system. The penalty is some extra (preallocated) storage that is wasted when the object size does not exactly match the slot size. Tuning the slot size and space allocated for each type of buffer minimizes this. Note that in Alltalk only the "working set" is in memory; in traditional Smalltalk the entire image (i.e., all objects) must be loaded into virtual memory.

## 17.4 Future work

We continue to examine ideas for performance improvements, including a change of the hardware platform. We have just ported our system from Sun 3 to Sun 4, reinforcing our determination to maintain portability. We are currently working on a prototype for a potential Kodak product to determine the utility of Alltalk as a delivery platform.

Additionally, we plan to improve the Alltalk development environment, add shareability, recoverability, and distribution to the database, and build an integrated logic programming facility into Alltalk.

## Summary

We have presented three of the performance optimization techniques in the Alltalk system: integer arithmetic instructions, message flattening, and our storage management scheme. Message flattening, by eliminating much of the overhead for message processing, has been shown to be very effective. Our storage management scheme, including the garbage collector, has eliminated the need for storage compaction in order to reuse storage.

## References

[Aho et al. 1983] A.V. Aho, J.E. Hopcroft, and J.D. Ullman, *Data Structures and Algorithms,* Addison-Wesley, Reading, MA, 1983.

[Ballard and Shirron 1983] S. Ballard and S. Shirron, "The Design and Implementation of VAX/Smalltalk-80," in *Smalltalk-80: Bits of History, Words of Advice,* G. Krasner, ed., Addison-Wesley, Reading, MA, 1983.

[Budd 1987] T. Budd, *Little Smalltalk,* Addison-Wesley, Reading, MA, 1987.

[Cohen 1981] J. Cohen, "Garbage Collection of Linked Data Structures," *ACM Computing Surveys,* September 1981.

[Decouchant 1986] D. Decouchant, "Design of a Distributed Object Manager for the Smalltalk-80 System," *Proceedings of the First ACM Conference on Object-Oriented Programming Systems, Languages and Applications, SIGPLAN Notices,* September 1986.

[Deutsch and Schiffman 1984] L.P. Deutsch and A.M. Schiffman, "Efficient Implementation of the Smalltalk-80 System," *Proceedings of the 11th Annual ACM SIGACT-SIGPLAN Symposium on Principles of Programming Languages,* Salt Lake City, UT, January 1984.

[Goldberg and Robson 1983] A.J. Goldberg and D. Robson, *Smalltalk-80: the Language and Its Implementation*, Addison-Wesley, Reading, MA, 1983.

[Horak 1985] W. Horak, "Office Document Architecture and Office Document Interchange Formats: Current Status of International Standardization," *Computer*, pp. 50–60, October 1985.

[Krasner 1983] G. Krasner, ed., *Smalltalk-80: Bits of History, Words of Advice*, Addison-Wesley, Reading, MA, 1983.

[Miranda 1987] E. Miranda, "BrouHaHa—A Portable Smalltalk Interpreter," *Proceedings of the Second ACM Conference on Object-Oriented Programming Systems, Languages and Applications, SIGPLAN Notices*, October 1987.

[Moss 1987] J.E.B. Moss, "Managing Stack Frames in Smalltalk," *Proceedings of the ACM SIGPLAN Symposium on Interpreters and Interpretive Techniques*, St. Paul, MN, June 1987.

[Ungar 1987] D. Ungar, *The Design and Evaluation of a High Performance Smalltalk System*, MIT Press, Cambridge, MA, 1987.

# 18

## Version Control in an Object-Oriented Architecture

Anders Björnerstedt, Christer Hultén

## INTRODUCTION

Conventional database systems work in terms of a single evolving logical state. Transactions are used to alter the database from one consistent state to the next. As soon as a transaction commits, the previous state is discarded for all practical purposes. The *system* has no memory with respect to prior states of the database. If the history of updates to an object is to be captured, an application data structure must be introduced to record the evolving state of the object.

If one departs from this model and allows the database to retain several states besides the current one, then several interesting possibilities arise: possibilities for additional functionality that exploit the retained information; possibilities to solve old problems in new ways, such as the problem of maximizing concurrency.

The departure from the traditional model involves the incorporation of *time* in one form or other as part of the explicit semantics of the system. In object-oriented systems, it would be useful to have version control at the object level. Each object is defined by a set of versions, usually ordered by time. The generation of new versions of an object could be associated with any of a number of different semantics, the simplest of which is perhaps that any update to an object will generate a new version. The set of versions is then subject to interpretations, depending on how (or whether) the versions are timestamped, labeled, or otherwise distinguished. An *object version* represents an identifiable state of an object. Object versions are either totally ordered as a function of time, or partially ordered in terms of a successor function. Object versions may be used for three different purposes:

1. To capture the history of an object.

2. To cope with the problem of changing type definitions. If a type definition is changed in a conventional system, instances of that type, as well as the programs that depend on that type, must all conform to the new definition. In many cases, this requires massive data reorganization as well as program changes. The problem of reorganization becomes even more difficult if the system is decentralized.

3. To use object versions for concurrency control and for reliability.

We distinguish version management on two levels: application-level and system-level. The first use of version management, to capture history, is at the application level. The third use is at the system level. The second use has aspects of both, since the type design application involves the evolution of the system. The version control mechanisms will be described in the context of the AVANCE[1] system [Björnerstedt and Britts 1988]. AVANCE is an object management system, primarily aimed at applications in the field of Office Information Systems, which uses version control on both the system and application levels.

Section 18.1 discusses motivations for different applications for version control. In Section 18.2 a short overview of the AVANCE system is given. Section 18.3 discusses object versions at the application level. Section 18.4 discusses object versions as used by the system.

## 18.1 MOTIVATION FOR OBJECT VERSIONS

Motivation for object versions can be discussed from two perspectives. The first is application-level problems, occurring in *design* applications, applications that require historical data, and so on. The second is system-level problems, such as concurrency control and crash recovery. Application-level

---

[1] AVANCE was previously named OPAL [Ahlsén et al. 1984]. It is under development at the University of Stockholm and SISU (the Swedish Institute for Systems Development).

version control can often utilize the lower system-level version control. This is possible if the needs of the application are compatible with the constraints of the system on its utilization of versions. When this is not possible, one must build a higher level version model, which is independent of the lower level model. It should be noted that the system *can* provide special support for both application- and system-level version management. The difference between system-level and application-level version control lies in "whom" the mechanism is primarily intended to support, the system or the user. System version control and application version control usually correspond to different time semantics. These are called *transaction time* and *valid time* in [Snodgrass and Ahn 1985]. In system-level version control, the version history of an object reflects a sequence of modifications to an object as perceived by the system. This history is by definition correct and does not need to correspond to the changes made to some "real" object outside of the system. It does not make sense to allow an external user to edit the *system version* sequence.[2] Furthermore, what is regarded as an "object" is determined by what is appropriate for the system.

On the other hand, in application-level version control, the aim is to support the representation of time- or sequence-dependent information as defined by the user or application. The user may be allowed to edit the version sequence (or graph) and even to modify an old version; that is, in general, versions need not be immutable.

## 18.1.1 Application-Level Version Control

**Object Versions**   The need for object versions arises in many application areas to keep track of the history of objects. This history tracking has traditionally been solved by the application. The application has included and managed object attributes, such as timestamps or version numbers.

One area that requires versions is design applications, in particular VLSI CAD and software development [Katz et al. 1986; Klahold et al. 1986]. Another area is document management, where version graph structures are needed. This issue has been addressed in [Zdonik 1984; Zdonik 1985]. Here, a particular version may be derived by several designers in parallel and parallel versions may coexist, possibly to be merged eventually into a single version. Document creation and management in an office information system may be seen as a form of design activity, and any activity that incorporates the design of objects in one form or another tends to need version control.

All mechanisms for version control at the application level presented in this chapter consider versions to be immutable after some specific operation (such as *freeze* in Section 18.3.1) has been applied. As a consequence of this

---

[2] Certain editing operations by the user, such as deleting a certain version, may be allowed when they do not conflict with the requirements of the system.

we are restricting ourselves to having *valid time* correlated with *transaction time*. Application-level version control still differs from system-level version control in that what is regarded as an "object" is determined by the application, and in that control over when a version becomes immutable resides with the application. This restriction is possible because we consider version support only for design applications. Design applications are characterized by the application objects being artifacts (such as a report or a drawing) undergoing a development process, *in* the system, and controlled by users. Version control may then be used to track the design process.

**Type Versions**   There is also a need for objects of the same conceptual type, but with different implementations or even different specifications, to coexist. As an example, consider an invoice form that has a number of instances. If a change is made to the invoice routine, which requires some changes to the data associated with the invoice form, it would be desirable to be able to keep the old instances and at the same time create new instances according to the new invoice definition. Furthermore, if one could introduce transformation functions (or filters [Zdonik 1985]) between the old and new versions of the invoice definition, it would be possible, in a number of cases, to process old invoice instances using the new version of the invoice definition, and vice versa. Of course, this holds only in the cases where it is logically possible to define such filters.

There are basically three different ways of coping with type changes in a system with persistent objects.

1. Conversion. When a type is changed, all instances of that type are changed in order to conform with the new type definition. This allows the old type definition to be dropped, and hence there is really no need for type version control. The conversion is typically done as an atomic operation, and all instances of the type are unavailable for use by others for the duration of the operation. This is the conventional database approach, which is also used in GemStone [Penney and Stein 1987].

2. Incremental conversion. Instead of converting all instances as soon as a type change is made, one could defer the conversion of each instance until some later, more suitable, time. This could be when an instance is updated, or on some other user-defined criterion.

3. Screening. Instead of converting instances, one may place a filter between the accessing routines and the instance versions that are accessed. The filter acts just like a database view in that it gives the user of an object the "illusion" that the object is of the type (version) that the user expects, yet no change has been made to the persistent representation of the object. This approach has been explored by Zdonik [Zdonik 1985; Zdonik 1986;

Skarra and Zdonik 1987], Banerjee et al. [Banerjee et al. 1987a; Banerjee et al. 1987b],[3] and ourselves [Ahlsén et al. 1983; Ahlsén et al. 1984].

The latter two approaches presume some form of version management of types, or at least the ability of the system to manage several representations of one type.

The advantage of the first approach is, of course, that it is more efficient once the conversion has been made. However, in AVANCE we have adopted the screening and incremental conversion approaches, because we assume a loosely coupled decentralized system. The immediate conversion approach conflicts not only with the principle of autonomy of nodes (see Section 18.2.2) and the authorization mechanism of our system,[4] but also with the fact that often it will not be known (in one place) where all instances of a type are located.

In view of the fact that in many object-oriented systems the type definitions are themselves objects, the mechanism of object version control can be extended to provide type version control. In an object-oriented system, the objects model both data and programs in a traditional system. Therefore, a type version control mechanism is applicable to typing of both data and programs.

## 18.1.2 System-Level Version Control

Reliability is one of the most important issues in a system. Guaranteeing the consistency of the database in a concurrent environment where parallel transactions change the state of the database is a problem that all builders of a multiuser system must face. The problem areas are basically concurrency control, transaction rollback, and database recovery. System-level version control offers solutions to these problems. In fact, system versions can provide more concurrency than is otherwise possible. Read transactions may be allowed to run concurrently with update transactions without interference even when they access the same objects. This is possible by making the read transactions access older versions while update transactions generate new versions. In certain cases it is also possible to have several concurrent update transactions operating on the same objects. This is possible if some update transactions perform only *independent* operations on the objects of contention. An operation on an object is independent if it does not need access to the previous state of an object in order to generate a new state.[5]

---

[3] ORION (the system built at MCC) also uses incremental conversion to some extent.

[4] As an example, a user (programmer) who is authorized to alter a type object should not necessarily be authorized to modify or access all instances of that type.

[5] We use the word *state* rather than *version* here because the definition of an independent operation does not require identifiable versions.

A formal treatment of the use of multiple versions for concurrency control appears in [Bernstein and Goodman 1983] and [Papadimitriou and Kanellakis 1984]. Papadimitriou and Kanellakis also point out its relation to reliability. Examples of the use of system version control to increase the performance of read-only transactions may be found in [Weihl 1987]. Carey and Muhanna have made a study of the overall performance of multiversion concurrency control algorithms [Carey and Muhanna 1986].

## 18.2 AN OVERVIEW OF THE AVANCE ARCHITECTURE

AVANCE [Björnerstedt and Britts 1988] is a research prototype that supports (among other things) sharing of persistent objects, nested transactions, object version management, decentralization of both data and control, and a strongly typed (compiled) programming language. The architecture is designed to provide three levels of abstraction to implementors: the object manager, the AVANCE virtual machine, and the high-level language PAL.

The object manager provides functions for identifying and manipulating a data abstraction called a *packet slice*. This concept will be explained later. It provides an interface suitable for building interpreters.

The second level of abstraction is the virtual machine interface provided by the pseudo-machine code (p-code) interpreter. It has similarities with the Smalltalk-80 virtual machine [Goldberg and Robson 1983]. The interface provided by the p-code interpreter is essentially a stack machine that understands a set of primitive datatypes and an instruction repertoire to operate on them.

The third level of abstraction is the high-level language PAL. A compiler translates PAL into the pseudo-machine code of the virtual machine. Most users and programmers would use only this level of abstraction.

### 18.2.1 Object Granularity

The world of objects in AVANCE is partitioned into two disjoint sets: *packets* and *datatype values*. Both packets and datatype values are instances of abstract datatypes. By this is meant that they have an internal hidden representation (consisting of instance variables) and the only way to operate on a packet or a datatype value is by using an operation defined for the type.

**Packets** Packets are associated with persistence, independent existence, synchronized sharing, resiliency, atomicity, and system version control. Packets are identified by non-reusable surrogates allocated when the packet is created. The identifier space is very large in order to allow global identification in a decentralized or distributed system. Packet identifiers are used only as components of packet references, and are not directly available for manipulation outside the object manager. Packets may be aggregated by the use of packet references into any directed graph structure. Packets may be shared between AVANCE processes.

A packet is roughly comparable to a *monitor* [Hoare 1974], in that it synchronizes processes that invoke operations on it. A packet operation invocation is a *remote procedure call*. In other words, arguments and return values are passed by value, the invoker is blocked until the invoked operation returns control, and the details of communication protocol and error detection are hidden from the programmer. Packets resemble Guardians in Argus [Liskov and Scheifler 1983] in that they are persistent objects with remote procedure call handlers. They differ from Guardians in that they are generally not active by themselves (they do not have their own thread of control).[6]

**Datatype Values**   Datatype values do not have independent existence. For a datatype value to be persistent, it has to be assigned to an instance variable of a packet. Datatype values never overlap, that is, every instance variable contains a "private" value, and assignment of values between variables entails copying of values. The only way for two or more objects[7] to share an object is by using references to a common packet.

Datatype values have significantly less overhead than packets. The operations of datatypes can be implemented rather efficiently, compared with the operations of packettypes, since no overhead for such things as persistency, synchronization, and version control is needed. Furthermore, datatype values are not assigned system unique identifiers (as are packets), since they are not persistent, independently existing objects. This also reduces space and time overhead. Depending on these differences in properties, the designer can decide whether to implement a type as a packettype or datatype. A datatype definition can be as complex as a packettype definition, and there is very little syntactic difference between the two.

The PAL programmer defines the internal representation of a type (both packet- and datatypes) in terms of datatypes, i.e., by declaring instance variables on datatypes. Packets cannot be directly incorporated in the internal representation of a type; instead, the reference datatype (explained later) is used.

**Packet Slices**   A packet represents an object meaningful to designers and users at the level of PAL. At the level of the object manager a packet is represented by a set of packet slices. The object manager provides a single-level store for packet slices, handles references to packet slices, and controls the execution of processes. What conceptually unites a set of packet slices into

---

[6] A thread of control is created in AVANCE by creating an AVANCE process. It is outside the scope of the chapter to go into the syntax and semantics of AVANCE processes.

[7] In the rest of this chapter, except for Section 18.4.1 which describes Reed's model, we use the term *object* to mean either a packet or a datatype value.

one abstract packet is a common identifier. A packet slice consists of a set of persistent instance variables (called attributes) belonging to one specific packettype. The usual reason a packet is represented by more than one slice is property inheritance. For each type of which a packet is an instance, there will correspond a slice containing exactly the instance variables belonging to that specific type. However, the slices of a packet are independent from each other from the perspective of the object manager, and it does not place any restrictions on which slices of a packet are created and destroyed. Restrictions, such as those implied by property inheritance, are defined and enforced at the PAL level. Only operations (methods) are explicitly inherited. Instance variables are always hidden. Inheritance is realized at the object manager level by a flexible invocation mechanism that allows type objects to delegate [Stein 1987] the implementation of operations to other type objects. A packet could in principle dynamically change its type structure or even consist of types that are unconnected by inheritance. A packet could also be distributed over a network by having slices at different locations. Datatype values, on the other hand, always have their representation kept together as one unit by the object manager.

## 18.2.2 The AVANCE Logical Network

An AVANCE system consists of a logical network of nodes. Each node provides a centralized information processing environment, suitable for an "organizational unit" requiring authority over processing and data. Authentication of users and protection of data is handled within a node. Each node resides on a physical *host* machine, although one host may support several nodes. Each node may become unavailable for communication with other nodes in the system. This may be because the administrator of the node has decided to close it, or because of a crash of the node or host, in which case the node closes without warning. Nodes are thus relatively autonomous; what unites a set of AVANCE nodes into a system is the adoption of

- a common identification scheme for all packets

- a common representation form for all packets and datatype values

- a communications protocol between nodes

- a common set of packettypes and datatypes

The predefined types (primitive datatypes and system-defined packettypes) form a substrate common to all nodes. The user-defined packettypes and datatypes in PAL are added incrementally on a per-node basis. A type is implemented as a special kind of packet, and thus one type maintains its identity over all nodes where it is installed.

## 18.2.3 The PAL Programming Language

PAL [Ahlsén et al. 1987] is a high-level, block-structured language primarily inspired by Simula [Birtwistle et al. 1973], Smalltalk-80 [Goldberg and Robson 1983], and CLU [Liskov et al. 1981]. It contains facilities for both defining and manipulating objects (packets and datatype values). In this chapter we shall only sketch the language in order to illustrate the version control aspects. Hence the examples are simplified and only things of interest for the example are included.

PAL supports typing, property inheritance, data abstraction, encapsulation, instantiation, and both dynamic and static binding within a homogeneous environment. Not only "data" but also "meta-data" are represented as objects.

Both datatypes and packettypes are organized in property inheritance "trees." As *multiple inheritance* is supported, the inheritance "tree" is actually a directed acyclic graph. In Fig. 18.1a, parts of the inheritance graph for primitive datatypes (strongly inspired by Smalltalk) is shown. Indentation means property inheritance.

Since datatypes and packettypes have different semantics, a datatype cannot be a subtype of a packettype and vice versa. Therefore, a separate inheritance graph is constructed for packettypes. In Fig. 18.1b, some system-defined packettypes are shown. All datatypes and packettypes must, directly or indirectly, be a subtype of **Value** or **Packet,** respectively.

Some datatypes are *type parameterized* (unlike Smalltalk), e.g., **List-(Integer)**, **List(Char)**, and **Array(List(Set(Integer)))**. The **Reference** datatype

**FIGURE 18.1** SOME PREDEFINED OBJECT TYPES

| (a) Primitive Datatypes | (b) System-Defined Packettypes |
|---|---|
| ● Value | ● Packet |
| ● ● Boolean | ● ● Node |
| ● ● Magnitude | ● ● DirectoryEntry |
| ● ● ● Date | ● ● ● User |
| ● ● ● Number | ● ● ● Directory |
| ● ● ● ● Integer | ● ● ● Application |
| ● ● ● ● Real | ● ● ● ● TypeDef[8] |
| ● ● Compiler | ● ● ● ● ● DatatypeDef |
| ● ● Parameterized | ● ● ● ● ● PackettypeDef |
| ● ● ● Collection | ● ● Checkpointable |
| ● ● ● ● Sequence | ● ● ● InstalledType |
| ● ● ● ● Bag | ● ● ● SpecDef |
| ● ● ● Reference | ● ● Version |
| ● ● ● Process | ● ● VersionSet |

[8] Packettype **TypeDef** is a subtype of both **Application** and **Checkpointable**.

(**Ref** for short) is a special case in that it is parameterized with a packettype, while most other parameterized types are parameterized with a datatype. An instance of **Ref** is a handle to a packet of the type the parameter specifies, e.g., **Ref(Directory)**.

Following the data abstraction philosophy, objecttypes (packettypes or datatypes) are defined in terms of a specification and an implementation. These parts are defined separately and may also be compiled separately. An application, consisting of several interconnected types, may be defined purely by specifications that may be compiled before the corresponding implementations exist. After this, several programmers may work independently on the implementations. The PAL compiler ensures that specifications are type-compatible with each other and that implementations conform to their specification.

**Specifications**   An objecttype specification consists of three optional parts: a context part, a public part, and a private part. In the *context part* the supertypes of the objecttype, and packettypes and datatypes that the objecttype references, are specified.[9] The *public part* contains declarations of operations that are available to all other objecttypes that use the type. The *private part* declares operations that are available only to subtypes of the objecttype and to itself for operating on itself and other intances of the same type. A specification thus defines two interfaces: the interface provided by the public operations for external use, and the interface provided by both the public and the private operations for use by subtypes and in its own implementation. The following is an example specification.

```
PACKETTYPE Report;
    SPECIFICATION
    CONTEXT
        SUPERTYPE Document;
        PACKETTYPE ReportSection;
        DATATYPE Author;
    PUBLIC
        OPERATION getTitle():Text;
        OPERATION getAuthors():List(Author);
        OPERATION editSection(SectionNumber:List(Integer));
            .
            .
            .
    PRIVATE
        OPERATION getSection(SectionNumber:List(Integer)):
            Ref(ReportSection);
END Report;
```

[9] Primitive datatypes need not be stated.

The context part of **Report** states that it is a subtype of **Document** and that it must have access to the **ReportSection** packettype and the **Author** datatype. The declarations of three public operations **getTitle**, **getAuthors**, and **editSection**, and one private operation, **getSection**, are shown. **Report** inherits the context and all public and private operations of **Document**.

**Implementations**   An objecttype implementation consists of two parts, a *representation* and an *operation implementation*. The representation defines instance variables used to hold the object state. The operation implementation defines operations. The implementation of **Report** is shown here.

```
PACKETTYPE Report;
    IMPLEMENTATION

    ATTRIBUTE
        authors:List(Author);      /*These are persistent*/
        title:Text;                /*instance variables.*/
        sections:List(Ref(ReportSection));

    OPERATION getTitle():Text;
    BEGIN
        RETURN(@title);
    END getTitle;

    OPERATION getSection(SectionNumber:List(Integer)):Ref(ReportSection);
    VARIABLE section:Ref(ReportSection);      /*These are temporary*/
        sectionNumberRest:List(Integer);      /*variables.*/
    BEGIN
    section:=@ sections.getNth(SectionNumber.first());
    sectionNumberRest:=SectionNumber.removeFirst();
    IF sectionNumberRest.isEmpty() THEN
      RETURN(section)
    ELSE
      RETURN(section$getSection(sectionNumberRest));
    END getSection;
      .

      .

      .

END Report;
```

All public and private operations declared in the specification must be defined in the implementation. The implementation of an operation simply adds to the operation heading optional temporary variables and a compound statement.

The representation of an object is defined in terms of instance variables. Instance variables in packettypes are called *attributes*. **Report**, above, has three attributes, **authors**, **title**, and **sections**. In statements, '@' must precede an attribute. This is to remind programmers of their semantics (persistence), and that there is generally a difference in access cost between attributes and other variables. Variables (and attributes, which are simply a special kind of variable) are distinct from datatype values in PAL. A variable should be seen as a container for a datatype value. When a datatype value is assigned to a variable, it replaces the previous datatype value. Hence, assignment is not an operation on a datatype value, but on a variable.

The expression:

```
section$getSection(sectionNumberRest)
```

means: invoke the **getSection** operation on the packet referenced by the variable **section** and pass the value of **sectionNumberRest** as a parameter. The '$' operator is used for packettype operations and '.' for datatype operations. This reminds programmers of the difference in semantics and cost between operations on packets and datatype values. The '$' operator may be applied only to packet references. The '.' operator may be applied to all kinds of datatype values, including packet references. The '.' operator is used on a packet reference when one wants to operate on the reference as such, and not on the packet it points to.

The **select** statement is a powerful declarative statement where conditional invocation of operations on objects in a **Collection**[10] is possible. The syntax is:

```
select {operation} from {Collection} where {boolean expression}
```

Omitting the operation between **select** and **from** means that a subcollection of the same type as the source collection is returned. If an operation is stated between **select** and **from**, then a **List** is returned containing the values returned by the operation applied to each element in the selected collection. Note that if a collection is defined on **REF**(*packet_type*), the collection will not contain packets, but references to packets.

---

[10] **Collection** is a datatype with subtypes such as **Set**, **Bag**, and **List**. Because datatype values are assigned or updated as one unit and because they are not persistent (unless assigned to a packet attribute), there are practical limitations to their size. Currently, the implementation of AVANCE cannot handle collections larger than a few hundred elements, with acceptable performance. Thus AVANCE currently does not have support for large database associative retrieval.

## 18.3 OBJECT VERSIONS AT THE APPLICATION LEVEL

In AVANCE there are three ways in which applications can use version control. The first, and simplest, utilizes the system-level version control of AVANCE to provide a packet state history. The second also builds on the system-level version control, but provides identifiable versions. The third is a version control application built on AVANCE, which is independent of the system-level version control. This application manages parallel version structures suitable for design applications, such as document development.

The management of type versions in AVANCE builds on the second form of object version management.

### 18.3.1 Object Versions

**Packet State History**   The system-level version control mechanism of AVANCE can be used for retaining information about old states of packets. This does not provide true version management at the application level, since it does not provide identifiable versions to applications. We have included it here because it may be used for the same purpose as true version management, that is, keeping track of the evolution of an object. The mechanism is essentially "free" since it builds on the version management of packet slices used by the object manager.

When some arbitrary update operation on a packet modifies that packet, the object manager will create new versions of only those packet slices which have been modified. Furthermore, only the differences (deltas) will be stored. Old versions of packet slices are normally retained only for as long as needed by the system (see Section 18.4). However, a user may request that older packet slice versions be retained indefinitely. The effect of this is not that there will be packet versions available as identifiable entities at the PAL level. Instead, the effect is to provide a memory of the state history of a packet (or part of a packet) over a continuous time. A packet reference may be bound to any time in the past and any read-only operation applied, reflecting the state of the packet as of that time. The following example illustrates the use of this mechanism.

```
rep:Ref(Report);                    /*1*/
    .
    .
    .
rep.retainAll();                     /*2*/
    .
    .
    .
rep.bindToDate(880212)$getTitle();  /*3*/
```

Statement 1 declares a reference of type **Report**. Statement 2 tells the object manager not to garbage collect old slice versions of the report that **rep** references. It is assumed that the variable **rep** has been assigned a reference value (identifying a report) between statements 1 and 2. A reference, such as **rep**, is by default bound to the current system time. Statement 3, which is assumed to be executed at a much later point in time (most likely after many updates), binds the reference to the time point of February 12, 1988 (assumed to be in the past with respect to current time) and executes the packet operation **getTitle** on the state of the report as of that time. Note that the reference datatype (**Ref**) is a primitive datatype. The operations **retainAll** and **bindToDate**, used in the example, are operations defined for this datatype.

**Simple Packet Versions**   The second form of versioning builds on the previous mechanism. It adds facilities for managing a sequence of identifiable points in time of the state history. These identifiable points we call packet versions. A designer of a new packettype may make it a subtype of the packettype **Checkpointable**. The specification for **Checkpointable** is:

```
PACKETTYPE Checkpointable;
    SPECIFICATION
    CONTEXT
        SUPERTYPE Packet;
    PUBLIC
        OPERATION checkpoint():Integer;
        OPERATION successor():Integer;
        OPERATION predecessor():Integer;
        OPERATION validfrom(id:Integer):Timepoint;
        OPERATION vid():Integer;
    END Checkpointable;
```

Instances of **Checkpointable** will have a sequence of identifiable versions. Versions are identified by an **Integer** value, which is guaranteed to increase for every checkpoint. The operation **checkpoint** will mark the state of the packet (as of the current transaction time) as being a version, and return the identifier of that version. Assuming a designer had made the type **Report** a subtype of **Checkpointable**, some examples of the use of packet versions might be:

```
rep:Ref(Report);
id:Integer;
.

.

.
id:= rep$vid();                              /*4*/
id:= rep.bindToDate(880212)$vid();           /*5*/
rep:= rep.bindToTime(rep$validfrom(id));/*6*/
rep$getTitle();                              /*7*/
```

Statement 4 finds the **id** of the most current packet version (since **rep** by default is bound to current time). Statement 5 finds the **id** of the packet version valid as of February 12, 1988.[11] Statement 6 creates a reference bound to the time when the version with the version **id** obtained in statement 5 was checkpointed. Statement 7 obtains the report title of this version. It is important to notice the difference between the effects of statement 7 of the current example and statement 3 in the example of the previous section. The state of the report as of February 12, 1988 is not necessarily the same as the state of the report associated with the checkpointed version valid at February 12, 1988. For example, the title might have been changed sometime between the checkpoint and February 12, 1988.

**Complex Packet Versions**    As we have shown, some version control is obtained by using the system-level version control mechanism of AVANCE. However, in some applications linear version structures are not adequate. Design document management is a case in point. Here, a particular version may be derived by several designers in parallel, and parallel versions may coexist, possibly to merge eventually into a single version. At a specific time, an object may have several "latest" versions. The version structure is, generally speaking, a graph (a network). In this case operations are needed to create and search the version graph. For this purpose a version control application has been built on top of AVANCE.

A designer may declare a packettype as a subtype of the packettype **Version**. Such packettypes inherit a number of operations for manipulating a set of **Version** packets. In this model each version is a different **Version** packet, and each such packet is also an entry point for accessing other **Version** packets in the set. A **Version** packet may be created either (as a first version) by the same **create** operation used to create packets of other types, or by a **derive** operation applied to an existing **Version** packet. The **derive** operation creates a new **Version** packet that is a copy of the packet to which the operation was applied. However, a **Version** packet will accept an invocation of the **derive** operation only if the operation **freeze** had been applied to it earlier. The **freeze** operation also has the effect of freezing the **Version** packet to which it is applied; that is, modifying operations are no longer accepted on that packet. A **Version** packet thus has two phases in its lifetime. In the first phase, after it is created but before the **freeze** operation has been applied, the packet may be modified and developed in any way the application requires. But the generation of new dependent **Version** packets by the **derive** operation is now allowed. In the second phase, after the **freeze** operation, the packet may not be modified, but it does allow the use of the **derive** operation to generate new

---

[11] Since the value of **id** obtained in statement 4 is replaced in statement 5, statement 4 is rather pointless and included only for the sake of the example.

versions.[12] Because the **derive** operation may be applied more than once to the same **Version** packet, there may be branching in the dependency graph.

A **Version** packet to which the **freeze** operation has been applied represents the state of a design at some time when it is considered stable enough to provide a basis for branching alternatives, or important enough to be frozen as a reference point. The **Version** packet is timestamped to reflect this time. This represents the system time (that is, the time from the system's point of view) when the **freeze** took place. In addition to the timestamp, a version also obtains a version number (from the system), and possibly (from the user) a version label. The specification of packettype **Version** is:

```
PACKETTYPE Version ;
    SPECIFICATION
    CONTEXT
        SUPERTYPE Packet ;
        PACKETTYPE VersionSet, User ;
    PUBLIC
        OPERATION time ( ) : Timepoint ;
        OPERATION label ( ) : Text ;
        OPERATION versionNumber( ) : Integer ;
        OPERATION first( ) : Ref(Version) ;
        OPERATION derive (MergeSet : Set(Ref(Version) ) ) : Ref(Version);
        OPERATION undoDerive( ) ;
        OPERATION freeze(label : Text) ;
        OPERATION last( ) : Ref(Version) ;
        OPERATION pred( ) : Set(Ref(Version) ) ;
        OPERATION succ( ) : Set(Ref(Version) ) ;
        OPERATION before(tp : Timepoint) : Ref(Version) ;
        OPERATION after(tp : Timepoint) : Ref(Version),
        OPERATION beforeOnPath(tp : Timepoint ; path : Text) : Ref(Version) ;
        OPERATION afterOnPath(tp : Timepoint ; path : Text) : Ref(Version) ;
        OPERATION predOfLabel(label : Text ; path : Text) : Ref(Version) ;
        OPERATION firstOnPath(path : Text) : ref(Version) ;
        OPERATION lastOnPath(path : Text) : ref(Version) ;
        OPERATION predOnPath(path : Text( : ref(Version) ) ;
        OPERATION succOnPath(path : Text) : ref(Version) ;
        OPERATION succOfLabel(label, path : Text) : Ref(Version) ;
        OPERATION versions( ) : Set(Ref(Version) ) ;
        OPERATION setArcName(predRef : Ref(Version) ; arcname : Text) ;
        OPERATION predPaths( ) : Set(Text) ;
```

---

[12] When an unfrozen **Version** packet is modified, the system will of course generate the needed slice versions of the **Version** packet for the purposes of reliability and concurrency control. Thus, there are two levels of version control in this case.

```
        OPERATION succPaths( ) : Set(Text) ;
        OPERATION vDelete( ) ;
        OPERATION derivers( ) : Set(Ref(User) ) ;
END Version ;
```

Every **Version** packet has an attribute that is a reference to a **VersionSet** packet. The **VersionSet** packet maintains a set of **Version** packets belonging to one generic (or abstract) design object. All **Version** packets that belong to the same version set will reference the same **VersionSet** packet. The **VersionSet** packet is a "bookkeeping" object, hidden from users. It contains a set of references to all **Version** packets that have been generated by a **derive** operation on some **Version** packet already belonging to the set. When a first **Version** packet is created, by a normal **create** operation, a corresponding **VersionSet** packet is created, and the set is initialized with the single reference to the first packet. When a dependent **Version** packet is created by a **derive** operation, then this packet is given a reference to the same **VersionSet** packet, and a reference to the new **Version** packet is added to the set. The **VersionSet** packet also maintains the labeled dependency graph.

We now give a short explanation of some of the operations in the specification of **Version**. The **derive** operation has already been explained, except for the parameter **MergeSet**. This parameter is an empty set, if the new version will depend only on the version to which the **derive** is applied. The set is nonempty if the **derive** is a merge of several versions. All the versions in **MergeSet** must be frozen. If a merge of several versions is to be made, then the user has to decide on one "main" version. It is to this main version that the **derive** is applied, and only this version is copied into the new version. It is left to the user to access the other "subsidiary" versions to be merged, and extract relevant information from them. A set of references to the predecessors in the graph is obtained by the operation **pred** on the new version.

The operation **undoDerive** is applicable only on unfrozen **Version** packets, and simply removes the version from the derivation graph. The operation **derivers**, when applied to a **Version** packet, returns a set of references to users that have applied the **derive** operation to this version but still have not done either **freeze** or **undoDerive**.

Information about the version structure (the graph) must be accessible. In general, a **Version** packet may have zero or more predecessors and successors. The version structure associated with a version set can conceptually be seen as a network of objects that have arcs between them. To make it easier to operate on the version structure, it is possible to name the arcs in the version structure. The predecessor arcs from a **Version** packet must be uniquely named (if the user doesn't name the arc, the system will), and the same applies to the successor arcs. Thus, it is always possible to uniquely access a previous or later version of a **Version** packet by arc name. A consecutive sequence of arcs with the same name constitutes a **path** to/from a given **Version**. The **pathname** coincides with the common arc names.

A set of operations makes it possible to examine the version structure. One subset is concerned with versions relative to a specific version. This includes operations that return all predecessors or successors, the immediate predecessor or successor (based on time), or predecessors or successors constrained by pathname or label, and also operations that return pathnames associated with a specific version. An example is **succOfLabel**, which returns the successor version (relative to "this" version) with the specified label on the path.

Another subset of the version-graph operations is concerned with the entire graph (i.e., the first, last, or all versions of a version set), possibly constrained by label and/or time (e.g., **after**, which returns the earliest version after the specified time).

Two operations are concerned with updating the graph: **setArcName**, which assigns a name to the arc between "this" version and a predecessor version, and **vDelete**, which deletes "this" version. All arcs associated with this version are erased.

For example, assume **r** is declared **r:ref(Report)** and that **Report** now has the packettype **Version** as a supertype. At some point in time, **r** has been assigned a particular **Report R**.

1. Find the previous version(s) of **R**:

```
r$pred( );   /*Returns a singleton version set if it is a linear
    version structure.*/
```

2. Find the latest version of **R** on path **pl** before some time **t**:

```
r$beforeOnPath(t,''pl'');
```

3. Find the version(s) with the label "Charlie's version":

```
vset:Set(Ref(Version));
vset:= select from r$versions( ) where $label( ) =
    ''Charlies version'';
```

4. Assume that the report's title was changed from "Version Management" to "Version Control" some time after January 1, 1986. Find the versions of **R** for which **R** had the title "Version Management" after January 1, 1986:

```
vset:= select from r$versions( ) where :Report$getTitle( )=
    ''Version Management'' and $time( )>860101;
```

This version control model is general and provides a basic set of concepts that may be refined by a user. The only classification of versions lies implicitly in the **Version** states "unfrozen" and "frozen." In contrast, some other version control approaches support a more fine-grained classification scheme for versions. An example of this is [Chou and Kim 1986], where versions are classified as *transient, working,* or *released,* and reside in *private, project,* and *public* databases. The operational semantics of the three classes of versions differ; e.g., a released version is not deletable. These semantics support one class of design applications with a certain organization. This model also supports change notification and a configuration hierarchy scheme. AVANCE is instead open-ended in the sense that it is fairly simple to extend the version control application to give this kind of support. New subclasses of **Version** can be introduced to enhance the semantics of the application.

## 18.3.2 Object Type Versions

One application that is very important in AVANCE is the design of new (packet or data) types. The aims of this application are to allow programmers to create and change types in the system with as much flexibility as possible, and to prevent the introduction of inconsistencies into the system (between different types and between types and their instances). These two aims conflict with each other, so one has to strike a compromise between them. The type design application is complex and still under development. As more is understood about the needs and possibilities of type evolution, the type design application can be improved. Thus even the type design application is an evolving application!

When analyzing mechanisms for handling type change in AVANCE, it is useful to distinguish not only between the *specification* and *implementation* of a type, but also between the two implementation components: *operation implementation* and *representation* (instance variables). A factor that significantly reduces the complexity of the type change problem in AVANCE is the encapsulation of the representation. A change to the representation (and the operation implementation), but not the specification, will affect *instances* of older versions of the type (including of course instances of subtypes to the type), but not other dependent types, not even subtypes.[13] A change to the specification (and the operation implementation), but not to the representation, will affect other dependent types, but not instances of older versions of the type. Finally, a change of only the operation implementation of a type (for example, a "debug" change) will affect neither other dependent types nor instances of older type versions. In terms of the ANSI/SPARC 3 level schema architecture [ANSI 1978], the type specification corresponds to (a component of) the conceptual schema, the representation corresponds to

---

[13] Subtypes are not affected because the code in the implementation of a subtype can depend only on the specification of the supertype. The code of the subtype is not allowed direct access to the instance variables in the supertype.

the internal schema, and the operation implementation corresponds to the conceptual/internal mapping.

**Detecting the Mismatch of Type Versions**   Currently, the type design application is constructed using the following packettypes:

- Packettype **PackettypeDef**
- Packettype **DatatypeDef**
- Packettype **SpecDef**
- Packettype **InstalledType**

These packettypes are meta objecttypes, since they define how to create new objecttypes in AVANCE. All of them are also subtypes to packettype **Checkpointable**.

When a designer wants to create a new packettype,[14] a new instance of **PackettypeDef** is created. The initialization operation for **PackettypeDef** also creates a **SpecDef** packet and an **InstalledType** packet. On the **Packettype Def** packet the designer then executes operations to define the specification and implementation (in terms of PAL source code). The compiled specification is maintained in the **SpecDef** packet. When the designer has successfully compiled the specification, and is prepared to make it official, an operation **InstallSpec** is executed on the **PackettypeDef** packet. This will checkpoint the **SpecDef** packet, giving the current version of the specification an identifier **SID**.

The two parts of the implementation (representation and operation implementation) are compiled together, but defined (updated) by different operations. The operation for updating the representation (and only this operation) will also checkpoint the **PackettypeDef** packet itself, effectively giving the current version of the representation an identifier **RID**. If the implementation has been compiled after the last checkpoint of the specification, and if neither the specification nor the representation has been updated after their respective last checkpoints, then the designer may install and checkpoint a new executable version of the type in the **InstalledType** packet. The current **SID** and **RID** are stored together with the executable code, linkage tables, etc. in the **Installed-Type** packet.

When a new instance of the newly installed type (version) is created, the **RID** of the **InstalledType** doing the creation is stored with the instance.

Finally, when the implementation is compiled, the compiler will append to the result the current **SID** of all types in the context.

If a type is to be installed at AVANCE nodes other than the one where it was created, then separate **InstalledType** slices are created at the other nodes

---

[14] The reasoning here is identical for datatypes, except that the packettype **DatatypeDef** is used.

for the type. A designer thus has freedom to choose whether and when to install a type (version) at the nodes of the system.

At runtime, when an invocation is made, the object manager will first look up the current version of the **InstalledType** and then, if necessary (see Section 18.4.2), the current version of the instance. A comparison is then made between the **SID** of the **InstalledType** with the **SID** expected by the invoker, and the **RID** of the **InstalledType** with the **RID** of the instance. If the two comparisons agree (the normal case), then the invocation is allowed to proceed. If the **SID**'s do not agree, then an exception **SpecificationMismatch** is raised. If the **RID**'s do not agree, then an exception **RepresentationMismatch** is raised.

**Handling the Mismatch of Type Version**    In a way similar to [Skarra and Zdonik 1987], we use exception handling to cope with type version mismatches. The **SID** expected by the invoker is supplied along with a **SpecificationMismatch** exception. The **RID**, together with values corresponding to the attribute values of the instance, is supplied along with a **RepresentationMismatch** exception. Of course, both kinds of exceptions may be raised in the same invocation.

Each operation implementation for an operation defined in the specification may be supplied with one or more exception handlers. Each exception handler declares either the **SID** or the **RID** (or both) that it is prepared to handle. If either the **SID** or the **RID** is omitted, then the current one is assumed. Thus the normal operation implementation, for the current **SID** and **RID**, omits both from its declaration.

Each handler definition must obey some constraints for declaring parameters. First, the handler must declare parameters corresponding exactly in number and type to the specification of the **SID** for which it is intended. Second, if the handler is intended for an **RID** other than the current one, then it must add a list of input parameters corresponding exactly in number and type to the attributes of the **RID**. Both of these constraints are checked by the compiler. The compiler also checks that the declared **SID/RID** combination exists.

The designer may also supply global handlers for certain **RID**'s. Such a handler is used only for converting old representations to the current one.

When one or both of the exceptions occur, the matching handler is invoked. If a **RepresentationMismatch** exception has occurred and there is a matching global handler for the **RID**, then this handler is invoked first, converting the instance to the new representation. After this, the handler for the proper **SID** is invoked, which can be the normal implementation if no **SpecificationMismatch** has been raised. If there is no matching handler, then the operation is aborted. The handler may convert the instance to conform with the new **RID** or it may simply emulate older specifications, or both. Currently the handler is not allowed to generate a new version of an old **RID**. Another limitation in the current design is that a designer may modify the declaration of supertypes in the context part of the specification only by adding new supertypes. A specification that has been checkpointed and that has declared some other type as supertype may not have this type removed from the list of supertypes.[15]

## 18.4 OBJECT VERSIONS AT THE SYSTEM LEVEL

The AVANCE system uses version management for:

1. Synchronizing access to packets (shared objects)

2. Providing rollback recovery from system crashes

3. Providing the means for greater concurrency than is possible without version management

A modification of Reeds' approach [Reed 1983; Reed 1978] is used. Reed's approach consists of a few concepts and mechanisms that are used to build *atomic actions*. Randell et al. [Randell et al. 1978] have pointed out that the *atomic action* concept is a generalization of the concept of *transaction* [Eswaran et al. 1976] as used in the database literature. Henceforth, we will use the two concepts of *transaction* and *atomic action* interchangeably. Atomic actions are useful for constructing fault-tolerant systems. If a failure occurs in the middle of an atomic action, then the states of all objects modified by the atomic action are restored by the system to the values they had before the atomic action. Version management at the system level may be used as the basis for providing such backward error recovery [Randell et al. 1978], since the versions of an object may be used as redundant checkpoints of the object state. In a decentralized system, fault-tolerance is important because of the lack of global knowledge of the state of the system. If a failure occurs, the user may not know whether the resulting state of the system is consistent or how to ensure that it becomes consistent.

### 18.4.1 Reed's Model

In this section we will describe a condensed and slightly modified version of Reed's model [Reed 1978; Reed 1983]. We will be speaking in general terms, and not in terms of the AVANCE system. In *simplified* form Reed's model

---

[15] The reason for this is that collections are type parameterized in AVANCE. If we allowed a type to drop supertypes, then it is unclear how this should affect old instances of the type. If they were allowed to also drop their instantiation of the supertype, then type checking would have to be applied on all instances of a collection, each time the collection is used.

adds to the basic object model[16] the concept of *versions, pseudo-time,* and *possibilities.*

An object is defined by a sequence of versions, where each version $v_{c,e}$ has a range of validity $[c,e]$ $(c \leq e)$. The range starts at $c$, the pseudo-time of creation, and ends at $e$, the pseudo-time of extension. Pseudo-time is an ordering that is correlated but not identical with *real* time. Each transaction $T_{i,j}$ is given an exclusive range of pseudo-time $[i,j]$ in which to logically perceive the system. A version $v_{c,c}$ is created by a **write** operation belonging to $T_{i,j}$ by associating it with a pseudo-time from the range $[i,j]$, that is $i \leq c \leq j$. After a version $v_{c,e}$ is created[17] it may have its range of validity extended to result in $v_{c,e'}$ by a **read** operation belonging to some transaction $T_{k,l}$ by associating it with a new pseudo-time of extension $e'$, where $e' > e$ and $k \leq e' \leq l$. One can think of this as each sequential (read or write) step in a transaction being assigned a "tick" of the pseudo-time clock.

Pseudo-time is then a concept for ordering the sequence of versions constituting an object and for ordering the actions (operations) on objects throughout the system. A transaction is executed in such a way that all bindings of references to objects are done to the object version valid at a pseudo-time associated with the transaction. Ordering the operations is only a basis for synchronization; it is not enough to make transactions atomic. Transactions must also be recoverable.

The concept of *possibility* is introduced by Reed to provide actions that are recoverable. With each transaction $T_{i,j}$ we now also associate an identifier $P$ called a possibility: $T_{i,j}(P)$. Every effect produced by $T$ that must be recoverable is made tentatively and is identifiable through $P$. A possibility groups a set of actions into an atomic action. Each version generated by a write operation and each extension of valid time generated by a read operation in a transaction is tentative until a commit or abort is made on the possibility. A commit is never allowed if it would make one version's range of validity overlap with another. A two-phase commit protocol [Gray 1978] is used to ensure atomicity in the face of hardware or software failure.

A write operation on an object defines a new (tentative) version with a pseudo-time of creation taken from the containing transaction. A read operation on an object is given access to the latest version valid before the current pseudo-time of the containing transaction, and the validity of the version is extended (tentatively) to this pseudo-time. An object is then not only a sequence of (committed) versions, but in addition may have one or more possible (uncommitted) *eductions*. An eduction of an object is either a version produced by a write, or an increase in pseudo-time of extension of

---

[16] Since we are not speaking in terms of the AVANCE system in this section (18.4.1), the term *object* should be interpreted only as something that has state, and where that state may be read, or a new state written.

[17] Here it does not matter whether we use *after* in terms of pseudo-time or realtime, since a version cannot be read before it is written.

a version produced by a read. An eduction *belongs* to some possibility. The system must synchronize transactions so that they observe only the known history (committed eductions) of objects plus eductions that belong to the same possibility as the transaction. This ensures that transactions observe a consistent state of the system.

Synchronization is achieved by sometimes delaying access to versions. The problem of deadlock must then be addressed. Deadlock can be handled in several ways [Bernstein and Goodman 1981], but in Reed's model timeouts are used to avoid it. Assume a read operation executing in $T_{i,j}(P)$ is associated with the pseudo-time $t (i \leq t \leq j)$. The system will attempt to provide the "latest" version as of $t$ for this read, that is, the version $v_{c,e}$ such that $c < t$ and there is no "newer" version $v_{c',e'}$ where $c < c'$ and $c' < t$. For a read operation there are three possible cases:

R1. $v_{c,e}$ is a tentative version not belonging to $P$. In this case the read must wait until the other possibility either commits or aborts, or until $P$ times out.

R2. $v_{c,e}$ either is committed[18] or belongs to $P$, and $e < t$. In this case the read is allowed to proceed and a tentative eduction is made under $P$ increasing $e$ to $t$. When $P$ is committed, then $v_{c,t}$ is made definite.

R3. $v_{c,e}$ either is committed or belongs to $P$, and $e \geq t$. In this case the read is allowed to proceed and no eduction need be made, since the pseudo-time of extension is already beyond the time of the read.

Similarly, for a write operation at $t$ there are three cases:

W1. If there is a committed version $v_{c,e}$ such that $c \leq t \leq e$, then $P$ is aborted.

W2. If there is a tentative eduction $v_{c,e}$ ($c < t < e$) not belonging to $P$, then the write must wait until the other possibility either commits or aborts, or until its own possibility $P$ times out.

W3. If there are no versions, or only versions $v_{c,e}$ ($e < t$) with no tentative eductions beyond $t$, then the write is allowed to proceed. $v_{t,t}$ is tentatively educed.

Of course, there are variants to this protocol; specifically, the waiting at R1 and W2 could be substituted with "optimistic" eductions and certification on commit [Sinha et al. 1985]. Notice that read operations are never directly aborted, although they may abort due to timeout. A read that lies within the range of a committed eduction (a read on the known history) will always proceed directly and always succeed (the read might fail for reasons other than synchronization). It should also be noted that in *real* time there may be concur-

---

[18] A version is committed if the possibility that created it has committed.

rent reads and writes on the same object. As long as the concurrent possibilities do not generate versions of the same object with overlapping pseudo-times of validity, we have what is called a *serializable schedule* [Eswaran et al. 1976]. However, for more than one concurrent write on the same object to be possible, all the writes (except the one with the lowest pseudo-time) cannot have reads with a lower pseudo-time on the same object within their possibility. Another way of saying this is that we must allow "holes" in the known history if we are to allow concurrent writes to the same object. Such transactions are of the form "give the object a value without regard to the value it had before" and may be unusual in practice.[19]

As defined so far, a transaction consists of some steps executed sequentially and associated with a possibility. To provide concurrency within transactions and for modularity in their construction, Reed allows the nesting of transactions. Instead of allowing only elementary reads and writes to be associated with a "tick" of the pseudo-time clock, one can allow any abstract operation to be a subtransaction. Transactions are then atomic in a relative sense, and a "tick" of the pseudo-time clock is to be taken at a relative level of resolution. If we have a transaction $T1_{i,j}(P)$, then a subtransaction $T2$ of $T1$ can be executed at time $t$ ($i \leq t \leq j$) and may be expressed as $T2_{t',t''}(Q(P))$, where $t' = t'' = t$ at the resolution associated with $T1$, yet $t' < t''$ at the increased resolution of $T2$. $T2$ has an associated possibility $Q$ that is *dependent* on $P$.

The synchronization protocol for elementary reads and writes must also be altered. The notion of eductions belonging to a possibility (cases R1 to R3 and W2) is altered in the following way: If a possibility $Q$ is dependent on $P$, then all eductions belonging to $P$ also belong to $Q$. If a commit is applied to $Q$, then all eductions belonging to $Q$ are still tentative but are added to the eductions belonging to $P$. If an abort is applied to $Q$, then all its eductions are forgotten, but the eductions belonging to $P$ are not affected. If a *top-level* (independent) transaction $P$ commits, then all eductions become permanent (and owned by all possibilities).

It has been pointed out that Reed's model is unnecessarily restrictive with respect to concurrency [Kohler 1981]. See for example [Schwarz and Spector 1984] for a model where the specification of a type includes synchronization information.

Another problem with Reed's model is that there is a risk of starvation. Specifically, transactions that are long in duration (in terms of real time) and that attempt writes late in their execution have a tendency to be repeatedly aborted. Jefferson has proposed a mechanism for synchronization called the *time warp* [Jefferson 1985], which has similarities with Reed's model but does not have the problem of transaction starvation.

---

[19] An example of such an operation is *initialization*, which should not try to read an object's value before writing it. If initialization is allowed more than once on an object, then many concurrent transactions writing to the same object are possible, if they all start by initializing the object.

Several subtransactions can execute concurrently, since they are given subranges of pseudo-time that are mutually exclusive. It is also possible for the parent transaction to continue in parallel with subtransactions, which would correspond to a process fork. A parent may then generate eductions that also belong to the possibility of the child in the sense described above, but that affect pseudo-times after the range of the child. This will not affect reads of the child but may abort writes. Of course, a parent must have a means of coping with the semantics of aborted subtransactions, since it is normally interested in the results produced by them.

A further problem with Reed's model and with version management at the system level is how to cope with an ever increasing amount of version data. Some means of pruning the version sequence or at least of moving infrequently accessed versions to archival storage is needed. Although a general discussion of this is outside the scope of this chapter, an outline of how the problem is attacked in AVANCE is given in the next section.

### 18.4.2 Reed's Model Adapted to AVANCE

The main advantage of Reed's model, and the reason we have built on it in AVANCE, is its relative conceptual simplicity.[20] It fits well with modular programming. The goal has been to make the construction of transactions very simple, if not transparent, to the programmer. We recognize that this may result in schedules that are not optimal with respect to concurrency.

Reed's model was chosen also because it was designed to deal with decentralized (and possibly distributed) systems. The idea of using system versions in a decentralized system is attractive for many reasons. One example is that we can move an object between the nodes of the system, without having to delete all information on the object in the node from which we are moving the object. An object may have a version history distributed over the nodes, and each node that the object has passed retains a first-class object described by a subset of the version history. In AVANCE at most one node at a time holds the right to update the object[21] (generate new versions). What is moved between the nodes is the *right* to update the object. Reed's model is just one example of a concurrency control model suitable for decentralized systems, and not essential to the operational semantics of AVANCE at the level of PAL. However, we do believe that a multiversion model has advantages for AVANCE, since many intended applications need versions anyway. In addition we believe a timestamp model (as opposed to a locking model) has advantages in addressing the problem of maintaining consistency in a decentralized system where the objects are not stationary.

---

[20] This does not necessarily mean it is easy to implement.

[21] In AVANCE a remote object may still be updated by a remote procedure call. A packet operation invocation is logically indistinguishable from a remote procedure call in AVANCE because of the encapsulation of attributes and because parameters are passed by value in packet operations.

In AVANCE, if a programmer wants to create a type with instances that are persistent and shared, a packettype is created. The type describes the persistent representation of instances as a set of attributes. Such a set is maintained in a packet slice (see Section 18.2.1). Since a type may have supertypes and subtypes, a packet may have several such slices associated with it. One may think of each packet as having a stack of slices, each slice corresponding to a type of which the packet is an instance. Packettype inheritance in PAL should be thought of as inheritance of specification; thus even though we have multiple inheritance, only one occurrence of a slice belonging to a type is allowed for each packet.

In AVANCE, Reed's model is applied at the granularity of slices: the unit of synchronization and system version management is the packet slice. The unit of action on packets is the packet operation. Synchronization is therefore applied to packet operations. Since each operation is bound to some type, this will give a binding to a corresponding slice of the packet.[22]

The AVANCE object manager caches versions of packet slices. Packet slice versions are fetched from secondary storage to the cache as they are needed for execution of packet operations. Thus, packet operations operate on the versions in the cache, and it is up to the object manager to maintain consistency between the cache and the repository on secondary storage. Each AVANCE process actually has its own cache, and there is a central coordinating process at each node that synchronizes the different cache managers in the AVANCE processes. Because each AVANCE process has its own cache, synchronization is needed only when versions are read and written between the repository and the different caches. The execution of packet operations in one AVANCE process is always sequential. Concurrency is introduced by generating more than one AVANCE process. The reads and writes of Reed's model are mapped in AVANCE to reads and writes of packet slices between the cache and repository.

It is the policy of the cache manager to minimize the traffic between secondary storage and the cache, and to ensure reliability and enable sharing (through the repository) when required. The cache manager writes new versions to secondary storage only when top-level transactions are to commit (for reliability), when a concurrent subtransaction is forked (for sharing), or when an AVANCE process terminates.

When a packet operation is invoked, the system normally prepares for access to three different packet slice versions in the cache.

1. The *InstalledType* version. This is where the code for the operation resides. The system must find the correct type version if there are several versions of the type object. This slice version is always made available. One cannot

---

[22] This does not mean that the binding of an invoked operation to a type is static. In AVANCE the binding can be made dynamic. We are saying that at either run-time or compile-time the binding will be made to one type and its corresponding slice.

execute an operation without having any instructions telling the system what to do! An operation will only read from the *InstalledType* version.

2. The read version. This is the latest version of the instance slice, created before the pseudo-time of this operation. An operation will only read from the read version. The read version may be omitted for some operations.

3. The write version. This is the new slice version to be generated by the operation. An operation may both read and write to the write version (in the cache). If the operation reads from an attribute it has not written, the value is taken from the read version. If the operation reads from an attribute it has already written, the value is taken from the write version. The write version may be omitted for some operations.

Since the read version and the write version may be omitted, there are four kinds of packet operations:

1. Read-only. The packet operation accesses attributes, but does not assign to them or apply modifying datatype operations to their values. The write version is omitted.

2. Independent. The packet operation only makes assignments to attributes, or assigns to attributes before using them. The read version is omitted.

3. Modifying (both read and write). The packet operation both reads and writes to attributes and makes some reads before writes. All three slice versions are needed.

4. No-instance. The packet operation does not access attributes. This means that it needs neither to see the previous version nor to write a new one. It does not use the persistency of the packet. Both the read version and the write version are omitted.

The first two classes of operation synchronize like the elementary reads and writes of Reed's model. Even though they are abstract operations executing what was (before compilation) perhaps hundreds of lines of code, they are in essence a simple read or a simple write of a packet slice version between the cache and the repository.[23]

The class of modifying operations needs both to access the current version for reading and to create a new version for writing. The basic synchronization protocol (R1 to R3 and W1 to W3) for both read and write is used.

The no-instance class does not need any synchronization. It is similar to what Hewitt has called an *unserialized actor* [Hewitt and deJong 1984],

---

[23] Many reads will not do an actual read on the repository, if the version is already present in the cache. Many writes may delay the actual write to the repository until necessary for reliability or sharing.

except that here it is not the packet (or actor) that is serializable or not, but the operation (or part of the behavior). Such an operation does not access the instance as such.

The classification of an operation into one of the four kinds is done automatically by the compiler, and this information is stored along with the code for the operation in the *InstalledType* slice version.

Both the read protocol (R1 to R3) and the write protocol (W1 to W3) are applied before execution of the operation starts. Thus, for the operations requiring a write version (modifying and independent operations) the write protocol (W1 to W3) is applied earlier than actually needed, and not when the actual write is done. This makes no difference for the class of independent operations, but for modifying operations it reduces the theoretical concurrency of the system.[24] We have made this choice because it simplifies the implementation, and because it easily provides for a seamless integration of a pessimistic concurrency mechanism [Penney et al. 1987]. It provides a means to get around the starvation problem mentioned earlier. A pessimistic concurrency mechanism is needed if we want to avoid the abort of long and complex operations, perhaps having interactive parts. It should be possible for a programmer to write applications, particularly interactive applications, so that access to some packets can be guaranteed (without aborts due to synchronization) before some part of the processing in an operation begins. Going through the write synchronization protocol when the modifying operation is invoked will either reserve a version of the packet slice itself or abort immediately. If the operation references other packets as part of its processing, it is possible for the programmer (if it is known which packets will be involved) to first execute a simple "touch" operation on the involved packets. This will logically create a new version of the referenced packet if the write protocol does not cause an immediate abort. If the touch operation succeeds, the programmer can invoke other modifying operations on all packets that have been touched (transitive closure) because:

- The programmer has been allowed to generate a version at some pseudo-time $t$ in the range of the current transaction $T_{i,j}(P)$; that is, $v_{c,t}$ and $v_{t,t}$ ($i \leq t \leq j$) have been accepted.

- No other transaction independent of $P$ will be allowed to make eductions overlapping the range $[i,j]$ before $P$ commits; they will either abort or wait on the outcome of $P$.

- Further operations in $T$ will have pseudo-times in the range $(t,j]$.

---

[24] Actually the situation is complicated by the possibility that a write operation may directly or indirectly invoke another operation on the same slice, creating the need for more than one write version for one invocation. The write protocol is then applied each time a new write version is needed.

- Operations of the independent class, executed in other independent transactions, may create versions of the involved objects at a pseudo-time later than $j$, but these will not interfere with $T$. There will always be a "hole" between $j$ and the pseudo-time of version creation for the versions generated by the other transactions.

**The Pseudo-Time Generator**    Since pseudo-time is an ordering correlated but not identical with real time, we do not need to have exact synchronization of the clocks on different hosts. It suffices that we always generate pseudo-time with an ever increasing value and an unambiguous ordering. In AVANCE pseudo-time is represented by a data structure having four components:

1. Clock-time. This is the time at a resolution of seconds as provided by the host physical machine. This time is set when a new pseudo-time range is generated. For example, when an independent top-level transaction is started, the clock-time is set to the current second. After it has been set, it is never altered for this pseudo-time range.

2. Process-id. This is an integer uniquely identifying an AVANCE process within a node. This value is set to the process-id of the AVANCE process creating a new pseudo-time range. After it has been set, it is never altered.

3. Node-id. This is an integer uniquely identifying a node in the decentralized AVANCE system. This value is set to the node-id of the node where the pseudo-time range is created. After it has been set, it is never altered.

4. Sub-id. This is a variable-length list of integers, initially of length one. As more resolution is needed, the length of the list is increased. Within a transaction, the currently least significant integer is incremented before and after the invocation of a subtransaction. The subtransaction does the same for its subtransactions. If the subtransaction is executed concurrently, then the resolution (the length of the list) is increased by one before the pseudo-time is given to the subtransaction. This ensures that the subtransaction will execute in an exclusive range of pseudo-time.

The process-id and node-id components are used to distinguish between transactions that "accidentally" started within the same second wherever they start in the system. A given node-id and process-id uniquely identify an AVANCE process in the overall decentralized system. Within an AVANCE process, clock-time is guaranteed to increase by at least one second for every new generation of a pseudo-time range. Thus the three components of clock-time, process-id, and node-id are guaranteed to define an exclusive pseudo-time in the global ordering. The sub-id component is then used to provide a monotonically increasing clock, where each "tick" can be taken at an arbitrarily deep level of resolution.

**Pruning the System Version Sequence**   Reed's model was used in the implementation of the distributed data storage system SWALLOW [Svobodova 1981]. This system was built assuming a large and inexpensive *write-once* storage as part of the repository, for example, an optical disk. In principle, the object versions were never to be deleted, but a mechanism for moving infrequently accessed objects and old versions offline was presented.

In AVANCE, the repository is designed without assuming write-once storage. The use of immutable system versions of packet slices was introduced mainly to provide reliability and consistency in a decentralized system. What is needed is not to keep all system versions forever, but only to keep them for as long as they are needed to make transactions reliable and consistent. Of course, it may still be useful for some applications to keep old system versions; and indeed they are allowed to do so, but in this case it is up to the application to prune versions. If no special action is taken by applications to save system versions, then they will be pruned sooner or later by the system.

The life of an AVANCE node cycles through a sequence of phases in which it is closed, initializing, open, or closing. The administrator responsible for a node decides when a node is to move from one phase to another unless the node crashes, in which case it effectively moves to the closed phase. It is only in the open phase that a node may accept requests to start new transactions, either local transactions or transactions that are initiated from requests on other nodes. While in the open phase, a node will keep all versions generated by committed transactions, and the repository will continually grow. In the closing phase the node waits for all on-going transactions to either commit or abort. In the initializing phase the node performs any recovery operations needed after a crash and, if the node administrator wishes, does a *cleanup*. This cleanup deletes all older versions of packet slices, unless they have been explicitly requested to be retained.

The *cleanup* operation solves the major part of the system version pruning problem, but not all of it. Furthermore, it does not solve the repository garbage-collection problem. The last version of a packet slice is always kept, even if the packet is "garbage" (not reachable). The repository garbage-collection problem is simplified by the packettype/datatype distinction. For transient objects needed for some computation, the programmer will often have used datatype values and only assigned them to variables (not the attributes of a packet). Such objects will not "pollute" the repository, since only packets are persistent.

A mark-and-sweep algorithm can be used for the repository garbage-collection problem. This algorithm could be executed either in the initializing phase as part of the cleanup operation, or in the open phase in parallel with on-going transactions.

We are also considering the introduction of a mechanism for moving infrequently used packets and versions offline to archival storage, in a way similar to SWALLOW [Svobodova 1981].

## SUMMARY

Several aspects of version control in the AVANCE architecture have been described. In particular, three kinds of version control have been discussed: how to keep track of the historical states of an object; how to cope with object-type changes; and how to use object versions at the system level for system reliability, specifically concurrent transaction management and recovery.

The motivation for these different aspects of version control were discussed, after which an overview covering central concepts in AVANCE was presented in order to set the context for the chapter. In the overview, the AVANCE object model and the PAL programming language were introduced.

Three different techniques were presented for control of user-defined objects: 1) packet state history, 2) checkpoint versions, and 3) complex versions. In addition, a technique for controlling evolving objecttype definitions was described.

Finally, a context for concurrency control and crash recovery was set by a description of Reed's synchronization model. Thereafter the AVANCE concurrency control scheme (based on Reed's model) was discussed.

## ACKNOWLEDGMENT

This work is supported by the National Swedish Board for Technical Development (STU).

## REFERENCES

[ANSI 1978] ANSI, "The ANSI/X3/SPARC DBMS Framework: Report of the Study Group on Data Base Management Systems," in *Information Systems 3*, ed. D.C. Tsichritzis and A. Klug, 1978.

[Ahlsén et al. 1983] M. Ahlsén, A. Björnerstedt, S. Britts, C. Hultén and L. Söderlund, "Making Type Changes Transparent," *Proceedings of IEEE Workshop on Languages for Automation*, Chicago, November 7-9, 1983. Also available as Syslab Report No. 22.

[Ahlsén et al. 1984] M. Ahlsén, A. Björnerstedt, S. Britts, C. Hultén and L. Söderlund, "An Architecture for Object Management in OIS," *ACM Transactions on Office Information Systems*, vol. 2, no. 3, July 1984. Presented at ACM SIGOA Conference 1984.

[Ahlsén et al. 1987] M. Ahlsén, A. Björnerstedt, S. Britts and S. Paulsson, "PAL Reference Manual," WP No 125, SYSLAB, University of Stockholm, Stockholm, Sweden, 1987.

[Banerjee et al. 1987a] J. Banerjee, H. Chou, J.F. Garza, W. Kim, D. Woelk, N. Ballou and H. Kim, "Data Model Issues for Object-Oriented Applications," *ACM Transactions on Office Information Systems*, vol. 5, no. 1, pp. 3–26, January 1987.

[Banerjee et al. 1987b] J. Banerjee, W. Kim, H. Kim and H. Korth, "Semantics and Implementation of Schema Evolution in Object-Oriented Databases," *ACM SIGMOD Proceedings*, pp. 311–322, San Francisco, May 1987.

[Bernstein and Goodman 1981] P.A. Bernstein and N. Goodman, "Concurrency Control in Distributed Database Systems," *ACM Computing Surveys*, vol. 13, no. 2, pp. 185–222, June 1981.

[Bernstein and Goodman 1983] P.A. Bernstein and N. Goodman, "Multiversion Concurrency Control—Theory and Algorithms," *ACM Transactions on Database Systems*, vol. 8, no. 4, pp. 465–483, December 1983.

[Birtwistle et al. 1973] G. Birtwistle, O-J Dahl, B. Myhrhaug, and K. Nygaard, *Simula Begin*, Auerbach, Philadelphia, 1973.

[Björnerstedt and Britts 1988] A. Björnerstedt and S. Britts, "AVANCE: An Object Management System," WP-124, SYSLAB, University of Stockholm, Stockholm, Sweden, March 1988.

[Carey and Muhanna 1986] M.J. Carey and W.A. Muhanna, "The Performance of Multiversion Concurrency Control Algorithms," *ACM Transactions on Computer Systems*, vol. 4, no. 4, pp. 338–378, November 1986.

[Chou and Kim 1986] H.T. Chou and W. Kim, "A Unifying Framework for Version Control in a CAD Environment," DB-066-86, MCC, February 1986.

[Eswaran et al. 1976] K.P. Eswaran, J.N. Gray, R.A. Lorie, and I.L. Traiger, "The Notions of Consistency and Predicate Locks in a Database System," *Communications of the ACM*, vol. 19, no. 11, pp. 624–633, November 1976.

[Goldberg and Robson 1983] A. Goldberg and D. Robson, *Smalltalk-80: The Language and its Implementation*, Addison-Wesley, Reading, MA, 1983.

[Gray 1978] J.N. Gray, "Notes on Database Operating Systems," in *Operating Systems*, ed. R. Bayer, R.M. Graham, and G. Seegmuller, pp. 393–481, Springer-Verlag, Berlin, 1978.

[Hewitt and deJong 1984] C. Hewitt and P. deJong, "Open Systems," in *On Conceptual Modelling*, ed. M.L. Brodie, J. Mylopoulos, and J.W. Schmitt, pp. 147–164, Springer-Verlag, New York, 1984.

[Hoare 1974] C.A.R. Hoare, "Monitors: An Operating System Structuring Concept," *Communications of the ACM*, vol. 17, no. 10, pp. 549–557, October 1974.

[Jefferson 1985] D.R. Jefferson, "Virtual Time," *ACM Transactions on Programming Languages and Systems*, vol. 7, no. 3, pp. 404–425, July 1985.

[Katz et al. 1986] R.H. Katz, E. Chang, and R. Bhateja, "Version Modeling Concepts for Computer-Aided Design Databases," *ACM SIGMOD Proceedings*, pp. 379–386, Washington DC, June 1986.

[Klahold et al. 1986] P. Klahold, G. Schlageter, and W. Wilkes, "A General Model for Version Management in Databases," *Proceedings VLDB*, pp. 319–327, Kyoto, Japan, August 1986.

[Kohler 1981] W.H. Kohler, "A Survey of Techniques for Synchronization and Recovery in Decentralized Computer Systems," *ACM Computing Surveys*, vol. 13, no. 2, pp. 149–183, June 1981.

[Liskov et al. 1981] B. Liskov, R. Atkinson, T. Bloom, E. Moss, J.C. Schaffert, R. Scheifler, and A. Snyder, *CLU Reference Manual*, Springer-Verlag, Berlin, Heidelberg, 1981.

[Liskov and Scheifler 1983] B. Liskov and R. Scheifler, "Guardians and Actions: Linguistic Support for Robust, Distributed Programs," *ACM Transactions on Programming Languages and Systems*, vol. 5, no. 3, pp. 381–404, July 1983.

[Papadimitriou and Kanellakis 1984] C.H. Papadimitriou and P.C. Kanellakis, "On Concurrency Control by Multiple Versions," *ACM Transactions on Database Systems*, vol. 9, no. 1, pp. 89–99, March 1984.

[Penney et al. 1987] D.J. Penney, J. Stein, and D. Maier, "Is the Disk Half Full or Half Empty? Combining Optimistic and Pessimistic Concurrency Mechanisms in a Shared, Persistent Object Base," *Workshop on Persistent Object Systems: Their Design, Implementation and Use*, Appin, Scotland, August 1987.

[Penney and Stein 1987] D.J. Penney and J. Stein, "Class Modification in the GemStone Object-Oriented DBMS," *Proceedings of the Second ACM Conference on Object-Oriented Programming Systems, Languages and Applications*, pp. 111–117, Orlando, FL, October 1987.

[Randell et al. 1978] B. Randell, P.A. Lee and P.C. Treleaven, "Reliability Issues in Computing System Design," *ACM Computing Surveys*, vol. 10, no. 2, pp. 123–165, June 1978.

[Reed 1978] D.P. Reed, "Naming and Synchronization in a Decentralized Computer System," MIT/LCS/TR-205, MIT Laboratory for Computer Science, Cambridge, MA, September 1978.

[Reed 1983] D.P. Reed, "Implementing Atomic Actions on Decentralized Data," *ACM Transactions on Computer Systems*, vol. 1, no. 1, pp. 3–23, February 1983.

[Schwarz and Spector 1984] P.M. Schwarz and A.Z. Spector, "Synchronizing Shared Abstract Types," *ACM Transactions on Computer Systems*, vol. 2, no. 3, pp. 223–250, August 1984.

[Sinha et al. 1985] M.K. Sinha, P.D. Nanadikar, and S.L. Mehndiratta, "Time-stamp Based Certification Schemes for Transactions in Distributed Database Systems," *ACM SIGMOD Proceedings*, pp. 402–411, 1985.

[Skarra and Zdonik 1987] A. Skarra and S. Zdonik, "Type Evolution in an Object-Oriented Database," in *Research Directions in Object-Oriented Programming*, ed. B. Shriver and P. Wegner, pp. 393–415, MIT Press, Cambridge, Massachusetts, 1987.

[Snodgrass and Ahn 1985] R. Snodgrass and I. Ahn, "A Taxonomy of Time in Databases," *ACM SIGMOD Proceedings*, pp. 236–246, 1985.

[Stein 1987] L.A. Stein, "Delegation Is Inheritance," *Proceedings of the Second ACM Conference on Object-Oriented Programming Systems, Languages and Applications*, pp. 138–146, Orlando, FL, October 1987.

[Svobodova 1981] L. Svobodova, "A Reliable Object Oriented Data Repository for a Distributed Computer System," *Proceedings of the Eighth Symposium on Operating System Principles*, pp. 47–58, 1981.

[Weihl 1987] W.E. Weihl, "Distributed Version Management for Read-Only Actions," *IEEE Transactions on Software Engineering*, vol. SE-13, no. 1, pp. 55–64, January 1987.

[Zdonik 1984] S.B. Zdonik, "Object Management System Concepts," *ACM SIGOA Conference on Office Information Systems*, pp. 13–19, Toronto, Canada, June 1984.

[Zdonik 1985] S.B. Zdonik, "An Object Management System for Office Applications," in *Languages for Automation*, ed. S.K. Chang, pp. 197–222, Plenum Press, New York, 1985.

[Zdonik 1986] S.B. Zdonik, "Maintaining Consistency in a Database with Changing Types," *ACM SIGPLAN Notices*, vol. 21, no. 10, pp. 120–127, October 1986. Reprints from the Object-Oriented Programming Workshop, June 9–13, 1986.

# 19

# A Distributed Object Manager for the Smalltalk-80 System

Dominique Decouchant

## INTRODUCTION

This chapter describes the design of a distributed object manager that allows several Smalltalk-80 systems to share objects over a local area network. This object manager is based on the following principles: location transparency and uniform object naming, unique object representation and use of symbolic links for remote access, possibility of object migration, and distributed garbage collection.

The object model has received considerable attention in recent years as a means for structuring distributed systems. The design of an experimental investigation of an object-based distributed system can be conceived along two main lines:

1. Design a new language (or even a whole operating system) based on an object model, and implement such a language (or at least the kernel of a distributed operating system).

After Decouchant, "Design of a Distributed Object Manager for the Smalltalk-80 System," OOPSLA '86, Special Issue of the SIGPLAN Notices Volume 22, Number 12, December 1987.

2. Extend an existing object-based language with the facilities that would allow its use in a distributed environment.

The first approach has been taken in several projects (e.g., Argus [Liskov 1982; Liskov 1984] and Eden [Almes et al. 1985; Black 1985]). These projects are large-scale, resource-consuming efforts. In an environment with limited resources, we decided to take the second approach, that is, to start with an existing language. The choice of Smalltalk-80 [Goldberg and Robson 1983] was motivated by two considerations: First, Smalltalk-80 may be regarded as a paradigm for the definition of an object model, and second, the language and its implementation are well documented, and the source code of an implementation of a Smalltalk system (Berkeley Smalltalk) was available.

The objective of the project was to design a distributed object manager, which could eventually be used on a network of personal workstations. This manager would replace the original object manager of the Smalltalk-80 system, thus allowing the users of several such systems to share objects, to perform remote execution, or to store objects in a repository.

As presented in [Bennett 1987; McCullough 1987], it is possible to define proxy objects as full-fledged Smalltalk objects. Thus, proxy objects are instances of a Smalltalk Class named "Proxy" (virtual image modifications). These solutions need few modifications of the standard standalone Smalltalk system, whereas the solution explained in this chapter implies important modifications of the interpreter and the object manager levels (no virtual image modifications). This choice prevents the Smalltalk user of a site from seeing and modifying proxy objects (Smalltalk does not manage object space protection). In addition to making object distribution invisible, it seems natural not to have to implement proxy objects as standard Smalltalk objects.

The general layout of the object manager is represented in Fig. 19.1. In the original Smalltalk-80 system, object management is integrated in the byte-code interpreter, which runs on a centralized operating system. Our design separates the interpreter from the object manager, while preserving the interface between the interpreter and the virtual image defined in [Goldberg and Robson 1983]. The object manager is now distributed over several nodes of a local area network.

This chapter is organized as follows. Section 19.1 presents the general problems of object management in distributed systems: naming, sharing, migration, and garbage collection. Section 19.2 describes the design principles of the distributed object manager. The main implementation features are described in Section 19.3. Some conclusions and directions for future work are presented in the summary.

## 19.1 PROBLEMS OF DISTRIBUTED OBJECT MANAGEMENT

The development of distributed systems has been partly motivated by the desire to extend the limited set of shareable resources of a particular computer system to a large set of network resources. Resource sharing poses the problems of

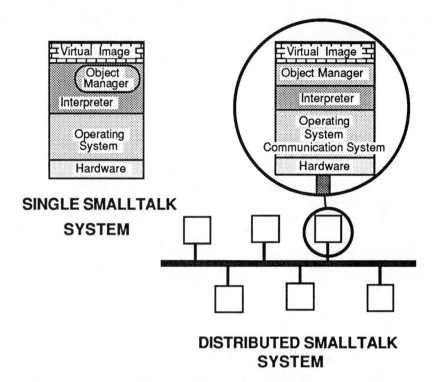

**FIGURE 19.1** ORGANIZATION OF THE DISTRIBUTED SMALLTALK SYSTEM

naming, protection, and consistency. While these problems have been resolved to a satisfactory extent for object-oriented centralized systems, they have not been adequately resolved for object-oriented distributed systems. In particular, the Smalltalk-80 system, initially designed for personal workstations, has no built-in facility for managing resources in a network of Smalltalk systems. Thus, this work addresses some Smalltalk-specific issues for object-oriented distributed programming.

In a Smalltalk system, the elementary manageable resource is an object. As a result, resource sharing in a Smalltalk network concerns the distributed management of objects. Distributed object management can be achieved by a collection of cooperating local object managers. Each local object manager runs on a particular workstation, is in charge of the objects that are local to the workstation, and cooperates with remote object managers to achieve the distributed sharing of objects.

Problems that result from object sharing, such as naming, protection, and consistency, are amplified by the facilities inherent in distribution. These are well-known problems in the area of distributed systems and databases (e.g., [Tanenbaum and Mullender 1983; Tanenbaum 1985; Stonebraker et al. 1976; Mohan et al. 1986]). In particular, facilities such as remote access, dynamic migration of objects, and dynamic connections and disconnections of workstations dramatically increase the complexity of distributed management of objects. In the following subsections, attention is focused on the problems we have identified so far.

### 19.1.1 Naming

In general, naming provides users with a mechanism for designating objects without any concern for their physical location. Similarly, naming in a distributed environment allows objects to be designated without specifying their actual site of residence. Such object naming is a type of virtual naming (as opposed to physical naming).

Although location independence is generally desirable, virtual naming removes the possibility of direct control of an object's location. For example, a user may want to force the migration of a particular object to a specific site for explicit transfer or for taking advantage of real parallelism. In short, an appropriate naming mechanism should be location-independent while providing the user with facilities for controlling object location when needed.

### 19.1.2 Access

Access to objects is either local or remote. An access is local when the object is at the same site as the caller. It is remote when the object is located at a different site from the caller. Problems related to local access have been resolved satisfactorily in our implementation of Smalltalk virtual memory (see Section 19.3). Remote access can be handled in two ways: either an effective remote access is performed and the object does not migrate, or a local access is performed and the object is forced to migrate between the calling and resident sites. Migrations used in this context are only temporary migrations needed to perform a local access on a shared remote object. Round trips can be avoided by migrating a copy of the object. Object replication induces an overhead whose cost in terms of space and computation may exceed migration costs (Smalltalk objects in particular being small). The choice between actual remote access or local access with migration depends on communication load, object size, and application requests.

### 19.1.3 Protection

Protection is usually concerned with detection of unauthorized access. Unauthorized access may be performed by a program that, maliciously or not, has confiscated some "strategic" data belonging to another program; to do so, the malicious program first reads data and acquires the capabilities of the victim program. Then, it can access some secret information or randomly perform some kind of sabotage. In distributed environments, the problem is amplified by resource migration. In particular, a resource may migrate to a new site, which must then be responsible for protecting this resource.

Protection in general purpose systems, such as time-sharing systems, is difficult to achieve. In these systems, entities are organized as large collections of information and tied to a unique entity, the process. As a result, once the capabilities of a process have been confiscated, unintended access can easily propagate through a large amount of information. Conversely, in object-oriented systems such as Smalltalk, the fine granularity of data and programs, in the form of independent objects, provides a natural framework for protection.

### 19.1.4 Memory Allocation and Garbage Collection

In the previous paragraphs, we observed that object-oriented systems are well suited to the management of resource sharing. However, these systems are intensive object consumers: objects are allocated and released with high frequency. Moreover, they are organized in graph structures that express reference relationships. As a result, a Smalltalk system can rapidly be congested by unused objects if these are not reclaimed by a garbage collector.

Garbage collection consists of detecting unused objects and reclaiming the memory space allocated to these objects. It implies costly graph traversals that may be prohibitive in the absence of optimization. In addition, garbage collection is interleaved with foreground processing. This interleaving may result in unexpectedly long response times for the user. Ungar [Ungar 1984a] has addressed this problem and proposed "generation scavenging." Generation scavenging is based on a hierarchy of object generations: if an object survives a garbage collection, it is made older and is classified in the immediate upper generation. It is no longer subject to on-line reclaiming if it belongs to the root generation. The root generation contains all the Smalltalk objects that are declared as persistent by the object manager. This solution has been investigated for centralized systems but needs to be adapted to deal with migrations.

## 19.2 OBJECT MANAGER DESIGN PRINCIPLES

So far, we have identified the problems posed by the management of objects in a local network of Smalltalk workstations. In this section, we present the design principles that we have adopted to solve these problems.

Our object manager is implemented as a collection of cooperating local object managers. A local object manager runs on each workstation and provides the programmer with a collection of primitives. These primitives allow objects to be named and shared objects without the programmer being aware of their actual location. In addition, the object manager provides such features as migration, garbage collection, and connection/disconnection of sites.

### 19.2.1 Basic Design Decisions

**Remote References and Proxy Objects**   The central design principle is physical location transparency. An object name is always a pointer to a local object. More precisely, if an object $O1$ holds a name $N$ to reference another object $O2$, $N$ always identifies an object localized at the same site as $O1$. For remote references, we introduce a particular type of object, the "proxy" object [Shapiro 1986], that locally represents a remote object. As shown in Fig. 19.2, $O2$ is located at site $B$ and a proxy object is created at site $A$ to serve as a local representative of the remote $O2$.

In addition, if $O3$ at site $A$ also references $O2$, it uses the same proxy object as $O1$. This solution has been adopted to ensure correctness and homogeneity of the Smalltalk-80 image. The migration algorithm, detailed in the next section, also enforces this property.

A proxy is part of the private data of the object manager. It has two fields that describe a remote object: the resident site of the remote object and the virtual pointer to the object in the resident site. When the referenced object migrates, the contents of the referencing object are not modified; instead, the proxy is updated by the object manager. In addition to physical location invisibility, the proxy preserves the local consistency of reference counts. A proxy is functionally equivalent to a UNIX link, except that a proxy is not visible to the programmer. It is a private data structure that is manipulated by the object manager like any other Smalltalk object for swapping, garbage collection, and memory relocation.

Given the notion of proxy for physical location independence, we now need to be precise about how to solve the following problems:

1. Migration of an object in a distributed system.

**FIGURE 19.2** PROXY OBJECT USAGE FOR REMOTE ACCESS

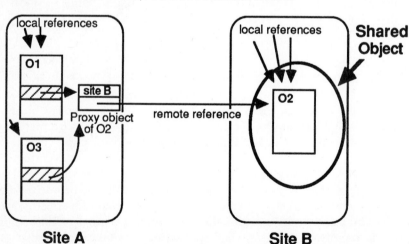

Site A                              Site B

2. Reference to a proxy object by another proxy object.

3. Distributed reclamation of circular structures. This is also an important task of a centralized object manager, but the problem is complicated by distribution. Figure 19.5 shows an elementary distributed circular structure.

4. Consistency of shared object access, and privileges of different systems to shared objects.

5. Dynamic system connection and disconnection protocols, and consistency of other systems connected to the network.

**Object Migration**   Several cooperating Smalltalk systems may need to share objects to implement a distributed application. Sharing can be achieved through remote or local access. Remote access is performed through the "proxy" mechanism. For efficiency reasons, access to a remote object may be transformed into a local access by replication or migration of the desired object. But, as in Fig. 19.3, in the case of the migrated object $O1$, previously local references can become remote references, and degrade performance of objects on site $B$ that reference it. The migration of an object is independent from changes in its ownership. In a Smalltalk environment, object replication is not appropriate. Given the object size and the high rate of object creation and deletion, the cost of managing replicated objects would be prohibitive.

Object migration consists of moving a real object from one workstation to another. A real object is an entity explicitly manipulatable by the user. When a real object migrates, it is replaced by a proxy object in the source workstation. A real object may come back to its previous site and then migrate again. Therefore, when migrating an object, it is necessary to check for the existence of a proxy object for the migrated object in the destination workstation. If a proxy already exists, the real object and its proxy are exchanged. The real object moves to its new site and takes the proxy object's name. A proxy object replaces the real object in the source workstation and references the real object through the network; this is necessary to avoid updating of objects that referenced the migrated object. As shown in Fig. 19.3, object $O1$ of site $B$ moves to site $A$. On site $B$, a proxy object replaces $O1$ and takes its name to keep the local references unchanged. It is important to note that the $O1$ references to $O2$ and $O3$ are modified in the same way: proxy objects for $O2$ and $O3$ are created on site $A$ to reference them.

In addition, when an object migrates from $A$ to $B$, then to $C$ and so on, all the proxy objects on each site should point to the current residence site. However, a particular site updating must be deferred until a remote access is attempted with its proxy object. Figures 19.6a, 19.6b, and 19.6c illustrate proxy automatic updating.

**Storage Management and Garbage Collection**   Functional and object-oriented languages impose a heavy load on storage management. In Smalltalk, memory

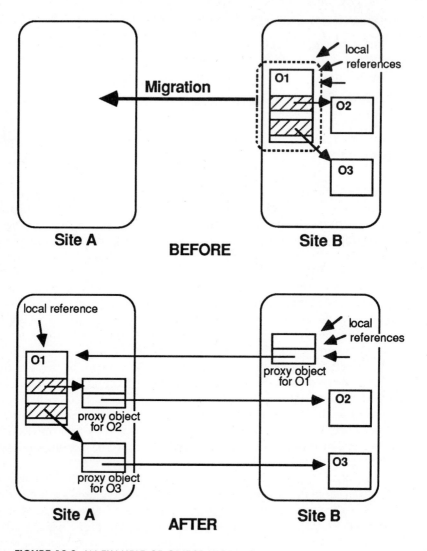

**FIGURE 19.3** AN EXAMPLE OF OBJECT MIGRATION

requests are very frequent and fragment the memory into a vast number of small pieces; paging systems being ill-suited to these types of request, the object is used as the unit for storage management. The main storage is allocated by using a buddy-system scheme. Free memory blocks are split up and recombined according to the rule

$$L(i) = L(i-1) + L(i-k)$$

where $L(i)$ represents the block size of level $i$, and $k$ is a parameter (the "splitting order") that allows us the selection from several algorithms:

$k = 1$ Binary buddy system:

$$L(i) = L(i-1) + L(i-1)$$

The block size series is: 1  1  2  4  8  16  32  64  128...

$k = 2$ Fibonacci buddy system:

$$L(i) = L(i-1) + L(i-2)$$

The block size series is: 1  1  1  2  3  5  8  13  21  34  55  79...

$k = 6$ Buddy system of order 6:

$$L(i) = L(i-1) + L(i-6)$$

The block size series is: 1  1  1  1  1  1  2  3  4  5  6  7  9  12  16  21  27  34  43  55  71...

By example, suppose that the "splitting order" is fixed to 2 (Fibonacci buddy system). For a request of 14 memory units, it is necessary to allocate a block of 21 memory units. If no block of the requested size exists, a big one may be split. Now suppose that a block of 79 memory units exists. First it is split into two blocks of 34 and 55 memory units. Next the smallest (34 memory units) is split into two blocks of 13 and 21 memory units, and the block of size 21 is allocated.

Large values of the splitting order allow a finer control over the size of the blocks. Since most Smalltalk objects are small, a fairly high order ($k = 9$ or 10) may be a good choice. This solution and its advantages are presented in [Peterson and Norman 1977; Shen and Peterson 1974]. This algorithm allows efficient allocation and deallocation, and reduces internal and external fragmentation. Internal fragmentation results from allocating memory in predefined block sizes. More precisely, it results from allocating a larger block size than the requested size because the requested size does not exist in the buddy-system series. External fragmentation results from splitting the free memory into blocks that can be recombined only if they are "buddies."

Our implementation of storage management is based on the following decisions:

- a hashing function over the pointer value of the objects, for the topography function (object localization in main memory)

- LRU (Least Recently Used) for the replacement algorithm

We need now to consider the effects of dynamic linking, remote object access, and object migration on the storage management policy.

In a Smalltalk system, an object exists if its reference count (i.e., the number of objects that are currently using it) is not zero. An object is garbage collected for the reclamation of storage when its reference count reaches zero. In a distributed Smalltalk system, an object may be used by local or remote objects.

In order to maintain the reference mechanism for managing object existence in a distributed system, it is necessary to introduce a new reference count for each real object: the remote reference count. The value of this count is the number of proxy objects that reference the real object. It is less than or equal to the total number of referencing objects. Figure 19.4 illustrates this. Thus, our approach introduces two levels of garbage collection: local and distributed storage reclamation.

**Local Reclamation**     In Section 19.1.4, we introduced a convenient solution for storage reclamation on a centralized Smalltalk system, generation scaveng-

**FIGURE 19.4** POSSIBLE STATES AND REFERENCE COUNTS OF AN OBJECT

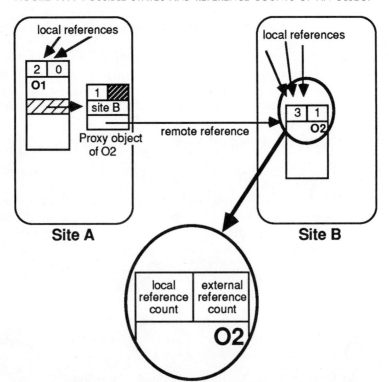

ing. This storage reclamation algorithm matches object evolution well and is convenient for local garbage collection. This algorithm has been implemented on the Berkeley Smalltalk (BS) version of Smalltalk-80 [Ungar et al. 1984b]. Other garbage collection techniques are explained in [Almes 1980; Bobrow 1980; Christopher 1984; Deutsch and Bobrow 1976; Dijkstra et al. 1978; Lieberman and Hewitt 1983].

**Distributed Reclamation**   A major problem with garbage collection is reclaiming distributed circular structures. As described in Fig. 19.5, distributed circular structures may result from object sharing and object migrations. Suppose that initially $O1$ and $O2$ are unique elements of a linked list located on site $B$. During execution, $O1$ moves to site $A$ (for example, to exploit the possibilities of parallelism), and later the application completes. This distributed circular structure remains, and must be reclaimed by a distributed garbage collection.

An elementary solution is based on distributed marking. Each workstation marks all accessible objects in its virtual image. When a proxy object is found, a marking request is transmitted to the resident site of the real object. The real object to which the proxy object points constitutes a new starting point of the marking process for its site. While remote marking may be done in the background, collecting is an expensive operation that degrades network performance.

Currently, no better solution to this problem has been reported. It constitutes an interesting and important topic for future research. Other solutions have been proposed in [Hughes 1985; Wiseman 1985; Shin and Malek 1985; Halstead 1985].

**FIGURE 19.5** EXAMPLE OF DISTRIBUTED CIRCULAR STRUCTURES

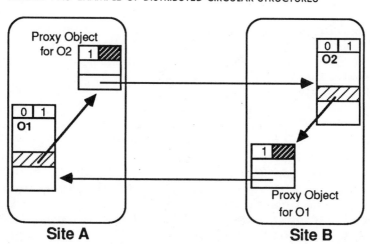

**Dynamic Connection and Disconnection**   One of the requirements for our distributed system is that individual workstations may be dynamically connected or disconnected. In order to ensure the global consistency of the system, specific operations must be performed at connect or disconnect time.

When a new site is connected, it broadcasts its readiness to communicate with the rest of the network. Thus the connection protocol is simple and easy to implement.

Site disconnection is more difficult for two major reasons. First, the disconnecting site may currently support objects owned by other sites. These objects need to be sent back to their owners, or to any other site ready to receive them for later use. Sending back objects is necessary to ensure a graceful disconnection; for traumatic disconnections, such as software or hardware errors, no satisfactory solution is available. Second, and more problematic, is the case where objects owned by the disconnecting site are currently present on other sites. Site $X$, one of these sites, may become disconnected later than the site that owns the object. What will happen if the owner site is reconnected before site $X$? In the same way as discussed previously, a trivial solution may be to send remote objects back to their owner site. However, this solution decreases object sharing possibilities. Solutions based on object read-only copy management or on object version management may be investigated.

A disconnecting site that owns a proxy to access a remote object is not informed of migration of the object that may take place after disconnection. So it is necessary for a site to update its proxy objects after reconnection. Two solutions are possible to satisfy this necessity:

1. An object migration automatically generates updates of all its associated proxy objects. Messages are sent to all sites (running or not). Messages to disconnected sites are stored until their reconnection. This solution may be expensive in terms of message storage.

2. Proxy updating is postponed until object access via each individual proxy. An access to an object with a proxy whose content is invalid (after the object migration) causes an automatic and transparent update of the proxy. This mechanism is illustrated by Fig. 19.6a, 19.6b, and 19.6c. Initially (Fig. 19.6a), site $X$ references a remote object $O1$ of site $B$ via a proxy object $P1$. During an eventual disconnection of site $X$, the real object $O1$ migrates from site $B$ to site $A$ (Fig. 19.6b). Thus, a proxy object $P1'$ now replaces $O1$ on site $B$ according to the migration mechanism presented earlier under "Object Migration." Proxy object $P1$ of site $X$ now is not correct because it references a proxy of site $B$ (not the real object $O1$). $P1$ remains incorrect while an access to $O1$ will be attempted. In this case, remote access to $O1$ via $P1$ will transparently update $P1$. Also, site $B$ may become disconnected between site $X$ disconnection and site $X$ reconnection. In this case, it is impossible to update $P1$.

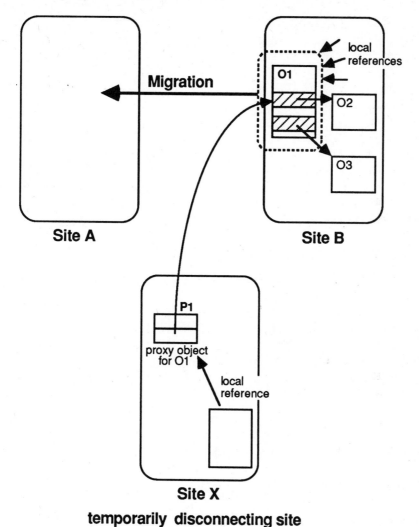

**FIGURE 19.6(a)** SITE STATES BEFORE O1 MIGRATION (SITE X BEING DISCONNECTED)

It is important to note that an individual site may not destroy one of its proxy objects without preliminary intersite consultations. Thus an individual proxy is a part of the global migration history and constitutes necessary information for proxy updating of other sites.

**Access Protection**  Access protection ensures that any access to an object is made in conformity with some stated rules of usage. Three levels of access protection may be defined:

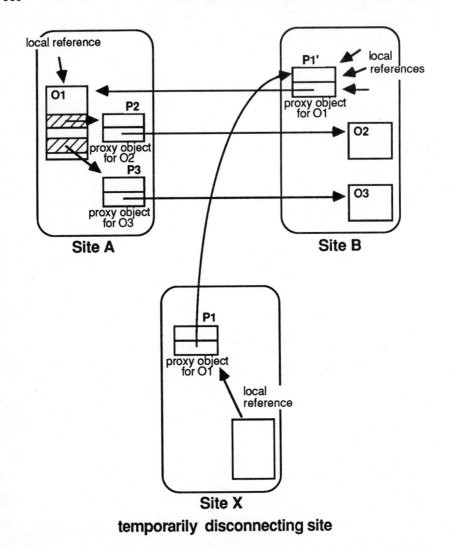

**FIGURE 19.6(b)** SITE STATES AFTER O1 MIGRATION (SITE X IS STILL DISCONNECTED)

1. Object protection provided by the Smalltalk access rules (i.e., the methods defined by the object's class), which is equivalent to abstract data type protection. This protection is ensured by the Smalltalk interpreter and will not be considered further.

2. Object rights for remote access control.

3. Protection of a site from unwanted remote access.

Object migration requires strict access control. To implement it, two additional fields are associated with each object. One of them represents read

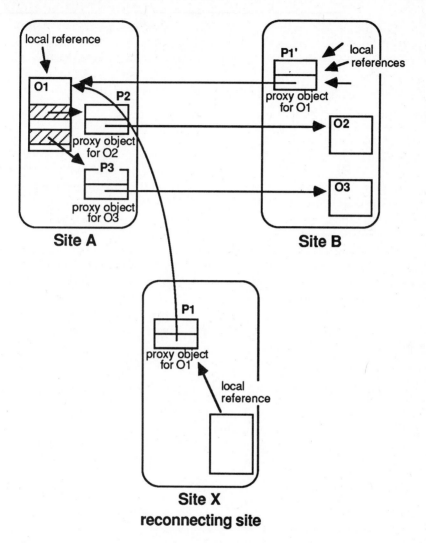

**FIGURE 19.6(c)** UPDATING OF SITE X PROXY AFTER ONE ACCESS

and write capabilities on this object by foreign sites. The second one is the name of the owner site. For homogeneity and performance reasons, a proxy object also has these two fields.

Thus, an access is correct if either the accessing site is the owner of the object, or the access rights (read, write, or execute) are sufficient for the attempted access when the site is not the owner site.

To protect each site against unwanted intrusion, we decided not to use the standard remote procedure call but to perform remote object access through a unique server process on each workstation. This process controls validity of the access and performs the access for the client site.

The protection indicators of the future instances are specified in the object model definition (class) and are automatically initialized at instantiation time. Protection rights are object attributes. This protection level is equivalent to the MULTICS [Organick 1972] or UNIX [Ritchie and Thompson 1974] protection systems in which access controls are performed for each elementary access.

However, a second level of protection that is better suited to the object-oriented execution model may be added to the first level. This protection is based on the observation that when a method (procedure) is executed on an object (receiver), only the fields of this object may be modified; modifications of other objects (parameters, local variables, and so forth) are possible only through message passing to these objects. Thus at compile time it is possible to detect whether a method modifies its receiver, and methods may be separated into two classes: read methods and write methods.

Access controls are then performed for each method invocation (object access fields are compared with access permissions needed by the method) instead of on individual access. If the system provides dynamic method linking, these controls must be performed at call time. If the system provides static method linking, these controls may be performed at compile time if modifications of object access rights are forbidden; otherwise, these controls must also be performed at run time.

### 19.2.2 Interface Specifications

The object memory level provides an interface to the objects that make up the Smalltalk-80 virtual image. The interpreter uses object pointers to access the objects. An object pointer is the system name of each object and is invisible at the application level. The interface provides the following types of primitives:

Internal and external reference counting

Access to the class pointer and length of an object

Access to elementary values (word, byte, integer)

Object creation

Object migration

Enumeration of the instances of a class

### 19.2.3 Organization of the Object Manager

Three processes cooperate to perform object management functions: the network manager, the main memory manager, and the secondary memory manager (see Fig. 19.7). In addition, several Smalltalk interpreter processes, which access the objects to perform Smalltalk actions, may be present at a site. These processes may be viewed as clients of the system.

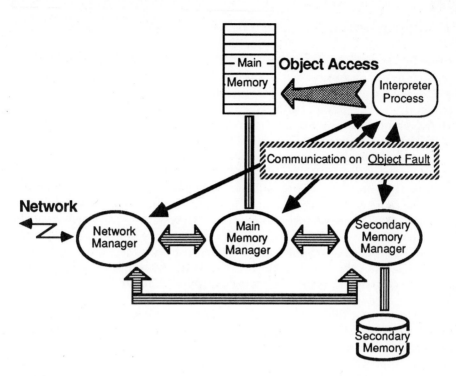

**FIGURE 19.7** SYSTEM PROCESSING MODEL

**The Network Manager (NM)**   The network manager is the master process of a Smalltalk site. It executes remote accesses on remote objects, performs and verifies local access requests from network manager of other sites, and controls the local processes.

**The Main Memory Manager (MMM)**   The main memory manager is in charge of object management in main memory (relocation, swapping, free space management, garbage collection, etc.). It resolves object faults by allocating free space for missing objects and sending object load requests to the secondary memory manager. After an object has been loaded, the main memory manager reactivates the Smalltalk interpreter process that caused the object fault.

**The Secondary Memory Manager (SMM)**   This process performs object management on secondary storage. This storage is actually represented by two files; one contains the Smalltalk object table (object descriptor table), and the other the object space (object information).

## 19.3 IMPLEMENTATION

In the above design, the objects located in main memory must be made accessible to all processes. A first implementation was done under UNIX 4.2 bsd, a system that does not allow memory sharing between processes. Consequently, it was not possible to implement this design by allocating one UNIX process for one Smalltalk process. The solution was to manage several "lightweight processes" in one UNIX process. Thus we implemented a UNIX process multiplexor MUX [Tricot 1987], which takes care of the scheduling among subtasks (lightweight processes). These processes communicate by messages through mailboxes. This solution [Decouchant 1986] was abandoned because of poor performance and the availability of UNIX System V [Thomas et al. 1986], which allows several processes to share memory and to be synchronized with semaphores. More precisely, the new implementation is developed on Sun2 and Sun3 computers that run with the Sun Operating System. This system is derived from Berkeley Unix 4.2 bsd to which some functionalities of UNIX System V (shared memory, semaphore, message queue, etc.) have been added.

The current implementation uses the shared memory mechanism: each Smalltalk process is represented by a UNIX process and accesses Smalltalk objects that are stored in a common block of shared memory. This block represents the real memory of the Smalltalk virtual machine. For this reason, the size of this block is fixed and allocated at system initialization. In addition, each process owns a message queue for communicating with other processes. This interprocess communication allows each message to be characterized by a type. For example, in a distributed object manager, the type of a message is the identifier of the sending process. The receiver process can select one or several message types; this is equivalent to selecting a subset of the senders.

This mechanism is sufficient to allow local communication within a Smalltalk site, but not communication with a remote site. For this reason, we use the UNIX 4.2 bsd "socket" mechanism [Leffler et al. 1983a; Leffler et al. 1983b] to provide the intersite communications. As a process cannot synchronize between these two communication mechanisms, an additional UNIX process (COM) is introduced to deal with network communications. This is necessary because network communication primitives (UNIX "recvFrom" and "select" primitives) may lock the receiver until information is available. This extra UNIX process takes charge of communications with other sites via sockets, and communicates with the Network Manager as follows.

The communications from the Network Manager to the COM process are done by a "socket" connection. Thus the COM process waits for communications from the network or from the Network Manager with a unique "select" operation, which allows a process to wait for information from several sockets. The "select" operation is a system call of UNIX 4.2 bsd.

The communication from the COM process to the Network Manager is done by message passing to the Network Manager message queue. The Network Manager waits for UNIX System V messages from the COM process.

The COM–Network Manager connection is dynamic and allows several Smalltalk implementations to run on the same computer. Thus, network communications may be simulated by "socket" communications, and workstation connections by mixed "socket/message queue" connections. Within each Smalltalk system, connections between managers are realized by "message queue" connections. Figure 19.8 illustrates interprocess communications within a distributed Smalltalk system, and the implementation of intersite communications.

### 19.3.1 Object Representation in Secondary Memory

In the initial version of the virtual image [Goldberg and Robson 1983], an object is identified by an object pointer, which is an index into the Object Table (OT). Each entry of this table is an object descriptor that contains the information that describes the object (pointers or immediate values, odd or even string size, and the location of the object value block), as in Fig. 19.9.

It is important to note that the original value block (defined in the standard Xerox implementation) includes two elements (the block value size and the object class pointer) that logically should be located in the object entry. The size is necessary for loading the object, and the object class pointer is required because it may be used to determine some specified processing on its state. For example, the state of an instance with a class pointer equal to "StringClassPointer" must be accessed by byte.

Our representation modifies the original implementation of Smalltalk (see Fig. 19.10) by moving the "size" and "classPointer" fields to the object descriptor (object entry in OT) and by adding the following new fields:

- **PX:** If this indicator is set, it means that the object is a proxy.

- **M:** This indicator is used during a garbage collection (either local to this site or global).

- **external reference count:** This is the number of sites that own a proxy for accessing the object. This count complements the internal reference count to define the object reclamation rule.

The internal reference count corresponds to the standard reference count of the centralized Smalltalk system. It allows an object to be reclaimed when it becomes zero. However, this rule is not sufficient for object reclamation in our system, because the object may be shared by other sites. The new reclamation rule must use the two reference counts, and may be defined as:

```
If isNotProxy(objectPointer)
    then
    /*Proxy objects must not be reclaimed because they
    make up the migration history*/
```

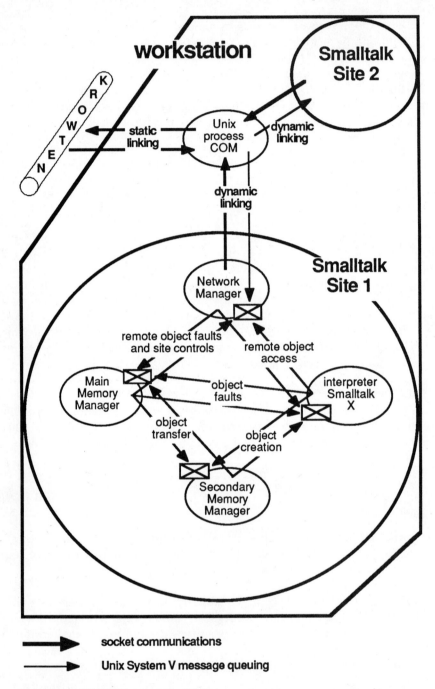

**FIGURE 19.8** SYSTEM IMPLEMENTATION

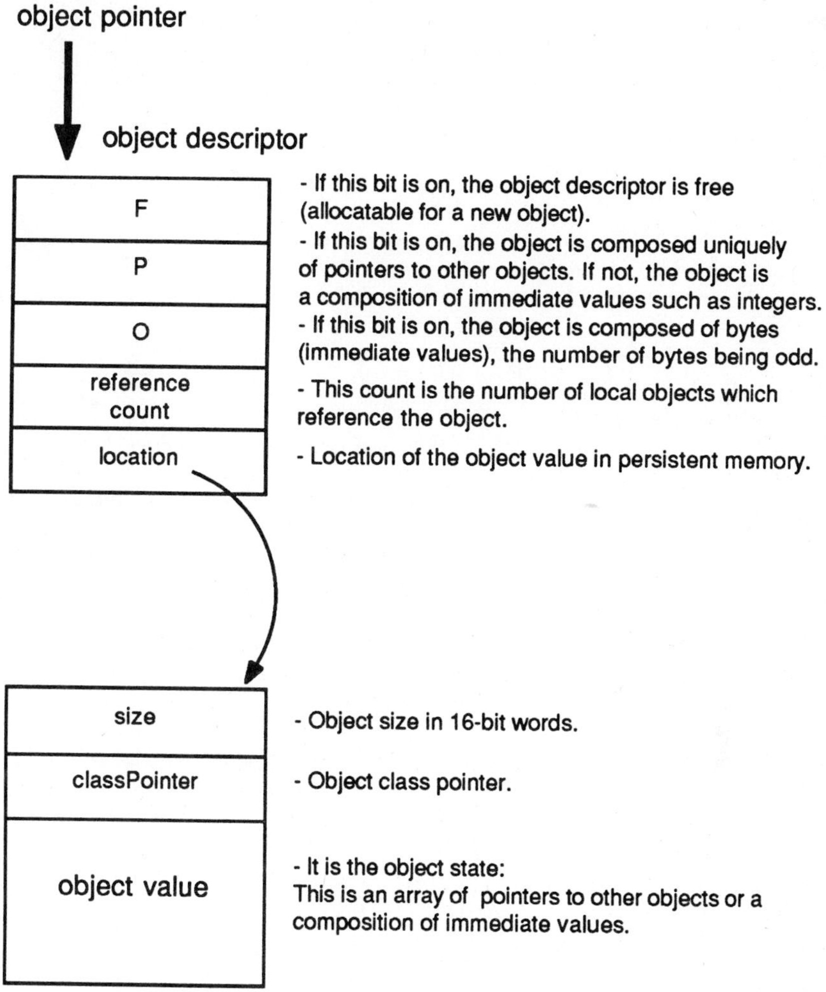

object pointer

object descriptor

| | |
|---|---|
| F | - If this bit is on, the object descriptor is free (allocatable for a new object). |
| P | - If this bit is on, the object is composed uniquely of pointers to other objects. If not, the object is a composition of immediate values such as integers. |
| O | - If this bit is on, the object is composed of bytes (immediate values), the number of bytes being odd. |
| reference count | - This count is the number of local objects which reference the object. |
| location | - Location of the object value in persistent memory. |

| | |
|---|---|
| size | - Object size in 16-bit words. |
| classPointer | - Object class pointer. |
| object value | - It is the object state: This is an array of pointers to other objects or a composition of immediate values. |

**FIGURE 19.9** INITIAL COMPOSITION OF THE VIRTUAL IMAGE

```
If externalReferenceCountOf(objectPointer) = 0
    then
    /* The object is no longer referenced and has never
    been referenced through the network. It is possible to
    reclaim it*/
    destroyObject(objectPointer);
    else
    /* Other sites use this object, but its actual resident
    site doesn't use it. This local reclamation comes down
    to its migration onto a new site which does use it. It
```

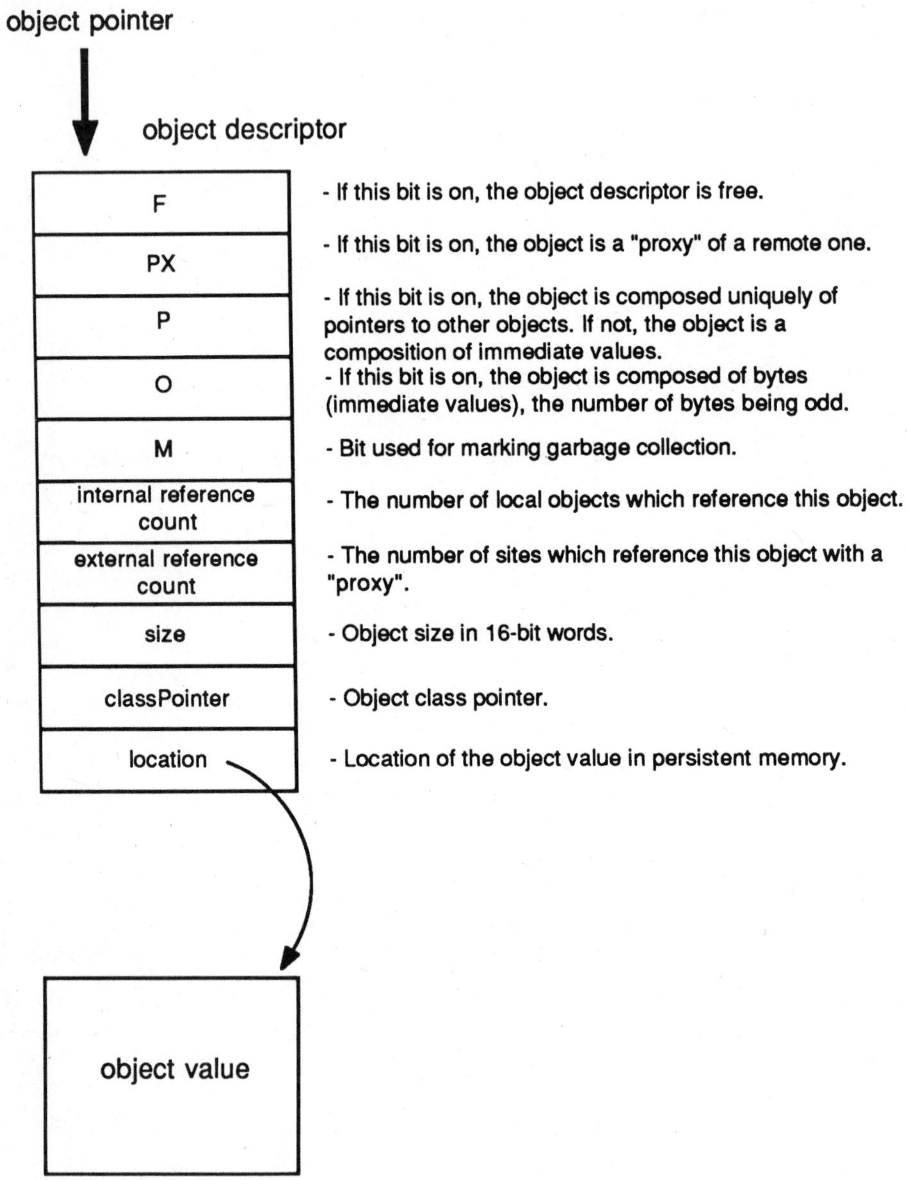

object pointer

object descriptor

| | |
|---|---|
| F | - If this bit is on, the object descriptor is free. |
| PX | - If this bit is on, the object is a "proxy" of a remote one. |
| P | - If this bit is on, the object is composed uniquely of pointers to other objects. If not, the object is a composition of immediate values. |
| O | - If this bit is on, the object is composed of bytes (immediate values), the number of bytes being odd. |
| M | - Bit used for marking garbage collection. |
| internal reference count | - The number of local objects which reference this object. |
| external reference count | - The number of sites which reference this object with a "proxy". |
| size | - Object size in 16-bit words. |
| classPointer | - Object class pointer. |
| location | - Location of the object value in persistent memory. |

object value

**FIGURE 19.10** THE NEW COMPOSITION OF THE VIRTUAL IMAGE

```
        is important to note that if the object is on its
        owner site then the site to which the object is
        migrated becomes the new object owner*/
        newSite:=determineANewLocationSiteFor(objectPointer);
        moveObjectTo(objectPointer,newSite);
    endIf
endIf
```

## 19.3.2 Object Representation in Main Memory

Objects are dynamically loaded into main memory upon access fault. Object moves between main memory and secondary memory are similar to segment moves in the standard segmented virtual memory. Thus a definition of an object management structure is needed for management of the object state, synchronization of accesses on each object, and object movements into main memory.

The object management structure is composed of two substructures: a set of object entries and a mapping structure. An object entry describes the object in memory and also includes additional information for object access synchronization and management. All the object entries are placed in an LRU (Least Recently Used) chain; during an access the object entry is moved to the head of the chain, and objects that must be swapped are chosen starting from the tail of the chain. The mapping structure is a standard hash table that associates an object pointer and an object entry memory address.

The object management and object entry structures are displayed in Figs. 19.11 and 19.12.

## 19.3.3 An Example of Proxy Use: the *fetchPointer* Primitive Realization

The "fetchPointer" primitive is a function of the object manager interface. This primitive executes a read operation of an object value block. The "fetch-Pointer" primitive format in Pascal-like form is:

**function** fetchPointer (anObject:objectPointer, fieldIndex:INTEGER): objectPointer;

It interprets the object value block as an array of object pointers and returns the *fieldIndex*-th object pointer field. This function is explained further in the next subsections. It is very important to note that a local object pointer must always be returned to the Smalltalk interpreter process in order to preserve the virtual image homogeneity and the local object naming of each site; the interpreter still runs inside a private local object set and does not see object distribution. In this way, the object manager executes hypothetical remote accesses, and returns the same results as if they were local.

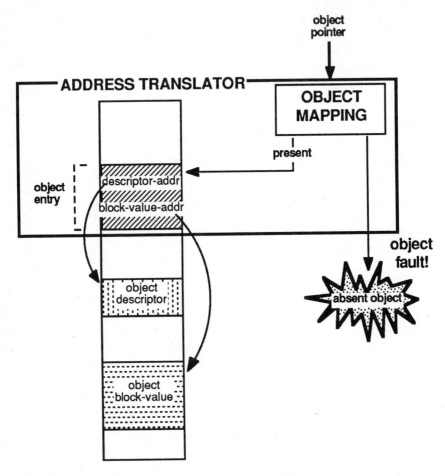

**FIGURE 19.11** OBJECT REPRESENTATION IN MAIN MEMORY

**The Object *anObject* is a Local (Real) Object**   This is the common case of the centralized Smalltalk-80 in which each object, except for the basic objects (integer, string, etc.), is an aggregate object. The returned object is simply the value of the *fieldIndex*-th object field, as shown in Fig. 19.13.

**The Object *anObject* is a Proxy**   Assume that "anObject" is a proxy object at site *A* that references the real object at site *B*. The problem is representing the result pointer (which is a local pointer of the remote site!) at site *A* (Fig. 19.14). This is made difficult by the fact that the result pointer may be stored in another object. Thus it is necessary to know the nature of the *fieldIndex*-th field of the remote real object. The Smalltalk process does not see the real object location, and accesses it as if it were local.

## object entry

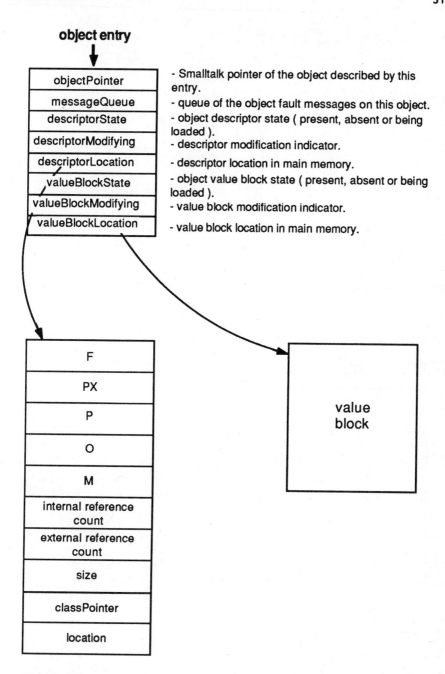

| | |
|---|---|
| objectPointer | - Smalltalk pointer of the object described by this entry. |
| messageQueue | - queue of the object fault messages on this object. |
| descriptorState | - object descriptor state ( present, absent or being loaded ). |
| descriptorModifying | - descriptor modification indicator. |
| descriptorLocation | - descriptor location in main memory. |
| valueBlockState | - object value block state ( present, absent or being loaded ). |
| valueBlockModifying | - value block modification indicator. |
| valueBlockLocation | - value block location in main memory. |

F

PX

P

O

M

internal reference count

external reference count

size

classPointer

location

value block

**FIGURE 19.12** OBJECT DESCRIPTION STRUCTURE

## LOCAL REFERENCE:

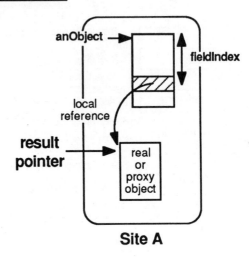

**Site A**

**FIGURE 19.13**

**FIGURE 19.14**

## REMOTE REFERENCE:

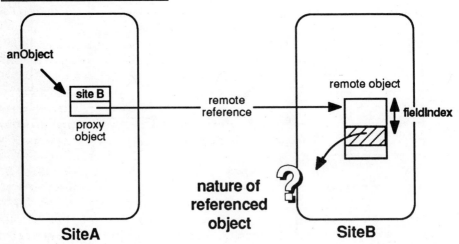

Three different cases are possible, depending on the nature of the value field:

1. a proxy object references a real object at site *A*

2. a proxy object references a real object at site *B*

3. a proxy object references a real object at a third site (*C*, for example)

These three possibilities are dealt with next.

**The Value Field References a Proxy of an Object at Site *A***   This is the simplest case. The value is a proxy of a real object located at site *A*. The result pointer returned to the Smalltalk process at site *A* is simply the pointer stored in the proxy object at site *B*. Figures 19.15 and 19.16 illustrate this case.

**The Value Field References a Local Real Object at Site *B***   The returned value of the "fetchPointer" primitive must be a local pointer at site *A*. Thus the value field of the object at site *B* may not be directly used at site *A*.

As shown in Figs. 19.17 and 19.18, it is necessary to create a proxy object at site *A* to reference the object named by the *fieldIndex*-th field of the remote object. This case illustrates the implicit creation and use of proxy objects. A read operation ("fetchPointer") may transparently create proxy objects to maintain the local homogeneity of each site.

**FIGURE 19.15**

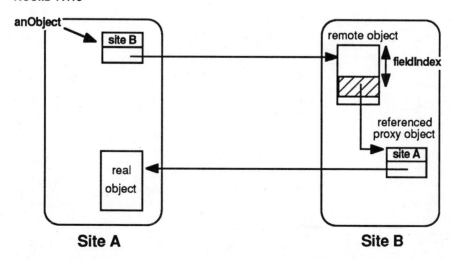

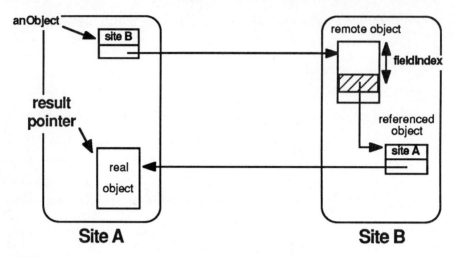

**FIGURE 19.16**

**The Value References a Proxy of an Object at Site C**   The *fieldIndex*-th field value is the pointer of a proxy object of site $B$ that references an object of another site $C$. As in the previous case, a proxy object must be created at site $A$ to reference the real object at site $C$ (Figs. 19.19 and 19.20).

**FIGURE 19.17**

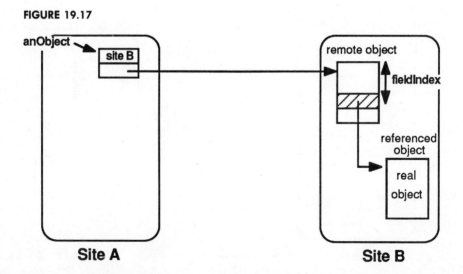

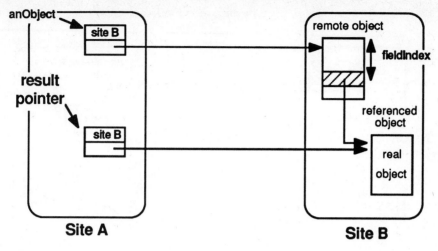

**FIGURE 19.18**

**FIGURE 19.19**

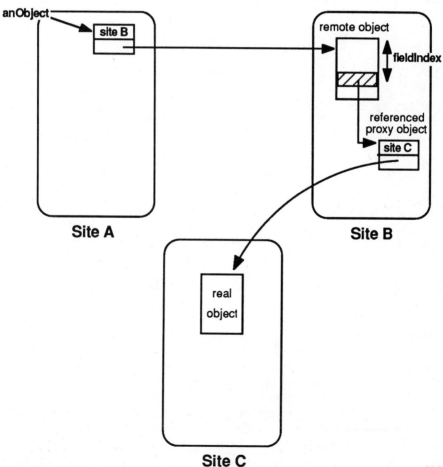

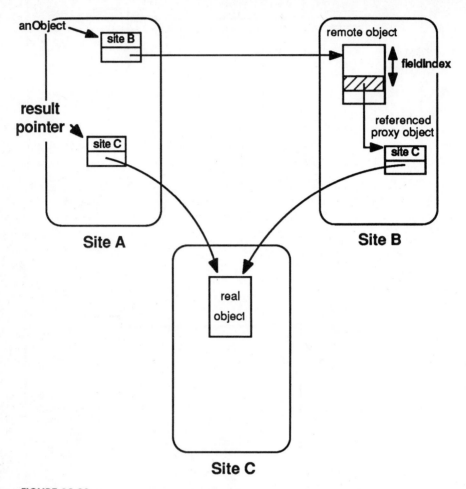

**FIGURE 19.20**

## SUMMARY

Our objective is to design a mechanism for object management in a distributed system composed of Smalltalk-80 workstations. Achieving this objective consists of two phases: a first phase in which we defined a centralized object manager, and a second phase that extends it to a distributed environment. This new object manager allows several Smalltalk systems to share objects on a local area network.

Smalltalk-80 is a very homogeneous system, and our goal was to maintain this homogeneity in a distributed environment. The distributed object manager design is based on the following guidelines:

- Location transparency, based on a uniform naming scheme

- Single copy objects, with remote access through symbolic links ("proxy" objects)

- Object migration, involving proxy updates

- Distributed garbage collection

A new object type, "the proxy object," has been defined. A proxy is a descriptor object that allows the real object to be located elsewhere in the network. The proxy notion may be viewed as an object-oriented extension of the standard remote procedure call mechanism [Birrell and Nelson 1984]. However, this mechanism allows objects in the network to be moved. In the virtual image, the proxy is managed in the same way as other Smalltalk objects. Basically, a Smalltalk object is a composition of object references. To maintain this reference structure, a proxy is accessed via a pointer as a real object. This allows access to a remote object as if it is local. Remote object access is automatically performed by an elementary proxy access and is invisible to the user. However, this homogeneity is not complete because proxy objects are not instances of a Smalltalk class; they are only internal and private objects of the object manager. This choice comes from two considerations: to make proxy objects invisible to the user, and to ensure shared object protection at each site.

Several problems related to proxy definition and use have been studied: proxy uniqueness, object migration mechanism, object protection, garbage collection, and dynamic connection and disconnection.

The garbage collection problem has been presented, but it was not a central aspect of the study. However, it is important to note that our (segmented) object management structure decreases the importance of object reclamation, because objects that are no longer used will sooner or later be moved to secondary storage. The object reclamation problem is now associated with object management on secondary storage. This does not require immediate garbage collection, but may be deferred to a more appropriate time, such as unused CPU time or the start or end of the user work session. However, garbage collection on the storage memory is always necessary in the event of saturation.

The implementation of the system is still under way. A complete version of the object manager is used on a two-node configuration, and will be integrated with the Smalltalk-80 system. The Smalltalk system still does not run, because the object manager was originally integrated with the interpreter level and their splitting implies considerable modifications to their definitions (interpretation, screen display, and virtual image translation). The final step of this study will be to design an interface enabling the user of the Smalltalk system to use object sharing capabilities; this interface will be in the form of Smalltalk classes. Preliminary experiments seem to show that the functionality of distributed object management can be achieved at a tolerable cost.

## REFERENCES

[Almes 1980] G.T. Almes, "Garbage Collection in an Object-Oriented System," Ph.D. Thesis CMU-CS-80-128, Carnegie-Mellon University, Pittsburgh, June 1980.

[Almes et al. 1985] G.T. Almes, A.P. Black, E.D. Lazowska, and J.D. Noe, "The Eden System: A Technical Review," *IEEE Transactions on Software Engineering,* no. SE-11, pp. 43–59, January 1985.

[Bennett 1987] J.K. Bennett, "The Design and Implementation of Distributed Smalltalk," *Proceedings of the Second ACM Conference on Object-Oriented Programming Systems, Languages and Applications, SIGPLAN Notices,* vol. 22, no. 12, pp. 318–330, October 1987.

[Birrell and Nelson 1984] A.D. Birrell and B.J. Nelson, "Implementing Remote Procedure Calls," *ACM Transactions on Computer Systems,* vol. 2, no. 1, February 1984.

[Black 1985] A.P. Black, "Supporting Distributed Applications: Experience with Eden," *Proceedings of the 10th ACM SIGOPS,* Washington, December 1985.

[Bobrow 1980] D.G. Bobrow, "Managing Reentrant Structures using Reference Counts," *ACM Transactions on Programming Languages and Systems,* vol. 2, no. 3, pp. 269–273, July 1980.

[Christopher 1984] T.W. Christopher, "Reference Count Garbage Collection," *Software Practice and Experience,* vol. 14, no. 6, pp. 503–507, June 1984.

[Decouchant 1986] D. Decouchant, "Design of a Distributed Object Manager for the Smalltalk-80 System," *Proceedings of the First ACM Conference on Object-Oriented Systems, Languages and Applications, SIGPLAN Notices,* vol. 21, no. 11, pp. 444–452, October 1986.

[Deutsch and Bobrow 1976] L.P. Deutsch, and D.G. Bobrow, "An Efficient Incremental, Automatic Garbage Collector," *Communications of the ACM,* vol. 19, no. 9, pp. 522–526, September 1976.

[Dijkstra et al. 1978] E.W. Dijkstra, L. Lamport, A.J. Martin, C.S. Scholten, and E.F.M. Steffens, "On-the-Fly Garbage Collection: An Exercise in Cooperation," *Communications of the ACM,* vol. 21, no. 11, pp. 966–975, November 1978.

[Goldberg and Robson 1983] A. Goldberg and D. Robson, *Smalltalk-80: The Language and its Implementation,* Addison-Wesley, Reading, MA, 1983.

[Halstead 1985] R.H. Halstead, "Multilisp: A Language for Concurrent Symbolic Computation," *ACM Transactions on Programming Languages and Systems* vol. 7, no. 4, pp. 501–538, October 1985.

[Hughes 1985] J. Hughes, "A Distributed Garbage Collection Algorithm," Lecture Notes in Computer Science, Functional Programming Languages and Computer Architecture, pp. 256–272, September 1985.

[Leffler et al. 1983a] S.J. Leffler, R.S. Fabry, and W.N. Joy, "A 4.2 BSD Interprocess Communication Primer," Computer Systems Research Group, Department of Electrical Engineering and Computer Science, University of California, Berkeley, CA, July 1983.

[Leffler et al. 1983b] S.J. Leffler, R.S. Fabry, and W.N. Joy, "4.2 BSD Networking Implementation Notes," Computer Systems Research Group, Department of Electrical Engineering and Computer Science, University of California, Berkeley, CA, July 1983.

[Lieberman and Hewitt 1983] H. Lieberman, and C. Hewitt, "A Real-Time Garbage Collector Based on the Lifetimes of Objects," *Communications of the ACM,* vol. 26, no. 6, June 1983.

[Liskov 1982] B.H. Liskov, "On Linguistic Support for Distributed Programs," *IEEE Transactions on Software Engineering,* no. SE-8, pp. 203–210, May 1982.

[Liskov 1984] B.H. Liskov, "Overview of the Argus Language and System," Programming Methodology Group Memo 40, MIT Laboratory for Computer Science, February 1984.

[McCullough 1987] P.L. McCullough, "Transparent Forwarding: First Steps," *Proceedings of the Second ACM Conference on Object-Oriented Programming Systems, Languages and Applications, SIGPLAN Notices,* vol. 22, no. 12, pp. 331–341, October 1987.

[Mohan et al. 1986] C. Mohan, B. Lindsay and R. Obermarck, "Transaction Management in the R* Distributed Database Management System," *ACM Transactions on Database Systems,* vol. 11, no. 4, pp. 378–396, December 1986.

[Organick 1972] E.I. Organick, *The Multics System: An Examination of Its Structure,* MIT Press, Cambridge, MA, 1972.

[Peterson and Norman 1977] J.L. Peterson and T.A. Norman, "Buddy Systems," *Communications of the ACM,* vol. 20, no. 6, pp. 421–431, June 1977.

[Ritchie and Thompson 1974] D.M. Ritchie and K. Thompson, "The Unix Time-Sharing System," *Communications of the ACM,* vol. 17, no. 7, July 1974.

[Shapiro 1986] M. Shapiro, "Structure and Encapsulation in Distributed Systems," *Proceedings of the 6th International Conference on Distributed Computer Systems,* Boston, MA, May 1986.

[Shen and Peterson 1974] K.K. Shen and J.L. Peterson, "A Weighted Buddy System for Dynamic Storage Allocation," *Communications of the ACM*, vol. 17, no. 10, pp. 558–562, October 1974.

[Shin and Malek 1985] H. Shin and M. Malek, "Parallel Garbage Collection with Associative Tag," *Proceedings of the 1985 International Conference on Parallel Processing*, IEEE, pp. 369–375, August 1985.

[Stonebraker et al. 1976] M. Stonebraker, E. Wong, P. Kreps and G. Held, "The Design and Implementation of INGRES," *ACM Transactions on Database Systems*, vol. 1, no. 3, pp. 189–222, September 1976.

[Tanenbaum and Mullender 1983] A.S. Tanenbaum and S.J. Mullender, "An Overview of the Amoeba Distributed Operating System," *ACM Computing Surveys*, vol. 15, no. 3, pp. 51–64, September 1983.

[Tanenbaum and Van Renesse 1985] A.S. Tanenbaum and R. Van Renesse, "Distributed Operating Systems," *ACM Computing Surveys*, vol. 17, no. 4, pp. 419–470, December 1985.

[Thomas et al. 1986] R. Thomas, L.R. Rogers, and J.L. Yates, *Advanced Programmer's Guide to UNIX SYSTEM V*, Osborne McGraw-Hill, Berkeley, CA, 1986.

[Tricot 1987] C. Tricot, "Mux: A Lightweight Multiprocessor Subsystem Under Unix," EUUG: European UNIX Systems User Group, Helsinki and Stockholm, May 1987.

[Ungar 1984a] D. Ungar, "Generation Scavenging: A Non-disruptive High Performance Storage Reclamation Algorithm," *First Symposium on Practical Software Development Environments, ACM Software Engineering*, pp. 157–167, April 1984.

[Ungar, et al. 1984b] D. Ungar, R. Blau, P. Foley, D. Samples, and D. Patterson, *Architecture of SOAR: Smalltalk on a RISC*, IEEE, Ann Arbor, MI, pp. 188–197, June 1984.

[Wiseman 1985] S.R. Wiseman, "A Garbage Collector for a Large Distributed Address Space," RSRE Report 85009, June 1985.

# 5 Future Research and Development in Object-Oriented Systems

# 20

---

# Directions in Object-Oriented Research

D.C. Tsichritzis, O.M. Nierstrasz

---

## INTRODUCTION

Object-oriented systems as an approach have inherited concepts, methods, and tools from many other areas in computer science. We can say that object-oriented systems consist of a repackaging and relabeling of a cross section of computer science. As a result, many researchers see projections of their ideas within object-oriented systems. This situation explains two phenomena. First, in a short period object-oriented systems evolved from an esoteric, exotic way of programming in certain artificial intelligence applications to a diverse and expanding area of research. Second, there are disagreements among researchers on basic definitions; for example, "What is an object?" Researchers coming from programming languages, artificial intelligence, and databases, among other fields, have conflicting ideas on when an "object" can be called an object. There is no reason to worry. Loose definitions are inevitable and sometimes welcome during a dynamic period of scientific discovery. They should and will become more rigorous during a period of consolidation that will inevitably follow.

Directions in object-oriented research to some extent follow the roots of the researchers. We see, therefore, object-oriented research related to programming languages, to operating systems, to databases, and so forth. This does not necessarily mean that object-oriented researchers are rediscovering the results already present in other areas. On the contrary, researchers in other areas are finding a new territory in which to apply their ideas. The net effect is, however, that the directions in object-oriented research can be clearly categorized according to the traditional areas in computer science to which they are related. In the first part of this chapter we shall discuss the directions that we will call *traditional*. They are advanced but closely related to areas already well understood. In the second part of the chapter, we will permit ourselves to dream. In this way we can explore some exciting problems that we consider very important for the success of the object-oriented approach. Some of these problems existed before, but an object-oriented setting gives them different emphasis and a new light. The solutions may therefore take on a very different flavor. We will call the research directions related to these problems *exotic*.

## 20.1 TRADITIONAL RESEARCH DIRECTIONS

Whenever a new technology becomes available, we must reevaluate what we already know with respect to these new ideas. With the gradual introduction and acceptance of object-oriented techniques, we find ourselves forced to pursue several directions of research along traditional lines, in order that we may understand how objects require us to reinterpret established results.

We can identify (at least) five major directions that researchers are currently investigating:

1. Programming languages

2. Concurrency and distribution

3. Object management

4. Software management

5. User environments

This list is not intended to be exhaustive, but rather to identify broad classifications of current research. We shall overview each of these areas and briefly discuss how object-oriented techniques pose new problems.

### 20.1.1 Programming Languages

Objects affect our understanding of programming languages in three fundamental ways. First, our languages have a different "look" to them; that is, we need and use different language constructs and mechanisms. Second, our programming methodology must adapt, since we must use different disciplines to build our applications. Third, we need to develop new formal models that can help us to describe and analyze the systems we build.

If object-oriented programming were simply an issue of substituting an entirely new programming paradigm, we should perhaps have an easier job of it. Instead, we have discovered that the idea of "objects" has always been around, except that it has been lurking in the shadows under various guises, and using obscure names. Now our big problem is that of *language integration*: we would like to continue to be able to do all the things we have discovered to be good in the past, and we want to be able to use the new object-oriented techniques that have become available as well. We can do this only if we discover how to integrate disparate object models into our programming languages cleanly and consistently.

The first major "discovery" of this sort is that Smalltalk-style objects look a lot like abstract data types. That is, perhaps we can identify object classes and object *types*. This identification introduces a host of problems. What does strong-typing mean in this context? How can (static) strong-typing cope with dynamic binding of variables to object instances? How can a type theory for objects adequately cope with single and multiple class inheritance? Should class inheritance be permitted to violate encapsulation by permitting subclass methods to access inherited instance variables? How can we understand type-casting and coercion in an object-oriented language? How can we exploit encapsulation to support heterogeneous objects, that is, environments in which different objects may be implemented in various languages with, say, a common object-oriented interface language? Various answers to these problems have been proposed, and even implemented [Meyer 1986; Nierstrasz 1987a; Schaffert et al. 1986].

We are a long way, however, from having standard solutions, because the object models supported by different languages emphasize different properties of objects. For example, another important "discovery" is the similarity between Smalltalk-style objects and active entities, or processes. However, not all concurrent object models view objects as active entities, as we shall see in the following subsection. We are still at the stage of enumerating the mechanisms supported by different object models, and attempting to understand their interactions [Wegner 1987].

Now that we have object-oriented programming languages that enable us to exploit encapsulation in various ways, we have discovered that we can no longer program in the way that we are used to. Our concerns with encapsulation in the past were mostly limited to problem decomposition and minimal interference between program modules. Now if we wish to exploit object reusability, polymorphism, class inheritance, parameterized types, and so on, we must organize our applications in such a way as to be consistent with these possibilities. We have developed techniques for decomposing problems into relatively independent components, but we still lack a methodology for viewing applications in terms of *objects*. Such a methodology will arise only through years of experience programming with these languages, followed by reflection and attempts to pass this knowledge on to other programmers. An extremely interesting research issue is whether it will be possible to construct software tools that encourage programmers to conform to such a methodology—this is related to the *object design* problem we shall discuss below.

Finally, we must reevaluate our formal models of computation with respect to object-oriented concepts. This is already happening with type theory [Cardelli and Wegner 1985], models of concurrency [Agha 1986; Hoare 1985], and semantics of programming languages and applications [Wolczko 1987]. As object-oriented languages and systems gain acceptance, we shall see a similar reevaluation of our models of security, distribution, and persistence, since in each of these cases we are concerned with the properties of environments that have been partitioned into interacting components, and with interaction across environments. In distributed object-oriented systems, we will have to be able to understand and model security and persistence of objects communicating across environments.

### 20.1.2 Concurrency and Distribution

We have already alluded to the importance of concurrent and distributed object-oriented applications. As in the past, object-oriented approaches to concurrency typically adopt one of two models of concurrency. The first is to view objects as passive entities manipulated and shared by concurrent application programs. The object management system controls and synchronizes access to these objects. This we call the "database" world-view of objects and concurrency.

The second approach is to consider objects as active entities themselves. Objects thus replace the notion of a "process." Passive objects are effectively "server" processes that do nothing except wait for and serve incoming requests. Objects communicate by passing "messages," and so synchronize themselves without the aid of an object manager. This is the "actors" world-view of objects and concurrency [Agha 1986].

Both these views have their advantages and disadvantages, but they are not so clearly at odds with one another as they might first seem. The database view offers explicit threads of control (encapsulated in the applications), and can support the abstraction mechanisms of passive objects (á la monitors, for example). The main difficulty with this view has to do with the separation of the world into passive entities (objects) and "applications," which are not objects. This means that applications cannot be described by such an object model. In particular, it is not possible for applications to communicate with one another directly, unless we invent an independent communication model for applications.

The active object model eliminates this problem by adopting a homogeneous view in which there is no distinction between objects and "applications." On the other hand, active objects lack an explicit notion of threads of control. (Despite our claims of homogeneity, threads are not objects!) We must restrict ourselves to specific communication protocols, or message-passing patterns, if we are to be able to program effectively. By analogy, programming with *send*s and *accept*s is as dangerous as undisciplined programming with *goto*s. Note also that the active object model does not say whether objects are persistent, whereas this is an implicit assumption of the database view.

Distribution is also viewed differently by the two models. The (traditional) database approach is to provide an illusion of a global shared database of objects, with communication between remote sites being handled automatically by the system. With active objects, it is more natural to expose the network, and even to allow objects to move themselves between sites. We can imagine, however, object-oriented databases that support migrations, or, conversely, active object systems that hide the network or automatically perform load-balancing.

More fundamental is the different approach taken to communication and synchronization. The database view is that applications perform operations on passive data and that the data must be protected from conflicts between concurrent applications. As a consequence it is natural to adopt a mechanism for mutual exclusion based on, for example, locks or transactions. Synchronization is viewed as orthogonal to an object's interface. With active objects, on the other hand, communication is modeled by message-passing, so there is no need for an explicit synchronization mechanism. Mutual exclusion is not an issue since objects themselves decide when they are ready to accept a message.

These differences have more to do with modeling than with implementation, however. Distributed transactions in an object-oriented database necessarily require message-passing between cooperating object managers. Similarly, active objects can be implemented in a centralized system by coroutines (representing execution threads) sharing passive object data structures. Message-passing between active objects is thus a communication paradigm rather than an implementation requirement.

Current research into concurrent object-oriented languages generally adopts either a database view [Moss and Kohler 1987] or an actors view [Yonezawa et al. 1986], though there have been attempts to integrate these approaches into a single model [Nierstrasz 1987b].

### 20.1.3 Object Management

As our object models and object-oriented languages evolve, we discover that it is useful to have object-oriented environments that provide us with run-time support for our objects. A sample of the kinds of support one might desire follows:

- *Persistence:* automatic saving of objects between sessions, through either persistent virtual memories or object-oriented databases

- *Garbage collection:* automatic deletion of unreferenced objects

- *Concurrency:* multiple concurrent threads; communication and concurrency control through message-passing or object-oriented databases

- *Distribution:* global object-naming, and remote message-passing or method invocation

- *Security:* ownership of objects; "access rights," or permission to invoke objects' operations

Depending on the intended application domains, these kinds of functionality can be provided either by operating systems or by object-oriented databases. The database approach is valid for data-intensive applications that deal with large numbers of similarly structured objects (the number of objects will be much larger than the number of object classes). Content addressability is fundamental in order to support querying and to provide a basis for organizing the object store (e.g., for indexing). For application domains that violate these assumptions, there must be a greater emphasis on providing support for non-database objects. There is clearly a need for object-oriented systems that can support a mix of these two application paradigms. We will eventually have to address an integration problem in bringing object-oriented databases closer to object-oriented programming languages. The basic choice will be whether we decide to maintain the barrier between "the applications" and "the database," thus viewing an object-oriented database as a strictly separate component that can be interfaced to the rest of the system, or whether we will move toward truly integrated object management systems that provide standard support (for persistence, etc.) for all applications, and additionally provide database support for the applications that need it.

## 20.1.4 Software Management

We mentioned the *object design* problem earlier in this section. This is the problem of deciding what objects one needs to put together an application. The strategy for decomposing an application into objects depends on the properties required of the resulting partitioning. Do we wish merely to write a minimum of code, or to produce a prototype in the shortest time possible; or do we need an extendible application whose objects are reusable and portable to other environments? For these questions there is no substitute for experience. The issue is whether we can take short cuts by learning from other people's experience. The development of a methodology for object-oriented programming will help in the object design problem.

We may now well ask what software tools would be useful to a developer of an object-oriented application. In other words, can we realistically speak of computer-aided design of software objects? If so, is object design similar to other design tasks? The first example that comes to mind is that of database design. Here too we are concerned with decomposition into semi-independent "objects." Can we develop tools (say, graphical tools) that drive the decomposition and design task?

Once we have a plan of our application in terms of objects, we must find ways to implement them. Again, experience is invaluable. But object-oriented programming heavily emphasizes reusability. That means we can expect extremely large collections of reusable objects to be available to us. "Browsing" tools are popular for navigating through a collection of object classes, but they may be severely limited when dealing with tens of thousands of reusable classes. Since the mapping from object specifications to plausible implementation components is effectively "expert knowledge," we should ask whether expert systems are appropriate tools for helping programmers to find their way through databases of reusable object classes.

At a more technical level, as software is being developed, we must keep track of the dependencies between object classes, and between instances and their realizations. In a distributed environment, we must also manage the distribution of evolving software. We already know how to manage evolving software written in traditional programming languages. In object-oriented systems, software not only evolves, but reusable software is expected to have a very long lifetime. Furthermore, we expect that objects with their well-defined boundaries will be easier to manage than traditional software. These points suggest that tools for managing object-oriented software will quickly become standard as their need arises.

## 20.1.5 User Environments

Object-oriented concepts have a very natural application in user interfaces. *Direct manipulation* is a fundamentally object-oriented idea that demonstrates both encapsulation and polymorphism (the "same" operation can apply to different kinds of objects). Instead of issuing a command to perform some function, and then later checking to see how that function was performed, one is presented with a view of the "object" one wishes to manipulate, and then one performs an action "directly" on the object (that is, on its presentation). The feedback is typically immediate. This approach is best seen in WYSIWYG ("What you see is what you get") applications, such as document editor-formatters.

Direct manipulation is well suited to object-oriented applications, since it is quite easy to identify the objects that must be presented to the user. *How* an object should be presented, however, is often not so easy! The paradigm of direct manipulation starts to break down when we have to perform complicated actions on objects. Inserting text at the current location by pressing the appropriate character key is straightforward enough, as is deleting the current object by hitting the *delete* key. But if we want to construct and remember a more complicated procedure, such as deleting obsolete addresses from several address lists of people on another list, then we must resort to "programming." If we can package this procedure in some convenient way, then we can apply it whenever the occasion recurs. To do this, we need a direct manipulation analogue of shell programming. This is what is often referred to as "programming-by-example" [Halbert 1984]. It remains to be seen how far object-oriented interfaces can be pushed to replace the need for command shells.

The development and popularization of window systems to a large extent solves the problem of managing multiple concurrent threads. Not only can we present to the user applications with concurrently executing objects, but the user can switch his attention between tasks by moving from window to window without interrupting or terminating the current one. We are also beginning to see "nested" windows (replacing directory hierarchies) and "remote" windows for distributed applications.

Perhaps with the continuing development of computer games, we will see the kinds of objects that we now play with begin to appear as characters in the interfaces we use for our work. As we become more desperate to find good paradigms for direct manipulation, we shall probably find that plausible solutions already exist in terms of presentation objects that jump, fight, crash, and blow up.

## 20.2 Exotic research directions

By *exotic* directions we do not necessarily mean impossible or unnecessary problems. We simply mean research directions that are particularly relevant when we think in terms of objects. We will present the direction as a series of interesting problems. Most of these problems manifest themselves when we deal with a distributed, open-ended environment of active objects.

### 20.2.1 Acquaintance Problem

The acquaintance problem is related to the binding problem in programming. Consider a population of independent objects that can move around in a network, a population that is continuously evolving and expanding. An object at its birth knows about a number of objects in its immediate environment. We can think that these objects' names have been passed down as capabilities from the creator of the object. For an object to be effective, however, especially in a network environment, the object may have to communicate with other totally unknown objects. The problem is how two objects unknown to each other can be introduced. We are not discussing the location problem (how you find an object already known to you). We are discussing how you obtain the name of an object you would like to talk to.

Two immediate solutions come to mind, one from the user and one from the object manager. They both have severe limitations. The user does not and should not know all the objects around. The object manager knows only the objects in its jurisdiction. We need, therefore, so solve a problem of context. We need to define a context in which we will try to select some interesting objects. Second, we need to specify the criteria according to which an object should be selected. An unknown object cannot be selected according to its internal structure or values, because they are hidden. Its methods do not have the proper selectivity, since many objects share them. We should probably select it according to its *past behavior*. We need, therefore, to define and implement a notion of past behavior. We can then select a new acquaintance within a context in terms of what it did (good or bad) during its lifetime.

### 20.2.2 Evolution Problems

Consider an object that can dynamically inherit new methods, i.e., that can *evolve*. Apart from the mechanics of changing an object, we have two very difficult problems. First, how does an object decide that it is advantageous to inherit or modify a method or a part of itself? The object may be forced to do so, which means that its independence was inherently limited (i.e., it was not fully encapsulated). Or the object may have no alternative, which means it has detected a malfunction. Finally, the object may inadvertently inherit a "bad" trait. In this case "bad" may mean incompatible, or inconsistent with some of its other characteristics. Evolving means not only adding but also rejecting methods and parts. This suggests another interesting problem: How does an object decide that a particular method or trait is disadvantageous and should be rejected? In special cases a metric may exist to evaluate new methods or shed existing ones. For instance, we have implemented objects for which rules relating to buying and selling stocks were evaluated according to their performance in the market [Tsichritzis et al. 1987]. In general, the situation is much more complex, unless we take the approach that each object is a total actor and its methods are always passed in the messages.

### 20.2.3 Global Behavior Problem

Consider a population of independent objects. The behavior of each object is defined by its methods. We can specify what an object is supposed to do by properly defining it and controlling it during its lifetime. The global behavior of the expanding and evolving population is implicitly defined by the behavior of its parts (the objects). This implies that we cannot specify global behavior. The notion of a formal specification of global behavior being used to generate the object population is in conflict with the idea of freewheeling, independent objects.

We may want, however, to *constrain* the global behavior. Consider, for instance, the notion of a flock of birds [Maruichi et al. 1987]. The global behavior of the flock results from the combined behavior of its independent objects (birds). We have, for example, a notion of a flock flying south. There are two ways, at least, to coordinate objects. In one approach we can define scripts that participating objects should follow [Fiume et al. 1987]. These scripts are constraint mechanisms comparable to a scenario in a play: an actor is capable of acting many different parts, any one of which can be performed in a variety of ways. But in any given play the actor must conform to the constraints of that play's script. Scripts are very valuable, especially for temporal coordination of objects.

Another way to coordinate objects is through the definition of fields [Pintado and Fiume 1988]. A field is a population of objects each of which is subject to a force defined in the point it occupies. In this way, we can define fields where objects can be attracted or repulsed. A field does not totally define the behavior of each object. It partially influences their collective behavior according to some desired overall goal.

## 20.2.4 Presentation Problem

Consider a dynamic, evolving object. We need to portray the different states that the object can reach in a suitable fashion. This is especially important for users to be able to visualize and monitor the progress and interplay of objects. An active object cannot be meaningfully portrayed by a static icon. We need to represent it by an animated character. In this way object states will be mirrored in the character's appearance. The animated character behaves in a fashion that reflects the progress of the object it represents and its coordination with other objects. The user can then be trained to look for abnormal object behavior. The same script that coordinates object behavior can define the behavior of the corresponding animated objects [Fiume et al. 1987]. We are readily immersed in problems of event-driven simulation and real-time animation. In addition, we have complete freedom in portraying animated objects. If they correspond to real-world objects, we can choose to represent them by animation of their real-world counterparts. For objects that are completely imaginary, we need to create an artificial reality that properly portrays them. Objects not only have to do the right things, but they have to look good.

## 20.2.5 Defense Problem

It is probably improper to talk about *protection* of objects. Dynamic, moving objects are not passive units that need protection. They can actively organize their own defense. An object can refuse to allow certain operations. It can hide information. It can provide disinformation. It can move outside a context where it cannot be reached. It can completely erase itself. An object can even defend itself by directly or indirectly attacking the intruding object. All these possibilities give protection mechanisms a new meaning.

We can consider special objects with proper defense mechanisms that guard more sedate but critical objects. There is no limit to the ways that objects may defend themselves, just as there is no limit to the ways that objects can attack other objects. Proper object behavior is not supervised by any one user, but by a combination of object managers who can watch out for signs of aggression.

### 20.2.6 Temporal Problem

So far objects operate independently, perhaps in coordination with other objects. We may, however, want to force objects to be at certain points or states at certain times. We need to introduce, therefore, a notion of time, real or artificial, to force not only ordering of operations but rendezvous of objects. This is especially important when objects are interfaced with machines and robots. Objects operating these processes need to abide by real-time requirements. Therefore, their interaction with the other freewheeling objects has to be subjected to some strict temporal constraints. An event-driven script controlled by independent samples is a plausible mechanism for forcing a rendezvous [Dami et al., 1988] (provided, of course, that the machines and the networks perform well enough to support object coordination). The same issues come up with the interfaces of video for the visualization of objects. The operations of the objects have to be rendered in animation with specific audiovisual characteristics (frames per second, voice or sound time delay, etc.). The only difference is that people for whom the objects are rendered may be more flexible in terms of real-time constraints than are machines.

## SUMMARY

The paradigm of object-oriented programming has proved its value in many areas, such as enhancing software reusability, maintainability, and reliability. Despite the obvious benefits of the object-oriented approach, it is often unclear how object models affect traditional issues such as strong-typing, security, concurrency, and distribution. Not only are we faced with the challenge of integrating object-oriented and traditional approaches, but we must constantly be prepared to discover new ways in which object models can help us to find better solutions to old problems. What we have classified as traditional research directions are the most immediate and obvious problems of fitting the object-oriented approach into the traditional body of known computer science.

All the exotic problems we have discussed carry connotations of science fiction. However, they are not really new. They all have counterparts in programming problems that are known and sometimes unresolved. We propose the following correspondence.

The acquaintance problem is related to selection and binding in programming. The evolution problem is related to software maintenance and modification. The global behavior problem is related to constraint specification and verification. The presentation problem is related to multimedia user interfaces. The defense problem is related to protection and security issues. The temporal problem is related to real-time issues in operating systems, simulation, and animation.

We should not dismiss the traditional directions as old and uninteresting just because the exotic directions are new and exciting. They are both equally important. The main difference is that the traditional directions emphasize getting an object right, whereas the exotic directions emphasize the societal problems in a population of objects, that is, getting a set of objects to do something together. It is well-accepted in computer science that getting autonomous objects, programs, people, or whatever to work together is far more difficult. Without mechanisms for cooperation, however, we are limited to what can be done by a single object, program, or person. Recent interest in computer-supported cooperative work points out that getting persons and programmed objects to cooperate for an overall goal can be a critical issue.

## REFERENCES

[Agha 1986] G.A. Agha, *ACTORS: A Model of Concurrent Computation in Distributed Systems*, The MIT Press, Cambridge, MA, 1986.

[Dami et al. 1988] L. Dami, E. Fiume, O. Nierstrasz, and D. Tsichritzis, "Temporal Scripts for Objects," in *Active Object Environments*, ed. D. Tsichritzis, pp. 144–161, Centre Universitaire D'Informatique, Universite de Geneva, June 1988.

[Cardelli and Wegner 1985] L. Cardelli and P. Wegner, "On Understanding Types, Data Abstraction, and Polymorphism," *ACM Computing Surveys*, vol. 17, no. 4, pp. 471–522, December 1985.

[Fiume et al. 1987] E. Fiume, D.C. Tsichritzis, and L. Dami, "A Temporal Scripting Language for Object-Oriented Animation," *Proceedings of Eurographics 1987*, (North-Holland) Elsevier Science Publishers, Amsterdam, 1987.

[Halbert 1984] D.C. Halbert, "Programming by Example," Ph.D. Thesis, Dept. of Electrical Engineering and Computer Science, University of California, Berkeley, CA, 1984.

[Hoare 1985] C.A.R. Hoare, *Communicating Sequential Processes*, Prentice-Hall, Englewood Cliffs, NJ, 1985.

[Maruichi et al. 1987] T. Maruichi, T. Uchiki, and M. Tokoro, "Behavioral Simulation Based on Knowledge Objects," *Proceedings of the European Conference on Object-Oriented Programming*, pp. 257–266, Paris, France, June 15–17, 1987.

[Meyer 1986] B. Meyer, "Genericity versus Inheritance," *Proceedings of the First ACM Conference on Object-Oriented Programming Systems, Languages and Applications, SIGPLAN Notices*, vol. 21, no. 11, pp. 391–405, November 1986.

[Moss and Kohler 1987] J.E.B. Moss and W.H. Kohler, "Concurrency Features for the Trellis/Owl Language," *Proceedings of the European Conference on Object-Oriented Programming*, pp. 223–232, Paris, France, June 15–17, 1987.

[Nierstrasz 1987a] O.M. Nierstrasz, "Hybrid—A Language for Programming with Active Objects," in *Objects and Things*, ed. D.C. Tsichritzis, Centre Universitaire d'Informatique, University of Geneva, pp. 15–42, March 1987.

[Nierstrasz 1987b] O.M. Nierstrasz, "Active Objects in Hybrid," *Proceedings of the Second ACM Conference on Object-Oriented Programming Systems, Languages and Applications, SIGPLAN Notices*, vol. 22, no. 12, pp. 243–253, December 1987.

[Pintado and Fiume 1988] X. Pintado and E. Fiume, "Grafields: Field-Directed Dynamic Splines for Interactive Motion Control," *Proceedings of Eurographics 1988*, pp. 43–54 (North-Holland) Elsevier Science Publishers, Amsterdam, 1988.

[Schaffert et al. 1986] C. Schaffert, T. Cooper, B. Bullis, M. Killian, and C. Wilpolt, "An Introduction to Trellis/Owl," *Proceedings of the First ACM Conference on Object-Oriented Programming Systems, Languages and Applications, SIGPLAN Notices*, vol. 21, no. 11, pp. 9–16, November 1986.

[Tsichritzis et al. 1987] D.C. Tsichritzis, E. Fiume, S. Gibbs, and O.M. Nierstrasz, "KNOs: KNowledge Acquisition, Dissemination and Manipulation Objects," *ACM Transactions on Office Information Systems*, vol. 5, no. 1, pp. 96–112, January 1987.

[Wegner 1987] P. Wegner, "Dimensions of Object-Based Language Design," *Proceedings of the Second ACM Conference on Object-Oriented Programming Systems, Languages and Applications, SIGPLAN Notices*, vol. 22, no. 12, pp. 168–182, December 1987.

[Wolczko 1987] M. Wolczko, "Semantics of Smalltalk-80," *Proceedings of the European Conference on Object-Oriented Programming*, pp. 119-131, Paris, France, June 15-17, 1987.

[Yonezawa et al. 1986] A. Yonezawa, J-P Briot, and E. Shibayama, "Object-Oriented Concurrent Programming in ABCL/1," *Proceedings of the First ACM Conference on Object-Oriented Programming Systems, Languages and Applications, SIGPLAN Notices*, vol. 21, no. 11, pp. 258-268, November 1986.

# 21

# A Proposal for a Formal Model of Objects

Yair Wand

## INTRODUCTION

The concept of an object emerged as a programming construct [Stefik and Bobrow 1986] and has been adapted to databases [Banerjee et al. 1987; Kronke and Dolan 1988], as we have seen in this book. In various discussions it is described as an outgrowth of abstract data types or as encapsulation of data and processes [Nierstrasz 1986, 1989]. The essence of the object paradigm of programming is the view that a program is composed of independent objects that communicate via messages.

Despite a considerable effort in object-oriented programming, there is still no commonly accepted definition of the object-oriented approach. For example, one article on objects begins with the words "There is much confusion about the term object-oriented" [Nierstrasz 1986]; another article states: ". . . there is no consensus about the object-oriented model" [Banerjee et al. 1987]. It is our premise in this chapter that much of this confusion surrounds objects because they emerged as programming concepts and, therefore, were driven by implementation considerations. Hence, we suggest a model that views objects as constructs for modeling the problem domain. In other words, our proposal is that the perspective of the object-oriented paradigm be shifted from implementation-driven to modeling-driven.

This suggestion is in line with recent views of programming. Thus, in his paper about abstraction in programming, [Abbott 1987] observes that there is a continuing evolution in programming, away from a computer-oriented view—how to implement a solution on the computer—toward a problem- or knowledge-oriented view—how to capture the problem domain. He proposes that the advent of object-oriented programming is a step in this evolution. On the same note, Brooks claims that the use of object-oriented concepts allows the designer "to express the essence of the design . . ." [Brooks 1987].

The discussion of objects can be examined in a wider context yet. In their Turing Award article, Newell and Simon suggest the view of computer science as an empirical study of symbolic systems. They claim that "One of the fundamental contributions to knowledge of computer science has been to explain, at a rather basic level, what symbols are" [Newell and Simon 1976]. Combining this with the notion that a program or a database is but a representation of our perceptions of reality [Borgida et al. 1985; Wand 1988; Wand and Weber 1988], we pose the question:

> Is the emergence of the object paradigm an *empirical indication* that humans find it easier to describe perceptions of the world through the notion of objects?

In other words, we propose that the significance of objects extends beyond the improvement of data and control transfer in programs, the portability and reusability of program components, and the advantages of information hiding [Banerjee et al. 1987; Nierstrasz 1986; Stefik and Bobrow 1986]. Rather, objects gain their importance because they reflect a "natural" view of the world we are modeling (abstracting) in our software. This being the case, if we view programs as models of some reality, the use of objects amounts to adopting programming and database design constructs that are direct mappings of real concepts.

The branch of philosophy of science that deals with modeling the existence of things in the world is ontology (or metaphysics). We turn, therefore, to an ontological view in the context of philosophy of science to seek a formal base for the notion of an object. The formalism we use is the one defined by Bunge in his "Treatise on Basic Philosophy," especially his volumes Ontology I and Ontology II [Bunge 1977; Bunge 1979].

Bunge begins his discussion of ontology by adopting the following definition: "Metaphysics studies the generic (nonspecific) traits of every mode of being and becoming, as well as the peculiar features of the major genera of existents" [Bunge 1977, p. 24]. Then, he claims: "Metaphysics can render service by analyzing fashionable but obscure notions such as those of a system, hierarchy, structure, event, information . . ." Thus, our purpose of formalizing the object concept is in accordance with Bunge's objectives of formalizing ontology.

The next section defines the main concepts of Bunge's ontology that we employ as formal foundations for the object concept. Section 21.2 maps the formal definitions of ontology onto commonly used concepts of objects and mentions some observations on similarities and differences. Section 21.3 proposes a formal model of objects and their dynamics. Finally, the Summary suggests some practical conclusions that emerge from the proposed formalism.

## 21.1 BASIC CONCEPTS

In this section we summarize the ontological concepts of Bunge's formalism that will be used as the basis for our model of objects. We begin by repeating some of the fundamental principles that Bunge states.[1] Next, structural concepts are introduced in the following order: things and properties, states and laws, and classes and kinds. The structural elements are then used to discuss dynamics: change and events. Finally, a comment is made about the inseparability of things and changes.

### 21.1.1 Ontological Principles

Most of this subsection is quoted from [Bunge 1977, pp. 16–17].

*The world is composed of things.* Consequently, the sciences of reality (natural or social) study things, their properties and changes.

*Forms are properties of things.* . . . (a) we study and modify properties by examining things and forcing them to change, and (b) properties are represented by predicates (e.g., functions) defined on domains that are, at least in part, sets of concrete objects.

*Things are grouped into systems* or aggregates of interacting components. There is no thing that fails to be a part of at least one system. There are no independent things: the borders we trace between entities are often imaginary. What there really is are systems—physical, chemical, living, or social.

*Every thing changes.*

*Nothing comes out of nothing and no thing reduces to nothingness.*

*Every thing abides by laws.* Whether natural or social, laws are invariant relations among properties.

### 21.1.2 Things and Properties[2]

The world is viewed as composed of things of two kinds: concrete things that are called *entities* or *substantial individuals,* and *conceptual things.* For our purpose we deal with substantial individuals, and it is important that they

---

[1] We repeat here only those principles that are related to the proposed view of objects.

[2] Exact page references to [Bunge 1977] in this subsection are: Postulate 1, definitions 1–3 are from pp. 28–31, definition 5 is from p. 72, Postulate 2 from p. 74, definition 6 from p. 111, definition 7 from p. 119, and Postulate 3 from p. 120.

are concrete things and not concepts or types of things. An individual may be either simple or composite, namely, composed of other individuals. The idea that objects can be combined to generate other objects is formalized in the following postulate:

**Postulate 1:**[3]    There exists a binary operation · called *concatenation* or *association* such that:

1. If $a_1$ and $a_2$ are individuals, then $a_1 \cdot a_2$ is also an individual.

2. $a \cdot a = a$ (substantial individuals are idempotent under association).

3. The association operation · is commutative.

4. The association operation is associative.

Basically, this postulate states that any collection of individuals can be viewed as an individual and that the order of combining them is not important. Whether a given collection makes sense is irrelevant. Also, an individual cannot be combined with itself to form something new.

A corollary of postulate 1 is that a string $a_1 \cdot a_2 \cdot ... \cdot a_n$ represents an individual. The following three definitions relate to the notion that individuals may be composed of other individuals.

**Definition 1:**    An individual $x$ is *composite* if and only if (iff) there exist substantial individuals $y$ and $z$ such that $y \neq x$, $z \neq x$, and $x = y \cdot z$. Otherwise, the individual is *simple*.

The meaning of definition 1 is that an individual is considered composite if it can be described as made of (at least) two other individuals. For example, if an electronic component can be disassembled into two subcomponents (where each might be disassembled further), then it is considered composite.

**Definition 2:**    Let $x$ and $y$ be substantial individuals. Then $x$ is-part-of $y$ iff $x \cdot y = y$.

**Definition 3:**    The *composition* of an individual is the set of its parts:

$$C(x) = \{y \mid y \text{ is-part-of } x\}.$$

A key notion is that entities possess *properties:* ". . . there are no bare individuals except in our imagination" [Bunge 1977]. Properties of substantial

---

[3] Bunge's definition was simplified and modified here for the sake of clarity and self-completeness. In particular, Bunge assumes the existence of a "null individual," which is not necessary for our purposes.

individuals are called *substantial properties*. A distinction is made between *attributes* and properties. An individual may have a property that is unknown to us. In contrast, an attribute is a feature assigned by us to an object. Some of the attributes of a thing will reflect their properties. Indeed, we recognize properties only through attributes. A known property must have at least one attribute representing it.

Properties do not exist on their own but are "attached" to entities. On the other hand, entities are not bundles of properties. Thus, it might be said that the fundamental components of the world are entities, that entities are "known" to us through their properties, and that properties materialize in terms of attributes.

The properties of composite things may be related to the properties of the things in their composition. Hence, properties of composite things are of two kinds: *hereditary*, that is, properties that belong to the components of a (composite) entity, and nonhereditary. The latter are called *emergent properties*.

**Definition 4:**   Let $P$ be a property of an entity $x$ with composition $C(x)$. Then:

1. $P$ is a *resultant* or *hereditary property* of $x$ iff there exists $y \in C(x)$, $y \neq x$, such that $P$ is a property of $y$.

2. $P$ is an *emergent property* of $x$ if there is no $y \in C(x)$, $y \neq x$, such that $P$ is a property of $y$.

To demonstrate this notion, consider a computer. The memory capacity of the computer is the same as its memory size, so it is an hereditary property. However, the processing power of the computer depends on how all its components function together and is therefore an emergent property.

**Definition 5:**   Let $T$ be a subset of substantial individuals. Let $P$ be the set of properties.

1. The set of *properties of individual* $x \in T$ is $p(x) = \{P \in P|\ x \text{ possesses } P\}$.

2. The set of substantial properties of the $T$'s is $p(T) = \{P \in P|\ \text{for all } x \in T, x \text{ possesses } P\}$.

It is important that no two concrete things can be the same. This is formalized in the following assumption:

**Postulate 2:**   No two substantial individuals have exactly the same properties.

If we perceive that two entities are identical, it is just because we do not assign attributes to all their substantial properties.

We can now summarize the main premises underlying the definition of a thing:

1. All things possess properties.

2. Properties do not exist independent of entities.

3. Entities are not sets of properties.

4. The totality of properties of an entity (substantial individual) is required to render it different from any other entity.

**Definition 6:** Let $x$ be a substantial individual and $p(x)$ the collection of its properties. Then the individual with its properties is called the *thing* (or *concrete object*) $X$: $X=<x,p(x)>$.

Things are perceived (in sciences, ontology, or other symbolic representations) as concepts or models. This is formalized via the notion of *conceptual schemata*. A conceptual schema of a thing will be called a *model thing*. A model thing is defined in terms of a *frame of reference*,[4] which is a "point of view," and a set of functions that represent the properties that are important for the purpose for which we model the thing. Bunge uses physics to demonstrate the concepts; for example, a mass point is viewed differently from various frames of reference, at different times, and it can be described by various sets of properties (such as <mass, position, force>). These concepts can be extended to the types of systems handled by business information systems. For example, consider a product that is manufactured, distributed, and sold through retailers. The same product is viewed differently by a manufacturer, a retailer, and a customer. Each of them may assign different attributes to it because for each, different properties (out of the totality of properties) are relevant.

**Definition 7:** Let $X=<x,p(x)>$ be a thing of class $T$.[5] A *functional schema* $X_m$ of $X$ is a certain nonempty set $M$, together with a finite sequence $F$ of functions on $M$, each of which represents a property of things in $T$. Briefly, $X_m=<M,F>$, where $F=<F_i | F_i$ is a function on $M$ and $1 \leq i \leq n < \infty>$.

In this definition $M$ stands for all possible frames of reference or points of view.

**Postulate 3:** Any thing can be modeled as a functional schema.

---

[4] Here we use the words "frame of reference" in a more general sense than its meaning in physics to include a full specification of the point of view, conditions of observation, and time (when applicable).

[5] Classes will be defined formally later. In this context a "class" refers to a set of objects that have similar properties.

### 21.1.3 States and Laws[6]

In a functional schema $F$ each component is $F_i: M \rightarrow V_i$ where $V_i$ is a domain of values for the property represented by $F_i$. The $F_i$ are called *state variables* or *state functions*. The set of all values of $F_i$ is called the *state* of the thing. Every thing is at a given time in some state. Formally:

**Definition 8:** In a functional schema $X_m = <M,F>$, $F_i$, for $1 \leq i \leq n$, is called the $i$th *state function* for $X$, $F$ is the *total state function* for $X$, and its value $F_m = <F_1,...,F_n>(m) = <F_1(m),...,F_n(m)>$ for $m \in M$ is said to represent the state of $X$ at $m$.

Note that there is no such thing as an absolute state function. The choice of the specific state function depends on knowledge, goals, views, etc.

In reality, not every conceivable combination of values of the state function can materialize as a state of a thing. Rather, the nature of a thing is such that only certain combinations are allowed. This notion is formalized via the concept of *laws*.

**Definition 9:** Let $X_m = <M,F>$ be a functional schema for a thing $X$. Any restriction on the possible values of the components of $F$ or any relation among two or more such components of $F$ is called a *law statement*.[7]

Since laws contain information about things, they are also properties of things. More formally, a law statement can be viewed as a mapping from the possible states of a thing (in a given functional schema) into the set {'lawful', 'unlawful'}. Being a function on values of properties that are functions on $M$, the possible frames of reference, a law is also a function on $M$.

The concept of a law is fundamental in modeling things because it contains the knowledge of what a thing can be or not be. In this sense, laws contain "dynamic" information of things. Further, laws define the part of the set of states that a thing can really be in, as opposed to the conceivable states that are the possible combinations of values of state functions. Hence, the following definition:

**Definition 10:** Let $X_m = <M,F>$ be a functional schema for a thing $X$, where $F: <F_1,...,F_n>: M \rightarrow V_1 ... V_n$ is the state function, and let $L(X)$ be the set of all law statements of $X$. Then the subset of the codomain $V_1 \times V_2 \times ... \times V_n$ of $F$ restricted by the conditions (law statements) in $L(X)$ is called the *lawful state space* of $X$ in the representation $X_m$, or $S_L(X)$:

$$S_L(X) = \{<x_1,...,x_n> \in V_1 \times ... \times V_n \mid F \text{ satisfies jointly every member of } L(X)\}$$

---

[6] The definitions in this subsection are based on [Bunge 1977, pp. 126–134].

[7] Bunge adds some ontological conditions on what is a law: that the restriction belongs to a consistent theory about the $X$'s and that it has been confirmed empirically to a satisfactory degree. For our purpose here, this definition suffices.

and every point of $S_L(X)$ is called a *lawful* (or *really possible*) *state* of $X$ in the representation $X_m$.

To demonstrate, consider the following example: the thing is an account and all related transactions. The law statements are: "Balance is the algebraic sum of transaction amounts" and "No transaction is dated prior to the date the account was created." In this case, the lawful state space of the account is the one in which all transactions pertain to dates after a given date and the balance is equal to the sum of transactions.

### 21.1.4 Classes and Kinds[8]

Since things are known via their properties, things that possess the same properties are "similar" in some sense. Hence, properties can be used to classify things. This notion is formalized in the following definitions:

**Definition 11:**   The *scope* of a substantial property is the collection of entities possessing it: $G(P) = \{x \mid P \in p(x)\}$.

**Definition 12:**   A subset $X$ of individuals is called a *class* if and only if there exists a substantial property such that $X$ is the scope of $P$.

**Definition 13:**   Let $R$ be a subset of properties. The set $\cap \{G(P) \mid P \in R\}$ is called the $R$-kind.

An $R$-kind is a class with respect to a "compound property" composed of all properties in $R$.

Recall that laws are also properties of things; hence the definition of an $R$-kind can be specialized to a set of properties that are laws. This leads to the following definition:

**Definition 14:**   Let $L^*$ be a subset of laws. The set $\cap \{G(L) \mid L \in L^*\}$ is called a *natural kind*.

All things of the same natural kind will have the same lawful state space. The lawful state space is, therefore, a way of describing the general properties of things of the same kind.[9]

To demonstrate the above definition, consider the students of a given university. They are a class since there are two properties that are common to all of them: 1) all are human beings, and 2) all are enrolled in the given university. Assume now that the university has regulations specifying which courses have to be completed in order to graduate. Then, for all graduating

---

[8] The definitions in this subsection are based on [Bunge 1977, pp. 140–146].

[9] If we assume that the things in a natural kind are taken from the same kind, then they all have the same properties and the same laws. From our perspective the distinction between natural kind and kind is unimportant and we shall refer to both as a "kind."

students, the state variables describing the courses taken will have values in accordance with the graduation requirements, that is, their states will be lawful with respect to the graduation rules. The graduates are a natural kind with respect to the graduation requirements.

According to the preceding definitions, a thing may belong to more than one kind; this is expressed in the following theorem.

**Theorem 1:** The collection of all kinds forms a complete lattice under inclusion.

Rather than proving this theorem, we provide the following intuitive explanation: The theorem states that the set of all kinds forms a multiple inheritence hierarchy. Let $k_1$ be a kind and let $k_2$ be a proper subset of $k_1$. Then all elements of $k_2$ have the common set of properties that the elements of $k_1$ possess. Also, a kind could be a subset of two kinds, and the inclusion relationship is assymetric. Hence, the set of all kinds can be described as a directed acyclic graph.


## 21.1.5 Changes, Events, and Interaction[10]

Full knowledge of a thing requires information about how the states of the thing can *change*. The following postulate assures the necessary condition for this.

**Postulate 4:** Every (concrete) thing has at least two distinct states.

When a thing undergoes a change, at least one property will have to change in value; hence, a change of a thing is manifested as a change of state. It follows that, for a change to be possible, the thing has to have more than one state. However, the question may arise: when a thing $x$ changes, could it stop being $x$ and become a new thing $y$? For example, if a "car" thing has been painted, is it still the same car? And if it were taken apart, is it still a car? To answer this, recall that a thing is described via a functional schema, and that the functional schema describes a view of a thing, and therefore is in the eye of the beholder. Bunge, therefore, adopts *the principle of nominal invariance* [Bunge 1977, p. 221]:

> A thing, if named, shall keep its name throughout its history, as long as the latter does not include changes in natural kind—changes which call for changes of name.

A change of state will be termed an *event*. An event can be described as an ordered pair $<s_1,s_2>$ where $s_1$ and $s_2$ are the states before and after the change, respectively. Consider the state space $S(X)$ of a thing $X$. The set of

[10]Exact page references to [Bunge 1977] in this subsection are as follows: Postulate 4 to definition 16 are from pp. 218–230, definition 17 is modified from that of p. 255, and Postulate 5 is based on pp. 259–260.

all conceivable events is $E(X)=S(X) \times S(X)$.[11] This includes the identity event that designates no change: $<s,s>$, $s \in S(X)$. Also, two events can be combined into another event if the first ends in a state that is the beginning of the second. This combination will be designated by $<a,b><b,c>=<a,c>$, and $<a,c>$ will be called a *complex* event.

Not all conceivable events can happen in reality, because the transition between two states (even if lawful) is not always allowed. This leads to the following definitions:

**Definition 15:**   Let $S_L(X)$ be a lawful state space for a thing $X$. Then the family of *lawful transformations* of the state space into itself is the set of functions:

$G_L(X)=\{g$ is a function $|g{:}S_L(X) \to S_L(X)$ and $g$ is compatible with the laws of $X\}$

**Definition 16:**   Let $G_L(X)$ be a family of lawful transformations on $S_L(X)$. Then the *space of lawful events* is

$E_L(X)=\{<s,s'> \in S_L(X) \otimes S_L(X) \mid s'=g(s)$ and $g \in G_L(X)\}$

To illustrate, consider again the university example. The family of lawful transformations is defined by the allowed transitions of a student's status, such as conditions for enrolling in a course, completing a course, completing a program of studies, and graduating. The space of lawful events will include pairs of states such as $<$ student is enrolled in course $a$, student completed course $a>$ provided the student has completed all requirements of the course (otherwise, there is no lawful transformation that can cause this event).

Recall the ontological principle "every thing changes." This principle requires that a thing changes its state with time. The states "traversed" by the thing can be described as a "trajectory" in the state space. This leads to the following definition:

**Definition 17:**   Let $F$ be a state function for a thing $X$ relative to a reference frame $f$. Let the set of states for the reference frame be $S(f)$. Assume that there is a one-to-one mapping $S(f) \to S(X)$, and let the states of $S(f)$ be denoted by $t \in S(f)$. The *history of $X$ relative to $f$* is the set of ordered pairs $h(X)=\{<t,F(t)>\mid t \in S(f)\}$.

The most common case is that the states of a reference frame $f$ refer to $f$ at different times. In this case, the mapping $S(f) \to S(X)$ means that for any

---

[11]The operations $\times$ and $\otimes$ (to be used later) designate external product on sets, namely, all pairs $(a,b)$ where $a \in A$, $b \in B$.

given time the thing $X$ is in a unique state. In our university example, at any given time the student will be in a state described by courses completed and presently taken. The history of the student will be the description of the student's states at different times.

The notion of history allows for defining the interaction of objects. Basically, if two objects interact, then at least one of them will not be traversing the same states as it would if the other did not exist. This is formalized in the following definition.

**Definition 18:** Let $X$ and $Y$ be two different things with state functions $F_X$ and $F_Y$, respectively. Let $h(X)$ and $h(Y)$ be their respective histories. $X$ *acts on* $Y$ if the history of $Y$, given $X$, is different from $h(Y)$: $h(Y|X) \neq h(Y)$.[12]

To demonstrate this notion, assume that students exchange information about courses. It might happen that a student will decide not to enroll in a course that he or she would have taken otherwise; therefore, the student's history will be different than what it would be without consulting other students.

**Definition 19:** Two different things *interact* iff each acts upon the other.

**Definition 20:** Two different things are *bonded* (or *linked* or *coupled*) together iff at least one of them acts upon the other.

An important principle is that no thing is *observable* if it cannot be "acted upon" by other things. This is expressed in the following postulate.

**Postulate 5:** Every thing acts on, and is acted upon by, other things.

## 21.1.6 Combining Things and Change

We conclude this section with a quote from Bunge in which he ties together the concepts of things and events [Bunge 1977, p. 273]:

"A basic polarity in traditional metaphysics is that of being and becoming: event is opposed to thing, process to stuff, change to structure. This opposition makes no sense in our system, where every change is a transformation of some thing or other, and every thing is in flux. This view . . . is consistent with science: the latter provides no ground for hypothesizing the existence of thingless events anymore than it suggests that there might be changeless things."

---

[12] This definition was simplified for the sake of clarity. It assumes some intuitive understanding of what $h(Y|X)$ means as opposed to $h(Y)$.

## 21.2 MAPPING ONTOLOGICAL CONCEPTS INTO OBJECT CONCEPTS

In this section we review the main principles of the object-oriented approach and compare them to the ontological notions of things discussed in the previous section. We begin with a statement from [Banerjee et al. 1987]: "In an object-oriented system all conceptual entities are modeled as objects." Each object has a "private memory" that holds its state information. This information is held as *instance variables*.

[Nierstrasz 1986] identifies five main categories of principles or concepts that are attributed to the notion of an object:[13]

Data abstraction or encapsulation

Independence and persistence

Message passing

Inheritance

Homogeneity

In the following we briefly repeat the definition of each of these principles and discuss the ontological concepts to which it is related.

### 21.2.1 Data Abstraction

According to [Nierstrasz 1986]: "By far the most important concept in the object-oriented approach is data abstraction. By this we mean that we are interested in the behaviour of an object rather than its representation." The behavior of an object is encapsulated in its methods. Methods are mechanisms that have access to and can change the "state" of an object. Thus, an object type is described in terms of the form (instance variables) of its instances and the operations (methods) applicable to its instance variables. The instance variables, together with the methods, are called the *properties* of the object [Banerjee et al. 1987].

In the ontological approach, things must change and changes cannot be described separately from things. In this respect, encapsulation is a fundamental principle. However, the notion of methods or any other mechanism for changing the state of an object does not exist. Instead, the concept of a law defines the lawful or "allowed" states (i.e., combinations of state variables). Laws are viewed as properties of things.

---

[13] Nierstrasz mentions a sixth principle, concurrency, but indicates that it is applicable to some systems only.

## 21.2.2 Independence

The notion of independence incorporates two characteristics of an object. One is related to the state of the object and the other to its existence. This is explained in [Nierstrasz 1986] as "Objects also have control over their own state. Once created, an object will continue to exist (or *persist*) even if its creator dies."

Independence implies that the only way an object can change its state is through the actions of its own methods, namely, through its dynamic characteristics. Therefore, encapsulation is a necessary condition for independence.

In ontology, the possible states of a thing are decided by the laws of the thing. These laws are considered properties of the thing. Persistence of a thing manifests through the principle of *nominal invariance* that enables changes of state without changing the essence of the thing. There are no explicit mechanisms for the creation or destruction of things.

## 21.2.3 Message Passing

In the object-oriented approach objects can communicate only through message passing. A message can cause an object to "behave" by invoking a method of the object. Thus, objects may affect each other through message passing and, since objects are independent, this is the only way they can do so. Indeed, methods can be viewed as definitions of responses to possible messages [Banerjee et al. 1987].

Ontology states the principle that every thing is acted upon by other things. The effect of things on each other manifests through the history of the things, namely, the states they traverse in time. Again, ontology is not concerned with the specific mechanisms through which the interaction between things is attained. A formalism for interaction will be suggested in the next section.

## 21.2.4 Homogeneity

Homogeneity implies that everything is an object. In particular, for complete homogeneity, messages and properties (instance variables) should be viewed as objects. Note that in both cases, this approach leads to circularity [Nierstrasz 1986]. For if messages are viewed as objects, then they should send messages to communicate with objects, and so on. Similarly, if attributes are objects, they should have their own attributes, which are objects, etc. Therefore, one has to stop arbitrarily at a certain level in order to break the circularity.

Ontology makes a clear distinction between things and their properties. In this sense, there is no complete homogeneity. Moreover, properties cannot exist independent of things; hence, there is an asymmetry in the fundamental characteristics of the two concepts. Ontology allows for things to be composed of other things, and also makes a specific assumption that there exist simple things that cannot be further decomposed. Thus, the existence of a basic level is a principle, and not an arbitrary decision. It is possible that certain properties belong to a thing that is in the composition of a given thing. Also, ontology adds the distinction between resultant and emergent properties, thus formalizing the idea that a thing may be totally different from the collection of things in its composition. This view implies that state variables of a thing belong either to its composing objects or only to the thing itself.

### 21.2.5 Inheritance

Objects can be grouped together into classes. A class is a definition of an object type. All objects in a class have the same instance variables and methods and respond to the same messages. "A class describes the *form* (instance variables) of its instances and the operations (methods) applicable to its instances" [Banerjee et al. 1987]. Objects can be categorized into *subtypes* or subclasses through *specialization*. Specialization forms an "IS-A" hierarchy. Objects in a subclass inherit all the instance variables and the methods from the superclass, but may have additional instance variables and methods. Multiple inheritance can exist; therefore, class hierarchy can be viewed as a directed acyclic graph (a lattice) [Banerjee et al. 1987; Nierstrasz 1986; Stefik and Bobrow 1986]. It is important to note that in the object-oriented literature, class hierarchy is viewed as a mechanism to provide for reusability of code [Nierstrasz 1986], savings of information in databases and programming, and simplicity [Banerjee et al. 1987].

In ontology, classes are defined based on the notion of the scope of properties. The concept of a class is extended to a kind by considering the combined scope of a set of properties, and further to a natural kind by considering the scope of a set of laws. Thus, both "static" properties (attributes) and dynamic properties (laws) are used in the definition of kind hierarchies. It can be proved that the collection of kinds forms a complete lattice under inclusion [Bunge 1977]. Hence, ontology's view of classes parallels the notion of classes in the object-oriented approach.

## 21.3 DEFINING OBJECTS IN ONTOLOGICAL TERMS

In this section we suggest a formalization of the object concept based on ontology. In doing so, we try to capture as much as possible of the concepts of the object-oriented approach to programming and database modeling.

### 21.3.1 Basic Principles

#### Statics: Encapsulation and Persistence

The world is made of *objects*. Objects describe concrete beings, that is, specific entities rather than types or classes.

For example, when considering people, each individual will be viewed as an object.

Objects are known (or observable) to the world through their *properties.*

Properties are of two kinds: *observable attributes* and *laws.* An observable attribute is a mapping from the set of objects that have this property into a given domain, namely, it is a property to which specific values can be assigned. Laws are constraints on the allowed combinations of the values of attributes.

The conclusion is that since both attributes and laws are properties, a representation of a property can be either a function assigning a value to a property or a predicate specifying whether state constraints hold.

The specific set of properties used to describe a given object depends on the point of view and the purpose of modeling. This set is called a *functional schema.*[14]

The value of an attribute at a certain time is called a *state variable.*

The set of state variables defines the *state* of the object.

The allowed states of an object are determined by the set of object laws. Laws are also properties of things. An object can only be in states consistent with its laws. Such states are called *lawful* states.

Two or more things can be combined through *association* to form another thing. An object that can be described as an association of other objects is called a *composite object.* An object that is not composite is called a *simple object.*

There exist simple objects.

The properties of a composite object are of two kinds:

1. *Resultant* or *hereditary*—when the property belongs also to an object in the composition of the composite object.
2. *Emergent*—when the property does not belong to any object in the composition of the composite object.

### Dynamics and Object Communication

Objects can stay only in lawful states.

An object that is in unlawful state will change its state to a lawful state, uniquely defined by the unlawful state.

Objects do not reach unlawful states spontaneously.

---

[14] Note that the notion of a functional schema can be interpreted as a formalization of the concept of perspective [Stefik and Bobrow 1986].

To demonstrate this notion, consider again the example of a bank account and transactions as a (composite) object. When a new transaction occurs, the balance will not equal the sum of transactions and hence it will have to change. Also, the balance will not change "spontaneously" unless a transaction happens.

It is important to note that objects do not "obey" laws. Rather, laws are the rules describing the states the object can assume. If an object remains in a state that is considered "unlawful," then the law is ill-defined.[15]

The following premise deals with interaction among objects:

An object can affect the state of another object. This is done via a law linking state variables of the two objects.

As an object affects the state of another object, it might place it in an unlawful state. Then, the affected object will change to a new lawful state. It follows that the last four principles are sufficient to describe the dynamics of objects interaction.

### 21.3.2 Formal Notation and Definitions[16]

The set of states of an object $i$ will be denoted by $S(i)$.

**Definition a:**  A law is a function on the set of states:

$$L : S(i) \rightarrow S(i).$$

A state for which $L(s) = s$ will be called a *lawful state*.
A state for which $L(s) \neq s$ will be called an *unlawful state*.

Note that while the concept of law specifies "allowed" states, or to what (lawful) state an unlawful state will change, it does not relate to the "how" of the state change; that is, it is an *assertional*, not a *procedural* concept.

**Definition b:**  Let $i, j$ be two objects. An *interface* or *interobject* law is a function:

$$A: S(i) \otimes S(j) \rightarrow S(i) \otimes S(j)$$

---

[15] Objects are viewed here as describing real things. However, if objects are viewed as implementations, then the situation reverses, that is, the laws are given and the object has to be implemented so that it "obeys" them.

[16] The definitions, lemmas, and theorems from this point onward will be denoted by letters to distinguish them from definitions, lemmas, and theorems taken from Ontology [Bunge 1977].

If two objects do not interact, then each of them may assume any (lawful) state in its set of states. However, if the objects interact, then not all possible combinations of their (lawful) states will be allowed. The idea of an interface law is, therefore, an extension of the law concept as defined for a single object.

In the following we use $s^k$ for the state of object $k$ (in its respective set of states) and denote $A((s^i, s^j)) = (s^i, s^j)$.

**Definition c:**   A state for which $(s^i, s^j) = (s^i, s^j)$ will be called an *interobject stable state*. If $(s^i, s^j) \neq (s^i, s^j)$ then the joint state will be called an *interobject unstable state*. Further, for $s^i \neq s^i$, we will say that object $j$ affects object $i$. For $s^j \neq s^j$ we will say that object $i$ affects object $j$.

To demonstrate the notions of an interobject state and objects' interaction, consider two workstations where station 1 sends signals to station 2. The state of workstation $k$ is defined by the pair $<I_k, O_k>$ where $I_k$ and $O_k$ are the input and output of the process running on the workstation. The interobject state is $(<I_1, O_1>, <I_2, O_2>)$. Assume that the following interobject law holds: $I_2 = O_1$. In terms of our notation this will be expressed as $A(<w, x>, <y, z>) = (<w, x>, <x, z>)$. Thus, if $y = x$, the interobject state is stable, and if $x \neq y$ then it is unstable.

The two types of laws, object laws and interobject laws, contain the information on which state changes will happen, and what these state changes are. Hence, laws capture the dynamics of objects. The dynamics of objects can be described in terms of their state changes. Such changes are called events.

**Definition d:**   A transition between two states will be termed an *event*. An event will be denoted by an ordered pair $e = <s_1, s_2>$ where $s_1$ and $s_2$ are the states before and after the transition.

Since a law describes the possible changes of state, a law can be stated explicitly by enumerating all the events that begin on unlawful states (lawful states are not changed by the law).

Using these notations and definitions, we can now describe the dynamics of interaction of objects. Assume that the object pair $i,j$ is in an unstable state $(s_1^i, s_1^j)$. Consider first object $i$ and assume that it is in a lawful state $s_1^i \in S_L(i)$. Suppose that due to interaction with object $j$ (i.e., the interface law between $i$ and $j$), $i$ now changes to a state $s_2^i$. If $s_2^i$ is lawful, then nothing more will happen. However, if $s_2^i$ is unlawful, then object $i$ will change its state to a new state $s_3^i$ that conforms with its laws $\{L^i\}$. The action of object $j$ on $i$ is therefore modeled in terms of a sequence of two events: $<s_1^i, s_2^i>$ due to the interface law, and $<s_2^i, s_3^i>$ due to the object laws. The state of object $j$ can be treated in the same way.

To demonstrate this, consider again the two communicating workstations. Assume that workstation $k$ is governed by a law describing the process running on it, relating the output to the input: $O_k = f_k(I_k)$. Now, if the output of workstation 1 changes, the interobject law will result in a change in the input of workstation 2. The state $<I_2,O_2>$ may now be unlawful, and hence it will change to $<I_2,f_2(I_2)>$.

Some comments should be made about this view in comparison with the usual notion of object dynamics conveyed through methods and messages. First, methods are viewed as operations that encapsulate the behavior of an object. Methods are capable of "responding" to specific messages. In contrast, in the present model there is no concept of an operation. The internal dynamics of an object is captured via an assertional concept, a law. The specific way a law is implemented is not included in the model. A law is "triggered" if the object is in an unlawful state. This may happen because of interface laws connecting it with other objects, namely, due to the effect of other objects. Second, no mechanism for object interaction has been specified. Indeed, more than one "implementation" can be suggested. Mechanisms in use usually adapt everyday communication metaphors. One possibility is to assume that a "message" is sent from one object to another and that this message might change the state of the latter to unlawful so it will have to respond by a further change of state. Another possibility is to introduce a public communication area ("bulletin board," "blackboard," or "common workspace") [Tsichritzis et al. 1987; Woo and Lochovsky 1986], and to assume that objects can place information in this area or read information from this area. In particular, the common message-passing paradigm can be viewed as an implementation of the special case where only one object changes its state when the joint state is unstable. Whichever approach is taken, the important point is that both message passing and common-area communication are viewed as either metaphors for object interaction or ways of implementation. Finally, since no direct parallel exists for methods and messages at the model level, the notion that methods can respond to specific messages cannot be accommodated.

The notion of encapsulation[17] is supported in several ways:

1. It is not necessary that an object knows the state of another object, although it is not an impossibility. All that an object can observe are changes to its own state as a result of interface laws. Such changes can be interpreted as obtaining information about the state of another object.

2. An object is not required to know that it has forced a change of state on another object.

3. An object does not have to be "aware" that the other object has further changed its state in accordance with its laws.

---

[17] The features discussed here can also be viewed as "information hiding" in the sense of [Parnas 1972]. This notion of information hiding differs from that of [Banerjee et al. 1987], where the concept is used to describe sharing of information via class variables.

### 21.3.3 Class Hierarchy and Inheritance: Formal Definitions

We begin by introducing some notation:

Let $X$ be a set of objects. Let $p(x)$ be the set of properties of $x \in X$. We denote by $P(X)$ the set of all properties possessed by objects in $X$: $P(X) = \cup \{p(x) \mid x \in X\}$ and by $2^x$ we denote the power set of $X$ (the set of all subsets of $X$).

**Definition e:** The *scope* of a property $P$ in $X$ is the subset of objects possessing the property $P$:

$$G(P;X) = \{x \mid x \in X \text{ and } P \in p(x)\} \in 2^x$$

Recall that properties include both observable attributes and laws. Hence, in our definition a scope is defined in terms of either. A class can now be defined on the basis of the notion of scope.

**Definition f:** Let $p = \{P\}$ be any subset of $P(X)$. A class with respect to $p$ in $X$ is the set of all objects possessing all properties in $p$:

$$C(p;X) = \cap \{G(P) \mid P \in p\}.$$

**Lemma a:** Let $p_1, p_2$ be two subsets of $P(X)$. Then $p_1$ is a (proper) subset of $p_2$ if and only if $C(p_2;X)$ is a (proper) subset of $C(p_1;X)$.

**Theorem a:** Let $2^{P(X)}$ be the set of all subsets of properties of the set $X$. Then the set $CL = \{C(p,X) \mid p \in 2^{P(X)}\}$ is a directed acyclic graph (a lattice) under inclusion.

Lemma *a* and theorem *a* provide the basis for the notions of class hierarchy and inheritance of properties. To understand this, consider two sets of properties $p_1$ and $p_2$ such that $p_1 \subset p_2$. Denote the set of all objects possessing $p_i$ by $C_i$. Every object possessing all properties in $p_2$ also possesses all properties in $p_1$, hence $C_2 \subseteq C_1$. Also, consider any subset of $C_1$. All objects in this subset have the properties $p_1$. Therefore, it can be said that $C_2$ is a subclass of $C_1$ or, alternatively, that $C_1$ is a superclass of $C_2$. In addition, assume also that $p_3 \subset p_2$. Then, $C_3$ is also a superclass of $C_2$. Hence, the definitions of classes create a multiple inheritance hierarchy. Since the inclusion operation $\subset$ is asymmetric, classes can be described as a directed acyclic graph where the existence of a link implies an inclusion.

### 21.3.4 Composite Objects

The basis for introducing composite objects is the following assumption:

Every pair of objects can be combined through a pairwise-association operation (denoted by $\cdot$) into another object. The operation $\cdot$ is commutative and associative.

Using this notion, an object may be composed of other objects.

**Definition g:**   Let $x$ and $y$ be objects such that $x \cdot y = x$, $x \neq y$. Then $y$ is a part of $x$, denoted as $y$ p-o $x$.

**Definition h:**   The composition of an object equals the set of its parts:

$$C(x) = \{y \mid y \text{ p-o } x\}.$$

**Definition i:**   $x$ is a simple object if and only if $y$ p-o $x \rightrightarrows y = x$.

**Theorem b:**   The set of all objects is partially ordered under the relation p-o.

**Definition j:**   Let $P \in p(x)$ be a property of object $x$. Then $P$ is a *resultant* or *hereditary* property if there exists $y \in C(x)$ such that $P \in p(y)$, $y \neq x$. On the other hand, $P$ is an *emergent* property if for all $y$ such that $y \in C(x)$ and $y \neq x$, $P \notin p(y)$.

The notion of an emergent property enables us to attribute to an object *holistic* properties. Recall, however, that the object can only be in lawful states, and that the lawful states are determined by the laws of the object. Since objects can have some state variables that are emergent and others that are resultant, the laws of the object link these two kinds. We therefore make the following observation:

The emergent properties of an object are linked by object laws to the properties of its composing objects.

Furthermore, we will assume that all properties of a composite object are related to the properties of its composing objects by laws:

Let $P$ be an emergent property of object $x$. Then there exists a law on the states of $x$ that uniquely determines the value of $P$ for every allowed combination of values of the properties of the objects in the composition $C(x)$ of $x$.

In this light, every state variable of a composite object is either "attached" to an object in the composition, or is a function of state variables that are attached to objects in the composition. This view of a composite object can be interpreted as a generalization of the concept of instance variables as objects. Moreover, since both emergent state variables and resultant state variables appear as part of the state, the objects that interact with the given object do not have to be "aware" of the composition of the object. This can be interpreted as encapsulation and independence.

## SUMMARY

The main premise of the object model of this chapter is that objects should be defined independently of any implementation considerations. The model supports the principles of encapsulation, independence and persistence, and inheritance. However, it differs from previous discussions of objects in two major areas. First, it does not rely on full homogeneity, but makes a clear distinction between the constructs of objects and properties. Secondly, the model's approach to object dynamics does not recognize the two common object-oriented concepts of message passing and methods. Instead, the model introduces the fundamental concept of a law for capturing dynamics.

This leads to the proposition that object characteristics discussed in other works may be categorized into two "levels": conceptual-oriented and implementation-oriented. In particular, the notions of encapsulation, independence and persistence, and inheritance belong to the conceptual level. In contrast, the message-passing paradigm and the method concept are implementation-oriented constructs. This might be somewhat a surprise, as message passing is usually introduced as a fundamental principle, while the notion of classes is justified on practical considerations.

It is of interest that in both areas in which the proposed model deviates from most of the previous discussions, there are recognized problems. First, the requirement for complete homogeneity leads to circularity problems that should be arbitrarily broken. Second, the dynamic concepts are a source of confusion. Thus, one author claims that "Every object has a clearly defined interface . . . The interface is a collection of operations, or 'methods' . . ." [Nierstrasz 1986]. In contrast, other authors claim that "Methods, as well as instance variables . . . are not visible from outside of the object" [Banerjee et al. 1987]. Finally, even message passing as a paradigm for object communication is replaced or amended, in some works, by the "workspace" or "blackboard" approach. Thus, we find in one article: "Independence of objects is supported conceptually by using message passing as a model for object communication" [Nierstrasz 1986]; in another [Tsichritzis et al. 1987] the authors suggest that their objects (called KNOs) ". . . communicate through the blackboard for reasons of *autonomy* and *resilience*"; and a third work employs both approaches [Woo and Lochovsky 1986].

In the model suggested in this chapter, these conflicts about dynamics do not arise because they belong to the implementation level, and thus are not dealt with by the model. Indeed, the differences can be settled by viewing the different approaches as different ways to implement the fundamental abstract concept of a law.

Some other differences between this model and common concepts of objects should also be noted. First, in the present model there is no mechanism for object creation. Second, the model does not assume full homogeneity, as it relies on constructs that cannot be viewed as objects. Finally, for composite objects the model introduces a distinction between resultant (hereditary) and emergent properties.

## Acknowledgment

I am indebted to my colleague Carson Woo for many enlightening discussions of the object concept. This work was supported in part by a Natural Sciences and Engineering Research Council of Canada operating grant, OGP0004105.

## References

[Abbott 1987] R.J. Abbott, "Knowledge Abstraction," *Communications of the ACM,* vol. 30, pp. 664–671, 1987.

[Banerjee et al. 1987] J. Banerjee, H. Chou, J.F. Garza, W. Kim, D. Woelk, and N. Ballou, "Data Model Issues for Object-Oriented Applications," *ACM Transactions on Office Information Systems,* vol. 5, no. 1, pp. 3–26, January 1987.

[Borgida et al. 1985] A. Borgida, S. Greenspan, and J. Mylopoulos, "Knowledge Representation as the Basis for Requirements Specifications," *IEEE Computer,* pp. 82–90, April 1985.

[Brooks 1987] F.P. Brooks, Jr., "No Silver Bullet, Essence and Accidents of Software Engineering," *IEEE Computer,* pp. 10–19, April 1987.

[Bunge 1977] M. Bunge, *Treatise on Basic Philosophy: Vol. 3: Ontology I: The Furniture of the World,* Reidel, Boston, 1977.

[Bunge 1979] M. Bunge, *Treatise on Basic Philosophy: Vol. 4: Ontology II: A World of Systems,* Reidel, Boston, 1979.

[Kronke and Dolan 1988] D.M. Kronke and K.A. Dolan, *Database Processing: Fundamentals, Design, Implementation,* Third Edition, SRA, Chicago, 1988.

[Newell and Simon 1976] A. Newell and H.A. Simon, "Computer Science as Empirical Inquiry: Symbols and Search," Turing Award Lecture, 1975, *Communications of the ACM,* vol. 19, pp. 113–126, 1976.

[Nierstrasz 1986] O.M. Nierstrasz, "What is an 'Object' in Object Oriented Programming?", in *Objects and Things,* ed. D. Tsichritzis, Universite De Geneve, Centre Universitaire D'Informatique, pp. 1–13, 1987. Reprinted from *The Proceedings of the CERN School of Computing,* Renesse, The Netherlands, August 31–September 13, 1986.

[Nierstrasz 1989] O.M. Nierstrasz, "A Survey of Object Oriented Concepts," in *Object-Oriented Concepts, Databases, and Applications,* ed. W. Kim and F. Lochovsky, Addison-Wesley, Reading, MA, 1988.

[Parnas 1972] D.L. Parnas, "On the Criteria To Be Used in Decomposing Systems into Modules," *Communications of the ACM,* vol. 15, pp. 1053–1058, 1972.

[Stefik and Bobrow 1986] M. Stefik and D.G. Bobrow, "Object-Oriented Programming: Themes and Variations," *The AI Magazine,* vol. 6, no. 4, pp. 96–112, 1986.

[Tsichritzis et al. 1987] D. Tsichritzis, E. Fiume, S. Gibbs, and O. Nierstrasz, "KNOs: Knowledge Acquisition, Dissemination, and Manipulation Objects," *ACM Transactions on Office Information Systems,* vol. 5, no. 1, pp. 3–26, January 1987.

[Wand 1988] Y. Wand, "An Ontological Foundation for Information Systems Design Theory," *Proceedings of the IFIP WG 8.4 Working Conference on Office Information Systems: The Design Process,* Linz, Austria, August 1988.

[Wand and Weber 1988] Y. Wand and R. Weber, "A Deep Structure Theory of Information Systems," Working Paper 88-MIS-003, Faculty of Commerce and Business Administration, The University of British Columbia, March 1988.

[Woo and Lochovsky 1986] C. Woo and F. Lochovsky, "Supporting Distributed Office Problem Solving in Organizations," *ACM Transactions on Office Information Systems,* vol. 4, no. 3, pp. 185–204, 1986.

# 22

---

# Active Objects: Realities and Possibilities

Clarence A. Ellis, Simon J. Gibbs

---

## INTRODUCTION

This chapter defines and explains the concept of *active object*. Justifications
and examples of active objects are presented. We briefly discuss several systems
that have been designed and implemented that incorporate active objects. We
also mention some of the research issues and future possibilities in this area.
We focus on the "active" aspects and issues of these systems, and do not discuss
other important issues such as interclass relationships and inheritance that
we feel are less related to the active object theme. At the end of the chapter,
we philosophize and argue that active objects are a natural mechanism for
making computing processes more generally understandable and accessible.
In the future, as we move beyond object-oriented programming, it is likely
that one of the useful enduring concepts is that of "active objects."

## 22.1 BACKGROUND, INTUITION, AND DEFINITIONS

Although active objects have not been implemented in many object-oriented systems, the notion has been around for a long time. One early reference to active objects is contained in the article "Hierarchical Program Structures" [Dahl and Hoare 1972]. The utility of active objects has been documented within the Simula language, the Smalltalk language, and other object-oriented systems. The definition that we offer here of "active object" is abstract and behavioral because different authors have interpreted this concept in different ways. All have tried to capture a notion of object intelligence, and of the object as an encapsulation of an asynchronous locus of activity. Thus we define an active object as an object in which a high degree of autonomous responsibility and control is vested. The active object is considered, within its usage, as an independent agent, and frequently a source of knowledge and activity. Many object-oriented systems have objects that must receive a message before performing any action—we would usually call these passive objects. A few object-oriented systems have objects that can initiate actions asynchronously without receiving a message—we would usually call these active objects. But the essence of the concept is the combination of the object's capabilities and its usage.

Active objects open new possibilities for modularization, and suggest that delegation of responsibility can be performed in nicer, more distributed, more natural ways. The ease with which this modularization can be obtained is a measure of the "level of activity" of an active object system. As an intuitive example, consider an electronic timecard system that records and tracks the amount of time worked by each employee (per week) in some organization. The timecards can be considered as objects (one instance per employee per week) that might receive messages updating the number of hours worked. This system can be enhanced if we consider the timecards as active objects. These objects actively seek information when necessary, autonomously check for exceptional conditions, spawn other processes when necessary, and independently move around the network to obtain approvals and other processing necessary for the employee to get paid. In this example, the concept of active object encourages a functional modularization of control and data that is difficult or impossible with most traditional systems and design methodologies. We reiterate that an object is active partly because of the capabilities with which it is endowed, but also because it is *used* in an active manner. In the remainder of this section, we explore further examples of active objects.

## 22.2 EXAMPLE SYSTEMS

We now examine a few examples of active object systems that have been designed, implemented, and fruitfully applied. Again, we restrict our focus to the highly "active," novel aspects of objects in these systems. These systems are generally intended for network architectures consisting of interconnected processors. In the following, "node" refers to a network node.

### 22.2.1 Actors

One of the earliest expressions of active objects is found in Hewitt's actor formalism [Hewitt 1977]. The basic properties of actor systems are:

1. Actors communicate with each other by sending messages, which are transferred by a *mail delivery system*.

2. Each actor consists of a mail address and a *behavior* [Agha 1986]. The behavior of an actor specifies the types of messages the actor will receive and the operations performed upon receipt.

3. Sender and receiver proceed *asynchronously* and in parallel during and after message transfer.

Using message passing between actors, one can represent common control structures such as request/reply and recursion. The actor formalism implies a very high degree of fine-granularity parallelism. Its encapsulation of data structure, procedure, and process identifies it as a forerunner of active object systems.

### 22.2.2 Argus

Actors can be described as *lightweight*; typically one would expect to find large numbers of actors present in an actor-based system and their creation or destruction should be inexpensive (comparable to the cost of a procedure call). Other systems provide much *heavier* active objects. One example is Argus [Liskov and Scheifler 1982]. Active objects within Argus are known as *guardians*. A guardian provides a set of operations that may be invoked by other guardians. Within a guardian are passive data objects and processes associated with either operation invocations or housekeeping activities of the guardian itself. Argus provides mechanisms for the synchronization of processes within guardians and for recovering a guardian's state in the case of node failure.

### 22.2.3 Emerald

Emerald is a programming language for distributed applications [Black et al. 1986]. An Emerald object is much like an actor except that the behavior is divided into two parts: *operations* that may be invoked by other objects via message passing, and an optional *process* that executes in parallel with operation invocations. Emerald objects containing a process are active, and the process is executed even in the absence of messages from other objects. Emerald objects with no process are passive—they merely respond to invocations.

Emerald supports a number of *object implementation styles*. For example, *global* objects may change location within the network and be invoked remotely, while *local* objects may be referenced only by a second, "enclosing," object. Furthermore, objects can be defined to be *immutable*, in which case the state of the object cannot change and multiple copies of the object are allowed. For example, frequently accessed static information could be encapsulated within an immutable object and replicated over the network.

Sometimes there is a tradeoff between flexibility of a system and uniformity of its underlying model. Although there is much flexibility in the Emerald system, a single object model provides a wide object spectrum from "lightweight" private objects to "heavyweight" mobile objects.

### 22.2.4 KNOs

A KNO [Tsichritzis et al. 1987] consists of an internal data state, a set of operations, and a set of *rules*. Operations are invoked by message passing, while rules, which are condition/action pairs, are continuously checked and fired if possible. KNOs exist in *environments* consisting of other KNOs and passive objects. A KNO may move from one environment to another. A KNO may also form *limb* KNOs; the system informs a parent KNO of the activities of its limbs. KNOs are intended for applications where objects must adapt their behavior or learn new behavior; this is possible with KNOs since a KNO's rule set is not fixed at specification time but may be dynamically modified.

### 22.2.5 Example Applications

Active objects are advantageously employed within applications where there is a desire to add decentralized control, parallelism, and/or distributed intelligence to enhance features such as extensibility, performance, or modularity of the system. Here are a few examples:

1. The System for Business Automation (SBA) developed an actor-based programming system to add intelligence to common business objects [Byrd et al. 1982]. The system extended the two-dimensional formlike "boxes" of SBA by enriching them with a set of behaviors and communication abilities.

2. Argus has been used in the implementation of the Collaborative Editing System (CES) [Grief et al. 1986]. CES allows a set of users to edit the same document concurrently. The concurrency control mechanisms provided by Argus greatly simplified the implementation.

3. KNOs have been used to specify "messenger" objects that aid in delivering electronic mail by searching for the intended destination [Tsichritzis and Gibbs 1987]. KNOs have also been used to specify the behavior of objects engaged in negotiation.

4. An actor-based language has been used to model the motion of animal groups such as flocks of birds and schools of fish [Reynolds 1987]. Each member of the aggregate (dubbed bird-like objects or "boids" in general) was represented by an actor. The model was used to drive an animation of the aggregate's motion.

## 22.3 ISSUES

The transition from passive objects to active objects has many implications for language design and implementation. Here we will review a number of issues that are particularly relevant to active object systems and discuss some of the alternatives that have been used in practice.

### 22.3.1 Method Invocation

The semantics of method invocation within active object systems is perhaps the most important difference between active and passive object systems. In the latter, method invocation has a procedure call semantics; that is, execution of the calling method is replaced by execution of the called method and resumes when the called method returns.

One form of active object method invocation, which mimics that used among passive objects, is the *blocking invocation*. In this case the object in which the method invocation originates is suspended until the method has been executed by the invoked object. When the invoking object resumes, it may be provided with a "return value" from the invoked object. Such a capability resembles a remote procedure call [Birrel and Nelson 1984]; it does not promote parallelism.

In contrast, during *nonblocking invocations*, the invoking object simply issues the method invocation and continues execution. This encourages parallelism but burdens the programmer with the responsibility for synchronization.

Related to method invocation are a number of subtle issues that in varying degrees are hidden from the programmer. For example, there is the entire area of error recovery: what happens if a node or the network fails during method invocation, if the invoked object does not exist, or if an inappropriate message is sent to a remote object. Most of these errors can be detected only at runtime, so some recovery mechanism is needed.

There is also the problem of scheduling the method invocation within the receiving object. Here it is useful to distinguish between *multithreaded* and *single-threaded* active objects. The first can support simultaneous method invocations (and may provide locks or monitors for controlling access to internal data), while the second allows only one invocation at a time. Furthermore, an active object may consist of methods only, and so be active only after invocation, or may also contain one or more internal processes that execute regardless of the object's interactions with other objects. Table 22.1 shows a number of method scheduling policies. For example, take the case of single-threaded objects containing both methods and an internal process. Here one approach is to interrupt the object's currently active process before servicing the method. If multiple method invocations arrive, then they must be queued. With multithreaded objects there is a *laissez faire* attitude toward scheduling invocations; however, the programmer must be aware of potential conflicts.

Both blocking and nonblocking method invocations are relatively simple extensions of standard method invocation. Active objects can also support forms of method invocation that do not resemble anything found among passive objects. One example is the *broadcast method* [Stefik et al. 1987]. Assume that objects may be replicated in some fashion. When a broadcast method is sent to such an object, it results in the method being executed by all copies of the object. This may be extended to *multicast methods,* which allow a set of objects to be specified as the target of a method invocation.

When a method is invoked, one must supply the method with its parameters. This raises a number of interesting questions when the parameters themselves are active objects. For example, Emerald allows parameters to contain references to objects. In certain cases when the invoked object and the parameter object are in different contexts, such as on different machines, the parameter object may be temporarily transferred to the context of the invoked object. This is termed "call-by-move" [Black et al. 1986]. When is it beneficial to perform such a transfer? Suppose, for instance, that the parameter object is a multithreaded active object and is already engaged in a number of invocations. It might be best to leave such a busy object as is, and transfer only those objects that are not active at the time of the invocation.

### 22.3.2 Concurrency Control

As mentioned in the previous section, some active object implementations allow both simultaneous execution of methods within the object and simultaneous execution of different objects. It is useful then to distinguish between what could be called "scheduling in-the-small" and "scheduling in-the-large." The first deals with scheduling within an object, while the second is concerned with scheduling a set of objects.

The possibility of two levels of concurrency has many ramifications on application design. Such issues as the partitioning of a distributed system and the choice of synchronization methods become more complex. However, the high degree of concurrency one obtains from the finer granularity of

**TABLE 22.1** METHOD INVOCATION SCHEDULING

|  | single-threaded | multithreaded |
| --- | --- | --- |
| **methods only** | queued | on demand |
| **methods and processes** | interrupt | on demand |

scheduling in-the-small is well suited to some applications (for example, multiobject simulations with real-time constraints).

Irrespective of the granularity of concurrency in the system, mechanisms are needed to protect the integrity of objects and to avoid or recover from deadlock within the system. For instance, Argus treats method invocations as transactions—either the invoked object receives the message and returns a reply, or the message is not received and the invoking object is so informed. In some cases, though, one does not want transactions hidden within method invocations. For example, the implementors of CES found it useful for the programmer to be explicitly able to commit or abort transactions. In general, mutual exclusion within an object may be provided by the method invocation scheduler, in the case of single-threaded active objects; or by the use of synchronization constructs within the methods of multithreaded objects.

## 22.3.3 Performance

There is a strong affinity between active object systems and multiprocessor architectures. The first needs computational resources on which to run objects, and the second needs a programming methodology that exploits parallelism. Perhaps the ideal architecture for an active object system would be one in which the number of processors is comparable to the number of objects (and where a single processor would be of sufficient power and flexibility to run an object). At present such an architecture cannot be realized, since current multiprocessor systems either are limited in the number of processors or contain processors of insufficient flexibility.

Furthermore, active object systems allow run-time creation of objects, so the number of objects can grow to exceed the number of processors. Thus the performance of active object systems is intimately related to scheduling and allocation policies. It follows that *load balancing,* which addresses the "democratic" allocation of processors to objects and the interplay with scheduling, is of great practical concern.

Performance in active object systems is further complicated by two factors. First, these are dynamic systems: objects are constantly being created, establishing new communication connections with other objects, and perhaps changing location. Second, there may be real-time constraints on the actions of particular objects. Little work has been done in optimizing the performance of active objects, although there are parallels with operating systems and transaction processing systems. As more flexible multiprocessor architectures become available, we can expect much progress in this area.

### 22.3.4 Contexts

Many active object systems, either implicitly or explicitly, make use of *contexts*. A context is a set of objects that are somehow more accessible or visible to each other than to those not in the context. Examples of what could constitute contexts include a set of mutually interacting objects, the objects located on a particular processor, or the objects under the jurisdiction of a particular object manager. Examples of operations involving contexts include populating contexts and transferring objects between contexts.

Given these examples, a distinction emerges—in certain cases contexts arise as artifacts of the implementation of the active object system; in other cases contexts are explicitly supported by the programming language. (And some systems may possess both notions of context.) Context mechanisms that are a side-effect of implementation may not appear desirable. It is often argued that the programming language should hide the underlying hardware, and so it would appear unsuitable for an active object system to reveal the hardware by providing contexts corresponding to particular processors. However, in some cases the application programmer may want control over the placement of objects, perhaps for reasons of performance or reliability. In some applications, notions of object placement are inherent in the user model. For example, the location of a "received electronic mail object" naturally corresponds to the receiver's context. Additionally, placement can sometimes be controlled implicitly rather than explicitly. As an example, consider a system that determines the placement of an object from frequency of use and criticality information specified by the programmer.

If one believes that control of object location is useful in active object systems, a number of issues immediately emerge:

1. What is the impact of object location on method invocation?

2. What is the impact of object location on load balancing?

3. How can one object find another?

4. Can objects change location?

5. How is the concept of object location expressed in the programming language?

Questions such as these expose a number of issues related to distributed object systems. Examples are distribution of the type hierarchy over contexts [Bennet 1987; Lee and Malone 1988] and minimization of the communication overhead among distributed objects.

## 22.4 THE FUTURE OF OBJECT-ORIENTED PROGRAMMING

Object-oriented programming in the 1980s can be compared to structured programming in the 1970s. Each is a useful and powerful way to construct and organize program modules. Each expands the capabilities of adherent programmers by imposing a carefully selected discipline upon the programmer. We have accumulated experience with structured programming, and can see in hindsight that it was not a panacea. However, it was extremely valuable in creating a cadre of programmers who have internalized this important discipline. After internalizing, it has been useful (no, necessary) to move beyond the structured programming discipline because the discipline is inherently constricting.

Another example is the seven communication layers of the ISO Open Systems Interconnection model. This paradigm has been very useful in structuring the complexity of communication network implementations. Again it can be observed that many of the advocates who have adopted and internalized this modularization are now moving beyond this model. Many of the realistically successful implementations skip several layers in the model altogether. Thus there is a modicum of cooperation within the computer science field in which designers build upon the work of others. Some of our great successes are predicated upon conceptual constructs that were invented, served a significant purpose, and died. In this section we hypothesize that object-oriented programming as we know it today is serving a significant purpose, but that it (as well as a set of other common computer concepts) is destined to die soon.

In what way is the object-oriented paradigm imposing restrictions upon the programmer? The primary imposition of this discipline is the choice of two relationships to make primary and explicit. (1) Instantiation—the relation "$a$ is an instance of $b$" implements the basic abstraction mechanism. Instances are concrete; classes are abstractions (i.e., conceptual groupings.) (2) Subclassing—the relation "$a$ is a subclass of $b$" implements the basic layering or hierarchy mechanism for modularization. There are many other relationships, such as the subpart relationship, that one may use heavily within an application; but just as structured programming generally does not advocate GO TO statements, object-oriented programming generally does not provide explicit facilities for these other relationships.

By restricting the programmer's freedom and providing a smaller number of conceptual foundation blocks, there is hope that the programmer can be more easily steered in the direction of producing code that has agreed-upon good properties. We note in passing that this hope is sometimes unfulfilled.

Languages such as Objective C [Cox 1986] conveniently allow a programmer to mix programming styles, thereby sometimes attaining the worst of each style. Even in cases where this unfortunate mix is avoided, these languages present a strong temptation NOT to use the less familiar object-oriented technique, but simply to inject a few message sends into a more familiar, non-object-oriented program.

Other restrictions imposed upon object-oriented programmers include not having attributes and relations available as first class citizens (objects). Also, the awkward conceptualizations necessary to understand constructs such as class Class (all classes are subclasses of this class) and metaclasses (classes whose instances are also classes) are intellectual burdens and a roadblock to the casual object-oriented traveller. See [Borning 1986], [Zdonik 1986], and [O'Shea 1986] for further discussion of cumbersome restrictions within object-oriented systems.

The object-oriented programming paradigm has evolved as a system and methodology to make quality programming less burdensome. It has been predominantly treated as a technique for programmers. We believe that the future of the object-oriented paradigm is to view it as a way of thinking and doing rather than simply as a way of programming. There are numerous nonprogramming situations that can benefit from object-oriented conceptualization and modularization. Thus many people who have neither time nor interest to study programming formally will be able to instruct active objects what to do for them. It is imperative that computer programming move out of the domain of the specialist and into use by the general public. Object-oriented programming with active objects may be a vital key that opens the door to this opportunity.

Personal computers, during their conceptual stage, were envisioned as the solution that would bring low cost, quality computing to the majority of people. Personal computers, in their current usage, have actually served to widen the gap between the haves and the have-nots. How can object-oriented systems with active objects help? If we can move beyond the current confusing systems, terminology, and programming languages, then people will be less reluctant to embrace (or at least to work with) computers. Simula, a language that pioneered the object-oriented paradigm, was really conceived for simulations. Similarly, within the early development team of Smalltalk, Alan Kay was fond of saying that programming is simply a subclass of the class of simulations. The Smalltalk and Logo [Papert 1980] object-oriented languages were designed to help school children to have an active education by trying and doing within an easy-to-learn, easy-to-use environment. Both languages have experienced some success in this domain. These perspectives have, unfortunately, been lost in many recent object-oriented languages.

Much of our creative work and problem solving can be assisted by mental simulations and thinking aids. Object systems can help here. Further, active objects can act as intelligent assistants who help us and do some of the tedious tasks that are subsidiary to the main creative work. Finally, we remark that one of the nicest aspects of object-oriented systems that have been created to date is their leading-edge user interfaces and graphics. Objects are thinking units, and further advances in multimedia user interfaces can make user objects self-evident. This is the step that needs to be taken to bring computers and programming to the people rather than forcing people to bend to the language and organization of the computer.

## Summary

Although we foresee that object-oriented programming, as we know it today, is close to its deathbed, we foresee tremendous possibilities in the future of active object systems. People will find it natural to think in terms of active objects; thus programming will be a natural extension of this way of thinking, and there will be lots of multimedia active objects around to help us organize and put our thoughts into actions. *Vive l'objet actif.*

## References

[Agha 1986] G. Agha, *Actors: A Model of Concurrent Computation in Distributed Systems*, MIT Press, Cambridge, MA, 1986.

[Bennet 1987] J.K. Bennet, "The Design and Implementation of Distributed Smalltalk," *Proceedings of the Second ACM Conference on Object-Oriented Programming Systems, Languages and Applications, SIGPLAN Notices*, pp. 318–330, 1987.

[Birrel and Nelson 1984] A.D. Birrel and B.J. Nelson, "Implementing Remote Procedure Calls," *ACM Transactions on Computer Systems*, vol. 2, no. 1, pp. 39–59, 1984.

[Black et al. 1986] A. Black, N. Hutchinson, E. Jul, and H. Levy, "Object Structure in the Emerald System," *Proceedings of the First ACM Conference on Object-Oriented Programming Systems, Languages and Applications, SIGPLAN Notices*, pp. 78–86, 1986.

[Borning 1986] A.H. Borning, "Classes versus Prototypes in Object-Oriented Languages," *Proceedings of the IFIP Fall Joint Computer Conference*, pp. 36–40, 1986.

[Byrd et al. 1982] R. Byrd, S. Smith, and S. de Jong, "An Actor-Based Programming System," *ACM Conference on Office Information Systems*, pp. 67–78, 1982.

[Cox 1986] B.J. Cox, *Object-Oriented Programming, An Evolutionary Approach*, Addison-Wesley, Reading, MA, 1986.

[Dahl and Hoare 1972] O.-J. Dahl and C.A.R. Hoare, "Hierarchical Program Structures," in *Structured Programming*, ed. O.-J. Dahl, E.W. Dijkstra, and C.A.R. Hoare, Academic Press, London, pp. 175–220, 1972.

[Grief et al. 1986] I. Grief, R. Seliger, and W. Weihl, "Atomic Data Abstractions in a Distributed Collaborative Editing System," *Proceedings of the 13th Annual Symposium on Principles of Programming Languages*, pp. 160–172, 1986.

[Hewitt 1977] C. Hewitt, "Viewing Control Structures as Patterns of Passing Messages," *Artificial Intelligence*, vol. 8, pp. 323–364, 1977.

[Lee and Malone 1988] J. Lee and T. Malone, "How Can Groups Communicate When They Use Different Languages," *ACM Conference on Office Information Systems*, pp. 22–29, 1988.

[Liskov and Scheifler 1982] B. Liskov and R. Scheifler, "Guardians and Actions: Linguistic Support for Robust, Distributed Systems," *ACM Transactions on Programming Languages and Systems*, vol. 5, no. 3, pp. 381–404, 1982.

[O'Shea 1986] T. O'Shea, "Why Object-Oriented Systems are Hard to Learn," *Proceedings of the First ACM Conference on Object-Oriented Programming Systems, Languages and Applications, SIGPLAN Notices*, 1986.

[Papert 1980] S. Papert, *Mindstorms: Children, Computers and Powerful Ideas*, Basic Books, New York, 1980.

[Reynolds 1987] C. Reynolds, "Flocks, Herds, and Schools: A Distributed Behavioral Model," *Computer Graphics*, vol. 21, no. 4, pp. 25–34, 1987.

[Stefik et al. 1987] M. Stefik, G. Foster, D.G. Bobrow, K. Kahn, S. Lanning, and S. Suchman, "Beyond the Chalkboard: Computer Support for Collaboration and Problem Solving in Meetings," *Communications of the ACM*, vol. 30, no. 1, pp. 32–47, 1987.

[Tsichritzis et al. 1987] D. Tsichritzis, E. Fiume, S. Gibbs, and O. Nierstrasz, "KNOs: KNowledge Acquisition, Dissemination, and Manipulation Objects," *ACM Transactions on Office Information Systems*, vol. 5, no. 4, pp. 96–112, 1987.

[Tsichritzis and Gibbs 1987] D. Tsichritzis and S. Gibbs, "Messages, Messengers, and Objects," *IEEE Office Automation Symposium*, pp. 118–127, 1987.

[Zdonik 1986] S. Zdonik, "Why Properties are Objects," *Proceedings of the Fall Joint Computer Conference*, pp. 41–47, 1986.

# 23

## Making Database Systems Fast Enough for CAD Applications

David Maier

## INTRODUCTION

Why are database systems infrequent components of computer-aided design (CAD) systems? The answer is lack of modeling power and performance. Record-based models are not up to handling complex design structures for very large scale integration (VLSI) or mechanical CAD. It's hard to design an arithmetic logic unit in a check register. The encoding involved greatly complicates application programs, and leaves too much room for misinterpretation of data. For flexibility, most CAD systems perform their own data management on top of the operating system's file system. Of course, a file system has no understanding of the structure of the data items in a design, and so is powerless to help with integrity or specialized storage mappings. Also, the data management features in a file system are minimal.

Those CAD systems that are built atop relational databases use them almost exclusively for selection, sometimes for projection, but perform or precompute joins in the program memory of the design tools. Such tools read the appropriate chunk of the database at startup, and build internal record and pointer structures from it in virtual memory. Thus, a design session starts by copying one part of the disk into another. At the end of the session, the internal structures are converted back to tuples and written to the database. This startup overhead gives a batch-processing flavor to doing design. Consider a VLSI designer who discovers a glitch in a layout while using a design rule checker. He or she must load the design into the layout editor, make the change, dump the design back into the database, then reload the design into the checker. The whole process can take up to half an hour, simply to reroute a wire. Furthermore, the virtual memory knows little about the structure of the design objects, and cannot be expected to give good paging performance.

Such CAD systems are using a database management system (DBMS) as an index package to support associative access. These systems forego the other data management features of the DBMS, such as recovery, concurrency control, integrity checking, and buffer management, during a design session. The ubiquitous reason is "Performance! Commercial database systems aren't fast enough to support simulators and interactive design tools."

A crop of object-oriented database (OODB) systems is emerging that greatly surpasses conventional record-based systems in modeling power [Atwood 1985; Banerjee et al. 1987; Landis 1986; Maier et al. 1986; Wegner and Zdonik 1986], and other new systems also support complex data items [Dittrich et al. 1986; Katz and Chang 1987]. These systems overcome the data model objections to using DBMSs for design support—but will they prove fast enough? The following sections give my opinion on what conventional database systems are too slow at, why they are slow at it, and why OODBs could deliver the required performance. My remarks are directed at conventional relational DBMSs, but most carry over to hierarchical and network models. I conclude with some areas for more research.

## 23.1 WHAT'S TOO SLOW?

Certainly, conventional relational systems are no slouches at associative retrieval. Their indexing routines are among the most sophisticated and highly tuned of any class of software systems. Associative access to disk is not the bottleneck—as I pointed out, when CAD tools do use a DBMS, it's for selection. No, conventional database systems are too slow at fetching and storing individual fields. A typical design task is unlike most data processing transactions. The latter involve either getting a few tuples from a relation and updating them, or selecting large groups of tuples from one or more relations and performing similar operations on the lot of them: taking a join to generate a report, updating a field in each to post interest. The design task also starts with a selection—to pull out the pieces of a design of interest—but then continues with many dissimilar fetch and store operations: move this strut a little to the right, propagate this signal to all inputs connected to the output of that NAND-gate. The access paths on the selected data follow the connectivity of the real-world entities, not the logical structures of the database.

The ideal is a database system in which field access is as fast for database items as for values in program memory. Field access in program memory can take as few as one or two machine instructions, if the proper addressing modes exist. While that speed may be unobtainable for database items, I believe coming within a factor of 10 is possible, rather than the factors of 1000 or 10,000 seen now.

## 23.2 WHY IT'S TOO SLOW

CAD tools use record structures from the application programming language to get the speed they need on fetching and storing single values. Why are those operations too slow in a relational database? I consider some of the reasons here. Not all these reasons are inherent in the relational model; some have to do with architectural tradeoffs made in current commercial systems, which are biased toward a data-processing application mix.

1. Each fetch or store incurs the cost of a procedure call from the application program to the database. That overhead is insignificant on a data processing transaction that accesses a field in every tuple from a relation, using a single query. The overhead *is* a burden for a query that accesses a single tuple. A procedure call cannot compete with simple offset addressing for accessing a field of a record in program memory. This overhead is largely a language limitation. Relational interfaces mostly do not allow packaging a sequence of data manipulation language (DML) commands in a single call to the database, much less providing more sophisticated control structures.

2. Connections between entities in a relational system are logical, through attribute values. At least one address translation is required to get from a key value to the location of a tuple. By contrast, in program memory, records can point to other records directly.

3. Normalization and other encoding of complex design structures pads the levels of indirection between an entity and a subcomponent even further. Reassembling the pieces of an entity in the database requires taking a join, but it is an odd type of join, as it involves one or a few tuples from many different relations. Invoking the same machinery to compute such a join as is used for a join of a few large relations takes us far away from memory access speeds. Certain useful data structures, such as arrays, just don't have any efficient encoding in record-based models. Implicit ordering information ends up being represented by explicit position numbers. Bitmaps and

long text strings are other examples of structures that are hard to represent efficiently in record-based systems.

4. The common strategies for concurrency and recovery that work well in commercial systems are locking and logging. Both put a lot of overhead on transactions that do individual updates to tuples. Neither has been validated as the optimal approach in an environment with long transactions and data fields that may change many times before commit. Commercial systems are optimized for high transaction throughput. High throughput means reducing the number of disk accesses during the critical section of the commit protocol. Write-ahead logging can reduce the number of writes in the critical section to one: the one that records the commit of the transactions. Some systems even commit multiple transactions with one write. The log and updated pages can be written to disk outside of the critical section. However, high throughput is not synonymous with fast response to individual transactions. Writing a log record on each update imposes delay, especially as transactions must contend for access to the log tail. However, slower response time during the transaction in exchange for faster commits does not make much sense in a design environment. Other schemes trade faster response time for more work at commit. A designer would gladly accept a several-second pause when saving a design in return for fast editing abilities.

Most concurrency and recovery schemes are aimed at applications where a data item is updated once in a transaction, which may not be characteristic of design transactions. (Consider pushing VLSI cells around to get a more compact layout.) Design transactions can also be long-lived. Conventional recovery schemes might degrade significantly when the log records for a transaction occupy more volume than the data items used by the transaction.

5. Answers are copied. The result of a relational query is a new relation, whose tuples must be composed of copies of other tuples or parts of tuples. Copying forces the database system to look at certain data items when it might not need to, such as when the tuples in a selection are located via an index.

Many of these problems are exacerbated in the distributed workstation environments common with design projects. Commercial database systems mainly run on a single processor. Such a system would occupy one node in a local network, and be accessed through messages over the network. Crossing the application-database boundary many times becomes even more prohibitive, because it involves a remote procedure call, and another layer of copying if the database does not include network communication features. Logging and locking deserve further scrutiny in a local network system, as both access a centralized resource during transaction execution, or at least require distributed agreement.

## 23.3 WHY CAN AN OBJECT-ORIENTED DBMS DO IT FASTER?

In this discussion, I am treating object-oriented databases with behavior, that is, ones that can associate methods or operations with classes of objects. Here are reasons an object-oriented database system could be made faster at fetching and storing fields than a relational system. The numbers correspond to items in the preceding section.

1. Having an execution model (methods in the database) means that one message sent from the application program can do multiple field accesses in the database, at the cost of one procedure call. Design operations are not really single fetches and stores, but typically involve following a path to another entity or filling in a new object in a class. OODB languages can express more complex operations on objects in a single method than a relational DML language can in a single command.

2. Objects can refer to subcomponents by identity, not state (key values). Thus, one level of mapping can be removed. However, even one level of mapping, from object identifier to main memory address, puts us more than a factor of 10 from straight memory-structure speeds. There are techniques to reduce the cost of this mapping. Global object identifiers can be swizzled (translated) to local memory addresses when an object resides in main memory, as in POMS [Cockshott et al. 1984] or LOOM [Kaehler and Krasner 1983]. POMS delays the translation until the first use of a field. Thus, the first use incurs the mapping cost, but subsequent uses are at program structure speeds. Direct translation has some drawbacks, as it is difficult to move objects back out to disk on a one-by-one basis to make room for other objects. Moving an object back to disk requires finding all references to it using the local memory address. LOOM avoids this problem by having local references go through an in-memory object table (using the reference as an index into the table) and allowing *leaf* objects that are in-memory "stubs" for objects whose state is only on disk. An alternative to external-to-internal reference replacement is maintaining a cache of main memory addresses for object identifiers. This mechanism requires a few more operations than replacement for object accesses subsequent to the first, but allows easier movement of objects back to disk, as the memory and disk formats of an object contain the same values.

3. Complex design entities can be represented more directly in an OODB, with less encoding, meaning fewer levels of mapping to access one conceptual entity, and the computation to the mapping at each level is simpler. In particular, many OODBs support array types directly. Some include large indexed objects with the ability to insert items in the middle, in time proportional to the size of the inserted section, rather than to the portion of the object past the insertion [Carey et al. 1986].

4. Long design transactions require that database users not be oblivious to each other and that the database support multiple versions of objects. These conditions, along with object identity, make optimistic concurrency control with shadowing for recovery an alternative to consider. If each application gets a "personal" copy of the database to operate on, there is no need to log changes or lock items centrally during the body of a transaction. (Of course, a transaction must keep track of objects that it touched for use by the commit protocol, but it can do that locally.) Also, less overhead is incurred while the transaction runs (at the expense of more I/Os at commit). In particular, an object can be updated many times without making a log entry each time. Object storage schemes that use an object table are especially amenable to shadowing [Maier et al. 1986].

5. Answers to queries can often be constructed by collecting references to objects in the database, rather than by copying the objects.

I believe all these advantages can combine to let OODBs handle individual object accesses quickly enough to keep design data under database control while being manipulated by tools. Actually, I expect they can give better performance than the current method of reading in a file or some relations and building structures in program memory. First, they avoid batch load. A designer does not have to wait until a tool loads in an entire design to begin work. Also, if the database system (rather than virtual memory) handles buffering, it should be able to achieve better hit ratios, as it knows more of the semantics of the data.

Many of the OODBs being developed also seem well suited to mapping onto a workstation-server architecture. Most behavioral OODBs are internally structured into a storage layer and an execution layer. The storage layer handles data management functions, and the execution layer provides a workspace for evaluating methods or operations. There is one instance of the storage layer, but an instance of the execution layer for each application session. It seems reasonable to move the execution layer up to the workstation, leaving the storage layer on a central storage server [Rubenstein et al. 1987]. For such a split to work, the communication between the two layers has to be minimized. Having method execution on the server avoids shipping the results of intermediate queries to the workstation to perform nonrelational computations. For data fetching and storing, after some initial conversation, an execution layer can read and write pages directly across the network to move objects between workspace and disk. This arrangement is preferable to having the storage layer do the mapping between pages and objects, since the latter makes the storage layer a bottleneck for concurrent transactions. Even functions that must be centralized in the storage server, such as allocating free pages and new object identifiers, can be batched to cut down on communication overhead. An application session can be given pages and identifiers in large chunks, returning to the storage server only when the chunk is exhausted. One question that remains for a local network architecture is how associative access support should work. If set queries are processed on the storage server, then an execution layer must push whatever portion of the state changed down in order to have such a query evaluated in the middle of a transaction. Perhaps it can just push down the identifiers of modified objects, and the storage layer can request the states of only those it needs to process the query.

## 23.4 RESEARCH QUESTIONS

There are still numerous problems to be solved in learning how to optimize OODB performance for design applications. I discuss several here.

1. What new tradeoffs exist in an architecture with one more level in the memory hierarchy (disk, to central server over a network, to local workstation memory, to processor cache)? What is the major bottleneck? Disk bandwidth? Server CPU? Network communication? To what uses can disks on the local workstation be put: recovery and checkpointing; scheme or method cache? Does it make sense to have execution capabilities in both the workstation and the storage server, or is the expense of maintaining state consistency too much?

2. Different design tools have different access patterns. Thus, any single scheme for clustering objects into pages is unlikely to suit all of them. A design goes through phases: initial creation, design rule checking, correction, extraction, simulation. Should the objects in a design be reclustered in each of these phases? If so, how? Batch reclustering? Adaptive reclustering based on currently active access paths? The latter course has the disadvantage of making the design data well clustered for the *last* thing you did, but not the current task.

3. Most object-oriented languages derive the storage layout of instances from the class definition. In a language with encapsulation, there exists the freedom for tuning the internal representation. Even if the basic building blocks for classes are sets, arrays, and records, there are multiple ways to lay out combinations of them on secondary storage. An array of records might be contiguous records in order, or it could be a list of offsets to the records. We need to look at mechanisms for specifying representations easily. We also may want to support different representations on disk and in memory.

4. Optimization and access planning techniques need to be extended for the types of operations that show up in design applications, such as single-object manipulation and traversals of logical object structure, as in connectivity checking or fault propagation in electrical CAD. Also, updates

are common during early parts of the design cycle, and we must understand how to optimize them as well.

5. The flexibility of dynamic binding of messages to methods is useful during system development. It means that the decision of the exact typing of the instance variables for a class can be delayed. Any value can be placed in an instance variable, as long as it responds to the messages sent to that variable by the methods of the class. Such flexibility is desirable in modeling a domain for the first time. Later, when the types of variables become apparent, we may want to declare them in order to do more static binding and get better performance. However, it is also desirable to return to dynamic binding if the system must undergo modification. The general problem is keeping track of binding environments, when they change, and what has been bound relative to a certain state of an environment. The goal is to figure out when an environment is changing slowly enough that binding relative to it is worthwhile. The range of variability runs from slowly changing, such as the connection of class names to class definitions, and of types to instance variables, to more quickly changing, such as the association of messages to methods, values to instance variables, and object identifiers to memory locations. But even in the most rapidly changing environments, binding may pay off. An object may reside only briefly in main memory, but it could still be worthwhile to map references to its identifier to references to its memory location, if the object is expected to be accessed several times before leaving memory.

6. It seems too early to settle on a single semantics of versions and configurations. Still, we can start to identify features that should be present in the database kernel to support a range of version semantics. Some such features might be cheap copies of large objects, support for compound identifiers (capturing both identity and version) and resolution of such identifiers, and partial objects, to be used for representing the common structure across multiple configurations [Zhu and Maier 1988].

7. There is a tension between encapsulation and maintaining auxiliary access paths. Databases conventionally index on structure. However, to respect encapsulation, an OODB should index on the results of an operation. That is, the operation is applied to all elements of a set, and the results of the applications are organized into an index. The problem is knowing, for an arbitrary operation, that it returns the same value when applied twice in a row and which other operations on an object can cause the result of the indexed operation to change. The current choices are to violate encapsulation and index on structure, or to trust the implementor of a class to ensure that certain operations behave properly for indexing. The latter choice runs counter to what is provided in relational systems, where index maintenance is guaranteed no matter how a relation is defined.

## Summary

I have tried to build the case that OODBs can be made fast enough to meet the needs of design applications. The real test of my arguments, come, of course, as such systems move out of the prototype stage and are employed in design systems. I have also put forth what I think are the important research questions in connection with performance of OODBs in design applications.

## Acknowledgments

My thanks to Arne Berre, Rod Butters, Craig Brandis, Goetz Graefe, and Jacob Stein for letting me try some of these ideas out on them. They can take credit for the good ones and disown the losers. Won Kim helped by poking holes in some claims no longer contained herein.

Some of the ideas in this chapter were first articulated in a position paper that appeared in the 1986 Workshop on Object-Oriented Database Systems [Maier 1986].

## References

[Atwood 1985] T.M. Atwood, "An Object-Oriented DBMS for Design Support Applications," *Proceedings IEEE COMPINT*, vol. 85, 1985.

[Banerjee et al. 1987] J. Banerjee, H.-T. Chou, J.F. Garza, W. Kim, D. Woelk, N. Ballou, and H.-J. Kim, "Data Model Issues for Object-Oriented Applications," *ACM Transaction on Office Information Systems*, vol. 5, no. 1, January 1987.

[Carey et al. 1986] M.J. Carey, D.J. DeWitt, D. Frank, G. Graefe, J.E. Richardson, E.J. Shekita, and M. Muralikrishna, "The Architecture of the EXODUS Extensible DBMS: A Preliminary Report," University of Wisconsin TR 644, May 1986.

[Cockshott et al. 1984] W.P. Cockshott, M.P. Atkinson, K.J. Chisholm, P.J. Bailey, and R. Morrison, "Persistent Object Management System," *Software—Practice and Experience*, vol. 14, pp. 49–71, 1984.

[Dittrich et al. 1986] K.R. Dittrich, W. Gotthard, and P.C. Lockemann, "DAMOKLES—A Database System for Software Engineering Environments," *Proceedings of the IFIP Workshop on Advanced Programming Environments*, Trondheim, June 1986.

[Kaehler and Krasner 1983] T. Kaehler and G. Krasner, "LOOM—Large Object-Oriented Memory for Smalltalk-80 Systems," in *Smalltalk-80: Bits of History, Words of Advice*, G. Krasner, ed., Addison-Wesley, Reading, MA, 1983.

[Katz and Chang 1987] R.H. Katz and E. Chang, "Managing Change in a Computer-Aided Design Database," *VLDB XIII*, September 1987.

[Landis 1986] G.S. Landis, "Design Evolution and History in an Object-Oriented CAD/CAM Database," *31st IEEE COMPCON*, March 1986.

[Maier 1986] D. Maier, "Why Object-Oriented Database Systems Can Succeed Where Others Have Failed," *Proceedings of the International Conference on Object-Oriented Databases*, September 1986.

[Maier et al. 1986] D. Maier, J. Stein, A. Otis, and A. Purdy, "Development of an Object-Oriented DBMS," *Proceedings of the First ACM Conference on Object-Oriented Programming Systems, Languages and Applications, SIGPLAN Notices*, September 1986.

[Rubenstein et al. 1987] W.B. Rubenstein, M.S. Kubicar, and R.G.G. Cattell, "Benchmarking Simple Database Operations," *Proceedings of the ACM-SIGMOD International Conference on Management of Data*, May 1987.

[Wegner and Zdonik 1986] P. Wegner and S. Zdonik, "Language and Methodology for Object-Oriented Database Environments," *Proceedings of the Nineteenth Annual International Conference on System Sciences*, Honolulu, HI, January 1986.

[Zhu and Maier 1988] J. Zhu and D. Maier, "Abstract Objects in an Object-Oriented Data Model," *Second International Conference on Expert Database Systems*, Tysons Corner, VA, April 1988.

# 24

---

# Object Orientation as Catalyst for Language-Database Integration

J. Eliot B. Moss

---

## INTRODUCTION

We explore the issue of unifying programming languages and databases to produce a coherent new way of building data-oriented applications. In so doing, we argue as to the benefits of such an approach and the obstacles to carrying it out, and show how object orientation makes significant contributions toward removing those obstacles. Finally, we suggest topics of research for resolving the remaining issues in achieving a marriage of programming languages and databases within an object-oriented framework.

## 24.1 THE BENEFITS OF LANGUAGE-DATABASE INTEGRATION

Programming languages, along with compiler and language technology and theory, have long been considered a subdiscipline separate from databases and the related field of operating systems. We contend that bringing these two specialties together to produce smoothly integrated software will be beneficial, even necessary. The fundamental issue is not one of ultimate power or functionality—it is easy to make languages as well as database systems Turing complete. Rather, the underlying point is our ability to produce suitable applications software. That is, software engineering is the ultimate challenge. Hence the thrust of our argument is that language-database integration will enable us to build, modify, and enhance more capable applications software than would otherwise be possible.

First, it is important to understand that we are interested in *data-oriented* applications: ones that access and/or maintain significant data. This covers a broad range of very useful programs, but excludes many real-time systems, such as control systems, which have little memory and whose main function is to observe and respond to real-world events. Likewise, many numerical applications serve to compute results, but do not manipulate stored data. However, the boundaries of data orientation are a bit fuzzy. Suffice it to say that if an application uses a database or a file system other than as a way of expressing the problem and recording the results, then the application is probably data-oriented.

The problem that language-database integration addresses is the interface between the part of the application that solves the problem (the "program," expressed in some programming language) and the part that is responsible for storing the data (typically a file system or a database manager). The interface is a problem because these two parts have different models of the data, of how to manipulate the data, and so forth. For example, in Pascal, the language provides integers, characters, arrays, records, pointers, and other data constructs. For data storage one has files, which cannot store arbitrary Pascal data structures, and have undefined sharing and recovery properties. In short, these are two vastly different worlds—and the *programmer* is responsible for making them communicate effectively. Using communications as a metaphor, the interface problem has been called *impedance mismatch* [Copeland and Maier 1984].

It is relatively obvious that forcing all persistent data (data that outlive the execution of the program) to be stored in a textual form is somewhat limiting, or at least inconvenient and frequently inefficient. The limitations of constructs such as the FILE data type in Pascal are perhaps a bit less obvious. Even if we somehow removed the requirement that data items in any given file be homogeneous (a typical constraint on record-oriented input/output in Pascal and other languages), there are still issues such as the order of items in a file, and insuring correct semantics of concurrent access and update. To see the problem more clearly, consider a complex linked data structure: the flow graph of a program as used in an optimizing compiler. Saving this information in a file and reconstructing it requires devising a complicated algorithm for "flattening" the data structure into a linear file, while somehow reflecting accurately the intricate pointer structure. Even if this is achieved, questions arise as to the handling of multiple graphs, separate files, and other matters. Using a database is little different: the information must still be passed across the interface between the application program and the database manager, and the problems are similar.

Achieving a "seamless" (coherent) integration of the language and database approaches to building applications would eliminate this interface from the programmer's consideration. This is a tremendous benefit since it avoids a large conceptual burden (keeping the two models in mind and translating between them appropriately), which is likely to be a source of complexity and errors in the system. Further, a unification would allow the problem solution to be expressed more naturally. For example, rather than many lines of rather obscure and tedious Pascal code to convert data structures for I/O to a file system, we could simply use the language structures directly.

Even a partially integrated language such as Pascal/R [Schmidt and Mall 1980] or an embedded query language goes only part of the way. Special data structures are provided for the permanent data and one must still explicitly move data back and forth between "language" variables and "database" variables. *Persistent programming languages* such as PS-Algol [Atkinson and Morrison 1985] achieve more complete integration. However, as we will discuss further, the persistent programming languages are only a step in the right direction. Database query languages—at least the traditional ones such as SQL [Astrahan and Chamberlin 1975]—also fall short, primarily in that they are not general purpose but are intended only to offer a notation for accessing databases and performing limited application-related functions.

Through a complete unification of language and database data models, execution semantics, and so on, we would be able to express data-oriented applications programs using a single language and single model. The software engineering benefits of dealing with one model to solve a problem, as opposed to two or more models, are obvious. Further, through an integrated design effort we may be able to perform important optimizations on the combined language-database whole, which neither component could realize and perform on its own in a partitioned design. This should *not* be taken to imply that a new "superlanguage" need be implemented in an entirely monolithic manner—just that it present a coherent unified view of the world to programmers using it.

## 24.2 PROBLEMS IN ACHIEVING INTEGRATION

There are three categories of problems that must be solved in order to achieve effective language-database integration. First, we must determine the appropriate *functionality* of such a system (how it is to act; what functions it is to support). Second, we need to figure out how to obtain acceptable *performance* in such systems. Finally, there are problems of system *acceptance* that go beyond the technical issues. We now consider each category of problems in turn.

One of the major functionality issues, that of data models, is the problem closest to resolution. In fact, it is here that object orientation comes in most directly. The object-oriented approach to languages, exemplified by Smalltalk [Goldberg and Robson 1983] and Trellis/Owl [Schaffert et al. 1986], offers models of data very similar to ones proposed for databases, such as VBASE [Andrews and Harris 1987]. On the other hand, while we claim that the data model issue may be closer to resolution than some of the other problems, it is far from being resolved. While objects provide a reasonable start, programming languages have not usually addressed semantic modeling issues such as integrity constraints. For further discussion of this point, see [Bloom and Zdonik 1987].

Of course, unifying the data model is not enough. A number of the other issues on which languages and databases typically differ are discussed in [Bloom and Zdonik 1987]. For example, we must settle on an execution paradigm, be it procedural, logic programming, equations, functions, rule-based, production systems, or some other approach—or we must find ways to use more than one of these paradigms together effectively and cleanly. This is an area of considerable current research, though most of it addresses language issues only, ignoring the additional database issues crucial to language-database integration.

The functionality issues other than data model and programming paradigm include: system modularization techniques; exception handling (arguably part of the data model, but typically separate in programming languages); parallelism, expression of concurrency, and concurrency control (to include means for dealing with cooperation, which goes beyond traditional database concurrency control techniques); crash recovery; and distribution and communication.

As can be seen, there is considerable work ahead in devising even one unified system that addresses all these functionality issues. However, there are performance problems that must be considered as well. These fall roughly into four groups. First there are the traditional database performance issues such as storage and access techniques (indexing, clustering, etc.) and query optimization. The Orion project, among others, is reporting progress on these issues [Banerjee et al. 1987; Kim et al. 1988]. Orion, though it represents a smooth integration of database features into a language, still has a separate submodel consisting of the database system's data model, with this data model distinct from and exhibiting somewhat different semantics from the host language's native data types.

In addition to database performance issues such as those just mentioned, we must deal with the problems of compiling and optimizing the integrated

database programming language. Of course, there are likely to be other performance problems of which we are as yet unaware.

It will be very important for performance to be considered carefully in
designing an integrated language-database. However, the functionality issues
should drive the design, not the performance problems; otherwise we will not
achieve as coherent and clear a result. In an effort of this magnitude, coherence,
clarity, and simplicity (at least in a relative sense) will be of utmost importance
because of their direct impact on whether the system can be used effectively
by everyday applications programmers.

Finally, we come to acceptance problems. Because of their commitment
to past approaches, tools, and technologies, many people and organizations
will not convert to an integrated system of the kind described. (There are
lots of FORTRAN and COBOL users still out there!) However, even if some
people might be willing to convert, we will not get many takers unless we can
reduce the cost of doing so, and make the benefits more clear and available.

One obvious thing that will encourage acceptance is the availability of
good implementations of an integrated system. Since any implementation will
be expensive to build, and a good one even more so, we cannot afford to
build many of them. Hence, the ones we do build must support a broad
enough range of applications to justify being built. This requires addressing
the particularly difficult tradeoff between generality and performance. Effort
also needs to be applied toward providing tools to convert old applications
to the new approach. These tools might be more narrow yet still quite
useful. Finally, and perhaps most importantly, we need to understand the
engineering methodologies appropriate for use in the proposed environment,
and to support those methodologies with both tools and training. In fact,
methodologies should be developed hand in hand with the design of the
integrated language-database system.

## 24.3 INTEGRATION AND OBJECT ORIENTATION

Object orientation provides significant contributions toward integration, and
perhaps provides the strongest evidence for feasibility of integration. As previously noted, the similarity of the data models of object-oriented programming
languages and object-oriented databases—which is by no means an accident,
the database models frequently having been patterned after the programming
language models—is a prime unifying factor. However, object orientation
contributes in other ways, too.

The object-oriented approach would appear to be one of the best-known
modularization techniques, when applied well. It must be admitted, though,
that our understanding of exactly how to apply it is as yet limited. Object
orientation seems to subsume data abstraction, with inheritance going farther
than data abstraction in supporting reuse. It is clear that object-oriented

systems incorporating inheritance offer considerable power and flexibility, and organize system components better than a flat set of modules. However, better organization and control mechanisms are needed for true programming-in-the-large, and most experience to date has been within the realm of single-user environments.

It is also encouraging that object-oriented systems are on the leading edge of programming environment design, as well as of programming language research and database technology. In particular, the views that have arisen from research on object-oriented systems have begun to illuminate more clearly some of the shortcomings of other approaches. An example of this is the notion of *object identity:* that every object created has an identity unique unto itself for its entire lifetime in the system, whether or not there are ever other objects with similar or identical states or properties [Khoshafian and Copeland 1986]. This provides additional perspective on the referential integrity problem in relational databases [Codd 1970; Smith and Smith 1977a; Smith and Smith 1977b]. Further, it helps indicate how relational database technology could be used in a more object-oriented way—inventing object identifiers (these have also been called *surrogates* [Abrial 1974; Hall et al. 1976; Codd 1979]) and adding them as keys in the appropriate relations. It is not surprising that object-oriented languages exhibit fewer semantic problems (such as object identity and referential integrity), since they bear more resemblance to conceptual and semantic modeling languages [King and McLeod 1985].

The demand for object-oriented programming languages and database technology seems to be coming from so-called "new" application domains, especially design areas such as VLSI, printed circuit board layout, electrical and mechanical CAD, document production and office automation, and software engineering. However, we believe that *all* data-oriented applications will benefit from language-database integration. In particular, traditional database applications would clearly benefit from better tools and approaches, especially if programming and maintenance costs can be reduced, and functionality improved. The big questions are, of course, performance and acceptance.

An integrated *object-oriented* system would be particularly good, for several reasons. First, object-oriented languages more closely model the real world, and a substantial part of most data-oriented applications is modeling of real (or extended or ideal) worlds. This can be seen both in their roots as simulation languages (notably Simula-67 [Dahl and Nygaard 1966]) and in their similarity to semantic data models [King and McLeod 1985], the entity-relationship model [Chen 1976], and conceptual modeling languages. This makes the object-oriented approach natural and comparatively easy to apply. Object orientation permits simple local views of the world (from the point of view of individual objects), as well as simple restrictions of these views (by considering appropriate subsets of the available operations and instance variables of objects). Also, the object-oriented approach supports extensibility well by allowing old algorithms to work with newly invented objects (provided the new objects support the appropriate interface).

## 24.4 REMAINING RESEARCH ISSUES

While the outlook for language-database integration is improving, as evidenced by systems such as Orion, and object orientation does indeed help point the way, there are obviously a number of research issues remaining to be solved. We have mentioned a number of these already, but wish to point out some more of them.

First, considerable work needs to be done in devising approaches and specific techniques for improving the performance of object-oriented programs. In great measure, we have yet to achieve in the domain of object-oriented languages the well-known optimizations of FORTRAN and other traditional languages. Better compile time handling of types—either through declarations and type checking, or through type inference, or possibly other (as yet undiscovered) approaches—is clearly necessary, as is expanded application of global optimization techniques.

However, careful language design, as well as hardware architectures more suited to object-oriented languages, might be of assistance. A chief example in this area is dealing with integers and integer arithmetic. Many object-oriented languages offer garbage collection; to support it, they tend to use tag bits in the data items. The tagging of integers significantly interferes with performing efficient integer arithmetic and optimization of integer operations on typical processors. Architectural support for tags would reduce or eliminate this problem. However, as the history and evolution of implementations of Smalltalk shows, there is probably a certain amount of cleverness yet to be discovered in solving such problems.

Going beyond the usual compiler issues, we should be working harder at unifying compiler and database optimization techniques. Both approaches tend to look for code patterns and replace them (possibly only under restricted circumstances) with equivalent sequences. However, database query optimization has generally been more sensitive to the statistics of the applications (e.g., selectivity) and data (e.g., key distributions), more adaptive to changing situations (existence of indexes, or ordering of base relations for scans), and more cognizant of multiple ways of achieving the same ends and of the tradeoffs among those ways. Both approaches have typically dealt with fixed sets of data types having well-understood semantics.

In the future, optimizers will need to adapt to new data types easily. This suggests relying more on rules (or other descriptions), quite likely combined with user specifications of properties of operations. Some of the work on automatic construction of code generators for programming languages is undoubtedly relevant, as is current research on rule-based query optimizers

[Graefe and DeWitt 1987]. A broad, unifying approach is needed, that takes statistics into account and addresses the issue of choice among competing representations.

In the transaction area we require good methods for supporting cooperation among many users. At present we are relying on either traditional database transactions, widely felt to be inadequate, or ad hoc extensions to traditional techniques (such as additional lock modes). While it seems likely that we will have no trouble devising mechanisms adequate to the problem, we lack an appropriate high-level model of the desired semantics to guide the design and use of such mechanisms.

We previously mentioned the need for software engineering methodologies. There are two new factors that must be handled. One is object orientation. We have yet to arrive at clear and accepted principles for designing systems in an object-oriented way, especially when inheritance is used. This issue falls within the scope of traditional research activities, so we expect it will be addressed. The other issue, which is less likely to be addressed, is how to use an integrated language-database system appropriately. Of course, it is hard to develop principles without a system to use as a basis for experiments. However, we have a chicken and egg problem: we desire to identify software engineering principles so as to guide the design of the integrated system.

Beyond the research issues just mentioned, there is the whole series of technical issues related to specific language features—the details of data model, execution model, syntax, persistence, transactions, etc. There is further the rather subtle issue of how to integrate such a wide variety of language features and functionality into a single coherent language—which is, of course, the point. But we want to avoid a language that "feels" too large, such as PL/1 or Ada. Perhaps appropriate discipline in the choice of basic data types and abstract syntax (e.g., statement and declaration forms for a procedural language) will help, but there is the issue of smooth *semantic* integration, which is much harder to evaluate, yet no less important.

## Summary

We believe that integration of programming languages and databases will have substantial benefits, not only to the challenging new application domains such as design, but also in traditional applications. Further, object orientation is leading the way, and is catalyzing efforts toward such integration through the development of object-oriented languages and object-oriented databases, which share many underlying concepts, most notably in data models. However, a number of hard problems remain to be solved. These include: improving the overall performance of object-oriented systems, unifying compiler and database query optimization techniques, incorporating the statistics of the application and the data, supporting cooperation from an understanding of its semantics rather than through ad hoc extensions, developing clear principles of object-oriented system design and development, and a whole series of technical details needed for smooth semantic integration of programming language and database features.

## REFERENCES

[Abrial 1974] J.R. Abrial, "Data Semantics," in *Data Base Management,* J.W. Klimbie and K.L. Koffeman, eds., North-Holland Publishing Company, 1974.

[Andrews and Harris 1987] T. Andrews and C. Harris, "Combining Language and Database Advances in an Object-Oriented Development Environment," *Proceedings of the Second ACM Conference on Object-Oriented Programming Systems, Languages and Applications, SIGPLAN Notices,* vol. 22, no. 12, pp. 430–440, 1987.

[Astrahan and Chamberlin 1975] M.M. Astrahan and D.D. Chamberlin, "Implementation of a Structured English Query Language," *Communications of the ACM,* vol. 18, no. 10, pp. 580–588, 1975.

[Atkinson and Morrison 1985] M.P. Atkinson and R. Morrison, "Procedures as Persistent Data Objects," *ACM Transactions on Programming Languages and Systems,* vol. 7, no. 4, pp. 539–559, 1985.

[Banerjee et al. 1987] J. Banerjee, W. Kim, and K. Kyng-Chang, *Queries in Object-Oriented Databases,* MCC Technical Report DB-188-87, Microelectronics and Computer Technology Corporation, Austin, TX, June 1987.

[Bloom and Zdonik 1987] T. Bloom and S.B. Zdonik, "Issues in the Design of Object-Oriented Database Programming Languages," *Proceedings of the Second ACM Conference on Object-Oriented Programming Systems, Languages and Applications, SIGPLAN Notices,* vol. 22, no. 12, pp. 441–451, 1987.

[Chen 1976] P.P.S. Chen, "The Entity-Relationship Model: Towards a Unified View of Data," *ACM Transactions on Database Systems,* vol. 1, no. 1, pp. 9–36, 1976.

[Codd 1970] E.F. Codd, "A Relational Model for Large Shared Databanks," *Communications of the ACM,* vol. 13, no. 6, pp. 377–390, 1970.

[Codd 1979] E.F. Codd, "Extending the Database Relational Model to Capture More Meaning," *ACM Transactions on Database Systems,* vol. 4, no. 4, pp. 397–434, 1979.

[Copeland and Maier 1984] G. Copeland and D. Maier, "Making Smalltalk a Database System," *SIGMOD '84, Proceedings of Annual Meeting, SIGMOD Record*, vol. 14, no. 2, pp. 316–325, 1984.

[Dahl and Nygaard 1966] O.-J. Dahl and K. Nygaard, "Simula—an Algol-Based Simulation Language," *Communications of the ACM*, vol. 9, no. 9, pp. 671–678, 1966.

[Goldberg and Robson 1983] A. Goldberg and D. Robson, *Smalltalk-80: The Language and its Implementation*, Addison-Wesley, Reading, MA, 1983.

[Graefe and DeWitt 1987] G. Graefe and D.J. DeWitt, "The EXODUS Optimizer Generator," *Proceedings of the ACM SIGMOD International Conference on the Management of Data, SIGMOD Record*, vol. 16, no. 3, pp. 160–172, 1987.

[Hall et al. 1976] P.A.V. Hall, J. Owlett, and S.J.P. Todd, "Relations and Entities," in *Modeling in Data Base Management Systems*, G.M. Nijssen, ed., North-Holland Publishing Company, 1976.

[Khoshafian and Copeland 1986] S.N. Khoshafian and G.P. Copeland, "Object Identity," *Proceedings of the First ACM Conference on Object-Oriented Programming Systems, Languages and Applications, SIGPLAN Notices*, vol. 21, no. 11, pp. 406–416, 1986.

[Kim et al. 1988] W. Kim, N. Ballou, J. Banerjee, H.-T. Chou, J.F. Garza, and D. Woelk, *Integrating an Object-Oriented Programming System with a Database System*. MCC Technical Report ACA-ST-089-88, Microelectronics and Computer Technology Corporation, Austin, TX, March 1988.

[King and McLeod 1985] R. King and D. McLeod, "Semantic Database Models," in *Database Design*, S.B. Yao, ed., Prentice-Hall, Englewood Cliffs, NJ, 1985.

[Schaffert et al. 1986] C. Schaffert, T. Cooper, B. Bullis, M. Kilian, and C. Wilpolt, "An Introduction to Trellis/Owl," *Proceedings of the First ACM Conference on Object-Oriented Programming Systems, Languages and Applications, SIGPLAN Notices*, vol. 21, no. 11, pp. 9–16, 1986.

[Schmidt and Mall 1980] J.W. Schmidt and M. Mall, *Pascal/R Report*, Report 66, Fachbereich Automatik, University of Hamburg, January 1980.

[Smith and Smith 1977a] J.M. Smith and D.C.P. Smith, "Database Abstractions: Aggregation," *Communications of the ACM*, vol. 20, no. 6, pp. 405–413, 1977.

[Smith and Smith 1977b] J.M. Smith and D.C.P. Smith, "Database Abstractions: Aggregation and Generalization," *ACM Transactions on Database Systems*, vol. 2, no. 2, pp. 105–133, 1977.

# Index

# Index

## A

ABCL/1, 14, 83, 100, 119
abstract data type, 12, 24
access message, 252
accessor, 56
acknowledgment, 109
acquaintance, 9, 90, 312
active entity, 525
active object, 9, 13, 561
    multithreaded, 565
    single-threaded, 566
Actor, 13, 31, 39, 40
    Act 1, 89
    Act 2, 89
    Act 3, 89
actor, 82, 85, 86, 88, 526, 563
    immutable actor, 89
    insensitive actor, 96
    mutable actor, 95
    nonprimitive actor, 90
    primitive actor, 89
    serialized actor, 95
    unserialized actor, 89, 478
Actra, 38
Ada, 12, 119
aggregation, 25
Alltalk, 422
alpha rule, 311
Argus, 15, 457, 488, 563, 567
assertion, 138

associative access, 295
atomicity
    dynamic atomicity, 407
    hybrid atomicity, 407
    local atomicity, 407
attribute
    complex attribute, 267
    scalar attribute, 266
    set attribute, 266
    simple attribute, 267
authorization, 292, 304
Avance, 13, 452

## B

backward chaining, 143
backward inference, 143
backward rule, 143
behavioral replacement, 92
binding, 10, 305
    dynamic binding, 10
    static binding, 10
binding variable, 136
boid, 565
browsers, 208
B-tree, 235; see B+tree
    B-tree index, 376
B+tree
    B+tree index, 348
    B+tree locking protocol, 359

buddy system, 446, 494
buffer group, 362
buffer management, 360
bytecode, 428
bytecode interpreter, 488


**C**


C++, 8, 11, 15, 37, 74, 76, 207
C*, 120
CAD application, 573
Cantor, 100
CBox object, 108
Cedar, 16
change-approval timestamp, 260
change notification, 260
change-notification timestamp, 260
Chorus, 15
class dictionary, 431
class-hierarchy, 370, 376
class-hierarchy index, 370, 376
class lattice, 274
client, 99
CLOS
    Persistent-CLOS (PCLOS), 243
Clu, 12, 459
clustering, 265
collaborative design, 399
collaborative editing system (CES), 564,
    567
collection, 462
Common LISP, 49
Common LISP Object System
    (CLOS), 49
Common Loops, 50
Common Objects, 8
commutativity, 408
    backward commutativity, 408
    forward commutativity, 408
compiler temporary, 429
complex object, 313, 316
composite object, 262
composite object hierarchy, 262
composite reference, 262
computer aided database design
    (CADD), 177
concurrency, 13, 79

concurrency control, 270, 286, 290, 304,
    345, 359, 364, 395, 404, 566
    concurrency control within objects,
        415
    concurrency control with
        transaction groups, 416
    local concurrency control, 406
    optimistic concurrency control, 287
    pessimistic concurrency control, 287,
        479
    semantic concurrency control, 399
Concurrent Sequential Process (CSP),
    83, 85, 119
Concurrent Smalltalk, 14, 82, 87, 107,
    110, 114, 119
conflict relation, 407
context, 429, 568
cooperative work, 151, 164
current behavior, 90
cut-path, 352


**D**


DAPLEX, 222, 237, 342
Darmstadt Database Kernel System, 344
database design, 180
    conceptual design, 180
    logical design, 180
    physical design, 180
data-directed inference, 147
datatype value, 457
default version, 259
delegation, 9, 33, 35, 40, 99
    delegation hierarchy, 41
Delegation, 32, 38, 39, 41
dependency between transactions, 402
dependency graph, 402
dependency specification, 402
design transaction 413, 576
direct manipulation, 529
dirty data, 270
display independence, 173
distributed circular structure, 497
distributed marking, 497
distributed object manager, 487
dynamic connection, 498
dynamic disconnection, 498

# E

Eden, 488
education, 473
Eiffel, 7, 207
electronic book, 204
Emerald, 27, 86, 120, 563
empathy, 31, 34, 37
Empress, 332
encapsulation, 3, 5, 80, 86, 200, 209, 210, 554
equivalence of history, 400
E-R model, 237
event, 321, 545
    event tree, 322
    lawful event, 546
EXODUS, 246, 294
expert system, 128
extensibility, 274
extension, 69

# F

field
    automatic field, 203
    modifiable field, 203
    nonmodifiable field, 203
    virtual field, 203
filter, 300
Flavors, 7, 33, 46, 50, 207
Formes, 120
forward chaining, 147
forward inference, 147
forward rule, 147
forward traversal, 267
fragmentation, 495
frame, 132
F-Tree, 235
function, 222, 225
    declaration, 225
    derived function, 227
    foreign function, 228
    implementation, 225
    materialized function, 228
    multi-valued function, 226
    predicate function, 226

single-valued function, 226
stored function, 227
functional dependency, 181
future, 101

# G

garbage collection, 439, 481, 491
    mark/sweep algorithm, 446, 481
    generation scavenging, 439, 491
GemStone, 15, 283, 343, 454
generic class, 11
generic function, 53, 54
generic instance, 233
generic reference, 233
generic software, 209
Genesis, 342
goal-directed inference, 143
Gordas, 237
GrafBag, 152, 157
granularity locking protocol, 265, 271
grouping, 25
guardian, 15, 457, 563

# H

hierarchical graphic, 153
hierarchy
    class hierarchy, 8, 13
    delegation hierarchy, 41
    type hierarchy, 33, 223
hierarchy locking; see granularity locking protocol, 271
homogeneity, 549
horizontal modifier, 186
HP-SQL, 244
Hybrid, 14, 32, 39, 42, 120
hypertext, 204

# I

iMAX-432, 343
impedance mismatch, 584

indexing, 297, 298, 370
    class-hierarchy index, 370, 376
    single-class index, 370, 376
individual method, 67
INGRESS, 178, 348
inheritance
    class inheritance, 6, 210
    dynamic inheritance, 9, 33, 35
    multiple inheritance, 7, 73
    partial inheritance, 8
    part inheritance, 9
    scope inheritance, 9, 204
    single inheritance, 7, 73
    static inheritance, 8
inheritance conflict, 60
in-list, 128
instance variable; *see* attribute
    anonymous instance variable, 295
instantiation, 5
Integrated Data Model, 222
integration
    integrating application, 210
    language-database integration, 583
    language integration, 525
intention mode lock, 271
introspection, 69
Iris, 15, 219


**J**

justification, 128


**K**

kind, 544
    natural kind, 544
KNO, 206, 557


**L**

lexical scoping, 106
LISP, 7, 15
Little Smalltalk, 436

load balancing, 567
lock variable, 111
locking granule, 271
log
    REDO log, 272
    UNDO log, 272
Logo, 570
long field, 245; *see* multimedia data
LOOM, 15, 288, 343, 577
Loops, 33
LRU algorithm, 447, 495


**M**

Mach, 15
mail-address, 90
mail-queue, 91
memory representation of object, 324
Mesa, 7
message flattening, 434
message passing, 5, 14, 80, 275
    asynchronous, 82
    buffered, 14
    express mode, 103
    future, 102
    now, 102
    ordinary mode, 103
    past, 102
    synchronous, 14, 83
    unidirectional, 14
metabase, 187
metaclass, 134
meta-display, 167
meta object, 68
metatype, 187
method, 5, 9, 55
    active, 116
    broadcast method, 566
    inactive, 116
    method selector, 428
    method temporary, 428
    multicast method, 566
    multi-method, 67
    primitive only method, 434
method combination, 63
    after method, 64
    around method, 65

auxiliary method, 64
before method, 64
daemon method, 64
declarative method combination, 64
imperative method combination, 64
primary method, 64
method invocation, 565
blocking invocation, 565
nonblocking invocation, 565
mixin, 46
Modula-2, 13
monitor, 457
multimedia data, 273
multimedia information management, 273

N

name space, 289
nonmonotonic reasoning, 129
notification-sensitive, 261

O

object, 221
atomic object, 109
dependent object, 262, 318
distributed object, 112
file object, 362
generic object, 259
immutable object, 564
independent object, 324
knowledge object, 114
large object, 294
large storage object, 343
messenger object, 565
meta object, 68
office object, 202
passive object, 13
permanent object, 318
persistent-CLOS (PCLOS), 243
presentation object, 210
small storage object, 347

storage object, 344, 347
user object, 318
object design, 208, 528
object identity, 588
object instantiation, 374
Objective C, 207, 570
object migration, 87, 498
object property, 222
Object SQL (OSQL), 237
object type version; see type version
object version, 453, 463
object version at the application
level, 463
object version at the system
level, 472
ODDESSY, 177
office activity, 310
Office Document Architecture (ODA),
438
office information system, 200, 309
office knowledge, 206
office modeling concept, 201
office procedure, 204
office task, 206
office tool, 204
omega rule, 311
ontological principle, 539
ontology, 538
OPAL, 284
optimizer; see query optimizer
Orient84/K, 114
Orion, 15, 152, 300, 370, 376, 455, 586,
589
OTM, 120
out-list, 128
overloading, 10, 70, 223
OZ, 310
OZ+, 309

P

packet, 456
packet slice, 457
packettype, 457
PAL, 456, 459
parallel version, 453

Parc Place Smalltalk-80, 295
Pascal/R, 585
path expression, 293
Persistent-CLOS (PCLOS), 243
PHIGS, 152
POGO, 151
polymorphism, 10
POMS, 577
POOL-T, 14, 119
possibility, 473
POSTGRES, 342, 344
POSTQUEL, 344
precedence list, 60
predicate, 142
    complex predicate, 267
    simple predicate, 267
premise, 129
premitive call, 428
PROBE, 342
programming-by-example, 205
protection, 490, 499, 532
Proteus, 128, 152, 251
prototype, 41
prototypical object, 6, 9
proxy, 99, 492
PS-Algol, 585
pseudo-time, 473


Q

query, 299, 372
    range query, 385
    single-key query, 385
query evaluation plan, 374
query graph, 267
query optimizer, 235, 374
query processing, 235


R

rapid prototyping, 207
recovery, 272, 290, 345, 359, 364
Reed's model, 476
reference-consistent, 261

reference count, 505
reference-inconsistent, 261
referential integrity, 222, 285, 588
region, 442
relational database, 178
relationship, 25
remote procedure call (rpc), 457
    blocking rpc, 84
    future rpc, 83, 103, 110
    nonblocking rpc, 83
replacement behavior, 90
resource management, 85
reusability, 5, 209
    extensibility, 71
reverse traversal, 267
rule, 190, 229, 316
rule-based, 235
rule firing, 147
rule triggering
    self-triggering, 312
run-time support, 207


S

scheduling
    scheduling-in-the-small, 566
    scheduling-in-the-large, 566
schema, 181
schema evolution, 8, 224, 253, 263
schema evolution invariant, 255
schema evolution rule, 257
schema modification; see schema
        evolution
    conversion, 300
    screening, 300
schema modification invariant; see
        schema-evolution invariant, 300
script, 90, 101
secretary, 109
segment, 292
SELF, 32, 37, 38, 39, 41
self, 90, 99
semantic concurrency control, 399
    data approach, 400, 412
    FIFO Queue semantics, 404

intertype synchronization, 401
transaction approach, 400
Weakly-FIFO Queue semantics, 405
semantic model, 24
Binary Model, 24
Entity-Relationship model, 24
functional model, 24
IFO model, 25
Semantic Data Model, 24
semantic pattern, 416
serial dependency, 410
serializability, 397
serializable schedule, 475
session
default session, 269
shadow-page, 272
shared memory, 80
sharing
anticipated sharing, 35
unanticipated sharing, 35, 45
Simula, 4, 11, 33, 37, 39, 40, 81, 459,
570, 588
slot; *see* attribute
local slot, 68
shared slot, 68
Smalltalk, 4, 13, 15, 16, 24, 26, 33, 37,
39, 60, 75, 284, 285, 286, 288, 295,
425, 496, 570, 586
Berkely Smalltalk, 488, 497
Smalltalk-80, 31, 107, 118, 177, 343,
459, 487, 489
Smalltalk/V, 295
software evolution; *see* reusability, 44
specific reference, 233
SQL, 585
SQL/DS, 253, 376
Starburst, 342
starvation, 475
storage reclamation
local reclamation, 496
distributed reclamation, 496
subclassing
dynamic subclassing, 9
super, 109
support-status, 128
supporter, 129
surrogate, 347
Swallow, 481

System for Business Automation
(SBA), 564
System R, 178

**T**

Taxis, 222
template, 31, 34, 37
minimal template, 39
nonstrict, 41
strict, 38
temporary object, 318
tenuring, 441
Thoth, 13, 83
Traits, 7
transaction, 268, 290, 396, 414
atomic transaction, 414
automicity, 396
cooperating transaction, 414
hypothetical transaction, 270
serializable transaction, 271
transaction atomicity, 272
transaction groups, 414
visibility, 396
transaction group, 415
transitive closure, 440
Trellis/Owl, 7, 13, 16, 586
truth maintenance system, 128
two-phase commit, 473
type, 136, 223
object type, 11
strong type, 26, 119
type check, 12, 286
type parameterized, 459
typing, 293
type change; *see* schema evolution

**U**

UNIX socket, 504
user interface, 210

**V**

variable, 136
Vbase, 586
version, 345, 355
   transient version, 258
   type version, 454
   working version, 258
versionable class, 259
version binding
   dynamic binding, 259
   static binding, 259
version control, 233, 451
   application-level version
      control, 453
   system-level version control, 455
version management; *see* version
      control

   application-level, 452
   system-level, 452
version set, 233
vertical modifier, 185
virtual image, 488, 505
Visage, 157
Visual Office, 157
V Kernel, 83
Vulcan, 120


**W**

WiSS, 344
workspace, 15, 290
write ahead log, 272, 333